Consumer
Behaviour

Consumer
Behaviour

Jim Blythe

THOMSON

Australia • Brazil • Canada • Maxico • Singapore • Spain • United Kingdom • United States

THOMSON

Consumer Behaviour
Jim Blythe

Publishing Director	**Publisher**	**Development Editor**
John Yates	Jennifer Pegg	Charlotte Loveridge
Content and Media Production Manager	**Manufacturing Manager**	**Senior Marketing Manager**
Alissa Chappell	Helen Mason	Angela Lewis
Typesetter	**Production Controller**	**Cover Design**
ICC Macmillan Inc., India	Maeve Healy	Design Deluxe, Bath
Text Design	**Printer**	
Design Deluxe, Bath, UK	Rotolito Lombarda, Milan, Italy	

Copyright © 2008
Thomson Learning

The Thomson logo is a registered trademark used herein under licence.

For more information, contact
Thomson Learning,
High Holborn House,
50-51 Bedford Row,
London WC1R 4LR

or visit us on the World Wide Web at:
http://www.thomsonlearning.co.uk

ISBN: 978-1-8448-0381-1

British Library Cataloguing-in-Publication Data
A catalogue record for this book is available from the British Library

Brief contents

Contents

List of figures

List of tables

Preface

Introduction

Marketing is about consumers if it is about anything. Marketers centre everything they do on consumers – developing products which will meet consumer needs, writing advertising copy which excites and motivates consumers, planning competitive moves which will make our brands more appealing than competitors' brands. Consumer behaviour is therefore the starting point for all marketing planning, and (which is perhaps more important) it is a really fascinating area of study.

This book has been written from a European perspective but also provides examples from elsewhere in the world – what is fascinating about people is not so much our differences, but rather our similarities. Throughout the world, members of our species have surprisingly similar needs, hopes, and wants.

Who Should Use this Text

This text has been designed for undergraduates on general business or marketing courses, but works equally well for HND Students and MBA students who have not studied consumer behaviour before. It should also provide an interesting read for practitioners looking to update their understanding of academic thinking about marketing.

Aim and Structure of the Text

The book begins by outlining some of the disciplines which have contributed to our understanding of consumer behaviour. Academics from a wide range of disciplines have found consumption behaviour to be a fascinating topic for study, so the book opens with a comprehensive overview of this research.

The first part looks at ways in which an understanding of consumer behaviour contributes to our ability to plan marketing activities. It covers consumers and the marketing concept, consumers and the seven P model, consumer behaviour and segmentation, consumer behaviour and relationship marketing, and the role of consumer behaviour in marketing planning. Parts Two and Three look at the contribution made by psychologists and sociologists to our understanding of consumer behaviour.

The final section of the book shows how the behavioural theories outlined in previous chapters affect the actual decision-making process. This section draws on research conducted by marketing academics and others, and covers decision-making, innovation, involvement, post-purchase behaviour, consumer behaviour in services markets, segmentation and the marketing mix.

Text Book Features

To help you get the most from your book, there are various features in the text. First, each chapter contains Consumer Behaviour in Action boxes. These are intended to give live, up-to-date examples of current consumer behaviour issues and practice. As such, they provide additional, more detailed explanations in the text.

Second, there are two case studies in each chapter. The Preview Cases open the chapter and flag up the issues. They are revisited at the end of the chapter to show how the company involved tackled the particular problem at hand. The second case offers an opportunity for you to test your understanding of the issues contained in the chapter.

Third, each chapter contains a set of Talking Points, which are boxed statements challenging accepted views. They are deliberately provocative and intended to stimulate argument and deeper thought about the issues.

Fourth, each chapter has a set of Chapter Review Questions at the end. These link to the key points in the chapter, and are for you to use to check your understanding of the chapter.

Supplementary Material

There is a website to accompany the text, the details of which are printed on the following page. This book and its accompanying materials are not a substitute for your lectures, but they should give you a solid basis on which to build your understanding of consumer behaviour.

Thanks

In writing this book I have incurred a number of debts to colleagues and others. First I would like to thank my friends at Thomson, who have remained calm in the face of missed deadlines, missing text, inconsistent headings, and last-minute disasters. Authors are an unreliable bunch at best. Second I would like to thank my colleagues at the University of Glamorgan who gave me advice, pointed me towards useful papers, argued with me, and generally made me think a bit harder.

Third I would like to thank the anonymous reviewers who sometimes praised, sometimes criticised, sometimes disagreed, but who always met their deadlines and thus helped me meet mine. Writing a book of this type would not be possible without reviewers to pick up on my mistakes, omissions, and plain stupidity – which is, of course, why they remain blissfully anonymous, to minimise the embarrassment factor for me.

Fourth, I would like to thank my many colleagues throughout the world who have carried out research into consumer behaviour. It is their work which is the foundation of all textbooks, yet for most of them it is a labour of love: their enthusiasm and diligence in research is what makes academic life so stimulating and rewarding.

Finally, I would like to thank my students, past and present. Apart from their ability to ask me difficult questions and thus make me go away and think about the subject more thoroughly, it is the students who taught me how to teach. Teaching is about explaining subjects in a way which is comprehensible, motivating and entertaining – three things which I have aimed to achieve in writing this book. Such success as I have achieved in this endeavour I owe to the students.

**Visit the supporting website at www.thomsonlearning.co.uk/blythecb
to find further teaching and learning material, including:**

Students

MCQs to test your learning
Links to useful companies, news and other relevant sites
Glossary explaining key terms
Internet exercises

Lecturers

Further case studies
Teaching notes
Instructors' manual
Downloadable PowerPoint slides
Varying course outlines
Further questions

Supplementary resources: Examview®

This testbank and test generator provides a huge amount of different types of questions, allowing lecturers to create online, paper and local area network (LAN) tests. This CD-based product is only available from your Thomson sales representative.

Virtual Learning Environment

All of the web material is available in a format that is compatible with virtual learning environments such as Blackboard and WebCT. This version of the product is only available from your Thomson sales representative.

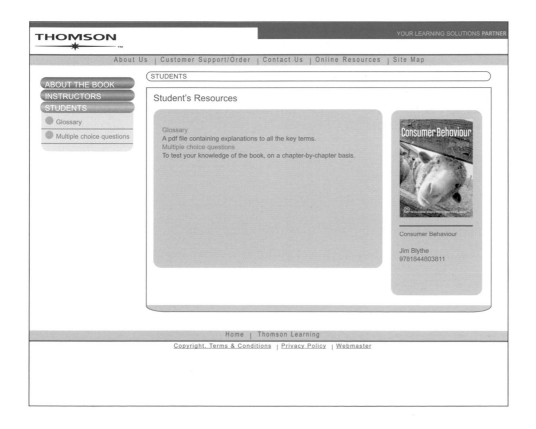

Walk through tour

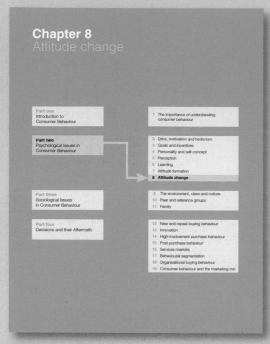

Road map Before each chapter begins, there is a "road map" which shows how the book is structured and how the chapters relate to each other.

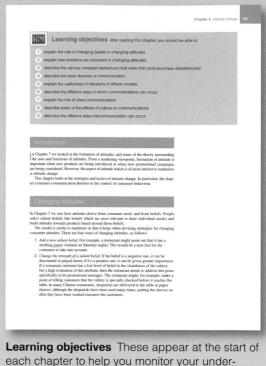

Learning objectives These appear at the start of each chapter to help you monitor your understanding and progress through each chapter. Each chapter also ends with a summary section that recaps the key content for revision purposes.

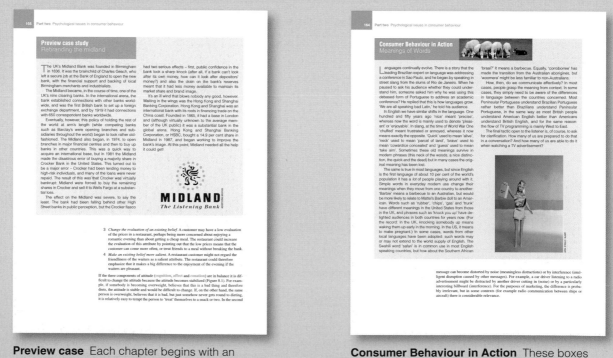

Preview case Each chapter begins with an in-depth case study which sets the scene for the chapter. This case study is then revised at the end of each chapter which shows the reader how the knowledge learnt within the chapter is integrated within the real world example.

Consumer Behaviour in Action These boxes are provided throughout the text and give extra examples of consumer behaviour in the real world.

Talking Points These are deliberately controversial and thought-provoking statements, provided throughout the text. Designed to challenge conventional opinions, they promote critical thinking and discussion in class.

Glossary Key terms are highlighted in colour throughout and explained in full in a Glossary at the end of the book, enabling you to find explanations of key terms quickly.

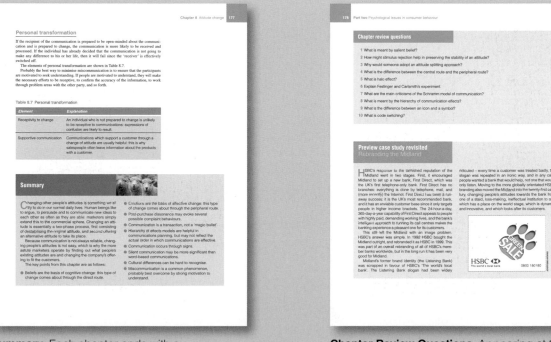

Summary Each chapter ends with a comprehensive summary that provides a thorough re-cap of the issues in each chapter, helping you to assess your understanding and revise key content.

Chapter Review Questions Appearing at the end of each chapter, these help reinforce and test your knowledge and understanding, and provide a basis for group discussions and activities.

Case study
The Scottish Road Safety Campaign

The Scottish Road Safety Campaign was founded in 1985, with the aim of reducing the death toll on Scottish roads. Funded by the Scottish Executive (later the Scottish Parliament) SRSC has five main objectives as of 2005:

1 To reduce the use of inappropriate and excessive speed on Scotland's roads.

2 To reduce the incidence of drunk driving on Scotland's roads.

3 To reduce the incidence of drug driving on Scotland's roads.

4 To reduce young driver casualties.

5 To increase the level of seatbelt compliance for all drivers and passengers.

Previous attempts to reduce average speeds on Scottish roads were less than successful: the campaigns were ad hoc and the effects were short term. SRSC planners therefore decided to take a long-term approach, using a campaign called Foolspeed. The first phase of this campaign, launched in November 1998, comprised a series of short TV advertisements backed up by widespread display of the Only Foolspeed message on buses, petrol nozzles, and motorway service station sites. Police forces, local authorities and even some commercial companies helped by displaying the Only Foolspeed logo on their publications as well as on their vehicles.

In 1999, 2000 and 2001 respectively three full-length 40-second TV advertisements were produced. The first advert, called 'Mirror', aimed to challenge drivers' existing beliefs about their speeding behaviour. The second advert, 'Friends and Family', showed how fast driving was stressful for passengers. The third advert, 'Simon Says', showed how drivers can sometimes be pressured by other drivers into speeding.

The overall effect was a marked change in drivers' attitudes towards speeding. The next advert in the series will address the issue of behavioural intentions about speeding.

For drink driving, the SRSC commissioned some research which showed that younger drivers were more concerned about losing their licences, whereas older drivers were more concerned about the moral aspects of drinking and driving. To tackle these differing attitudes, SRSC began by trying to change the attitudes of the younger drivers with a campaign called 'Wheel of Misfortune'. In this campaign a young driver was featured being caught drinking and driving, and winning a series of 'prizes' including higher insurance premiums, loss of independence, and so forth. The advertisements went out on radio, since young drivers typically listen to the radio while driving: the campaign was backed up by 'Wheel of Misfortune' stickers in pub toilets.

Research also showed that drug driving was more typical of younger drivers. The evidence was that these drivers did not believe that the police had simple ways of detecting the drugs, and that therefore they were less likely to be caught than they would if they were driving while drunk. The campaign therefore concentrated on showing young drivers that the police can, and do, use quick and effective roadside tests for drug use. Follow-up research on this campaign found that drivers believed that police had the means to test for drugs, but drivers did not believe that the police actually used the equipment, since nobody had seen them actually testing somebody (even though breathalyser tests for alcohol are often seen). SRSC believed that this problem would reduce as the police use the tests more often.

Reducing the casualty rate among young drivers presented a particularly difficult problem, as young drivers are (almost by definition) over-confident in their own abilities. They are therefore unlikely to regard the advertising as applying to them, and will consequently ignore the messages. SRSC planned to attack this on two fronts: first, by targeting new drivers. Having just passed their tests, these drivers are less likely to have developed an over-confident attitude, and are probably more open to communication. Second, and perhaps controversially, SRSC found that attitudes to driving are formed much earlier than had previously been thought – by primary-school age, most children had formed attitudes about driving, some of which were inappropriate. SRSC targeted the parents of primary-school children with a view to engaging their help in getting the road safety message across. Secondary schools were also targeted so as to reach older children, but in this case the message came from the SRSC education officer rather than from parents.

To increase seat belt usage, SRSC developed a campaign called 'Good Egg'. This showed cartoon eggs wearing seatbelts: aimed at children, the campaign also conveyed the subtle message to adults that their children are fragile, and should be protected by wearing seatbelts.

All these campaigns are ongoing. The aim is not just to change behaviour (by threatening prosecution) but to change basic attitudes so that people monitor their own behaviour, and want to be safer on the roads.

Case study questions

1 How does the theory of planned behaviour apply to SRSC's campaigns?

2 What is the relevance of the elaboration likelihood model to the Foolspeed campaign?

3 How might the young driver campaign be strengthened?

4 How does personal transformation theory apply to the young driver campaign?

5 How might metacommunication affect the campaign in secondary schools?

References

Aronson, E., Chase, T., Helmreich, R., and Ruhnke, R. (1974) A two-factor theory of dissonance reduction: the effect of feeling stupid or feeling awful on opinion change. *International Journal of Communication Research*, 3: 340–52.

Bakamitsos, Georgios, and Siomkos, George (2004) Context effects in marketing practice: the case of mood. *Journal of Consumer Behaviour*, 3(4): 304–14.

Berney-Reddish, I.A., and Areni, C.S. (2005) Effects of probability markers on advertising claim acceptance. *Journal of Marketing Communications*, 11(1): 41–54.

Bhatnagar, Namita, and Aksoy, Lerzan (2004) Et tu, Brutus? A case for consumer skepticism and backlash against product placements. *Advances in Consumer Research*, 31(1).

Costa, Janmeen Arnold, and Pavia, Teresa M. (1992) What it all adds up to: culture and alpha-numeric brand names. *Advances in Consumer Research*, 19, eds. John F. Sherry Jr. and Brian Sternthal (Provo, UT: Association for Consumer Research).

Deetz, S.A. (1992) *Democracy in an Age of Corporate Colonization: Developments in Communication and the Politics of Everyday Life* (Albany, NY: State University of New York Press).

Engel, James F., Warshaw, Martin R., and Kinnear, Thomas C. (1994) *Promotional Strategy* (Chicago, IL: Irwin).

Festinger, L. (1957) *A Theory of Cognitive Dissonance* (Stanford, CA: Stanford University Press).

Festinger, L., and Carlsmith, J.M. (1959) Cognitive consequences of forced compliance. *Journal of Abnormal and Social Psychology*, 58: 203–10.

Case Studies These close each chapter and show how each chapter's main issues are applied in real-life situations. Each case is accompanied by questions to help you test your understanding of the issues.

References Comprehensive references at the end of each chapter allow you to explore the subject further, and act as a starting point for projects and assignments.

Part one
Introduction to consumer behaviour

Consumer
Behaviour

Acknowledgements

The publisher acknowledges the contribution of the following lecturers, who provided invaluable feedback on the manuscript:

Anne Danguilaume, CERAM Business School

Sylvie Laforet, University of Sheffield Management School

Peter Murphy, Teesside University Business School

John Temperley, Leeds Business School, Leeds Metropolitan University

The following lecturers are acknowledged for their role in reviewing the proposal:

Jeremy Baker, London Metropolitan University

Mike Cant, UNISA

Mark Gabbott, Monash University

Gillian Hogg, University of Strathclyde

Dale Littler, Manchester Business School

Bilal Moosa, Hogeschool van Amsterdam

Mike Pretious, University of Stirling

Darach Turley, Dublin City University

Helen Woodruffe-Burton, Lancaster University

Consumer behaviour is an area of marketing which has received attention from many different directions. Academics from a wide range of disciplines have found consumption behaviour to be a fascinating topic for study – and as a result the literature on consumer behaviour is rich and varied.

Part 1 outlines some of the disciplines which have contributed to our understanding of consumption behaviour. It also looks at ways in which an understanding of consumer behaviour contributes to our ability to plan marketing activities: it covers consumers and the marketing concept, consumers and the seven P model, consumer behaviour and segmentation, consumer behaviour and relationship marketing, and the role of consumer behaviour in marketing planning.

Although the part's topics are covered in greater depth later in the book, it gives the overview which shows how the various elements fit together. It also shows how the study of consumer behaviour has developed from simple economic models to complex models drawing on psychology, sociology, anthropology and microeconomics.

Chapter 1
The importance of understanding consumer behaviour

Part one
Introduction to
consumer behaviour

**1 The importance of understanding
consumer behaviour**

Part two
Psychological issues in
consumer behaviour

2 Drive, motivation and hedonism
3 Goals, risk and uncertainty
4 Personality and self-concept
5 Perception
6 Learning
7 Attitude formation
8 Attitude change

Part three
Sociological issues
in consumer behaviour

9 The environment, class and culture
10 Peer and reference groups
11 The Family

Part four
Decisions and their aftermath

12 New and repeat buying behaviour
13 Innovation
14 High involvement purchase behaviour
15 Post-purchase behaviour
16 Services markets
17 Behavioural segmentation
18 Organizational buying behaviour
19 Consumer behaviour and the marketing mix

Learning objectives After reading this chapter, you should be able to:

1. explain how the study of consumer behaviour has evolved

2. show how consumer behaviour relates to marketing decision-making

3. explain why relationships are harder to establish in business-to-consumer situations than in business-to-business situations

4. explain the role of consumer research in studying consumer behaviour

5. describe the scope and nature of psychology and sociology

6. describe the scope and nature of anthropology

7. describe the relationship of economics with the study of consumer behaviour

8. explain the role of exchange in improving people's welfare

9. explain how the terms 'luxury' and 'necessity' relate to consumer behaviour

Introduction

Every day we buy things. We exchange our money for goods and services, for our own use and for the use of our families: we choose things we think will meet our needs on a day-to-day basis, and we occasionally make buying decisions which will affect our lives for years to come. At the same time, we make decisions about disposing of worn-out or used-up possessions. All these decisions and exchanges have implications for ourselves, our families, our friends, the environment, the businesses we buy from, the employees of those businesses, and so on in ever-widening ripples.

For marketers, understanding the processes involved in making those decisions is central to establishing policy. The key concept of marketing is customer centrality: we cannot ignore customer decision-making.

Consumer behaviour, and industrial buyer behaviour, have been studied by marketers since the times before marketing itself became an academic subject. The academic subjects which preceded marketing include economics (the study of supply and demand), sociology (the study of group behaviour), psychology (the study of thought processes) and anthropology (the study of what makes us human). Each of these disciplines has looked at the problem from a different angle, and each will be discussed in greater detail throughout the book. The study of consumer behaviour combines elements from all these disciplines: as marketers, we relate our understanding of consumer behaviour to everything we do.

Defining consumer behaviour

All of us are consumers; all of us behave. This does not mean that all of our behaviour can be defined as consumer behaviour, of course. Specific consumer behaviour has been defined as follows:

> Consumer behaviour is the activities people undertake when obtaining, consuming and disposing of products and services. (Blackwell, Miniard and Engel 2001, p. 6)

Preview case study
Just AAsk

In 2005 the Automobile Association (AA) celebrated its first 100 years of existence. Founded in the days when cars were unreliable, rare novelties, the AA was founded in order to offer motorists assistance with what was then a hobby for the wealthy. The original aim of the AA was to help motorists avoid police speed traps, but within a few years AA mechanics were hired to make roadside repairs to broken-down vehicles, the organization lobbied Parliament on behalf of motorists, and AA inspectors even made recommendations for suitable hotels for motorists far from home.

As time has moved on, so has the AA. Nowadays cars are more reliable, and of course much more common, but the AA still offer a roadside repair service. The organization also offers legal help, help starting the car even when it is outside the member's property, and help with insurance. One area which still vexes many motorists, though, is choosing a car in the first place. Here the AA can help in two ways: first, for a small fee a prospective buyer can have a car inspected by an AA mechanic, a useful reassurance for the less mechanically minded driver. Second, the AA offers a car-buyer's website which provides prospective buyers with all the information they need to find a suitable used car.

The site, at www.theaa.com/cbg/home.jsp, leads the prospective buyer through the whole decision-making process. Buyers are first asked to say whether they already know exactly the type of car they want, whether they want help finding a car that will suit their needs,

whether they need help finding a car that will suit their budget, or whether they want to know how much their own car might be worth in part-exchange. Buyers who want help finding a car that suits their needs are asked such questions as the size of car required, whether petrol or diesel engined, whether they need a car with high fuel economy, and so forth. At the next stage buyers are allowed to say how important each factor is, and finally they are asked which 'optional extras' such as air-conditioning and CD players they would like. The website then automatically generates a recommended guide price so that the buyer knows exactly what specification to look for, and what the forecourt price should be.

Talking point

This definition is widely used, but it still leaves some questions to answer. First, what do we mean by 'obtaining'? This presumably includes all the activities which lead up to making a purchase, including searching for information about products and services, and evaluating the alternatives. 'Obtaining' may not involve an actual purchase, but most consumer behaviour researchers and writers ignore this angle: a child who promises to

From a manufacturer's viewpoint, shoplifting can only be a good thing. If the product is attractive to shoplifters, more of it will leave the retailer's premises, and since the retailer has already paid the manufacturer for the goods, the manufacturer doesn't care whether the goods are bought or stolen from the retailer. Leaving ethical considerations aside (and who doesn't, from time to time?) wouldn't it be in manufacturers' best interests to make their products as easy to swipe as possible?

On the other hand, would retailers continue to stock products which were easy to steal? For the manufacturer, the retailer is the customer, not the consumer, so the manufacturer needs to focus on industrial buyer behaviour rather than consumer behaviour! Or, better still, consider the needs of both.

keep his room tidy in exchange for a new video game is clearly obtaining a product, but this is not usually regarded as part of a study of consumer behaviour. Likewise theft is usually ignored as an aspect of consumer behaviour, for ethical reasons.

Other issues in the 'obtaining' category might includes the ways in which people pay for the products (cash, credit card, bank loan, hire purchase, interest-free credit, and so forth), whether the product is for themselves or is a gift, how the new owner takes the purchases home and how the decisions are affected by branding and by social elements such as the respect of friends.

'Consuming' refers to the ways in which people use the products they buy. This includes where the product is consumed, and when (in terms of what occasions the product might be used) and how the product is used. In some cases, people use products in ways which were not intended by the manufacturer: this is called re-invention. For example, a biologist might buy a turkey-basting syringe to use for taking water samples from a river, or a gardener might buy a china serving-dish to use as a plant-pot. Consumption is necessary for our health and well-being: obviously some consumption is not good for us (over-consumption of alcohol, drug abuse, or even using a mobile telephone while driving) but most of our consumption is essential for living and relating to other people (Richins 2001).

Disposal of products when they are worn out or no longer needed has become a 'hot topic' in recent years due to environmentalism. Disposal includes the disposal of packaging – whether it is recycled, burned, or goes into landfill, packaging represents a major problem for the twenty-first century. Knowing how people dispose of products can be crucial to marketing them. For example, in most of Africa empty metal cans are used to make oil lamps, ash trays, drinking vessels and so forth. Changing the design or size of the can may well affect sales. Likewise, a system for trading in used or worn-out items can be a major boost for sales of new items: second-hand car trading is based entirely on this principle.

Another definition of consumer behaviour runs as follows:

> The dynamic interaction of affect and cognition, behaviour, and environmental events by which human beings conduct the exchange aspects of their lives. (Bennett 1989)

This definition has the advantage that it regards consumer behaviour as dynamic, and emphasises the interaction of many different elements in determining consumer behaviour. This is the main reason why strategy needs constant review: a strategy which worked well in the past may not work nearly as well in the future, because the forces which shape behaviour may have changed out of all recognition. The definition also includes the concept of marketing as the management of exchange, which is not accepted by all marketers: few people would argue, for example, that a mother who promises a child some sweets in exchange for good behaviour is engaging in a marketing process. On the other hand, marketing-as-management-of-exchange has a lot to recommend it when considering not-for-profit marketing.

The general model of consumer behaviour shown in Figure 1.1 shows that basic attitudes (formed of thought, emotion and intended behaviour) are influenced by personal and

Recycling in action – growing roses in an old toilet.

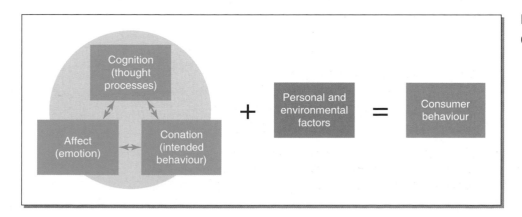

Figure 1.1

Consumer behaviour dynamics

environmental factors to create actual behaviour. Marketers are able to influence this process at several points – they can influence thought processes by providing relevant information at the right time, they can influence emotion by using appealing communication and imagery, and they can provide suitable environmental stimuli (for example pleasant shops or user-friendly websites) to stimulate purchase. On a more subtle level, marketers can even encourage greater consumption of the product – good marketing does not stop at the point of sale.

From the viewpoint of academic researchers, consumer behaviour might be considered as the field of study which concentrates on consumption activities. In the past, the study of consumer behaviour has mainly focused on why people buy. More recently, the focus has moved to include looking at consumption behaviour – in other words how and why people consume.

Studying consumer behaviour is clearly of interest to marketers, but it is an interesting study in itself, even for non-marketers, because we are all consumers. Ultimately, consumers hold all the power in the business world – as Sam Walton, founder of Wal-Mart, famously said, 'There is only one boss – the customer. And he can fire everyone in the company, from the chairman on down, simply by spending his money somewhere else.' Walton always regarded himself as an agent for his customers, finding them the best value for money: this simple philosophy moved Wal-Mart from one small store in Arkansas to the world's largest retailer within Walton's lifetime.

The world's biggest retailer – an agent for consumers?

KATHY DEWITT/ALAMY

Consumer behaviour in action
Trade-in

Trading in old cars for new ones was reputedly invented by General Motors dealers in the 1930s as a way of stimulating the market for new cars. The second-hand cars that were traded in could be sold to people who could not afford a new car, and so the number of people who were driving could be increased dramatically. Trade-in also solved the problem of what to do with a car once it was a few years old and perhaps not looking as new as it once had.

In 1995 Mrs Katherine Freund of Portland, Oregon, had an idea for extending the trade-in concept and at the same time improving road safety. Her son was run over by an elderly driver in 1988 (the son recovered fully) and it occurred to Katherine that there were many elderly people on the road who really shouldn't be driving, but who felt that they had little choice in a world (and especially in a country) dominated by cars. So Katherine instituted a scheme whereby senior-citizen drivers can trade in their cars in exchange for rides. The elderly people are credited with rides, but the cars are operated by volunteers supplemented by a few paid drivers, and the scheme is self-financing. The rides are very much cheaper than using taxis so the credit in the scheme lasts a long time, and the service runs 24 hours a day, seven days a week.

One of the main advantages of the scheme is that it allows elderly people to remain part of the community and continue to do everything they used to do when they were still driving. The other advantage is that the roads are much safer – the over-75 age group has more accidents than any other group except teenagers.

This novel approach to trade-in has created an entirely new opportunity for older drivers: at the same time, it maintains their mobility and makes life safer for others. As a way of disposing of no-longer-needed cars it is second to none!

Consumer behaviour in context

The fundamental basis for marketing thinking is that the customer (or consumer) should be at the centre of everything the firm does. While there may be some dissent about whether the marketing concept always applies, for marketers customers are the key concern. This means that an understanding of how and why people make purchasing decisions is crucial to formulating a marketing plan.

In the first instance, purchasing behaviour relates strongly to segmenting the market. The whole purpose of segmentation is to determine which potential buyers are most likely to behave favourably towards the company and its products: most segmentation methods bear at least some relationship to consumer behaviour issues.

First, geographic segmentation breaks the market down according to the location in which the potential customers live. Where someone chooses to live, or is forced to lived, is either an example of decision-making or dictates decision-making. Someone living in a cold climate is compelled to buy warm clothing, heating equipment, insulation products for the home, and so forth.

Psychographic segmentation and behavioural segmentation clearly relate very directly to consumer characteristics and behaviour. Demographic segmentation is based on consumers' wealth, age, gender and education levels (among other things), each of which relate directly to purchasing decisions.

People in hot climates may need special clothing, housing – and even camels!

Consumer behaviour and the marketing mix

Marketing management is usually considered to consist of controlling the marketing mix. The original four-P model of the marketing mix was suggested by McCarthy in 1960, although many other writers contributed to the concept both before and after this time.

Table 1.1 on page 10 shows how consumer behaviour relates to the seven-P model of the marketing mix developed by Booms and Bitner (1982).

Although the marketing mix has been widely criticized by academics because it tends to imply that things are being done *to* consumers rather than that things are being done *for* consumers, it is still widely taught because it offers a relatively simply way to understand what marketers do. Putting each element of the mix into a separate 'silo' is one way of simplifying the real world, but looked at from the consumer's viewpoint the distinctions between the elements may not be valid at all. For example, price is regarded as a cost from the consumer's viewpoint, but might also be regarded as a promotion – a money-off special offer could be regarded as a major incentive to buy now rather than postpone the purchase. In other words, the seven-P model may be fine for the marketers to understand, but may not be appropriate from the consumer's viewpoint.

Consumers and relationship marketing

Relationship marketing seeks to establish long-term relationships with customers rather than focusing on the single transaction. The differences between relationship marketing and transactional marketing are shown in Table 1.2 on page 11.

Establishing a relationship in a business-to-business (B2B) context turns out to be a great deal easier than establishing a relationship in a business-to-

Loyalty cards are a way of fostering relationships with consumers.

Table 1.1 Consumer behaviour and the seven Ps

Product	The bundle of benefits which consumers acquire is the basis of their decision-making. Deciding which benefits are essential, which are desirable, which do not matter and which are actually not benefits at all but drawbacks is the starting point for all rational decisions.
Price	The cost of a product goes beyond the price tag in most cases. If the product is complex, there will be a learning cost attached to figuring out how to use it: if the product is dangerous, there may be a cost attached to consequent injury. If the product is visible to others, there may be an embarrassment cost. In some cases, these extra costs may exceed the price tag – consumers will take account of them, and will weigh them in the decision, but producers will only be able to obtain the price on the tag.
Place	Convenient locations for making purchases are essential; in fact it would not be too much to say that the easier the marketers make it for consumers to find the product conveniently, the more product will be sold. Like price, the location can affect the decision in ways which do not benefit the producer – equally, producers can sometimes charge a premium for delivering location benefits. Corner shops (convenience stores) are a good example: although they are invariably more expensive than supermarkets, being within easy reach of home offers a clear advantage which is worth paying for.
Promotion	Promotion is not something which is done to consumers, it is something which they consume. People buy magazines, watch TV shows, go to the cinema and ride on public transport. Although they do not usually do these things in order to be exposed to advertisements, they usually pay at least some attention to them and frequently they enjoy the experience. Furthermore, people often use media such as classified advertisements and directories in an active search for information about goods they might like to buy.
People	Business is not about money, it is about people. The people who run businesses and deal with the public need to understand how other people react in purchasing situations. In some cases, the product is the person: people become loyal to the same hairdresser, the same doctor, the same restaurant chef.
Process	The way services are delivered affects the circumstances in which people buy as well as their propensity to buy. A meal out might be a ten-minute lunch stop at a fast-food outlet, or it might be a romantic dinner for two in an upmarket restaurant. The process is completely different in each case, and so is the price: in the first case, the consumer may only go through a limited problem-solving process, in the second case the process may well be longer because the need to get it right is greater. This is called 'involvement'.
Physical evidence	Physical aspects of the service experience often relate to the pleasure one feels from receiving the service rather than the practical aspects. The surroundings in a restaurant, the food itself, the décor, the table linen and cutlery all form part of the service and provide part of the pleasure of dining out.

consumer (B2C) context. The reasons for this are currently obscure, but may include the following:

1 Businesses change their needs less often than do consumers.
2 There are fewer suppliers and customers in B2B markets.
3 B2B transactions almost always involve the personal relationships between salespeople and buyers, whereas B2C relationships are often impersonal.
4 The possibilities for mutual advantage in establishing a relationship are often much greater in a B2B context.

Table 1.2 Relationship marketing vs. transactional marketing

Transactional marketing	Relationship marketing
Focus on single sale	Focus on customer retention
Orientation on product features	Orientation on product benefits
Short time-scale	Long time-scale
Little emphasis on customer service	High emphasis on customer service
Limited customer commitment	High customer commitment
Moderate customer contact	High customer contact
Quality is the concern of the production department	Quality is the concern of all

Source: Christopher, M., Ballantyne, D. and Payne, A. (1991) *Relationship Marketing* (Oxford: Butterworth-Heinemann).

Relationship marketing is rooted in the idea that it is cheaper to retain an existing customer than to recruit a new one. There is a certain appeal to this idea: acquiring new customers is a difficult business, whereas keeping someone on board should only be a matter of making sure their needs are met.

In consumer markets, this is a great deal harder than it sounds. First, consumer needs change relatively rapidly: the needs of someone aged 18 are likely to be somewhat different from those of the same individual aged 25. Likewise, a childless couple's needs might change quite dramatically should they have a baby together, quite apart from the probable change in their financial circumstances. Second, there is a great deal more choice of supplier in consumer markets, and a great many more ways to spend one's money. People can easily be tempted away from an existing supplier and towards a new supplier. Third, there

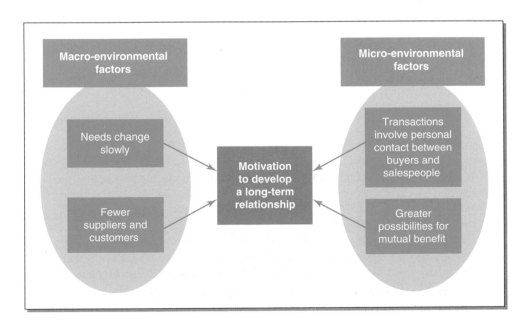

Figure 1.2

Businesses and relationship marketing

is little incentive for most consumers to remain loyal to a given supplier when there are so many tempting offers around and little to keep them on board: extra-nice service is really not enough.

Relationship marketing has become closely associated with direct marketing, simply because the best way to establish a relationship with a customer is to have direct dealings. Unfortunately, direct marketing has also become associated with direct mail and direct telephone marketing, both of which are extremely unpopular with the public in general: this is probably another reason why relationship marketing is less successful with consumers than with industrial buyers.

Understanding how people create and maintain relationships in their personal lives is obviously useful when considering how people create and maintain business relationships. Businesses are not about profits: they are about people.

Talking point

If businesses are about people, why is it that companies consistently report their successes and failures in financial terms? Why not report on how pleased their customers were, or on how loyal they were? Why not report on how many customers recommended them to their friends?

Or is it that it would be difficult to do these things? How do we know whether people are recommending them anyway? The market researchers should be able to find out – but it's obviously easier to just count up the money!

Consumers and marketing planning

Marketing planning has often been considered in terms of managing the product portfolio, developing new products, launching products, managing the product life cycle, and so forth. This involves planning communications which explain the product features and benefits, and which seek to persuade consumers to buy the products. It involves deciding which distributors the products should be sold from, what price will provide the company with a good return on its investment, and so forth.

This way of looking at marketing suffers from a serious flaw in that it is not customer-centric. Suppose we were to act in a completely customer-centred manner. We would then be seeking to manage the customer portfolio, considering which customers (or groups of customer) we can serve profitably and which we cannot. We would consider which marketing communications would appeal most to the groups we want to keep, and which would be off-putting to the groups we want to lose. We might consider the customer's life cycle (see pages 9–12 on relationship marketing) rather than the product's life cycle, and consider price in terms of what consumers will think is fair.

Talking point

Can we really let consumers run the business? After all, if we ask people what they are willing to pay for a product, they are likely to pitch the price as low as they think they can get away with. The same applies to service – everybody wants a lot, but is only prepared to pay a little!

Not to mention the competitive arms race. As one company offers one level of service, everyone else has to match it at least, and exceed it at best. Before long we get to the point where we are grovelling to the customers!

For example, in France one would never argue with the chef. If one likes one's steak well done, the waiter will suggest the idea to the chef, but after muttering something about 'Les sales anglais!' the chef will produce a steak which looks as if it needs a sticking-plaster. Contrast with America, where the customer tells the chef exactly what to put in and leave out of the food: 'No salt, hold the mayo, just a little Tabasco' and so forth. No doubt the American chef is much more customer-centred, but aren't we, as the customers, paying for his expertise? What's the point of going to a restaurant where we have a trained chef with years of experience, and then second-guessing the guy?

So where is customer centrality really located? In France, or in America?

Marketing strategies should therefore not only seek to influence consumers, they should also be influenced by them. Planning for a customer-led future means planning with consumer behaviour at the centre of the firm's planning. In the twenty-first century, consumers hold the power: there is evidence that people consider their spending power to be a form of voting, a way of expressing approval for what the supplier is offering (Shaw, Newholme and Dickson 2006). People are aware that they have choice: at first, when choice became widespread, people might have found this confusing and daunting, but as time has gone on people have found it empowering, and they do not hesitate to use their power (Davies and Elliott 2006).

For example, consumer research might show that a specific group of our customers is more profitable than another simply because they are more loyal. This means that we do not need to recruit new customers to replace those who drop out, which is of course substantially cheaper. We might therefore seek (a) to ensure that we continue to retain these customers and (b) try to find more like them. Their loyalty comes from their purchase behaviour – their propensity to repeat purchases on a regular basis – which in itself may be a function of their personalities, their degree of involvement with the products, and so forth.

Consumer research

Although there is a great deal of research conducted into competitors, stakeholders, and so forth, researching consumer behaviour is probably the main topic of interest for marketing researchers. Finding out what consumers intend to buy, have already bought or are planning to dispose of is fundamental to marketing planning and control.

Academic researchers are usually interested in the basics of creating a body of knowledge about this aspect of human behaviour. In most cases these researchers have backgrounds in the behavioural sciences, and seek to explain exchange phenomena. This type of research comprises the major part of published research because it appears in academic journals, and is the body of research on which this book is based.

Commercial market research is not usually published because it is commercially sensitive: firms do not want their new knowledge to leak out to their competitors. Some research is conducted by commercial market research companies such as Mintel or Keynote and is sold to interested parties; the reports tend to cover areas of general interest to as large a number of potential buyers as possible, of course, so they may not be as tailored as the purchasing firms would wish.

Traditional street surveys are being phased out in favour of focus groups.

In recent years, survey-type consumer research has begun to be replaced by in-depth interviews, focus groups and so forth. This is largely because surveys have not proved to be as reliable as they were thought to be in the past: people do not always tell the truth when they are surveyed, and in some cases the surveys are poorly conducted or even faked by unscrupulous interviewers.

There have frequently been calls for academic and commercial research to move closer together, and even to remove the distinction between consumer theory and practice (Marsden 2001). In practice, such a movement is difficult to implement, since academics and practitioners operate under different sets of pressures.

A full account of marketing research is beyond the scope of this book, but some of the commonest techniques and their strengths and weaknesses are shown in Table 1.3 on page 14.

There is a counter-argument to the 'let's understand consumers' approach: some observers believe that there is no need to understand people's inner drives, attitudes and thought processes – all we need to look at is how people behave. Alan Mitchell offers the analogy of a cat and a mouse: the cat does not study the mouse's thought processes, it simply tries to anticipate the mouse's next movements (Mitchell 2002). This viewpoint has, currently, few adherents among marketing academics, but it has a certain logic to it.

Table 1.3 Research techniques

Technique	Advantages	Disadvantages
Questionnaire-based interviews	A large number of opinions can be obtained quickly. A good understanding of what people can be determined. The results can be analysed numerically.	People often lie on questionnaires. It is difficult to formulate questions without either leaving out important details or leading the respondents to a particular answer. Analysis requires a fairly good level of mathematical and statistical understanding. Sometimes interviewers bias the responses, either consciously or unconsciously.
Self-completion questionnaire	Administered by post, this offers a cheap way of obtaining responses.	It is extremely difficult to write the questions so that they are clear and unambiguous, but still obtain the necessary information. Often has a very low response rate (less than 10% is not unusual) so that the sample may be biased.
In-depth interviews	Face-to-face interviews on an 'open-ended' basis, i.e. without specific questions. This allows the respondents to explore topics in greater depth, and to discuss issues which are of importance to them, rather than issues which are of importance to the interviewer. An excellent technique for finding out why people behave as they do (as opposed to how they behave).	Difficult to analyse. Requires a great deal of judgement on the part of the researchers, so may lead to bias. Difficult to conduct the interviews without leading the respondents towards specific answers.
Focus groups	Similar to in-depth interviews, but conducted with a group of respondents. Has the advantage that the group members lead each other, so there is less interviewer input. Good for finding out why people behave as they do.	Difficult to analyse. Some group members might dominate the group, reducing the range of answers obtained. Requires considerable skill in controlling the group.
Observation	Watching how people behave allows researchers to obtain direct and unbiased data.	Impossible to infer motivations from behaviour. No way of knowing why people are behaving as they do.
Experiment	Can provide data from a controlled environment so that outside influences do not bias the results.	Is expensive and difficult to perform correctly. Can only apply to a relatively small sample.

Antecedents of consumer behaviour

The study of consumer behaviour is, like marketing itself, a combination of other disciplines. As a study, it draws from economics, sociology, psychology and anthropology for its basic theories and research approaches (see Figure 1.3). Researchers aim to develop a body of specifically consumer-based research, but the influence of the other disciplines will always be at the forefront of the theory that develops.

All of these areas will be discussed in much greater detail throughout the book, but a quick overview of the basic contributions of each discipline should be helpful in understanding how consumer behaviour has developed as an academic study.

Economics is the study of demand. Economists study demand in the individual transaction, at the level of the firm and its customers, and also the overall level of demand in

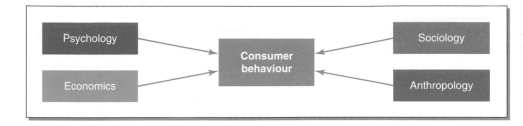

Figure 1.3
Antecedents of studying
consumer behaviour

the economy. The former study is called 'microeconomics', the latter is called 'macroeconomics'. Although microeconomics appears at first sight to explain consumer behaviour, in fact it only really explains *rational* behaviour. Economists consider such concepts as utility, value for money and economic choice, not such nebulous ideas as whether one's friends will admire one's new outfit.

Economics has provided consumer behaviour theorists with a number of useful concepts which help to explain the rational side of consumer behaviour.

Supply and demand

The laws of supply and demand explain how prices are set (at least in theory this is so). According to the theory, as prices rise more suppliers will enter the market, but fewer consumers will want the goods: as prices fall, more people will want to buy, but suppliers will be less willing to provide the goods. There is a point at which supply and demand form an equilibrium where exactly the same amount of the product will be supplied as the amount the consumers want to buy (see Figure 1.4) This is an interesting concept in one sense, since it shows that consumers have a strong role in setting prices, but it does suffer from a number of weaknesses. First, it assumes that all the suppliers are providing identical products, which is rarely (if ever) the case. Second, it assumes that people have perfect knowledge of the market, which again is unlikely to be the case. Third, it assumes that people are rational in their decisions – that they do not remain loyal to a particular supplier, that they do not take account of any branding issues, that they are not influenced by their friends or relatives, and so forth.

The demand curve (the line which tells us how much of the product will be bought at different prices) is useful in planning production. Marketers can develop a demand curve for a particular product by carrying out market research or by experience: the latter method is obviously more reliable, but may be problematic in practice.

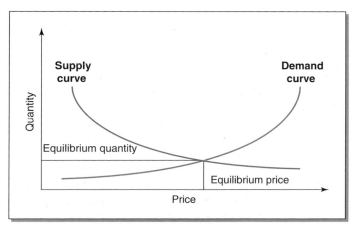

Figure 1.4
Supply and demand

What firms try to do is to minimise the effects of competition by differentiating their products. If each firm is producing identical products, the consumer will control the price: if the firm produces something which the competitors cannot offer, the price can be set by the supplier.

The economic choice

This simply means that someone cannot spend money on something if he or she already spent the money somewhere else. This implies that all companies are competing with all other companies for the consumer's money: people have only a certain amount of money they can spend, or commit to borrowing. In fact economic choice is somewhat blurred by the existence of credit. People can easily be persuaded to borrow the money to buy whatever they want, which means that other factors than money might come into the equation. The theory still holds true, though, if we consider the economic choice of how we spend our time, or how we use other resources such as our cars or our homes. The theory really talks about use of limited resources in aiming to satisfy one's needs.

Marketers have certainly taken on board the concept of the economic choice, broadening out the spectrum of competitors to include anyone who aims to satisfy similar needs in consumers. This means that cinema owners recognize theatres, restaurants, bowling alleys and other entertainment places as competitors, and in recent years have developed complexes where all leisure activities can take place under one roof: this is not just an example of taking over competitors, it is also an example of how a firm can help people make the best use of limited leisure time. With time as the constraining variable, such complexes can make best use of economic choice theory.

Indifference curves

People typically own portfolios of products. Some people like to have large numbers of some products (for example, some people have several TV sets) and few of something else. Indifference theory says that people might have a 'trade-off' in their minds about how much of a given product they consider is equivalent to a quantity of another product.

Figure 1.5 shows an indifference curve comparing money and turkeys. Someone who has no turkeys but plenty of money might decide to buy a turkey: if he or she is a particular lover of roast turkey, the temptation might arise to buy one or two extras for the freezer.

Figure 1.5

Indifference curve

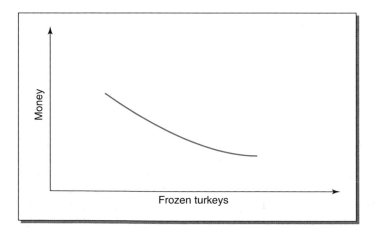

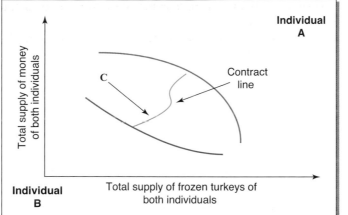

Figure 1.6
Edgeworth Box

As the freezer fills, though, there will come a point where the turkeys would have to be a real bargain to be worth buying, and of course eventually the individual will reach the point where he or she would not buy any more no matter how good a deal the marketer offered. Likewise, someone who is desperate to buy a turkey might be prepared to spend more money than usual on one. At one end of the curve we have a mood of 'What's the use of having all this money if I can't enjoy a turkey?' and at the other end of the curve the mood would be 'How many turkeys does one person need?'

For example, if you are in a pub and a friend goes to the bar, you might want a pint of beer and two packets of sandwiches. If the friend mixes up the order and brings back two pints of beer and one packet of sandwiches this may not matter to you, but if he brings backs no beer and three packets of sandwiches (or vice versa) this might not be acceptable. In those circumstances, you would have moved beyond the limits of your indifference curve: one way of returning to a satisfactory arrangement would be to swap some of your sandwiches for someone else's beer – in other words to trade.

Indifference curve theory leads on to the Edgeworth Box, which tells us that trade always makes people better off because both parties move onto a higher indifference curve.

In Figure 1.6, we have a situation where two roast-turkey lovers meet and decide to trade. Each has some turkeys and some money: the axes of the box show the total amount of each that the two people have between them. Each person would be quite happy with any combination of turkeys and money along the line of the indifference curve, but obviously would be even happier with more of both. If the people concerned trade, they will each end up with a turkey–money combination situated somewhere along the contract line; where each person ends up is a matter for negotiation.

The idea that trade is always good is actually fairly obvious: if both parties were not better off, one or other would not be prepared to make the trade. The degree to which each party is better off depends largely on negotiation skills: some people are better negotiators or are in stronger negotiating positions than others.

Elasticity of demand

While a rise in prices generally means a reduction in demand (although there are some exceptions), there is a question about the degree to which demand is affected by price. In some cases, a rise in price appears to make very little difference to demand – salt is the example usually given for this, because salt is extremely cheap and is rarely purchased, so even a doubling of the price would probably go unnoticed. On the other hand, some products seem to be dramatically affected by even small changes in price: this usually

Figure 1.7

Inelastic demand curve

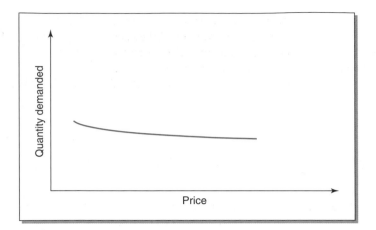

happens if there is a close substitute available. An example might be if the price of beef rose relative to the price of pork or lamb. In these circumstances, price calculations need to be carried out extremely carefully as a mistake could result in a dramatic loss of business.

Figure 1.7 shows a product which sustains much the same demand whatever happens to the price. As the price rises, demand does fall slightly but overall demand remains fairly constant.

There are elasticities other than price. For example, income elasticity of demand tells us that some products are affected by increases in the individual's spending money. In some cases, this will produce an increase in demand – as people become richer, they are likely to buy more clothes and more entertainment products, for example. In other cases the demand for an individual product might reduce as people become wealthier: a higher income might lead someone to buy a BMW rather than a Ford. In some cases a general rise in income reduces demand fairly dramatically, and here bread is an example. As people become richer, they tend to buy less bread and more meat and vegetables.

Figure 1.8 shows an elastic demand curve. Here the demand for the product is affected greatly by the price – even a small increase in price has a fairly profound effect on the demand for the product.

One point which arises from the elasticity concept is that there is no product which has a completely inelastic demand curve. In other words there is no product which has a demand curve which is entirely unaffected by price. This means that there is no product which is an absolute necessity of life – if this were the case, the producer could charge anything at all for the product and people would have no choice but to pay, since the alternative would be death. This is an important issue for marketers, because it shows us that there is no theoretical basis for considering some products as necessities and other products as

Figure 1.8

Elastic demand curve

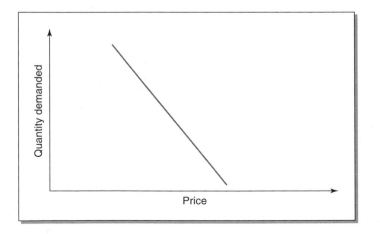

luxuries. The difference exists only in the minds of consumers. To some people, a car would be a luxury; to others it is a necessity. Likewise, water might be considered as a necessity of life, yet some people rarely (if ever) drink just plain water. They drink tea, beer, orange juice, Coca Cola, or any one of many different products containing water, all of which are substitutes for plain old tap water.

Water-based products – necessities of life?

Psychology

Psychology is the study of mental processes. Psychologists study the ways people think, which is of course basic to understanding how people think about the products they buy (see Figure 1.9). This includes learning about products, developing an overall perception of products and brands and fitting it into one's overall perception of the world, and the basic drives which encourage people to seek solutions for their needs.

Each of the contributions made by psychologists will be covered in more detail in Part 2 of this book, but for the time being here is a brief overview of the main issues.

- **Drive** and **motivation** – Drives are the basic forces which make us want to do things. A drive is created when the desired state of the individual is different from the actual state: the greater the difference, the stronger the drive. A drive which has a definite target becomes a motivation. Part of the marketer's job is to encourage drives to develop by encourages shifts in the desired state (it is pretty much impossible to develop shifts in the actual state). The other part of the marketer's job is to direct drives towards a specific target. For example, a marketer might encourage a shift in the desired state by saying, 'Isn't it about time you bought yourself a better car?' and follow this by saying, 'Why not treat yourself to a new Jaguar?'

- **Goals** and **incentives** – A goal is the rational element of motivation. Motives are largely emotional: goals are the rationalisation of a motivation. For example, someone might decide that they really want to learn to fly (a largely emotional motivation, based on reading adventure stories or on an unspecified emotion). The goals which derive from this might be concerned with finding an appropriate flying school, saving up the money to pay for lessons, and freeing up the time to learn. The incentive for achieving these various goals is the satisfaction of the need.

- **Personality** and **self-concept** – Personality is a combination of the various traits that determine who we are. The type of person we are dictates what we like and what we dislike, our preferred ways of dealing with our consumption problems, our

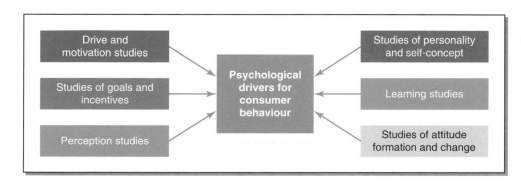

Figure 1.9

Contributions from psychology

preferred lifestyles, and so forth. Self-concept is about how we see ourselves – this includes how we see ourselves in terms of consumption patterns, branding and other consumption-based aspects. For example, each of us has favourite brands which we feel express our personalities. Some of us are Ford drivers, some of us BMW; some of us are Nike wearers, others Adidas, and so forth. What we buy and wear expresses who we are.

● Perception – This is about the way we make sense of the world. Each of us has a particular view of the world, a perceptual map, which enables us to make sense of what is happening around us. We assemble this map by taking in information through our senses and using it to develop an understanding of how the world works and where different things fit into it. Psychologists study the ways in which people filter out unnecessary information, group information together in useable 'chunks', and arrange the information to create the perceptual map. Marketers are interested in these processes in order to ensure that their brand is mapped into the most effective place in the consumers' perceptions.

The word 'perception' is often used to mean 'untrue' but in fact this is not the case. The only truth we have is what we hold in our minds, so a person's perceptual map is the truth for that person. Even though we each have different perceptual maps, they are near enough to each other for us to be able to communicate and cooperate.

● Learning – Learning is the behavioural changes that result from experience. How we learn is critical to marketing communications, because marketers want people to remember the messages and act upon them in ways which are favourable to the organization.

● Attitude formation and change – Attitudes consist of knowledge, feelings, and proposed behaviour. An attitude is a tendency to behave in a consistent manner towards a given stimulus: in other words, people tend to react the same way every time towards something about which they have an attitude. For marketers, understanding how attitudes are formed and are changed is useful in creating appropriate attitudes towards brands and products: sometimes attitudes need to be demolished and rebuilt if the brand is to continue.

Psychology is not the only behavioural science, however. It is mainly concerned with the individual, but human beings are herd animals: we operate in groups. In prehistoric times, being part of a group meant the difference between surviving and not surviving: even today, people who do not fit in with one or more groups often lead unhappy lives, and there is medical evidence to suggest that they do not live as long as other people either. The behaviour of people in groups is the province of sociology.

Sociology and anthropology

Group behaviour is crucial to human beings, and therefore is crucial to understanding what motivates people to buy specific brands (see Figure 1.10). Buying the wrong brand can be embarrassing: we are all aware of how, in our early teens, we have to have the right brand of trainers, play the right video games, see the right films and enjoy the right music to fit in with the desired group. Even adolescent rebellion is actually a drive to join a group. Again, the following topics will be covered in much greater detail in Part 3 of the book.

● Peer and reference groups – People identify groups which they would like to join, and also groups which they would prefer not to be associated with. Almost all such groups involve some type of consumption: clothing to wear, things to use

Figure 1.10 Contributions from sociology and anthropology

in the group activities, or shared consumption of group-owned items. Most of us define ourselves at least in part by the groups we belong to, whether it is our work group, our group of friends, our family group, our religious group or our group hobbies.

- **Family** – The family is probably the most important reference group because it exerts the most influence on us. Families share consumption of many items (food, housing, energy, etc.) and our upbringing also influences our behaviour in later years.

- **Class** and **culture** – The study of culture and class is part of the study of anthropology. Anthropology is a wide-ranging discipline, covering everything that makes us human: anthropologists consider archaeology as part of their discipline as well as cultural anthropology. Culture is the set of beliefs and behaviours which distinguishes one large group of people from another, and it includes such issues as religious beliefs, language, customs, class distinctions and accepted norms of behaviour. For marketers, culture is one of the driving forces of behaviour including consumption behaviour, but perhaps more importantly it is a minefield in which communications and brands can cause offence to people from other cultural backgrounds. In particular religious beliefs can create problems for marketers since people are often inflexible about religious taboos or restrictions. Cognitive anthropology has been used to study the problem solving behaviour of green consumers (Wagner-Tsukamoto and Tadajewski 2006).

- **Self-image** and **role** – The images we form of ourselves are almost entirely derived from feedback from other people. This feedback is derived in turn from the images we project as part of our role in life. In fact, we each perform many roles in our dealings with others: as friends, work colleagues, children, fathers, mothers, professionals and so forth: we judge ourselves as being good at each of these roles by the feedback of the people we deal with every day. The only way one can know if one is a good work colleague is by the feedback from fellow-workers.

  People often define themselves, at least in part, by the products they consume. Possessions become an extension of the individual – an extended self – and thus project who the person is to others (Mittal 2006). Indeed, many acts of consumption are tribal and role-supporting, even when they do not define the self (Ryan, McLoughlin and Keating 2006).

Consumer decision-making is therefore not isolated from all other human behaviour. People behave in ways which enable them to enjoy their lives, to relate to their friends and families, and to contribute to society at large. In almost all cases this behaviour is likely to involve consumption of products and services produced by other people: this is the province of consumer behaviour.

Summary

Consumer behaviour studies derive from many different academic disciplines, as well as from direct studies by marketing academics. As a field of study, it has an appeal to most of us because it is, after all, about people. For marketing practitioners, understanding the ways in which people make decisions about their purchasing behaviour is clearly of crucial importance in planning almost every aspect of managing the exchange process.

The key points from this chapter are as follows:

- The study of consumer behaviour is largely derived from other disciplines.
- Consumer behaviour is at the centre of all marketing decision-making.
- Relationships are harder to establish in business-to-consumer situations than in business-to-business situations.
- Consumer research is the starting point for studying consumer behaviour.
- Psychology is about internal thought processes: sociology is about behaviour within groups.
- Anthropology is the study of what makes us human.
- Sociology is the study of behaviour in a group context.
- Economics is the study of demand.
- Exchange always makes both parties better off.
- 'Luxury' and 'necessity' are subjective terms: they have no objective reality.

Chapter review questions

1 How might marketers use knowledge of indifference curves to affect consumer choices?

2 Would you expect salt to have an inelastic demand curve or an elastic demand curve? Why?

3 If a product has an inelastic demand curve, what does that imply for marketers?

4 If a product has an elastic demand curve what are the implications for marketers?

5 How might group behaviour affect purchasing behaviour?

6 How might consumer research inform marketing decisions?

7 Why does exchange always make both parties better off?

8 What is the importance of the concept of perception to marketers?

9 Why is learning important to marketers?

10 Why are customers more important to a firm than, say, employees?

Preview case study revisited
Just AAsk

The AA website provides in-depth information which allows drivers to find out which car would best suit their needs: it does not recommend a specific car, but it does tell prospective buyers which make, model and year of manufacture would meet their requirements in terms of price, reliability, seating capacity, insurance costs and so forth. Armed with this information, the buyer can now hit the local car dealers and find the model and make required, armed with all the necessary negotiating tools. More importantly, the website helps people to think through their decision, and choose the most suitable car for their needs.

The website has proved extremely popular with motorists, and since the service is free and is available to all drivers it has even proved popular with non-AA members. Naturally, this raises the question of why the AA should provide this service for people who are not members – in other words for those who are not existing customers? The answer is simple: it is a way of recruiting new customers to the AA fold.

The website also offers prospective buyers access to AA insurance, AA car inspections, AA car loans and of course breakdown cover. All these services are available for a fee, but members either receive the services free as part of their membership, or can obtain a discount on the service.

Facilitating the number of people who drive can only be good for a motoring organization, especially one with

the history and reputation of the AA: the cost of providing the service is very small compared with the benefits it brings, and the development of a closer relationship with motorists can only increase memberships and help to 'lock in' existing members.

Case study
The Financial Services Authority

The UK's Financial Services Authority (FSA) is the regulatory body for all financial services. It is funded entirely by the firms it controls, but it has a supervisory board which is appointed by the Government, via the Treasury. Its primary purpose is to protect consumers by regulating the market to provide fair trading in financial services.

The FSA has a wide remit – it regulates banks, brokers, credit card companies, hire purchase companies, and indeed anyone providing loans or other financial services to the public. It regulates industry advertising to ensure that it is clear and fair, it regulates financial services contracts, it lays down guidelines for the selling of financial services, and it reprimands firms who infringe the rules.

In 2003, the FSA commissioned consumer research with the aim of finding out how consumers identify their financial needs, and what their decision-making process is in finding the right financial package to meet those needs. The aim of the exercise was, in the FSA's words, to find out how consumers navigate the financial services maze, with a view to enhancing how the industry thinks about the maze itself, and to change the way the industry fulfils its responsibilities. The research was regarded:

as a contribution to the FSA's wider retail strategy, which aims to:

- Create capable and confident consumers who have access to clear, simple and understandable information on which to base financial decisions.
- Encourage well-managed and soundly capitalized firms to treat their customers fairly and offer appropriate products, and
- Deliver risk-based regulation. (FSA 2005, p. 4)

The research found that there were many possible reasons for a consumer recognising a need for financial services products. The ones identified by the research came under three headings, as follows:

1 *Personal triggers*. These are life events such as the birth of a child, redundancy, moving home and so forth.
2 *External trends*. This would include Government legislation, changes in the economic climate or financial services industry initiatives (such as the introduction of a new type of credit card or bank account).
3 *Financial traits*. These are the personal attitudes and approaches of the individual, for example the degree of risk-taking, the planning horizon, the decision-making style and the degree of interest the person has in financial planning.

These categories subdivided in each case. Under personal triggers, the researchers found that people were typically triggered by six sub-categories: family events such as marriage, divorce, children, or elderly parents; occupation events such as new job, promotion, redundancy, self-employment or retirement; health events such as long-term illness or illness of a dependent; housing events such as moving house, renting a room or downsizing; leisure events such as travel or hobbies; and windfall or loss events such as winning a lottery prize, inheritance or robbery.

None of these categories would come as a surprise to anybody involved in financial services, but what the research did do was enable the industry to focus effort on finding ways of ensuring that people know where to go for advice when faced with these triggers.

The external trends triggers were not of much use to the FSA since it has little influence over either the Government or the industry's new product development policies, but understanding how they work was thought to be useful in educating consumers to make the best use of financial advisers in general.

The main lesson the FSA obtained from the data on personal traits was that they should consider tailoring their messages to each group separately. The FSA recognizes that people may have conflicting attitudes, and may change their attitudes over time in any case, but they recognize that it is not possible to treat every consumer the same. This led to an initiative to ensure that financial advisers are aware that consumers may not be financially literate enough to make their own decisions, they may not in fact be very interested in planning their finances, and they may need much better-tailored communications than they have been getting.

Overall, the research was not exactly rocket science but it did provide the FSA (who, after all, are financial people rather than marketers) with a clear framework for decision-making as well as some ideas for educating consumers.

Case study questions

1 Why might some people not be interested in financial planning?

2 Why would someone wait for a major life event to overtake them before considering their financial position?

3 What is the role of the financial adviser in helping people to plan ahead?

4 How might the FSA pitch its advertising messages in future?

5 What should the FSA be doing to re-educate financial service providers?

SEAN POTTER/ALAMY

References

Bennett, P.D. (1995) *Dictionary of Marketing Terms* (Chicago, IL: American Marketing Association).

Blackwell, Roger D., Miniard, Paul W., and Engel, James F. (2001) *Consumer Behaviour*, 9th ed. (Mason, OH: Southwestern).

Booms, B.H., and Bitner, M.J. (1982) Marketing strategies and organizational structures for service firms. In J.H. Donnelly and W.R. George (eds) *Marketing of Services*. (Chicago, IL: American Marketing Association): 47–52.

Davies, Andrea, and Elliott, Richard (2006) The evolution of the empowered consumer. *European Journal of Marketing*, 40(9/10): 1106–21.

FSA (2005) *Consumer Needs Research: Informing Our Future Work.* (London: Financial Services Authority) (www.fsa.gov.uk/pubs/other/consumer_needs.pdf).

Marsden, David (2001) Deconstructing consumer behaviour: theory and practice. *Journal of Consumer Behaviour*, 1(1): 9–21.

McCarthy, E.J. (1960) *Basic Marketing: A Managerial Approach.* 2nd ed. (New York: Richard D. Irwin).

Mitchell, Alan S. (2002) Do you really want to understand your customer? *Journal of Consumer Behaviour*, 2(1): 71–9.

Mittal, Banwari (2006) I, me, and mine: how products become consumers' extended selves. *Journal of Consumer Behaviour*, 5 (Nov–Dec): 550–62.

Richins, Marsha (2001) Consumer behaviour as a social science. *Advances in Consumer Research*, 28(1): 1 5.

Ryan, Conor, McLoughlin, Damien, and Keating, Andrew (2006) Tribespotting: a semiotic analysis of the role of consumption in the tribes of Trainspotting. *Journal of Consumer Behaviour*, 5 (Sept–Oct): 431–41.

Shaw, Deirdre, Newholme, Terry, and Dickson, Roger (2006) Consumption as voting: an exploration of consumer empowerment. *European Journal of Marketing*, 40(9/10): 1049–67.

Wagner-Tsukamoto, Sigmund, and Tadajewski, Mark (2006) Cognitive anthropology and the problem-solving behaviour of green consumers. *Journal of Consumer Behaviour*, 5 (May–Jun): 235–44.

Part two
Psychological issues in consumer behaviour

This section looks at the contribution made by psychologists to our understanding of consumer behaviour. Psychology is (basically) the study of how people think, but the discipline also considers emotions and their effect on people's decision-making processes.

Chapter 2 looks at the fundamental reasons which underlie behaviour: the basic motives, drives and emotional needs which power our actions. Motivational models are discussed, along with the building blocks of motivation – drive and hedonism.

Chapter 3 is about the ways in which motives (which are often largely emotionally based) are translated by rational thought into goals. Problems with goal setting, issues of risk and uncertainty, ways in which goals might have to be revised and the reasons for doing so, and what happens when goals are not reached are also discussed.

Chapter 4 outlines the effect on consumer behaviour of one of the most fundamental concepts in psychology: personality. Our personality is what makes us who we are, so it is scarcely surprising that it has a profound effect on our purchasing and consumption behaviour. Some people even define their personalities by what they consume, whether (for example) as supporters of a particular sports team or as owners of a particular motorcycle. The chapter therefore also considers self-concept, or how we see ourselves.

Chapter 5 is about the way in which we process information. Perception is a key issue for marketers, because it affects the ways in which people process marketing communications. It also affects the ways in which brands are rated against competing brands, and the ways in which information is linked to existing knowledge – a factor of crucial importance in designing targeted campaigns.

Chapter 6 looks at learning. This goes beyond formal classroom-style learning to cover all the ways in which people retain information. Every type of learning from classical conditioning (which assumes little or no thought or choice) to cognitive learning (which assumes an active participation in the process) is covered. From a marketing viewpoint, an understanding of how people remember facts about products is certainly very useful, probably crucial in many marketing scenarios.

Chapter 7 considers attitudes and their formation. Attitudes are learned – we are not born with them, and part of the fun of being human is that we all have different attitudes to things. Attitude has a number of dimensions, and is by no means a simple concept: it also has a profound effect on people's choice behaviour.

Chapter 8 is about changing people's attitudes. It outlines ways in which attitudes can be measured, techniques for destablising existing attitudes, and strategies for shifting attitudes. The chapter also looks at involvement, or the ways in which people fall in love with products.

Chapter 2
Drive, motivation and hedonism

Learning objectives After reading this chapter, you should be able to:

1. explain the role of the subconscious in motivation

2. understand the difference between needs and wants

3. explain how drives are generated

4. explain the role of needs and wants in marketing

5. explain the relationship between motivation and behaviour

6. critique the concept of hierarchy of need

7. explain how motivations change with changes in wealth

8. explain the role of hedonism in purchasing behaviour

Introduction

Dissatisfaction is the beginning of all behaviour. If we were not dissatisfied, we would simply stick with what we have – there would be no need to change what we do. The gap between where we are now and where we want to be is what drives us to make changes in our lives, and of course this is what makes us change the products we own and the services we consume.

Understanding what motivates people has clear implications for marketers. If we know what drives people to buy particular products and services we are in a much better position to ensure that our products have the features and benefits that people want. If we understand how the pressure to buy develops, we can communicate better with people to show how we can meet their needs (before the need actually arises, in some cases). If we know how people rank their needs, we know when they are likely to be ready to buy our products. Of course, marketing practitioners do not yet have all the answers, so we are a long way from being able to predict consumption behaviour with anything like real accuracy.

Sometimes our need for excitement and pleasure overrides our need for security and survival.

Much of what drives us as individuals is the desire for pleasure. In the wealthier countries of the world, our basic survival needs have long been taken care of. We no longer need to eat in order to survive, for example: we eat more than enough simply for pleasure, so that few of us have ever experienced real hunger. The same applies to our housing, our clothing, our heating, and so forth. We therefore look to satisfy our emotional, aesthetic needs – in other words, we look for things which are pleasurable or fun.

This chapter examines the forces which drive behaviour. Beginning with drive (the basis of all motivation) the chapter goes on to look at different studies of motivation, and the role of pleasure-seeking in consumer behaviour.

Drive

Drive is the force that makes a person respond to a need. It is an internal stimulus caused by a gap between someone's actual state and their desired state. In other words, drive is created when the position someone is in at that moment differs from the position they would

Preview case study
Chocolate

At the height of the Mayan empire, in Central America, chocolate was regarded as an aphrodisiac. The Aztecs only gave it to warriors, nobility and priests because it was supposed to confer wisdom and vitality. It was so valuable that 100 cacao beans were enough to buy a slave.

Chocolate has a mild euphoric effect, somewhat like marijuana, and it has been said that it replicates the same feelings one has when one is in love. It also contains polyphenols, which are thought to protect against heart disease, and it is interesting to note that several supercentenarians (people who live beyond 100) were confirmed chocoholics. Jeanne Calment (1875–1997), for example, ate a kilo of chocolate a week until her doctor advised her to give up sweets when she was aged 119. She died three years later, aged 122.

When the first Aztec crushed the first cacao pod and extracted the dark-brown, fatty substance within, one could imagine an advertising man standing by ready to weave fantasies about chocolate. Chocolate is, above all, the stuff of fantasy: it has virtually nothing to recommend it in terms of healthy eating since it is composed almost entirely of sugar and fat, it has no practical purpose in that it does not make you stronger, fitter, faster or more beautiful, and it is not even particularly cheap, so all that is left is the flavour and the euphoria.

The pioneers of chocolate technology have become household names – the man who found out how to make solid chocolate was the Swiss chemist Rudolph Lindt; milk chocolate was invented by Henri Nestlé; Fry invented the first commercial chocolate bar; Frank Mars invented the first chocolate-covered snack, the Milky Way (his son Forrest invented the Mars bar). In the early years, chocolate manufacture and dealing was a license to print money, and even today 70 per cent of the profit from the chocolate trade remains in wealthy Western countries. Of the top 20 chocolate-consuming countries, 16 are European, and 80 per cent of the world trade is controlled by just six companies.

Chocolate's Latin name (*Theobroma cacao*) means 'food of the gods'. This is bound to make it a popular choice. Chocolate sales worldwide amount to US$50 billion per annum, yet still the majority of the world's population have never tasted chocolate. For the rest of us, chocolate pervades our lives – every holiday, feast or celebration involves chocolate in some way (Valentine's Day sees a huge upsurge in sales, and what would Easter be without chocolate eggs?)

So what makes people buy chocolate? Why is it that chocolate is predominantly consumed by women? (Some studies report that more than half of all women prefer chocolate to sex – whether this is a comment about chocolate or about men is open for debate.) Why is it that the world's most famous chocolate manufacturing countries (Switzerland and Belgium) are not those which actually grow the stuff themselves?

© iStockphoto.com

like to be in. A typical example would be someone becoming thirsty. The actual state is 'thirsty'; the desired state is 'not thirsty'; so a drive to go for something to drink is created. Other more subtle drives are apparent in human beings, of course: if the actual state is 'not accepted by your work colleagues' and the desired state is 'to be accepted by work colleagues' the drive might be even more powerful than that of thirst.

The greater the gap between the actual state and the desired state, the greater the drive to do something about it (see Figure 2.1). Once the gap between actual and desired states has closed, the drive disappears: our thirsty person, having had a drink, now no longer feels any pressure to look for a drink. The energy formerly devoted to finding something to drink can now be channelled elsewhere. In some cases, achieving the desired state may lead the individual to raise his or her sights and aim for something even better. For example,

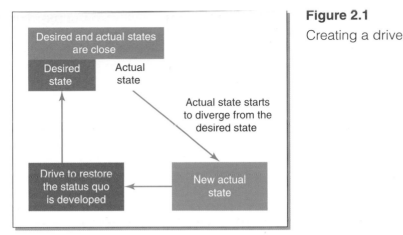

Figure 2.1
Creating a drive

someone who has saved for years to buy a BMW may finally buy the car, but immediately start saving for an even more expensive car.

Marketers cannot usually do very much about the actual state. We cannot make somebody thirsty or hungry, or remove their possessions: what we can sometimes do is encourage people to revise their desired state; in other words, encourage people to aspire to something new. Most of the effort marketers put into generating drives is directed at changing the desired state – encouraging people to feel that they deserve something better than whatever they currently possess. Marketers can also remind people about their actual or desired states in order to encourage them to move a purchasing decision forward.

If the drive state is at a high level (i.e. the gap between the actual and desired states is large) the individual is more open to the idea of trying a new way of satisfying the need. This is fairly obvious: if a thirsty person finds that his or her favourite brand of soft drink is out of stock at the corner shop, there are two choices available. Either the person can buy a different brand, or he or she can go to a different shop. If the person is not feeling especially thirsty, he or she might be prepared to make the trip to the next shop, but if the thirst is very strong the individual will be much more likely to buy the new brand. Most people are familiar with the problem of food shopping when hungry – most of us tend to overbuy when we are in that position because our drive level is high.

If the drive state is at a low level, a reminder might stimulate the individual to take action. For example, it is common to see signs saying 'Teas, Coffees, Sandwiches, Burgers 150 Yards' when driving. These signs are placed at the right distance from the vendor so that passing drivers have time to be reminded that they are growing hungry or thirsty before they pass the vendor.

Working up a thirst always makes a drink more enjoyable.

The owner of the burger van is unlikely to have studied consumer behaviour or the psychology of drive, but will have found out by trial and error that the sign needs to be 150 yards (or 250, or 350) away from the van in order to give drivers enough time to think, discuss with a passenger and pull over safely. Reminding people that they may have a need is called 'activating the need'. Although the motorist is not actively looking for a cup of coffee or a snack, the sign acts as a reminder that a cup of coffee is enjoyable, and helps to strengthen a low-intensity drive by moving the desired state further from the actual state. Motorists whose drive state is at zero (perhaps because they just had lunch) will simply drive straight past.

Allowing the drive to become stronger can make the consumption experience more enjoyable. Delayed gratification increases the pleasure of satisfying the need – although it is not always the case that this is worth the wait (Nowlis, Mandel and Brown 2004). Most of us enjoy a meal much more if we are really hungry, and even saving up for a special treat increases the pleasure when the goal is finally attained. Each of us has a level at which the drive provides a pleasant stimulus without being uncomfortable or threatening: this is

called the 'optimum stimulation level' or OSL. If the drive goes above the OSL, the individual will seek to make an immediate adjustment by satisfying the need. If stimulation falls below the OSL, the individual is likely to allow the drive to strengthen before acting on it. In fact people often enjoy the anticipation more than they do the actual consumption (Ragunathan and Mukherji 2003).

Marketers are constantly telling us about how customer-orientated they are. To hear most of them talk, you would think they are engaged in some kind of charity work – meeting the customers' needs, listening to the customers, helping consumers achieve a lifestyle, and so forth.

So what's all this about 'activating' a need? Either the need is there or it isn't – and if it isn't, should we really be trying our best to put it there? Should we be messing around with people's drive states, trying to raise them and make them dissatisfied with life? In short, are we in the business of creating a need, then (just by chance) happening to have the solution to hand?

OSL is subjective, that is to say it varies from one individual to another. Research has shown that people with high OSLs like novelty and risk taking, whereas those with low OSLs prefer the tried and tested. People with high OSLs also tend to be younger (Raju 1980).

Drive acts as the basic component for motivation: motivation is drive directed at a specific objective. If we consider drive as a general feeling that things are not as they should be, we can see that motivation is a drive which has crystallized into a definite decision to do something about the problem. Marketers are able to help people (or direct people) towards specific ways of satisfying the drive by giving them a specific solution which they might be motivated to adopt.

Motivation

Motives can be classified according to the list shown in Table 2.1. Although it is difficult to separate out people's motivations for making a particular purchase, emotional and dormant motives often take precedence over rational and conscious motives.

Motives should be distinguished from instincts, which are automatic responses to external stimuli. A motive is simply a reason for carrying out a particular behaviour: instincts are pre-programmed responses which are inborn in the individual, and are involuntary. Although behaviour may result from an instinctive source (for example, ducking when a helicopter appears to fly out of a cinema screen), virtually all consumer behaviour is non-instinctive, or volitional.

Figure 2.2 shows the dimensions of motives. Motives can be classified across three dimensions, with the rational/conscious/primary ends relating to each other, as do the dormant/emotional/secondary ends. Any given motivation can be placed within the three-dimensional space represented by the diagram.

There have been many psychological studies of motivation, and several which have focused on consumer behaviour issues. **Needs** are the basis of all motivation, so it may be worth remembering that needs are a perceived lack of something, whereas **wants** are specific satisfiers. In order for someone to recognize a need, the individual not only should be without something, but should also perceive this as something which would make life more pleasant or convenient. Unless the individual understands how the proposed product will make a positive difference to his or her lifestyle, the product will not be perceived as filling a need and the individual will not want it.

There have been many attempts on the part of psychologists to develop lists of needs. Some of these lists run into the dozens: Murray (1938) listed 20 separate need categories, for example. These are as follows: succourance, nurturance, sentience, deference,

Table 2.1 Classification of consumer motives

Primary motives	The reasons that lead to the purchase of a product class. For example, an individual might look for a new car to replace one which is becoming old and unreliable.
Secondary motives	These are the reasons behind buying a particular brand. Our prospective car buyer might have reasons for buying a Toyota rather than a Ford, or a Ford rather than a BMW.
Rational motives	These motives are based on reasoning, or a logical assessment of the person's current situation. The car purchaser may need a car which will carry four children and a large amount of camping equipment, for example.
Emotional motives	Motives having to do with feelings about the brand. Sometimes emotions get the better of us – our prospective car buyer may end up with a sports car, despite having four children and a tent to accommodate!
Conscious motives	These are the motives of which we are aware. Because our car buyer knows he needs a new car, this element of his motivation is conscious.
Dormant motives	These motives operate below the conscious level. The car buyer's desire to buy a sports car may be linked to his approaching middle age, but he may not be aware of this.

abasement, defendence, infavoidance, harm avoidance, achievement, counteraction, dominance, aggression, affiliation, autonomy, order, rejection, sex, understanding, exhibition and play. Murray developed this list from his extensive clinical experience rather than from a programme of organized research, so much of the evidence for the list is anecdotal.

Virtually all these needs have marketing implications. The need for rejection is used by brand owners when the exhort consumers to reject own-label products, and the need for nurturance is emphasised in advertisements for cold cures and soup. The need for sentience is appealed to by cable stations such as Discovery Channel and History Channel. Murray's list is long, but probably not definitive – there are probably many other needs which are not included in the list. Also, some needs on the list conflict with each other, for example dominance and deference.

Because human beings are complex creatures with strong social bonds, we tend to have a wider range of needs than animals, and we also have many needs which go beyond mere

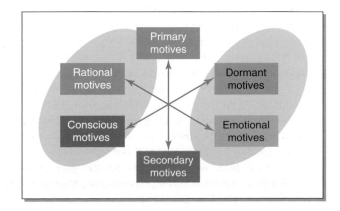

Figure 2.2

Dimensions of motives

Perceiving a need
The Yamana tribe

Tierra del Fuego lies at the southernmost tip of South America. It is buffeted by gales from the Antarctic, and is so far south that much of the land is covered in snow throughout the harsh winters. It is inhabited largely by penguins, and by a small number of hardy farmers who use the short summers to grow their crops, then batten down the hatches to survive the winter.

The Yamana tribe inhabited this harsh country for thousands of years, but lacked something that most cold-country people discovered very early on: clothes. The Yamana never invented clothing, apart from tiny loincloths and a few strips of cloth worn for decorative purposes. They spent their days canoeing in the icy waters, hunting penguins (which formed a large part of their diet) and fishing. They had, however, invented fire, so when the weather got really bad they would cluster round large bonfires to keep warm. It was the light of these fires that caused the early European explorers to call the country Land of Fire – Tierra del Fuego.

There is some evidence that the Yamana underwent a biological adaptation to the conditions. European explorers (including Captain Cook) reported that Yamana tribes people would often be sweating in conditions which the Europeans found cold even when fully dressed in winter clothing. Even so, following on from contact with Europeans the Yamana began to wear clothes, and within a relatively short period of time they went the way of most aborigines – disease, deliberate murder by settlers and the disappearance of the penguins on which they depended for their diet combined to kill them.

For thousands of years the Yamana had felt no need whatsoever for clothes. Standing round their fires cooking penguins in the winter they had perfectly comfortable and happy conditions for living: although this may seem strange to us, their early contacts with Europeans must have seemed even stranger to them. Once the concept of clothing was explained, they suddenly recognised the need for clothing, and when the last pure-blooded Yamana died in the late 1990s this people were certainly fully clothed and indistinguishable from any other Argentineans. Their traditional way of life, however, represents an extreme example of not recognizing something as a need until a solution is presented.

survival: some commentators divide needs into primary needs, which are concerned with biological functions and survival, and secondary needs, which are concerned with everything else. In some cases, researchers have concentrated heavily on the idea that most needs are biologically determined. Internal genetic stimuli are driven by homeostasis, which is the tendency for any living entity to try to maintain a state of equilibrium: in the natural world, change is death. The drives which maintain homeostasis are involuntary, as is the behaviour which results from it. If one becomes too hot, for example, one begins sweating, and if one becomes too cold one develops goose pimples and one may even begin shivering. A sudden shock will result in adrenaline entering the bloodstream, which may be exciting (a positive outcome which is often generated by white-knuckle rides at theme parks) or may be merely frightening (a negative outcome which may be generated by a near-accident or a threatening situation such as a street robbery).

Hunger and thirst are obviously biologically generated, but most eating and drinking happens as a result of social or aesthetic demands. Socially motivated eating might include dinner parties, meeting friends for a meal, business lunches, and picnics. Curiosity is often supposed to be socially generated, and there is certainly evidence that exploration of the

Marketing in practice
Sky TV

Sky TV, as the name suggests, had its beginnings in the satellite TV business. In 1989 Sky Television began broadcasting via the Astra satellite direct to homes in the UK and Western Europe: at that time, viewers needed a satellite dish mounted on their houses to receive the signal. The following year, Sky merged with rival British Satellite Broadcasting (BSB) to form BSkyB. Currently the company offers over 140 channels of television.

So who needs 140 channels of TV? Answer: nobody. However, a large number of people have common interests in packages selected from the 140 channels. Sky offers a Children's Mix, which includes channels such as Nickelodeon, Boomerang and Jetix; it offers a Knowledge Mix, which includes Discovery, National Geographic and Animal Planet; a News and Events Mix, including Sky News Eurosport, and Bloomberg. Each mix includes many other channels, and there is even a Variety Mix which has an across-the-board selection.

Subscribers can also pay for premium channels such as movies and major sports channels. Although television stations appear to be meeting a need solely for entertainment, Sky offers solutions for a wide variety of subdivisions of need.

world has a connection with particular countries and cultures, but we also know that some curiosity is biological. Most carnivorous animals display an innate tendency to explore and investigate their environment: cats, dogs and humans all display this behaviour, and bears in zoos are generally happier if their food is hidden from them so that they have to explore and find it.

The best-known biological motivator is, of course, sex. Marketers have used mild sexual imagery in advertising throughout its history, and at various times there have been advertisements which have overstepped the boundaries of good taste and have been attacked

Talking point

Humans are born with a fear of falling, yet we often go to theme parks and fun fairs, and even go bungee jumping. Falling off a bridge with lengths of elastic round your ankles might be thrilling, but isn't it also pretty stupid? And if we like to be thrilled by such things, why isn't it fun if someone pushes you off a cliff?

Sometimes, of course, it *is* fun. If your friend playfully pushes you into a swimming pool, the correct response is to laugh – but if a complete stranger did it, or an aggressive bully, you'd probably call the police.

So where do we draw the line? How do we decide what is fun and what is frightening? Why do we put our lives in danger (threatening our survival needs) just for esteem or self-actualization needs?

Going for a drink with friends – the alcohol stimulates conversation by reducing inhibitions.

or withdrawn. There is certainly evidence that Valentine's Day gift-giving is associated with power relationships between the genders (Rugimbana *et al.* 2003).

The arousal theory of motivation (Zuckerman 2000) proposes that people need to be aroused if they are to become motivated. People seek to maintain an optimum level of arousal: too little, and they become bored, too much and they become stressed. Zuckerman developed a 'hierarchy' of stimulation, as follows:

1 Thrills, adventure-seeking, risk taking through extreme sports, or adventure travel. The highest level of arousal.

2 Experience-seeking through travel, walking, the arts, books. The second highest level.

3 **Disinhibition** (removing the internal inhibitors which control behaviour). Social stimulation, parties, drinking alcohol, etc.

4 Boredom. The need to change things around, perhaps to buy new products, try new things, etc.

At the lower end of the hierarchy, boredom, the individual has a risk-free but also stimulation-free existence: at the highest level, thrill-seeking, the individual has an exciting but dangerous life. Most people establish a balance between the quiet life and the stimulating life, at some point on the continuum which is specific to themselves.

Probably the best-known motivation theory is Maslow's hierarchy of needs (Maslow 1954), which sought to show that people are motivated to fulfil different needs in a specific order, beginning with survival needs (as the most pressing needs to satisfy) and ending with **self-actualization** needs (the need to fulfil a long-held ambition, or to act independently of the pressures and opinions of other people, or to act for action's sake). The reasoning behind the model is that needs cannot always be met all at once. Sometimes one need must be fulfilled at the expense of another, creating motivational conflict.

At the lowest level of the hierarchy, survival needs, marketers offer houses, clothes and food. However, in most cases these are not sold as survival items – more commonly the marketing communications emphasize other aspects of the products such as their appearance, flavour or location. Relatively few products are offered purely on the basis of survival, and most of these are in the category of safety equipment for sports such as aviation or boating.

At the security level, people buy insurance policies, savings plans, burglar alarms, and breakdown memberships. In recent years, we have developed new safety needs: we need to secure our computers against fraudsters and malicious viruses. This has led to the development of whole new industries, developing software to combat such dangers. People also

Figure 2.3

Zuckerman's hierarchy of stimulation

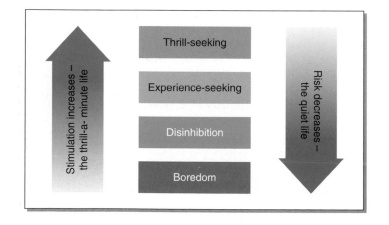

spend money safeguarding their health, hence the huge sales of products designed to help people lose weight or give up smoking. The popularity of such products in the period immediately following the New Year celebrations indicates the degree to which people believe they should safeguard their health (but not yet). Survival needs might also be satisfied through health-care products or even slimming products.

At the belonging level people buy a wide range of products: fashion clothing, club memberships, sports equipment, and so forth. In order to be accepted at the golf club, members not only need to pay their membership fees, green fees and so forth, they also need to buy the right set of clubs, the right clothing and the right magazines. Belonging needs are therefore of considerable interest.

Esteem needs include anything which someone buys as a status symbol (see Chapter 10). Products which make a statement about oneself include fashion; cars; expensive hobbies such as flying; holidays and houses. Almost any product might have an esteem value in the right quarters, and there are even circumstances in which a lack of consumption generates esteem – backpackers may have more respect for someone who has managed to cross Asia for less money than anyone else, for example. Esteem needs may also play a part in seemingly altruistic behaviour – people who buy the *Big Issue* (the UK magazine devoted to helping homeless people) do so not so much for the actual magazine content, but because there is a dimension of helping others in the purchase (Hibbert, Hogg and Quinn 2005). This may be coupled to the fact that the magazine is a visible purchase, whereas a contribution to a charity would not be.

Aesthetic needs can be met in many ways. In the main, such needs are traditionally associated with the arts: paintings, sculptures, books, theatre, film and music being the main ways aesthetic needs have been met. However, a hiking holiday in an area of outstanding natural beauty is also a way of meeting aesthetic needs, as is a microlight aircraft or a yacht.

At the self-actualization level, needs might be fulfilled in a great many ways. In some cases self-actualization needs are met by reducing consumption, for example if the individual decides that a 'green' lifestyle should be adopted. Someone who has worked in a city for many years might, for example, buy a smallholding in the country and grow his or her own food, use solar power for electricity and run a wood-burning stove for heat.

Maslow's hierarchy (see Figure 2.4) has been widely criticised for being too simplistic, and for ignoring the many exceptions which can easily be seen in everyday life. For example, an artist starving in garret is clearly placing aesthetic or self-actualization needs ahead of survival needs, and someone who gives up a good career in order to work with poor people in the Third World is giving up security in favour of esteem needs or self-actualization needs. Such anomalies are commonplace. Another criticism of the hierarchy is that it is largely irrelevant to the vast majority of people in the wealthy countries of Europe and North

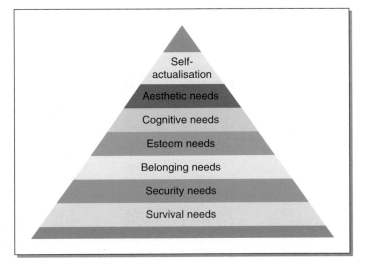

Figure 2.4
Maslow's hierarchy of needs

America because they already have their survival and security needs taken care of, and indeed many of them are operating at the self-actualization level already (McNulty 1985).

A further criticism is that an individual may move to different parts of the hierarchy even within a single day: for example being primarily concerned with esteem needs during the working day, with aesthetic needs when enjoying an evening meal at a good restaurant, and with belonging needs when meeting friends for a drink afterwards.

These criticisms notwithstanding, Maslow's model is widely taught and widely referred to: there is little doubt that the needs themselves exist and can be categorized in this way, but whether they truly operate as a hierarchy is open to question. There may be evidence that the hierarchy operates for large groups of people, so that there will be a prevailing social paradigm in which some needs are brought to the forefront. Research by McNulty (1985) showed that an increasing number of people in the UK were operating at the self-actualization level, presumably as a result of rising living standards. In the intervening 20 years, it would appear to the casual observer that this trend has not reversed, and has (if anything) accelerated. Another use of the Maslow hierarchy has been the VALS model (Mitchell 1983), which describes nine different lifestyles, as shown in Figure 2.5.

The model supposes that people at the lower levels (which correspond with Maslow's survival and security needs) are controlled by their basic needs for food, shelter and a measure of security. After these very basic needs have been met, there is a divergence: some people become inner-directed (driven by internal motives) while others become outer-directed (motivated by the opinions of others). Inner-directed people may become selfish and uncaring of other people's well-being, they may become interested in new experiences or they may fulfil a burning ambition to change the world for the better despite opposition. Outer-directed people may seek to copy other people whom they regard as successful or may seek to impress other people by achieving or by conspicuous consumption. Finally, Mitchell postulates that people may adopt an integrated position, where concern and respect for others is combined with knowledge of their own needs and desires.

Mitchell's model has been used for market segmentation purposes, and the lifestyle types have been identified both in the United States and in Europe. As wealth increases, more people operate at the higher levels: we might reasonably expect that, as countries

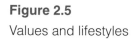

Figure 2.5

Values and lifestyles

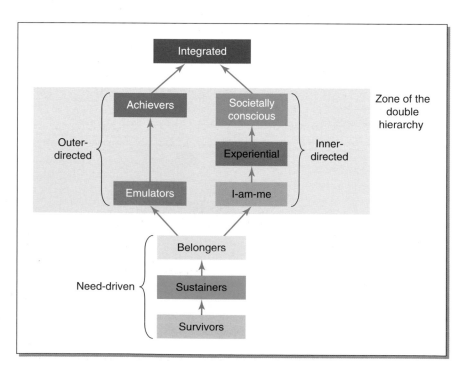

become wealthier, levels of consumption increase but so do levels of social concern, and levels of crime increase as more people become inner-directed. This may account for levels of crime committed by people who are already wealthy.

Talking point

Mitchell's categorizations are all very well for segmentation, but what happens when we are dealing with people at the self-actualization level? By definition, these people might do *anything*! They are professional individualists.

Also, how clear are the boundaries? To say that someone is outer-directed means that they care about the opinions of other people – but do they care about the opinions of everyone else or just a few people? Are they attracted to or repelled by the opinions of the other people in question?

Finally, if someone acts rebelliously, is this because they don't care what other people think – or because they care very deeply? Being a rebel is a statement made to impress other people, is it not?

The basic problem here is that people consistently refuse to be categorized!

An alternative approach to considering motivation was that advanced by Herzberg (1966). Herzberg was a medical researcher who developed the idea that some factors in life are motivational, while others are simply expected as a matter of course: the absence of these factors would be demotivating, but more of the same would not be motivational. Herzberg called the first group of factors 'motivators', and the second group '**hygiene factors**' (he was a medical researcher, remember). The hygiene factors needed to be present in order to prevent the 'disease' of demotivation. Herzberg's findings were considered revolutionary at the time of their publication because he claimed that salary is not a motivator – people expect a fair rate of pay for the work they are expected to do, so it is a hygiene factor, and only affects motivation if it is seen to be unfair in some way. For marketers, Herzberg's work is interesting in that it explains product **differentiation**. For example, anyone buying a car expects that it will have wheels, an engine, an enclosed space to sit in and space for luggage. Nowadays, people would expect it to have a radio and probably a CD player as well. These are hygiene factors, the basic core product features which any car would have. Lack of any of these would demotivate the customer. To generate motivation to buy, though, the vehicle manufacturer would need to add features as motivators: air conditioning, smarter upholstery, in-car refrigerator etc.

Herzberg's theories are also applied to sales force management, which is outside the scope of this book. As a way of categorizing needs, Herzberg's theory is undoubtedly useful, but part of the problem in applying the theory is that people have differing views on what should be a hygiene factor. Once again, it is difficult to make generalizations about people because we all have different priorities.

In Figure 2.6, the motivation line rises somewhat as the individual recognizes that the hygiene factors are improving, but this is really a reduction in demotivation. Motivation as

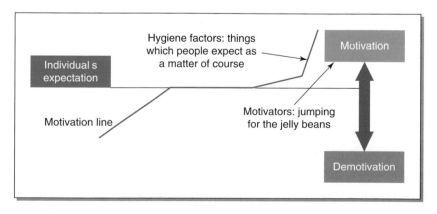

Figure 2.6

Dual-factor theory

Marketing in practice
Differentiation

The history of the automobile has been one of continuous adaptation, additional features and added inducements to buy. The basic need is for transportation: ever since the first human being jumped on the back of a horse we have wanted to travel further, faster and more comfortably, and although the earliest cars were less reliable (and sometimes slower) than horses, they at least had the convenience of starting fairly quickly (without the need for saddling and bridling) and of going pretty much where the driver wanted them to go rather than setting off into a field with the other horses.

Starting with Daimler and Benz's first practical automobile in 1885, manufacturers have added optional extras on a regular basis ever since. For example, in 1890 Canadian Thomas Ahearn invented the car heater. In 1901 disc brakes were added (invented by Lanchester). In 1911 Charles Kettering invented the starter motor, which eliminated the need for hand cranking the engine to start it (Kettering also invented Freon, the gas which has been identified as a major cause of holes in the ozone layer). In 1929, Paul Galvin invented the car radio, although it had to be bought as an optional extra: car manufacturers did not fit radios as standard until the 1970s. Galvin called his new radio 'the Motorola'. Daimler introduced electric windows in 1948, and in 1966 British engineers developed electronic fuel injection.

Not all the inventors were men, incidentally. Mary Anderson invented windscreen wipers (hand-operated at first), and Helen Blair Bartlett, a geologist, invented alumina ceramic insulators for sparkplugs in 1930.

Why all this innovation? Simple. Any car manufacturer could meet the basic hygiene factor of transportation. In order to motivate people to buy a specific model, manufacturers had to add extras, making the car more comfortable, safer, more reliable or more fun than the competitors' vehicles. Every so often someone will go back to basics and produce a car with 'no frills' for a low price, but the optional extras soon cease to be optional because price is not a good motivator – it is a hygiene factor!

such does not start until the motivators begin to arrive, but even so there is no sharp rise until the motivators go beyond expectations. At this point, further increases in hygiene factors have no real effect.

A third approach to analysing motivation is Vroom's expectancy theory (Vroom 1999). Vroom suggested that motivation is the result of rational calculations made by individuals, taking into account the value of the reward itself, the expected likelihood of being able to obtain the reward, and the effort needed to achieve the reward. The trade-offs between these factors are the subject of the calculation, and if the reward is not adequate compared to the effort needed to win it, the individual will simply not bother to try for it. Equally, if the likelihood of gaining the reward is perceived as being small, the individual will not be motivated to try. Vroom's theory has much to offer – it is more comprehensive in its approach than other theories, and it takes much greater account of individual differences than do either Maslow's or Herzberg's models. As we saw already, individuals may believe that aesthetics needs are more important than survival needs, and (in terms of Herzberg) individuals may have different ideas of what constitute motivators and hygiene factors.

An aspect of motivation that is not considered in Vroom's model is the idea of pain avoidance. Although needs are the basis of all motivation, there is a difference between the need to avoid bad consequences and the need to acquire a benefit. In most cases, someone who wishes to obtain a positive benefit from a purchase has only one way to obtain the benefits, whereas there are many ways to avoid a negative outcome. This was demonstrated by Skinner in his famous experiments with rats, in which rats were taught to push buttons in complex sequences in order to obtain food and avoid electric shocks: the rats became very inventive in the ways they avoided the shocks, but were unable to find any other way to obtain food (Skinner 1953). Human beings are, of course, not rats: we are probably better able to understand the longer-term consequences of our behaviour than a rat would be, so we may be more susceptible to pain-avoidance messages. On the other hand, we may be even more inventive in avoiding the pain.

For example, **cautionary-tale** advertising in which the negative consequences of an action are shown may result in someone behaving in the desired manner, or it may (and perhaps is more likely to) result in the individual avoiding the advertisement. This may be part of the reason why Government campaigns against smoking or drinking often fail – shocking people by telling them about the diseases their habit might cause simply results in people not reading the warnings.

One way in which marketers can use pain avoidance in motivating consumers is by modelling. This is a process whereby people are shown the negative consequences of a given action through an actor who demonstrates the behaviour and suffers the consequences. For example, an advertisement might show a commuter who has been prosecuted for fare dodging, complete with a detailed account of the consequences of the action ('It was the embarrassment of having to stand up in court and admit fiddling a £2 fare. And I lost my job, because I now have a criminal conviction.') Another example might be a housewife who 'Can't shift those greasy stains'. In each case the consumer is invited to see the potential negative consequences of fiddling the fare or using the wrong washing powder. Modelling can also be used for positive reinforcement, of course (see Table 2.2).

Models should be as similar as possible to the target audience, but at the same time need to be seen as attractive: this may appear to be a contradiction in some cases, but models show us ourselves as we wish we were, rather than as we actually are.

For human beings, and especially human beings living in the wealthier countries of the world, most physical needs have been met long ago. We are therefore driven much more by social, aesthetic or psychological needs than by physical needs. This manifests itself most clearly in our eating habits. We eat for pleasure (the flavour and texture of the food) for social purposes (going for a meal with friends, sharing a snack, going to a dinner party), and even as a means of self-expression (cooking a special meal for friends or family). These needs sometimes override our need to live a healthy lifestyle: we become obese and

Table 2.2 Using modelling for positive reinforcement

Modelling employed	*Desired response*
Instructor, expert, salesperson using the product (in an advertisement or at the point of purchase)	Use product in the correct, technically competent way
Models in advertisements asking questions at the point of purchase	Ask questions at the point of purchase that highlight product advantages
Models in advertisements receiving positive reinforcement or punishment for performing undesired behaviours	Extinction or decrease of undesired behaviours
Individual (or group) similar to the target audience using the product in a novel, enjoyable way	Use the product in new ways

Source: Walter R. Nord and J. Paul Peter (1980) A behaviour modification perspective on marketing, *Journal of Marketing*, 44 (spring): 36–47.

develop hardening of the arteries, bad teeth and many other diseases caused by eating the wrong things.

When needs conflict, motivational conflict occurs (Figure 2.7). This can take any one of three basic forms, as follows:

1 Approach–approach conflict. This happens when the individual is faced with two or more desirable alternatives. For example, the person might have been invited to a party on a weekend when his or her football team is playing an away match 300 miles away. Approach–approach conflicts are common, since most people have limited financial resources and often have to choose between spending money on one item, or spending it on a different item.

2 Avoidance–avoidance conflict. This occurs when the individual is faced with two or more equally unappealing choices. For example, someone might be faced with the choice of either buying new shoes to replace an old, comfortable pair, or continuing to wear the old pair despite the fact they are now letting in water and coming apart at the seams.

3 Approach–avoidance conflict. This occurs when the course of action has both positive and negative consequences. For example, some drugs have dangerous side-effects. Most purchases have an element of approach–avoidance conflict since they involve spending money or giving up something else: many purchases of new products involve a switching cost, i.e. the effort and sometimes cash expenditure involved in moving from the old product to the new one. Anyone who has bought a new DVD player to replace their old VCR knows about switching costs.

In many cases, the situation is far more complex than a simple dichotomy. This is because we are usually faced with several possible courses of action, each of which has both positive and negative consequences. If the motivational conflict is to be resolved, the individual needs to prioritize his or her needs. This is largely a matter for the individual concerned: even though Maslow tried to produce a general model for this, we have already seen that the model is far from perfect.

The intensity of the motivation is sometimes strong enough to override all other considerations, whereas at other times it may be much weaker. Sometimes motivational intensity is high due to a high level of drive (a 13-year-old who is being teased at school for wearing the wrong kind of trainers will be highly motivated to obtain the right kind, for example), and sometimes motivational intensity is high due to personal involvement with the product category. Involvement means that the individual places a high importance on having exactly the right product: for example, a pilot would place great importance on obtaining exactly the right spares, fuel and oil for the aircraft, since this affects the safety of the plane (and, of course, the pilot). Similarly, a musician might be very concerned to

Figure 2.7

Motivation conflict

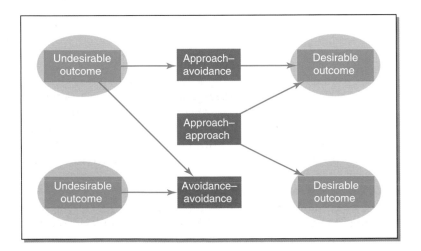

obtain the right instrument, a film star would be concerned to wear the right clothes, and so forth. Each of us has at least some products with which we are highly involved.

From the viewpoint of marketing, generating involvement is clearly crucial to establishing loyal customers. The greater the involvement, the greater the degree to which consumers make an effort to satisfy the need, and the greater the propensity to remain loyal in future. In some cases firms are able to run loyalty programmes to keep customers involved; supermarket loyalty cards and airline frequent flyer programmes are the usual examples. In other cases involvement is generated by the way the products are promoted, or by celebrity endorsement. There is more on involvement in Chapter 14.

Motivations can be divided into positive and negative. People may act to obtain a reward, or may act to avoid an unwanted outcome. For example, someone may buy aspirin in order to treat a headache (obtain a positive outcome) or to take one aspirin per day to prevent a heart attack (negative motivation). Other commentators divide motivation into internal motivations, which are those originating inside the individual, and external motivations, which are those resulting from an external stimulus or reward. An internal motivation may arise from a self-actualization need (such as the desire to learn to fly), whereas an external motivation might arise from social needs or physical needs (such as a need to be accepted by a new group of people or to move to a larger house).

Alternatively, motives might be divided into rational, emotional and instinctive motives. Rational motives are those resulting from a conscious thought process; emotional motives are those resulting from an irrational source such as anger, love, pride, jealousy and so forth. Instinctive motives arise from deeper drives and may result in obsessive behaviour: in most cases, though, instinctive motives simply drive the occasional impulse purchase.

Hedonism

Hedonism is the cult of pleasure. In consumer behaviour, it refers to the pleasurable aspects of consumption: the flavour of food rather than its nutritional value, the comfort of a car rather than its performance, the appearance of clothing rather than its ability to keep out the cold (Holbrook and Hirschmann 1982). Hedonic purchases are sometimes about a need for being cheered up, and can be triggered by feeling unhappy as well as by a normal day-to-day desire for comfort and pleasure. There is even evidence that a near-death experience can encourage greater pleasure-seeking behaviour, as well as encouraging people to change their lifestyles (perhaps by dieting, or sometimes by stopping a diet) (Ferraro *et al.* 2005).

Marketers put a great deal of effort into designing products which not only work well, but also give pleasure to their owners. This is an important way to differentiate the product from those of the competitors, and for some products hedonic content is virtually the entire product: fashion wear, cosmetics, holiday travel and many service industries such as restaurants and hairdressing rely heavily on hedonism to sell their products.

Hedonism is sometimes regarded as the opposite of **utilitarianism**, which is the cult of practicality (see Figure 2.8 on page 44). In marketing, most products have utilitarian aspects, and some are almost entirely utilitarian: most business-to-business products are utilitarian (there is little hedonic value in a bag of cement, although what a builder builds with it might be extremely hedonic). Utilitarian consumer products might include cleaning products, energy (electricity and gas), basic foods and most municipal services such as street cleaning and sewage removal.

In most cases, products have both hedonic and utilitarian features. Even a basic, cheap car has comfortable seats, a radio, a heater and so forth. This is because such comforts have become regarded as hygiene factors by most people. This means that manufacturers are in a constant race to add even more hedonic features to their products in order to stay ahead

Figure 2.8

Hedonism vs. utilitarianism

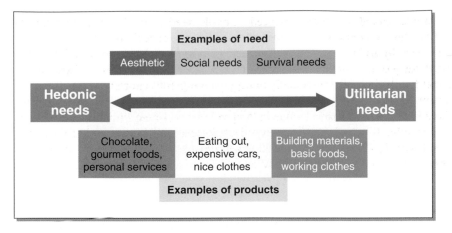

of the competition. Periodically, a company may produce a 'no frills' version of the product at a much-reduced price, and the process starts again. An example of this is low-cost airlines, some of whom now offer extra services such as rapid check-in or choice of seats as a competitive measure.

Marketing in practice
The Transit

Think of hedonism and probably the last thing you would think of is the light commercial vehicle. At first sight, a vehicle for delivering groceries, building materials, and furniture has to be as utilitarian as it gets – and for 60 or 70 years that was what manufacturers thought as well.

Then in 1965 the industry was revolutionised by the Ford Transit. The Transit handled like a car, had comfortable seats, was relatively quiet, and had good heating and ventilation systems. It was easy to load and a real pleasure to drive.

Within a few years Ford had captured 30 per cent of the UK light van market. The Transit became known as the People's Van: it was owned by small businesses, by budding rock bands, by hippies who slept in the back, by builders, by couriers and even by private citizens. Camper van versions, minibus versions, open truck versions and high-roof versions were all produced by Ford for the burgeoning market. The comfort and ease of handling made it ideal for drivers who were non-professionals, i.e. drivers who delivered goods as part of their normal business rather than drivers who deliver for a living.

Even delivery companies switched to Transits as they found that their drivers performed better when they were comfortable and not tired out by wrestling with heavy steering, or trying to coax some power out of a commercial engine. Transits were fast and manoeuvrable – so much so that some police authorities had to upgrade their own vehicles to be able to catch them. Quickly the police adopted Transits as well, to use as Black Marias, as dog-carrying vehicles, or as scene-of-crime vehicles. In September 1985 stunt man Steve Mathews jumped a Transit over 15 vehicles as a fundraiser for cancer research.

Throughout its 40-year life the Transit has been the market leader. It still retains its core values: it is the People's Van because it is designed for people, not for companies. The Transit, more than any other van before it, caters to people's hedonic needs.

burrows   3_TRV_M_RC_11647_NV   Ford

ALLAN BURROWS LIMITED

Hedonism also includes experiential needs. People need to have stimulating experiences: we have this in common with most other mammals, especially carnivorous ones. The need to learn by trying new things, the need to have something new to think about, and the need for excitement all stem from the need for new experiences. Experiential needs are met by playing sport (especially unusual or dangerous sports), by travel, and by taking up new hobbies. Often such activities are in conflict with utilitarian and functional needs – there is really no utilitarian value in bungee jumping or crossing India on a Royal Enfield motorcycle, but both fulfil an experiential need for someone. McAlexander, Schouten and Koenig (2002) suggest that competitive advantage can be gained by marketers if they concentrate on the consumers' experience of owning the product.

Talking point

Is it realistic to make a distinction between hedonic needs and utilitarian needs? After all, what is a pleasure to some people is a necessity to others. For example, take sport: for many people, playing a sport such as squash or tennis is a fun thing to do, a real pleasure, whereas for others it is simply sweaty activity that they don't have to do. But supposing somebody had been told by the doctor to exercise more or risk heart failure? Such a person might take up squash as the 'least worst' alternative, in other words exercise rather than die, but in fact hate every minute of it.

Equally, for most people driving a car is a necessity, purely a means of getting from one place to another conveniently. For others, it might be a real delight – and certainly car manufacturers plug the hedonic aspects of driving far more than they talk about the utilitarian aspects.

Maybe the old saying about one man's meat being another man's poison has some truth in it!

Hedonism also accounts for the utopian marketplace. This is the place where people dream (Manuel and Manuel 1979). Utopia has been deconstructed as follows (McLaran and Brown 2002):

- *Sensory No-Place:* This brings feelings of a world apart from the consumer experience.
- *Creating Playspace:* This provides the open-ended playful nature of the utopian text contained within it.
- *Performing Art:* This evokes the active life of people in the creation of utopian meanings.

Our dreams and fantasies do not, of course, always turn into reality, and in many cases people prefer to keep their fantasies as simple fantasies – remaining within utopia. This does not prevent marketers from feeding the fantasies – custom car magazines frequently have average readerships aged below the minimum age to have a driving licence, for example.

In general, hedonic needs account for a large proportion of consumer spending. The current trend towards service industries (as opposed to manufacturing industries) is largely fuelled by hedonic needs, as people travel more, eat out more and enjoy services such as hairdressing, beauty therapy, cinema, theatre, music concerts and sports facilities.

Understanding motivation

One of the difficulties with understanding consumer motivation is that people are often unable to be specific about what has driven them to a specific action. In some cases this is because the motivation operates below the subconscious level, and in other cases it is because the person is not willing to admit to a particular motivation. This is easily observable in everyday life: people often lie about their reasons for taking, or not taking, a particular action since it would involve admitting to something they would prefer to keep to themselves. For example, someone may turn down the opportunity to go to a concert on the grounds of being unwell, when in fact the individual is afraid of meeting up with an ex-girlfriend who likes the same band. This might be embarrassing to admit to. In some cases, people are motivated by some need which is illegal or immoral, so would be extremely unlikely to admit to being motivated by the need. Equally, someone might be genuinely unaware, at a conscious level, of their real motivation – a reluctance to go to a concert might be a fear of crowds, but the individual might believe that actually he or she is too tired to go and would prefer a quiet night in.

In general, people are not so much rational as rationalizing. A middle-aged man who is thinking about buying a sports car might actually want it because he wants to recapture his lost youth, but might rationalize the decision by talking about the car's fuel economy and good looks. 'I need a decent car to impress my clients' is a common rationalization.

In the 1950s and early 1960s there was considerable interest in motivational research. Motivational researchers thought that they had discovered underlying reasons for consumer behaviour, and many of their propositions were seized on by marketers. Unfortunately, some of the propositions were so peculiar they could not reasonably be used – the ideas that housewives were symbolically washing away their sins when they did the laundry or were symbolically giving birth when they baked a cake were among the less credible ideas of the motivational researchers.

A further complication is that any given action is likely to be the result of several different motivations, some of which may even conflict with each other. Some actions are the result of a decision to take the 'least worst' alternative, or may be rationalized in some way in order to maintain an attitude. Sometimes people make wrong decisions, and rationalize their motives afterwards rather than admit their mistake.

Overall, then, it is difficult to penetrate the layers of motivations to find the nugget of true motivation within.

Motivation research

Identifying consumer motivation is clearly far from simple. Finding out the true motivation for someone's behaviour is similar to finding out a hidden attitude (see Chapter 7). Projective techniques in which respondents are asked to explain the motivation of a fictitious third party will often draw out the individual's real reason for behaving in a specific way: the respondent might be asked to fill in speech bubbles in a cartoon, or be asked what the 'typical' person might think, and so forth.

A classic study carried out in the 1950s sought to establish the reasons for poor sales of instant coffee. Housewives were shown two shopping lists which were identical except that one list had instant coffee on it, while the other list had ground coffee. The respondents were asked to describe the type of housewife who would have drawn up each list: the instant-coffee list was seen to belong to a housewife who is lazy, badly organized and not a good housewife (Haire 1950).

Means-end chain analysis (laddering) involves asking people to explain what each benefit of the product means to them (Gutman 1982: Reynolds and Gutman 1988). The respondent works through a series of 'so what?' questions to arrive at the underlying motivation. For example, someone might be asked about the motivation for buying a bottle of wine, with the questioning going as follows:

'Why did you buy that bottle of wine?'
'Because it's a good Rioja.'
'What does that mean to you?'
'It will taste good.'
'Why is that important?'
'I'm cooking dinner for my girlfriend.'
'Why is the wine important?'

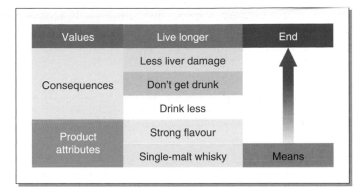

Figure 2.9
Means-end chain

'I want to impress her, and I want her to enjoy the evening.'
'Why is that important?'
'I want her to be in a good mood.'
'Why?'
'Because I'm going to ask her to marry me.'

The questioning could, of course, carry on if we wanted to know why the wine-purchaser wants to marry this specific person, but for most marketers (apart, perhaps, from those running dating agencies) this would not be especially important.

In Figure 2.9, the purchase of a single-malt whisky might be explained superficially by the purchaser as being about the quality of the whisky and its flavour. Further investigation shows that the individual finds that he or she drinks less of the product because the flavour is much stronger than that of a blended whisky, which means that he or she is less likely to get drunk quickly and therefore is less likely to suffer liver damage. This enables the individual to achieve a core value, that of living a longer (and presumably healthier) life. The product attributes (quality and flavour) lead to consequences which address core values.

Summary

This chapter has considered the forces which encourage people to buy. Needs are the basic generators of drive, and consequently of motivation, so it might be true to say that need is the basis of virtually all behaviour. Drives develop when there is a gap between where we are and where we want to be – motivation develops when we can see a possible solution (or solutions) to the need problem. Some motivation relates to our physical, utilitarian needs, but as human beings we also have powerful social, aesthetic and pleasure needs, so much of our buying behaviour relates to hedonism.

The key points from this chapter are as follows:

● Many motives are irrational or unconscious.

● Need is a perceived lack: want is a specific satisfier.

● Drive is caused by the gap between actual and desired states.

● Most marketing is about activating needs and directing wants.

● Motivation is complex, and cannot always be inferred from behaviour.

● Needs can be ranked, but there is considerable overlap.

● As wealth increases, motivations change.

● Many, even most, purchases are motivated at least in part by hedonic needs.

Chapter review questions

1 Why do some people have higher OSLs than others?

2 What is the difference between primary and secondary motivations?

3 What are the main difficulties in categorizing needs?

4 What are the main criticisms of Maslow's hierarchy?

5 Why is punishment a poorer motivator than reward?

6 What is the purpose of modelling?

7 What is meant by approach–approach conflict?

8 Why is hedonism an important factor for marketers?

9 How might marketers find out which factors are regarded as hygiene factors in a product and which are motivators?

10 In which areas of marketing would Vroom's expectancy theory have most relevance?

Preview case study revisited
Chocolate

Chocolate purchase and consumption meets a great many needs, and is the solution to a great many drives. Purchase of chocolate as gifts meets a need for belonging and for esteem, and in some cases (especially around Valentine's Day) may also meet a mating need. It even meets some of our aesthetic needs – handmade chocolates with intricate decorations, chocolate animals, cake decorations in chocolate and other artistic creations made of chocolate have a great appeal to our senses. The recent development of chocolate fountains, available for hire or sale for parties and corporate events, highlights the association of chocolate with fun.

Chocolate, above all else, speaks to hedonism. No one consumes chocolate for practical, utilitarian reasons, except perhaps soldiers or mountaineers who sometimes use it as an emergency ration. Chocolate is used as a mood changer, as a mild narcotic and to cheer oneself up when times are hard.

The drive to consume chocolate may also arise from an addiction, since it is a mildly addictive substance, or may arise from stress – the need for a treat. Advertising for chocolate products almost always uses models to show the reward aspects of the product. Interestingly, women make up the majority of chocolate consumers, so some manufacturers (notably Rowntrees of York) have made considerable efforts to persuade men that eating chocolate is not only a female occupation.

Chocolate appeals to the id, so advertising aims to weaken the superego's arguments and push the ego towards agreeing with the id. Above all other things, chocolate shows how many of our needs are divorced from the practical – a substance which speaks to so many needs, yet has no practical significance at all, says a lot about the human condition.

Case study
Toys and play

Most of us had favourite toys when we were children, and most of us had favourite games. Playing is an important part of childhood – and it carries on into adulthood, too. As children we might have played with other children, kicking a football around or acting out fantasies: mock battles, cowboys and Indians, playing with dolls, playing hide and seek, and so forth.

It is common knowledge that play is preparation for adult life. For example, dolls might give girls practice in looking after babies, or (in the case of Barbie and Sindy dolls) preparation in choosing clothing and (in more recent years) considering career options. Playing games such as cowboys and Indians gives boys valuable lessons in cooperation with others, negotiating, and both giving and taking orders. Active sports play builds coordination and physical fitness as well as developing team spirit. Dressing up allows children to develop their imaginations and practise adult roles.

Playing also helps to create bonds between parents and children. Parents who play with their children have the opportunity to relive their own childhoods (either repeating what they enjoyed doing, or doing things they never had the chance to do), and they can share a good time with their kids.

Of course, the main point of play is that it is fun. Parents who try too hard to direct their children's play into 'educational' or 'useful' channels usually fail – most parents are familiar with buying the child an expensive 'educational' toy, only to watch the child play with the box it came in and

ignore the toy. Toys need to be interesting, but they mainly need to be interactive – a toy truck that has to be pulled along and steered is much more interesting than a toy truck with an electric motor and a self-steering mechanism. Essentially, children need to play with toys, not merely watch them.

As with any other human activity, marketers have an input into play. Children are quite capable of playing with almost anything, or indeed with nothing: children can (and do) make their own toys, everything from soap-box carts to dolls (although such industry is rare nowadays in wealthier countries). Parents, on the other hand, like to treat their children to things: Christmas and birthdays are traditionally times when parents give their children toys (in fact 80 per cent of toys are sold in the six weeks leading up to Christmas). Some toys are simple, others are complex; some are old-fashioned, traditional toys, others use Space Age technology. In each case marketers aim to produce the toys that parents want to buy for their children, and that children will want to play with.

This naturally involves a great deal of promotional activity, especially in the period leading up to Christmas. Sometimes this advertising generates 'pester power' as children pester their parents for the latest toys and games as a result of seeing them advertised on TV. Most parents have come to expect this, and most have coping mechanisms in place (commonly based around using the promise of the toy as a lever in persuading the child to be good, tidy the bedroom, not pester, write to Santa Claus, and so forth).

Toys touch our lives on many levels: we remember favourite toys from when we were children, we learn how the world works through toys, we buy toys for our children, we use toys to bond with our children and with each other, we learn how to be adults through play. Though the nature of toys changes with each year that passes, the basic principles remain the same.

SCOTT CAMAZINE/ALAMY

Case study questions

1 How might a drive develop for buying a new toy?

2 How might a parent reduce the drive a child feels for a new toy?

3 How do toys fit into Maslow's theory?

4 How might toys relate to Herzberg's dual-factor theory?

5 What is the balance between utilitarianism and hedonism in toy purchase?

References

Ferraro, Rosellina, Shiv, Baba, Bettman, James R., Iacobucci, Dawn, and Kahn, Barbara (2005) Let us eat and drink, for tomorrow we must die: effects of mortality salience and self-esteem on self-esteem on self-regulation in consumer choice. *Journal of Consumer Choice*, 32(1): 65–75.

Gutman, J. (1982) A means-end chain model based on consumer categorisation processes. *Journal of Marketing*, 46 (spring): 60–72.

Haire M. (1950) Projective techniques in marketing research. *Journal of Marketing*, 14: 649–56.

Herzberg, F. (1966) *Work and the Nature of Man* (London: Collins).

Hibbert, Sally A., Hogg, Gillian, and Quinn, Theresa (2005) Social entrepreneurship: understanding consumer motives for buying the *Big Issue*. *Journal of Consumer Behaviour*, 4(3): 159–72.

Holbrook, Morris P., and Hirschmann, Elizabeth C. (1982) The experiential aspects of consumption: consumer fantasies, feelings and fun. *Journal of Consumer Research*, 9 (Sept): 132–40.

Manuel, Frank E., and Manuel, Fritzie P. (1979) *Utopian Thought in the Western World* (Oxford: Blackwell).

Maslow, Abraham (1954) *Motivation and Personality* (New York: Harper and Row).

McAlexander, J.H., Schouten, J.W., and Koenig, H.F. (2002) Building brand community. *Journal of Marketing*, 66(1): 38–55.

McLaran, Pauline, and Brown, Stephen (2002) Experiencing the Utopian marketplace. *Advances in Consumer Research*, 29(1).

McNulty, W. Kirk (1985) UK social change through a wide-angle lens. *Futures* (August): 42–9.

Mitchell, A. (1983) *The Nine American Lifestyles* (New York: Macmillan).

Murray, Henry A. (1938) *An Exploration in Personality: A Clinical Experimental Study of Fifty Men of College Age* (London: Oxford University Press).

Nowlis, Stephen M., Mandel, Naomi, and McCabe, Deborah Brown (2004) The effect of a delay between choice and consumption on consumption enjoyment. *Journal in Consumer Research*, 31(1): 502–510.

Raghunathan, Raj, and Mukherji, Ashesh (2003) Is hope to enjoy more enjoyed than hope enjoyed? *Advances in Consumer Research*, 30(1): 85–6.

Raju, P.S. (1980) Optimum stimulation level: its relationship to personality, demographics and exploratory behaviour. *Journal of Consumer Research*, 7 (December): 272–82.

Reynolds T.J., and Gutman, J. (1988) Laddering theory, method, analysis, and interpretation. *Journal of Advertising Research* (Feb/Mar): 11–31.

Rugimbana, Robert, Donahay, Brett, Neal, Christopher, and Polonsky, Michael Jay (2003) The role of social power relations in gift giving on St. Valentine's Day. *Journal of Consumer Behaviour*, 3(1): 63–73.

Shiv, Baba, Ferraro, Rosellina, and Bettman, James R. (2004) Let us eat and drink for tomorrow we shall die. Mortality salience and hedonic choice. *Advances in Consumer Research*, 31(1).

Skinner, Burris F. (1953) *Science and Human Behaviour* (New York: Macmillan).

Vroom, V.H. (1999) *Management and Motivation* (Harmondsworth: Penguin Business).

Zuckerman, M. (2000) Are you a risk-taker? *Psychology Today* (Nov/Dec): 54–87.

Chapter 3
Goals, risk and uncertainty

Learning objectives After reading this chapter, you should be able to:

1. explain the relationship between drives and goals
2. describe the various ways in which goals adopt hierarchies
3. explain risk avoidance behaviour
4. understand what is meant by heuristics, and explain how they help reduce risk
5. explain the role of interrupts in problem-solving
6. explain how dissonance arises
7. understand complaining behaviour

Introduction

As we saw in the last chapter, behaviour is driven by needs. Needs develop drives, and drives are focused into motivation, but motivation achieves nothing unless it is backed up by action. The process of converting a motivation into concrete action is one of developing goals. A goal is a concrete objective, one which dictates a specific plan of action, and one which carries with it its own decision-making, risks and rewards.

Any plan of action carries with it a degree of risk. Individuals will usually try to reduce the risks to an acceptable level, sometimes by developing rules of behaviour which have proved to be successful in the past. This type of decision-making is important to marketers because it enables practitioners to put risk-reducing measures in place. The lower the risk to consumers, the more likely they are to buy the product and the less likely they are to complain afterwards.

Goals

A goal is an external object towards which a motive is directed (Onkvisit and Shaw 1994). Goals differ from drives in that the goal is external, and pulls the person in a given direction; a drive is internal and pushes the individual.

In this way the goal acts as an incentive to take a course of action (or refrain from taking a course of action, as the case may be). Having goals improves task performance: people are more risk-seeking when they have a specific, challenging goal (Larrick, Heath and Wu 2002). If someone has a drive which needs to be addressed, there may be several possible goals which would satisfy the drive. For example, if an individual feels the need for entertainment, this may lead to a drive to find something to do, which in turn causes the person to set some goals which would lead to some kind of entertainment. In these circumstances, several possible alternatives exist, and marketers clearly need to remember that consumers have a choice. Some examples are shown in Table 3.1.

The basic consequences, needs or values that consumers want to achieve are called 'end goals'. These end goals can be concrete or abstract. Concrete end goals derive directly from the product purchase, whereas abstract end goals derive indirectly from the purchase.

Going to university can be a challenging experience. For some students, it's their first experience of living away from home; for others, it's a set of new challenges in a much less structured learning environment than they have been used to. For mature students, there is the added challenge of combining education with existing commitments and responsibilities, such as children or career. For all concerned, there is the difficulty of being sure that one has chosen the right course, and is choosing the right subjects within the course, for one's chosen career.

None of this is new, of course. Nor are these challenges necessarily confined to universities – anybody leaving home to start a new job is going to find similar challenges, and we are all familiar with the feeling of being the 'new kid' whether it's in a job or in a school, or indeed in a university.

Since the huge increase in the numbers of students at UK universities, there has been a marked reduction in the amount of time teaching staff have been able to devote to individual students. Guiding students through the university experience has become less and less the province of the lecturers and has become much more formalized, with students expected to find their own way round, or (if really stuck) to find their way to an advice shop or student support unit where they can be put back on course. Unfortunately, some of those most in need of help are not even aware that they need help – and in some cases they simply fall by the wayside.

Getting students to focus on what is most important, and getting them to become self-motivated, is of course part of the problem. Another part of the problem is simply getting them to think through what it is they actually need to do in order to get the most out of what is, for the vast majority, a one-off experience.

For example, someone might buy a bottle of wine in order to go to a party. The party is the end goal, not drinking the wine (which is probably why so much cheap wine arrives at parties). The goal is abstract: it is intangible, and relates to hedonic and even irrational motives. Abstract goals need not be irrational or hedonic: someone buying a new suit to achieve the end goal of getting through a job interview has a practical purpose in mind.

Buying a new car because of a need for transport to get to work is a concrete goal; buying a car to impress the neighbours is an abstract goal. In most cases, abstract goals can be achieved in many different ways – the neighbours might be equally impressed by a new swimming-pool, or by an expensive holiday.

Different goals are satisfied by different cars – a sports car addresses different goals to a truck.

Table 3.1 Goal choices

Goal	Possible sub-goals	Action
Go to the cinema	Choose a film	Look in the evening paper, make a choice
Visit friends	Decide which friends to see	Phone around to see who is available
Watch TV	Which channel?	Look in the TV guide
Rent a DVD	Which DVD?	Visit the DVD rental shop
Read a book	Which book?	Choose a book from the shelf

Goals develop for various reasons. There is clearly a relationship between consumer values and means-end chains (Pieters *et al.* 1995; Reynolds and Gutman 1988): in other words, the individual's basic values will translate into systems for obtaining an end result by specific methods. Research in this area has tended to assume that the goal structures are static, which is unlikely to be the case since people's needs evolve. Means-end theory also does not explain how the gap between higher-level ('being') goals and lower-level ('having') goals can be bridged.

Talking point

How easy is it to categorize goals this way? How do we know where the end of the line is with goals? For instance, take the person who buys a bottle of wine in order to go to a party. Perhaps the party is an end goal, but why do we go to parties in the first place? To have a good time? To meet a potential new girlfriend/boyfriend? To network, and thus improve our career prospects? To make new friends? To show off our nice new clothes?

Even then the goal hierarchy may not stop. Why do we want a new boyfriend/girlfriend? Perhaps with a view to marrying, settling down and having children, enjoying a happy domestic life and eventually some grandchildren, setting ourselves up for a happy and fulfilling retirement, perhaps living longer than we otherwise might (there is research evidence on this), and having a long and meaningful trip through this vale of tears.

And we get all this for a buying a bottle of wine?

Social identity theory (see Chapter 10) is based on two main concepts. First, we assume that people take actions (and buy products) in order to enact roles within society and for their own self-image (Kleine *et al.* 1993; Sirgy 1982). Second, social identity theory states that people do not have a single identity, but in fact have separate identities for each social situation they find themselves in (for example, as friend, employee, volunteer worker, and so forth). Again, this body of research does not tell us how the higher-order abstract goals translate into lower-order concrete goals.

Behavioural decision theory may help to resolve this problem. This body of theory suggests that choice processes and outcomes relate to the context in which the behaviour occurs, for example on the number of choice alternatives which are available, and task factors such as available time (Bettman *et al.* 1998).

Combining these theoretical approaches, Huffman *et al.* (2000) produced two models showing how goals relate and how they are determined. Figure 3.1 shows the first of these.

In Figure 3.1, the individual's goals begin with life themes and values. These are concerned with the kind of person we want to be, or the kind of person we are, and are unlikely to change very greatly in the course of our lives. At the 'doing' level, we have immediate concerns which lead to consumption intentions. Finally, at the 'having' level, we would be concerned with specific benefits from products, which in turn leads to a search for specific features in the products we consume.

For example, an individual might have a life theme of being a world traveller. This might translate into a life project to visit every continent in the world. In the process, current concerns (such as earning a living in a profession which allows plenty of time off for travel) might provide a set of goals; the consumption intention might be to have at least one long-haul trip each year. Finally, the individual would be looking for specific benefits from each trip (the possibility to learn about the local culture, for example), which would require specific features when planning each trip.

This model shows a clear sequence from the general needs of the individual through to the final purchase goals for each individual product (in this case, each trip). There are likely to be many products and many sub-goals involved in leading a life which is dedicated to travel: the same would apply to someone whose life is based around being surrounded by artworks, or around having a large family, or having a high-powered working career.

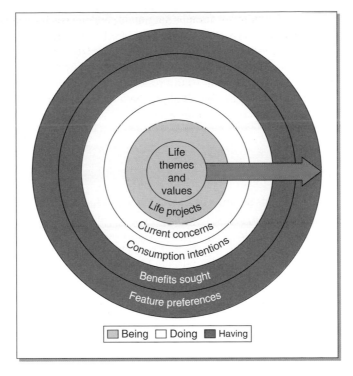

Figure 3.1

A hierarchical model of consumer goals

The model shows the sequence of events which occurs, and also the relationship between the goals, but it does not illustrate the actual processes involved. These are shown in Figure 3.2.

In Figure 3.2, 'incorporation' refers to the top-down process whereby higher-level goals shape goals at lower levels. Incorporation helps the individual to ensure that all the goals fit together in a logical and sensible way, and also it enables the individual to translate a set of ill-defined and possibly subconscious needs into a coherent set of choice problems.

'**Abstraction**' refers to the bottom-up process whereby lower-level goals help to determine what the higher-level goals must be if there is to be consistency between the various goals.

'**Adaptation**' is the process by which goals are influenced by contextual issues such as the cultural and social environment, current concerns and consumption intentions. Contextual factors appear to operate in two ways: first, the context may activate a pre-existing set of sub goals in the individual's memory. Different contexts generate different goals; for example, one's goals when planning a visit to one's parents are very different from one's

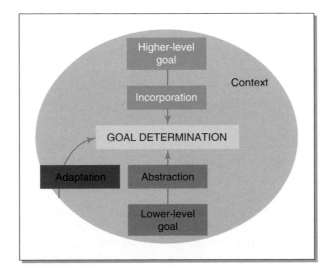

Figure 3.2

A model of goal-determination processes

goals when planning a friend's stag night. Second, the context may influence the individual's thinking on what is actually possible. If someone does not believe, for example, that there is any chance whatsoever of being promoted at work, then he or she might not bother to 'dress to impress'. In the case of 'being'-level goals, someone might decide that their circumstances prevent them from ever becoming a particular type of person. At the 'having' level, someone might decide that, much as they would enjoy driving a Porsche, this is unlikely to happen because of financial constraints.

Problems with goals

Some end goals are too general for the individual to make any real decisions. For example, someone who says 'I just want to be happy' may not have any idea how to achieve this. On a more concrete level, saying 'I want to buy a decent computer' is not much help to the salesperson who is trying to find a machine that will meet the customer's needs. In this case, the customer clearly does not know enough about the technical aspects of computers to be able to make an informed decision alone. 'I want to be respected' is also a difficult goal for which to develop a strategy.

Sometimes goals will conflict. In these circumstances, the strongly active goal will inhibit competing goals until the stronger goal has been achieved, at which point the weaker or less active goal will re-emerge (Brendl *et al.* 2002).

Table 3.2 gives some purchase end goals and motivations, with examples (see also Figure 3.3). In practice, marketers have little influence over consumers' main goals, since these often derive from basic values. Marketers can try to influence the less abstract end goals, such as the desired functional or psychosocial consequences, through promotional strategies. For example, although it may be difficult to persuade someone that he or she ought to dress well in order to impress other people, we can much more easily influence those who already believe in dressing to impress, perhaps encouraging them to shop at a specific retailer or buy specific clothing brands.

Table 3.2 Examples of purchase end goals

Dominant end goal	Basic purchase motivation	Examples
Optimization satisfaction	Seek maximum positive consequences	Buy dinner at the best restaurant in town rather than risking a cheap diner
Prevention	Avoid potential unpleasant consequences	Buy weatherproofing for a house so as to maintain the good appearance of the house, and protect its value
Resolution of conflict	See satisfactory balance of positive and negative consequences	Buy a moderately expensive car of very good quality so as to avoid high maintenance costs and unreliability, while still keeping within a reasonable expenditure
Escape	Reduce or escape from current aversive circumstances	Buy an anti-dandruff shampoo, in order to avoid embarrassment
Maintenance (satisfaction)	Maintain satisfaction of a basic need with minimal effort	Buy bread at a local shop. This satisfies the need for bread without having to go to the out-of-town hypermarket where you do your main weekly shopping

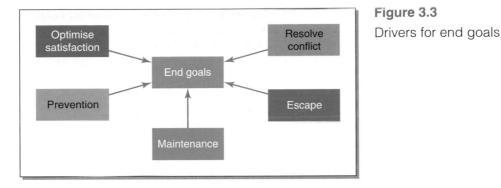

Figure 3.3
Drivers for end goals

Examples of this are common, as the following list shows:

- *If you want to get ahead, get a hat.* This slogan was thought of in the 1930s when the wearing of hats by men was going out of fashion. In fact the slogan was not very successful: hats still went out of fashion, and it was not until the 1990s that they returned to the fashion scene.
- www.howtolookgood.com/askcaryn_2_feb.html This website offers fashion advice and hyperlinks to online fashion and cosmetics retailers.
- www.net-a-porter.com/About-Us/Our-Company This is another fashion website, but this time at the top end of the market. It provides an information service for people with £3000 to spend on a new dress.
- *Just do it!* This slogan for Nike nudges people towards making a decision on the spot, although it appears to be about taking a determined approach to sports participation. Nike athletic shoes are primarily a fashion item – only a small proportion of the shoes are worn for actually playing sports.

It is not always feasible for an individual to go straight for an end goal. In fact, it is far more common for people to establish a series of subsidiary goals which will lead, eventually, to the end goal. Goal hierarchies are series of sub-goals which provide a structure for decision-making. In other words, people set priorities. If the individual has previous experience this will help, because consumers without previous experience will have more trouble establishing goal hierarchies and are likely to go by trial and error. For example, someone who has never bought a car before will not really know what to look for because he or she will not have been able to prioritize needs or form a hierarchy of goals. A simple goal hierarchy for buying a car might run as follows:

1 Find out which car would best suit your needs.
2 Find out which is the cheapest way of funding the purchase.
3 Find out who has the right type of car for you.
4 Do the deal and buy the car.

Many slogans are designed to encourage a quick decision.

To translate this into an action plan, the person will have to establish a series of activities to meet each sub-goal. Here is an example of the buying process for the second-hand car:

1 Buy a used-car guide.
2 Decide which car looks like the make and year that would best suit your needs.
3 Decide what price range is affordable.
4 Telephone banks and loan companies to obtain the best terms for a loan.
5 Buy the local paper as soon as it hits the news stands.
6 Telephone car dealers (or private sellers) who seem to have the right kind of car, go to see the car, and make the purchase.

Figure 3.4

Creation of sub-goals

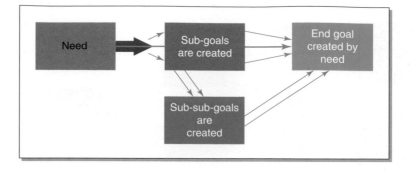

In Figure 3.4, the end goal is created by the need, but the path to meeting the need is not direct. Sub-goals are created, and even sub-sub-goals, and these sub-goals must be achieved on the way to achieving the final goal.

The experienced consumer – for example someone who buys second-hand cars regularly, or who is a real car enthusiast – will already know how to go about this process and will establish the goal hierarchy and action plan immediately. Inexperienced consumers have to establish the goal hierarchy from scratch, often by trial-and-error approaches, and develop a decision plan for each sub-goal. Marketers, and especially salespeople, can help here because they can guide individuals through the process. This is the most effective kind of selling activity since it addresses the consumer's need for assistance.

Problem-solving processes are greatly affected by the amount of product knowledge the consumer has already acquired through past experiences, and by the level of involvement with the product (and indeed with the choice process itself). In other words, if the individual has a great deal of knowledge about the product category, or has a strong interest in the product category, the process of finding a suitable product or brand will proceed along very different lines. The inexperienced car buyer might follow a plan such as this:

1 Decide to buy a car.

2 Ask around among family and friends to find out which car might be most suitable. This might involve some discussion to decide what the individual's needs are: an experienced car buyer might be aware of needs which the inexperienced buyer would not think of. The financing of the purchase might also be discussed at this point.

3 Go to used-car showrooms to examine the different makes and models.

4 Find a helpful salesperson who appears honest and trustworthy.

5 Tell the salesperson what the needs are.

6 Listen to the salesperson's advice about the particular models in stock. Again, the financing of the purchase might also be discussed at this stage.

7 Make the decision based on the closeness of fit between the salesperson's description of the car and the needs that have been identified.

8 Buy the car.

Consumers' relevant knowledge about the product category (or, if you prefer, the problem category) is obviously important in problem solving (Crosby and Taylor 1981), so inexperienced purchasers are likely to take a knowledgeable friend with them when they go to make a major purchase such as a car. Sometimes relevant knowledge is brought forward from the individual's memory, and some knowledge is acquired during the purchasing process (Biehal and Chakravarty 1983). Any brands which have simply been remembered are part of the evoked set, and for regular purchases or familiar product categories these may be the only brands which are considered. The result of the information search process is to create choice alternatives, which are further refined into a consideration set. The consideration set is the group of products which will be actively considered.

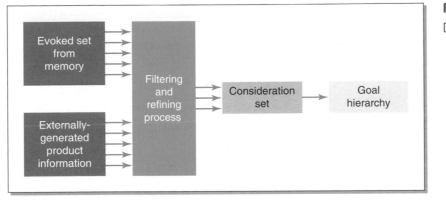

Figure 3.5
Developing goals

In Figure 3.5 the many brands which are in the evoked set, and the even more numerous brands which might be brought to the individual's attention, are filtered and refined to create the consideration set, which may only comprise a few brands. The individual will then usually select one or possibly two brands to feed into the goal hierarchy as being the desirable brands for solving the need problem.

There is an old joke about someone who has a lot of debts, and who writes to a particularly persistent creditor to say that each month all the bills are put in a pile, three are drawn out at random and paid, and the rest have to wait. 'If you continue to threaten me,' wrote the debtor, 'your bill will not go into next month's pile.'

It would appear that marketers are operating on the same basis. We try to get our product into the pile of products in the consideration set, otherwise there is no chance of it being purchased.

Does this analogy stack up, though? What if the creditor were simply to send hundreds of bills, so that most of the bills in the pile are his, and therefore (statistically) his bill is more likely to be paid? Is this what marketers do when they saturate the media with advertising? Do people simply throw away the excess information, in the same way that the debtor would throw away the red reminders?

From the viewpoint of marketing, ensuring that one's brand is in the evoked set, and more especially is part of the consideration set, is an important objective of marketing communications activities. If the brand is not going to be evaluated, it is impossible for it to be purchased: if it is already in the evoked set, it is likely to become part of the consideration set. The potential for a brand to be included in the consideration set is called its 'top of mind awareness', and this is influenced by several factors: first, past experience of the brand in terms of previous purchase and use experience; second, the level of marketing communications devoted to the brand – the amount of advertising out there (Baker *et al.* 1986); and third, the distribution strategy of the brand – if the brand has been seen in a large number of places, it is more likely to be purchased, especially since some estimates state that 65 per cent of purchase decisions are made in the shop. Fourth, package design will influence both the consideration set (due to its impact on the individual's consciousness) and the probability of the brand entering the consideration set. Packaging also provides important information about the formulation of the product, its use, and its probable effectiveness for the purpose for which the consumer wants to use it.

The probability that existing knowledge about the brand will be used in the evaluation process is influenced by the means-end relevance of the knowledge to the goal involved (Grunert 1986). People will try to predict what the outcomes of purchase will be (i.e. will try to predict whether the purchase will meet the goals) but we cannot always do this directly, unless it is possible to

Most fruit stalls do not allow people to taste the fruit, so people use substitutes such as colour and texture to judge quality.

test the product beforehand as one does when test-driving a car. For example, it is not usually possible (at least in the UK) to taste fruit and vegetables before buying them, so people use other criteria such as the colour, shape and texture of the fruit to judge what it will taste like. Likewise, items such as cleaning products can only be judged from the packaging, smell and consistency of the product.

Achieving each sub-goal in the purchase process may not always be straightforward: finding a suitable time to visit car showrooms (for example) might be difficult, establishing which salespeople are reasonably trustworthy and which are not may take considerable judgement, and identifying one's needs correctly can be a major task in itself.

Risk and uncertainty

In the case of the inexperienced buyer there is a greater risk attached to making the purchase. Inexperienced buyers have, by definition, less knowledge of the product category they are trying to buy into. Most consumers will try to reduce risk in this situation, and of course this is part of the reason for establishing goal hierarchies. By doing so, individuals can break down the task into manageable portions which can each take a share of the risk. People are more prepared to take risks with later goals if the earlier goals in the sequence were accomplished successfully (Dhar and Novemsky 2002).

Risk can be categorised in different ways, as shown in Table 3.3.

The amount of risk an individual perceives depends on two factors: first, how serious the downside is. If the possible negative consequences of buying the product will have a strong effect on the individual's well-being, the risk is high. Second, risk will be perceived as higher if the negative outcomes are thought to be highly likely.

For example, someone buying a light aircraft knows that faults with the airframe would be extremely serious, but also knows that such faults are fairly unlikely. Someone buying a lottery ticket knows that the chances of losing the purchase price are extremely high, but the loss of the money is not serious compared with the possible gain.

The main tactic for reducing risk is to increase one's knowledge about the product category. Our prospective aircraft purchaser is likely to seek a great deal of advice from a great many sources, and is likely to have the aircraft thoroughly inspected by a qualified engineer. If the risk is still perceived to be high the consumer will simply not make the purchase. This is why most retailers offer money-back guarantees or no-quibble return policies: such guarantees reduce risk for the consumer, so making purchase more likely. Since most purchases work out reasonably well (at least they do if the manufacturers have done their work properly) the products seldom need to be returned.

Table 3.3 Categories of risk

Type of risk	Explanation	Examples
Physical risk	The risk of injury from using the product	Buying a car which is faulty, or perhaps buying a medicine with unpleasant side-effects
Financial risk	The risk of losing or wasting money	Buying a car that depreciates quickly, or buying a computer and finding that the price drops dramatically when a new model comes out
Functional risk	The risk of finding that the product is not fit for purpose	Buying a product that breaks down regularly, or buying a painkiller that does not stop a headache
Psychosocial risk	The fear of looking foolish	Buying clothes that your friends think look weird on you, or buying a make of car with a poor reputation

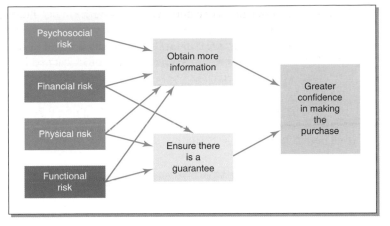

Figure 3.6
Reducing risk

Mood can have an effect on risk-taking behaviour: people tend to buy more lottery tickets if the weather is bad, but whether this is a way of making life more exciting in dull weather or whether it is a way of cheering oneself up with the prospect of a big win is debatable (Bruyneel *et al.* 2006).

People often spend considerable time shopping around, increasing their knowledge of the product categories in order to reduce risk (see Figure 3.6). This has been compared to the hunter-gatherer behaviour of our ancestors, and may account for the fact that the vast majority of retail purchases are still made in High Street shops rather than through mail order or the Internet. The need to inspect products personally as a way of reducing risk has been identified as a barrier to Internet purchase (Dailey 2003). On the other hand, some aspects of Internet purchase appear to reduce people's aversion to risk: online investing has been shown to lead to greater risks being taken: the theory is that the online experience is less 'real' than a live experience of dealing with a live stockbroker, so people are prepared to take more risks (Zwick 2004).

People will frequently choose the middle-ranked or mid-priced brand as a compromise between buying the worst alternative on the one hand and risking spending too much by buying the 'best' brand on the other. This means that, in a two-choice situation, a brand's chances of being bought are helped if a third brand is available which places it in the middle range (Sheng, Parker and Nakamoto 2003). Presumably this implies that a company which finds itself in second place to a major brand should consider introducing a third, cheaper, brand into the market in order to boost sales of its existing brand.

Shopping with friends helps to reduce risk.

Heuristics

Another way of reducing risk and simplifying the decision-making process is to establish rules for buying. These are called '**heuristics**', and they consist of simple 'if . . . then' decision-making rules which can be established before the search procedure begins. Heuristics are also subject to alteration in the light of new knowledge, so sometimes they are established as the search procedure continues. Heuristics can be divided into three groups, as follows:

1 *Search heuristics.* These are rules for finding out information. For example, someone might establish a rule to the effect that they will always ask advice from a friend when making a major purchase.

2 *Evaluation heuristics.* These are rules for judging products. For example, someone might have a rule that they never buy products made in Eastern Europe.

3 *Choice heuristics.* These are procedures for comparing evaluations of alternatives. For example, someone might have a rule of never buying the cheapest (or never buying the most expensive). In fact, most people do tend to go for the middle-priced product when offered a choice of three products at different price levels.

Some examples of these heuristics are given in Table 3.4.

Heuristics are used to simplify decision-making. They may be stored in memory, or constructed on the spot based on information received, but in either case they allow the

Table 3.4 Examples of heuristics

Search heuristics	Examples
Store selection	If you are buying meat, always go to the butcher across the street.
Source credibility	If a magazine accepts advertising from products it tests and reports on, the tests may be biased in favour of the advertiser.
Evaluation heuristics	**Examples**
Key criteria	If comparing processed foods, examine the sugar content.
Negative criteria	If a salient consequence is negative (for example high sugar content) give this choice criterion extra weight in the integration process.
Significant differences	If the alternative is similar on a salient consequence (for example all the alternatives are low sugar) ignore that choice criterion.
Choice heuristics for familiar, frequently purchased products	**If choosing among familiar products . . .**
Works best	Choose the product that you think works best – the one that provides the best level of performance on the most relevant functional consequences.
Affect referral	Choose the alternative you like best (in other words select the alternative with the most favourable attitude).
Bought last	Select the alternative you bought last time (assuming it proved satisfactory).
Important person	Choose the alternative that an 'important person' such as a spouse, friend or child likes.
Price-based rule	Buy the least expensive alternative, or perhaps the most expensive alternative, depending on your beliefs about the relationship between price and quality.
Promotion rule	Choose the alternative for which you have a special-offer coupon, or that you can buy at a reduced price (due to a sale or special offer).
Choice heuristics for new, unfamiliar products	**If choosing among unfamiliar products . . .**
Wait and see	Do not buy a new product until someone you know has used it for a while and recommends it. In the case of electronic products, wait until the next year or year after its introduction, when the price is likely to have reduced considerably.
Expert consultant	Find an expert or more knowledgeable person, have them evaluate the alternatives in terms of your goals, then buy the alternative that the expert suggests.

individual to reach rapid decisions without over-stretching his or her cognitive capacity (or brainpower). In the extreme, the use of heuristics leads to habitual behaviour. For example, someone might go to the same pub every Friday night and order the same drinks and sit at the same table each time. Routine choice behaviour such as this is comforting and relaxing since it does not involve any decision-making at all. In fact, most people find it disturbing if their routines cannot be carried out for whatever reason.

In most cases heuristics are simple rules which reduce risk in purchasing situations (for example, 'When choosing a restaurant in a foreign country, always eat where local people eat').

Interrupts

Sometimes the goal hierarchy cannot be followed exactly because events occur which force the individual to re-think the situation. These events are called 'interrupts', and they fall into four categories:

1 *Unexpected information which is inconsistent with established beliefs*. For example, if the shop which the consumer had expected to buy from has changed hands or closed, the consumer has to rearrange the goals to encompass finding a new supplier.

2 *Prominent environmental stimuli*. An in-store display might offer an alternative to the original purchase (perhaps by offering a large price discount on a similar product). This may divert the consumer away from his or her usual brand choice, or at the very least cause the consumer to consider switching.

3 *Affective states*. Hunger, boredom or tiredness during a shopping trip might lead to a change in goal. This may be a change away from looking for a new suit, and towards looking for the coffee shop.

4 *Conflicts*. These are the motivational conflicts discussed in Chapter 2. If an individual is confronted with an approach–approach conflict, or an approach–avoidance conflict, there will be a temporary cessation of goal attainment while new goals are formulated and the conflict resolved.

The effect of interrupts will depend on how consumers interpret the interrupting event (see Figure 3.7). On the one hand, the interrupt may activate new end goals (as when the shopping trip turns into a search for a cup of coffee). On the other hand, a choice heuristic might be activated – for example, if the unexpected information is a friend recommending a brand, this may activate a heuristic about acting on friends' recommendations. Sometimes the interrupt is severe enough that the individual shelves the problem-solving behaviour indefinitely (for example if the unexpected information is that the person has lost his or her job, or if a prominent environmental stimulus such as an anti-fur protest is taking place outside the fur emporium).

Talking point

In recent years we have been hearing a lot from politicians about increasing people's choice. Choice of schools, choice of hospitals, choice of public services in general have all come into the realm of politics. But how true is it that people actually want more choices? Surely the more choices we have, the more difficult it is to make decisions?

The more possible ways of achieving our goals there are, the more possibilities for conflict there will be. Wouldn't it be more accurate to say that what people actually want is products and services which work and which are not too expensive? And doesn't this apply as much to public services as it does to things we buy in shops?

Or perhaps people need choice because each of us has different needs and therefore we need to be able to select the solution that best suits our own situation?

Figure 3.7

Temporary effects of an interrupt

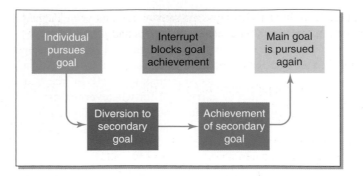

Figure 3.8

Goal and interrupt strengths

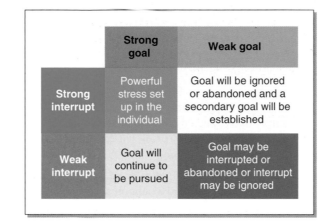

The strength of the interrupt is also important (Figure 3.8). If the goal is a strong one, and the interrupt weak, the individual is unlikely to be diverted from the main goal (for example, consider a husband who has forgotten his wife's birthday, and who is shopping in the last ten minutes before the store closes. He is unlikely to take a break for a sandwich, no matter how hungry he is). A weak goal and a strong interrupt will clearly result in a break in the problem-solving behaviour (for example, the intention to check the prices on GPS units for a possible purchase when one's bonus comes through is unlikely to take precedence over a desperate need for the toilet). A weak goal and a weak interrupt may or may not result in a divergence from the planned behaviour, and a strong interrupt and a strong goal are likely to lead to considerable stress on the individual.

In most cases people tend to resume an interrupted task fairly quickly. Even though a marketer might be able to distract somebody away from their shopping to have a cup of coffee or a snack, the shopping task will be resumed fairly quickly afterwards. Once a goal hierarchy is established, it usually takes some effort to dissuade an individual from following it.

Post-purchase dissonance

Post-purchase dissonance occurs when the product turns out to be not quite what was expected (Figure 3.8). It can come about through misunderstanding, mistake or deception, or sometimes through plain old second thoughts or new information arising.

The mechanism by which dissonance arises is simple. When working through the goal hierarchy, the consumer will form a view of what it will be like to own the product, and will develop a perceptual map of the anticipated benefits (see Chapter 5 for more on perception). The perceptual map is a mental picture of what life will be like with the product included. The expectancy disconfirmation model (Oliver 1980) says that satisfaction and or dissatisfaction is the result of comparing pre-purchase expectations and post-purchase outcomes.

Pre-purchase expectations fall into three categories, as follows:

1 *Equitable performance*, which is a judgement regarding the performance one could reasonable expect given the cost and effort of obtaining the product (Woodruff *et al.* 1983).

2 *Ideal performance*. This is what the individual really hoped the product would do, if the world were a perfect place (Holbrook 1984).

3 *Expected performance*. This is what the product probably will do (Leichty and Churchill 1979).

Maybe we complain too much . . . .

If later experience shows that the product actually has different attributes, and the expected benefits do not materialize, the purchaser experiences a discord (or dissonance) since there is a clash between anticipation and actuality.

The level of dissonance depends on the following factors:

● the degree of divergence between the expected outcome and the actual outcome;
● the importance of the discrepancy to the individual;
● the degree to which the discrepancy can be corrected;
● the cost of the purchase (in terms of time, money and risk).

For example, if someone buys a DVD player which turns out to have a scratch on the case, this is probably only a minor fault which does on affect the working of the equipment and is, in any case, easily corrected. In many cases, the customer would simply accept the scratch without bothering to seek redress from the supplier: if the scratch is a small one, it probably is not worth the effort of taking the DVD player back to the retailer for replacement, especially as the retailer might claim that the customer might have scratched the case while unpacking it or installing it. Some studies have shown that only one-third of dissatisfied customers will complain or seek redress: the remainder will boycott the products in future, or simply complain to others (Day *et al.* 1981). In the case of minor dissonance, or in cases where there is a high cost of complaint (for instance, returning goods to the duty-free shop at Istanbul Airport), the reluctance to complain is perfectly understandable.

On the other hand, if the DVD player has a major fault (failing to play DVDs effectively being the main one) there is a major discrepancy between the expected outcome and the actual outcome. The problem area is when the product does not live up to expectations (for example it breaks down after the warranty has expired) but there is no available redress.

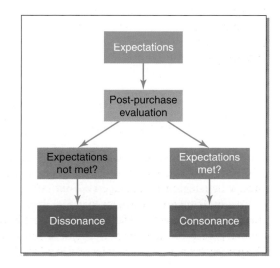

Figure 3.9

Dissonance and consonance

In these circumstances, the dissonance is likely to be considerable since the original goal has been frustrated.

A major study of dissonance was carried out by Festinger and Carlsmith in 1957. These researchers found that people are capapble of holding two dissonant pieces of information in their minds at once, but will try to reduce the dissonance. In their experiment, Festinger and Carlsmith offered students an incentive to lie to other students: apparently paradoxically, students offered a small bribe were more likely to begin to believe the lie themselves, whereas students offered a large bribe were less likely to believe the lie. The conclusion was that the students offered the small bribe could not justify the lie on the basis of being paid to do it, so had to resolve the dissonance by accepting the lie as being true (Festinger and Carlsmith 1957).

From a marketer's point of view, it is important to reduce post-purchase dissonance. The evidence is that people will try to do so themselves, often by complaining about the product. If they do not win redress from the supplier, they will complain about the product to their friends and family. If people experience dissonance, there are four general approaches they take to minimise the problem. These are as follows:

1 Ignore the dissonant information and look for positive (consonant) information about the product. For example, a newly purchased car may be slower than expected, but on the plus side it is solidly built and reliable.

2 Distort the dissonant information. The car may be slow, but at least it's faster than taking a bus.

3 Play down the importance of the issue. The car is slow, but it goes from A to B eventually.

4 Change one's behaviour. Perhaps the consumer will sell the car, trade it in for something else, or buy a bicycle.

Marketers are able to back up these general approaches. Some car manufacturers, aware that their cars are reliable rather than exciting, will make use of this in their advertising. For example, Volkswagen have used the slogan, 'If only everything in life was as reliable as a Volkswagen' for some years now. In general, it is better to avoid the occurrence of post-purchase dissonance by ensuring that the purchaser has accurate information about the product and its performance: in other words, ensuring that the customer's perceptual map conforms as closely as possible with later experiences of using the product.

Volkswagen use this slogan to reassure consumers – buying a VW will not cause post-purchase dissonance.

If post-purchase dissonance does occur, the consumer may take action against the producer to redress the situation. For this reason it would be foolish to assume that the marketing job has finished once the sale is completed. Consumers' actions tend to fall into one of three general categories:

● *voice responses*, where the consumer comes back to the supplier to complain;

● *private responses*, where the consumer generates negative word-of-mouth by complaining to family and friends;

● *third-party responses*, where the consumer takes legal action or complains to a consumer rights organization (Singh 1988).

Figure 3.10 shows the outcomes that may arise when a consumer feels dissonance as a result of a purchase. Voice responses are the only ones with any chance of a positive outcome for the supplier.

When faced with a voiced response, the supplier and the consumer may have differing views on the legitimacy of the complaint. Managers may sometimes feel that the consumer wants something for nothing, or may feel that there is an implied criticism in the complaint (this is not unreasonable, of course – any complaint means that the customer thinks that the supplier has done a bad job). Consumers will always feel that that there should be some response to the complaint, and the way in which the complaint is handled affects satisfaction

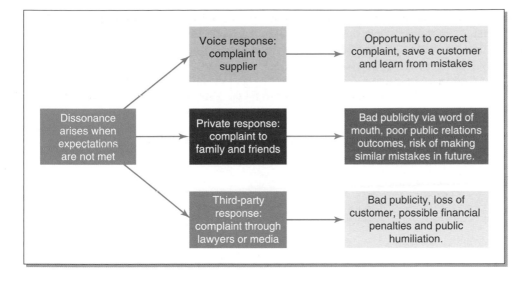

Figure 3.10
Complaining behaviour and its outcomes

and dissatisfaction (Cobb *et al.* 1987). One study has shown that, as the level of complaints increases, the willingness of managers to listen decreases (Smart and Martin 1991). This naturally tends to lead to an increase in the number of complaints, since managers are less likely to put right whatever is going wrong, and a vicious circle develops.

Third-party responses can range from a complaint to a regulatory body such as the UK's Trading Standards Office, through legal action in the courts, to a complaint to a consumer rights TV programme or newspaper column. In virtually all such cases the consumer will already have tried a voice response, and if he or she has not done so the third party will urge him or her to do so: a court case is unlikely to succeed if the supplier has not been given an opportunity to make amends.

From a marketer's viewpoint, it is better to cooperate with the third party than to be obstructive. For example, using a blanket 'no comment' response to a consumer affairs reporter is likely to be construed as an admission of guilt.

The following factors appear to affect whether or not a complaint will be made (Day 1984):

- *The significance of the consumption event.* This is likely to be a combination of product importance, cost, social visibility and time required in consumption. Consumers will be unlikely to complain if the product is cheap and unimportant, and was not expected to last long anyway.

- *The consumer's knowledge and experience.* The number of previous purchases, level of product knowledge, self-perception of one's ability as a consumer and previous complaining experience are all factors in consumer experience. People who have successfully complained in the past are more likely to do so in the future, and people who have a high level of knowledge about the product category are more likely to complain, presumably because they have much better-defined expectations of the product.

- *The difficulty of seeking redress, in terms of time, cost and nuisance.* People are unlikely to complain if the product was purchased a long way away, or if complaining would result in a disproportionate amount of time and trouble.

- *The perceived probability that a complaint will lead to a positive outcome* (Halstead and Droge 1991). Complaints are far more likely if the consumer has a guarantee or feels that he or she is dealing with a reputable supplier who will resolve the problem. Also, consumers are less likely to complain if the problem is perceived as being incapable of being put right or compensated for. For example, someone staying in an hotel where other guests have gone out for the evening, leaving a noisy dog in their room, might feel that there is little the hotel management can do about the problem until the dog owners return.

Since there is ample evidence to show that putting a complaint right actually increases the likelihood of the consumer remaining loyal to the producer, and consequently purchasing in future, it would seem sensible to encourage people to voice their complaints rather than use private responses or (worse still) third-party responses (Power 1993).

Complainers appear to be members of higher socio-economic groups than those who do not complain (Francken and van Raaij 1985), and the more people blame someone else for their dissatisfaction, the more likely they are to complain (Richens 1983).

Summary

Goal-setting is often a subconscious activity which arises from our deepest feelings about who we want to be, what we want to do, and what we want to own. In the course of meeting our goals, we may find obstacles in our path: the goals may not be possible, we may need to achieve other goals before we are in a position to achieve the main goal, or we may be interrupted in the task by more pressing matters.

Part of the problem in achieving goals is the fact that life is uncertain. We try to mitigate the problem by assessing the risks and taking measures to minimize them, often by following decision rules. When things go wrong, we become dissatisfied and this in turn leads to complaining behaviour.

The key points from this chapter are as follows:

- Goals are external: drives are internal.
- Goals operate in hierarchies.
- Choice processes and outcomes relate to the context in which the behaviour occurs.

- Themes relate to being: life projects and current concerns relate to doing; features and benefits relate to having.
- Brands need to be in the evoked set, and subsequently in the consideration set, to have any chance of being bought.
- People usually act in ways which minimize risk.
- Perceived risk depends on the seriousness of the negative outcome as well as on the likelihood of the negative outcome happening.
- Heuristics are decision rules intended to reduce cognitive effort and risk.
- Interrupts usually only delay problem-solving behaviour, but the delay depends on the strength of the interrupt and the strength of the goal.
- Dissonance occurs when there is a discrepancy between expectations and outcome.
- Complaints may not always be directed to the supplier.

Chapter review questions

1 How might a marketer seek to make an interrupt more effective?

2 How are drives converted to goals?

3 What is the difference between the evoked set and the consideration set?

4 What mechanisms are available for reducing risk?

5 How might heuristics help someone who is buying a product he or she has no experience of?

6 How might someone assess the risk of buying a new car?

7 How do life goals derive from life themes?

8 How does context affect choice in, say, the travel industry?

9 How might a marketer try to ensure that a brand is in the consideration set?

10 What are the key features of 'having' as opposed to 'themes'?

Preview case study revisited
Getting the most from university

One of the ways in which universities try to motivate and direct students is by getting them to think through their personal goals. This is usually done by providing information in the students' starter packs on how to establish one's life goals, but sometimes it is done as an exercise during the induction process.

The University of Aberdeen provides a good example of personal development goal-setting. The university's personal development plan is available online, not just for students but for anyone who cares to access it – which in itself is a good way of bringing the university's courses to the attention of anyone who searches Google under 'achieving life goals'. Beginning with life goals, the document goes on to invite students to state their university goals, asking questions such as 'How will other people know that you are performing differently?' The next stage in the process is to ask students to consider whether their goals are realistic. Many students start out with unrealistic goals, and then become disillusioned and demotivated when they are unable to achieve them. Equally, and perhaps more importantly, students who set their sights too high are often unable to feel pleased with

what they do achieve – a 2:1 is a respectable degree which most students would be delighted with, but someone who has been determined to obtain a First would be disappointed with a 2:1.

The next stage in the Aberdeen process is to get students to consider their opportunities. The questions now focus on the individual's strengths and weaknesses – using questions such as 'What are you good at?' and 'What are some other ways of achieving your goals?'

Moving on, students are asked to work out what they are going to do about their goals, how they are going to record their outcomes, and what their time scales are. Finally, they are led through the evaluation and monitoring process.

Whether this approach to goal-setting and problem-solving works remains to be seen. Probably a large number of students will work their way through the plan, then file it away and forget about it – after all, life gets in the way of all our plans! On the other hand, most students will undoubtedly benefit from the experience of really thinking about who they are, where they want to be, and how they are going to get there, even if the action plan blows a fuse!

Case study
Last-minute everything

Package holidays have been around for literally hundreds of years – even mediaeval pilgrims would contract with a guide to take them to the holy sites of Europe, usually on foot and perhaps taking several months. What we commonly think of as a package holiday (a flight to a holiday resort combined with accommodation on arrival, and sometimes with excursions or other activities) only really began in the 1960s, as an antidote to the high fares being charged by national airlines.

During the 1980s overcapacity in the industry led to slashed prices, and eventually to the 'last-minute' holiday. Because tour operators have to contract with the airlines and hotels to buy a specific number of seats and rooms, the operators can easily find themselves paying for empty space if they can't sell the packages. In an industry where profit margins are notoriously tight, this often spells disaster, and there is nothing as perishable as a package holiday – once the aircraft takes off, there is no

way of selling the seats, or even the hotel rooms at the other end of the flight.

The industry response to this was to introduce last-minute deals. Since the seats and rooms were already paid for, anything the company could get for them would be better than nothing: it's all about minimizing losses, not about making profits. Travel agents' windows became full of last-minute bargains, so that anyone with sufficient flexibility could pick up a real bargain.

In the UK, the traditional time for booking a summer holiday is during the cold and wet months of January and February. Tour operators traditionally advertise over the Christmas period, and people book their holidays during the post-Christmas lull, when they feel the need for something to look forward to. In recent years, however, this traditional approach has changed dramatically: people resent paying for a holiday six months ahead of time, thus giving the tour operator a free loan, when people who book later have been given impressive discounts. The result of this is that most people wait until the last minute, in some cases even buying from brokers at the departure airport, in the hope of securing a real bargain.

The advent of low-cost, easily-booked air travel has added to the problem, because people have found that booking the flight and the hotel independently is not only cheaper, but allows them to change their hotel on arrival if they don't like it.

The result of this has been a crisis in the travel industry. As the risks of travel have reduced, the tendency for people to 'go independent' has increased. However, the same has not necessarily been true of other service industries – so many others (theatres, restaurants, cinemas, hotels and so forth) have jumped on the 'last-minute' bandwagon, often through Internet-enabled agents such as lastminute.com. In effect, people are accepting the risk that they may not be able to enjoy a night out or a weekend away in exchange for a discount on the usual price. The service firm, on the other hand, can fill its capacity (albeit at a reduced price) which enables it to use its resources more effectively. Eventually one might expect that these industries will begin to face the same problems which have decimated the package holiday business: no one will be prepared to pay the full price.

The key factor in the last-minute revolution is the Internet. Rapid dissemination of information about deals, coupled with automated booking systems, mean that the burden of determining demand is moved away from managers. Pricing can be calculated automatically so that demand is matched with supply (for example, as the popularity of the offer rises, as evidenced by increased numbers of bookings, the price can be raised automatically). On the plus side, for suppliers, the work of making the booking (and the cost of printing the tickets or vouchers) is passed on to the customer, which does mean that some savings can be made on staffing costs. Of course, these savings do not come anywhere near to matching the discounts on offer, so firms will lose out if the trend continues. There is no question but that the Internet is here to stay, and that streetwise consumers will try to get the best deal they can from companies – the problem for companies lies in how they respond to those pressures.

Case study questions

1 What is the role of risk reduction in last-minute bookings?

2 How might companies encourage people to book earlier and pay the full price?

3 How might goal conflict affect a last-minute purchase?

4 How can restaurants and hotels avoid the pitfalls suffered by the package holiday industry?

5 What problems might be created for a firm in a three-firm market when prices start to fall?

References

Bettman, J.R., Luce, M.F., and Payne, J.W. (1998) Constructive consumer choice processes. *Journal of Consumer Research*, 25 (December): 187–217.

Biehal, Gabriel, and Chakravarti, Dipankar (1983) Information accessibility as a moderator of consumer choice. *Journal of Consumer Research*, June: 1–14.

Brendl, Miguel, Markman, Arthur, and Irwin, Julie R. (2002) Suppression and activation of competing goals. *Advances in Consumer Research*, 29(1): 5.

Bruyneel, Sabrina, DeWitte, Siegfried, Franses, Philip Hans, and DeKimpe, Marnik G. (2006) Why consumers buy lottery tickets when the sun goes down on them. The depleted nature of weather-induced bad moods. *Advances in Consumer Research*, 33(1): 46–50.

Cobb, Kathy J., Walgren, Gary C., and Hollowed, Mary (1987) Differences in organizational responses to consumer letters of satisfaction and dissatisfaction. In *Advances in Consumer Research*, 14, eds Melanie Wallendorf and Paul Anderson (Provo, UT: Association for Consumer Research).

Crosby, Lawrence A., and Taylor, James R. (1981) Effects of consumer information and education in cognition and choice. *Journal of Consumer Research*, (June): 43–56.

Dailey, Lynn (2003) Understanding consumers' need to personally inspect products prior to purchase. *Advances in Consumer Research*, 30(1): 146–7.

Day, Ralph L. (1984) Modelling choices among alternative responses to dissatisfaction. In *Advances in Consumer Research*, 11, ed. Thomas C. Kinnear (Provo, UT: Association for Consumer Research).

Day, Ralph L., Brabicke, Klaus, Schaetzle, Thomas, and Staubach, Fritz (1981) The hidden agenda of consumer complaining. *Journal of Retailing*, 57 (Fall): 86–106.

Dhar, Ravi, and Novemsky, Nathan (2002) The effects of goal fulfilment on risk preference in sequential choice. *Advances in Consumer Research*, 29(1): 6–7.

Festinger, L., and Carlsmith, J. Merrill (1959) Cognitive consequences of forced compliance. *Journal of Abnormal and Social Psychology*, 58: 203–10.

Francken, Dick A., and van Raaij, F. (1985) Socio-economic and demographic determinants of consumer problem perception. *Journal of Consumer Policy*, 8(3): 303–14.

Grunert, Klaus G. (1986) Cognitive determinants of attribute information usage. *Journal of Economic Psychology*, 7: 95–124.

Halstead, Diane, and Droge, Cornelia (1991) Consumer attitudes towards complaining and the prediction of multiple complaint responses. In *Advances in Consumer Research*, 18, ed. R. Holman and M. Solomon (Provo, UT: Association for Consumer Research).

Holbrook, Morris P. (1984) Situation-specific ideal points and usage of multiple dissimilar brands. In *Research in Marketing*, 7, ed. Jagdish N. Sheth (Greenwich, CT: JAI Press).

Huffman, Cynthia, Ratneshwar, S., and Mick, David Glen (2000) Consumer goal structures and goal-determining processes: an integrative framework. In *The Why of Consumption*, eds S. Ratneshwar, David Glen Mick, and Cynthia Huffman (London: Routledge).

Larrick, Richard P., Heath, Chip, and Wu, George (2001) Goal-induced risk taking in strategy choice. *Advances in Consumer Research,* 29(1).

Leichty, M., and Churchill, Gilbert A. Jr. (1979) Conceptual insights into consumer satisfaction and services. In *Educator's Conference Proceedings*, eds Neil Beck *et al.* (Chicago, IL: American Marketing Association).

Oliver, Richard L. (1980) A cognitive model of the antecedents and consequences of satisfaction decisions. *Journal of Marketing Research*, 17 (Nov): 460–9.

Onkvisit, Sak, and Shaw, John J. (1994) *Consumer Behavior: Strategy and Analysis* (New York: MacMillan).

Power, Christopher (1993) How to get closer to your customers. *Business Week*, Enterprise 1993 edition: 44.

Richens, Marsha (1983) Negative word of mouth by dissatisfied consumers: a pilot study. *Journal of Marketing*, 47(1): 68–78.

Sheng, Shibin, Parker, Andrew M., and Nakamoto, Kent (2003) Decision uncertainty, expected loss minimisation, and the compromise effect. *Advances in Consumer Behaviour*, 30(1): 47.

Singh, Jagdip (1988) Consumer complaint intentions and behaviour: definitions and taxonomical issues. *Journal of Marketing*, 52 (Jan): 93–107.

Sirgy, Joseph M. (1982) Self-concept in consumer behaviour: a critical review. *Journal of Consumer Research*, 9 (Dec): 287–300.

Smart, Denise T., and Martin, Charles L. (1991) Manufacturer responses to consumer correspondence: an empirical investigation of consumer perceptions. *Journal of Consumer Affairs*, 26 (Summer): 104–28.

Woodruff, Robert B., Cadotte, Ernst R., and Jenkins, Roger L. (1983) Modelling consumer satisfaction using experience-based norms. *Journal of Marketing Research*, 20 (Aug): 296–304.

Zwick, Detlev (2004) Online investing: derealization and the experience of risk. *Advances in Consumer Research*, 31(1): 58.

Chapter 4
Personality and self-concept

Learning objectives After reading this chapter, you should be able to:

1 describe the various ways in which personality is studied

2 define personality

3 explain the role and purpose of self-concept

4 describe the derivation of self-concept

5 explain the mechanisms of inner and outer direction

6 explain the reasons for an increase in inner-directedness

7 explain self-monitoring

Introduction

This chapter is about some of the factors which make up the individual person. People are complex and individual – our mental make-up affects what we buy, how we respond to marketing communications, and how we plan our future lives. From a marketing viewpoint, understanding personality is useful in segmenting markets and also in planning marketing communications.

Personality

Personality is the collection of individual characteristics that make a person unique, and which control an individual's responses and relationship with the external environment. It is a composite of subordinate processes, for example attitude, motivation and perception. It is the whole of the person, and is the system that governs behaviour rather than the behaviour itself.

The elements that make up personality are called **traits**. Considerable research effort has been made towards linking individual personality traits to buying behaviour, but with limited success. This is despite the apparent logic that people would buy products that reflect their personality traits (for example, outgoing, flamboyant people might be expected to buy more colourful clothing). In fact, there is some evidence that personality relates to new product purchasing behaviour, and there is more on this in Chapter 13; there is also some evidence that the degree to which someone is influenced by what other people think affects some buying behaviour. Overall, though, it is the total personality that dictates buying behaviour rather than each individual trait.

Personality has the following features:

1 It is integrated. That is to say, all the factors making up the personality act on each other to produce an integrated whole.

2 It is self-serving. The characteristics of personality facilitate the attainment of needs and goals. In other words, the personality exists to meet its own needs.

3 Personal characteristics are individualistic and unique, in degree and intensity as well as presence. Although many personal characteristics are shared with other people, the possible number of combinations of traits is huge, and therefore each individual is different. This is what makes each person a separate and unique being.

Preview case study
Ads on cars

Something new is hitting the streets of Britain: advertising on private cars. For years now public transport has carried advertising: buses, taxis and even trains have had advertising printed on them. The new idea is that private motorists can be paid for carrying advertising on their cars.

If the idea of being paid for driving around in your own car appeals, the company concerned (AdsOnCars) is happy to help. The company was established in 2003, following on from the success of a similar venture, Ads2Go, in the United States. Payments to motorists can be enough to cover their motoring for the entire year, although AdsOnCars are careful to point out that nothing is guaranteed, and it depends on the needs of the advertisers. In any event, many people who are involved find that the money they are paid covers a large part of their motoring costs.

The system is simple to operate. The car is wrapped in printed vinyl, which carries the advertising. The car owner then drives around as normal, travelling to work, going shopping or wherever the driver needs to go. Drivers are not required to drive specific routes, but they are vetted beforehand for driving convictions and according to their location and typical car use.

Drivers can, of course, refuse to carry any advertising that they feel is offensive or unethical or which does not meet with their own values. A vegetarian would not be required to carry advertising for meat pies, for example, nor would a green activist be expected to drive around advertising a cheap airline.

For advertisers, the service offers something new and potentially very eye-catching. Edie Lyons, the head of the American company, says that it allows for advertising to be taken to places where it otherwise might not go, such as supermarket car parks and golf clubs. Lyons goes on to say that, far from avoiding the advertising, people can often be seen crossing car parks to read what is written on the cars.

In the UK, drivers are sometimes offered an additional income if they are prepared to drive to specific events and hand out leaflets or otherwise help promote the companies they advertise on their cars. Again, this is optional: for people who want a little extra income, and who have the time to do it, handing out leaflets can be a useful way of earning some extra cash.

The main issue, of course, is whether people feel happy driving around in a car which is covered with advertising.

COVERED UK LTD

4 Personality is **overt**. External behaviour is affected by personality. In other words the personality can be observed (albeit indirectly) and deduced from the person's behaviour.

5 Personality is **consistent**. Once a person's basic personality has been established, it will change only slowly and with some difficulty; for practical purposes, an individual consumer's personality will stay constant throughout the buying process.

Because people are individuals it is difficult for marketers to take a standardized approach, yet the exigencies of the business world require standardization. For this reason, many attempts have been made to establish groupings of personality types which can be approached with a standardized offering. This is one of the bases of segmentation (the process of dividing the market into target groups of customers with similar needs). For this reason, and of course for the purposes of treating abnormal personalities, there is a long history of studying personality.

Approaches to studying personality

There are four basic approaches;

1 The psychoanalytic approach. Here the emphasis is on psychoanalysis, or studying the processes and events which have led to the development of personality traits. The focus is on the individual. This approach is typified by Freudian psychiatry, which seeks to help patients to confront the life events which have shaped their personalities.

2 Typology. Here the individuals are grouped according to recognized personality types.

3 Trait and factor theories. The individual traits of personality can be examined as factors making up the whole person, and each trait can be categorized.

4 **Psychographics**. The consumers are measured using their behavioural tendencies in order to infer personality traits.

These four basic approaches deserve a more comprehensive explanation.

The psychoanalytic approach

The psychoanalytic or Freudian approach is very much centred on the individual. Here the researcher (or, more usually, psychologist) asks the patient or subject to talk about anything regardless of logic, courtesy, self-defence etc. A Freudian would analyze these statements in terms of id, ego and superego.

According to Freud, the **id** is the underlying drive of the psyche. It is the source of the most basic, instinctive forces that cause people to behave in particular ways, and is largely operating below the conscious level; it may be responsible for some of the compulsive behaviour exhibited by some individuals. There is some evidence to show that compulsive behaviour such as buying lottery tickets and scratchcards is linked to other compulsive behaviour such as smoking, and negatively linked to agreeableness and intellectual dimensions of personality (Balabanis 2002). The **ego** is the conscious self, the part of the mind that makes the day-to-day decisions which lead to the satisfaction of the id; the **superego** is an internalized parent, the conscience that holds us back from selfish gratification of the id's needs. The superego is also operating mostly below the conscious level, and is the 'brake' on behaviour; in a sense, the ego is constantly making compromises between the id's demands and the superego's restraints. This is shown in Figure 4.1.

In simple terms, the id acts like a spoilt child, demanding instant gratification regardless of consequences; the superego acts like a stern parent, urging self-restraint and devotion to duty; and the ego acts like a good lawyer, arranging compromises and settlements between the two parties which will not lead to bankruptcy. Hedonic needs (see Chapter 2) largely

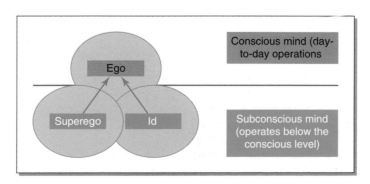

Figure 4.1

The id, the ego and the superego

Talking point

derive from the id, so advertising with a hedonic appeal is intended to strengthen the id's demands and encourage the ego to find in favour of the id. Some advertising also weakens the effects of the superego.

How much of what we think and do is really unconscious? Are we really so easily swayed by things that happened in our childhood? After all, we have the largest brain (relative to our size) of any known animal, so we ought to be able to think a bit, surely!

Or maybe we are not so much rational, as rationalizing. Perhaps we make our decisions on gut instinct, then justify them afterwards. In other words, perhaps we put our big brains to use to persuade ourselves that we are doing some real thinking!

The Freudian approach led to motivation research, which purported to explain the underlying reasons for buying. Motivation research was at its most popular in the 1950s and was, for a time, believed to be able to predict consumer behaviour in terms of basic drives which supposedly came from the id. Some of the claims made for motivational research now seem fairly ridiculous; for example, it was claimed that crunching cornflakes appealed to the killer instinct because it sounds like crunching animal bones, and that baking a cake is a substitute for giving birth. Convertible cars were thought to be a substitute for a girlfriend, and so forth. Motivational research became somewhat discredited because of the extravagant claims made, but still has something to say to marketers.

The **depth** (or **guided**) **interview** is an example of a motivational research method which is still widely used. A small number of respondents (50 or fewer) is interviewed without the use of a formal list of questions. Interviewees are encouraged to express their innermost thoughts and feelings about the object of the research (perhaps a new product). The interviewer needs considerable skill to keep the interview on course without leading the interviewee into expressing beliefs that are not his or her actual beliefs: it is easy to give the interviewee the impression that there is a 'right' answer.

A variation on this is the **focus group**, in which a group of ten or so respondents is invited to discuss their feelings and motivations collectively. The advantage of this method is that the respondents will tend to stimulate each other, and therefore there is less risk of the interviewer introducing bias into the results.

Projective tests are widely used in psychological counselling and psychiatry, and occasionally have applications in market research. They are based on the assumption that the individual may sometimes have difficulty in answering questions directly, either because the answers would be embarrassing or because the answers do not readily come to mind. In effect, a projective technique requires the respondent to say what somebody else might think about a given topic. Sometimes this is done by showing the respondent a cartoon strip of people in a relevant situation, sometimes the respondent is asked to complete a sentence, sometimes the respondent will be asked to draw a picture describing his or her feelings about the attitudinal object. In all cases the intention of the research is to allow the respondents to convey their innermost feelings in a non-personal way.

In Figure 4.2, the person on the left is expressing an opinion which may be controversial: the respondent in the research is asked to fill in what the person on the right might say

Figure 4.2
Cartoon projective technique

in response. In theory, the respondent will fill in his or her own opinion, but without the social risk of expressing the opinion openly. This method is particularly useful for uncovering hidden attitudes, perhaps where the individual has an attitude which might be regarded as antisocial or offensive.

Motivational researchers tend to be interested in the id, claiming that this dictates the individual's basic drives. The assumption is that knowledge of the id's demands will enable the marketers to shape arguments for the ego to use in overcoming the superego's restraining influence.

The typology approach

Freud was the earliest of the scientific psychologists. In subsequent years, additional beliefs to Freud's grew up; the followers of Jung, who (in addition to Freudian belief) also categorize people as **introverts** (preoccupied with themselves and the internal world) or **extroverts** (preoccupied with others and the outside world). This was an early attempt to classify people into broad types, and this process has continued ever since, with different researchers discovering different ways of grouping people according to personality types.

The mother and daughter team of Kathryn Briggs and Isabel Myers developed the Myers-Briggs Type Indicator (Briggs and Myers 1992) with four personality dimensions (Figure 4.3):

1 extrovert/introvert
2 sensing/intuitive
3 thinking/feeling
4 judging/perceptive.

The combinations can define people into 16 different types; for example, an extrovert-sensing-feeling-judging person is warm-hearted, talkative, popular and likes harmonious relationships. An introvert-intuitive-thinking-judging person is likely to be quiet, intelligent, cerebral and reclusive.

Note that most of us are on a continuum in terms of the Myers-Briggs dimensions. Relatively few people would be at the extremes of any of the dimensions, but the model does provide us with a means of classifying people across a range of characteristics.

Karen Horney defined people across three dimensions (Horney 1945):

1 *Compliant* – Moves towards people, has goodness, sympathy, love, unselfishness and humility. Tends to be overapologetic, oversensitive overgrateful, overgenerous and overconsiderate in seeking for love and affection.

2 *Aggressive* – Usually moves against people. Controls fears and emotions in a quest for success, prestige and admiration. Needs power, exploits others.

Extroverts like to be the centre of attention.

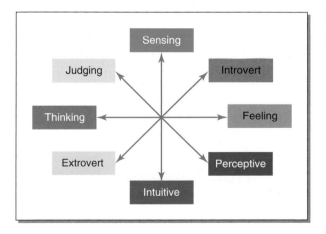

Figure 4.3
Myers-Briggs type indicators

3 *Detached* – Moves away from people. Conformity is repugnant to the detached person. Distrustful of others, these people are self-sufficient and independent, and value intelligence and reasoning.

There is some empirical evidence to show that these categorizations have some effect on people's buying behaviour. For example, it has been shown that compliant people use more mouthwash and toilet soap, and prefer branded products; aggressive people use more cologne and after-shave. Detached people show low interest in branding (Cohen 1967).

Reisman (1953) categorized people against three characteristics, in terms of the sources of their basic drives (Figure 4.4):

1 Inner-directed people are essentially driven from within, and are not too concerned with what other people think.

2 Other-directed people get their motivation and take their cues from other people.

3 Tradition-directed people get their cues and motivations from the past, from traditional beliefs and sources. These people are nowadays in a very tiny minority.

Reisman's categories have been used for marketing purposes. Inner-directeds, for example, tend to be innovators for cars and foodstuffs (Donnelly 1970), whereas outer-directeds

Decreasing respect for authority has led to tougher responses from the police.

have tended to be fashion victims (Zhinkan and Shermohamad 1986). There appears to be a change in the social paradigm, however, which is turning these views in a different direction. Broadly speaking, it would appear that more and more people are becoming inner-directed; according to some researchers the current figure is around 40 per cent of the population (McNulty 1985). This has led to a shift in the prevailing social paradigm away from the basically conformist attitude of the Victorian era towards a more individualistic, free-thinking society.

As with all the other classifications, most people are on a continuum. To some extent we are all driven by all three factors: Reisman's model is intended to show that some people may lean more towards one type of influence than towards others.

This shift in the social paradigm is having several effects. First, the fashion market has fragmented and almost anything goes (Evans and Blythe 1994). Second, there is a declining respect for authority and an increase in the crime rate. Third, and more positively, there is an increase in the tendency for people to espouse causes and work towards altruistic goals, even in the face of opposition from the establishment. The shift in the social paradigm is coming about as a result of increased wealth and security in the Western world; as consumers move up Maslow's Hierarchy of Need (see Chapter 2) more of them are operating at the self-actualizing level (McNulty 1985).

The movement towards a more inner-directed population has given rise to the VALS typology described in Chapter 2.

Overall, the type approach has much to offer marketers. There is little doubt that personality type affects buying behaviour, and since such types are easily identified and appealed to through marketing communications, it is not difficult to approach those groups.

Figure 4.4
Reisman's typologies

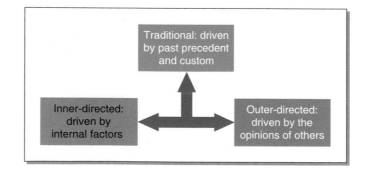

Trait and factor theories

Personality is composed of traits, or individual 'atoms' of personality. These individual predispositional attributes exert influences on behaviour, so the traits must be identified before people can be typed or classified.

Traits tend to be enduring facets of personality. In other words, traits tend not to change much over time, and even when they do change they tend to do so rather slowly. Those that might tend to change with age are anxiety level (which tends to go down as the individual gets older), friendliness (which can change either way) and eagerness for novelty (which tends to go down) (Goleman 1987). A few traits may vary throughout life, but studies show that adult personalities do not vary significantly as a person ages. This is not to say that behaviour and attitudes never change; merely that the underlying personality tends to stay very much the same. Changing roles, responsibilities and circumstances have much more effect on behavioural changes.

Traits can link to consumer behaviour; research has shown that computer adopters in the early 1980s were more likely to be homebodies who think of themselves as opinion leaders, were more intelligent than average, were cognitively structured (i.e. they think a lot), and tended to be introverted and not socially active (Dickerson and Gentry 1983). Presumably a similar study, if conducted now, would show a different result since computer ownership has become so widespread.

The number of personality traits is very large indeed. There has been an estimate that there are almost 18,000 identifiable personality traits (Allport and Odbert 1936) and more are being discovered daily. Traits are clearly interrelated with each other, but the study of this is still in its infancy, and this is scarcely surprising given the number of traits that have been identified.

Currently, however, the study of individual traits as they relate to buying behaviour is yielding few concrete results. This is probably because personality is interdependent; studying a few traits in isolation gives an insufficiently complete view of the whole person (*Marketing News* 1985).

Psychographics

Psychographics is sometimes known as 'lifestyle studies', since it is concerned with people's values and approaches to life. Essentially, it is a quantitative study of consumer lifestyles for the purpose of relating those lifestyles to the consumers' purchase behaviour. For example, somebody who has a 'green' set of values is likely to have an eco-friendly lifestyle, which in turn means that the individual will be more likely to buy a bike than a car, be more likely to be a vegetarian than eat red meat, and so forth. These ethical values can be powerful forces in decision-making (Shaw *et al.* 2005, Fraj and Martinez 2006). By knowing what a person's basic lifestyle is we can make a fair prediction as to their purchasing behaviour, and the kind of products and promotions that will most appeal to that individual.

The psychographic approach to personality study combines strengths of motivation research on the one hand with those of trait and factor theories. The assessment of lifestyle often involves very lengthy and involved studies of large samples of the population; the Target Group Index annual research programme, which is run by BMRB, asks people to respond to 246 lifestyle statements. From this survey, different lifestyles can be identified and consequently different purchasing patterns can be predicted.

An example of this approach is the VALS breakdown referred to in Chapter 2. A UK equivalent was developed by Taylor Nelson, as shown in Table 4.1 on page 80.

Psychographics approaches have in common that they all try to predict behaviour from knowledge of lifestyle and attitudes. The drawback with this approach is that the necessary research is complex and time-consuming, and ultimately relies heavily on the judgement of the researchers to decide which factors are appropriate to a particular lifestyle.

Table 4.1 Lifestyle types

	Lifestyle type	Characteristics	% of population
Sustenance-driven groups, motivated by the need for security	Belonger	People who believe in the establishment, traditional family values and patriotism. Averse to change.	19%
	Survivor	People who are fighting a 'holding action'; accept authority, hard-working, quiet, traditional. Strong class consciousness.	16%
	Aimless	Two main categories; young unemployed whose main motivation is short-term 'kicks', and the very old, whose motivation is simply day-to-day existence.	5%
Outer-directed group	Conspicuous consumer	Interested in material possessions, taking cues from reference groups (friends, family). Followers of fashion.	18%
Inner-directed group.	Social resister	Caring group, motivated by ideals of fairness and a good quality of life at the societal level. Altruistic, concerned with social issues like the ecology and nuclear disarmament.	11%
Motivated by self-actualization	Experimentalist	Materialistic and pro-technology, individualistic and interested in novelty.	14%
	Self-explorer	Motivated by self-expression and self-realisation. Tolerant, able to think big and look for global, holistic solutions.	16%

Source: Adapted from W. Kirk McNulty, 'UK Social Change through a Wide-Angle Lens' *Futures,* August 1985.

Talking point

The psychographics approach appears to have strong potential to tell us about what people will buy, since clearly most purchases are related to a chosen lifestyle. The problem is therefore not conceptual, but rather one of definition.

Trying to infer personality types from behaviour seems to be fraught with risk. Someone who describes themselves as environmentally friendly might still drive a car, for example – running your car on biodiesel might be greener than running it on mineral diesel, but does that make you environmentally friendly? Someone might be a humanitarian, but still join the Army because being a soldier might be seen as a way of fighting for the greater good of humanity.

The list goes on. People behave in all sorts of funny ways, so aren't we pushing our necks out by trying to guess *why* they behave the way they do? Maybe we can predict behaviour from knowledge of personality traits, and maybe we can analyze personality traits by observing behaviour, but isn't it just as likely that personality and behaviour have no connection whatever? Or maybe what we are talking about is not something which is absolute, but rather is something which is subjective!

Self-concept

Of all the personality concepts which have been applied to marketing, self-concept has probably provided the most consistent results and the greatest promise of application to the needs of business firms. (Foxall 1980:140)

Self-concept is the person's ideas and feelings about him/herself. It has an important role to play in understanding consumer behaviour, since people will buy products which contribute to the self-concept. For example, a woman who thinks of herself as a 'femme fatale' will choose chic clothes to enhance that image; a man who thinks of himself as a handyman will equip himself with the most sophisticated tools.

Essentially, people project a role and this is confirmed (or denied) by the people around. In order for the role to be confirmed, the person will try to develop all the exterior accoutrements appropriate to the role. In this sense, the person becomes a work of art; a sensory stimulus to other people which is intended to generate affective responses. The person may well use all five senses to generate the affective response: sight (by dressing appropriately, wearing make-up, etc.), hearing (by speaking with the right accent, or using the voice well), smell (by wearing perfume or deodorant), touch (by looking after the skin, perhaps by wearing clothes that feel good), and even taste (flavoured lipstick, mouthwashes) (Figure 4.5).

Some of these sensory stimuli will, of course, only be available to the individual's closest friends, and often only available to lovers, but most people at some time or another will consciously set out to create a work of art of themselves in order to 'make a good impression' on somebody. The extent to which people do this depends on the following factors;

1 The degree of importance attached to impressing the other person (or people).
2 The degree to which the individual anticipates that the 'target audience' can be impressed.
3 The cost in time and money of creating the desired image.

Clearly, though, the fact that people do create these works of art has led to the invention of whole industries to cater for the need; the cosmetics industry and fashion industry, to name but two. The forces involved can be very strong indeed: even in Nazi concentration camps people were prepared to trade food for clothing and cosmetics, thus placing their survival at risk for the purpose of maintaining their dignity (Klein 2003). In some cases, fashion items also represent personality determinants and even rite-of-passage symbols. Research by Russell Belk showed that shoes can represent a rite of passage (a girl's first high heels, for example) and that people often define themselves by their footwear (brands of trainer, for example) (Belk 2003). African Americans sometimes wear African clothing as a way of identifying themselves with their roots (deBerry-Spence and Izberk-Bilgin 2006).

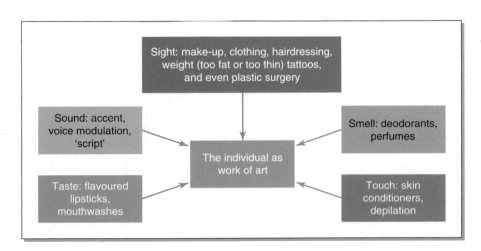

Figure 4.5

The person as artwork

Self-concept is a learned construct. Children tend to look for role models to imitate; these may not always be the same people, and the child may try several different role models before settling on one that is appropriate. Children can be crushed by a denial of the role being projected, for example if people laugh while the child is imitating a favourite auntie or uncle. During the teenage years, a further refinement occurs as the individual tries to develop an adult role, and again the role models may shift, typically away from the family members towards a hero (pop star or sporting personality) or sometimes to an individual within a peer group (a school friend, for example). Usually the role model will be an adult a few years older.

Talking point

Re-inventing ourselves is a common event. We change our hair, or our clothes, and effectively become someone else. But are we justified in considering this to be a work of art? Art is supposed to make people re-think the world around them – does this really happen when someone gets a haircut?

Or perhaps the person-as-artwork idea only applies at the extremes, where someone undergoes radical cosmetic surgery to (for example) give themselves a cat-like face or a body shape which is so extreme as to be a caricature?

Also, who is the artist here? The individual, or the cosmetic surgeon/hairdresser/beautician who carries out the work?

Self includes gender, and there are many studies on how the individual's perception of gender affects purchasing behaviour. People typically form a view on the gender-appropriateness of brands: there is evidence that men are more concerned about this than women, being less prepared to adopt a brand extension which they perceive as coming from a 'feminine' brand (Jung and Lee 2006). Men also tend to define masculinity in part through

Consumer behaviour in action
The Divine Image

The Divine Image is a consultancy with a strong foothold in a growing market – that of personal image.

Managing director Camelia Fredericks is a former lawyer now turned image consultant. She is a member of the Federation of Image Consultants, and has built The Divine Image on a foundation of sleek, upmarket chic (to quote the corporate website).

The Divine Image will, under the direction of Camelia and her staff, carry out a personal analysis of what colours the client should wear, what style of clothes, and what hairstyle and cosmetics are appropriate. What the consultancy does goes further than the TV makeover cliché – The Divine Image will advise on correct body language, and 'personal branding' to project the right image. The company is quite upfront about what they are aiming to do for clients: they aim to develop confidence, develop dress sense and style, improve self-esteem and overall improve self-image.

The service does not stop with advice, either. Consultants will go shopping with clients and help them find the right clothes, and will even precede this with a visit to the client's wardrobe to see what is already suitable and (more importantly) what is not. Consultants are available to advise on dating – everything from making the first approach to making a good impression on the night, and making the other person fall head over heels in love. Heaven on earth, for only £50 an hour for a consultation.

The service is not, as one might imagine, confined to women. Exactly the same service is available to men, and The Divine Image has a great many male clients.

Why do people use services like The Divine Image? Simple – most of us know that we would do better in our careers, in our love lives and in our social lives if we could only project the right image. Few of us are experts in this, and we envy people who seem always to wear the right clothes, say the right things, and influence the right people. Any money invested in image consultancy will come back tenfold in improved job prospects and less time and money wasted on unsuitable clothing and dating. After all, the investment is in something which can never be lost, repossessed or taken away – yourself.

advertisements they see (although they may interpret what masculinity means in different ways). Extensions from a 'male' brand are much more likely to be adopted (Tonkay 2006).

Self-concept has four attributes, as follows;

1　It is learned, not innate.

2　It is stable and consistent. Self-perception may change; self-concept does not. This accounts for brand loyalty, since self-concept involves an opinion about which products will 'fit the image'.

3　It is purposeful; in other words, there is a reason and a purpose behind it. Essentially, self-concept is there to protect and enhance a person's ego. It is therefore advisable not to attack a person's beliefs directly; people often become angry or at least defensive when this happens.

4　The self-concept is unique to the individual, and promotes individualism.

Self-concept breaks down into different components, or dimensions (Walker 1992). These are shown in Table 4.2.

There is some overlap, but the differences are quite marked between the dimensions. Each dimension has some relevance for marketers, and the implications are as shown in Table 4.3 (page 84).

For marketers, the differences are useful. Ideal self predicts attempts at upward mobility; purchases of courses, self-improvement classes, upmarket products, cosmetic surgery, etc. Looking-glass self is relevant for other-directed people.

In Figure 4.6 (page 85), self-concept is generated partly by internal factors such as looking-glass self, ideal self, and self-image, but these are modified (particularly through looking-glass self) by the real self. This is because those around us give us feedback on how we are coming across, either by showing approval of what we do or by showing disapproval.

Self can also be categorized as actual self, ideal self, and worst self (Banister and Hogg 2003). This is a simpler model, but it includes the concept of the worst self – the self we are ashamed of. For marketers, products can be promoted as being good for avoiding the worst self, or can be promoted as being good for appeasing the worst self.

Self-image is relevant to what we think we deserve; what is the 'right' product for us. People are swayed by what is promoted as being 'just right for people like you' – children

The person as artwork.

© iStockphoto.com

Table 4.2 Components of self-concept

Component	Explanation
Real self	This is the actual, objective self, as others see us. There is a problem with this definition, since other people never know the whole story. This means that the 'real' self may be something other than the face shown to the world.
Self-image	This is the subjective self, as we see ourselves. Self-image is likely to differ radically from the real self, but to an extent this is modified over time because of feedback from others. We modify our self-image in the light of the reactions of others.
Ideal self	How we wish we were; this connects to the self-actualization need that Maslow identified. This self is often the one that provokes the most extravagant spending, as the individual tries to make up the gap between self-image and ideal self.
Looking-glass self	The social self, or the way we think other people see us. This does not always coincide with the way people actually see us, since we are not able to read minds. Feedback from others will be constrained by politeness or by a desire to project a self-image on the part of the respondent, so we are not always aware of what other people really think we are like.
Possible selves	These are the selves we might become, or the selves we wish we could become.

Table 4.3 Relevance of self-image

Dimension	Relevance to marketers	Examples
Real self	As the face that is shown to the world, this is the one that people most wish to influence	Conspicuous consumption of cars, houses, etc. Cosmetics, fashion, and hairdressing.
Self-image	Useful in two ways; firstly, the negative aspects of self-image influence the ideal self, and secondly the positive aspects influence purchases to reinforce the self-image	Somebody whose self-image is 'cool' will not want to jeopardize that, and will buy appropriate products to match that image. Somebody whose self-image is poor will want to correct discrepancies.
Ideal self	The aspect that leads to the greatest purchases of self-improvement products	Correspondence courses, cosmetics, cosmetic surgery, musical instruments, and any number of other products that lead to self-development.
Looking-glass self	The way we *think* others see us; this influences us in making changes to those views, or reinforcing views that are perceived as positive	A man who thinks his friends see him as being staid or boring might be prompted to buy a sports car in order to correct the image. Conversely, somebody more outer-directed might deliberately buy a car to fit in with the image he thinks he has with his friends; perhaps to buy a Ford Focus or Volkswagen Golf because his friends see him as a solid, down-to-earth person. ALLAN BURROWS LIMITED
Possible selves	The selves we might become, or the selves we wish to become, are not necessarily the same. We may fear what we might become (for example being afraid of becoming overweight, or of contracting a serious disease, or of becoming an alcoholic)	In some cases marketers have a role in helping people to formulate and fulfil their dreams – education and training courses are an example. In other cases marketing techniques are used to enable people to avoid becoming what they fear being: social marketing campaigns encourage people to eat healthily, take exercise, cut down on smoking and over-eating, and control their alcohol intake.

can be told they are having 'the special children's meal'; students can be swayed by a 'special student discount', elderly people by the special 'senior citizen's service'. Sometimes this type of promotion can backfire – there may be fears about the quality of the service or product, for instance, and (especially in the case of older people) the self-image of the person might differ from the image the marketer has of their group. This is why advertising aimed at elderly people often uses actors in their fifties and sixties rather than actors in their seventies or eighties. An interesting piece of research showed that people tend to relate more strongly to brands which contain letters from their own names: this is probably a subconscious association with the brand (Brendl *et al.* 2003).

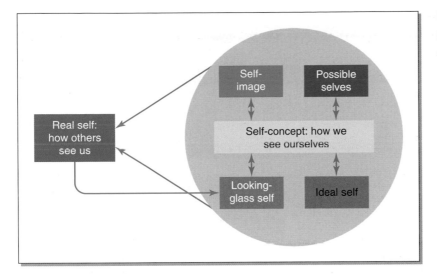

Figure 4.6

Relationship between components of self-concept

The real self is not known to the consumer, although it is one of the greatest motivators in consumer behaviour. In the words of Burns, 'To see ourselves as others see us' is not in our gift – and this may be just as well.

Achieving the ideal self is very much about getting appropriate applause and critical acclaim, so that we know whether we are getting it right; but perhaps more importantly there is the element of learning the lines and getting the production right in terms of costume, makeup and script. People therefore modify their behaviour according to the feedback obtained; this is called **self-monitoring** (Snyder 1974). Self-monitoring has three forms of expression (Figure 4.7): concern for the appropriateness of behaviour, attention to social comparison as cues for appropriate self-expression, and the ability to modify self-presentation and expression across situations (Nantel and Strahle 1986). Another example is people's attitude to credit: people with strong self-monitoring mechanisms, and people with low price-consciousness, are less likely to rely on credit cards than are people with low self-control or high price sensitivity (Perry 2001). Such self-monitoring mechanisms only have a limited amount of mental resources backing them up: often people who normally exhibit great self-control will 'snap' and buy something entirely on impulse (Vohs and Faber 2003).

In other words, people ensure that their behaviour is appropriate for the occasion by observing what others are doing and by acting in harmony with that behaviour. Rather like the inexperienced diner who watches others to see which knife and fork to use for each course, people take cues from those around them in order to ensure polite behaviour. Low self-monitors are more likely to behave according to some inner drive, and may even prefer to be seen as being different from the rest of humanity; high self-monitors are more likely to conform with those around them, and are therefore more susceptible to appeals to be fashionable.

Felix has a definite personality.

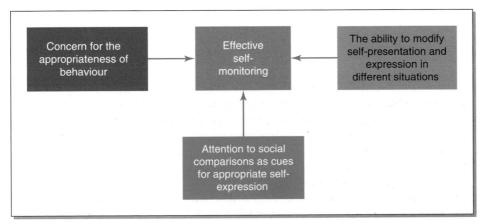

Figure 4.7

Self-monitoring

Summary

In this chapter we have looked at what constitutes peoples' personalities and self-concepts. We have also looked at role-playing, and have looked at some of the ways these elements affect consumers' buying behaviour. Car manufacturers still sell on personality; perfumes such as Jean-Paul Gaultier and Calvin Klein, and even pet food advertisements also rely on personality. The Felix cat is lively, inquisitive, a little mischievous, and always affectionate to its human. The implication is that feeding the cat Felix will make it into this type of cat, even if it starts out as a less-than-perfect house pet.

Here are the key points of the chapter:

● Personality is made up of traits; so far 18,000 possible traits have been identified.

● Personality is a self-serving, individualistic, unique, overt and consistent gestalt.

● Self-concept is concerned with one's feelings about oneself.

● Self-concept is learned, stable, purposeful and unique.

● As wealth increases, more people are becoming inner-directed.

● High self-monitors take their cues from others; low self-monitors take their cues from an inner drive.

Chapter review questions

1 Why are personality traits an important concept for marketers?

2 Why is self-concept such a useful way of segmenting markets?

3 What might be the impact of increased inner direction on fashion in the future?

4 How might high self-monitors respond to an increase in inner direction in the rest of the population?

5 How might the Myers-Briggs type dimensions be used by marketers for a perfume company?

6 What are the marketing implications of the possible self?

7 What are the marketing implications of the gender perception of brands?

Preview case study revisited
Ads on cars

So what kind of person would want to drive around in a car plastered with advertising? First, someone who is keen to save money on motoring costs, and is not too worried what other people think. Second, someone who likes the products being advertised. One of the American drivers said that she was advertising a hot-dog place that she takes her kids to, and she was more than happy to carry the advertisement and even answer people's questions about the advertisers. This was despite the fact that she reported being embarrassed at first by driving around with advertising on her car.

Third, people might join the scheme as a way of making a statement about themselves. In some cases this will be a statement connected with the product, in other cases it might be a statement about being a frugal person, in yet other cases it might simply be that the car looks smarter and more interesting than it does without the advertising.

There is, of course, a risk to the advertisers if the drivers behave badly in some way, as this might reflect badly on the brand. Motorists who drive inconsiderately, park the car in an inappropriate place (outside a sex shop, for instance) or do not clean their cars regularly might create a problem. AdsOnCars are careful about selecting drivers, but this is no guarantee that the driver will continue to be well behaved or will not lend the car to someone (a son or daughter perhaps) who behaves badly.

The idea of branding private vehicles is an interesting example of how brand personality and individual personality overlap. From the advertiser's viewpoint, the driver should have an appropriate personality for the brand (a sportswear manufacturer would obviously like to advertise on a car which goes to sports club car parks, for example) and from the driver's viewpoint the brand should be one which says something about the driver's lifestyle. Provided each party has a similar viewpoint, the arrangement has many advantages, since there are personality synergies as well as the simple financial gain for the driver against the novel advertising opportunity for the brand owner.

The country is unlikely to be aswarm with liveried private vehicles, however: most people probably prefer to keep their car the way it was when they bought it. What will happen is that more people will make statements about their lifestyles through associating themselves with brands – and getting paid for it into the bargain.

COVERED UK LTD

Case study
Cerebos Pacific Limited

Cerebos Pacific Ltd is the Asian subsidiary of Rank Hovis McDougal. The company manufactures food and health supplements for sale throughout the Asia-Pacific region. Brands include Fountain, Gregg's, Gravox and Brand's, as well as the salt for which the company first became famous. Brand's Essence of Chicken is probably the company's best-known brand in the region: originally developed as a health supplement for King George IV in 1820, Brand's Essence of Chicken became popular throughout what was then the British Empire, but nowhere more so than in the Asia-Pacific region. Cerebos Pacific now produce nine different varieties, with additives such as ginseng, tangkwei and lingzhi.

Building on its reputation, the company went on to develop the Asian Home Gourmet range of products. Asian Home Gourmet is a range of spice and herb pastes which can be used to create authentic dishes (everything from curries to stir fries to desserts) quickly and easily at home. Unlike many such products sold in Western countries, Asian Home Gourmet products are aimed at Asian consumers who simply do not have the time to spend on cooking, but who want to eat traditional food from the region.

The Asian attitude to food is generally considerably different from the attitude prevalent in Britain and the United States, and indeed in much of the rest of Europe. Cooking for family and friends is very much an act of love and respect in Asia, rather than simply another household chore as it tends to be in the UK and USA. With an increase in the number of career women, and increasing pressure in the workplace, people simply lacked the time to cook elaborate dishes or grind and mix spices and herbs in the correct proportions. This inevitably led to feelings of guilt and inadequacy on the part of many Asian women.

Because most Asian cultures tend to repress overt emotion, there are relatively few outlets for demonstrations of affection. Food has certainly traditionally been one of the ways in which people can express themselves. Guy Murphy, the strategic planning director for Bartle Bogle Hegarty (the ad agency that created the brand platform) expressed this well when he said, 'In Asia food is a proxy for showing emotion. While people the world over have an emotional relationship with food, that relationship appears to be most intense in the Asian region.' The agency created a campaign in which typically Asian ingredients such as chillies and herbs interwine and hold hands. Double-page magazine advertisements show the intertwined ingredients on the left-hand page, and the words on the right.

The campaign was called 'Recipes made with love' and the brand personality is very much family-orientated. Cerebos Pacific Ltd tapped into this cultural phenomenon very successfully by telling people:

> Our SpicePastes are made from fresh herbs and spices. You can use them to create any one of a range of authentic Asian dishes. All you have to do is add one important ingredient, a little of yourself.

recipes made with love

CEREBOS PACIFIC LIMITED

The line 'add a little of yourself' enables the consumer to feel that the most important part of the meal, the emotion, is coming from themselves even if the rest of the ingredients (and much of the skill, of course) is coming out of a jar. The product range itself was originally only available in Asia, but the company has since expanded its market to include most Western countries as well. Some of the driver for this has come from expatriate Asian families, but the Asian Home Gourmet brand has found its way into mainstream supermarkets as well as the traditional Chinatown retailers.

By linking the brand personality to a particular personality trait, Asian Home Gourmet has positioned itself, in less than ten years, as the world's leading brand of high-quality Asian convenience foods.

Case study questions

1   What is the role of the superego in creating demand for Asian Home Gourmet spices?

2   How does the ego resolve the conflict set up by a consumer being unable to spend the time on cooking that her or his ancestors did?

3   Why does the 'add a little of yourself' strap line work so well with an Asian audience?

4   Why might this strap line work less well on a UK audience?

5   Which of the Myers-Briggs personality types would be most attracted to this product range?

References

Allport, G.W., and Odbert, H.S. (1936) *Trait Names: A Psycholexial Study.* Psychological monograph 47, No. 211 (Princeton, NJ: American Psychological Association).

Balabanis, George (2002) The relationship between lottery ticket and scratchcard buying behaviour, personality and other compulsive behaviours. *Journal of Consumer Behaviour*, 2(1): 7–22.

Banister, Emma N., and Hogg, Margaret K. (2003) Possible selves? Identifying dimensions for exploring the dialectic between positive and negative selves in consumer behaviour. *Advances in Consumer Research*, 30(1).

Belk, Russell (2003) Shoes and self. *Advances in Consumer Research*, 30(1): 27–33.

Brendl, C. Miguel, Chattopadhyay, Amitiva, Pelham, Brett W., Carvalho, Mauricio, and Prichard, Evan T. (2003) Are brands containing name letters preferred? *Advances in Consumer Research*, 30(1): 151–2.

Briggs, Kathryn, and Myers, Isabel (1992) The Myers-Briggs type indicator. *San Jose Mercury News*, 23 September.

Cohen, Joel B. (1967) An interpersonal orientation to the study of consumer behaviour. *Journal of Marketing Research*, 6 (August): 270–8.

deBerry Spence, Benet, and Izberk Bilgin, Elif (2006) Wearing identity: the symbolic uses of native African clothing by African Americans. *Advances in Consumer Research*, 33(1): 193.

Dickerson, Mary Lee, and Gentry, James W. (1983) Characteristics of adopters and non-adopters of home computers. *Journal of Consumer Research*, 10 (Sept): 225–35.

Donnelly, James H. Jr. (1970) Social character and the acceptance of new products. *Journal of Marketing Research*, 7 (February): 111–13.

Evans, Martin, and Blythe, Jim (1994) Fashion: A new paradigm of consumer behaviour. *Journal of Consumer Studies and Home Economics*, 18.

Foxall, Gordon (1980) *Consumer Behaviour: A Practical Guide* (London; Routledge).

Fraj, Elena, and Martinez, Eva (2006) Influence of personality on ecological consumer behaviour. *Journal of Consumer Behaviour*, 5 (May–June): 167–81.

Goleman, Daniel (1987) Basic personality traits don't change, studies say. *New York Times* (18 June).

Horney, Karen (1945) *Our Inner Conflict* (New York: WW Norton).

Jung, Kwon, and Lee, Winston (2006) Cross-gender brand extensions: effects of gender of the brand, gender of the consumer, and product type on cross-gender extensions. *Advances in Consumer Research*, 33(1): 67–74.

Klein, Jill G. (2003) Calories for dignity: fashion in the concentration camp. *Advances in Consumer Research*, 30(1): 34–7.

Marketing News (1985), 13 September: 56.

McNulty, W. Kirk (1985) Personality: Major traits found stable throughout life. *Futures*, 9 June.

Nantel, Jacques, and Strahle, William (1986) The self-monitoring concept: a consumer perspective. *Advances in Consumer Research* 13 ed. Richard E. Lutz (Provo, UT: Association for Consumer Research): 83–7.

Perry, Vanessa Gail (2001) Antecedents of consumer financing decisions: a mental accounting model of revolving credit usage. *Advances in Consumer Research*, 28(1): 13.

Reisman, David (1953) *The Lonely Crowd* (New York, Doubleday).

Shaw, Dierdre, Grehan, Emma, Shiu, Edward, Hassan, Louise, and Thomson, Jennifer (2005) An exploration of values in ethical consumer decision-making. *Journal of Consumer Behaviour*, 4(3): 185–200.

Snyder, Mark (1974) Self-monitoring of expressive behaviour. *Journal of Personality and Social Psychology*, 34.

Tonkay, Linda (2006) Men's responses to depictions of idea masculinity in advertising. *Advances in Consumer Research*, 33(1): 64.

Vohs, Kathleen, and Faber, Ronald (2003) Self-regulation and impulsive spending patterns. *Advances in Consumer Research*, 30(1): 125–6.

Walker, Beth Ann (1992) New perspectives for self-research. *Advances in Consumer Research*, ed. John H. Sherry Jr. and Brian Sternthal (Provo, UT: Association for Consumer Research, 417–23.

Zhinkan, George M., and Shermohamad, Ali (1986) Is other-directedness on the increase? An empirical test of Reisman's theory of social character. *Journal of Consumer Research*, 13 (June): 127–30.

Chapter 5
Perception

Learning objectives After reading this chapter, you should be able to:

1 explain the role of analysis and synthesis in perception

2 explain the role of synergy in creating a perceptual impression

3 understand the problem created for marketers by selectivity

4 explain how past experience affects perception

5 describe Weber's law

6 describe the relationship between perception and reality

7 explain the conscious and unconscious aspects of perception

8 explain the difference between internal and overt perceptual responses

9 discuss subliminal advertising

10 explain the role of colour in perception

Introduction

How we analyze the environment around us and develop a picture of the world is of great interest to marketers. Ensuring that the company's brands become part of the world view of the potential consumers is the main purpose of marketing communications: understanding perception processes is what puts the product there.

Perception is the keystone of building knowledge, not just about products but about everything else in the world. Although it is common to refer to perception as if it were somehow different from the truth, this is not the case: perceptions may differ between individuals, but for each person their own perception is the whole truth.

Perception

There are eight main conventions regarding perception, as shown in Table 5.1 on page 93.

Perception is a process of converting sensory input into an understanding of how the world works. Because it involves combining many different sensory inputs, the overall perception is complex to analyze. Human beings have considerably more than five senses. Apart from the basic five (touch, taste, smell, sight, hearing) there are senses of direction, sense of balance, a clear knowledge of which way is down, and so forth. Each sense is feeding information to the brain constantly, and the amount of information being collected would seriously overload the system if one took it all in. The brain therefore selects from the environment around the individual and cuts out the extraneous noise.

In effect, the brain makes automatic decisions as to what is relevant and what is not. Even though there may be many things happening around you, you are

© iStockphoto.com

In a busy environment we ignore much of what is happening around us.

Preview case study
Car noise

For years, car buyers have slammed the doors to check on the quality of the car. A satisfying thump denoted a good quality, solidly made car: a tinny rattle showed that the car was poorly built. Of course, slamming the door is no real indication of the quality of the vehicle, but everyone slammed doors anyway as part of the choosing ritual.

As overall vehicle quality has improved, people have become more adept at using other surrogates to judge the quality of the vehicle. Sound still plays an important part, though: the many sounds the car makes all go towards giving the customer an overall impression of the vehicle, and car manufacturers have not been slow to recognise this. Sports drivers who hear the roar of the engine believe the car's performance to be suitably lively; luxury car buyers who are able to have conversations with rear-seat passengers believe the car to be high quality; and lower noise levels generally relate to a perception of good engineering and solid construction.

The difficulty for manufacturers lies in knowing exactly which sound signatures they need to engineer in for each type of customer. The sound patterns within the vehicle are not something which is easily customised – and people are easily affected by the sound of the car, without always realising that they are affected. Another problem is that, as sound levels within the car decrease, other sounds become more noticeable, so that a clunky gear change or squeaky suspension becomes much more audible above the reduced engine noise. For example, on one vehicle the engineers found that, at certain speeds, there was a vibration from the power steering pump. This was cured by re-routing the hydraulic line and changing the pump mountings, but the engineering consultants who cured the problem stated that the sound would have gone unnoticed in earlier models of the car because of the much higher noise levels in the passenger compartment.

Manufacturers therefore have to tread warily when making changes which might affect customer perceptions of the vehicles – after all, people are making a large investment when they buy cars, and they are likely to shop around and go as much on gut feeling as on practical considerations.

unaware of most of them; in fact, experiments have shown that some information is filtered out by the optic nerve even before it gets to the brain. People quickly learn to ignore extraneous noises; for example, as a visitor to someone else's home you may be sharply aware of a loudly ticking clock, whereas your host may be entirely used to it and unaware of it except when making a conscious effort to check that the clock is still running.

Perception is, in part, a process of analysis in which the outside world is filtered and only the most important (as defined by the individual) or interesting (as defined by the individual) items come through. Therefore the information entering the brain does not provide a complete view of the world.

In Figure 5.1, most of the stimuli surrounding the individual are filtered out. The remaining stimuli are combined and interpreted, then included with memory and imagination to create an overall perception.

Talking point

It looks as if we are all just making this up as we go along. If perception is reality, and we are imagining most of the world, why don't we imagine somewhere a great deal pleasanter?

We could imagine an earthly paradise, with free beer and sandwiches for all, if we just filter out the bad parts and keep the good bits. So why not do this? After all, there are plenty of lunatics about who seem to be perpetually cheerful and optimistic.

Or perhaps we need to let some of the threatening aspects of life enter in order to defend against them?

Table 5.1 Conventions about perception

Convention	Explanation
Perception is about more than the substantive part of the message	Messages may be expressed directly in words, but the observer 'reads between the lines' and creates new meanings from what is seen or read.
The law of similarity says that we interpret new information in a similar way to information we already hold	If we read a newspaper report in a paper we trust to be accurate, we will tend to assume that the new report is also accurate. If we see packaging (for example a brown coffee jar) we will associate this with similar brown packaging on other brands of coffee.
Expectations	If we expect a particular sequence of events, or a particular message, then we tend to see that message and interpret accordingly.
'Figure–ground' relationships influence interpretation	An individual will interpret a printed message differently according to which part of the image is interpreted as the message and which part as the background.
The Law of Closure	This means that people can only obtain the whole message if they have all the components of the message. This particular applies in advertisements which are intended to intrigue the consumers: and advertisement which contains a puzzle or a visual joke will not be understood be the observers unless they are in possession of enough information to infer the punch line.
The Law of Continuity	Gestalt perception is based on the idea that the elements of the overall message form a continuum rather than a set of separate elements. In other words, even when a particular stimulus (for example an advertisement) is composed of music, speech, pictures, and moving images the person watching it will still form an overall impression. Of course, someone who is asked to analyze an advertisement will be able to separate out the various elements, but in normal behaviour few people would do this.
The whole is greater than the sum of its parts	When the message consists of a number of elements, the elements often combine to create a stronger message.
Colour influences perception	Because human beings have a well-developed colour sense, colours are often influential in creating an overall image of a product. This may be due to the need, in prehistoric times, for hunter-gatherers to assess the ripeness or nutritional value of fruit.

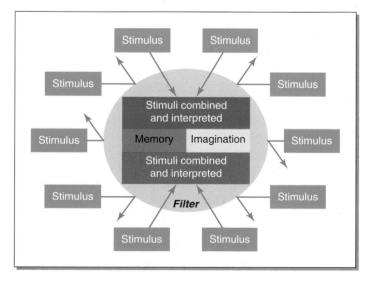

Figure 5.1

Selectivity and synthesis

When the individual constructs a world view, he or she assembles information to map what is happening in the outside world (Figure 5.2). Any gaps (and there will, of course, be plenty of these) will be filled in with imagination and experience. The cognitive map is therefore not a 'photograph'; it is (at least in part) a construct of the imagination. This mapping will be affected by the following factors:

1   **Subjectivity**. This is the existing world view within the individual, and is unique to that individual.

2   **Categorization**. This is the 'pigeonholing' of information, and the prejudging of events and products. This can happening through a process known as **chunking** whereby the individual organizes information into chunks of related items (Miller 1956). For example, a picture seen while a particular piece of music is playing might be chunked as one item in the memory, so that sight of the picture evokes the music and vice versa.

3   **Selectivity** is the degree to which the brain is selecting from the environment. It is a function of how much is going on around the individual, and also of how selective (concentrated) the individual is on the current task. Selectivity is also subjective; some people are a great deal more selective than others. Recent research shows that people judge the authenticity of Irish-themed pubs by the behaviour of the employees and the patrons rather than from the décor, showing that people are being selective in the factors they use to judge the pub (Munoz, Wood and Solomon 2006).

4   **Expectations** lead individuals to interpret later information in a specific way. For example, look at this series of numbers and letters;

A 13 C D E F G H J

10 11 12 13 14 15 16

In fact, the number 13 appears in both series, but in the first series it would be interpreted as a B because that is what the brain is being led to expect (the B in Matura MT Script looks like this: *B*).

5   **Past experience** leads us to interpret later experience in the light of what we already know. This is called the Law of Primacy by psychologists. Sometimes sights, smells or sounds from our past will trigger off inappropriate responses; the smell of bread baking may recall a village bakery from 20 years ago, but in fact the smell could have been artificially generated by an aerosol spray near the supermarket bread counter.

Granny Smiths.
What's the difference between ours and our competitors'?
Not much really.
They're the same quality as Waitrose.
And the same price as Asda.

TESCO | *Every little helps*

ADVERTISING ARCHIVES

Supermarkets often need to explain how they differ from each other.

An example of cognitive mapping as applied to perception of product quality might run as follows. The consumer uses the input selector to select clues and assign values to them. For quality, the cues are typically price, brand name and retailer name. There are strong positive relationships between price and quality in most consumers' perceptions, and brand name and quality; although the retailer name is less significant, it still carries some weight. For example, many consumers would feel confident that a major department store such as Harrod's would sell higher-quality items than the local corner shop, but might be less able to distinguish between rival supermarket chains such as Sainsbury's and Tesco.

The information is subjective in that the consumer will base decisions on the selected information. Each of us selects differently from the environment, and each of us has differing views. In the case of distinguishing between rival supermarket chains, each individual will have a slightly different view of the supermarkets concerned. If this were not so, we would rapidly develop a situation in which only one supermarket chain existed. The individual's previous experience also has a bearing – for example, research shows that adolescents

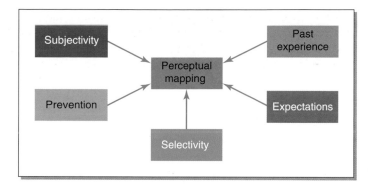

Figure 5.2

Influences on perceptual mapping

who live in areas where there are high levels of drug use and sexual promiscuity overestimate their own knowledge of these things (Parker, Fischhof and deBruin 2006).

Information about quality will be pigeonholed or categorized so that products from different categories might be placed next to each other in the cognitive map. For example, an individual may put Jaguars in the same category as BMW, but might also include Sony or Grundig in the same grouping. It is common to hear people refer to a product as 'the Rolls Royce of . . . ' whichever product category is under consideration.

Selectivity will depend on how much is going on in the environment, on the individual's interest and motivation regarding the subject area, and on the degree of concentration the individual has on the task in hand. People with a highly developed ability to concentrate select less from the environment, because they are able to 'shut out' the world much more.

Expectations of quality play a huge part; if the individual is expecting a high-quality item, he or she will select evidence which supports that view and tend to ignore evidence that doesn't.

Past experience will also play a part in quality judgement. If the consumer has had bad experiences of Japanese products, this might lead to a general perception that Japanese products are poor quality.

Price has a strong effect on people's view of quality. There is a general belief that the higher the price, the better the quality in some way; often this view will be justified, of course. The downside from a marketer's viewpoint is that price has a negative effect on perceived value and on willingness to buy. The problem lies in knowing how big a price reduction will increase sales without leading to a negative perception of quality.

Weber's Law states that the size of the least detectable change depends on the size of the stimulus. This means that a very intense stimulus will require a bigger change if the change is to be perceived by the consumer. For example, three pence off the price of a morning newspaper is a substantial discount, and would attract attention in advertising; three pence off the price of a BMW would go unnoticed. Clearly at this level of intensity (a price of a few pence compared with a price of thousands of pounds) Weber's Law may not work very precisely (Britt and Nelson 1976), but in the middle range of prices the law appears to work well. Incidentally, reducing the price from £10 to £9.99 is very noticeable even though the actual reduction is only 0.01 per cent of the initial price. The important element here is that the reduction be noticeable.

Weber's Law also applies to product differentiation. The law can be applied to determine how much better the product has to be for the difference to be noticeable (Britt 1975), or conversely to determine how similar the product needs to be indistinguishable from the leading brand.

It should be noted here that perception and reality are not different things. There is a popular view that perception somehow differs from reality; in fact, reality only exists in the heads of individuals. If there is an objective reality, it is not accessible to us as human beings; we only have what our senses tell us, and for each of us reality is different because each of us selects and synthesises in a different way. Figure 5.3 may help to illustrate this.

Figure 5.3

Perception and reality

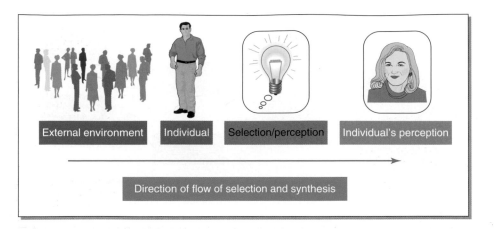

The individual in the diagram is in a crowded room, yet he only has eyes for the lady. His synthesis of what she looks like may not be accurate, of course; somebody else may have a differing perception. We often say that someone is 'looking through the eyes of love' or that 'beauty is in the eye of the beholder'. These phrases accurately sum up what perception is all about.

The perception process

The perception process is a social-psychological phenomenon. It involves cue selection and cue interpretation, and combining these cues to create an overall impression. There are six components of perception, as follows (Warr and Knapper 1968):

1 Stimulus.
2 Input selector.
3 Processing centre.
4 Consumer's current state.
5 Consumer's stable characteristics.
6 Response.

The stimulus is the object which is being perceived. In this sense, the object could be a person, a product, an event, a situation, a communication, or anything which catches the individual's attention. For marketers, the stimulus on offer is likely to be a brand, a product, a retail shop, or a marketing communication.

Some experiments have been conducted in the use of multisensory brands. Nike found that people who tried out the trainers in a floral-scented room preferred them to the same trainers when they tried them in a non-scented room (Lindstrom 2005). Using senses which (at first sight) appear to be unrelated to the primary senses to which the product relates can be extremely powerful: for example, the 'snap, crackle and pop' of Rice Krispies relates sound to the brand, whereas one would normally expect a food product to be primarily concerned with flavour and (perhaps) texture. Another example is the way in which store atmospherics are manipulated to generate perceptions about the products on offer. There are three factors in the information processing of store atmospherics: proxemics, kinesics and paralanguage (see Figure 5.4).

Obviously if the fragrance is an inherent part of the product (for example, soap) any changes in the fragrance will have a profound effect on perception of the brand, even when the primary function of the brand is unaffected (Milotic 2003).

Proxemics refers to the use of physical space in conveying a perceptual stimulus. In a retail environment, for example, a shop assistant might stand too far away (which might be

The sound of the cereal is a key element in the perception of Rice Krispies.

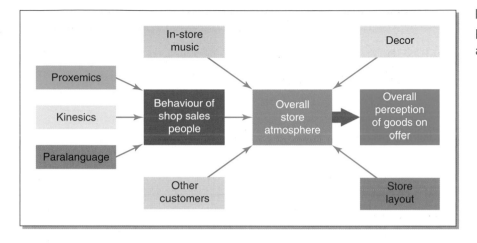

Figure 5.4
Perception and store atmospherics

interpreted as dislike for the customer) or too close (suggesting a threatening invasion of personal space). Kinesics is about body language, eye contact and gesture: greater eye contact between buyers and sellers would indicate positive feelings between them.

Paralanguage refers to the way words are used. Use of 'here' and 'this' is more positive than using 'there' and 'that'. Some other sound cues such as yawning, speaking too loudly or too softly, or speaking too quickly or too slowly also convey messages about how the individual feels about the product.

Talking point

We are all aware that body language makes a great deal of difference to communications. Gestures and subtleties of facial expression can completely change the meaning of words used. Yet most of this happens without us even being aware of it. We operate on gut feeling – we get a sense of when someone's lying, for example, without necessarily being able to say what particular facial expression or gesture gave the game away.

So how can we possibly expect to train shop assistants to behave in a particular way? Aren't we liable to make poor play-actors out of them, and thus give customers the impression that we are lying to them?

Or maybe we should just hire nice people to begin with?

The input selector is the mechanism by which the individual selects cues from the stimulus and assigns a meaning to each one. For example, someone seeing an advertisement for a car might remember the shape of the car but not the make, or might remember the background detail of the advertisement (the scenery against which the car is filmed, perhaps) and remember nothing about the vehicle itself. This is a perennial problem in marketing communications. Knowing which cues people most often select is clearly of great interest, especially if we are considering a specific factor such as quality. In some cases people judge quality on the basis of price, in other cases on the physical attributes of the product, but the current view is that the use of an extrinsic cue such as price and intrinsic cues such as physical and performance attributes depend on prior knowledge (Rao and Monroe 1988). As consumers become more familiar with the product's intrinsic attributes, price becomes less important as a surrogate for judging quality. In some cases, products are consumed almost entirely for their symbolic value: in emerging economies such as China products are often bought simply because they are Western brands, and symbolise a desirable lifestyle. These brands are sometimes desired even when the consumer has never seen the actual product (Clark, Micken and Hart 2002).

In a noisy, stimulating environment we have to focus more, so we ignore most of what is going on around us.

Figure 5.5

Information processing types

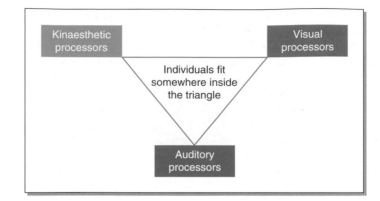

The input selector takes the various environmental factors and processes them one at a time: the processing centre has the task of integrating the cues to generate an overall perception. The input selector and the processing centre are not actually separate functions: they almost certainly operate at the same time, because the cues are delivered simultaneously or at least very closely after one another. Individuals process information in individual ways, of course; neuro-linguistic programming theory tells us that some people prefer to process visual information, some prefer auditory information, and yet others prefer tactile or kinaesthetic processing. Most of us are on a continuum in which we absorb and process cues from all three areas: it is simply that we prefer one route over another.

Visual processors are likely to respond better to advertising with strong graphics or visual content. Auditory processors prefer the spoken word, or music; kinaesthetic processors prefer to touch or try out products, so would be most likely to respond to advertising which offers a trial or free sample. As shown in Figure 5.5, most people fit somewhere inside a triangle formed by the three processing methods, favouring one or other but still able to process information in all three ways.

The processing centre is likely to be influenced by the individual's current state. The current state includes factors such as mood, motivation, goals and the physical state of the individual at the time the cues come along.

A mood is transitory: it will pass, no matter how strongly it is felt at the time. When we are in a good mood we tend to feel favourably towards more cues, whereas if we are in a bad mood we tend to be negative about cues. This is partly responsible for the halo effect (or horns effect) in which we tend to think that, if one thing is bad about something, everything is bad about it. Positive moods tend to create less elaboration (i.e. people think less when they are in a good mood) and decisions are often made much more automatically than would normally be the case (Batra and Stayman 1990). There is evidence that marketing messages which express positive outcomes are much more effective than those which stress negative outcomes, presumably because the former create good moods whereas the latter create fearful or worried moods (Zhao and Pechmann 2006). Moods can be manipulated to an extent by store atmospherics, which in turn affect purchasing behaviour – mood also affects processing of information from advertising (Bakamitsos and Siomkos 2004). Brand extensions are received more favourably if the individual is in a good mood (Griefeneder, Bless and Kuschmann 2007), and even the way the message is framed can affect perception: researchers found that smokers who read that almost 1000 people die of smoking every day found the message more powerful than saying that 440,000 people a year die of smoking. This is apparently because the shorter time-frame means that the message has more immediacy (Chandran and Menon 2003).

Time frames may have other effects – positive cues are often overrated when considering a future event because people broaden the range of factors they take into account when considering the future (Grant and Tybout 2003). Dates are regarded as abstract, whereas time intervals are concrete: in other words, 'six months' interest-free credit' sounds a great deal better than 'interest-free credit until 30th November' (LeBoeuf 2006).

Consumers' stable characteristics are the basic factors about an individual which do not change, or which change only slowly. Gender, personality, social class, age, educational level and intelligence all affect perception. Such differences can and do produce differences in the accuracy of interpretation of cues, and also in the selection of cues. Therefore wide differences in processing ability, and consequently in perception itself, should be expected between different individuals (Henry 1980).

Some demographic variables may be responsible for misunderstanding of cues; however, although the stable characteristics of the consumer might be expected to have a strong effect on perception, the interplay of the various factors is such that researching the effect of each one proves difficult. So far, therefore, research has been somewhat inconclusive on this issue.

Responses are not necessarily overt or external. In terms of perception, a response can just as easily be internal and non-behavioural. The perceptual response has three components: attribution, expectancy and affection (Figure 5.6, page 100).

Attribution is about applying a certain characteristic to an object. For example, someone who is scowling might be perceived as being angry. It is possible that the person is actually deep in thought about a problem which has just arisen, but the observer has attributed the

Consumer behaviour in action
Wolff Olins and Orange

When mobile telephones first appeared in the 1980s they were heavy, expensive and unreliable, but like all new technologies they quickly became more refined and sophisticated. The UK market for mobile telephones was seen in the industry as one of the more lucrative ones – a country with a relatively small geographical area and a densely packed wealthy population offered advantages both technically and economically.

The Hong Kong conglomerate Hutchison Whampoa had not failed to see the implications, and had tried to enter the UK market with a brand called Rabbit. This disappeared without trace; a second attempt, in 1994, used branding consultants Wolff Olins to manage the brand. The consultants came up with a concept which changed marketing history – the Orange brand.

The aim of the brand was to move mobile telephones away from being the preserve of business people and yuppies and move them into the mainstream of everyday life. The brand was conceived as being warm and friendly, energetic and optimistic. The philosophy behind the Orange brand was that landlines only connect one place to another – mobile telephones connect people with people.

Using the strap line 'The future's bright – the future's Orange', the consultants developed a series of eye-catching advertisements. Using the colour orange meant that marketing communications became even more powerful and memorable – within two weeks of the launch the brand had achieved an unprecedented 45 per cent awareness with the British public, and within

two years awareness was over 70 per cent (considerably higher than its rivals, Vodafone and Cellnet).

Wolff Olins managed the Orange brand from 1994 until 2000 (when the brand was sold to Mannesmann). At that time, the brand sold for the equivalent of £5,000 per customer, which perhaps shows that perception of brands affects more than just consumers.

speak without dialling. Orange believe that the most natural way to communicate is simply to speak. That's why Wildfire, the new virtual personal assistant from Orange, responds to the sound of your voice. She can help you by taking care of all your calls and messages. She can even greet all your friends. Advanced technology? Or the most natural thing in the world?

Call us on 0800 80 10 80.

The future's bright.

The future's Orange.

www.orange.co.uk

Figure 5.6

Perceptual responses

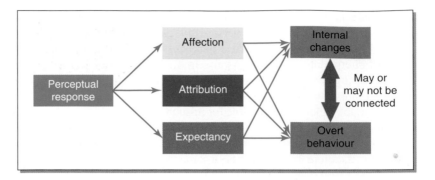

characteristic of anger based on the cue of the facial expression. The same process happens when people are confronted with a product or brand: they attribute characteristics to it, based on the cues received.

Expectancy is about what the individual thinks the object will do. In the case of the scowling person, the observer might expect that the person might shout or even become violent. In marketing, expectancy is what leads people to believe that a well-known brand is better than the generic brand, even though the formulation is the same. One of the best-known examples of this is analgesics (painkillers). Branded aspirin actually works better than generic aspirin, even though the active ingredient (acetylsalicylic acid) is identical in each case.

Affection is about emotional responses. In ordinary language, affection implies a positive response, but in psychology affection merely describes any emotional effect, whether positive or negative. Such responses to a given stimulus might be liking, sympathy, fear, respect, disapproval, disgust, and so forth. An affective response is what we refer to when we talk about gut feeling or instinct: it is not a rational response, but that does not necessarily mean that it is wrong or ill conceived.

Combining factors

The processing centre combines the various cues to create an overall impression. This is likely to include attribution, expectation and affection components, but there are three basic models which seek to explain how this happens in practice. There are as follows:

1 *The linear additive model* – This states that the inferences from each clue will build towards an overall perception. This means that the implications which attach to a particular characteristic will become stronger with the addition of each cue, regardless of how intense each cue is. A strong cue will not be weakened by a subsequent weak cue, in other words. See Figure 5.7.

2 *The linear averaging model* – This is a refinement on the previous model, since it assumes that the implication of a particular characteristic will be strengthened or

Figure 5.7

Linear additive model

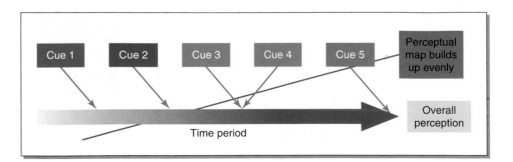

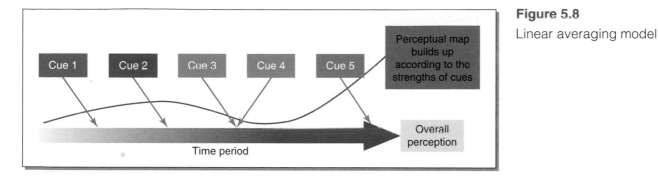

Figure 5.8

Linear averaging model

weakened by subsequent cues, according to their strength. This means that the quality of the information may be more important than the quantity of the information, so that marketers who try to provide people with very large amounts of positive information may find that the effect is weakened if people regard some of the information as being of less interest than other information. Salespeople generally understand this phenomenon well: they are trained to find out first what the customer is interested in about the product, then to talk only about those aspects. There is also some (rather elderly) research evidence to show that the linear averaging model fits the facts better than the linear additive model (Anderson 1965). See Figure 5.8.

3 *The configural model* – Linear models have the underlying assumption that the meaning of each cue remains the same when other facts are revealed. This is not necessarily the case: as cues are brought together, the meanings of previous cues are likely to be revised in the light of the new information. The configural model is intended to address this issue. The problem with this model is, of course, that it is virtually impossible to calculate what may or may not happen in a particular individual's mind as a result of being presented with a number of cues, and it is even difficult to know what will happen across a target audience of potential customers, which makes advertising difficult. See Figure 5.9.

As with any models, all three of the above are simplifications of reality, and therefore do not tell the whole story. It seems likely that people perceive the whole of a given object, rather than breaking it down into individual cues, but this (naturally) varies according to circumstances. Someone choosing a new car might well want to consider every aspect individually – the comfort of the seats, the sound of the door closing, the quality of the interior finish, the space in the back seats and in the boot, the shape of the steering wheel, the layout of the various controls, and so forth. The motive for including the car in the consideration set in the first place might be an overall impression offered by the firm's advertising, however.

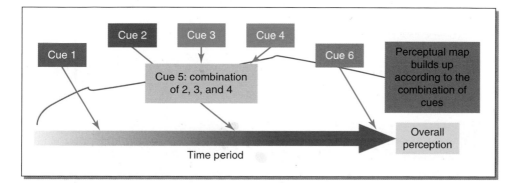

Figure 5.9

The configural model

Equally, the purchase of a brand of biscuits is unlikely to involve the same level of analysis. Few people would trouble to read the list of ingredients and the nutritional information on the packet, or ask a friend's advice or go online and investigate the company's history and manufacturing methods.

An interesting area of research, therefore, is to try to find out which rules people use at particular times. Sometimes people will use a linear rule, at other times they might use a configural method and at still other times people might use a combination of rules to form an overall opinion. Research carried out by Meyer in 1987 seemed to indicate that people tend to use configural methods, but later on in the process the decisions moved towards additive rules (Meyer 1987).

It may be that the more utilitarian aspects of the product are judged against a linear set of rules, whereas the hedonic or affective aspects are judged against the configural model (Holbrook and Moore 1981).

Subliminal perception

Perception is not necessarily a conscious process. Much of what happens in our minds happens below the conscious level (see Chapter 4), and we know that often people have a 'gut feeling' about something without being able to define why. Most of us have had the experience of falling in love at first sight – with people or with products. This happens without our having any real facts to go on, and without our having any way of analysing the reasons.

Subliminal perception has a controversial history in marketing. During the 1950s it was claimed that subliminal advertising, as it was called, could make people do things they otherwise would not do. The theory was that a brief exposure to a message (for example, flashing 'Drink Cola' onto a cinema screen during a film) would cause people to experience a sudden mysterious desire to drink a cola. The theory was that the message would appear and disappear much too quickly for the input selector mechanism to operate, so the message would bypass the normal perceptual safeguards and enter the person's consciousness unedited (Figure 5.10). These claims were so powerful that subliminal advertising was banned in some countries and was regulated in others: in fact, the general air of paranoia in the 1950s may have contributed to the scare, since there is little evidence to support the claims made for subliminal advertising. One widely publicised 'experiment' in 1957 was later found to have been faked by the researcher, but the story still circulates about the effectiveness of flashing messages onto cinema screens.

Wilson Key has published several books on the subject of subliminal perception in advertising (Key 1973, 1976, 1980 and 1989) in which he claims that advertisers have

Figure 5.10

Subliminal advertising

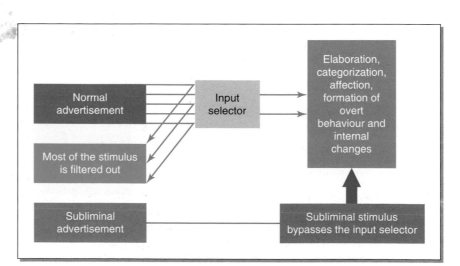

airbrushed in words such as 'U Buy' into the shadows around a bottle of rum, and various sexual images in advertisements for cigarettes and even cake mix. In 1957, Vance Packard published a book called *The Hidden Persuaders*, in which he analyzed the various ways in which the media industry manipulate opinion: he included subliminal advertising in his analysis (Packard 1957). However, in both cases the authors have been criticized for failing to produce solid evidence, and for making too many assumptions and suppositions.

The evidence for and against subliminal perception, at least as far as marketing goes, is mixed to say the least. There is some evidence that drive and behaviour may be influenced (Hawkins 1970), and there is also some evidence that flashing brand names onto cinema screens has impact when the stimulus is related to right-brain processing (Cuperfain and Clarke 1985). Other studies have failed to find any evidence for subliminal perception (Kelly 1979; Gable *et al.* 1987; Beatty and Hawkins 1989).

Subliminal perception, and from that subliminal advertising, is supposed to work in the same way as self-hypnosis tapes. Such tapes are often sold as a means of losing weight, giving up smoking, and so forth, yet there is no evidence that they have any effect whatsoever (Anon 1991). People's attitudes towards subliminal perception are ambivalent: on the one hand, people tend to fear it, since they are afraid that marketers (and others) might use it to manipulate them unfairly, and on the other hand people often hope that it does work when they buy self-hypnosis recordings (Spencer, Strahan and Zanna 2003).

Talking point

Subliminal advertising has been dismissed as a figment of the imagination, a product of Cold War paranoia and people's general paranoia about marketing. But of course marketers would say that, wouldn't they?

We know that a lot of our impressions of the world come from deep below the conscious level, from cues we are not really aware of, so why wouldn't this be true of advertising? If self-help hypnosis tapes don't work, why do people keep buying them? Is it simply that there is a widespread belief that they will work (and therefore people subconsciously act on the belief but not on the tape) or is it more likely that the tapes do have some effect on the individual's thought processes?

Even worse – are marketers for faceless corporations using subliminal advertising to make us into robots?

Even if subliminal advertising were shown to work, it seems probable that it would be ineffective: first, different people have different perception thresholds, so some people might be aware that the message has flashed onto the screen. Second, there is a very high risk of misunderstanding: after all, people frequently misunderstand or misinterpret advertising which is in plain language, so the potential for missing the point in an advertisement which is flashed onto a cinema screen for a fraction of a second must be very much greater. Finally, the selective nature of perception means that most stimuli are ignored or rejected by the input selector, even when the stimulus is strong. The fleeting nature of subliminal messages is likely to mean that they never register with the observer. This view accords with Weber's Law (explained earlier in the chapter).

In Japan, white is the appropriate colour for mourning at funerals.

Colour

Colours are used to attract attention, but they also convey particular emotions and meanings (Figure 5.11). These meanings are culturally specific: for example, in Japan white is the colour of funerals, whereas in the United States and most of Europe it is black; in China, bright colours symbolize high quality, whereas in the UK they are often associated with low price, low quality articles.

Figure 5.11

Colour in marketing

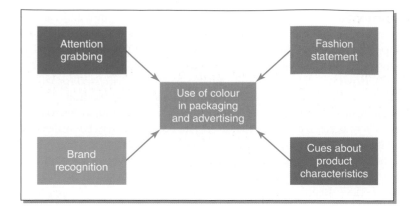

The contrast between the colour of the label and the colour of the beans makes the beans look good.

BP have protected their right to use an exact shade of green.

A study by Madden, Hewett and Roth (2000) found that red is perceived as hot, active and vibrant across all cultures, while black and brown are perceived as sad and stale. Black and brown are also perceived as formal in Brazil, Colombia, China and Taiwan, and as masculine in Austria, Hong Kong and the United States.

Table 5.2 shows some common colour perceptions, particularly as they relate to packaging and advertising.

Colours have a strong effect on perception. Research conducted in the 1960s showed that people believed that coffee from a dark brown container was stronger than coffee from a blue container, and that coffee from a yellow container was weak in both flavour and aroma (Dichter 1964). In fact, the coffee in each container was identical. This research is not generalizable across cultures, and it also suffers from the major weakness that (not unnaturally) respondents will try to find a difference between the coffees if they are asked to do so. Having said that, the differences that Dichter found were remarkably consistent between the respondents, with 87 per cent of them agreeing that the coffee from the yellow container was too weak. Had people been inventing differences simply to please the researcher, the differences would have been much less consistent. In packaging colour often has a profound effect on people's perceptions of the actual product: for example, Heinz uses turquoise for their baked beans (even though most other Heinz products have different colours): turquoise makes the beans look brighter orange when the can is opened.

These perceptions may not, of course, translate into other countries or cultures. In some cases, colour may be a fashion statement – Goths wear black, for example. Each year has its 'fashionable' colours – for 2006 it seemed to be white and gold, and for other years different colours have predominated.

Colour also has a dramatic effect on search times for products. Bright colours and contrasting colours make a product stand out, but people also use colour as a way of identifying brands rapidly (Jansson, Marlow and Bristow 2004). Companies often therefore adopt a corporate colour, or a colour denoting specific brands in the range. Coca Cola uses red and white, Heinz uses red for its range of soups, Kodak uses yellow for its films, and so forth. In the UK, firms have (in recent years) been able to include corporate colours in their trademark registration, so that (for example) the shade of green used by BP on its forecourts is now protected by law. This does not mean that other people cannot use the same shade of green, but it would mean that other oil companies would not be able to use it as part of their forecourts if the result might be to confuse the public into thinking that they were actually buying from BP. So far, there has been very little litigation based on infringements of corporate colours, although Orange and easyGroup have disputed the use of the colour orange for mobile telephone networks and the low-cost airline respectively.

Deliberate attempts to confuse consumers are called 'passing off', because one company is trying to pass off its products as being from the other company. This is illegal in most countries, since it is obviously against consumer interests as well as against the interests of the brand owner.

Table 5.2 Colour perceptions

Colour	Perceived meaning
Yellow	A strong attention-grabber, yellow often symbolizes summer. It works well as a background colour for black print, because it makes the print stand out, but it can sometimes be perceived as 'cheap and cheerful'. Some people associate yellow with warmth, novelty or caution.
Orange	Orange is a sociable colour, but in packaging it is mainly used for products such as orange juice which actually contains oranges. Some products (and many billboard posters) use dayglo orange as an attention-grabber: in the UK, this was successfully used in billboard advertising for the washing powder Radion.
Red	This is a strong attention-grabber because it can stand for most human emotions. It is often regarded as hot, exciting, passionate and strong.
Purple	Purple was formerly associated with royalty, and it has retained its upmarket image. Because it is the most expensive colour to reproduce, and has poor resistance to fading, its use in packaging is limited.
Blue	Blue is rarely associated with food packaging, because very few foods are blue. It is commonly used to denote coolness or cleanliness, and it is often perceived as having authority and commanding respect. This is why many countries use blue as the colour for police uniforms.
Green	The rise of environmentalism has increased the use of green for packaging and advertising. It carries connotations of naturalness, security and calmness. For some people, green can denote Irishness since green is the national colour of Ireland: for many Americans, green is the colour of money, since all American banknotes are green on one side.
Pink or magenta	Pink has always been regarded as a feminine colour, so it has been widely used on cosmetics, but in recent years it has been used for baby products and some categories of household goods. It is also becoming associated with the gay movement.
White	In most European countries and the United States, white is the colour of purity and cleanliness. In Japan it is the colour of mourning, however.
Brown	In food packaging, brown usually denotes strong flavours such as pickles and sauces. For gardening products, it conveys a rich earthiness.
Black	Black is usually associated with death, but combined with gold it can denote exclusivity and premium prices.
Grey	Grey can symbolize sadness, transition, compromise, depression, boredom, and monotony, but in recent years it has become a fashionable colour for high-tech products and modern design.

The naming of colours is a crucial factor in the marketing of products such as paint or fabrics. Names such as midnight blue, dawn pink, apple green or corn yellow have a positive effect on consumer perception because there is an underlying assumption that the information must be useful in some way, which leads people to put a positive 'spin' on the colour name (Miller and Khan 2003).

Summary

From a marketing viewpoint, the fact that perception is so nebulous and individual a thing is probably helpful in the long run. People's views of products and services rely heavily on perceived attributes, some of which have no objective reality; the difficulty for marketers lies in knowing what will be the general perception of the members of the market segments with whom we are attempting to do business.

Perception is, if nothing else, an individual thing. The way one person selects and interprets information will be very different from the way someone else selects and interprets the same basic cues. This chapter has dealt with the processes which lead up to the formation of a view of the world: the selection, processing and interpretation of information and the subsequent keying-in of new information to existing knowledge is what enables us to understand our surroundings and deal with problems.

The key points from the chapter are as follows:

● Perception is both synthetic and analytic.

● Stimuli combine synergistically to create the whole impression.

● Selectivity is a key issue in perception, and is a key problem for marketers.

● Past experience contributes to the way new stimuli are interpreted as well as to the overall impression.

● Changes in the stimulus will go undetected if the stimulus is a large one.

● Perception and reality are not intrinsically different.

● Most perception happens below the conscious level.

● Perceptual responses may be internal or overt.

● Subliminal advertising is unlikely to be effective.

● Colour speeds search times as well as attracts attention.

Chapter review questions

1 What effect does selectivity have on an integrated marketing communications campaign?

2 How might colour perceptions be complicated in a global market?

3 Why is subjectivity a problem for marketers?

4 How do internal responses create problems for marketers?

5 What is the difference between the linear additive model and the linear averaging model?

6 Explain Weber's Law.

7 What is the difference between kinaesthetic processing and visual processing?

8 What is the Law of Primacy?

9 What is the role of expectancy in branding?

10 What are the arguments for the effectiveness of subliminal advertising? What are the arguments against?

Preview case study revisited
Car noise

Interior noise levels in cars have fallen dramatically in recent years. The average sound level inside a car travelling at 55 miles per hour dropped from 72 decibels in 1980 to only 62 decibels in 2000. Because the decibel is a logarithmic scale, this is actually a 30 per cent drop in noise levels.

It isn't only about reducing overall noise levels, though. For the luxury car market, the ability to hold conversations easily inside the car is one of the key factors in perception of quality, so manufacturers seek to eliminate sounds in the 300 to 3400 herz range, which is the range of human speech. This consideration has achieved even greater prominence with the advent of mobile telephones – after all, if someone has trouble hearing what is being said when they are in a room at home, the problem can only be greater in a moving vehicle.

Manufacturers use specialist consultancy firms such as Roush Anatrol to solve their noise problems for them.

Roush Anatrol have specialized testing equipment for finding noise and vibration problems in everything from an airliner to a baseball bat.

Collins and Aikman, another acoustic engineering firm, uses advanced computer modelling systems to predict where problems might arise. The company also supplies lightweight soundproofing materials to automobile manufacturers, and is able to supply materials which block out particular frequencies so that the 'right' sound signature is created.

Using these sophisticated measures to affect customer perception of the car is only one part of creating an overall image. After all, sound is only one of our five senses: getting the right design, colours and even interior smell is an entirely separate, and equally complex, set of problems.

Case study
David Blaine

In September 2003, American magician and illusionist David Blaine had himself suspended from Tower Bridge in London in a transparent box. He was to remain in the box without food for 44 days, with only water (supplied through a tube) to sustain him.

Blaine certainly has a talent for startling stunts. In a press conference he apparently cut off part of his ear, even showing the assembled journalists the ear with a piece cut out of it. In previous stunts he has had himself encased in ice for three days, and spent 35 days standing on top of a pole. Such stunts have certainly done his career no harm at all: sales of his DVD have skyrocketed, and his TV appearances and stage shows have broken all records for magicians.

Of course, not everyone saw his Tower Bridge stunt in the same way. Ken Livingstone, the Mayor of London, said that it would be offensive to the families of IRA hunger strikers (which apparently Blaine thought was funny). The Guinness Book of Records refused to endorse his claim (on the grounds that they discourage record attempts which might be fatal, and also on the grounds that Blaine was not planning to fast longer than previous record holders).

In the ensuing weeks, crowds gathered at Tower Bridge either to cheer him on (supporting the 'yank in a tank', as he came to be known) or to provide him with entertainment (Keep Blaine Sane) or, perhaps less creditably, to throw things at him. During his six weeks in the tank he was pelted with eggs, golf balls, fruit, half-eaten fast food, and indeed anything else Londoners could think of. Blaine baiting almost achieved the status of a national sport: at one point the exercise went a little too far, when a man climbed up to Blaine's water supply tower and tried to cut the tube. The water supply failed for a while, and the man was arrested and subsequently fined £1000.

Other distractions included frying burgers immediately below the box, and three young women tried to destroy his concentration by flashing their breasts at him. Drummers played all night in order to keep him from sleeping, and journalists were less than kind – the *Sun* referred to him as 'that total twerp currently dangling in a glass box over the Thames'.

In the United States, newspapers and TV shows were astounded at the British response. Sarah Lyall, writing in the *New York Times*, could not understand the British reaction to Blaine, whom she described as a 'dazzling magician'. The *Chicago Tribune* said that 'Brits have no respect for David's high art' and the *Los Angeles Times* said that Blaine could not have realized that Brits enjoy a savage public spectacle.

From the British viewpoint, the joy of being creative in Blaine baiting probably overcame the normal British reticence: taking a driver and some golf balls onto Tower Bridge and seeing who can hit the box probably seemed like harmless, though rather naughty, fun at the time. Likewise, sending up a remote-controlled helicopter with a cheeseburger dangling from it probably also seemed gleeful. The fact that a miniature 'Yank in a tank' was set up at the Legoland theme park, complete with golfers and burger van, says a lot about the British sense of humour, and the prevailing view that sitting motionless in a Perspex box is not, in the scheme of things, high art.

For Blaine, the outcomes were mixed. It is unlikely that he expected such an outpouring of derision for his stunt: in his native America he was widely supported. On the other hand, any publicity is good publicity, and his stunt certainly made the news. The physical effects were extreme – he could not eat solid food for a long time after the event, and he was extremely emaciated when he left the box. Returning to full health and strength is likely to take months if not years, and the strain on his relationship with his girlfriend, model Manon von Gerkan, will also need to be addressed. On the plus side, Sky reputedly paid him a million pounds for his efforts – no small pickings, even after deducting the costs of his support team and hospital bills.

Ultimately, the Yank in a tank was subject to a variety of perceptions – artist, illusionist, or idiot, according to the viewpoint of the audience. Their responses were equally mixed – admiration, contempt, or outright hostility all came into play among one group or another.

Case study questions

1 What role did expectations play in establishing overall perceptions?

2 How did different groups select the stimuli presented by Blaine?

3 How might Blaine have improved his image?

4 Why did American journalists have a different perception of the stunt from that of British journalists?

5 Why might Blaine have found Ken Livingstone's comments funny?

© 2007 LEGOLAND WINDSOR

References

Anderson N.H. (1965) Averaging versus adding as a stimulus combination rule in impression formation. *Journal of Experimental Psychology*, 70: 194–400.

Anon (1991) Self help tapes are worthless, study says. *San Jose Mercury News*, 25 September.

Bakamitsos, Georgios, and Siomkos, George (2004) Context effects in marketing practice: the case of mood. *Journal of Consumer Behaviour*, 3(4): 304–314.

Batra, Rajeev, and Stayman, Douglas M. (1990): The role of mood in advertising effectiveness. Journal of Consumer Research 17 (September): 203–14.

Beatty, Sharon E., and Hawkins, Del (1989) Subliminal stimulation: some new data and interpretation. *Journal of Advertising*, 18(3): 4–8.

Britt, Steuart Henderson (1975) How Weber's Law can be applied to marketing. *Business Horizons*, 18, 1 (February): 27–9.

Britt, Steuart Henderson, and Nelson, Victoria M. (1976) The marketing importance of the 'just noticeable difference'. *Business Horizons*, 19, 4 (August): 38–40.

Chandran, Sucharita, and Menon, Geeta (2003) When am I at risk? Now, or now? The effects of temporal framing on perceptions of health risk. *Advances in Consumer Research*, 30(1): 108.

Clark, Irvine III, Micken, Kathleen S., and Hart, H. Stanley (2002) Symbols for sale – at least for now. Symbolic consumption in transition economies. *Advances in Consumer Research*, 29(1): 25–30.

Cuperfain, R., and Clarke, T.K. (1985) A new perspective of subliminal perception. *Journal of Advertising*, 14(1): 36–41.

Dichter, E. (1964) *Handbook of Consumer Motivations: The Psychology of the World of Objects* (New York: McGraw Hill).

Gable, Myron, Wilkens, Henry T., Harris, Lynn, and Feinberg, Richard (1987) An evaluation of subliminally embedded sexual stimuli in graphics. *Journal of Advertising*, 16(1): 26–31.

Grant, Susan Jung, and Tybout, Alice M. (2003) The effects of temporal framing on new product evaluation. *Advances in Consumer Research*, 30(1).

Greifeneder, Rainer, Bless, Herbert, and Kuschmann, Thorstein (2007) Extending the brand image on new products: the facilitative effect of happy mood states. *Journal of Consumer Behaviour*, 6 (Jan–Feb): 19–31.

Hawkins, Del (1970) The effects of subliminal stimulation on drive level and brand preference. *Journal of Market Research*, 7 (August): 322–6.

Henry, Walter A. (1980) The effect of information processing ability on processing accuracy. *Journal of Consumer Research*, 7 (June): 42–8.

Holbrook, Morris P., and Moore, William I. (1981) Feature interactions in consumer judgement of verbal versus pictorial presentations. *Journal of Consumer Research*, 8 (June): 103–13.

Jansson, C., Marlow, N., and Bristow, M. (2004) The influence of colour on visual search times in cluttered environments. *Journal of Marketing Communications*, 10 (September): 183–93.

Kelly, J.S. (1979) Subliminal imbeds in printing advertising: a challenge to advertising ethics. *Journal of Advertising*, 8 (summer): 43–6.

Key, W.B. (1973) *Subliminal Seduction* (Englewood Cliffs, NJ: Signet).

Key, W.B. (1976) *Media Sexploitation* (Englewood Cliffs, NJ: Prentice Hall).

Key, W.B. (1980) *The Clam-Plate Orgy and Other Subliminals the Media Use to Manipulate Your Behaviour* (Englewood Cliffs, NJ: Prentice Hall).

Key, W.B. (1989) *The Age of Manipulation: The Con in Confidence, the Sin in Sincere* (New York: Henry Holt & Co.).

LeBoeuf, Robyn A. (2006) Discount rates for time versus dates: the sensitivity of discounting to time-interval description. *Advances in Consumer Research*, 33(1): 138–9.

Lindstrom, M. (2005) Sensing and opportunity: sensory appeal. *The Marketer*, 10 (February): 6–11.

Madden, T.J., Hewett, K., and Roth, M.S. (2000): Managing Images in Different Cultures: A Cross-National Study of Colour Meanings and Preferences. *Journal of International Marketing* 8(4): 90–107.

Meyer, Robert J. (1987) The learning of multiattribute judgement policies. *Journal of Consumer Research* (September): 155–73.

Miller, George A. (1956) The magical number seven, plus or minus two: some limits in our capacity for processing information. *Psychological Review* (March): 81–97.

Miller, Susan Gelfand, and Khan, Barbara (2003) Shades of meaning: the effects of novel colour names on consumer preferences. *Advances in Consumer Research*, 30(1): 12–13.

Milotic, Daniel (2003) The impact of fragrance on consumer choice. *Journal of Consumer Behaviour*, 3(2): 179–91.

Munoz, Caroline L., Wood, Natalie T., and Solomon, Michael R. (2006) Real or blarney? A cross-cultural investigation of the perceived authenticity of Irish pubs. *Journal of Consumer Behaviour*, 5 (May–June): 222–34.

Packard, Vance (1957) *The Hidden Persuaders* (New York: D. MacKay & Co.).

Parker, Andrew M., Fischhof, Baruch, and deBruin, Wandi Bruine (2006) Who thinks they know more – but actually knows less? Adolescent confidence in their HIV/AIDS and general knowledge. *Advances in Consumer Research*, 33(1): 12–13.

Rao, Akshay R., and Monroe, Kent B. (1988) The moderating effect of price knowledge on cue utilization in product evaluations. *Journal of Consumer Research*, 15 (September): 253–64.

Spencer, Stephen J., Strahan, Erin J., and Zanna, Mark P. (2003) Subliminal priming and choice. *Advances in Consumer Research*, 30(1): 152.

Warr, Peter B., and Knapper, Christopher (1968) *The Perception of People and Events* (London: Wiley).

Zhao, Guangzhi, and Pechmann, Connie (2006) Regulatory focus, feature positive effect, and message framing. *Advances in Consumer Research*, 33(1): 100.

Chapter 6
Learning

Learning objectives

Learning objectives When you have read this chapter you should be able to:

1. explain what constitutes learning and what does not
2. explain the role of classical conditioning
3. describe how operant conditioning works
4. describe how cognitive learning can be used by marketers
5. understand the role of motivation in learning
6. show how experiential learning is more effective than vicarious learning
7. describe the various components of consumer knowledge and their importance to marketers

Introduction

Learning is not only about classroom-type learning. Most behaviour is learned as a result of external experiences; most of what people know (and almost certainly many of the things they are most proud of knowing) they learned outside school. People learn things partly through a formalized structure of teaching (or of self-teaching, perhaps by correspondence course) and partly through an unconscious process of learning by experience.

Consumption habits particularly are learned. British people were not born with a liking for fish and chips, any more than a Bangladeshi is born with a liking for curries or a Frenchman for horsemeat. Learning is highly relevant to marketing, since consumers are affected by the things they learn, and much consumer behaviour is actually based on the learning process. Persuading consumers to remember the information they see in advertisements is a major problem for marketers; for example, some years ago a series of advertisements were produced for Cinzano vermouth. The ads starred Leonard Rossiter and Joan Collins, and were widely screened throughout the UK, yet they were ineffective in increasing sales of the product. The reason for this was made clear when market research discovered that consumers actually thought the ads were for Martini vermouth, Cinzano's main competitor.

This chapter is about the ways in which the brain orders and stores information.

Even the most engaging advertising can fail.

Defining learning

Learning is defined as 'the behavioural changes that occur over time relative to an external stimulus condition' (Onkvisit and Shaw 1994:66). According to this definition, activities are changed or originated through a reaction to an encountered situation. We can therefore say that someone has learned something if, as a result, their behaviour changes in some way (Figure 6.1, page 113).

The main conditions that arise from this definition are as follows:

1. There must be a change in behaviour (response tendencies).
2. This must result from external stimulus.

Preview case study
Bayer educates consumers

Medicines, especially over-the-counter medicines, offer special problems for marketers. The market is very much need-driven: people do not buy medicines unless they have symptoms, and in the case of over-the-counter medicines they often need to know a great deal about what they are buying: after all, unlike prescription drugs, they are not getting advice from their doctors in most cases.

Obviously for simple painkilling drugs such as aspirin or paracetamol there is not much of a problem. These products are widely advertised, and it would be an unusual person indeed who did not know what aspirin does. For other products, however, there is clearly a problem in getting detailed information across to customers. For example, someone with a high cholesterol level would be unlikely to know which drugs to take, and even someone with a simple skin rash might not know whether to take anti-histamines or anti-inflammatories.

In most cases, drug companies can run advertising which helps to educate its potential customers. The usual approach is to use factual, content-laden advertisements, coupled with detailed point-of-sale and on-package information. In some cases this is difficult to achieve, however: sometimes people suffer from illnesses which they feel are embarrassing, and it is those very illnesses which they do not like to discuss with their doctors or indeed the pharmacist.

One group of diseases that people often feel embarrassed about is the fungal infections caused by the Candida strain of yeast. These include thrush, sweat rash and nappy rash, all caused by a change in the pH balance of the body. Other diseases with a high embarrassment factor include haemorrhoids, impotence and flatulence.

Bayer is a major German chemical company which manufactures both prescription medicines (called ethical medicines) and over-the-counter (OTC) medicines. The company has 93,000 employees worldwide, but conducts 40 per cent of its business in Europe, and has annual sales of over £1bn in the UK and Ireland alone. Bayer is nothing if not switched on in a marketing sense – the company operates in many different markets, and has an active and creative marketing department.

So how could the company rise to the challenge of educating people about products most of us do not want to think about?

CLYNT GARNHAM/ALAMY

Learning has not taken place under the following circumstances:

1 *Species response tendencies* – These are instincts, or reflexes; for example, the response of ducking when a stone is thrown at you does not rely on your having learned that stones are hard and hurt the skin.

2 *Maturation* – Behavioural changes often occur in adolescence due to hormonal changes (for example), but again this is not a behavioural change as a result of learning.

3 *Temporary states of the organism* – Whilst behaviour can be, and often is, affected by tiredness, hunger, drunkenness, etc. these factors do not constitute part of a larger learning process (even though learning may result from those states; the drunk may well learn to drink less in future).

4 *Damage to the brain* – Changes in behaviour due to surgery, disease or injury are also not a result of learning.

Regarding the study of learning there are two main schools of thought: first the stimulus-response approach, which further subdivides into classical and operant conditioning; and second, cognitive theories, where the conscious thought of the individual enters into the equation.

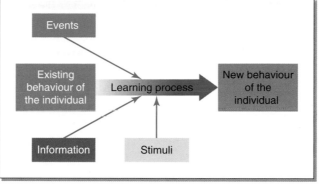

Figure 6.1

Learning

The stimulus-response approach

Classical learning theory

The classical theory of learning was developed by, among others, the Russian researcher Pavlov (1927). Pavlov's famous experiments with dogs demonstrated that automatic responses (reflexes) could be learned. What Pavlov did was present a dog with an **unconditioned stimulus** (in this case, meat powder) knowing that this would lead to an **unconditioned response** (salivation). At the same time Pavlov would ring a bell (the conditioned stimulus). After a while the dog would associate the ringing of the bell with the meat, and would salivate whenever it heard the bell, without actually seeing any meat. This mechanism is shown in Figure 6.2.

   Classical conditioning like this occurs with humans; many smokers associate having a cup of coffee with having a cigarette, and find it difficult to give up smoking without also giving up coffee. Likewise the use of popular music in advertisements for Levi's jeans is an example of classical conditioning. Repeated exposure to the advertisement leads the individual to associate the music with the product. This leads to two results: first, if the consumer likes the music, that extends to liking the product, and second, the

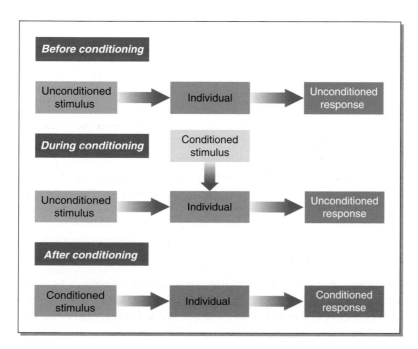

Figure 6.2

Classical conditioning

consumer will tend to think of Levi's whenever she or he hears the music. Assuming the song used actually becomes (or is already) a hit, Levi will obtain some free exposure whenever the song is played on the radio. Likewise, Christmas music played in retail shops during December tends to create a mood in which consumers are more likely to buy presents and seasonal items.

This all sounds rather depressing. We are apparently very easily led – our buttons can be pushed by the ringing of a doorbell, or the clink of a coffee cup. Does this really happen quite so automatically?

One product which might give us the answer is the Tinkle Toonz Musical Potty. An American product which has been available since 1986, this is an aid to toilet training: if the child pees in the potty, he or she is rewarded with a tinny rendition of 'Old Macdonald Had a Farm.' If Pavlov was right, then adults who were trained on the Tinkle Toonz Musical Potty would presumably be conditioned to pee every time they hear 'Old Macdonald Had a Farm'. Since those original babies are now in their late teens and early twenties, just the age for practical jokes, one can envisage all sorts of fun.

So does it happen? Do we have students, Army recruits, trainee warehouse staff, check-out operators, and young people in general avoiding 'Old Macdonald Had a Farm'? Or worse, *not* avoiding it? Or are human beings capable of overcoming their conditioning?

Try whistling 'Old Macdonald Had a Farm' and find out!

For this to work it is usually necessary to repeat the stimulus a number of times in order for the **conditioned response** to become established. The number of times the process needs to be repeated will depend on the strength of the stimulus and the receptiveness (motivation) of the individual. Research has shown that, although conditioning has been reported for a single conditioning event (Gorn 1982), perhaps as many as 30 pairings may be required before conditioning is maximized (Kroeber-Riel 1984).

Before conditioning, the unconditioned stimulus feeding into the brain causes the unconditioned response. During the conditioning both the conditioned stimulus and the unconditioned stimulus are presented, so that after conditioning the **conditioned stimulus** alone will produce the response.

Behaviours influenced by classical conditioning are thought to be involuntary. If the doorbell rings, it is automatic for most people to look up, without consciously thinking about whether somebody is at the door. Most people are familiar with the start of recognition that sometimes occurs if a similar doorbell is rung during a TV drama. Classical conditioning also operates on the emotions: playing Christmas music will elicit memories of childhood Christmases and advertisements evoking nostalgic feelings will generate warm feelings towards the product.

Another factor in the effectiveness of classical conditioning is the order in which the conditioned stimulus and the unconditioned stimulus are presented. In **forward conditioning** the conditioned stimulus (CS) comes before the unconditioned stimulus (US). This would mean that the product would be shown before the music is played.

In **backward conditioning** the US (unconditioned stimulus) comes before the CS (conditioned stimulus). Here the music would be played before the product is shown. **Simultaneous conditioning** requires both to be presented at the same time (Figure 6.3).

It appears that forward conditioning and simultaneous conditioning work best in advertising (McSweeney and Bierley 1984). This means that it is usually better to present the product before playing the popular tune, or play both together; the responses from this approach are usually stronger and longer-lasting. If classical conditioning is being used,

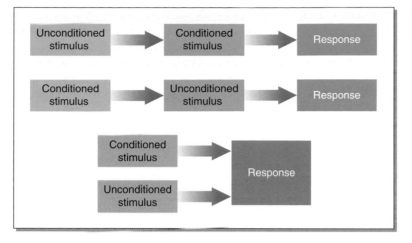

Figure 6.3
Ordering of stimuli

clearly the broadcast media will be better suited since it is easier to control the order in which the stimuli are presented; with print media this is not necessarily the case. For example, not everybody reads newspapers from front to back. Many people would start with the sports pages (at the back) and work forward, or perhaps read the headlines on the front pages then go straight to the TV pages before coming back to the local news. Even if the conditioned stimulus and unconditioned stimulus are placed in the same ad on the same page it is still possible that the reader's eye will be drawn to each stimulus in the wrong order; in other words, people do not necessarily read each page from top to bottom, either.

For these reasons the print media are not as effective for classical conditioning as are the broadcast media such as radio and TV, where the order of presentation of the stimuli is controllable.

Extinction occurs when the conditioned stimulus no longer evokes the conditioned response. This occurs in the ways shown in Table 6.1.

Generalization happens when a stimulus that is close to the existing one evokes the same response. Pavlov found that a sound similar to the bell he used could also stimulate

Table 6.1 Extinction

Reason for extinction	Example	Explanation	Techniques to avoid extinction
The conditioned stimulus is encountered without the unconditioned stimulus	The product is shown without the background music	Seeing the product without the music tends to reduce the association of the music with the product; other stimuli will replace the music	Ensure that all the advertising uses the same music, or imagery associated with the music
The unconditioned stimulus is encountered without the conditioned stimulus	The background music is heard without the product being present	In this case, other stimuli may be evoked by the music; it will become associated with something other than the product	Either ensure that the music is not played anywhere other than when the product is being shown, or ensure that the product is available when the music is played. For example, if the product is a drink to be sold in clubs, ensure that the clubs have an ample supply of the drink being advertised

HSBC makes good use of its global coverage.

Sometimes advertising slogans are learned so well they become part of daily conversation.

'Soapy' used to be a nickname for anyone called Hudson.

salivation, and it is often the case that a similar brand name can evoke a purchase response. A very common tactic in marketing is to produce similar packaging to that of one's competitor in order to take advantage of the generalization effect. For an example of this, observe the similarity in the packaging between Tesco's Premium coffee and Nescafé Gold Blend.

Discrimination is the process by which we learn to distinguish between stimuli, and only respond to the appropriate one. Consumers quite quickly learn to distinguish between brands, even when the design of the packaging is similar. Advertisers will often encourage discrimination by pairing a positive US with their own product, but not with the competitor's product. For example, the HSBC slogan, 'The world's local bank', conveys a clear image of a bank with worldwide experience coupled with familiarity with local customs and banking practice. Other banks are clearly excluded from this slogan. Even greater discrimination occurs when the competitor's product is paired with a negative US, for example by using phrases such as 'Unlike our competitors, we do not charge you a service fee'.

Classical conditioning is responsible for many repetitive advertising campaigns, and for many catchphrases which are now in common use; some advertising fosters this, as in the 'Does exactly what it says on the tin' campaign for Ronseal, which has resulted in the slogan entering the language. In some cases these stimuli can be very long-lasting: for many years, people with the surname Hudson were nicknamed Soapy, after Hudson's Soap which ran a series of advertising campaigns in the nineteenth century (one of which featured writing the brand name on a balloon, which was probably the earliest use of aerial promotion).

Classical conditioning assumes that the individual plays no active role in the learning process. Pavlov's dogs did not have to do anything in order to be 'conditioned', because the process was carried out on their involuntary reflex of salivation. Although classical conditioning does operate in human beings, people are not usually passive in the process; the individual person (and most higher animals, in fact) is able to take part in the process and cooperate with it or avoid it. This process of active role-playing is called **operant conditioning**.

Operant conditioning

Here the learner will conduct trial-and-error behaviour to obtain a reward (or avoid a punishment). Burris F. Skinner (1953) developed the concept in order to explain higher-level learning than that identified by Pavlov. The difference between Pavlov's approach and the operant conditioning approach is that the learner has choice in the outcome; the modern view of classical conditioning is that it also involves a cognitive dimension. In other words, Skinner is describing a type of learning that requires the learner to do something rather than be a passive recipient of a stimulus. The modern view is that even Pavlov's dog would have thought 'Here comes dinner' when the bell rang.

The basis of operant conditioning is the concept of **reinforcement**. If someone buys a product and is pleased with the outcome of using it, then he or she is likely to buy the product again. This means that the activity has had a positive reinforcement, and the consumer has become 'conditioned' to buy the product next time. The greater the positive reinforcement, the greater the likelihood of repeat purchase.

If the reward works, the consumer will try to think of a way to make it even better. 'If a little will help, a lot will cure.' This can lead to over-indulgence in food or alcohol, or indeed almost any other pleasurable activity. Typically this will happen if the consumer's need cannot be totally met by the product, but will be helped; a person with a serious psychological problem may well find that alcohol helps, but doesn't cure. An increasing intake of alcohol will never result in a complete meeting of the person's psychological needs because eventually sobriety will begin to set in again.

Talking point

How active are people in learning? Do we really seek out knowledge and consider everything that comes our way? Or does most of it go in one ear and out the other?

How many times have you been able to answer (say) a quiz question without having any idea where that nugget of information came from? How often do you say, 'Oh, that's common knowledge'. So were you born knowing this stuff? Games such as Trivial Pursuit are based on this kind of mental fluff – useless facts that just happen to have lodged in your brain, not through repetition (classical conditioning) nor through operant conditioning, but just through some kind of alien implanting process.

So is there something missing from the theory?

An example of operant conditioning is the recent growth of loyalty cards in retail stores, for example Tesco's Clubcard. Customers who remain loyal to Tesco are sent extra discounts and offers, and also their purchasing behaviour can be traced through the electronic point-of-sale systems so that offers can be targeted to those Tesco customers who will really be interested in them.

Airline loyalty schemes have also seen huge growth in recent years. These are aimed at reinforcing the frequent flyers, whose loyalty is desirable since they are likely to be the most profitable customers. The airlines offer free flights to their most regular customers, and for many business travellers these free flights offer an attractive reason for choosing the same airline every time. Loyalty cards are especially attractive to business customers because their flights are often paid for by their firms, so they are less likely to have to shop around for cheap deals.

Loyalty cards work through operant conditioning.

The problem with this type of loyalty scheme is that it is perfectly feasible for people to carry loyalty cards for several stores (or join the frequent flyer clubs of several airlines) and thus reap the rewards without actually having to remain loyal to any supplier. In effect, people have been taught to play the system, gaining the benefits without actually having to contribute anything.

Figure 6.4 charts three forms of operant conditioning.

In the first example, positive reinforcement, the individual receives a stimulus and acts upon it. This action works, and the individual gets a good result; this leads to the behaviour being repeated if the same antecedent stimulus is presented at a later date. For example, if you are in a long queue at a retailer such as the DIY store B&Q, you might notice that the customer service counter is empty, and go there to make your purchases instead of the usual tills. This gets you through quicker, so if you're in B&Q again and the queue is over-long, you would try the same tactic again.

The second example in the diagram shows a negative stimulus; this time the operant behaviour relieves the problem, and again the individual has learned how to avoid bad consequences when faced with a difficulty.

The third example shows how punishment fits into the learning process. If the operant behaviour leads to a bad result, for example the customer service counter won't serve you and you lose your original place in the queue, you will not try that tactic again. The problem with punishment as a motivator is that it may lead to the individual not shopping at B&Q again. (See Chapter 2 for a discussion of pain avoidance.)

Figure 6.4

Operant conditioning

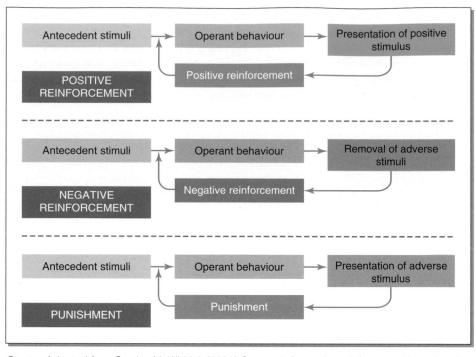

Source: Adapted from Stanley M. Widrick (1986) Concept of negative reinforcement has place in classroom. *Marketing News*, 20 (18 July): 48–9.

Operant conditioning does not necessarily require a product purchase; marketers will frequently give away free samples in the hope that a positive experience from using the product will encourage consumers to purchase in future. Likewise, car dealers always offer

Consumer behaviour in action
Pizzaland

Although pizza appeared on a menu dated 1934, it was virtually unknown in Britain before 1965, when the first Pizza Express restaurant opened in London. Within a few short years, pizzerias were springing up all over the UK, and in the 1970s Pizzaland made its first appearance.

Pizzaland positioned itself as a cheaper version of Pizza Hut (although at first, bizarrely, the restaurants had a Tyrolean-themed décor). The restaurants offered all-you-can-eat promotions, special two-for-one offers and themed evenings. This aggressive approach meant that the chain grew rapidly until there were Pizzalands in every major town in the UK.

On the other hand, an overuse of incentives can lead to negative consequences for the producer. Pizzaland's discount vouchers, which were given away in newspapers, on bus tickets and even on cans of tuna resulted in a major reeducation of customers. Many people would not eat at Pizzaland unless they had a discount voucher. In this way, the positive reinforcement backfired on the company, since there is an implied *negative* reinforcement in *not* going in with a voucher.

Of course, the company was now giving away so many pizzas that profits dropped dramatically: if the two-for-one offer stopped, people simply went elsewhere until the offer was re-instated, so Pizzaland were effectively selling all their pizzas at half price. In these circumstances, the company would hope to make up the difference by selling more desserts, beverages and starters, but since their clientele were mainly bargain hunters (some might say cheapskates) it was not unusual for people to have just the pizza, then go to the pub to buy a beer or a glass of wine afterwards.

Eventually Pizzaland disappeared altogether, a monument to the learning abilities of consumers.

a test drive; some go even further, and allow the customer to borrow a car for 24 hours or more in order to get a very clear reinforcement of the car's merits.

Operant conditioning is helpful in explaining how people become conditioned, or form habits of purchase; however, it still does not explain how learning operates when people become active in seeking out information. To understand this aspect of learning, it is necessary to look at the cognitive learning process.

Cognitive learning

Not all learning is an automatic response to a stimulus. People analyze purchasing situations taking into account previous experiences, and make evaluative judgements. Learning is part of this, both in terms of informing the process as a result of earlier experiences, and also in terms of the consumer's approach to learning more about the product category or brand.

When considering **cognitive learning**, the emphasis is not on *what* is learned (as in stimulus-response theories) but on *how* it is learned. Classical learning and operant conditioning theories suppose that learning is automatic; cognitive learning theories assume that there is a conscious process going on. For most people this is true in many cases of consumer behaviour.

The classical and operant theories assume that what goes on inside the consumer's head is a 'black box' in that we know that a given stimulus will prompt a particular response, but for most practical purposes we have no real way of knowing what is happening inside the black box. Within the cognitive learning paradigm, however, we are concerned with what happens inside the box, and we try to infer what is going on by analyzing behaviour and responses from the individual. Figure 6.5 illustrates this.

The black box contains the cognitive processes; the stimulus is considered in the light of the individual's memory of what has happened in the past when presented with similar stimuli, his or her assessment of the desirable outcome, and an assessment of the likely outcome of any action. Following this processing the individual produces a response.

Cognitive learning expertise has five aspects:

● cognitive effort
● cognitive structure
● analysis
● elaboration
● memory

Cognitive effort is the degree of effort the consumer is prepared to put into thinking about the product offering. This will depend on such aspects as the complexity of the product, the consumer's involvement with it, and the motivation for learning.

Cognitive structure is about the way the consumer thinks, and the way the information is fitted into existing knowledge.

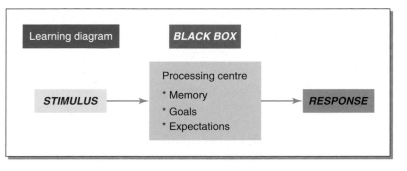

Figure 6.5

Cognitive learning

Figure 6.6

Factors in cognitive learning

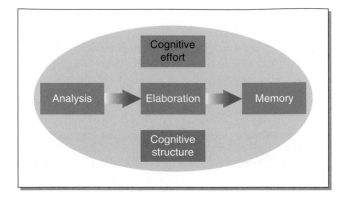

The **analysis** of information is first concerned with selecting the correct, relevant information from the environment, and second with interpreting the information correctly in order to obtain a clear action plan.

Elaboration is the structuring of the information within the brain, and adding to it from memory in order to form a coherent whole.

Memory is the mechanism by which learned information is stored. In fact, nothing is ever truly forgotten; information will eventually become irrecoverable by the conscious mind (forgotten) but the brain still retains the information and can be stimulated to recall it, either by hypnosis or by association of ideas.

Cognitive learning processes are important to marketers since they are helpful in predicting consumer responses to advertising. Stephen J. Hoch and Young-Won Ha (1986) say that consumers view advertisements as tentative hypotheses about product performance that can be tested through product experience. Early learning about a product will affect future learning; this is called the Law of Primacy. For this reason first impressions count for a great deal.

According to Hoch and Young-Won, advertising will tend to be ignored if there is unambiguous objective evidence to hand; if you can test the product for yourself, the adverts won't affect you as much. If the evidence is ambiguous or unobtainable at first hand (as is often the case) the advertising might sway you, and in fact advertising appears to have dramatic effects on consumers' perceptions of quality.

For example, it is possible for somebody to test out a new computer before making a commitment to buy. Thus advertising plays a small part in computer purchase, only serving to alert the consumer to what is available within the current technology. Conversely, somebody spending a similar amount on a holiday has no chance to try out the holiday before buying it, and is therefore more likely to be swayed by the advertising or other communications (brochures, salespeople, etc.). One of the main considerations for a consumer in that position is the reputation of the tour operator, since the consumer is, after all, buying a promise. Chapter 16 has more on the topic of services marketing.

Learning from experience is a four-stage process, as Table 6.2 shows.

In most cases people prefer to learn by experience, especially for major product purchases; few people would buy a car without having a test-drive first, and still fewer would buy one by mail order unless they were people with previous direct experience of the car. It is for this reason that mail-order companies have a no-quibble money-back guarantee; if this were not the case, few people would be prepared to buy by post rather than visit a high-street shop where they can see and feel the goods.

There are also three moderating factors in the cognitive learning process;

1 Familiarity with the domain. This is the degree to which the consumer has pre-existing knowledge of the product category. For example, an IT enthusiast would go through a different, and probably shorter, learning curve for buying a new laptop than would a complete novice. Familiarity with the components of a brand name makes it more memorable (Lerman 2003).

Very few restaurants allow customers to try the food first.

Table 6.2 Learning from experience

Stage	Explanation	Example	Marketing response
Hypothesizing	Developing a rough estimate as to what's happening or what's available.	Getting information from a friend, or reading some advertising material; getting some brochures.	Have clearly written brochures and advertising, don't use too much jargon especially if your product is a complex one, or can be 'test-driven'.
Exposure	Having a look at the product, trying one out, getting direct experience of it.	Visiting a computer shop to try the product and ask questions about it.	Ensure that the product is on display, and allow plenty of opportunity for hands-on testing.
Encoding	Making sense of the information.	Translating the jargon into something comprehensible, perhaps getting some clarification; understanding what the product is and does in terms which fit in with previous experience.	Have salespeople who can explain things in lay terms, and who don't frighten the customer off by using too much technical language.
Integration	Fitting the new information into the existing knowledge bank.	Thinking about the new information gained about computers and discarding previous misconceptions.	Ensure that customers feel able to come back for further explanations if they still have problems. Make sure that customers understand everything before leaving the shop.

2 Motivation to learn. If the purchase is an important one, or the possible effects of making a mistake would be serious, the consumer is likely to be highly motivated to obtain as much information as possible.

3 Ambiguity of the information environment. If the information is hard to get, contradictory, or incomprehensible this will hinder the learning process. Sometimes consumers give up on the process if this is the case.

Figure 6.7 (page 122) illustrates these moderating factors in terms of classifying readiness to learn from experience.

If someone is highly motivated to learn (for example, someone who has committed to buying a holiday home in Spain might be highly motivated to learn Spanish) the learning process is most susceptible to management. The individual would probably want to follow a formal course of study (evening classes or a distance learning course) and would welcome help in managing the learning process. If the individual already speaks Spanish, but has bought a house in Catalonia, the motivation to learn Catalàn might be just as strong, but familiarity with the domain (learning a foreign language) might cause the individual to form beliefs which are unrealistic.

People who are only weakly motivated to learn are obviously less likely to want their learning managed, or indeed to manage it themselves. If the person is unfamiliar with the domain, he or she is unlikely to be interested in learning at all; if, on the other hand, the domain is all too familiar, complacency sets in and the person is likely to say 'I already know all that stuff' and thus will have no interest in managing learning. Motivation has an effect on the tendency to 'zap' TV advertisements: if the advertisement is unpleasant or uninformative, the advert is more likely to be zapped, but at higher levels informativeness and pleasantness are incompatible because of a reduced motivation and ability to process information (Elpers, Wedel and Pieters 2002)

Figure 6.7

Managing the learning process

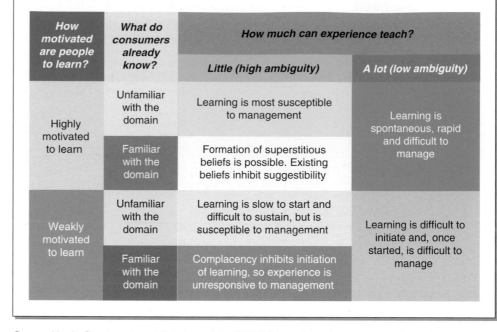

Source: Hoch, Stephen J. and Deighton, John (1989) Managing what consumers learn from experience. *Journal of Marketing*, 53 (April): 11.

If people are unable to learn much by experience, the situation becomes ambiguous: if learning by experience is the main way of learning, the situation is unambiguous but learning is difficult to manage. From the viewpoint of marketers, encouraging people to learn about products is easiest when the individuals are motivated to learn, and where the situation is ambiguous and therefore needs careful explanation.

Cognitive lock-in occurs when there is a high cognitive cost to obtaining information. This happens on the Internet: people tend to stick with the sites they are familiar with rather than going to the trouble of learning how to navigate a new site, especially if the initial setting up or the ongoing usage is difficult (Murray and Haubl 2002; Zauberman 2002). The result is that searches carried out online are (perhaps surprisingly) limited, with an average of only 1.1 book sites, 1.2 CD sites and 1.8 travel sites being visited (Johnson *et al.* 2002).

Incidentally, people who respond most favourably to Internet advertising are those with a high motivation to learn, high social escapism and high Internet ability due to its perceived informativeness (Zhou and Bao 2002). Evidently a desire to learn affects the ways people learn as well as their capacity for learning.

Cognitive theories recognize that consumers influence the outcome in an active manner, so the learning process is not always easy for an outsider (i.e. a marketing person) to manage. This may be some of the reason why new products fail so frequently; weak motivation to learn about new products leads to difficulty for marketers in starting the learning process.

Cognitive learning can also be viewed as having five elements, as shown in Figure 6.8.

Figure 6.8

Five elements of cognitive learning

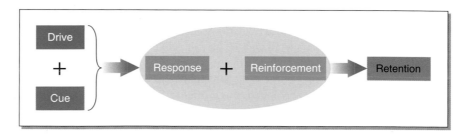

1 **Drive** – As seen in Chapter 2, drive is the stimulus that impels action. It is strong, internal and general. The impulse to learn can be driven by a fear of making an expensive mistake, or by a desire to maximize the benefits of the purchase.

2 **Cue** – This is some external trigger which encourages learning. It is weaker than a drive, is external and is specific. For example, a public service such as the Health and Safety Council might exhort employers to send for a leaflet on safety in the workplace. Sometimes firms will use advertisement retrieval cues to trigger responses.

3 **Response** – This is the reaction the consumer makes to the interaction between a drive and a cue. With luck, this results in a sale; but humans learn and will base future purchases on their concrete experience of the product rather than on the marketer's cues.

4 **Reinforcement** – Purchase response should be rewarded with a positive experience of the product. The object of reinforcement is to get consumers to associate the product with certain benefits.

5 **Retention** – This is the stability of the learned material over time, or in other words how well it is remembered. For example, advertising jingles have very high retention. People can often recall jingles that have not been broadcast for 30 years or more. This is particularly true for advertisements that were popular when the consumer was a child. (The opposite of retention is **extinction**.)

Cognitive learning usually involves some form of reasoning – people need to think about what they are seeing or hearing in order to remember the information. If the person has a low involvement with the product or brand, it will take a long time for the information to sink in, whereas if the individual has a high involvement with the product the information is processed and absorbed much more effectively, presumably because the person is thinking about the product much more (Krugman 1965).

Part of the problem for marketers is that they have little or no control over how people think about the messages they are shown. For example, an advertisement may be designed to be as interesting as possible in order to cut through that advertising clutter and attract attention, but the people who see the ad may become more interested in the cleverness of the advertising than they are in the brand. (Pieters, Warlop and Wedel 2002). This is exemplified by the Cinzano adverts mentioned earlier in the chapter – enjoyment of a clever and entertaining advertisement detracted from people's understanding of what was actually being advertised.

A further possibility for cognitive learning is vicarious learning, in which we learn from the experiences of others. This is an extremely useful way of learning, since it requires much less effort and risk than learning directly by trial and error. It requires either direct observation (watching what happens to someone else when they buy a product or behave in a particular way) or effective communication (as when someone describes their learning experiences). Because human beings are excellent communicators compared with most other species, we are particularly good at vicarious learning. In the marketing context,

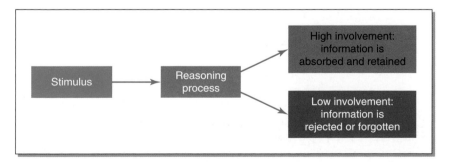

Figure 6.9

Reasoning and cognitive learning

Talking point

advertisers use models to show how products are used, and to show (or describe) the benefits of using a specific product. Having said that, learning by doing is generally much more effective than vicarious learning – imagine how far you would get in learning to drive a car if all you were ever allowed to do was to observe other drivers and read an instruction book.

So learning by doing is more effective than thinking about things. If that's so, why do we still sit in classrooms, read books, and (eventually) get a degree or other qualification? Why don't we do all our learning at work? Whatever happened to getting oneself apprenticed at 14 and spending seven to ten years becoming a master craftsman?

I suspect most of us can remember assignments we have written a great deal better than we can remember any lectures we ever attended – and we can remember how to play cricket, football, netball, hockey and so forth a great deal better than we can remember Shakespeare's plays (unless we acted in them, of course). So much for school-room lessons!

Maybe it's just about motivation to learn, but maybe it's something wrong with the way the education system operates: perhaps sitting through an hour-long monologue delivered by someone in a beige cardigan is not the best way to learn!

Learned responses are never truly unlearned. The brain remembers (stores) everything, but rather like a computer with a faulty disk drive it may not always be able to recall (re-trieve) everything. Also, the human memory is huge; the Encyclopaedia Britannica contains 12,500 million characters, but the brain has approximately 125,000,000 million characters' storage capacity. This is enough storage to hold 10,000 Encyclopaedia Britannicas, which makes the human brain easily the world's most powerful computer.

The need for knowledge

The purpose of learning about products is mainly to reduce risk. The more one knows about the product and the product category, the lower the level of risk (Figure 6.10). In many cases, less knowledgeable buyers will ask a more knowledgeable friend to help in making the purchase. In some cases, people will spend considerable time researching information about the product category and individual brands (this is mainly true where there is high involvement with the product or where there is a high risk).

Lack of knowledge may lead to a purchase which is inappropriate: for example, an inexperienced car buyer might miss a sign of potential engine problems, whereas more

Figure 6.10
Knowledge and risk

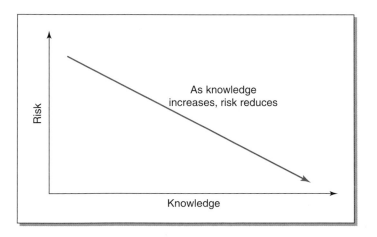

experienced and knowledgeable buyers would not. Knowledgeable people have a better understanding of what attributes to look for, and how to evaluate the product against those attributes (Alba and Hutchinson 1987).

The key point here, however, is that people understand that they need to know about the products they buy, especially when a major commitment is involved. This means that there is a motivation to learn, arising from a need for knowledge (see Chapter 2). This need is met through the same ways as any other need – goals are set, heuristics are developed, and the process is as subject to interrupts and dissonance as the actual purchase itself.

Talking point

If we have such a drive to learn, why is it that so many people dislike school? How come truancy rates are the highest they have ever been – and university classes are not always as well attended as they might be! And even more to the point, this is in a situation where attendance and learning affects one's capacity to earn money – a project dear to most people's hearts!

Perhaps it isn't so much that we don't want to learn as that we don't want to be told what to learn? Or maybe we just don't like to be taught!

This drive to extend knowledge about products accounts for the widespread sale of specialist consumer magazines. For example, a magazine aimed at sport pilots will contain flight tests of new light aircraft, information about flying schools and detailed tests of auxiliary equipment such as radios and GPS units. In most cases, the products are supplied to the magazines by the producers in order to gain publicity for the products: this is clearly a marketing communications activity, but the magazine's readers are eager to learn about products which may make their flying easier, safer and more enjoyable.

Each individual has many different types of knowledge, as shown in Figure 6.11. This is far from being a comprehensive list of an individual's knowledge categories, but some

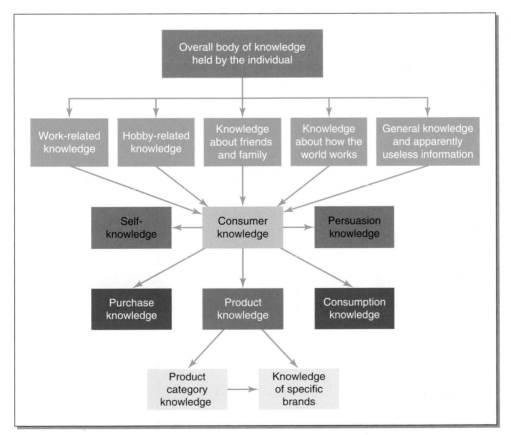

Figure 6.11

Categorizing knowledge

knowledge in each category will relate to marketing issues. The main types of knowledge of interest from a marketing point of view are as follows:

1 *Product knowledge* – This subdivides into product category knowledge and brand knowledge. Product category knowledge is the information an individual remembers about all the possible solutions to the need problem.

2 *Purchase knowledge* – This is about how to buy, what things cost and where to buy from.

3 *Consumption or usage knowledge* – This is about how to use the product, how to dispose of whatever is left after use and what the risks are in using the product.

4 *Persuasion knowledge* – This is an understanding of the goals and tactics of people who might be trying to persuade us to buy – in the main, this is knowledge about marketers, but it includes knowledge about friends who might be recommending a product to us.

5 *Self-knowledge* – This is knowledge about one's own needs, including knowledge about one's own failings. For example, a novice golfer might be well aware of his or her lack of knowledge about the game, and therefore be more prepared to buy books about the game, extra coaching and equipment suitable for novices.

Product category knowledge

This type of product knowledge is fairly general. For example, we all know what a television set is, and, broadly, we all know how to operate one and know what it will do for us in terms of entertainment. Relatively fewer of us would know the difference between plasma and LCD screens, even if we know that both terms refer to flat screens. Few of us would really understand what digital TV is or what it does, even though this is projected to be the only available TV system in the UK within a relatively few years' time. If we head into the technical detail of different types of microchip almost all of us would be lost. The risk for a UK television purchaser is that the new standard is likely to make most existing televisions obsolete, which will be somewhat annoying for someone who had bought a set which is not digitally compatible. Someone who has basic product knowledge is called a 'product novice': someone who has a large amount of product knowledge is a 'product expert' (Figure 6.12).

Knowledge about these different factors would be chunked in the individual's memory under the category of 'TV sets'. For most people, information is frequently cross-referenced, so that information about the microchips might also be contained in the category of 'things I know about electronics' or, in some cases, 'things I deal with in work'.

A product expert would also have extensive knowledge of the members of a product category (the brands). A product expert would be able to judge unknown product attributes by reference to known attributes (for example, knowing that the product's components are reliable would give an indication of the longevity of the product as well as its reliability), and would influence acceptance of a price for a product since the expert would be aware of the

Figure 6.12

Product expert knowledge

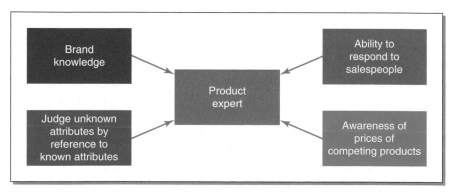

prices of competing products. Knowledge influences responses to salespeople, which places a burden on salespeople to judge quickly and accurately how much the prospective customer already knows.

Brand knowledge

Brand knowledge is concerned with what people know about a specific product within the general product category. From a marketing viewpoint, the starting point of brand knowledge is whether people remember the brand at all. The next level is whether people associate the brand strongly with the product category: further increases in knowledge about the brand may follow, but without knowing that the brand exists and that it relates to a particular product there is no chance whatever that the brand will be included in the consideration set.

To test whether individuals have this level of knowledge, market researchers have two main tools. The first is a recall test, which tests top-of-the-mind awareness. Respondents might be asked to list all the breakfast cereals they can think of, for example, and the researcher would be able to tell first whether the brand being tested is included in the list, and second where it stands in relation to the other brands. The second method is a recognition test, in which people are shown a list of brand names and are asked to say which ones they recognize. The problem with this test is that people may claim to recognize brands which they have never heard of rather than appear to be ignorant: sometimes researchers will include fictitious brands in the list to test for this.

The tests are used for different circumstances. A recall test might be useful for testing advertising effectiveness or to determine the product's position in consumers' perceptual maps. A recognition test might be more useful when testing merchandising success, since it is important that people recognize the brand when they see it in store.

Both recall and recognition are enhanced when the brand has a strong symbol attached to it. The Michelin Man, the Nokia ring tone and the Volkswagen VW logo are all powerful symbols, each in a different way. Each one provokes instant recognition, and a clear image of what the product is and what it does.

Encouraging people to learn about brands is a major part of advertising, and certainly of the more information-based, cognitive approaches to advertising. Many sales promotions are aimed at increasing people's knowledge about brands, encouraging them to learn more: for example, the tourist boards of countries sometimes run informative advertisements about their countries, linked to a competition for which the prize is a holiday in the country. In order to win the prize, participants have to complete a questionnaire about the country, which means that they need to read the advertisement to find out the answers.

Brand associations (Figure 6.13, page 128) are the connections people make between the brand and other concepts (Blackwell *et al.* 2006). Brand associations include beliefs and perceptions about what the brand will do, in other words the consumption benefits. Brand associations are important to marketers because they tend to influence the degree to which consumers will adopt the product, and also the degree to which they will accept brand extensions and recommend the product to others (Belen del Rio, Vacquez and Iglesias 2001). The higher the consumer's perception of brand quality, the more likely he or she is to recommend the brand (no surprises there) and also to buy brand extensions.

Some symbols are instantly recognizable . . .

In other words, brand association tends to mean that people will buy a different product, perhaps with no associated characteristics, simply on the basis that the brand is the same as another product which is tried and tested. Brand extensions may, of course, be in products which have some related production similarities, so that one might assume that a firm which is good at making the one product would also be good at making the other. Saab have played on this assumption in their advertising: since the company manufactures fighter aircraft as well as cars, it might be reasonable to assume that the engineering capabilities within the company would be high.

. . . and thus make the brands memorable.

Figure 6.13

Brand association

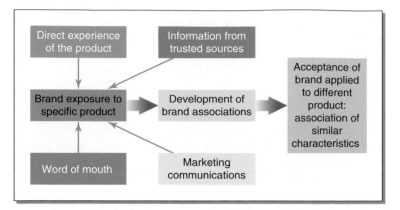

SAAB builds fighters as well as cars – so we can assume they are good engineers.

There is absolutely no reason to suppose that Virgin would be good at running airlines, commissioning new bands, running an insurance company and manufacturing cola drinks. Yet the fact that the Virgin brand appears on the products is apparently seen as a signal of quality, and people who have been happy with one Virgin product seem to accept that other Virgin products will have similar quality values.

Developing appropriate brand associations for new products is an especially challenging task (there is more on this in Chapter 13). An almost equally challenging task is that of moving an existing product into a new market, and this is precisely the problem firms have when they move to Internet trading. A brand which is well known in its home market might be entirely unknown in the rest of the world, so apart from the logistical problems of arranging physical distribution the firm faces the challenge of establishing a consistent brand image across a wide spectrum of foreign cultures.

Purchase knowledge

Purchase knowledge is the information people have about buying products. This includes where the product can be bought, whether discounts apply at some times or in some places, how much the product should cost and what the procedure is for buying the product.

Price is an important issue, because it is the measure of what the consumer has to give in return for the product benefits (Figure 6.14). This judgement is made not only on the basis of the cost of the brand from different sources, but also on the cost of products which provide similar benefits (Rao and Seiben 1992). If one has little knowledge of the pricing within the product category, one might assume that a reasonable price is far too high (or be delighted to find that the actual price is lower than expected). In some cases, marketers (and especially salespeople) will try to give an impression that the price will be higher than it actually is, in order to delight the customer with the real price. This is called price conditioning. For example, a salesperson selling fitted kitchens might, at an early stage of the presentation, suggest that the new kitchen might cost £10,000 or more. When the actual price turns out to be only £8500 the customer is delighted, but if the customer had been expecting a price of £6000 the delight would have been replaced by an entirely different feeling.

It is useful if marketers have knowledge of what people think is a reasonable price for a product. This will be a combination of what people believe is reasonable when they see the actual product, and what people already know about the price of competing products. Relative price knowledge is what people know about one price relative to another (Barone, Manning and Miniard 2004). For example, one American study found that people thought that buying books online was about 3 per cent cheaper than buying them from a bricks-and-mortar

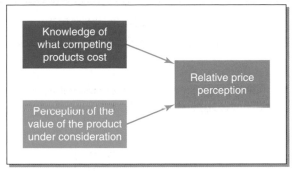

Figure 6.14

Relative price information

retailer, whereas in fact the price difference was an average 10 per cent (Tedeschi 2005). This is clearly bad news for the online retailers, who are apparently cutting their profit margins without effectively communicating the price savings to their customers.

Marketers may decide prices (at least in part) on how well informed they believe customers to be about competitors' prices (Figure 6.14). If the products are rarely purchased, consumers will be unlikely to have very precise knowledge of prices (although this is a major motivator for customers to learn about prices before committing to a purchase). A further factor would be the ease of finding out about prices – in the case of home improvements, for example, it might prove extremely time-consuming to obtain quotes from different contractors, even if the contractors are willing to provide quotes (which they are often unprepared to do, given that this is a time-consuming activity for them and most builders have more than enough work as it is). In this respect, the Internet represents something of a threat to marketers since price comparisons are relatively easy to make, especially in such areas as booking flights or ferries.

Knowing when to buy is also an important part of purchase knowledge (Figure 6.15). In some cases purchases are seasonal: for example, flights are cheaper at off-peak times and so also is hotel accommodation. For those with the flexibility to travel at any time, there are considerable savings to be made. Buying in advance may also save money.

Another example is consumer electronics. Most people are well aware that when a new product is launched the price is high: for example, plasma-screen TV sets started off priced in the thousands of pounds, but prices dropped dramatically as the sets gained in popularity. Partly this is due to reduced manufacturing costs on longer production runs, and partly it is due to the need for manufacturers to recoup development costs, but it is also due to manufacturers knowing that some people are prepared to pay a premium price for the pleasure of being the first to own a new, exciting product.

Knowing where to buy the product is a more complex issue than it once was, due the increasing number of possible retail outlets from which products can be purchased. Fifty years or so ago retailers were much more specific in the range of products they carried:

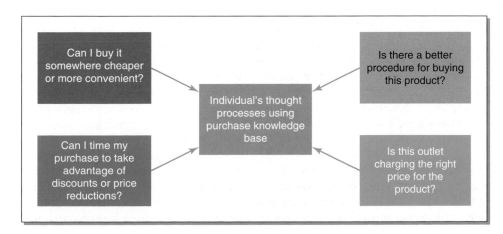

Figure 6.15

Advantages of having purchase knowledge

stationers only sold stationery, chemists only sold medicines and so forth. Nowadays, products are available from a wide range of stores, and also online. Items such as soy sauce or curry spices are often cheaper from specialist Chinese or Indian grocers than they are from supermarkets, for example. In addition, someone may need a specific product and have no knowledge of where to buy it: specialist products for motor or building work might not be available from normal hardware stores, but might instead need to be bought from specialist outlets or ordered from the manufacturers. In these circumstances manufacturers need to be sure that people are aware of where the products can be bought.

Consumption knowledge

This type of knowledge is the information which consumers have about how a product's benefits can be obtained in use. Lack of such knowledge would mean that people would be unlikely to buy the product in the first place: mobile telephones suffered from this problem for some time, since people found the systems and choices confusing (many still do). Other high-tech products suffer from similar problems – most people have trouble using their DVD players properly, digital cameras are in general complex to operate and download pictures, and many people have trouble understanding how to programme their washing machines correctly. A product which is used incorrectly is unlikely to perform to the required standard, which in turn is likely to lead to consumer dissatisfaction or even injury (Staelin 1978).

In Figure 6.16, ignorance about the correct use of the product can lead to two outcomes: either the consumer uses the product incorrectly, which leads to dissatisfaction with the product's performance, or the consumer reads the producer's information about the product (the manual) and learns how to use the product correctly. This should lead to satisfaction. In some cases, consumers effectively re-invent the product, failing to use it according to the manufacturer's instructions, but are still satisfied with the performance. The final possibility is that the consumer knows how to use the product, uses it according to the instructions and is thus satisfied with the product.

At an obvious level, it is difficult to sell cars to people who do not have driving licences, and difficult to sell computers to people who have no idea how to use one. At a more subtle level, there may be uses for the product which are not obvious to consumers – using baking powder for deodorizing fridges is a well-known example, but using bath oil to remove tar spots from cars is less obvious. Whether a manufacturer would want to promote this use for a bath oil is doubtful, but consumers do invent ways of using products in novel ways and this knowledge enters the product experts' minds even when it is not put there by the producers.

Persuasion knowledge

Persuasion knowledge is what people know about the goals and tactics of those trying to persuade them (Friestad and Wright 1994). People are often sceptical about the motives of

Figure 6.16

Consumption knowledge

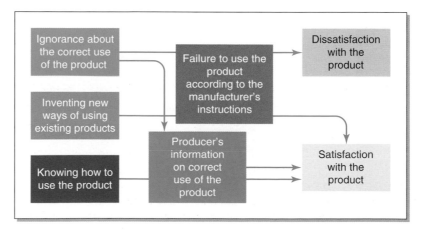

marketers, with good reason: marketers are not in business to do consumers a bit of good, they are in business for their own ends, and aim to manage the exchange between consumers and the firm. Since most of us resent being managed, we tend to seek out information about marketing tactics in order to strengthen our own negotiating position.

In recent years, people have become more marketing aware, and marketing jargon is commonly heard being used by people who are not marketers. Understanding how marketers (and perhaps especially salespeople) operate has been shown to affect consumers' opinions of marketer sincerity adversely (Brown and Krishna 2004). A study by Bearden, Hardesty and Rose (2001) showed that people were able to make the following statements about their understanding of persuasion:

1 I know when an offer is 'too good to be true'.
2 I can tell when an offer has strings attached.
3 I have no trouble understanding the bargaining tactics used by salespeople.
4 I know when a marketer is pressuring me to buy.
5 I can see through sales gimmicks used to get consumers to buy.
6 I can separate facts from fantasy in advertising.

This clearly has implications for the marketing approach. Marketers cannot naively assume that consumers can be led around by the nose or can be easily persuaded by a glib sales patter: people are suspicious, and are able to see through many marketing ploys.

Self-knowledge

This area of knowledge is about the individual's understanding of his or her own mental processes (Alba and Hutchinson 2000). People who understand their own strengths and weaknesses as well as what they like and do not like are in a better position to make realistic purchasing decisions than people who are not in touch with their own personalities. Self-knowledge is important to market researchers, since much commercial market research is based on self-reports by consumers.

For example, knowing that one likes cream cakes and doesn't like chicken pies is a useful piece of knowledge for choosing lunch. Knowing that one cannot eat just one cream cake without going on to eat the whole box is a useful piece of self-knowledge which might prevent a dietary disaster.

Sources of consumer knowledge

People gather information about products from a large number of sources both personal and impersonal. The sources may be controlled (or at least influenced) by marketers or may be entirely independent. Figure 6.17 (page 132) shows some of the sources.

In fact, even the non-marketer-controlled sources can be influenced by marketers. Product placement in films and TV programmes is common (although in the UK it is illegal for programme makers to accept payment for placing products, this does not prevent brands appearing on TV).

People are naturally suspicious of marketer-controlled information sources, but will use them and will often base most of their decision-making on the rival claims of different producers. Word-of-mouth and impartial articles in newspapers and magazines are trusted much more, because people feel that there is no purpose to be served by the source lying to them. It is for this reason that marketers try to influence word of mouth, word of mouse (the use of e-mail, blogs and chatrooms to discuss products) and the opinions of journalists (who are, after all, powerful influencers).

The most useful source of information is, of course, the actual consumption of the product itself. Actually using a product and forming a judgement about it is clearly far and away

Figure 6.17

Classifying sources of knowledge

	Marketer-controlled	*Non-marketer-controlled*
Personal sources of information	Sales people Service people Paid product endorsers	Family and friends Work colleagues Other shoppers Experts, opinion leaders and influentials Internet forums and bulletin boards
Impersonal sources of information	Products Point-of-purchase materials Advertising Catalogues Corporate websites Yellow pages	TV and radio shows Non-corporate websites Books Government reports Newspapers Magazines

Source: Adapted from Blackwell, Roger D., Miniard, Paul W. and Engel, James F. *Consumer Behavior*, 10th ed. (Mason, OH: Thomson): 355.

the best route for gaining information. Obviously this is not always possible, but for cheap, low-risk products it is often the best choice.

Sometimes a lack of knowledge can be an advantage. Research shows that surprising people (i.e. providing information for which there are no antecedents) can lead to them evaluating the surprising brand higher than do people to whom the information was not a surprise (Vanhamme and Snelders 2003).

Summary

Learning is something that we all do, every day of our lives, and the bulk of what we learn comes from outside the classroom. Learning comes about in many ways: sometimes it happens subconsciously, as in the case of classical conditioning; sometimes it requires conscious effort as in cognitive learning. We never really forget anything we have learned, however.

From a marketing viewpoint, how people find out about products and brands, and more especially what drives people to do so, is the basis of our thinking when developing communications strategies. How people store the information in memory, and where they store it, is the basis of our communications strategies. Even though people flip past advertisements, we do have a natural desire to learn, and we also have considerable pressures on us to know about the products we buy – the downside of not knowing varies from losing our money, through social embarrassment, to physical injury.

The key points from this chapter are as follows:

● Learning is behavioural change over time relative to an external stimulus.

● Classical conditioning is largely involuntary on the part of the learner.

● Operant conditioning assumes that the learner has choice in the process: 'good' behaviour is reinforced by reward, 'bad' behaviour is reduced by punishment.

● Cognitive learning involves conscious thought and effort.

● Motivation is a key factor in all learning.

● Learning by experience is more powerful than learning vicariously.

● Consumer knowledge breaks down into product knowledge, purchase knowledge, consumption knowledge, persuasion knowledge, and self-knowledge.

Chapter review questions

1 How might a marketer use music in classical conditioning?

2 What methods of operant conditioning are available to marketers?

3 What is the role of cognitive learning in major purchases?

4 How might a marketer motivate a consumer to learn about a product?

5 How can learning by experience be used in selling high-value products such as stereo systems?

6 How might product experts be recruited for a word-of-mouth campaign?

7 What effect does persuasion knowledge have on marketing communications?

8 How can self-knowledge be enhanced by marketers?

9 How can marketers encourage people to improve their purchase knowledge?

10 What should marketers do to ensure that consumers have adequate consumption knowledge?

Preview case study revisited
Bayer educates consumers

Bayer's corporate slogan is 'Science for a better life.' The company prides itself on creating a better life for its employees, shareholders and customers through applying good scientific research to meeting everyday problems.

The problem of thrush is one of them. Thrush is an irritation of the genital area caused by the Candida yeast. Candida lives on the skin all the time, but is normally controlled by the body's own pH balance: if this is altered, for example by using perfumed soaps or by excessive sweating, the yeast multiplies beyond the body's capacity to control it and infections set in. Although thrush affects women in the main, men are far from immune and are often carriers of the yeast. Bayer's answer to the problem is a combination of cream, pessaries and tablets called Canesten. Canesten restores the body's natural balance and kills the yeasts.

From a marketing viewpoint, this is hardly something that can easily be promoted on TV. What Bayer have done is produce a website dedicated to Canesten: the site is a sponsored link to Google, keyed to the word 'thrush' and also to similar key words. The website has a large amount of information on it about the disease, the symptoms, the prevention of it and of course the cure. The site is designed to be reassuring and matter-of-fact with its visitors: since three out of four women suffer from thrush at one time or another, there is really no need to feel embarrassed, but reassurance is helpful.

The website does advise people to see their doctors, since it is important to ensure that the diagnosis is correct – similar symptoms might be connected with other, more serious diseases. Once the diagnosis is sure, the individual can order Canesten online, can obtain advice from the 'Canesten hot line', and can read up about preventative measures for the future. The site even has a section on myths about thrush – also very reassuring!

Bayer have followed a similar approach for their websites on haemorrhoids, period pain, flatulence and cystitis, all of which can be embarrassing for some people. Each site contains thousands of words, far more than could be contained in an advertisement: although few people would read everything, the need for knowledge is amply met by this approach.

Comco Ikarus is a German manufacturer of light aircraft, based at Hohentegen in south-western Germany. The company has two main products: the Breezer, a two-seat light aircraft of aluminium construction, and the C42, a three-axis microlight.

The C42 is something of a breakthrough in the microlight world. It looks and flies like an ordinary light aircraft: people who see it for the first time cannot believe that it is a microlight, but since it comes under the 450 kg maximum take-off weight restriction, it can fly under the much less stringent rules that apply to these very small aircraft. It cruises at almost 100 mph, has a wider cabin than a Cessna, and has a cabin heater and all the home comforts one expects from a small car. It can take off from a farmer's field or from an airport runway, and it outperforms many aircraft that have much higher price tags. Running costs are also at microlight level: the aircraft uses ordinary petrol, not aviation fuel, and it burns about 12 litres per hour on average, giving it the fuel costs of a small car.

For Comco Ikarus, the problem is one of conveying several ideas to potential customers. These are as follows:

1 That flying is not solely the province of the wealthy.

2 That a microlight is not necessarily something that looks like a cross between a motorbike and a tablecloth.

3 That you don't need to wear leather flying helmets and scarves anymore.

4 That you can use a microlight aircraft as serious transportation for two people and a reasonable amount of luggage and go anywhere in Europe with minimal regulatory constraints.

For people who already fly, this information may or may not come as a surprise (although a great many light aircraft pilots are unaware of how far microlights have developed in

PAUL HEINRICH/ALAMY

recent years). The problem here is that these people are likely to be members of clubs (and hence have access to club aircraft when they want to fly) or already to own an aircraft. Pilots do not buy and sell aircraft nearly as frequently as motorists change cars: the working life of an aircraft is measured in decades rather than years, so there is little pressure to trade an aircraft in for the latest model – in any case the second-hand market for aircraft is poorly developed.

For people who do not fly, there is a general impression that flying is expensive, dangerous and far too complex to understand – not to mention that it is widely regarded as a young person's activity.

The UK importer of the Ikarus, Aerosport Limited, is based at Wolverhampton Airport. Getting the aircraft into the market and in front of the general public is a priority, since this is where future sales are likely to be generated. A major breakthrough for the company was the certification by the UK Civil Aviation Authority of the Ikarus as a training aircraft. Aerosport's strategy was to encourage flying schools to use the aircraft for training so that new pilots would see the advantages of the aircraft and would be more likely therefore to buy one. Additionally, most flying schools offer people trial lessons, and these are commonly given as birthday gifts, especially for 'milestone' birthdays such as fortieth or fiftieth birthdays.

Someone going for a trial flight is thus exposed to the aircraft, and has a considerable amount of information offered by the flying school: from the school's viewpoint, the majority of people who can easily afford to learn to fly are likely to be in their forties, fifties or even older. These people have paid off their mortgages, educated their children, and are likely to be at their peak earnings. Finding out that microlights require less stringent medicals, are cheaper to buy and fly, and are relatively simple to fly can be a real eye-opener for men who were brought up on Biggles books. In fact, one school (Swansea Sport Flying) had large boards made up saying 'Yes, This Is A Microlight!' to place by the parked aircraft so that they can be seen from the airport car park. Aerosport give a commission to the flying school on any aircraft sales, so there is an incentive to discuss buying an aircraft.

The end result is that many people who have not seriously thought of having flying lessons have gone on from their trial flight to obtaining a license. Of those, many have bought Ikarus aircraft, either as sole owners or in a syndicate.

Educating people about such a complex purchase as an aircraft, and (perhaps even more difficult) overcoming pre-existing prejudices about microlights, is no mean feat.

So what better place to start than with teaching establishments such as flying schools?

Case study questions

1 Why not simply send out brochures to prospective customers?

2 What type of learning is being encouraged?

3 How is cognitive effort encouraged?

4 What potential difficulties might arise from targeting an older audience?

5 What is the role of the product expert in the purchase decision for an aircraft?

References

Alba, Joseph A., and Hutchinson, J. Wesley (1987) Dimensions of consumer expertise. *Journal of Consumer Research*, 13 (March): 411–54.

Alba, Joseph A., and Hutchinson, J. Wesley (2000) Knowledge calibration: what consumers know and what they think they know. *Journal of Consumer Research*, 27 (September): 123–56.

Barone, Michael J., Manning, Kenneth C., and Miniard, Paul W. (2004) Consumer response to practical price comparisons in retail environments. *Journal of Marketing*, 68 (July): 37–47.

Bearden, William O., Hardesty, David M., and Rose, Randall L. (2001) Consumers' self-confidence: refinements in conceptualisation and measurement. *Journal of Consumer Research*, 28 (June): 121–34.

Belen del Rio, A., Vacquez, Rodolfo, and Iglesias, Victor (2001) The effects of brand association on consumer response. *Journal of Consumer Marketing*, 18: 410–25.

Blackwell, Roger D., Miniard, Paul W., and Engel, James F. (2006) *Consumer Behaviour* (Mason, OH: Thomson South-Western).

Brown, Christina L., and Krishna, Aradhna (2004) The skeptical shopper: a metacognitive account for the effects of default options on choice. *Journal of Consumer Research*, 31 (December): 529–39.

Elpers, Josephine Woltman, Wedel, Michel, and Pieters, Rik (2002) The influence of moment-to-moment pleasantness and informativeness on zapping TV commercials: a functional data and survival analysis approach. *Advances in Consumer Research*, 29(1): 57–8.

Friestad, Marian, and Wright, Peter (1994) The persuasion knowledge model: how people cope with persuasion attempts. *Journal of Consumer Research*, 21(1): 1–30.

Gorn, Gerald J. (1982) The effects of music in advertising on choice behaviour: a classical conditioning approach. *Journal of Marketing*, 46 (winter): 94–101.

Hoch, Stephen J., and Ha, Young-Won (1986) Consumer learning: advertising and the ambiguity of product experience. *Journal of Consumer Research*, 13 (September): 221–33.

Johnson, Eric, Moe, Wendy, Fader, Peter, Bellman, Steven, and Lohse, Jerry (2002) On the depth and dynamics of on-line search behaviour. *Advances in Consumer Research*, 29(1): 7–8.

Kroeber-Riel, Werner (1984) Emotional product differentiation by classical conditioning. *Advances in Consumer Research 11*, ed. Thomas C. Kinnear (Provo, UT: Association for Consumer Research).

Krugman H.E. (1965) The impact of television advertising: learning without involvement. *Public Opinion Quarterly*, 29: 349–56.

Lerman, Dawn (2003) The effect of morphemic familiarity and exposure mode on recall and recognition of brand names. *Advances in Consumer Research*, 30(1): 80–1.

McSweeney, Frances K., and Bierley, Calvin (1984) Recent developments in classical conditioning. *Journal of Consumer Research*, 11 (September), 2: 619–37.

Murray, Kyle B., and Haubl, Gerald (2002) The fiction of no friction: a user skills approach to cognitive lock-in. *Advances in Consumer Research*, 29(1): 8–9.

Onkvisit, S., and Shaw John J. (1994) *Consumer Behaviour, Strategy and Analysis* (New York: Macmillan).

Pavlov, Ivan P. (1927) *Conditioned Reflexes* (London, Oxford University Press).

Pieters, Rik, Warlop, Luk, and Wedel, Michael (2002) Breaking through the clutter: ad originality and familiarity effects on brand attention and memory. *Advances in Consumer Research*, 29(1): 89.

Rao, Akshay R., and Seiben, Wanda A. (1992): The effect of prior knowledge on price acceptability and the type of information examined. *Journal of Consumer Research*, 19 (September): 256–70.

Skinner, Burris F. (1953) *Science and Human Behaviour* (New York: Macmillan).

Staelin, Richard (1978) The effects of consumer education on consumer product safety behaviour. *Journal of Consumer Research*, 5 (June): 30–40.

Tedeschi, Bob (2005) Cheaper than it seems. *New York Times* (10 January).

Vanhamme, Joel, and Snelders, Dirk (2003) What if you surprise your customers – will they be more satisfied? Findings from a pilot experiment. *Advances in Consumer Research*, 30(1): 48–56.

Zauberman, Gul (2002) Lock-in over time: time preferences, prediction accuracy and the information cost structure. *Advances in Consumer Research*, 29(1).

Zhou, Zheng, and Bao, Yeqing (2002) Users' attitudes towards web advertising: effects of internet motivation and internet ability. *Advances in Consumer Research*, 29(1).

Chapter 7
Attitude formation

Learning objectives After reading this chapter, you should be able to:

1 describe what is meant by attitude

2 show that attitude is not neutral

3 explain how attitudes can be inferred from behaviour

4 explain why behaviour cannot be assumed from knowing attitude

5 describe the components of attitude

6 explain the role of salient beliefs in forming attitudes

7 explain the purpose of attitudes

8 explain the relationship between attitude and behaviour

9 describe the factors which determine the strength of attitude

10 explain the difference between public and private attitudes

11 show the effect of situation on attitude

Introduction

Attitudes are what put us in the right position for behaviour. We each have attitudes towards many things – our friends, our possessions, our families, Government policies, other people's behaviour, and so forth. Our differing attitudes are (in part) the differentiators between us as human beings, and since attitudes are the precursor to any consumption behaviour they are of great interest to marketers, both in terms of finding out what they are and in seeking to change them.

This chapter is about how attitudes are formed; the next chapter looks at how they are changed.

Defining 'attitude'

Attitude can be defined as 'a learned tendency to respond to an object in a consistently favourable or unfavourable way' (Onkvisit and Shaw 1994). Whether a product will be bought or not depends to a large extent on the consumer's attitude towards it, and therefore much marketing effort is expended on finding out what consumers' attitudes are to product offerings, and in seeking to change those attitudes where appropriate.

To break down the definition and make it easier to handle:

1 Attitude is learned, not instinctive.

2 It is not behaviour, it is a predisposition towards a particular behaviour.

3 It implies a relationship between a person and an object. The object of the attitude could be another person, an institution, or a physical article; 'object' is used here in the sense of 'an objective'.

Preview case study
Brand attitudes

It turns out that many people have become disillusioned with the whole idea of brands. According to research by Fitch, the global brand design consultancy, 68 per cent of consumers do not believe that brands are interested in improving their lives: 62 per cent do not trust organizations to meet their daily needs, and 66 per cent do not believe that organizations have changed for the better in recent years.

On the positive side, 80 per cent of customers said that they think it is realistic to talk about having a relationship with a brand, but 61 per cent think that they should have a more interactive relationship with the brand: 40 per cent think that consumers can act collectively to change the brand's values and marketing approach, and 56 per cent believe that collective action can affect prices.

So what changes do people want? What brand values do people look for? It turns out that honesty, trust, transparency and reliability are high on the agenda, and 68 per cent of people say that they trust brands with a 'tell it like it is' philosophy.

'This research reveals a sea-change in the way consumers are relating to brands' claims Pearse McCabe, Planning Director at Fitch. 'We believe recent events have forced people to question the world they live in, and in turn, their relationships with brands. Where previously brands have been accepted as paternalistic voices of authority, now consumers are seeking more mature, grown-up relationships with brands, based on honesty, openness and equality. Consumers have come of age and brands need to recognise and respond to that if they are to remain relevant in the future.'

Much of this is depressing news for marketers. After all, it is so much simpler to operate on the basis that people will buy into brand values without too much arguing. In the good old days, marketers developed the brand values and consumers accepted them without question – and certainly did not start thinking about ganging up on organizations to affect (i.e. reduce) prices! The sixty-four-thousand-dollar question for marketers, then, is how did people develop these attitudes? And what can be done about it?

4 Attitudes are fairly stable; they do not change much with physical states or circumstances. For example, if someone's favourite painkiller is Panadol, that attitude remains whether or not the individual has a headache. The behaviour (actually taking the tablets) may not happen, but the attitude remains.

5 The relationship between a person and an object is not neutral. It is a vector, having both direction and intensity; if you express an attitude about something, you either like it or you do not. If you are neutral about it, or indifferent, you would say you don't have any attitude towards it.

Attitude has to be inferred from statements or behaviour; it is intangible and not directly observable. In other words, although we can observe and measure behaviour, we have to ask people about their attitudes to various things, and hope that their replies are honest ones. This can cause difficulties if we are researching a sensitive topic.

The formation of attitude is based on experience with the object, normally from direct experience; driving a particular make of car or trying a particular brand of beer will lead to the formation of an attitude. The individual builds up a mental picture (perception) of the object, and forms an attitude accordingly. First impressions are important, since they colour our later information-gathering (see Chapter 5) – this is why people behave themselves on the first date, so that the other person forms a favourable attitude.

Some experience is indirect; recommendations and the communicated experiences of friends or relatives are important when forming attitudes towards objects of which we don't have direct experience. This can sometimes lead to superstitious beliefs and prejudices due to the **synthetic** nature of perception. If your friends have all told you that a particular film is boring, you are likely to maintain that attitude, even if you have not seen the

Talking point

film yourself. Negative attitudes are often formed in this way. Advertising, and indeed marketing communications generally, can help a lot here by providing additional sources of information (public relations has a particularly important role in this, since it is an activity which deals mainly with attitude formation and change).

So attitudes form through experience. And yet we often base our beliefs on very limited experience, do we not? Someone who travels by sea for the first time and is seriously seasick is unlikely to want to travel on a ship ever again – even though the seasickness might have been caused by the worst storm ever!

Are we really that stupid when it comes to developing attitudes? Is this some weakness in the human brain? Or is it, perhaps, a sign of one of our great talents – the ability to develop a working hypothesis based on limited data?

Either way, we seem to form attitudes almost spontaneously, and often make little effort to review them later!

There is a perceptual component in attitude. The manner in which an object is perceived is affected by the consumer's stable characteristics (personality, intelligence, previous knowledge, culture, gender, etc.) and by current characteristics, such as mood, state of the organism, etc.

Dimensions of attitude

Attitude has three dimensions, as shown in Figure 7.1.

Table 7.1 explains the relationship between each of these components.

It is important to note that attitude and behaviour are separate things. Simply because an individual has a particular attitude about something does not mean that the individual will act on the attitude.

For example, someone might hear that his bank is investing in a country with an oppressive regime. This is cognition. He may think that this is unethical, he does not like the bank doing this (affect). He therefore decides to move his account elsewhere (conation). Conation may not always lead to behaviour; our ethical bank customer may have second thoughts later and decide to leave the account where it is, perhaps on the basis that switching to another bank is just too complicated. Other factors often prevent us from taking the course of action we had originally planned.

The three elements are interrelated in a complex way (Figure 7.2). Purchase intentions relate to beliefs and brand evaluations, and likelihood of buying a brand has been shown to be influenced by attitudes towards advertising as well as attitudes towards brands (Homer and Yoon 1992).

The traditional view of attitude is that affect towards an object is mediated by cognition; in other words, emotional responses about something are controlled to a marked extent by

Figure 7.1

Dimensions of attitude

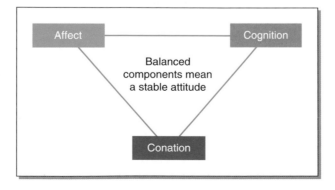

Table 7.1 Dimensions of attitude

Dimension	Definition	Explanation	Example
Cognition	The perceptual component of attitude	This is the individual's awareness, knowledge, beliefs and images of the object of the attitude. It is the conscious, thinking part of attitude.	An individual's attitude towards a car may be composed of comparative information, e.g. the Ford Focus has a tighter turning circle than the Vauxhall Astra, or the Vauxhall has better acceleration. These are the facts (or beliefs) informing the attitude.
Affect	The evaluative component of attitude	These are the emotions, the feelings of like and dislike which do not always have a basis in objective fact.	Drivers frequently have affective relationships with their first cars. The car is given a name, and often the driver will speak to it.
Conation	Behavioural intention	Conation is about what we intend to do about the attitudinal object; whether to approach it, reject it, buy it, etc. It is not the actual behaviour; merely an intention.	Having formed an attitude about a car ('I love the bodywork, it really looks great, and it does 40 to the gallon as well') the consumer forms an intention ('I'm going to take out a loan and buy one') This intention is the conation.

rational evaluation. This has been challenged by Zajonc and Markus (1985) who assert that affective responses do not have to be based on prior cognition. People can develop a 'gut feeling' about something without conscious evaluation, and even on limited information, then rationalize the decision afterwards. This may sometimes be due to classical conditioning; for example, the individual may form a favourable attitude towards a product because the advert uses a favourite song as background music (see Chapter 6). Affect also influences information processing: there is a 'meddling-in' effect in which cognition is influenced by the way in which information is processed, which is in turn influenced by emotions (Mishra, Mishra and Nayakankuppam 2006). In fact, forming an attitude about a product might start with any of the three components, with the others coming into play afterwards. Also, if the outcome of any action is expected to be affect-rich (pleasurable, unpleasant, emotionally moving etc.) the individual will evaluate the action by its effect on feelings. Affect-poor outcomes trigger evaluation by calculation (Hsee and Rottenstreich 2002). In other words, putting a strong emotional bias into marketing communications is likely to lead to emotionally based decision-making.

Although it may seem illogical or dangerous to form an attitude without first finding out a lot about the attitudinal object, most people are familiar with the feeling of having 'fallen in love' with a hopelessly impractical purchase. Likewise, most people are familiar with

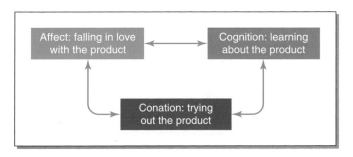

Figure 7.2

Starting points for attitude formation

We might fall in love with a car for its looks alone.

the feeling of having taken an instant dislike to somebody without first getting to know the person.

Attitude contains components of belief and opinion, but it is neither. Attitude differs from belief in that belief is neutral, not implying good or bad. Belief is concerned with the presence or absence of an attribute, and is usually based on a judgement of the available evidence. Attitude contains an element of affect, and evaluates whether the existence of an attribute will result in satisfaction or dissatisfaction. For example, a consumer might believe that a Volvo is a reliable, well-engineered car but have no particular feelings about this either way. Conversely, another consumer might feel that the Volvo is a good car, or a desirable car, because it is well engineered and reliable.

Attitude differs from opinion in that opinion is an overt, vocalised expression of an attitude. Attitude can also be expressed non-verbally (facial expressions, body language, etc.), or indeed may not be expressed at all. While opinions may arise from attitudes (i.e. be expressed as the result of an attitude) and attitudes may arise from hearing the opinions of others, the two are in fact separate entities.

Attitude formation

A more complete model of the formation of attitudes about brands shows that it is a somewhat complex process. Figure 7.3 gives an overview of the complete process.

The diagram begins with the consumer's needs, both utilitarian (practical) and expressive (emotional). This feeds into the consumer's motivation to process information, as does advertising; motivation and exposure feed into the processing, but the consumer also needs to have the ability and the opportunity to process the information.

Within the processing 'black box' the consumer's level of processing is affected by attention and capacity for processing; in other words, by the degree of interest the consumer has, and his/her ability to process the information. The result of the processing is both cognitive and affective, feeding into the formation of attitudes about the brand.

Situational variables surrounding the brand or product will also affect the attitude formation process. For example, an unpleasant salesperson or an inconveniently located dealership may affect the way we perceive brands. Exposure to ad stimulus plays a major part in encouraging learning and the formation of attitudes, but the main drive comes

Figure 7.3

Attitude formation

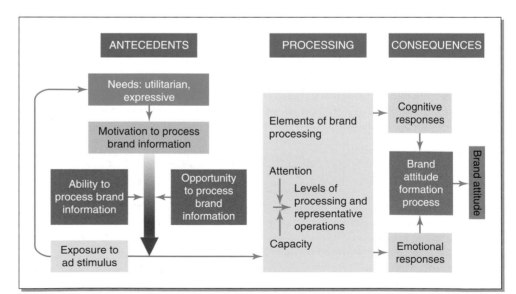

Source: Deborah J. McInnis and Bernard J. Jaworski (1989) Information processing from advertisements: toward an integrative framework. *Journal of Marketing*, 53 (October): 3.

Table 7.2 Example of a belief set

Attribute	Strength of salient belief (out of 10)	Level of importance (out of 10)
Convenient parking	5	7
Good food	6	8
Friendly waiters	?	4
Pleasant decor	7	5
Clean cutlery	3	7
Reasonable prices	?	3
Open on Wednesdays	?	5

(as always) from the consumer's needs (Berger and Mitchell 1989). Pre-existing attitudes may colour the formation of attitudes about a particular situation: researchers have found that people can be categorized according to their attitudes about Christmas, for example: these attitudes are themselves formed by attitudes about religion, about gift-giving, and about commercial influences (Gurau and Tinson 2003).

Consumers acquire **salient beliefs** about products. Because the cognitive system can only hold a relatively small number of facts in mind at once, the salient beliefs are the ones which are used by the consumer to make a judgement. Usually the salient beliefs will be those that the consumer holds most important, but they may be merely the ones that have been most recently presented (Fishbein and Ajzen 1975).

A consumer's overall attitude towards an object is a function of many attributes of the object. The attitude forms as a result of the consumer's strength of feeling, or the strength of the salient beliefs, about the attributes and also the evaluation of those beliefs. Table 7.2 shows an example of a belief set about a restaurant.

The question marks represent areas where the consumer has no knowledge, or has the knowledge but is not taking it into consideration. In other words, only the salient beliefs are taken into account.

This multiattribute attitude model attempts to explain how the consumer's salient beliefs help to form the final attitude. The attributes listed are integrated to form an overall attitude; in this example, the consumer will form an attitude about the restaurant as to whether it is a good restaurant or a bad one. The attitude may be qualified in some way; the restaurant may be regarded as a good one for lunch, but a bad one for dinner, or perhaps as a good one for a quick meal when one doesn't feel like cooking, but a bad one for special occasions.

Attitude formation is clearly affected by context: conation in particular may be affected by the feasibility of carrying out a particular behaviour or the need to modify it to take account of what is happening around the individual (Bless, Wanke and Schwartz 2002).

Attitude measurement

Measuring attitudes is clearly a subject of some interest to marketers, since attitudes play such a major role in consumer purchasing behaviour. It is obviously of importance for manufacturers to know what the consumers' attitude is to the product, but it is difficult to quantify. This is because attitude contains elements of both cognition and affect. Here are two contrasting models for attitude measurement: the Rosenberg model and the Fishbein model (Figure 7.4, page 144).

The Rosenberg model (Rosenberg 1960) says that an individual's attitude towards an object represents the degree and direction of the attitudinal effect aroused by the object. Put

Figure 7.4

Strength of attitudes

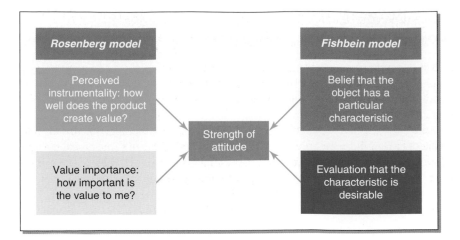

more simply, attitude is composed of a quantity of feeling, and a direction, and has two main components:

1 **Perceived instrumentality** – this is the subjective capacity of the object to attain the value in question, in other words the usefulness of the object.

2 **Value importance** – this is the amount of satisfaction the person derives from the attainment of a particular value. More simply, this is the importance of achieving the result that the consumer is hoping to achieve by buying and using the object of the attitude.

Perceived instrumentality means the degree to which the person believes that the product will work as it is supposed to. Value importance is the degree to which getting the job done is important to the consumer.

Theoretically perceived instrumentality and value importance are actually independent, and taken separately they don't predict responses well, but taken together they are good predictors of behaviour which is illustrative of attitude.

The Fishbein model (Fishbein 1980) takes a different perspective on the problem by focusing on the consumer rather than on the product. For Fishbein, attitudes can be predicted from beliefs and evaluation. Belief is the probability that the object possesses a particular attribute; evaluation is whether that attribute attracts or repels. This is not compatible with the value importance concept in the Rosenberg model.

In this model, the consumer's belief in the product's capabilities replaces the perceived instrumentality aspect. For example, it may be useful for a car to have a large boot (Rosenberg model) but whether a particular car's boot is large or not is a relative term and relies on the consumer's beliefs (Fishbein model). Furthermore, the belief that a car's boot is large does not necessarily mean that the prospective owner will like that attribute (Fishbein model). This will depend on how important the attribute is to the customer (Rosenberg model).

Combining the two models, there are three distinct aspects of the importance of attitude:

1 Perceived instrumentality.

2 Evaluative aspect (affect).

3 Value importance.

Examples of these aspects are as follows:

1 I believe the Ford Mondeo is the most comfortable car in its class.

2 I like comfort.

3 Comfort is very important to me.

Note that the second two are not identical. Someone can like something without it being very important to him or her.

Functions of attitudes

Attitudes have a function in helping consumers make decisions about their purchasing practices, and also serve other functions according to the individual's circumstances. Four main categories of function have been identified, as shown in Figure 7.5 and Table 7.3 (Locander and Spivey 1978).

These functions of attitude may not all be present at the same time: a given attitude may only serve one or two of these functions, while still being valuable. In some cases, the ego-defensive function and the value-expressive function might conflict with each other. If the individual has beliefs which go against the majority, the ego-expressive function may not protect the person from attacks by others. Equally, having attitudes which accord with those of other people may conform well with the ego-defensive function.

Table 7.3 Functions of attitudes

Function	Definition	Explanation	Example
Instrumental function	The individual uses the attitude to obtain satisfaction from the object	The individual thus aims to maximize external reward while minimizing external punishment.	An individual might develop an attitude towards a particular pub because his friends go there and the beer's good.
Ego-defensive function	Protects against internal conflicts and external dangers	Here the attitude shields the individual from his/her own failings.	Someone who is unable to understand how to use the product might have the attitude that manufacturers make products too complex.
Value-expressive function	Opposite of ego-defensive; the drive for self-expression	The attitudes expressed often go against the flow of opinion.	Most radical political viewpoints are examples of the value-expressive attitude in action.
Knowledge function	The drive to seek clarity and order	Related to the need to understand what the object is all about. Comes from the belief that if you know what you like and dislike, decision-making is easy.	Somebody who has an interest in hi-fi systems is likely to read magazines about them, to visit exhibitions, and to discuss them with friends so as to know what the latest products are.

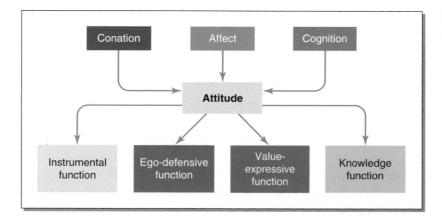

Figure 7.5

Functions of attitudes

Consumer behaviour in action
From stage to screen

Sooner or later in a pop star's career his or her agent suggests making a movie. This is often a quick way to leverage a star's fame to generate earnings from box-office receipts – and in most cases the stars sing in the movie, which generates record sales.

In some cases it works fine – the Beatles made *Hard Day's Night* and *Help!* which were considerable successes, but went on to make *Magical Mystery Tour* and *Yellow Submarine,* both of which virtually disappeared without trace. Later outings by the individual band members were equally poorly received: John Lennon's films (with Yoko Ono) scarcely saw the light of day, and Paul McCartney's *Give My Regards to Broad Street* sank like a stone. The greatest success has probably been Ringo Starr's voiceovers for Thomas the Tank Engine. Others have not even achieved this limited success – Elvis Presley made a string of low-budget, tacky movies which undoubtedly tarnished his image as a controversial and innovative musician, and more recently Madonna, the Spice Girls, Britney Spears and Mariah Carey have all made films which have been listed among the Top Ten

Worst Films of All Time. Newsday said of Madonna's *Swept Away*: 'New ways of describing badness need to be invented to describe exactly how bad this movie is.'

So why does this happen? No doubt these people are talented individuals, capable of holding an audience's attention and capable of performing a role. They already have a substantial fan base, most of whom are likely to go to see the movie. They have good, capable managers, and they already know the entertainment business.

Is it, perhaps, that we have already developed an attitude towards these stars as singers and musicians, and find it hard to relate to them when they are playing a part? The Beatles' successful movies both showed them purely as a band, to some extent mocking their own success and image, whereas the flops showed them acting a part. Fans want to see their idol, not someone who looks like the idol but is actually supposed to be somebody else! The willing suspension of disbelief is essential for enjoying a night at the cinema, and somehow this is damaged if one is unable to believe in the lead character.

Attitude and behaviour

The theory of reasoned action (Ajzen and Fishbein 1980) says that consumers consciously evaluate the consequences of alternative behaviours, and then choose the one that will lead to the most favourable consequences. Figure 7.6 shows the four main components of the theory – behaviour, intention to behave, attitude towards the behaviour, and subjective norm. The subjective norm is the component which reflects the social pressures the individual may feel to perform (or avoid performing) the behaviour being contemplated.

The individual's beliefs about the behaviour and the evaluation of the possible main consequences will combine to produce an attitude about the behaviour. At the same time, the individual's beliefs about what other people might think, and the degree to which he or she cares about what other people think, goes towards developing a subjective norm about the contemplated behaviour. The individual will then weigh the relative importance of the attitude and the norm, and will form an intention of how to behave. This may, in turn, lead to the behaviour itself.

The theory of reasoned action assumes that consumers perform a logical evaluation procedure for making decisions about behaviour, based on attitude towards the behaviour, which in turn derives from attitudes towards the product or brand.

Logically attitude should precede behaviour. In other words, we would expect that the consumer would form an attitude about something, then act on that attitude. In fact much

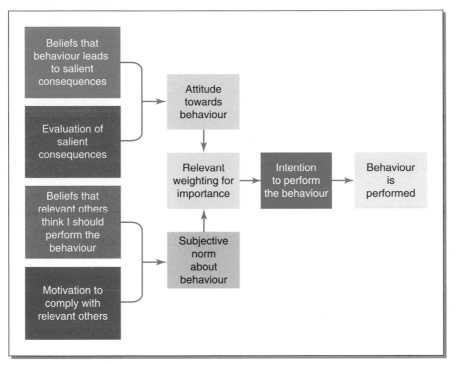

Figure 7.6
The theory of reasoned action

Source: Martin Fishbein (1980) An overview of the attitude construct. *A Look Back, A Look Ahead*, ed. G.B. Hafer (Chicago, IL; American Marketing Association): 8.

of the evidence points the other way. It appears in some cases that people behave first, and form attitudes afterwards (Fishbein 1972).

An extension of the theory of reasoned action is the theory of planned behaviour (Ajzen and Madden 1986, Ajzen 1988). Planned behaviour assumes that the individual also takes account of the ease or difficulty of performing the planned behaviour, in other words the degree of control the individual has over the behaviour and its outcomes. This depends in part on past experience, and in part on the anticipation of future obstacles.

Talking point

If attitudes are formed as the result of a logical thought process, how come we often take a sudden dislike to someone or something for no apparent reason? Is the theory wrong, or is there some other mechanism at work?

Perhaps we form our attitudes below the conscious level, so that there is some kind of logical process going on without our being aware of it. Equally possible, of course, is that we rationalize a decision we made originally on gut instinct – which may or may not be a logical process.

Even if we do go through a thinking process to form our attitudes, how good a process is it? How reliable are the factors on which we base our decisions? How reliable are our brains anyway?

Essentially, the model attempts to predict behaviour based on conation (intent to commit the behaviour). The overall attitude towards the behaviour is predicted by the salient beliefs about the behaviour and its possible outcomes, and the subjective norm is determined by the individual's beliefs about what salient others (friends and family) would think about the behaviour, coupled with the level of motivation to comply with the views of others.

Marketing efforts often encourage people to try products first, then form attitudes; free samples, test drives, demonstrations and coupons are all more powerful in forming attitude and behaviour consistency than are advertisements (Smith and Swinyard 1983). Attitudes

Figure 7.7

The theory of planned behaviour

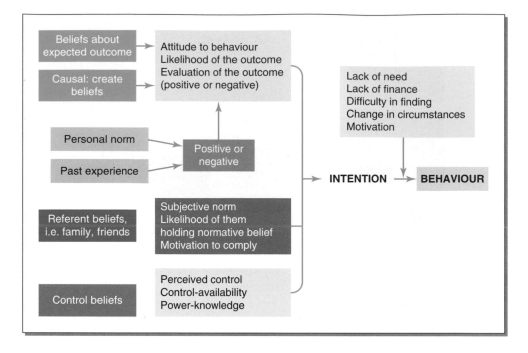

Although they know that smoking is unhealthy, people continue to enjoy a cigarette.

formed without trial experience are probably weak and easily changed. In this context, the Pepsi Challenge represents a way of persuading people that Pepsi is better than Coca Cola. Each summer, stands are set up in shopping malls and at seaside resorts and passers-by are offered the chance to compare Pepsi with Coke in a blind taste test. People are frequently surprised to find that they actually prefer the Pepsi.

Part of the reason for this is that the two drinks do, in fact, taste very similar and without the visual cue of the packaging, the consumers often cannot tell the difference between the two. Since Pepsi has a smaller market share than Coke, the company only needs half of the respondents to prefer the Pepsi in order to gain a greater market share than it currently holds. In fact, there is a slight preference for the Pepsi, since around 65 per cent of people state that they prefer it in blind taste tests.

The trial of a product is so much more powerful than advertising in forming favourable impressions that car manufacturers are prepared to give special deals to car rental companies and driving schools in order to encourage hirers and learners to buy the same model at a later date.

It may not matter greatly whether attitude precedes behaviour or not. Attitude is not always followed by the proposed behaviour; most people are familiar with having proposed doing something, then doing something else instead. This may be because attitude and behaviour are not always consistent. For example, a smoker may take the attitude that smoking is unhealthy and anti-social, but may still not give up smoking. Dieting is a similar example; even though an overweight person may believe that being fat is unhealthy and unattractive, losing weight may not be the end result. Many other examples abound; in Freudian terms, the attitude may have come from the superego, but the demands of the id result in a failure to act.

In fact, it seems more likely that, at least regarding fast-moving consumer goods (FMCG) the process of attitude formation and behaviour are interwoven. Figure 7.8 illustrates this.

In this model, there is a feedback loop that allows the consumer to re-evaluate and reconsider his or her attitudes. The formation of attitude is thus seen as a dynamic process, with the behaviour itself forming part of the process.

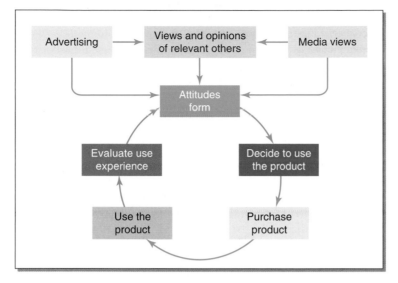

Figure 7.8
The cycle of attitude and behaviour

Private vs. public attitudes

Often people hold attitudes that they are reluctant to admit to in public. This is particularly true in recent years due to the fashion for political correctness. This makes attitude measurement difficult because respondents will give a rational or acceptable answer rather than a true one; few people would be prepared to admit openly that they have racist attitudes, for example, yet it is undoubtedly the case that many people do have such attitudes.

In marketing terms, people are often reluctant to admit to buying products which are embarrassing (or illegal). Many people would be reluctant to admit, for instance, that they like pornography and therefore it is easier to sell such products over the Internet than it is to sell them through retail outlets. Mail order preserves the anonymity of the customer.

Clearly there are implications for market research, since any questions which enquire into these attitudes are likely to meet with evasive answers or just plain lies. Most people will have some private attitudes and some opposing public attitudes, and therefore measurement of these private attitudes can best be carried by using projective techniques such as sentence completion or cartoon tests. In a sentence completion test the respondent is asked to complete a sentence such as, 'I think people who buy pornography are . . .'. In a cartoon test, the subject is asked to fill in the speech bubbles on a cartoon picture of somebody in a purchasing situation. In theory, the subject will state what he or she would say in that situation, but is not put in the (embarrassing) position of actually having to express the opinion first-hand.

In Figure 7.9, the person on the left is expressing an attitude which is controversial, and which many people would find objectionable. The respondent is asked to fill in the 'thought bubble' for the other person in the cartoon, on the basis of what the respondent thinks the 'average person' would think. The theory is that the respondent will actually put his or her own opinion in the 'thought bubble'.

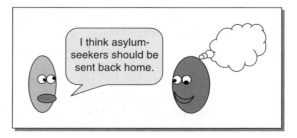

Figure 7.9
Projective technique

Often people's private attitudes do not have a logical basis, and therefore the individuals concerned are even more reluctant to admit to holding those views. Sometimes there is a reluctance to express an opinion when it has no logical basis; attitude, as we have seen, has a strong affective component.

Attitude vs. situation

During the 1930s, in a hotel in the south of France, a strange ceremony was acted out daily. One of the Romanoff princes (from the Russian royal family) would ask his chauffeur to mash up a plate of strawberries, and then eat them. This ceremony took place every day, even when the strawberries had to be specially flown in for the purpose. The reason was that the prince loved the smell of strawberries, but was allergic to them and therefore couldn't eat them. His attitude towards the 'product' therefore could not result in his consuming it, due his situation.

In Figure 7.10, the thwarted conation feeds back information to the cognition element of attitude, which may cause a slight shift in the attitude itself.

Positive attitude towards the product may not equate to positive attitude about the purchase of the product. A consumer may have a strong positive attitude towards light-coloured clothes, but not buy them because she works in the city and light-coloured clothes show the dirt.

Talking point

Presumably if one had an attitude which was permanently thwarted by one's situation, the attitude would have to change. For example, most of us have academic subjects we dislike – many people do not enjoy maths, as an example. Yet we often have to study something we dislike in order to be given a particular qualification, or as the precursor to studying something we do like.

Does this ever make us like the actual subject? Or do we simply like the outcome? How can we maintain an attitude in the face of its unpleasant aspects?

Fishbein suggests that the model be modified to take account of this (Fishbein 1972). The attitude to be measured should, under the extended model, be the attitude towards performing a given act (e.g. purchase or consumption) rather than an attitude towards the object itself. The evidence is that this model is a better predictor of purchasing behaviour than merely measuring attitudes towards the brands themselves, but of course there is greater complexity involved in understanding why a consumer has a particular attitude, since more variables are involved.

Figure 7.10

Effect of situation on attitude

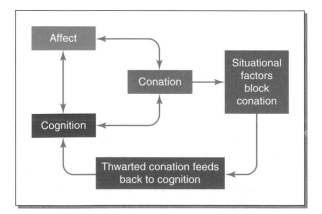

Attitudes can be changed due to situational changes. For example, a sudden drop in disposable income might lead somebody to think that a product is too expensive, even if it was seen as good value for money previously. Intentions can be checked against later performance by means of garbage analysis or self-report; Cote, McCullough and Reilly found that 'behaviour-intention inconsistency is partly attributable to unexpected situations' (Cote, McCullough and Reilly 1985: 188).

Attitude towards ads vs. attitude towards the brand

An individual may love the ads and hate the product, or vice versa. Although there is an assumption that a positive attitude towards the advertisement will lead to a positive attitude about the product, the two are actually separate hypothetical constructs (Mitchell 1986).

This is because the attitude towards the brand is affected by many more factors than the advertisement, whereas attitude towards the advertisement is only affected by the ad itself. The perception of the brand is much more likely to have a major cognitive element in it, whereas most advertising is intended to produce an affective response.

The evidence is that liking the advertisement relates to whether the product is meaningful and relevant to the consumer at the time (Biel 1990). There is some evidence that food and beverage advertisements are more likeable than non-food advertisements (Biel and Bridgewater 1990). Liking the advertisement will tend to spill over into liking the product, and the combination of the two is also likely to lead to an increase in sales (Biel 1990; Stapel 1991). This situation can be reversed in the case of some financial services products (e.g. insurance) because the advertising is often of the 'cautionary tale' type in which the advertisement shows what can go wrong if the individual does not buy the insurance. This naturally means that the advertisement is unpleasant and worrying. There is more on advertising and attitudes in Chapter 8.

People often become loyal to specific varieties of wine.

General vs. specific attitudes

It is necessary to look at specific attitudes when attempting to predict behaviour. It is possible to hold one attitude generally, but an opposing attitude in a specific case; for example, it is possible to dislike children while still loving one's own children, or to like wine in general but dislike Pinot Grigio. For marketers, the important attitude to measure is, of course, the attitude to the specific brand rather than the attitude to the product class as a whole.

Having said that, there is an issue regarding brand switching. If a consumer has a generally negative attitude about a product class, but will use a specific brand within that class, it may be possible to switch the consumer towards another brand which is similar to the one that is already acceptable. Consumers may already be prepared to do this in the event that the desired brand is out of stock; the difficulty lies in knowing why the individual consumer has made the decision to keep to only one brand of a class of products that he or she dislikes.

For example, a consumer may feel that, generally speaking, mayonnaise is thoroughly disgusting, with the exception of Hellman's. It is possible that the consumer could be switched to Heinz if the Hellmann's is out of stock, but this would only happen if the consumer can be persuaded that the Heinz is just as good. If it turns out that the consumer is allergic to every other brand but Hellmann's, however, there will not be any way of achieving a brand switch.

Someone who likes low fat mayonnaise is unlikely to switch to another brand.

Summary

In this chapter we have looked at attitudes and how they are formed and maintained. We have also looked at ways of changing attitudes, and at the some of the theories of attitude measurement. The key points from the chapter are as follows:

- Attitude is a learned construct which shows a person's tendency to respond to an object in a consistently favourable or unfavourable manner.
- Attitude is not neutral.
- Although attitude is not behaviour, it can be inferred from behaviour.
- Likewise, behaviour can be inferred from attitude, but the relationship is not reliable.
- Attitude is multidimensional, comprising affect, cognition and conation.
- Consumers only use salient beliefs when forming attitudes, not all the facts.

- Attitudes serve four useful purposes; instrumental, ego-defensive, value expressive and knowledge.
- Behaviour affects attitude more than attitude affects behaviour.
- Attitude has three dimension: affect, cognition and conation.
- The strength of an attitude is determined by perceived instrumentality, evaluative aspect, and value importance.
- People may also assess the difficulty of carrying out the behaviour when establishing an attitude.
- Attitudes may be public or private.
- Situation may prevent behaviour without altering attitude.

Chapter review questions

1 What is the role of belief in forming attitudes?

2 How might marketers appeal to the cognitive element in attitude formation?

3 What is the difference between the ego-defensive role of attitude and the value-expressive role?

4 How might a marketer increase the strength of an attitude?

5 What is the purpose of measuring private attitudes?

6 How does situation affect attitude?

7 What processes might be important in forming attitudes?

8 What is the relationship between affect and the evaluative aspect of attitude strength?

9 What difficulties might exist when trying to infer attitude from behaviour?

10 How might beliefs be formed?

Preview case study revisited
Brand attitudes

If brands are not trusted, and organizations are regarded with suspicion, marketers are presented with an uphill struggle to persuade people to part with their money. The attitude at Fitch is that brands (and organizations) need to become more generous. This does not mean that they should offer more 'buy one get one free' type offers or add extra features to the products: it merely means that they should become more human in their dealings with people, and more open about what they do.

This is not always easy, because it implies a move away from the straight management of exchange model that most marketers subscribe to. Examples of generous brands, cited by Fitch, include the following:

- Mobile telephone supplier Orange provide rechargers in the backs of London cabs, useable by anyone regardless of network.
- Innocent Drinks runs the Fruitstock free music festival.
- Amazon allows people to review books on sale, and publishes the reviews on the website including any negative comments.
- The Apple Store in London provides free advice on software problems.

Obviously these activities could all be viewed as mere public relations gimmicks, but there is an underlying regard for the needs of people as people. There is a message about the corporate attitude, rather than just a wish to change the consumer's attitude, which underpins the approaches taken – almost a wish to 'put something back' into society.

The last word on the topic goes to Fitch's Planning Director. '[This is] about brands becoming more human and real in the way they deal with people,' explains Pearse McCabe. 'Generosity needs to be viewed in terms of human gestures with no strings, rather than free offers with brand purchases. We believe brands which take this kind of leap of faith will enjoy far stronger brand loyalty in the long run, as our research shows this is exactly what consumers are looking for.'

Case study
April Fool!

Humour has been used in advertising for many years. Partly it is a way of getting people's attention, partly it is a way of making the advertising memorable, but largely it is a way of putting a human face on a large, anonymous corporation.

Nowhere is humour used more often than on April Fool's Day. Throughout the Western world, news media run spoof stories, people play jokes on each other, and at least some advertisers let their hair down and crack a joke with the customers.

April Fool's Day advertisements have become a tradition at the normally sober-sided BMW corporation, for example.

Famous for making serious cars for serious people, BMW's agency, WCRS, have produced some extremely witty spoof advertising over the years. Here are some examples:

- *BMW Uninvents the Wheel* – In response to a fictitious EU ruling that right-hand drive cars were to be banned from Continental European roads, BMW engineers had supposedly produced a car with no steering wheel, so that the driver simply needed to swap seats with the passenger during the ferry crossing, and direct the car by voice and head movements. BMW said in the advert that they had

had problems with the prototype suddenly doing a U-turn if the driver turned to yell at the kids of the back seat, but that these teething problems had been overcome.

● BMW *Ensures the Camera Always Lies* – This time, the fictitious ruling was that legislation was to be introduced to fine drivers who drive too slowly. BMW

Introducing BMW Instant Messaging.

WCRS LTD AND BMW

To avoid the proposed penalties for slow driving BMW ensures the camera always lies.

WCRS LTD AND BMW

technology would make the car appear to be going faster than it actually is, to fool the slow cameras.

● *No Flies* – In this one, the non-existent BMW technician Jurgen Afalfurit develops a special windscreen coating that makes flies bounce off. The company claim to be working on a version for the headlights and number plates.

● *Midnight in the City* – This was a supposed model of a BMW sports car, manufactured in beautiful 'Fralpooli' glaze, and designed by Prussian ceramicist Loof Lirpa. Apart from the fact that the artist's name is April Fool spelled backwards, the give-away was the actual size of the masterpiece: 15 feet by 5 feet.

● *Shef Technology* – This supposedly allowed the car to communicate with the microwave at home so that the driver's dinner would be perfectly cooked on arrival, even if he or she was delayed by traffic.

WCRS works for other major brands, including the Prudential and Carling Black Label. For Carling, the agency also produces humorous advertising, but it is only for BMW that they design April Fool advertising.

BMW state their brand values as being technology, quality, performance and exclusivity. Fun seems to be missing from the list, so maybe running the April Fool advertising helps to redress the balance a little. BMW drivers tend to be in their middle to late forties, with high incomes and high levels of education; they also tend to work in stressful, high-powered jobs. Many of them are company directors or own their own businesses, so their days are filled with serious matters and troubleshooting. BMW believe that the car owners appreciate the advertising even more than do the non-owners, because they feel as if they are in on the joke.

In terms of helping to form attitudes about the brand, BMW's light-hearted approach (albeit only once a year) undoubtedly helps. It may not directly sell cars, but it does help alleviate the stodgy image that BMWs could easily otherwise engender.

Case study questions

1 How does BMW's campaign relate to the affective component of attitude?

2 How does the theory of reasoned behaviour relate to BMW?

3 Which values of attitudes might be addressed by the April Fool campaign?

4 What might be the consequences of someone believing the April Fool advertisements?

5 How might liking the advertisement translate into an attitude about the brand?

References

Ajzen, Icek (1988) *Attitudes, Personality and Behaviour* (Milton Keynes: Open University Press).

Ajzen, Icek, and Fishbein, Martin (1980) *Understanding Attitudes and Predicting Social Behaviour* (Englewood Cliffs NJ: Prentice Hall).

Ajzen, Icek, and Madden, T.J. (1986) Prediction of goal-directed behaviour: attitudes, intentions and perceived behaviour control. *Journal of Experimental Social Psychology*, 22(5): 453–74.

Berger, Ida E., and Mitchell, Andrew A. (1989) The effect of advertising on attitude accessibility, attitude confidence, and the attitude-behaviour relationship. *Journal of Consumer Research*, 16 (December): 269–79.

Biel, A.L. (1990) Love the ad. Buy the product? *ADMAP* (September), 299: 21–5.

Biel, A.L., and Bridgwater, C.A. (1990) Attributes of likeable television commercials. *Journal of Advertising Research*, 30(3): 38–44.

Bless, Herbert, Wanke, Michaela, and Schwartz, Norbert (2002) The inclusion/exclusion model as a framework for predicting the direction and size of context effects in consumer judgments. *Advances in Consumer Research*, 29(1): 86–7.

Cote, Joseph A., McCullough, James, and Reilly, Michael (1985) Effects of Unexpected Situations on Behaviour-Intention Differences: A Garbology Analysis. *Journal of Consumer Research*, 12(2), September: 188–94.

Fishbein, Martin (1972) The search for attitudinal-behavioural consistency. *Behavioural Science Foundations of Consumer Behaviour*, ed. Joel E. Cohen (New York: Free Press).

Fishbein, Martin (1980) An overview of the attitude construct. *A Look Back, A Look Ahead*, ed. G.B. Hafer (Chicago, IL: American Marketing Association).

Fishbein, Martin, and Ajzen, Icek (1975) *Belief, Attitude, Intention and Behaviour: An Introduction to Theory and Research* (Reading, MA: Addison-Wesley).

Gurau, Calin, and Tinson, Julie (2003) Early evangelist or reluctant Rudolph? Attitudes towards the Christmas commercial campaign. *Journal of Consumer Behaviour*, 3(1): 48–62.

Homer, Pamela M., and Yoon, Sun-Gil (1992) Message framing and the interrelationships among ad-based feelings, affect and cognition. *Journal of Advertising*, 21 (March): 19–33.

Hsee, Christopher K., and Rottenstreich, Yuval (2002) Panda, mugger and music: on the affective psychology of value. *Advances in Consumer Research*, 29(1): 60.

Locander, William B., and Spivey, W. Austin (1978) A functional approach to the study of attitude measurement. *Journal of Marketing Research*, 15 (November): 576–87.

Mishra, Arul, Mishra, Himanshu, and Nayakankuppam, Dhananjay (2006) Meddling-in of affect in information integration. *Advances in Consumer Research*, 33(1): 48.

Mitchell, Andrew A. (1986) The effect of verbal and visual components of advertisements on brand attitudes and attitudes towards the advertisements. *Journal of Consumer Research*, 13(1): 12–24.

Onkvisit, Sak, and Shaw, John J. (1994) *Consumer Behaviour, Strategy and Analysis* (New York: Macmillan).

Rosenberg, Milton J. (1960) An analysis of affective-cognitive consistency. *Attitude Organisation and Change*, eds. Milton J. Rosenberg, C.I. Hovland, W.J. McGuire, R.P. Abelson, and J.W. Brehm (New Haven, CT: Yale University Press).

Smith, Robert E., and Swinyard, William R. (1983) Attitude-behaviour consistency: the impact of product trial versus advertising. *Journal of Marketing Research*, 20(3): 257–67.

Stapel, J. (1991) Like the advertisement but does it interest me? *ADMAP* (April): 30–1.

Zajonc, Robert B., and Markus, Hazel (1985) Must all affect be mediated by cognition? *Journal of Consumer Research*, 12 (December): 363–4.

Chapter 8
Attitude change

Learning objectives After reading this chapter, you should be able to:

1 explain the role of changing beliefs in changing attitudes

2 explain how emotions are important in changing attitudes

3 describe the various complaint behaviours that arise from post-purchase dissatisfaction

4 describe the basic theories of communication

5 explain the usefulness of hierarchy of effects models

6 describe the different ways in which communications can occur

7 explain the role of silent communications

8 describe some of the effects of culture on communications

9 describe the different ways miscommunication can occur

Introduction

In Chapter 7 we looked at the formation of attitudes and some of the theory surrounding the uses and functions of attitudes. From a marketing viewpoint, formation of attitude is important when new products are being introduced or when new promotional campaigns are being considered. However, the aspect of attitude which is of most interest to marketers is attitude change.

This chapter looks at the strategies and tactics of attitude change. In particular, the chapter examines communication theories in the context of consumer behaviour.

Changing attitudes

In Chapter 7 we saw how attitudes derive from consumer need, and from beliefs. People select salient beliefs (the beliefs which are most relevant to their individual needs) and build attitudes towards products based around those beliefs.

The model is useful to marketers in that it helps when devising strategies for changing consumer attitudes. There are four ways of changing attitudes, as follows:

1 *Add a new salient belief.* For example, a restaurant might point out that it has a strolling gypsy violinist on Saturday nights. This would be a new fact for the consumer to take into account.

2 *Change the strength of a salient belief.* If the belief is a negative one, it can be discounted or played down; if it's a positive one, it can be given greater importance. If a restaurant customer has a low level of belief in the cleanliness of the cutlery, but a high evaluation of this attribute, then the restaurant needs to address this point specifically in its promotional messages. The restaurant might, for example, make a point of telling customers that the cutlery is specially checked before it reaches the table. In many Chinese restaurants, chopsticks are delivered to the table in paper sleeves: although the chopsticks have been used many times, putting the sleeves on after they have been washed reassures the customers.

The UK's Midland Bank was founded in Birmingham in 1836. It was the brainchild of Charles Geach, who left a secure job at the Bank of England to open the new bank, with the financial support and backing of local Birmingham merchants and industrialists.

The Midland became, in the course of time, one of the UK's nine clearing banks. In the international arena, the bank established connections with other banks worldwide, and was the first British bank to set up a foreign exchange department, and by 1919 it had connections with 650 correspondent banks worldwide.

Eventually, however, this policy of holding the rest of the world at arm's length (while competing banks such as Barclay's were opening branches and subsidiaries throughout the world) began to look rather old-fashioned. The Midland also began, in 1974, to open branches in major financial centres and then to buy up banks in other countries. This was a quick way to acquire an international base, but in 1981 the Midland made the disastrous error of buying a majority share in Crocker Bank in the United States. This turned out to be a major error – Crocker had been lending money to high-risk individuals, and many of the loans were never repaid. The result of this was that Crocker was virtually bankrupt: Midland were forced to buy the remaining shares in Crocker and sell it to Wells Fargo at a substantial loss.

The effect on the Midland was severe, to say the least. The bank had been falling behind other High Street banks in public perception, but the Crocker fiasco had two serious effects – first, public confidence in the bank took a sharp knock (after all, if a bank can't look after its own money, how can it look after depositors' money?) and also the drain on the bank's reserves meant that it had less money available to maintain its market share and brand image.

It's an ill wind that blows nobody any good, however. Waiting in the wings was the Hong Kong and Shanghai Banking Corporation. Hong Kong and Shanghai was an international bank with its roots in financing trade on the China coast. Founded in 1865, it had a base in London and (although virtually unknown to the average member of the UK public) it was a substantial bank in the global arena. Hong Kong and Shanghai Banking Corporation, or HSBC, bought a 14.9 per cent share in Midland in 1987, and began working to improve the bank's image. At this point, Midland needed all the help it could get!

3 *Change the evaluation of an existing belief.* A customer may have a low evaluation of the prices in a restaurant, perhaps being more concerned about enjoying a romantic evening than about getting a cheap meal. The restaurant could increase the evaluation of this attribute by pointing out that the low prices means that the customer can come more often, or treat friends to a meal without breaking the bank.

4 *Make an existing belief more salient.* A restaurant customer might not regard the friendliness of the waiters as a salient attribute. The restaurant could therefore emphasize that it makes a big difference to the enjoyment of the evening if the waiters are pleasant.

If the three components of attitude (**cognition**, **affect** and **conation**) are in balance it is difficult to change the attitude because the attitude becomes stabilized (Figure 8.1). For example, if somebody is becoming overweight, believes that this is a bad thing and therefore diets, the attitude is stable and would be difficult to change. If, on the other hand, the same person is overweight, believes that it is bad, but just somehow never gets round to dieting, it is relatively easy to tempt the person to 'treat' themselves to a snack or two. In the second

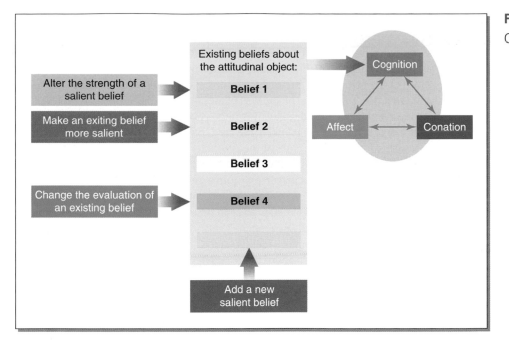

Figure 8.1
Changing beliefs

case, the attitude is not consistent because the conation does not match with the affect and cognition (Figure 8.2).

Inconsistency between the three components of attitude may come about when a new stimulus is presented. New information might affect the cognitive or conative aspects or a bad experience might change the affective aspects. When the degree of inconsistency between the three components exceeds a certain tolerance level, the individual will be compelled to undertake some kind of mental re-adjustment to restore stability. This can come about through three main defence mechanisms:

1 Stimulus rejection.
2 Attitude splitting.
3 Accommodation for the new attitude.

Stimulus rejection means that the individual discounts the new information. For example, an overweight person might reject advice that slim people live longer than fat people, on the grounds that the research does not examine people who used to be fat but are now slim and have kept the weight off. By rejecting the new information, the individual is able to maintain the status quo as regards the cognitive element of attitude. Sometimes stimuli are rejected simply because they come from a marketing source – there is evidence that consumers remember products which have been placed in movies and TV shows, but will often reject them because of a feeling of being manipulated (Bhatnagar and Aksoy 2004). People are generally much more marketing literate nowadays, and often know what

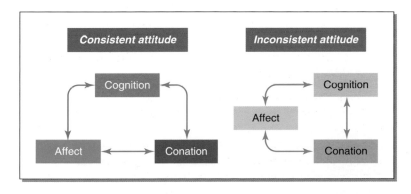

Figure 8.2
Consistent vs. inconsistent attitude

marketers are trying to do as well as understanding how they intend to do it: marketers would do well to remember this.

Attitude splitting involves only accepting that part of the information that does not cause an inconsistency. Here, the individual might accept that the new information is basically true, but that his or her own circumstances are exceptional. For example, if an individual finds out that the company he or she was planning to sue has gone bankrupt, this will alter the conative element of attitude since it is impossible to sue a bankrupt company. The individual might agree that this is *generally* the case, but decide that the circumstances are such that he or she can sue the directors of the company instead.

Accommodation to the new attitude means, in effect, changing the attitude to accommodate the new information. The fat person may join a gym and start dieting; the smoker may cut down or give up altogether; the prospective litigant may just chalk it up to experience.

The three elements are so closely related to each other that a change in one element will usually cause a change in the others (Rosenberg 1960). New information causing a change in cognition will change the consumer's feelings about the product, which in turn is likely to change the consumer's intentions about the product.

The elaboration likelihood model (Petty, Caccioppo and Schumann 1983) describes two routes by which attitude might be changed. The **central route** involves an appeal to the rational, cognitive element; the consumer makes a serious attempt to evaluate the new information in some logical way. The **peripheral route**, on the other hand, tends to involve the affective element by associating the product with another attitudinal object. For example, if a rock star appears in an ad for a soft drink this might cause the star's fans to change their attitudes towards the drink. This has nothing to do with the attributes of the drink, but everything to do with the attributes of the star. Peripheral cues such as this are not relevant to a reasoned evaluation, but because of the interdependence of the components of attitude, change will occur. In effect, the affect felt towards the star 'rubs off' on the product.

Changing existing attitudes relies heavily on market research, but in particular the teasing out of the factors which go to make up the attitude can be a demanding task. This is because of **halo effect**. Halo effect is the tendency for attitudes about one salient belief to colour attitudes about another. For example, if a diner had a bad meal at a restaurant, this is likely to lead to a view that everything else about the restaurant was bad, too. Likewise a favourable view of some factors often leads to respondents reporting a favourable view of other factors.

Talking point

Using the peripheral route to attitude change means working on the affective component of attitude. Research has shown that emotional appeals often work a great deal more

Halo effect is said to be the process by which attitudes about one aspect of a product (or person) tend to colour the whole perception of the product (or person). Apparently if we think our new car is really comfortable and cosy we will also think its fuel consumption is good.

How about the reverse case? If we think something is really bad, perhaps the car is unreliable, do we then think its performance is bad as well? Probably so, if the theory is correct. In that case, what happens if something is brought to our attention? If the rock star we loved and admired turns out to be a paedophile, do we stop liking the music? If so, where does that leave the company that used that rock star in their advertising?

Figure 8.3
Peripheral and direct routes to attitude change

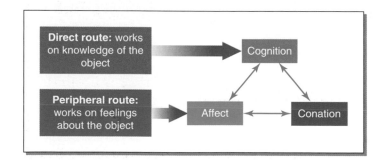

effectively than do cognitive, logical appeals: emotional appeals also appear to have a greater effect on explicit memory, so people remember the advertisement better (Williams 2003). Much depends on the group of individuals being studied. For example studies have shown that campaigns to discourage smoking among teenagers work best on boys if they use emotional 'cosmetic' appeals (for example, telling boys that the smell of smoke on their clothing is repellent to girls) whereas long-term health appeals (a logical, cognitive approach) work better on teenage girls (Smith and Stutts 2003). Mood also has an effect on the interpretation of information: people in a good mood tend to process and remember brands better (Bakamitsos and Siomkos 2004).

Cognitive dissonance theory states that holding two competing cognitions leads to discomfort and an eventual readjustment (Festinger 1957). The readjustment can take two forms: rejecting one or other of the competing cognitions, or introducing a third idea which resolves the conflict between the other two.

Telling boys that girls don't like smokers works better than telling them that smoking kills.

The most interesting aspect of dissonance theory is that attitudes can apparently be changed more easily by offering a low reward than by offering a high reward. In a famous experiment conducted in the 1950s, researchers induced students to lie to other students about a task they were being recruited to undertake. The actual task was to place round pegs into holes, turn the pegs one-quarter turn, then remove the pegs. The students were told that this was a psychological experiment, and were then asked to recruit other students primarily by telling them how interesting and fun the task was. Since it would be difficult to imagine a more tedious task, these students obviously had to lie: the experimenters offered a recruitment reward, but some students were only offered $1 to lie, whereas others were offered $20 (a substantial sum of money in 1959). The students being paid the lower amount were found actually to believe the lie, whereas the higher-paid students simply told the lie as a lie without changing their own attitudes. The theory is that the higher-paid students justified lying on the basis that they were being well paid for it, whereas the other students could not use this justification and therefore needed to find another reason for lying – in this case, they decided that what they were saying must be at least partly true (Festinger and Carlsmith 1959). This is shown in Figure 8.4.

Cognitive dissonance is a powerful force in attitude change because the individual is, almost by definition, personally involved in the process. Reduction in dissonance always involves some kind of internal debate and (ultimately) some self-justification (Aronson et al. 1974). This happens because the individual tends to believe that the dissonance has arisen through an act or thought that is immoral or stupid. The most common manifestation of cognitive dissonance in consumer behaviour is post-purchase dissonance, in which someone who has just made an important purchase finds out that the product is not quite what was expected. In other words, the individual has been presented with new information which contradicts his or her pre-purchase expectations. In most cases, actual experience with the product conflicts with information obtained in the pre-purchase information search. For example, someone buying a new flat-screen television set might have expected

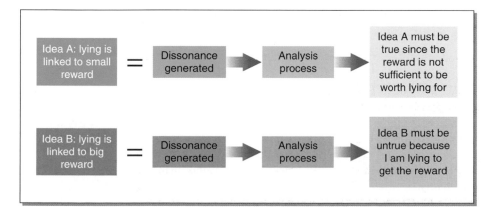

Figure 8.4
Cognitive dissonance

Figure 8.5

Post-purchase dissonance

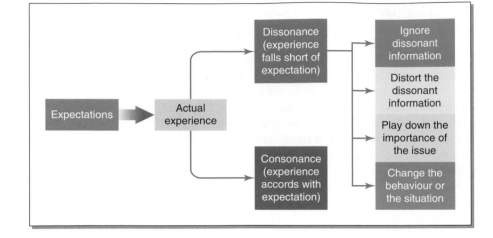

it to be wall-mountable, like a picture. On opening the packing, our new purchaser finds that the wall-mounting bracket makes the TV stand out six inches from the wall, and that this is a necessary factor because of the wiring, controls and air vents at the back of the set. At this point, the buyer has four basic choices (see Figure 8.5):

1 Ignore the dissonant information and look for positive (consonant) information about the product. In the case of the TV, the buyer might just accept that the TV will stick out from the wall a bit and will instead admire the quality of the picture, the excellent stereo sound, the ease of tuning the set, and so forth.

2 Distort the dissonant information. In this case our buyer might convince himself or herself that the TV really does not stand away from the wall too much after all. With some careful lighting, no one will notice.

3 Play down the importance of the issue. Here the buyer simply says that the distance from the wall is really not that important anyway.

4 Change the behaviour or the situation. Our TV buyer might take the TV back to the shop and ask for a refund, or might decide to put the TV on a table instead and buy a picture for the wall.

If post-purchase dissonance occurs, the individual might take action against the vendor (as in the last example above). If the buyer feels that the dissonance is caused by something which is the vendor's fault, for example if the vendor was less than truthful in describing the product in the first place, the buyer might complain. These responses fall into three categories (Singh 1988):

● *Voice responses* – This is a direct complaint to the vendor.

● *Private responses* – These are complaints to family, friends and anyone who will listen. These private responses constitute negative word-of-mouth, and can be extremely damaging to the vendor.

● *Third-party responses* – These are complaints voiced through a third party such as a consumer protection organization, a lawyer, a trade body or even a campaigning journalist or TV show.

From the vendor's viewpoint, voice responses are the least damaging. They give an opportunity for the vendor to put matters right, or at least pacify the buyer, before word spreads. Considering the widespread use of the Internet, word can spread extremely quickly, and particularly for e-tailers (companies marketing through websites) word-of-mouse (damaging comment spread by e-mail) can be disastrous.

For marketers, changing attitudes usually means using marketing communications effectively.

Communication

Communication is a transactional process between two or more parties whereby meaning is exchanged through the intentional use of symbols (Engel, Warshaw and Kinnear 1994).

Communication is one of the things human beings do much more than most other creatures. Conversation is still the most prevalent form of entertainment on the planet, and we communicate by many other methods – television, pictures, radio, letters, books, magazines, newspapers, Morse code, even jungle drums. As a species, we love to exchange our thoughts and feelings at every opportunity, whether verbally (conversation), by the written word or by pictures. Marketers are no exception, and in fact most of us not only expect to receive marketing communications, we often welcome them (Madden and Perry 2003). This is also true in business-to-business markets, where effective communication between firms is vital to the development and maintenance of relationships (Holden and O'Toole 2004).

© iStockphoto.com

People love to communicate even via Morse code.

The key elements in the definition are as follows:

1 Communication is intentional. This means that a deliberate attempt is made to generate some kind of response, usually a behavioural change as a result of learning (see Chapter 6).

2 It is a transaction, so that all the parties involved are active. This applies even if the person receiving the communication does not respond: however, if the person on the receiving end ignores the communication (for example, flips the page of the magazine to continue reading an article) then communication has not taken place.

3 Communication is carried out through symbols. Human beings are, as far as can be proven, not telepathic so we need to convert our thoughts into symbols in order to convey the original meaning. These symbols then need to be interpreted by the recipient of the message in order to understand what is being said.

Any communication needs to be reduced to a set of symbols (encoded) by the person initiating it, and decoded by the recipient. This means that both parties need to agree on what the symbols mean: if we do not agree on the meaning of a word, for example, the meaning is lost and can even be reversed.

Probably the best-known and most widely taught model of communication is the Schramm model, shown in Figure 8.6 (Schramm 1948, 1971).

In the Schramm model, communication requires a transmitter, a receiver, a message and a medium. The medium might be a newspaper, a TV set, a radio, even just the air which carried the sound of a voice. A message implies some kind of intelligent meaning. The

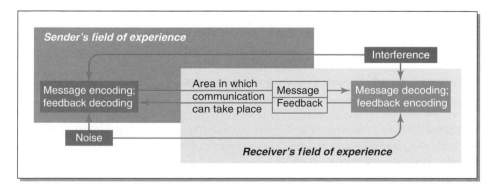

Figure 8.6

Schramm model of communications

Consumer behaviour in action
Meanings of words

Languages continually evolve. There is a story that the leading Brazilian expert on language was addressing a conference in Sao Paulo, and he began by speaking in street slang from the slums of Rio de Janeiro. When he paused to ask his audience whether they could understand him, someone asked him why he was using this debased form of Portuguese to address an academic conference? He replied that this is how languages grow. 'We are all speaking bad Latin,' he told his audience.

In English we have similar shifts in the language. One hundred and fifty years ago 'nice' meant 'precise', whereas now the word is mainly used to denote 'pleasant' or 'enjoyable'. In slang, at the time of World War One 'chuffed' meant frustrated or annoyed, whereas it now means exactly the opposite. 'Quick' used to mean 'alive', 'neck' used to mean 'parcel of land', 'brave' used to mean 'cowardice concealed' and 'guess' used to mean 'take aim'. Sometimes these old meanings survive in modern phrases ('this neck of the woods', 'a nice distinction', 'the quick and the dead') but in many cases the original meaning has been lost.

The same is true in most languages, but since English is the first language of about 10 per cent of the world's population it has a *lot* of people playing around with it. Simple words in everyday modern use change their meanings when they move from one country to another: 'Barbie' means a barbecue to an Australian, but would be more likely to relate to Mattel's Barbie doll to an American. Words such as 'rubber', 'chips', 'gas' and 'trunk' have different meanings in the United States from those in the UK, and phrases such as 'knock you up' have delighted audiences in both countries for years now. (For the record: in the UK, knocking somebody up means waking them up early in the morning. In the US, it means to make pregnant.) In some cases, words from other local languages have been adopted: such words may or may not extend to the world supply of English. The Swahili word 'safari' is in common use in most English speaking countries, but how about the Southern African

'braai?' It means a barbecue. Equally, 'corroborree' has made the transition from the Australian aborigines, but 'woomera' might be less familiar to non-Australians.

How, then, do we communicate effectively? In most cases, people grasp the meaning from context. In some cases, they simply need to be aware of the differences in language between the countries concerned. Most Peninsular Portuguese understand Brazilian Portuguese rather better than Brazilians understand Peninsular Portuguese, in the same way as most British people understand American English better than Americans understand British English, and for the same reason: the flow of TV programming is mainly West to East.

The final tactic open to the listener is, of course, to ask for clarification. How many of us are prepared to do that in a conversation? And how many of us are able to do it when watching a TV advertisement?

AVRIL O'REILLY/ALAMY

message can become distorted by noise (meaningless distractions) or by **interference** (intelligent disruption caused by other messages). For example, a car driver listening to a radio advertisement might be distracted by another driver cutting in (noise) or by a particularly interesting billboard (interference). For the purposes of marketing, the difference is probably irrelevant, but in some contexts (for example radio communication between ships or aircraft) there is considerable relevance.

For communication to work well, the transmitter needs to encode the message comprehensibly and the receiver needs to be able to decode it accurately. This means that there must be an overlapping field of experience, at least to the extent of sharing a language: this language need not be spoken, of course. For example, for thousands of years written Japanese and written Chinese were the same language, because both written languages use pictograms rather than an alphabet: the fact that the two spoken languages have absolutely nothing in common did not matter. Equally, the sign language of the Plains Indians enabled tribes to communicate throughout North America, despite profound differences in the spoken languages.

The final element in the Schramm model is feedback. Feedback is a response from the receiver by which the transmitter can judge whether the message was decoded accurately. In some cases (for example in some communications between pilots and air traffic controllers) the receiver is required to repeat the message back to ensure that it has been correctly received. In other cases, the receiver's response might be so inappropriate that the transmitter would be able to recognize that the original message has not been correctly deciphered.

The Schramm model is essentially a one-step model, which may of course be an oversimplification. Katz and Lazarsfield (1955) postulated a two-step communication model in which messages are filtered through opinion leaders, so that the message reaches the receiver by more than one route: this model is clearly of more relevance to marketers, since they often encourage word-of-mouth communications. Sending essentially the same message by more than one route (called 'redundancy') is thought to increase the reliability of communication: this is the rationale behind the integration of marketing communications. Redundancy is shown diagrammatically in Figure 8.7.

An alternative view

The Schramm model has been criticized in recent years because it tends to ignore the interactive nature of communication: in short, people are not radio sets, and the receiver undoubtedly thinks about the communication and interprets it in the light of previous experiences. The model implies that communication is something that is done to people, rather than something which comes about as a result of a cooperative effort. In fact, human conversations are not as neat as the Schramm model implies, since people often talk 'past' each other, each one eager to make his or her own point without really listening to what the other person has to say (Varey 2000). Having said this, the Schramm model is widely taught, and is also accepted instinctively by most people as the way communications work.

Communications theorists such as Deetz (1992) and Mantovani (1996) regard communication as a co-creation of meaning through a social process. Each person has an individual

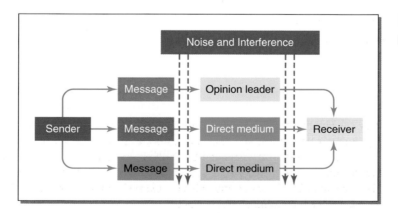

Figure 8.7

Redundancy in communication

Figure 8.8

Pool of meaning

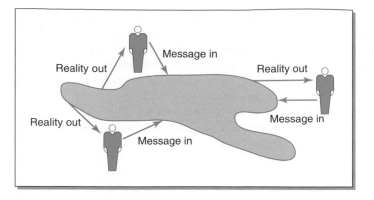

view of reality, and each is trying to move the other person's view closer to their own. In this model, communication is not something which is done to recipients: it is something which is shared with recipients.

This view of communication can be thought of as a co-creation of a pool of meaning. Reality can be thought of as a pool of shared meaning into which people have an input: people stand around the pool, each putting something in and each taking something out. What is put in mixes with what is already in the pool (existing concepts of reality) so what is taken out is not necessarily what went in (see Figure 8.8).

If this view of communication is accepted, it has potentially far-reaching consequences for marketers as well as for management in general. For example, the Internet is (above all) an interactive medium, so some of the current approaches to e-marketing are doomed to failure since they are, in the main, one-way communications. Other direct marketing approaches might also prove problematical: for example, an insurance company might decide to send out a mailing offering a free gift with every car insurance quote, without obligation to take out the insurance. The recipient of the mailing might respond to this communication in several ways, as follows:

1 Throw the mailing away immediately (recipient's reality: These people are wasting my time and the world's resources with yet another piece of junk mail. They are stupid and annoying).

2 Respond to the mailing, on the basis that the offer is a good one (recipient's reality: These people are clearly looking after their customers. I'll give them a try).

3 Respond to the mailing, with the intention of keeping the free gift without taking out the insurance (respondent reality: These people are stupid. I can something for nothing here).

4 Examine the exact wording of the address to work out which mailing list has been used (recipient reality: These people can't fool me. I know how they're doing this).

All except the second outcome are negative, from the insurance company's perspective. However, except for the second outcome, all the other responses lie outside the Schramm model.

Information is therefore not a fixed object which can be transferred from one mind to another. It is subject to interpretation, and is not so much distorted by outside influences as integrated with other information to create a new (and perhaps more accurate) view of reality. It is therefore unrealistic to talk about transmitters and receivers, at least in this alternative view. Varey (2000) suggests that it is more realistic to refer to **initiators** (those who start the communication process), **apprehenders** (those who receive and understand the communication) and appreciators (those who react to the communication in some way). Acceptance of the communication arises from the apprehender's choice to become an appreciator, not from the initiator's intentions or need to communicate.

Whether operating according to the Schramm model or to the 'pool of meaning' model, marketers need to consider the effects of their communications in terms of the recipient's pre-existing ideas, capacities, attitudes and experiences. This is because customers and consumers are not only recipients of information, they are also consumers of information as part of their learning process about products and brands (see Chapter 6). In either model, people decode and encode messages based on what they already know, and on what they perceive about the marketer. The result of this analysis is that people may or may not change their attitudes as a result of a marketing communication, since the overall result may not be a change in the individual's world view.

The hierarchy of communications effects

A single communication is unlikely to have an instant effect in terms of changing attitudes. A series of communications, on the other hand, may move the recipient up a 'ladder' of effects, as shown in Figure 8.9.

The model shows that at the bottom of the hierarchy the individual has virtually no knowledge of the brand. Initial communications might make the individual aware of the brand, and later communications build knowledge. At this point the person becomes much more involved in the process, because further communications are intended to generate liking for the product, which may or may not happen. Generating preference and conviction are unlikely to happen without a trial of the product (which is, of course, a form of communication) and the final level, purchase, might be better thought of as adoption of the product (i.e. building it into one's lifestyle).

A major criticism of the hierarchy of effects model (and of others like it) is that it assumes that the process is invariably linear, which is unlikely to be the case. As we saw in Chapter 7, people can form an attitude about a product through the affective route, i.e. can like and prefer a product before knowing very much about it, or even knowing about the brand. For example, imagine being on a picnic with a friend. The friend offers everyone a new type of dessert bar to try. Some of the people on the picnic might well like and even prefer the bar without knowing the brand or having any knowledge of the product whatsoever apart from its taste and texture.

The main use to which the hierarchy of effects model is put is planning communications campaigns. The first stage in the campaign is to build awareness by using high-impact advertising which features the brand name prominently. Such advertising may well not say much about the product's attributes. The next stage might be to use advertising which says more about the brand, the product and its uses. Eventually the advertising can move on to affective issues, such as the pleasure of owning the product or the pride one might feel in front of one's friends and colleagues.

Whatever the drawbacks of the hierarchy of effects model, it is certainly true to say that brand awareness has to be the first step in building an attitude about the brand in the minds of its potential consumers.

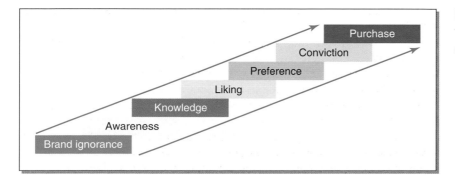

Figure 8.9

The hierarchy of communications effects

The Statue of Liberty is an effective icon for New York.

Each of these symbols is instantly decipherable by most people, irrespective of language.

Signs and meaning

A sign is defined as follows:

Anything that stands for something (its object) to somebody (its interpreter) in some respect (its context). (Peirce 1986)

Signs fall into the following three categories:

1 *Icon* – This is a sign that looks like the object itself, or represents it visually in a way that most people would recognise. For example, the Eiffel Tower is an icon for Paris, and often for France in general. Most people in the world would understand that an advertisement or a package showing the Eiffel Tower relates to something French.

2 *Index* – A sign that relates to the object by a causal connection. For example, an image of someone chopping wood on a hot day would equate to thirst. Most people are familiar with the idea that hard physical work in hot conditions builds up a thirst, so such imagery is often used in advertising beer, cider or soft drinks.

3 *Symbol* – An artificial sign which has been created for the purpose of providing meaning. For example, the logo used to indicate recyclable or recycled materials (the intertwined arrows) conveys a meaning of environmental friendliness to most people.

The most commonly used symbols are words. As we saw earlier, words can change their meanings, and can only have meaning as they are interpreted by individuals. The same word can mean different things in different languages – the Dutch word for chicken, 'kip', is a slang term for sleep in English, for example. Meanings of words can be the same for everybody who speaks the language (this is called denotative) or can have specific meanings which are unique to the individual (which is called connotative). For example, although everyone knows what 'rabbits' are (the denotative meaning of the word), someone who is allergic to rabbit fur might associate the word with the symptoms of the allergy (connotative).

Because connotative meanings vary so much among individuals, responses will be difficult to predict. In some cases, a connotative meaning will be common to a substantial group, so a marketer targeting that group might be able to establish a rapport with the group and be correspondingly cautious in the use of specific terms. This is easiest when the marketer and the audience are as similar as possible in terms of background and outlook. Semiotics, syntactics and semantics are fields of study which enable us to ensure that the correct meanings are attributed to symbols (Figure 8.10).

Figure 8.10

Semiotics, semantics and syntactics: structuring communication

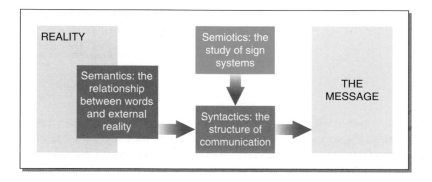

Semiotics

Semiotics is the study of sign systems. It is more a theoretical approach than an academic discipline (O'Sullivan *et al.* 1983). It uses spoken language as the main example of a sign system, although the study of semiotics is not limited to language. Semiotics regards meaning as being derived socially, so as a study it concentrates on the reader or observer. Meaning is derived as the result of an interaction between the reader and the text. Texts are created by manipulating signs, codes and symbols within the sign system to generate myths, connotations and meanings. The theory is that the social process involved generates pleasure as well as cognitive, rational outcomes.

For example, a television advertisement uses the sign systems of the spoken word, actions and gestures of actors, soundtrack music and the conventions of film direction and production to generate its meanings. Someone seeing the advertisement is able to add the various signs to his or her existing knowledge and interpret the overall meaning. The meaning is therefore not produced by the advertiser, but is co-produced by the advertiser and the viewer: it is subject to power plays, struggle and interpretation, much like any other social interaction. Because these social contexts affect the recipient of the communication, the recipient's world view will be affected, in other words the person's attitude is likely to change somewhat. Semiotic theory accords well with the 'pool of reality' model discussed earlier in the chapter.

In fact, words are far from being the only way in which communication is carried out: only about 30 per cent of communication is based on words. People communicate by pictures, non-verbal sounds, smell, touch, numbers, artifacts, time and kinetics (movement). Many of these media are used by marketers, even smell: the aroma of baking bread might remind you of a village bakery from ten years ago, but may in fact have been generated by an aerosol spray in a supermarket without a bakery being involved at all.

Some of these silent communications are as follows:

Henry Heinz thought the number 57 sounded impressive.

- *Numbers* – The famous Heinz 57 Varieties brand implies a wide variety of products in the range. In fact, although there may at one time have been 57 different products under the brand name, the number was applied simply because Henry John Heinz thought it sounded impressive.

- *Space* – If people are shown standing close together, the implication is that the relationship is an intimate one. Images of open spaces can imply freedom and adventure: pictures of enclosed spaces can imply confinement, or (if the furnishings are appropriate) cosiness.

- *Artefacts* – Images of people's possessions give a clear idea of their wealth and social status. Small business gifts or sales promotion items might place the recipient under a small obligation, or might make them feel warmer towards the giver.

- *Time* – Concepts of time vary from one culture to another. Someone in a hurry might signify success and energy (to Americans and Britons), but in other cultures it might imply someone who is disorganized and panicking (Germany) or someone who is arrogant and has no time for other people (parts of Africa).

- *Kinetics* – This is the study of movement. People who are gesticulating with their hands and arms and talking expressively might appear to be southern European; people running or cycling denote a fit and active lifestyle.

Syntactics

Syntactics is about the structure, or syntax, of communication. The way that the various signs and symbols are arranged will affect their meaning. At an obvious level, 'dog bites man' has a different meaning from 'man bites dog', but the differences may be a great deal more subtle. For example, the image of a fierce dog might seem threatening taken on its

Talking point

own. The same image of the dog would have an entirely different meaning if it were shown that the dog is defending its owner from an attack by a mugger. The meaning would change yet again if the sequence showed that the dog was injured in some way.

If only 30 per cent of communication is carried out using the spoken word, why do we bother learning foreign languages? Surely some kind of gesticulation or sign language would get us through nicely anywhere in the world!

After all, if the Plains Indians were able to develop a sophisticated sign language that could be understood everywhere from the Rockies to Florida, shouldn't we be able to cope just as well? And wouldn't that save us a lot of trouble?

Of course we would have to standardize our body language – which may be harder than just all learning English, which is what seems to be happening now!

Advertisements and other communications can change their meanings when seen in different circumstances. An advertisement for a retail store's sale might have one meaning when printed in an upmarket glossy magazine, and entirely different connotations when printed in a free-sheet or tabloid newspaper.

Semantics

Semantics is concerned with the way words relate to the external reality to which they refer. It is not actually about the study of meaning (although this is a common misconception) but is actually concerned with the appropriateness of the words themselves. We have seen already how words can change their meanings over time, and how new words are invented, but semantics also considers the interpretations placed on the use of particular words. For example, copywriters often 'hedge' their statements by using words such as 'could', 'may' or 'probably' in advertising. This is to avoid accusations of false or misleading advertising, but in fact there is evidence that the target audiences for these advertisements regard such hedges negatively, and do not trust advertisers who use them (Berney-Reddish and Areni 2005).

Using such words does not change the meaning of the words themselves, but the words now convey a different reality to the viewer.

Culture

The main problem with silent languages is that they are not culturally universal. Most gestures (and even involuntary body language) do not transfer well to other cultures, sometimes with humorous or offensive results. Some examples include the two-fingers gesture which is highly offensive to Britons, but which simply denotes 'two' to the rest of the world, the circled thumb and index finger gesture which means 'OK' to Americans but which is insulting to Brazilians, and showing the soles of the feet to Thais. Even numbers which are considered lucky in some cultures are considered unlucky in others (Costa and Pavia 1992).

These cultural differences are so subtle that people often do not recognize them as cultural differences, but instead regard the inappropriate use of the gestures as rude or crazy on the part of the foreigner. The tendency to believe that one's own culture is the right one, and that all other cultures are merely poor imitations, is called 'ethnocentrism' (Shimp and Sharma 1987). Ethnocentrism is probably one of the few cultural attributes that is common to all cultures: since people use their own cultural background as a yardstick for measuring foreigners, judgements will always be made and many of them will be negative.

From a marketing viewpoint, HSBC (the Hong Kong and Shanghai Banking Corporation) have run a very successful advertising campaign for several years now based on their knowledge of cultural differences between different countries. Using the strapline 'The world's local bank', the company highlights the misunderstandings which can occur through a lack of knowledge of local conditions. The other side of the coin is that very few marketing campaigns can be conducted, unchanged, globally: simply changing the language is rarely sufficient. Recent exceptions include the markets for pop music and fashion aimed at the youth market, since there is evidence for the existence of a global youth market (powered by MTV) which responds to these products in a fairly consistent manner (Steen 1995).

There is more on culture in Chapter 9.

Miscommunication

Failure to communicate is probably as common, or possibly more common, than successful communication (Figure 8.11). The causes are as follows:

1 *Implication* – The recipient 'reads between the lines' and develops an inaccurate view of the communication through a perceptual process.

2 *Distortion* – The message changes its meaning as a result of outside forces.

3 *Disruption* – This is damage to the message caused by circumstances and (sometimes deliberate) misconstruction of the message.

4 *Confusion* – If the message is ambiguous or poorly phrased this can be confusing for the recipient.

5 *Agreement/disagreement* – Disagreement arises because of discrepancies between the perceptual maps of the sender and the recipient.

6 *Understanding/misunderstanding* – Misunderstandings might arise because of cultural differences (especially in the case of different languages) or differences in respective codes of understanding between the parties trying to communicate.

7 *Personal transformation* – The recipient may not be receptive to the idea of changing or learning from the communication, and might therefore simply ignore it or only pay attention to part of it.

The consumer behaviour implications of each of these sources of miscommunication are outlined in the following sections.

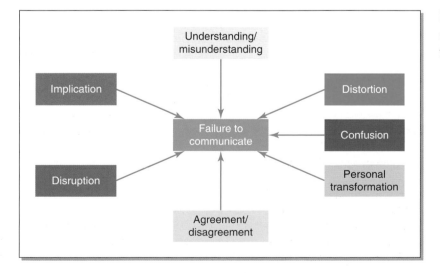

Figure 8.11

Causes of communication failure

Implication

The implications of a communication are the expected consequences that are attached to it by the recipient. If a message raises painful implications, it is less likely to be acted on – so in some cases the sender distorts the message to reduce the negative aspects. Equally, sometimes the recipient will distort the message to avoid painful aspects. For example, an advertisement for an exotic holiday destination might be extremely attractive, but for some potential travellers the fact that it is being advertised at all might imply that it will be over-run with tourists and therefore 'spoiled'. The main elements of implication are shown in Table 8.1.

Distortion

Internal distractions and external interference often lead to distortions in the message. For example, someone who has a bad impression of a chain restaurant might well decide that

Table 8.1 Elements of implication

Element	Explanation
Assumption	A failure to understand the message fully will lead to the recipient making assumptions about what was actually said. The assumptions are made based on previous experience, so might be slanted positively or negatively, and may or may not be open to inspection or revision in future when a clearer message is received.
Inference	The recipient may add extra ideas to the message by 'reading between the lines' and looking for implications which are in fact not there. Even when the original message is clear and unambiguous, the recipient can find meanings which were never intended. For example, someone receiving a direct mailing promoting a new credit card might spend some time trying to work out where the finance company bought the name and address, and may find inferences about the security of information supplied to another company.
Expectation	People tend to hear what they were expecting to hear. In direct marketing, people will often make the decision about whether to open the letter or simply bin it based on the appearance of the envelope.
Reflection	Consideration of past communications affects the way people respond to future communications, especially from the same source. Bad experiences of responding to a mailing would affect the way the individual responds to future mailings.
Attribution	If the communication is interactive, the outcome is jointly produced but there may be disagreement regarding responsibility for a failed outcome. For example, in the case of personal selling a salesperson might attribute a failed sale to the stupidity of the customer, whereas the customer might attribute it to dishonesty on the part of the salesperson in overstating the product's benefits.
Metacommunication	Metacommunication is concerned with how something is said rather than what is actually said. The style of the communication can affect the way it is interpreted by the recipient – for example, a mailing sent out on cheap paper with a poor print quality might contain the same wording as a better-produced mailing, but would not generate the same impression on the recipient.
The search for common ground	Communication fails if there is no overlap between the parties' fields of experience. Curiosity on the part of the recipient, and the need to communicate on the part of the sender, will lead to a search for the common experience which enables the communication. This in turn creates a new set of meanings.

Table 8.2 Elements of distortion

Element	Explanation
Interference	Outside distractions are likely to prevent the recipient from concentrating sufficiently on the communication. Other messages might be inadvertently included in the overall impression given, or may mean that parts of the main message are missed.
Bias	The mindset of the recipient may affect the message in some way. This is not necessarily as a result of bigotry or prejudice: it can simply be a result of previous ideological, ethnocentric or egocentric predispositions.
Miscalculation	This occurs when a message is wrongly interpreted through an error of cognition. This may be due to ignorance or simple mistakes, but sometimes it comes about because of a desire for an alternative truth to prevail. For example, someone might misinterpret the terms of a special offer because he or she is unable to meet the actual terms of the offer, and hopes that the achievable alternative will be available.
Pseudo-communication	Some communications are generated in order to cover up a true state of affairs. This is sometimes the case when companies suffer a PR disaster and take a 'spin doctoring' approach rather than a more long-term confidence-building approach.

all chain restaurants are suspect. Messages sent out by burger restaurants and pizza parlours will be distorted by this internal distraction.

Table 8.2 shows the main elements of distortion.

Disruption

Disruption in communications can be caused by outside interruptions (not necessarily deliberately) or by internal conflicts or misgivings on the part of the recipient. For example, a sales presentation may be in progress when the fire alarm is sounded, thus bringing the presentation to an abrupt halt. This would be an outside interruption. The same presentation could be halted by the prospective buyer in the event of him or her developing a dislike for the salesperson, however, which would be an example of an internal interruption. Disruption can only happen when the communication is interactive, either a sales presentation or an online interaction being the typical situations in which disruption can occur. Table 8.3 shows possible elements of disruption.

Confusion

Confusion arises from distortion, mistakes, disruption and conflict. If a potential customer receives conflicting information (for example from a salesperson on the one hand, and an advertisement on the other) confusion is the most likely outcome. Avoidance of confusion is one of the key difficulties in integrated marketing communications, since integration should (in theory at least) minimize the incidence of conflicting messages.

The elements of communication confusion are shown in Table 8.4.

Table 8.3 Elements of disruption in communications

Element	Explanation
Unmanageable circumstances	If the recipient begins to feel that the situation is becoming uncontrollable, he or she is likely to withdraw from it. For example, somebody confronted by a pushy salesperson might decide simply to walk away from the presentation.
Relational instability	Someone finding themselves in an awkward or unfamiliar situation may not be able to respond adequately to the message. For example, someone who is not very confident in the use of computers might find it difficult to navigate a website.
Conversational irregularities	Conversation is a multi-directional activity consisting of statements from one party, consideration and responses from the second party. If a statement meets with no response or with an inappropriate response, the communication breaks down. For example, if a customer telephones to complain about a product and is offered a sales pitch for another product, the dialogue breaks down.
Lack of reciprocity	A failure to give some concessions in the course of a negotiation, or a failure to allow the other party to state their case, will cause a breakdown in communication.
Mutual misconstruction	Mutual misconstruction occurs when the parties to the discussion are unable to translate their interpretations of self and other into a coherent vocabulary. Sometimes people lack the ability to understand why the other person's viewpoint seems sensible to themselves: it is sometimes the case in sales negotiations, where one or both parties has a hidden agenda.
Threat of dissolution	The knowledge that the relationship might end is one that can affect both parties. In the relationship marketing situations found in many business-to-business markets this can be crucial: if either party feels that the relationship might end, there might be considerations of confidentiality to take into account.

Table 8.4 Elements of confusion in communications

Element	Explanation
Conflict	Disputes between the parties will inevitably create confusion. Tension tends to rise, and people are likely to overstate their positions: in an argument, it is easy to stray away from the actual topic of discussion and become entrenched in side issues. In most marketing situations serious conflict will end the communication altogether rather than merely cause confusion.
Ambiguity	If there is more than one possible interpretation which can be placed on the communication it is ambiguous. This can easily happen in advertising, because there is pressure on copywriters to make the message as intriguing as possible within a very few words. There is no room for explanations or lengthy descriptions.
Equivocation	If two messages are received at the same time, and they conflict with each other, there is equivocation. This is a very real problem when trying to integrate a range of marketing communications.
Vagueness	Inevitably there will be some vague aspects of any communication, but some marketing communications (especially in advertising) are so vague that the meaning is lost. In some cases this is simply because advertising copywriters have very little scope for making detailed descriptions, in other cases it is because legal constraints make the copywriters hedge their statements.
Paradox	A paradox is a statement which is logically impossible (for example, 'Disregard everything I say.'). A sales promotion with a specific cut-off date is logical provided the goods are available before the deadline. If the goods will not be available, a paradox is created.
Contradiction	Similar to equivocation and paradox, contradiction is the appearance of irreconcilable differences in the communication received. Again this might be overcome by integrating marketing communications, but it is also one of the most difficult aspects of integration.

Table 8.5 Agreement and disagreement in communications

Element	Explanation
Relational ties	If the relationship between the parties is not a close one, disagreement is more likely than if the relationship is close. Close association between the parties means that they have greater knowledge of each other and are less likely to have misunderstandings: less needs to be explained, so there is less to argue about.
Commonality of perspectives	If the parties are starting out with a similar point of view on most issues, there is less scope for disagreement.
Compatibility of values	If the personal beliefs and attitudes of the parties are close, there is less scope for disagreement. Salespeople typically try to establish common ground with buyers because there is a greater probability of agreement if the buyers perceive the salesperson as being someone like themselves.
Similarity of interest	If both parties stand to gain from the discussions (and in any marketing situation this will be the case) there is likely to be more agreement. Disagreements will still arise around the issue of who is gaining the most from the transaction, but the communications should move fairly smoothly.
Depth of involvement	The more involved the parties are (in other words, the more important the issues) the less likely they are to concede points and therefore the more likely are disagreements. On the other hand, agreements will be a great deal more powerful, and the greater involvement is likely to lead to a greater propensity to continue the discussions until agreement is reached overall.
Quality of interaction	Disagreement will make the interaction unpleasant and therefore more likely to terminate early.
Equality of influence	In a relationship of equals, genuine agreement is more likely than if the relationship is unequal and one party is able to force a decision on the other party.

Agreement and disagreement

Disagreement occurs when the recipient understands the message, but does not accept it. This may occur for many reasons: a difference in perception between the sender and receiver, a problem with the style of the message or a bias against the sender.

Table 8.5 shows the elements of agreement and disagreement.

Disagreement with a message from a marketer can lead to different effects, depending on whether the individual concerned actually argues against the persuasion or simply remains silent. Someone who argues against the communication often becomes even more entrenched in their opposition to the proposal, even if they lose the argument (Rucker and Petty 2004) whereas those who do not voice objections will often be somewhat persuaded and will be less certain of their ground even when there is no apparent change in attitude (Tormala, Brinol and Petty 2004).

Understanding and misunderstanding

The main problem with understanding and misunderstanding is that it is difficult for the recipient of the message to be sure that he or she has understood it correctly. Only when the individual tries to act on the information will a misunderstanding come to light. Since misunderstanding is a common cause of consumer complaints, marketers are clearly concerned to minimize misunderstandings as far as is possible.

On some cases disagreement might lead to misunderstanding, although it is perhaps more common for misunderstandings to lead to disagreements. It is easier to determine

Table 8.6 Elements of understanding

Element	Explanation
Recognition of intent	Knowing what the other party means to achieve is helpful in understanding what it is they are trying to say.
Multiple perspective taking	The more possible ways the information is presented, the more likely it is that the recipient will understand. This is the principle behind redundancy in communications, and is also the idea behind integrated marketing communications.
Warrants and reasons	A warrant is an explanatory mechanism that connects acts of observation to a given conclusion. It is the reasoning process the individual goes through to arrive at an understanding. Reasons are the elements that serve as a basis for the warrant to operate.
Tests of comprehension	Understanding can be tested by using the knowledge in a real-world situation. If the information can usefully predict outcomes, it has been correctly understood: if not, the information is either incorrect or it has been misunderstood.
Code switching	If the participants in the communication are able to switch easily from one style of communication to another, the likelihood that the communication will be understood is significantly greater. This is another driver for integrated marketing communication: sending essentially the same message by several different routes greatly improves understanding, provided the messages do not become distorted by the use of different media.
Synchrony and alignment of communicative styles	Understanding is improved if both parties can remain synchronized and aligned throughout the process. In other words, if both parties follow through the dialogue at the same pace (synchronization) and both remain focused on the dialogue without getting sidetracked into other issues (alignment) there is less chance of misunderstanding.
Working through problematic concerns	More commonly found in personal selling situations, a preparedness to work through problems together is more likely to lead to a mutual understanding. Provided there is a mutually beneficial outcome from such cooperation, there should be a common understanding.
Mutual struggle to minimize miscommunication	If both parties are prepared to spend time on checking the messages, misunderstanding will be greatly reduced.

Talking point

whether people agree or disagree with each other rather than determine whether they actually understand each other: sometimes people will act as if they understand each other in order to reach an agreement more quickly. Since understanding is itself a socially constructed concept, there are degrees of understanding, and the process of interpretation of messages is potentially inexhaustible.

Table 8.6 shows the elements of understanding.

There seems to be so much that can go wrong with communication, it seems incredible that we manage to speak to each other at all! As marketers, why are we even trying? Why not just pile the goods up in the retail shops and let people help themselves, leaving the money on the counter?

There are some companies which appear to operate very well without advertising at all – British Home Stores rarely (if ever) advertise, and it doesn't seem to have done them any harm. Maybe marketing communications, with all their subtle references and half-statements, are more likely to go wrong than to go right!

Personal transformation

If the recipient of the communication is prepared to be open-minded about the communication and is prepared to change, the communication is more likely to be received and processed. If the individual has already decided that the communication is not going to make any difference to his or her life, then it will fail since the 'receiver' is effectively switched off.

The elements of personal transformation are shown in Table 8.7.

Probably the best way to minimize miscommunication is to ensure that the participants are motivated to seek understanding. If people are motivated to understand, they will make the necessary efforts to be receptive, to confirm the accuracy of the information, to work through problem areas with the other party, and so forth.

Table 8.7 Personal transformation

Element	Explanation
Receptivity to change	An individual who is not prepared to change is unlikely to be receptive to communications: expressions of confusion are likely to result.
Supportive communication	Communications which support a customer through a change of attitude are usually helpful: this is why salespeople often leave information about the products with a customer.

Summary

Changing other people's attitudes is something we all try to do in our normal daily lives. Human beings like to argue, to persuade and to communicate new ideas to each other as often as they are able: marketers simply extend this to the commercial sphere. Changing an attitude is essentially a two-phase process, first consisting of destabilizing the original attitude, and second offering an alternative attitude to take its place.

Because communication is not always reliable, changing people's attitudes is not easy, which is why the more astute marketers operate by finding out what people's existing attitudes are and changing the company's offering to fit the customers.

The key points from this chapter are as follows:

- Beliefs are the basis of cognitive change: this type of change comes about through the direct route.

- Emotions are the basis of affective change: this type of change comes about through the peripheral route.
- Post-purchase dissonance may evoke several possible complaint behaviours.
- Communication is a transaction, not a 'magic bullet'.
- Hierarchy of effects models are helpful in communications planning, but may not reflect the actual order in which communications are effective.
- Communication occurs through signs.
- Silent communication may be more significant than word-based communications.
- Cultural differences can be hard to recognize.
- Miscommunication is a common phenomenon, probably best overcome by strong motivation to understand.

Chapter review questions

1 What is meant by salient belief?

2 How might stimulus rejection help in preserving the stability of an attitude?

3 Why would someone adopt an attitude splitting approach?

4 What is the difference between the central route and the peripheral route?

5 What is halo effect?

6 Explain Festinger and Carlsmith's experiment.

7 What are the main criticisms of the Schramm model of communication?

8 What is meant by the hierarchy of communication effects?

9 What is the difference between an icon and a symbol?

10 What is code switching?

Preview case study revisited
Rebranding the Midland

HSBC's response to the tarnished reputation of the Midland went in two stages. First, it encouraged Midland to set up a new bank, First Direct, which was the UK's first telephone-only bank. First Direct has no branches: everything is done by telephone, mail, and (more recently) the Internet. First Direct has been a runaway success: it is the UK's most recommended bank, and it has an enviable customer base since it only targets people in higher income brackets. The 24-hour-a-day, 365-day-a-year capability of First Direct appeals to people with highly paid, demanding working lives, and the bank's intelligent approach to running its call centres makes the banking experience a pleasant one for its customers.

This still left the Midland with an image problem. HSBC's answer was simple. In 1992 HSBC bought the Midland outright, and rebranded it as HSBC in 1999. This was part of an overall rebranding of all of HSBC's member banks worldwide, but in the long run it has been very good for Midland.

Midland's former brand identity (the Listening Bank) was scrapped in favour of HSBC's 'The world's local bank'. The Listening Bank slogan had been widely ridiculed – every time a customer was treated badly, the slogan was repeated in an ironic way, and in any case people wanted a bank that would help, not one that would only listen. Moving to the more globally orientated HSBC branding also moved the Midland into the twenty-first century, changing people's attitudes towards the bank from one of a staid, loss-making, ineffectual institution to one which has a place on the world stage, which is dynamic and innovative, and which looks after its customers.

Case study
The Scottish Road Safety Campaign

The Scottish Road Safety Campaign was founded in 1985, with the aim of reducing the death toll on Scottish roads. Funded by the Scottish Executive (later the Scottish Parliament) SRSC has five main objectives as of 2005.

1 To reduce the use of inappropriate and excessive speed on Scotland's roads.

2 To reduce the incidence of drunk driving on Scotland's roads.

3 To reduce the incidence of drug driving on Scotland's roads.

4 To reduce young driver casualties.

5 To increase the level of seatbelt compliance for all drivers and passengers.

Previous attempts to reduce average speeds on Scottish roads were less than successful: the campaigns were ad hoc and the effects were short term. SRSC planners therefore decided to take a long-term approach, using a campaign called Foolsspeed. The first phase of this campaign, launched in November 1998, comprised a series of short TV advertisements backed up by widespread display of the Only Foolsspeed message on buses, petrol nozzles, and motorway service station sites. Police forces, local authorities and even some commercial companies helped by displaying the Only Foolsspeed logo on their publications as well as on their vehicles.

In 1999, 2000 and 2001 respectively three full-length 40-second TV advertisements were produced. The first advert, called 'Mirror', aimed to challenge drivers' existing beliefs about their speeding behaviour. The second advert, 'Friends and Family', showed how fast driving was stressful for passengers. The third advert, 'Simon Says', showed how drivers can sometimes be pressured by other drivers into speeding.

The overall effect was a marked change in drivers' attitudes towards speeding. The next advert in the series will address the issue of behavioural intentions about speeding.

ROAD SAFETY SCOTLAND

ROAD SAFETY SCOTLAND

For drink driving, the SRSC commissioned some research which showed that younger drivers were more concerned about losing their licences, whereas older driver were more concerned about the moral aspects of drinking and driving. To tackle these differing attitudes, SRSC began by trying to change the attitudes of the younger drivers with a campaign called 'Wheel of Misfortune'. In this campaign a young driver was featured being caught drinking and driving, and winning a series of 'prizes' including higher insurance premiums, loss of independence, and so forth. The advertisements went out on radio, since young drivers typically listen to the radio while driving: the campaign was backed up by 'Wheel of Misfortune' stickers in pub toilets.

Research also showed that drug driving was more typical of younger drivers. The evidence was that these drivers did not believe that the police had simple ways of detecting the drugs, and that therefore they were less likely to be caught than they would if they were driving while drunk. The campaign therefore concentrated on showing young drivers that the police can, and do, use quick and effective roadside tests for drug use. Follow-up research on this campaign found that drivers believed that police had the means to test for drugs, but drivers did not believe that the police actually used the equipment, since nobody had seen them actually testing somebody (even though breathalyzer tests for alcohol are often seen). SRSC believed that this problem would reduce as the police use the tests more often.

THE SCOTTISH GOOD EGG GUIDE TO IN-CAR

ChildSafety

ROAD SAFETY SCOTLAND

Reducing the casualty rate among young drivers presented a particularly difficult problem, as young drivers are (almost by definition) over-confident in their own abilities. They are therefore unlikely to regard the advertising as applying to them, and will consequently ignore the messages. SRSC planned to attack this on two fronts: first, by targeting new drivers. Having just passed their tests, these drivers are less likely to have developed an over-confident attitude, and are probably more open to communication. Second, and perhaps controversially, SRSC found that attitudes to driving are formed much earlier than had previously been thought – by primary-school age, most children had formed attitudes about driving, some of which were inappropriate. SRSC targeted the parents of primary-school children with a view to engaging their help in getting the road safety message across. Secondary schools were also targeted so as to reach older children, but in this case the message came from the SRSC education officer rather than from parents.

To increase seat belt usage, SRSC developed a campaign called 'Good Egg'. This showed cartoon eggs wearing seatbelts: aimed at children, the campaign also conveyed the subtle message to adults that their children are fragile, and should be protected by wearing seatbelts.

All these campaigns are ongoing. The aim is not just to change behaviour (by threatening prosecution) but to change basic attitudes so that people monitor their own behaviour, and want to be safer on the roads.

Case study questions

1 How does the theory of planned behaviour apply to SRSC's campaigns?

2 What is the relevance of the elaboration likelihood model to the Foolsspeed campaign?

3 How might the young driver campaign be strengthened?

4 How does personal transformation theory apply to the young driver campaign?

5 How might metacommunication affect the campaign in secondary schools?

References

Aronson, E., Chase, T., Helmreich, R., and Ruhnke, R. (1974) A two-factor theory of dissonance reduction: the effect of feeling stupid or feeling awful on opinion change. *International Journal of Communication Research*, 3: 340–52.

Bakamitsos, Georgios, and Siomkos, George (2004) Context effects in marketing practice: the case of mood. *Journal of Consumer Behaviour*, 3(4): 304–14.

Berney-Reddish, I.A., and Areni, C.S. (2005) Effects of probability markers on advertising claim acceptance. *Journal of Marketing Communications*, 11(1): 41–54.

Bhatnagar, Namita, and Aksoy, Lerzan (2004) Et tu, Brutus? A case for consumer skepticism and backlash against product placements. *Advances in Consumer Research*, 31(1).

Costa, Jamneen Arnold, and Pavia, Teresa M. (1992) What it all adds up to: culture and alphanumeric brand names. *Advances in Consumer Research*, 19, eds. John F. Sherry Jr. and Brian Sternthal (Provo, UT: Association for Consumer Research).

Deetz, S.A. (1992) *Democracy in an Age of Corporate Colonization: Developments in Communication and the Politics of Everyday Life* (Albany, NY: State University of New York Press).

Engel, James F., Warshaw, Martin R., and Kinnear, Thomas C. (1994) *Promotional Strategy* (Chicago, IL: Irwin).

Festinger, L. (1957) *A Theory of Cognitive Dissonance* (Stanford, CA: Stanford University Press).

Festinger, L., and Carlsmith, J.M. (1959) Cognitive consequences of forced compliance. *Journal of Abnormal and Social Psychology*, 58: 203–10.

Holden, M.T., and O'Toole, T. (2004) Affirming communication's primary role in a manufacturer-retailer context. *Journal of Marketing Management*, 20(9/10): 1047–73.

Katz, E., and Lazarsfield, P. (1955) *Personal Influence: The Part Played by People in the Flow of Mass Communications* (New York: New York Free Press).

Madden, K.M., and Perry, C. (2003) How do customers of a financial services institution judge its communications. *Journal of Marketing Communications*, 9 (June), 2: 113–27.

Mantovani, G. (1996) *New Communications Environments: From Everyday to Virtual* (London: Taylor and Francis).

O'Sullivan, T., Hartley, J., Saunders, D., and Fiske, J. (1983) *Key Concepts in Communication* (London: Methuen).

Peirce, C.S., quoted on p. 198 of Mick, David G. (1986) Consumer research and semiotics: exploring the morphology of signs, symbols and significance. *Journal of Consumer Research*, 13 (Sept): 196–213.

Petty, Richard E., Caccioppo, John, and Schumann, David (1983) Central and peripheral routes to advertising effectiveness. *Journal of Consumer Research*, 10 (Sept): 135–46.

Rosenberg, Milton J. (1960) An analysis of affective-cognitive consistency. In Milton J. Rosenberg, C.I. Hovland, W.J. McGuire, R.P. Abelson and J.W. Brehm (eds) *Attitude Organization and Change* (New Haven, CT: Yale University Press).

Rucker, Derek D., and Petty, Richard E. (2004) When counterarguing fails: effects on attitude strength. *Advances in Consumer Research*, 31(1): 87.

Schramm, W.A. (1948) *Mass Communication* (Urbana, IL: University of Illinois Press).

Schramm, W.A. (1971): The nature of communication between humans. In Schramm, W.A., and Roberts, D.F. (eds) *The Process and Effects of Mass Communication* (Urbana, IL: Illinois University Press).

Shimp. T., and Sharma, S. (1987) Consumer ethnocentrism: construction and validation of CETSCALE. *Journal of Marketing Research* (Aug): 280–9.

Singh, J. (1988) Consumer complaint intentions and behaviour: definitions and taxonomical issues. *Journal of Marketing*, 52 (January): 93–107.

Smith, K.H., and Stutts, M.A. (2003) Effects of short-term versus long-term health fear appeals in anti-smoking advertisements on the smoking behaviour of adolescents. *Journal of Consumer Behaviour*, 3(2): 155–77.

Steen, J. (1995) Now they're using suicide to sell jeans. *Sunday Express* (26 March).

Tormala, Zakary L., Brinol, Pablo, and Petty, Richard E. (2004) Hidden effects of persuasion. *Advances in Consumer Research*, 31(1): 75–6.

Varey, R. (2000) A critical review of conceptions of communication evident in contemporary business and management literature. *Journal of Communication Management*, (4): 328–40.

Williams, Patti (2003) The impact of emotional advertising appeals on implicit and explicit memory: an accessibility/diagnosticity perspective. *Advances in Consumer Research*, 30(1): 87–8.

Part three
Sociological issues in consumer behaviour

Sociology is the study of how people behave in groups. Sociologists and anthropologists have contributed a great deal to our understanding of behaviour, since human beings are nothing if not group creatures. Our friends, families, work colleagues, and casual acquaintances all have their influences on how we behave (and of course we influence their behaviour in turn). Nowhere is this more so than in consumption behaviour: sometimes it appears that no group can exist without consuming something.

Chapter 9 looks at the contexts in which behaviour takes place. Culture, subculture and cultural change are all the province of anthropology: social class is one of the key concepts of sociology, and continues to have meaning even in a so-called 'classless' society. These components of the human environment are important in understanding influences on behaviour.

Chapter 10 is concerned with the groups to which we all belong – our friends, our workmates, our professional associates, the other members of clubs we belong to, and the behavioural pressures that arise from being a member of these groups. We benefit from membership of such groups in many ways, not just in terms of social interaction. On the other hand there is a price to pay in terms of behavioural constraints, many of which involve buying particular products or paying for particular services.

Chapter 11 is concerned with the most influential group of all, the family. Our families influence us from our earliest childhood through to our old age, and in addition we frequently share consumption with family members. Within our families we play out roles both in day-to-day life and in consumption behaviour, and it is through our families that we learn how to be effective consumers within the society in which we live.

Chapter 9
The environment, class and culture

Introduction

This chapter is about the contexts within which behaviour takes place. Individual decision-making always occurs with a social, cultural, environmental or class context, since human beings interact and need to consider the responses of others. Also, the physical environment within which decisions are made can affect the outcomes dramatically: some environments are conducive to paying higher prices, or buying more of a specific type of product, whereas others encourage greater thrift.

Culture provides the social environment within which people live. This chapter also considers what happens when people change culture, or when their own culture shifts around them; it also considers the variations within a culture which are called subcultures.

Environmental influences

The environment refers to the physical surroundings in which decision-making takes place. It includes physical objects (the products themselves, the display stands in stores, and even the stores themselves), spatial relationships (the location of products in stores, the amount of space available within the stores, the locations of the stores) and the behaviour of other people within the environment.

For example, the shopping experience in an upmarket department store such as Harrod's in London, El Corte Ingles in Madrid or David Jones in Sydney is a great deal different from the shopping experience in markets such as Brick Lane in London, the Rastro market in Madrid or the Kirribilli market in Sydney. The actual goods on offer may even be the same in many cases, but the level of service, the behaviour of fellow shoppers and the general atmosphere will be totally different, as of course will be the prices.

Figure 9.1 (on page 187) shows some of the relationships between elements of the environment. The level of service, décor, presence or absence of music, and the other customers in the store all affect the store's brand image, but other factors over which the store management have little or no control will also affect the functional environment, which in turn affects the buying behaviour of the individual shoppers.

At a more subtle level, people may be influenced by factors such as music played within the store, the use of colour in the store and the perceived social class of other store users. For a marketer, the difficulty lies in assessing which

Shopping in a major department store is part of the consumption experience.

Preview case study
Hard Rock Café

Hard Rock Café first opened its doors in 1971, on Piccadilly in London. The founders were two Americans, Isaac Tigreet and Peter Morton, both believers in the idea that the environment of a restaurant is at least as important as the food. The original concept was to decorate the restaurant with general Americana, but the two entrepreneurs quickly discovered that what interested the customers was the collection of rock'n'roll memorabilia on display. As a result, they concentrated on collecting more items: a guitar that Jimi Hendrix once owned, John Lennon's handwritten lyrics for 'Help!' (reputedly his favourite Beatles song), one of Madonna's bustiers, and many platinum and gold records are all to be found in Hard Rock's premises.

In 1982 the founders decided to go their separate ways and open up Hard Rock Cafés elsewhere in the world. At first they concentrated on the United States, but later included Canada. By 1990, they original founders had sold their interests to Rank Organization: Rank extended the concept to 42 countries and 138 restaurants. Much of this expansion was achieved by franchising the original idea, but Hard Rock Café still owns all the rock memorabilia on display, leasing it to the franchisees for a proportion of its market value. With over 70,000 pieces in the collection, Hard Rock has the world's largest collection of rock'n'roll memorabilia.

The problem for the company has several dimensions. First, the original concept was distinctly anti-establishment and quirky – the company says that it was 'anti-established in 1971' – but this does not sit well with the idea of operating a global franchise. Second, and perhaps more importantly from a consumer's viewpoint, the whole atmosphere and environment of Hard Rock is about the memorabilia on display. Just how much rock memorabilia is there in the world, and how can Hard Rock expect to buy it all? Third, the concept relies on serving American fast food – burgers and sandwiches – while the ambience encourages customers to stay and admire the exhibits. This means that seats remain occupied while eager would-be diners have to wait outside or (worse) go elsewhere.

GUY SOMERSET/ALAMY

factors are crucial, and how those factors might affect different people: some people like to have in-store music playing, for example, whereas others are irritated by it. Likewise, some people enjoy the buzz and bustle of shopping in a street market, whereas others might find it distracting or even threatening.

The concept of store **atmospherics** was first described by Kotler (1973). Atmospherics are all the factors which go to make up the atmosphere and general 'feel' of a retail store: the décor, the music, the temperature and humidity, and so forth. Atmospherics go a long way towards determining whether a customer remains in the store longer, spends more (or less) money, and returns at a later date. Since Kotler, researchers have taken two basic approaches to researching atmospherics. The first approach concentrates on the factors which make up store atmosphere, whereas the other approach regards atmosphere in a holistic way and concentrates instead on its effects on consumers. Under the first approach, studies have been made of colour and lighting (Bellizzi, Crowley and Hasty 1983), social factors (Baker, Levy and Grewal 1992), music and lighting (Kellaris and Kent 1992), crowding (Eroglu and Harrell 1986) and point-of-purchase displays (Philips and Bradshaw 1990). There are two common findings in these studies: first, that manipulating these various elements correctly can result in outcomes favourable to the retailer, i.e. people stay in

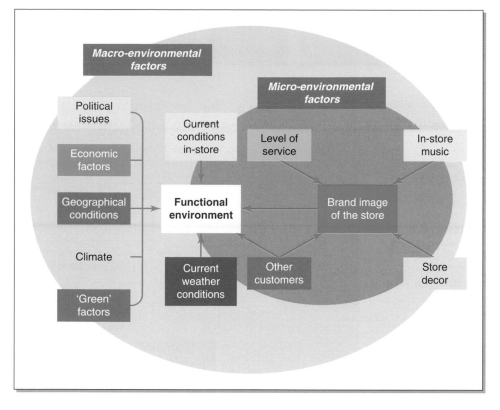

Figure 9.1

Elements in the environment

the store longer and spend more money, and second these elements have been shown to affect people's physical and psychological states, and hence their behaviour.

The second main thrust of research, an examination of the kind of effects atmospherics have on people, has produced some interesting results. Several researchers have used the Mehrabian-Russell Environmental Psychology Model to explain some of the features of store atmospherics (Mehrabian and Russell 1974). The M-R model says that environmental stimuli lead to emotional states (e.g. pleasure or arousal) which then lead to approach or avoidance responses. In a study of CD shops in Hong Kong, researchers were able to expand and modify the model to provide the example shown in Figure 9.2 (page 188) (Tai and Fung 1997).

The left-hand box in the model refers to the information rate. This is the degree to which the shopper is exposed to novelty and surprise – the more novel the environment, the greater the information rate. Likewise, the more complex the environment the higher the information rate. Mehrabian and Russell (1974) postulate that an individual's propensity to develop approach or avoidance behaviours is a function of three elements – pleasure (or displeasure), arousal (or boredom) and dominance (or submission). In the study of CD stores, the researchers found that information rates have a marked effect on arousal, but not necessarily on pleasure: in other words customers did not necessarily like having a high information rate, even though they found it stimulating or exciting. The researchers further found that in-store behaviour contributed more to the pleasure of the experience, so from a marketer's viewpoint it would seem sensible to allow people plenty of latitude to examine goods, interact with staff, and so forth.

The environment as perceived by the consumers themselves is called the functional (or perceived) environment (Block and Block 1981). The functional environment will be different for each individual, because individuals differ in their knowledge, beliefs, experience and (of course) preference. Since marketers generally deal with groups of people rather than individuals, subtle differences and idiosyncrasies are likely to be ignored in favour of creating a generally acceptable environment for the target group of customers.

Figure 9.2

Adapted M-R model

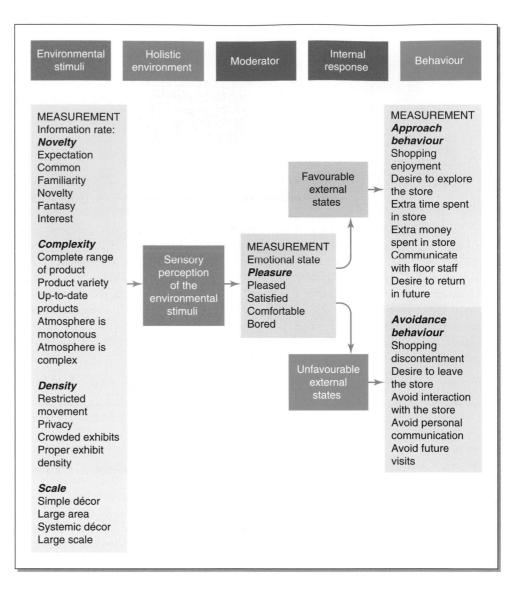

Figure 9.3 shows some of the elements of the functional environment. The **macro-environment** affects everything else, including the store and its branding: store décor, music, service levels and other customers all affect the store's brand image, but the behaviour and number of other customers also affect the functional environment directly. The current conditions in the store (crowding, cleanliness, availability of assistants) and the current weather (whether it is hot, rainy, cold) have a direct bearing on the functional environment. There are of course many other factors which may affect the individual: situational factors such as time pressures, physical interrupts such as hunger or thirst, and so forth. Since the functional environment is subjective, the individual's personality, tastes, moods and behaviour act as moderating factors.

Talking point

It sounds as if the functional environment is really difficult to deal with. It's subjective, it's easily affected by factors over which we have absolutely no control, and it changes with every passing minute. So why do we bother? Why not just pile everything up on the counter, and hope people buy it?

Maybe that's a bit of an exaggeration, though. Maybe we should influence the bits we can influence, and live with the bits we can't influence. At least we'll be able to make *some* difference to people's perceptions!

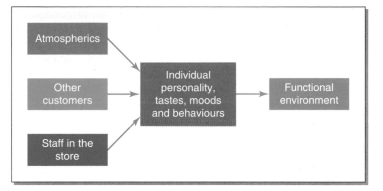

Figure 9.3
The functional environment

The subjective nature of the functional environment can be problematical in an international context, because there are often marked differences between individuals in different countries: even with the European Union this is a problem, despite the relative similarities between member states in terms of wealth, aspirations and product availability (Askegaard and Madsen 1995). Because of this, it is tempting for marketers to treat each country as a separate segment, whereas in fact this can be inappropriate since new transnational segments are appearing as people travel more and the European Union converges (Brunso, Grunert and Bredahl 1996). Recent research identified four consumer styles which transcend national boundaries (McCarty, Horn and Szenasy 2007):

1 *Price-sensitive consumers* – These are people who check prices, shop around for special offers, and are not brand-loyal.

2 *Variety seekers* – These people like to try new things and are the first to buy new products.

3 *Brand-loyal consumers* – These people buy known brands, and are likely to be brand loyal even when this costs more; they are less likely to check prices or shop around for bargains.

Consumer behaviour in action
Queues at Tesco

Tesco, the giant UK supermarket chain, has an interesting approach to reducing queues at its checkouts. The aim of each store is to allow no more than one person to be ahead of each customer in the queue. Although in practice this is impossible, Tesco have managed to use modern computer technology to minimize the waiting time of its customers.

Every 15 minutes each till freezes and can only be unlocked by the checkout operator entering the number of people waiting in the queue. This process takes a moment, but it provides store managers with instant information. The managers can then open up more checkouts, using back-up operators, until either the queues have reduced or all the tills are open and no more can be done. At the same time, the tills send the data through to the central Tesco computer, which calculates the average number of times in the day that there is a longer queue than two people. Store managers are expected to reach their targets 95 per cent of the time, so if there are more than two people in the queue on more than 5 per cent of the times the operators enter the number, the managers are asked to account for themselves. This leads them to try to anticipate potential bottlenecks and organize staff breaks and so forth accordingly – one simple method is to observe how many people enter the store, since this gives an advance warning of how many of them are likely to be at the checkouts in the near future.

This system means that Tesco have shorter queues at the checkouts than almost any other supermarket – a real benefit to customers, and one which does not cost the company anything beyond a few seconds spent by checkout operators in entering a single number.

4 *Information seekers* – These people exchange information with other people, are more receptive to advertising, and will try new products but tend to stick to known brands.

Other styles identified in the research differed across cultural boundaries – German consumers are less brand loyal and more price sensitive than consumers from some other countries, but they tend to enjoy shopping more than the French do, for example.

In the context of consumer behaviour, the environmental factors can be divided into macro-environmental factors (climate, economy, politics, geography and so forth) and micro-environmental factors such as the shop assistant, the store's cleanliness and décor, the current weather conditions, or the other shoppers. Each of these factors is relevant: macro-economic factors will dictate what people need to buy in terms of clothing, housing, transport and so forth, as well as what they are able to buy either as a result of their wealth or as a result of legal restrictions or requirements. Micro-economic factors influence decision-making at the point of purchase: people are unlikely to linger in noisy, crowded or dirty stores, and they become frustrated if there are long queues at checkouts (Park, Iyer and Smith 1989).

The social environment

The social environment includes all the behavioural inputs received from other people. In some cases, these may be direct interactions (a conversation with a salesperson, advice from a friend, an encounter with someone unpleasant) and in other cases they may be indirect (observing how a friend negotiates with a vendor, seeing an advertisement on TV, seeing how other people act in a new social situation).

The social environment can also be divided into macro and micro environments. The macro environment has three components: culture, subculture and social class. Each of these has profound influences on behaviour because they have been powerful drivers in the formation of attitudes, beliefs and values. Although people from the same cultural background differ considerably among themselves, there will still be similarities. Each of these elements will be dealt with in more detail later in this chapter.

As shown in Figure 9.4, the micro social environment comprises the face-to-face social interactions we have with our friends, work colleagues, family and others in the groups of which we are members. These micro-environmental interactions will be dealt with in more detail in the next two chapters. The macro environment comprises those factors which are common to everyone living within the same country or region, in other words those factors which affect all of us.

Figure 9.4

The social environment

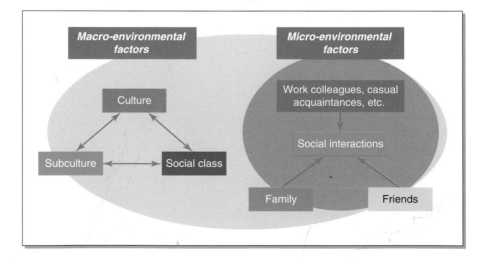

Culture

Culture is the set of shared beliefs, attitudes and behaviours associated with a large and distinct group of people. Culture is learned, but it is often so deeply ingrained in people that they imagine that the rules of their particular society or group have the status of natural laws. As a result, culture is one of the main drivers of behaviour, and influences almost everything we do, including (of course) our consumption behaviour.

The main elements of culture are as follows (see also Figure 9.5, page 193):

- *Religion* – Religious beliefs colour people's behaviour in many ways, from laying down rules about clothing to prescribing which foods are permissible and which are not. For example, for many years Catholics were officially forbidden (as a fast or a penance) to eat meat on Fridays, which many interpreted as an injunction to eat fish instead. Even after the original religious injunction was relaxed (on the basis that eating lobster Thermidor could hardly be considered a fast or a penance) people continued the tradition of having at least one fish meal on a Friday. The stricter restrictions on Muslims and Jews against eating pork, and the symbolic meal taken by Christians during Communion, are other examples.

- *Language* – Language clearly affects purchasing behaviour in many ways. First, the ability to understand and act on marketing communications relies not only on understanding the specific language (English or French for example) but also on understanding specific words and sentence constructions within the language. For example, slang terms and puns might not be accessible to all the observers of the communication, and communications written in dialect might not be understood by non-native speakers of the language. Second, some products (such as books and newspapers) are clearly of no use to someone who does not understand the language in which they are written. The market for books in Welsh, for example, is confined to Wales and parts of Argentina, with few (if any) sales elsewhere. The structure and rules of languages can affect consumer perceptions: in languages where brand names acquire gender (Spanish and French, for example) this will affect consumer perception of the product as being either masculine or feminine. In languages which include a neuter gender (English and Greek, for example) this is not an issue unless the marketer deliberately uses a masculine or feminine ending on the brand name (Yorkston and deMello 2004).

- *Customs* – These are norms of behaviour handed down from the past. Some customs grow out of religious beliefs (for example many of the traditions associated with Christmas have come from Christian belief, although some are pagan or pre-Christian), while others come from traditions associated with climate or shared experiences. For example, throughout most of southern Spain villages and towns celebrate the fiesta of 'Moros y Cristianos' which refers to the overthrow of the Moorish invaders in the twelfth century. The date varies in each village, as each village overthrew its Moors on a different date, but for most it is a spectacular celebration involving fireworks (symbolizing the fighting and also the traditional destruction of remaining ammunition to show that the shooting really is over) and a great deal of dancing and celebration throughout the night.

- *Food* – Food is strongly linked to culture. For example, while cheese is regarded as an essential part of any meal in France, and each region of the country produces several distinct examples, in Japan it is regarded as being as appealing as rotted milk and is rarely eaten. In Britain, people will not eat insects but will happily eat prawns, while in Zambia deep-fried caterpillars are a delicacy. In Mexico, the tortilla has a cultural significance which is bound into what it means to be a Mexican, but (paradoxically) there is an underlying belief that everything emanating from the United States is better than anything Mexican, and there is evidence that even American tortillas are somehow better than Mexican ones

(Gabel and Boller 2003). These differences in tastes are explained by culture rather than by random differences in taste between individuals: the behaviours tend to be shared by people from the same cultural background.

- *Mores* – A more is a custom with a strong moral incentive. In most societies, cannibalism is regarded as immoral and is not part of the cultural mores: in other societies (most of them in the past) cannibalism is not only moral but is regarded as a necessary and respectful way of dealing with dead people. Violation of mores often results in strong reactions from other members of the culture: in some cases these can be abusive or even violent, in other cases the law becomes involved and the individual receives a formalized punishment.

- *Conventions* – These are norms regarding the conduct of everyday life. For example, in the UK a dinner guest would normally be expected to bring a bottle of wine, and many dinner guests would also bring flowers. Some spoken phrases are conventional: someone who asks you 'How are you?' is expecting the answer, 'Fine, thanks' rather than an actual description of the other person's current circumstances. Table manners, appropriate clothing for formal occasions and rules about when it is permissible to make a noise (for example play loud music) and when it is not are also subject to conventions.

- *Myths* – A myth is a story which contains symbolic elements expressing the shared emotions and ideals of a culture. The outcome of a myth might illustrate a particular moral pathway, and it thus serves to provide a guideline to the world. An example might be the 'urban myths' which have grown up in recent years to warn people of inappropriate behaviour, or to provide entertainment.

- *Rituals* – A ritual is a set of symbolic behaviours which occur in a fixed sequence. For example, weddings follow a fairly well-defined path in most cases, and there are many rituals attached to sporting events such as football matches. The singing of specific songs, the consumption of specific foods or beverages (few football fans would watch the match while drinking a glass of Chardonnay – beer is the ritual drink), and the wearing of specific clothing are all ritualistic. Many people have grooming rituals (brushing one's hair 100 times each day, showering to a specific pattern, and so forth) and these rituals serve to transform the individual from the private persona to the public persona. Gift-giving is another example of a ritual – in most Western cultures, gifts should be wrapped in attractive paper, and should contain an element of surprise: the price tag should be removed, and the recipient has to look pleased to receive the gift. Deviation from this ritual causes discomfort for one or the other party to the transaction. In China, on the other hand, giving a gift imposes an obligation on the recipient to do the other person a favour at some time or to reciprocate: over-effusive thanks for a gift can be interpreted as an attempt to avoid this obligation.

- *Rites of passage* – A rite of passage is an event or a set of behaviours which moves an individual from one state to another. The Fresher's Ball at university is an example, as is the traditional twenty-first birthday party, which of course relates to the time when 21-year-olds were regarded as full adults. This has been diluted somewhat by changes in legislation, which now confers full responsibilities and rights at different stages during an individual's teenage years. Some rites of passage are more individual in nature: marriage or divorce ceremonies are rites of passage between the single and married states, but may occur at almost any stage in the individual's adult life, or may not occur at all. Rites of passage are important to people as statements of status, and new rites are invented periodically to take account of new status: recent legislation in the UK has allowed same-sex 'marriages' through the Civil Partnership rules, and at a more mundane level there are definite rituals which are observed when someone changes job.

- *Sacred consumption* – Some places are set apart as special because something of great significance happened there. In some cases, these places have mystical or

The Millennium Stadium has an almost religious status for some people.

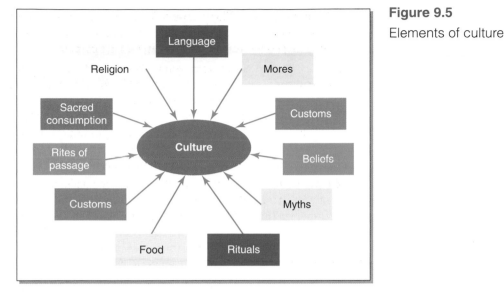

Figure 9.5
Elements of culture

religious significance, for example Stonehenge or Bethlehem, while in other cases the place might have no religious significance as such but acquires sacred qualities. A prime example is the Millennium Stadium in Cardiff, UK. The actual pitch is often referred to as 'the hallowed turf' and there have been numerous attempts (some successful) to scatter the ashes of deceased fans on the pitch.

These elements of culture are common to all cultures, but vary in type and importance between cultures. For some cultures, religion is almost the defining factor: Islamic states which operate under Sharia laws as laid down in the Koran, and countries such as Spain where fiestas, public holidays and many aspects of daily life are conducted with reference to the Catholic church, are prime examples. For other cultures, other aspects may contribute more.

To an extent, national characteristics can be identified. The most famous (and widely taught) study of national characteristics is that of Hofstede (1980). This research reports on a study of 6000 respondents in 66 countries, all of whom worked for IBM. Hofstede initially identified four cultural dimensions, as follows (Figure 9.6, page 194):

● *Individualism vs. collectivism* – This is the degree to which the culture values individualism and individual freedom above that of the group.

● *Uncertainty avoidance* – This is the degree to which the culture adheres to rules and customs to avoid risk.

● *Power distance* – This is the degree to which power is centralized in the culture.

● *Masculinity–femininity* – This is the degree to which the culture exhibits 'masculine' qualities of assertiveness, achievement and wealth acquisition rather than the 'feminine' attributes of nurturing, concern for the environment and concern for the poor.

Hofstede later revisited the data and the problem, and came up with a fifth dimension. This is long-term versus short-term orientation, and is a dimension which is particularly relevant to Oriental cultures.

These categorizations are interesting, and may be useful for planning the overall tone of a communications campaign, but it would be dangerous to make assumptions about individuals based on these broad generalisations. The average Taiwanese may be more collectivist than the average American, but the most individualistic Taiwanese is likely to be a great deal more individualistic than the most collectivist American.

Hofstede's research has been widely criticised for several reasons. First, the research was conducted with IBM employees, and since IBM has a strong corporate culture it seems

Consumer behaviour in action
Football violence?

In some cultures, football seems to have acquired religious status. Feelings run high when people build their entire self-images around supporting a particular football team, and football matches worldwide have often been accompanied by riots and violent behaviour on the part of fans. Often this is thought of as a particularly British activity, but even the most violent British fans would be hard put to keep up with Latin American fans.

The most violence ever attributed to football occurred in 1969 when Honduras and San Salvador were competing in the qualifying rounds of the World Cup. The San Salvador team were set to play the Honduran team at the Tegucigalpa stadium in Honduras. The night before the match, the Salvadoran team was besieged in their hotel by a hostile crowd of Hondurans letting off fireworks, sounding their car horns and throwing stones at the windows. Not unnaturally, after having had a poor night's sleep, the Salvadorans lost 1–0 the following day. This might have been a minor incident had not one of the Salvadoran fans, 18-year-old Amelia Bolanios, shot herself through the heart with her father's pistol after witnessing the Honduran goal. She was accorded a state funeral with the President of the Republic among the mourners.

Unfortunately the two teams ended up tied on points so the match had to be replayed, this time at the Flor Bancal stadium in San Salvador. The Salvadorans were ready for the Honduran team – this time the hotel windows were shattered and rotting animal carcasses thrown into the rooms. At the match, the Hondurans were delivered by armoured car and a military cordon armed with machine guns surrounded the pitch. The match organizers burned the Honduran flag in front of the players and ran a dirty dishcloth up the flagpole in its place, so the Hondurans were in no doubt as to the feelings of the Salvadorans. Honduras lost 3–0 this time, and the team were rushed away to the airport and flown home.

The Honduran fans were not so lucky. Fleeing for the border, many were caught and killed and hundreds were seriously injured. Within hours the border was sealed off. At dusk the next day, an El Salvadoran military aircraft bombed the Tegucigalpa stadium and the city was blacked out. Cross-border gunfire developed during the night, and border villages were shelled and destroyed. On both sides of the border nationals of the other country were rounded up and imprisoned (ironically) in football stadiums. The war only lasted five days, due to pressure from neighbouring Latin American countries, but during that period over 6000 people were killed and 15,000 seriously injured: thousands were left homeless.

A peace treaty between the two countries was finally signed in 1980, 11 years after the war began, but there is still ill-feeling between the countries and the occasional shot is fired across the border.

In the immortal words of Bill Shankly: 'Some people believe football is a matter of life and death. I'm very disappointed with that attitude. I can assure you it is much, much more important than that.'

Figure 9.6

Dimensions of culture

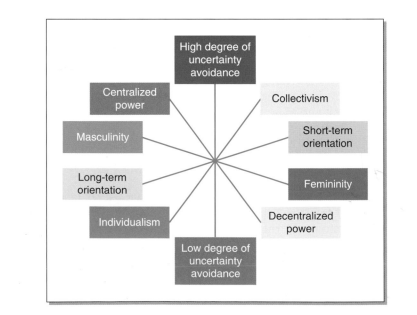

likely that this will have affected the results. Second, the actual survey was conducted in the late 1960s, almost 40 years ago, and the world has become considerably more globalized since then. Third, Hofstede was concerned mainly with work-related values rather than with consumer behaviour, yet the research has often been used to justify marketing communication activities.

Talking point

Hofstede might be getting a critical hammering these days, but there is little doubt that different cultures do generate different behaviours and attitudes – that's sort of the point! So why can't we identify and classify these differences? Is it a fear of being politically incorrect? Or is it just that these differences are notoriously difficult to pin down?

Maybe it's just that we are daunted by the prospect of carrying out a research project on that scale!

There are three main approaches to studying culture, as follows:

1 *Taxonomies of culture* – This involves dividing cultures into different levels and/or into high-context or low-context cultures (Figure 9.7, page 196).

2 *Lifestyle analysis.*

3 *Identification of cultural universals* – These are aspects of culture found in all societies. For example, all cultures use some form of bodily adornment (tattooing, cosmetics, jewellery, clothing, etc.). All cultures have sexual taboos (who is 'permissible' for sexual activity and who is not), all cultures have gift-giving rituals, and all cultures have differences in status between members.

High-context cultures are those in which norms of behaviour and values are deeply embedded in the members of the culture, and thus do not need to be explained in any specific way (Hofstede 1980). Members communicate easily, because they share the same basic beliefs and reference points – there is no need to explain, so people can communicate non-verbally relatively easily. Characteristics of high-context cultures are as follows:

● Communication is rapid and efficient within the group, but rapidly breaks down with outsiders because the group members find it harder to explain matters which they think of as obvious.

● Behaviour within the group is stable and predictable.

● The nature of the group is such that outsiders are likely to stereotype the group, as the only way they have of understanding the culture.

● All parties within the group share much the same perceptual field.

High-context cultures are therefore totalitarian, orthodox and conservative. There is little room for personal expression or change, but each member has a clear (and perhaps reassuring) understanding of their role and responsibilities as well as what they can expect from the other members of the culture. Rigidity gives a degree of security in a high-context culture.

Low-context cultures are much less rigid, but require more effort of their members. They have the following features:

● They are individualistic rather than collectivistic.

● Members communicate using clearly coded messages.

● Members' values, attitudes, perceptions and patterns of behaviour are diverse and liable to change quickly.

The United States and most of Western Europe have low-context cultures, because of mass migrations and world travel, which have combines to expose the members of the cultures to many diverse cultural influences. Countries such as Japan, which have relatively few foreigners living in them, tend to have high-context cultures.

Figure 9.7

High-context vs. low-context cultures

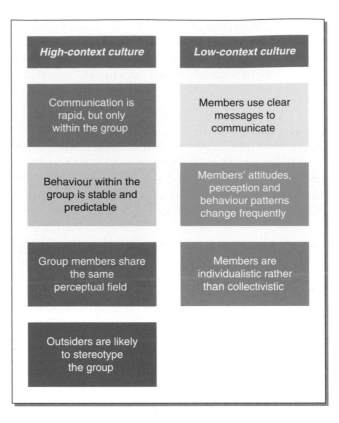

Consumer culture

In the developed world, we have cultures which are almost defined by what we consume rather than by what we believe. The concept of the consumer society has been around for some time now, and refers to the way in which most human activity in the developed world centres around consumption. We define ourselves by what we consume rather than by what we produce, we spend a large amount of our time consuming things or learning about things to consume (which is itself a form of consumption) and it is impossible for us to have a social life without at the same time being a consumer. Even such activities as kissing and making love cannot come about without elaborate dating rituals and consequent consumption – it would be hard to imagine someone successfully acquiring a girlfriend or boyfriend without first going on a date, eating at a restaurant, buying nice clothes and perfume, or even going to a dating service.

Problems with consumer culture have been identified. First, consumer culture tends to erode national cultures because the culture associated with specific brands becomes more important than the 'naturally occurring' cultural identity of the individual. For example, there is strong evidence for a worldwide 'youth' culture based on consumption of music (via MTV) and fashion items. This culture means that young people worldwide tend to wear similar clothing and listen to similar music rather than wearing the clothing typical of their countries and listening to traditional music. Second, consumer culture creates superficial social interactions and encourages people to be competitive rather than cooperative. Third, consumerism is regarded as bad for the environment because it encourages excessive use of natural resources.

These criticisms do not in fact stand up very well (Miller 1995) but they do indicate that the consumer society is not necessarily an unmitigated force for good in the world. No doubt debate will continue on this topic.

The degree to which culture affects behaviour has been questioned.

Consumer behaviour in action
Gift giving behaviour

Everybody likes getting a gift – but human beings also seem to like giving gifts as well. Every human culture contains some kind of gift-giving behaviour, from small gifts to oil the wheels of our working lives to major gifts to family and friends on special occasions. We give gifts as a way of apologizing, as a symbol of respect, as a 'thank-you', or because we feel obligated to by social conventions.

Although gift giving is common to all cultures, the connotations of some gifts can be different in different cultures. For example, in China it is common practice for someone to give a small gift to a superior or someone in power. The gift is not intended to influence the person especially, although it is intended as an ice-breaker: if the superior makes a decision which goes against the gift-giver, there would not be any special feeling of resentment. However, to a Westerner these gifts look suspiciously like bribes. In the West, one might offer a gift after the business has been concluded, but even this is fraught with social risks: one does not tip one's superiors. In Western cultures, it is more likely that the gifts would come from the superior to the subordinate, not the other way round.

Bribery is, of course, a horse of a different colour. A bribe is a gift given on the explicit understanding that some advantage will be conferred on the donor as a direct result. This also happens in China, but the rules are different and the outcomes are also different. This is a business transaction rather than a true gift.

In many Western cultures, the period around Christmas is the main time of year for exchanging gifts. Typically, people aim to spend about the same amount on each other (so as to avoid embarrassment) and sometimes even agree an approximate figure beforehand. For small children, parents maintain that the gifts do not in fact come from the parents at all, but from Santa Claus (also known as Papa Noel, Pére Noel, Kris Kringle, Sinter Klaas, Babbo Natale, Joulupukki, and many other names). The gifts are supposed to be a surprise, although among adults people often ask each other what would be a suitable present. Recipients of the gifts have to look surprised and pleased as they open the gifts (on Christmas Day for the UK and USA, or at Epiphany, or on Christmas Eve, or on whatever date is appropriate to the local culture), even if they knew in advance what the gift was, or (worse) if it is something they do not want. All this is regarded as normal, polite behaviour.

A study by Joel Waldfogel (1993) showed that the giving of gifts at Christmas destroyed anything up to 30 per cent of the monetary value of the gift. This was because the recipient of the gift frequently ascribed a cash value to it well below the actual price paid by the donor. What Waldfogel's research did not take into account is all the social aspects of the gift itself – the choosing, the wrapping, the performance rituals attached to the actual exchange of presents. For most people, it seems that these are far more important than the actual gift itself.

Subcultures

Subcultures are distinctive groups of people within a society that share common cultural meanings, behaviours and environmental factors. Although a subculture shares most of the mainstream culture within which it is embedded, its members have a distinct and identifiable set of behavioural norms, customs, scripts and so forth which distinguish them from the rest of the culture. In some cases, the subculture requires members to buy specific items, and members will often not buy items from outside the subculture (Richardson and Turley 2006).

Subcultures might be based on age, ethnic background, gender type or special interests. For example, Goth culture is distinct from mainstream UK culture, but has a distinct set of behaviours and beliefs. Likewise second-generation immigrant populations often develop subcultures which are combinations of the new country's culture and elements from the parents' home country culture. Some subcultures are defined by the ways they interpret messages: these are called 'interpretive communities' (Kates 2002). For example, a subculture of conspiracy theorists would tend to interpret all official statements as evidence of a

Figure 9.8

Culture and subculture

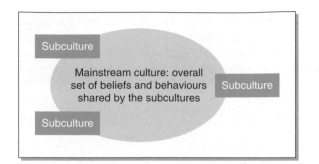

cover-up. An anti-globalization interpretive community would respond with deep suspicion or even hostility to any marketing messages, which makes marketing to such communities difficult: however, they are still consumers.

In Figure 9.8, the main culture's beliefs are shared by the subcultures but each subculture has beliefs and behaviours which lie outside the mainstream. Often the behaviours associated with the subculture can create problems for its members as members of the mainstream culture see them as outsiders or rebels, and therefore a threat to the mainstream.

Geographic subcultures can be very significant for marketers. Most countries have geographical subcultures: Friesland in the Netherlands has a distinct language and traditions, Bavarians regard themselves as culturally different from the neighbouring 'Prussian' culture (and often feel closer to their Austrian neighbours in Salzburg than they do to their fellow Germans in Stuttgart). In the UK, Wales and Scotland regard themselves as separate, and have different food, language and customs from those of England, and Ulster has (as is well known) a different culture either from the UK of which it is legally a part or from Eire of which it is historically a part. The significance for marketers lies in the possibilities for causing offence – for a Welshman, Wales is not, and never has been, part of England. There is also a positive significance in terms of recognizing the differences between the subcultures, perhaps by referring to local events or using local dialects in advertising.

Age subcultures sometimes exist because the members have differing attitudes and values. This is often called the generation gap. In some cases people retain behaviours and attitudes which were current in their youth – this is typically the case with popular music, for example. In other cases people change their views as they age, for example becoming more politically right wing as they become wealthier and less inclined towards radical changes.

Teenagers form a distinct, and often international, subculture. They are important not only because of their own spending power (which can be substantial) but also because they have a strong influence on their parents' spending. Often teenagers have at least some responsibility for the household shopping, and undoubtedly influence family choices about food brands, environmental issues and media consumption. The teen market is notoriously difficult to deal with, since brand preferences change with each year: each group of teenagers wants to have its own favourite brands, so that 14-year-olds are unlikely to be loyal to the same brands as their 16-year-old brothers and sisters. This means that producers need to be at the forefront of what is going on. Teenagers are often very communications-literate, and understand that they are being 'marketed to'.

Baby boomers are people born between 1946 and 1964. These years saw an unprecedented number of births, following on from the Second World War as soldiers returned to civilian life and began raising families. This period was also one of rising prosperity and improved health care, so that more people survived into adulthood and had greater expectations from life.

Baby boomers are now aged between 40 and 60, and are in their peak earning and spending years. They represent the largest and most affluent market in history, and will continue to have a major economic and social impact for the next 40 years at least. Since baby boomers have tended to have smaller families than did their parents, the spend per child has been much higher, and in the longer term the levels of inheritance that baby boomers' children will receive will also be higher.

A phenomenon which is of increasing importance within Europe, Japan and the United States is the ageing population. As life expectancies increase, there are progressively more people in the over-50 age group. This is commonly called 'the grey market', but it should not be assumed that it is homogeneous: it is unlikely that a 55-year-old man would have a lot in common with his 80-year-old mother, at least in terms of consumer behaviour. By 2025 it is estimated that 22 per cent of Europe's population will be aged over 65 (compared with 15.4 per cent in 1995), and this has dramatic implications for pensions, prosperity and of course marketing (Eurostat 2002).

The assumption has always been that these older consumers would be prime candidates for walking frames, stairlifts, hearing aids, and little else. However, the rising life expectancy has been accompanied by a rise in the level of fitness of older people, due to better nutrition and health care. Obviously products such as over-the-counter medicines, hearing aids, spectacles and the like will become even bigger markets, but the grey market also consumes holidays, leisure activities such as golf or aviation, restaurant meals, recreational vehicles, education, and so forth.

The market for the over-50s is extremely diverse – considering that it will shortly comprise almost half of all adults, this is not surprising (National Statistics Office 2005). At the younger end, most of this group are at the peak of their earning power and often have paid off their mortgages and are free of commitments to children. Their discretionary income is therefore higher than it has ever been. As we look at older members of the group, many have retired or are semi-retired and have a great deal more leisure time, while frequently enjoying generous private pensions and savings. Many older people use this time to take holidays, enjoy new hobbies, improve their education, and so forth. These new activities are not necessarily those traditionally associated with elderly people: the holidays on offer in the Saga brochure are just as likely to include windsurfing, mountaineering or ski-ing as they are to include bridge playing or coach tours. Some flying schools report that the majority of their students are over 50, and Open University applications from the over-sixties run into the thousands.

Equally, some other members of the segment fit the more traditional pattern, happy to dig the garden and perhaps do an evening class. This is far from being a homogeneous subculture.

A World of Holidays

SAGA
Exclusively for people aged 50 and over

Saga has successfully tapped into an older market by offering adventures as well as traditional holidays.

Talking point

Apparently many older people are not ready for the rocking-chair and daytime TV just yet! We see plenty of people in their fifties, sixties and even seventies joining the gym, taking flying lessons, canoeing up the Amazon, and generally behaving like teenagers. At the same time the rising divorce rate sees older people at the disco, or using dating services, or chatting each other up on holiday.

Is nothing sacred? Is Granny going to be dancing until two in the morning and getting thrown out of nightclubs at four a.m.? Perhaps there is no such thing as an age-related product. Perhaps we should ignore age altogether in our planning!

On the other hand, Granny isn't what she used to be in many ways. Physically, older people are not going to be as fit as they were when they were young, and mentally things begin to deteriorate as well – greater experience might be a fine thing, but when you can't remember what you came upstairs for experience may not help a lot. So perhaps there will still be a few things we can sell specifically to older people – if only we can get them off the windsurfer.

Ethnic subcultures are a growing group within Europe. Ethnic marketing is much more advanced in the United States, probably because the US is composed of a wide variety of cultures, whereas within Europe ethnic minorities usually account for less than 5 per cent of the population. These groups are growing as immigration continues, and tend to fall into two main groups: those who have emigrated from their country of origin, and are therefore perhaps best considered as members of their home-country culture, and those whose parents came from another country but who were born in the host country. The latter group often develop a distinct culture which is part way between their parents' national culture and the culture of the host country. Research conducted in Canada, for example, showed that Muslim women used the *hijab* (the face-covering material used by some Muslim women) as a way of indicating that they are traditional and therefore respectable when using an on-line dating service (Zwick and Chelariu 2006). This is a distinct move away from the cultural origins of the *hijab* in the Middle East, showing a willingness to comply with religious norms of conduct rather than a genuine belief in those norms.

Clearly these groups have specific purchasing behaviour: specific foods to meet religious restrictions or personal tastes, non-Christian greetings cards, clothing, cooking utensils, and products from the country of origin. On the other hand, most immigrants are happy to embrace at least some aspects of the host country culture, and in some cases deliberately seek out local products as a way of expressing a desire to integrate (Bann 1996).

How these groups should be addressed by marketers is a matter for considerable thought. At present, advertising largely ignores ethnic minorities, and attempts to include minorities (or advertise directly to them) have sometimes been interpreted as patronizing or even offensive (Sudbury and Wilberforce 2006). Part of the difficulty here is that what some people regard as offensive can be regarded as totally acceptable by others: the UK Advertising Standards Authority, which responds to examples of offensive advertising, will take action even if a relatively small number of people complain. This may cause advertisers to avoid the issue by not including ethnic minorities in their advertising at all.

The degree to which individuals from ethnic minorities differ in their behaviour from the rest of society depends largely on their degree of **acculturation**. Acculturation refers to the degree to which people from one cultural background adapt to the meanings, values, beliefs, behaviours, rituals, and lifestyles of another culture or subculture (Faber, O'Guinn and McCarty 1987). For marketers, consumer acculturation is clearly of more interest: this refers to the process of becoming a skilled consumer in a different culture or subculture (Penaloza 1989).

For example, a British citizen who buys a retirement home in Spain might at first believe that everything is cheaper in Spain. Alcoholic drinks, cigarettes, meals in restaurants, petrol and many other daily items are much cheaper in Spain than in the UK. Some items, however, are more expensive or unobtainable (fresh milk is almost impossible to find, and of course British food such as pork pies or brown sauce are unobtainable outside British enclaves). The new immigrant therefore has to learn how to function within the new consumer environment. Obviously these problems are multiplied if the individual moves to a consumer environment which is further removed from the UK – a British immigrant to India would find that supermarkets as they are known in Britain hardly exist at all, that toilet paper is almost unknown, and that bartering is commonplace even for everyday purchases. Acquiring the skills to become an effective consumer in India would take considerable time and effort, and one would have to assume that immigrants coming the other way would face the same steep learning curve.

The degree to which someone can adapt to the new culture will depend on the level of cultural interpenetration he or she experiences. The more the individual interacts socially with members of the host culture, the more he or she is able to adapt. This does not necessarily mean giving up one's original cultural norms and beliefs: it does mean understanding and being sympathetic to the cultural norms and beliefs of the host culture (Andreasen 1990).

There are four stages in acculturation (Figure 9.9), as follows (Oberg 1960):

1 *Honeymoon stage* – The individual is fascinated by the culture or subculture, but because interpenetration is shallow and superficial, there is very little acculturation. The honeymoon stage is typical of tourists travelling in another country: on their return from holiday, they may feel a desire to go and live in the country, having only seen the positive aspects of life there.

2 *Rejection stage* – After further cultural interpenetration, the individual realizes that previous cultural norms are not adequate for dealing with the new culture, and that new norms and behaviours will need to be adopted. Often people become hostile to the new culture at this point, seeing the drawbacks rather than the advantages. Cultural conflicts are at a maximum in this stage.

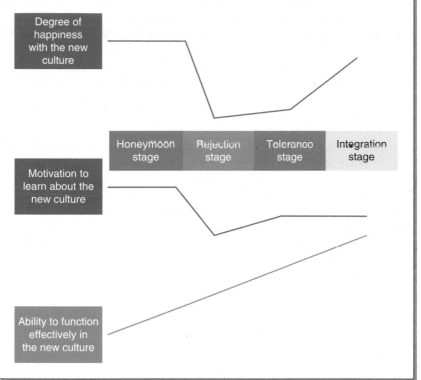

Figure 9.9

Stages in acculturation

3 *Tolerance stage* – Here the interactions have increased to the point where the individual accepts the new culture with all its drawbacks. This stage is reached by a process of cultural interpenetration, learning more about the new culture and reducing the level of cultural conflict.

4 *Integration stage* – At this stage the individual has made the necessary adjustments, valuing the new culture for its good qualities while still retaining important elements of the old culture. The new culture is seen as a perfectly viable way of life, as valid in its own way as the old culture.

In Figure 9.9, the individual's initial degree of happiness with the new culture is high in the honeymoon stage, as is motivation to learn about the culture: actual knowledge of the culture (and therefore ability to function well within it) is low. At the rejection stage, satisfaction with the culture drops dramatically, as does motivation to learn, but ability to function is still rising. With the tolerance stage comes a renewed interest in the culture, and also greater satisfaction with it: finally, in the integration stage the individual is functioning well, knows about the culture, and is consequently much happier within the culture. The initial disappointment at the rejection stage may account in part for the fact that the majority of immigrants return home within a few years.

Recent research has indicated the existence of cultural fractures caused by crossing borders (Davies and Fitchett 2004). These are as follows:

1 *Emotional fracture* – This can lead to feelings of loneliness and lack of a support infrastructure from friends and family left behind, or could be characterized by a willingness and ability to make new friends in the new country.

2 *Symbolic fracture* – This is characterized by running out of things to say in everyday conversation, not knowing what are the appropriate greetings for different people and having a difficulty in 'reading the signs' to understand what people are thinking or feeling. There is also a difficulty in understanding how people socialize in the new country.

3 *Functional fracture* – This is about the ease or difficulty of carrying out functional tasks such as opening a bank account, using trains and buses, or buying and preparing food.

4 *Culture shock* – This is how life in the new country differs from expectations.

5 *Consumer behaviour* – This is the gap between what one would buy at home and what one buys in the new country.

6 *Demographic fracture* – This is the disparity between the socioeconomic structure one was part of in the old culture, and the socioeconomic structure one finds oneself in in the new culture. Sometimes immigrants move down the social scale, sometimes up, depending on the relationship between the host country and the old country.

Gender may also be the basis for a subculture. Although there are relatively few products which are gender specific, there has been a growing re-acceptance in recent years that men and women's consumption behaviours are different in many ways. In the post-feminist era, women have developed 'girly' activities, and 'new laddism' has grown up as an exclusively male subculture. It would be a serious mistake to stereotype either gender: most men are not 'new lads' and most women do not spend their free time on girls' nights out or marathon shopping expeditions. However, these subcultures have become acceptable and are a part of the twenty-first century mainstream.

Brand-based subcultures also exist – Harley Davidson owners, football fans, World Wrestling fans, and so forth have an entire set of rules, beliefs and language surrounding the products they consume (Deeter-Schmelz and Sojka 2004).

Class

Some sociologists regard class as being one of the central concepts of the discipline, yet it is an ill-defined and ambiguous concept. For non-sociologists the concept of class is beginning to seem outmoded: at the beginning of the twentieth century, around 75 per cent of people in industrialized countries were manual workers of one sort or another, quite clearly distinct in behaviour and wealth from the better-educated white-collar workers and (of course) the aristocracy. As machines have largely taken over from muscle power, education has become universal and differential taxation has eroded differences of wealth, the differences between 'working class' and 'middle class' are almost undetectable. Even aristocrats now work for a living.

In the 1911 Census in the UK, the Government decided to record socioeconomic groupings for the first time. The system used is shown in Table 9.1.

This system of classification worked fairly well for several decades, but shifts in social patterns made much of its assumptions irrelevant: the table assumes that incomes are lower

Table 9.1 UK socioeconomic groupings

Social grade	Social status	Head of household's occupation
A	Upper middle class	Higher managerial, administration or professional
B	Middle class	Intermediate managerial, administrative or professional
C1	Lower middle class	Supervisory or clerical, junior managerial, administrative or professional
C2	Skilled working class	Skilled manual workers
D	Working class	Semi-skilled and unskilled manual workers
E	Lowest level of subsistence	Unemployed, casual or lowest-grade workers, state pensioners

further down the scale, but in the twenty-first century plumbers earn more than doctors (at least in much of Western Europe) and changing patterns of working life mean that today's labourer is tomorrow's film star (and vice versa). The basic lifestyles and indeed standards of living do not vary greatly between the groups – Group D individuals probably still own cars and have foreign holidays, even if Group A individuals run bigger cars and go to more exotic destinations. The classification, sometimes known as the ABC classification, is still used in a great deal of published market research: partly this is because it is familiar to researchers, and partly it is because researchers sometimes need to make comparisons with previous studies, but it is well-known that the system is seriously flawed.

In 2001 the UK Government introduced an alternative classification method, the Socioeconomic Classification System. This classification system has eight categories, the first of which can be subdivided: there is a ninth category, 'Not classified' which is reserved for students and people whose occupations have not been adequately described. The categories are as shown in Table 9.2.

Although this classification system is a better reflection of early twenty-first century society, it still suffers from a number of weaknesses common to all such classification systems. First, it does not take account of the possibility of rapid social movement: someone might change occupations very rapidly, without (presumably) changing lifestyle very much. Equally someone might change lifestyle rapidly without officially changing occupation – a teacher who decides to leave the inner-city school for a less stressful life in the country would be an example. Third, the classification usually refers to the head of the household, which might have been a reasonable concept in 1911 but which has many possible interpretations now. In 1911, the head of the household would almost certainly have been the father of the family, the main (and probably only) earner. In 2008, several people in the household are likely to be earning, and decision-making is likely to be shared in many different ways.

There is, of course, more to social class than occupation. Class implies a position in the power hierarchy: the further up the class ladder an individual is, the more power and influence he or she will have. This can vary from the small powers and discretions exercised by a warehouse manager up to the hire-and-fire decisions made by a managing director. Early sociologists such as Karl Marx and Max Weber examined social class: Marx saw class as being essentially about the power to set the prevailing intellectual climate: he said that 'The

Table 9.2 Socioeconomic classification system

Group	Occupation
1	Higher managerial and professional occupations
	1.1 Large employers and higher managerial occupations
	1.2 Higher professional occupations
2	Lower managerial and professional occupations
3	Intermediate occupations
4	Small employers and own account workers
5	Lower supervisory and technical occupations
6	Semi-routine occupations
7	Routine occupations
8	Never worked and long-term unemployed

Figure 9.10
Studying social class

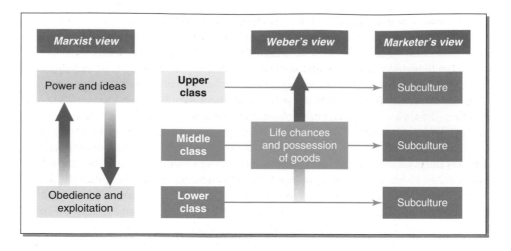

ideas of the ruling class are, in every epoch, the ruling ideas, i.e. the class which is the ruling material force of society, is at the same time its ruling intellectual force' (Marx and Engels 1848).

Weber defined class in terms of life chances (Weber 1946). For Weber, a class is a group of people who have in common a specific causal component of their life chances which is represented by possession of goods and opportunities for income, and which operates under the conditions of the commodity or labour markets. In other words, the individual's class is determined by the opportunities presented to that individual in terms of earning opportunities and the level of possession of goods.

Looked at in this way, it would appear that the individual's consumption pattern is as much a determining factor of social class as it is the result of social class. Those individuals who are able to accumulate possessions and improve their opportunities to earn money can move up the social scale. For example, a bricklayer would clearly be classified as working class (skilled manual worker). Yet if that same bricklayer saves some capital and sets up his own business he could eventually become a wealthy property developer or house builder and thus be redefined as middle class (managerial) or even upper middle class (higher managerial, larger employer). His basic attitudes and values might change a little during this process, but he would probably still define himself as working class. This type of social mobility is become more common as class barriers break down and educational opportunities increase.

Talking point

Social class seems to be a bit problematic. People move up and down the social scale, they have trouble defining their own social class never mind anybody else's, and changes in the structure of society in general mean that we have trouble now identifying classes anyway.

Is it still realistic to talk about social class at all? Can we really predict someone's behaviour based on how they earn a living? And if we take more factors into account, are we really looking at social class, or are we defining people in different ways?

In short, given that people in the twenty-first century are not only individuals but are also individualistic, is social class a concept that still has any relevance?

From the viewpoint of marketers, social class is more a reflection of the existence of a set of subcultures based on the education level, occupational requirements and economic power of the individual members. In this context, marketers use class-related imagery in advertising in order to involve the consumer. Although the old social class distinctions are disappearing, new social classes are emerging and new ways of categorizing people have appeared: the basis is still wealth, societal power, social skills, status aspirations, community participation, family history, cultural level, recreational habits, physical appearance and social acceptance (Kroeber-Riel and Weinberg 1996). Social class represents a set of subcultures because the class distinctions are generally agreed upon within the main culture, and the members of each class share most of their meanings and behaviours. The assumption is that people from one social class are less likely to mix socially with people from other social classes, preferring the company of members of their own class.

Social class is measured in two basic ways. People can be asked which social class they belong to (self-assignment), or their social class can be inferred from objective criteria. In market research, the latter approach is much more common, but in most cases respondents are only asked about their income, occupation and education level, which may not be the only determinants of social class. Certainly there is likely to be some discrepancy between a self-assignment and an objective measure in cases where there has been upward social mobility – an individual who comes from a working-class background but who has become educated, professional and wealthy might still self-assign him- or herself to the working-class category. Likewise the same might be true of someone who has been downwardly mobile, for example someone who dropped out of university to become a train driver.

More useful measures of social class have emerged in recent years, notably geodemographic measures such as ACORN and MOSAIC. These measures work by classifying people according to the area in which they live, which is likely to be a better indicator of social class than income or occupation data.

Overall, social class still has some relevance to marketing activities, but increasing social mobility and a steady reduction in wealth concentration are eroding the old distinctions between classes.

Summary

Consumer behaviour (and indeed all behaviour) happens against a backdrop of environmental and cultural factors. These vary from place to place and from time to time, and some of these variations are greater than others, but as consumers we have to learn to operate within the environment and culture we inhabit.

The environment of consumer behaviour includes the social environment as well as the physical environment. The social environment is the sum total of the human interactions that surround us, both those we are directly involved in and those we are not. Some of these interactions involve social class as well as personal behavioural preferences.

The physical environment includes store atmospherics, climatological elements, and so forth. These have a bearing on the mood of the customers – we are all affected by our physical surroundings, and clearly our moods affect our purchasing behaviour. What is difficult from a marketing viewpoint is to make accurate predictions of how the environment will affect our target group of customers.

The key points from this chapter are as follows:

- Atmospherics affect the degree of pleasure people obtain from the shopping experience, which in turn affects their approach-avoidance behaviour.

- The functional environment is subjective: it is affected by objective environmental factors, but the effects may not always be predictable.

- Cultural factors colour all our behaviour, not just our purchasing behaviour.

- High-context cultures have deeply embedded norms of behaviour.

- Low-context cultures are individualistic and characterized by change.

- Moving from one culture to another is almost always problematic in terms of learning to be a consumer.

- Class is as important now as it has ever been, but class distinctions are not the same as they were 50 years ago.

Chapter review questions

1 Why is it that other customers have an effect on store atmospherics?

2 What might be the problems for someone emigrating from a low-context culture to a high-context culture?

3 What might be the problems for someone emigrating from a high-context culture to a low-context culture?

4 How might social class affect consumption behaviour?

5 Which aspects of purchasing environment can be controlled by the store management, and which cannot?

6 What special marketing approaches might be useful at traditional gift-giving times?

7 What are the main problems with the ABC system of social classification?

8 What special difficulties might arise for a firm seeking to export products to a high-context culture?

9 What are the main criticisms of Hofstede's work?

10 How should marketers approach marketing to a subculture?

Preview case study revisited
Hard Rock Café

For Hard Rock, the biggest problem is ensuring that demand is evened out across the day's opening hours. Restaurants usually open around midday for lunch, then stay open until late into the evening, so inevitably there will be dead spots when customers will be few, and busy times when the customers flock in.

In many restaurants and bars, managers use price as a way of encouraging more customers during the quiet times, but Hard Rock pioneered using the restaurant environment as a way of flattening out the peaks and troughs of trade. Hard Rock's environment is all about music – music on the walls, music over the loudspeakers, and music in the waiters and waitresses. During the busy lunch period the restaurants play fast, loud rock (which is largely what the customers came for). The effect of this is to make the customers eat faster, and the waiters and waitresses move faster. The staff almost literally dance to the music, and the frenetic activity encourages an eat-and-run approach to lunch, while at the same time providing the diners with a seriously exciting lunch break. After lunch, the pace slows down: those who do not have to go back to work are treated to slower, ballad-like music and a less lively ambience. This encourages them to order another coffee or a dessert, and to chill out for a while.

Having people staying on for the afternoon serves two purposes: first, the customers are likely to spend more money on coffee or drinks, and second the restau-

rant always has customers in it. Restaurants always appear more inviting if they have people already in them, so passers-by are more likely to be attracted in for a snack or a drink.

Varying the music is the perfect way for Hard Rock to control its customer levels: it fits with the restaurant's image, it provides a unique experience, and it doesn't cost anything. Understanding consumer behaviour has certainly helped Hard Rock to grow into a global business – provided the supply of rock memorabilia doesn't run out, the restaurants are set to continue growing indefinitely.

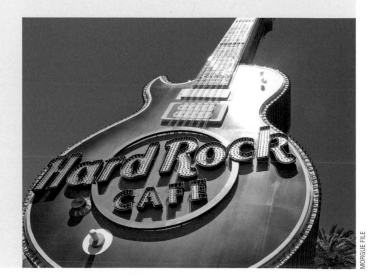

Case study
Tweenager fashion victims

In recent years a new consumer phenomenon has hit Britain: the tweenager. Tweenagers are children aged between 8 and 13 – out of babyhood, not yet teenagers – and in previous years they have been a negligible force in consumerism. Now, though, with increasing prosperity of their parents and themselves, tweenagers are becoming a market segment in their own right.

In some cases the children have enough money of their own (supplied by generous parents) to make any purchases they want. In other cases parents supply the cash, either in exchange for good behaviour or simply because they do not want their child to feel left out or be ridiculed by the other children. A recent study by academics at Leicester University found that tweenagers were becoming obsessed by fashion: 'It's just Kookaï mania at our school' one girl said.

The trend is not just confined to girls. Dean, aged 10, takes an hour to get ready for school each morning, and not because he is playing with his train set. He wears designer labels such as Diesel and Lacoste, and uses DKNY aftershave even though he does not, technically, need to shave yet. He goes on to recount an episode in which his friends made fun of him because he was wearing last year's trainers, but instead of bursting into tears or fighting, Dean went home and changed into his 'good stuff', including this year's trainers.

The research also showed that middle-class parents were more likely to accept the idea of dressing their children in hand-me-downs than were working-class parents, who tended to dress their children in the latest fashions. Middle-class parents looked for quality and durability rather than fashion trends, and seemed more likely to be able to withstand the pressure from their children.

Datamonitor, the research organization, says that three social trends are driving the tweenager revolution. First, people are having children later and having fewer of them (often only one child). This means that they have more money to lavish on the children. Second, with both parents working there is less time to spend with the children, so spending money on them is (at least potentially) a way of feeling less guilty. Third, the rising divorce rate means that children are better able to wheedle money out of one or other parent (or even both), especially if the wheedled parent is the one who spends the least time with the child. Another possible driver for the tweenager phenomenon is the 'trophy child' syndrome in which the children are dressed expensively as a way of showing how wealthy the family is. This theory moves away from the idea that it is the children who pester the parents for the latest fashions – it may be that the parents are encouraging the children to dress in designer outfits, or at least are complicit in the process.

Targeting tweenagers is far from easy – if marketers pitch their advertisements too low, the tweenagers will feel patronized, but if they pitch them too high tweenagers might feel that the product is aimed at an older audience. In most cases the marketers are likely to score well by apparently targeting the communication at teenagers, because tweenagers are so keen to grow up quickly.

Of course there is a downside to all this. Manufacturers of dollies and toy trucks might find themselves out in the cold as children go from age 7 to age 25 in one leap. Second, tweenagers are extremely marketing-literate: they know that they are being manipulated, and at present they are prepared to go along with it, but as future consumers they may turn out to have already done all the consuming they want to do. Third, because tweenagers are the result of a falling birthrate and a rising divorce rate there will be fewer adults in future markets, in particular relatively fewer young adults. Many people who work with children (teachers, social workers and so forth) believe that becoming such avid consumers so early is damaging children's development.

From a marketing viewpoint, tweenagers are a shrinking market: according to the Datamonitor report, there were 16.7 million tweenagers in Europe in 1997, compared with 15.4 million in 2007. Also, tweenagers are notoriously fickle: this year's 13-year-olds are not interested in products their 15-year-old siblings bought two years ago. This makes for a very volatile market. Finally, there is some evidence that

YVES SAINT LAURENT
enfants

ADVERTISING ARCHIVES

parents are seeking to limit their children's pocket money, on the basis that they do not approve of what the children are buying.

Whatever the long-term effects, though, tweenagers are a phenomenon to be reckoned with, and will certainly be a major target market in the fashion industry for several years to come.

Case study questions

1   What is the role of social class in the tweenager phenomenon?

2   What social changes have driven the changes in buying habits of pre-teens?

3   What cultural effects might result in the long term as tweenagers grow up?

4   How might demographic changes affect the tweenager market?

5   Why might fashion be the main focus for tweenager buying rather than (say) expensive toys?

References

Andreasen, Alan R. (1990) Cultural interpenetration: a critical consumer research issue for the 1990s. *Advances in Consumer Research*, 17 eds Marvin E. Goldberg, Gerald Gorn and Richard W. Pollay (Provo, UT: Association for Consumer Research): 847–9.

Askegaard, Soren, and Madsen, Tage Koed (1995) *European Food Cultures: an Exploratory Analysis of Food Related Preferences and Behaviour in European Regions*. MAPP Working Paper no. 26 (Aarhus: The Aarhus School of Business).

Baker, J., Levy, M., and Grewal, D. (1992) An experimental approach to making retail store environmental decisions. *Journal of Retailing*, 68: 445–61.

Bann, Graham (1996) Race for opportunity. *New Impact Journal*, Dec 1996–Jan 1997: 8–9.

Bellizzi, J.A. Crowley, A.E., and Hasty, R.W. (1983) The effects of colour in store design. *Journal of Retailing*, 59: 21–45.

Block, Jack, and Block, Jeanne H. (1981) Studying situational dimensions: a grand perspective and some limited empiricism. *Toward a Psychology of Situations: An International Perspective*, ed. David Magnusson (Hillsdale, NJ: Lawrence Erlbaum).

Brunso, Karen, Grunert, Klaus G., and Bredahl, Lone (1996) *An analysis of national and cross-national consumer segments using the food-related lifestyle instrument in Denmark, France, Germany and Great Britain*. MAPP Working Paper no. 35 (Aarhus: Aarhus School of Business).

Davies, Andrea, and Fitchett, James (2004) Crossing culture: a multi-method enquiry into consumer behaviour and the experience of cultural transition. *Journal of Consumer Behaviour*, 3(4): 315–30.

Deeter-Schmelz, Dawn R., and Sojka, Jane Z. (2004) Wrestling with American values: an exploratory investigation of World Wrestling Entertainment as a product-based subculture. *Journal of Consumer Behaviour*, 4(2): 132–43.

Eroglu, S., and Harrell, G.D. (1986): Retail crowding: theoretical and strategic implications. *Journal of Retailing*, 62: 346–63.

Eurostat (2002) *The Social Situation in the European Union 2002*. (Luxembourg: Office for Official Publications of the European Union).

Faber, Ronald J., O'Guinn, Thomas C., and McCarty, John A. (1987) Ethnicity, acculturation, and the importance of product attributes. *Psychology and Marketing*, summer: 121–34.

Gabel, Terrance G., and Boller, Gregory W. (2003) A preliminary look into the globalization of the tortilla in Mexico. *Advances in Consumer Research*, 30(1): 135–41.

Hofstede, G. (1980) *Culture's Consequences* (Beverley Hills, CA: Sage).

Kates, Steven (2002) Doing brand and subcultural ethnographies: developing the interpretive community concept in consumer research. *Advances in Consumer Research*, 29(1): 43.

Kellaris, J.J., and Kent, R.J. (1992) The influence of music on consumers' temporal perceptions: does time fly when you're having fun? *Journal of Consumer Psychology*, (1): 365–76.

Kotler, P. (1973) Atmospherics as a marketing tool. *Journal of Retailing*, 49 (winter): 48–64.

Kroeber-Riel, Werner, and Weinberg, Peter (1996) *Konsumentenverhalten* 6th ed. (Munich: Vahlen).

Marx, Karl, and Engels, Frederick (1848) *The Manifesto of the Communist Party*. (London: The Communist League).

McCarty, John A., Horn, Martin I., and Szenasy, Mary Kate (2007): An exploratory study of consumer style: country differences and international segments. *Journal of Consumer Behaviour*, 6 (Jan–Feb): 48–59.

Mehrabian, A., and Russell, J.A. (1974) *An Approach to Environmental Psychology.* (Cambridge, MA: MIT Press).

Miller, Daniel (1995) Consumption as the vanguard of history. *Acknowledging Consumption,* ed. D. Miller (London: Routledge).

National Statistics Office (2005) *Focus on Older People* (London: National Statistics Office).

Oberg, Kalervo (1960): Cultural shock: adjustment to new cultural environments. *Practical Anthropologist*, 7: 177–82.

Park, C. Whan, Iyer, Easwar S., and Smith, Daniel C. (1989) The effects of situational factors on in-store grocery shopping behaviour: the role of store environment and time available for shopping. *Journal of Consumer Research*, March: 422–33.

Penaloza, Lisa N. (1989) Immigrant consumer acculturation. *Advances in Consumer Research*, 16, ed. Thomas K. Skrull (Provo, UT: Association for Consumer Research): 110–18, 121–34.

Philips, H., and Bradshaw, R. (1990) How customers actually shop: customer interaction with the point of sale. *Journal of the Market Research Society*, 35: 51–62.

Richardson, Brendan, and Turley, Darach (2006) Support your local team: resistance, subculture and the desire for distinction. *Advances in Consumer Research*, 33(1): 175–80.

Sudbury, Lynn, and Wilberforce, Fiona (2006) The portrayal of black people in UK television advertising: perception and reality. *Journal of Consumer Behaviour*, 5 (Sept–Oct): 465–76.

Tai, Susan H.C., and Fung, Agnes M.C. (1997) Application of an environmental psychology model to in-store buying behaviour. *International Review of Retail, Distribution and Consumer Research*, 7 (October), 4: 311–37.

Waldfogel, Joel (1993) The deadweight loss of Christmas. *American Economic Review*, 83(5): 1328–36.

Weber, Max (1946) Class, status, party. Published posthumously in Hans H. Gerth, and C. Wright Mills (eds) *From Max Weber.* (Oxford: Oxford University Press).

Yorkston, Eric, and deMello, Gustavo (2004) Sex sells? The effects of gender marking on consumers' evaluations of branded products across languages. *Advances in Consumer Research*, 31(1): 148–9.

Zwick, Detlev, and Chelariu, Cristian (2006) Mobilising the hijab: Islamic identity negotiation in the context of a matchmaking website. *Journal of Consumer Behaviour*, 5 (Jul–Aug): 380–95.

Chapter 10
Peer and reference groups

Learning objectives After reading this chapter, you should be able to:

1. explain how reference groups influence individual members

2. explain what is meant by normative compliance

3. describe the main drivers for normative compliance

4. explain the role of word of mouth communication

5. describe ways of handling complaints

6. explain the importance of e-mail communication

Introduction

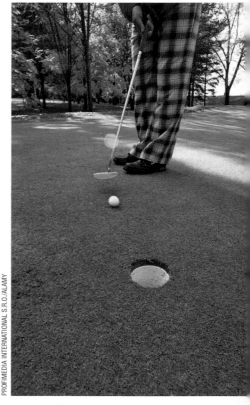

PROFIMEDIA INTERNATIONAL S.R.O./ALAMY

Human beings are social animals: we form ourselves into groups, and in fact most of us are members of several different groups, formed for different purposes. In most cases, we join groups because we can achieve more as part of a group than we can as an individual, but there are some groups which we belong to without ever having made a voluntary decision to join. Examples are our gender group, our ethnic or racial group and our family group. Because the family is such an important group it has a chapter to itself: this chapter deals with other groups which affect consumption.

Groups have considerable influence on our buying behaviour, either because we need to own certain items in order to join the group (there is no point in joining a golf club if one does not own a set of golf clubs, for example, although the loud check trousers are usually optional), or because we have joint consumption within the group for the purposes of saving ourselves time, money or effort. For example, a yacht club is able to share facilities such as berthing, a club house, maintenance facilities, and so forth.

Sociology is the study of human behaviour in groups, so much of the research into groups comes from sociologists rather than from marketing academics. Marketers are, of course, mainly interested in how group behaviour affects purchasing behaviour.

Peer and reference groups

A group is two or more persons who share a set of norms and whose relationship makes their behaviour interdependent. A **reference group** is 'A person or group of people that significantly influences an individual's behaviour' (Beardon and Etzel 1982, p. 184). The reference groups provide standards or norms by which consumers judge their attitudes and behaviour.

Originally groups formed for the purpose of cooperating on survival activities. Because human beings could cooperate in such activities as hunting, food-gathering and defence from predators, we were able to increase the chances of survival for the species as a whole. Interestingly, this still appears to hold true: social researchers have reported that socially isolated people have mortality rates between 50 per cent and 300 per cent higher than people who are strongly integrated into groups (Koretz 1990). For all of human history we have cooperated with each other to survive and prosper, and we continue to do so for both practical and social reasons.

Loud check trousers are not compulsory for golf club members, but many still prefer them.

Preview case study
Children and Youth Health Service

South Australia is an amazingly diverse place. As the jumping-off point for the Outback, it has a significant proportion of wild country as well as the sophisticated city of Adelaide. It has one of Australia's premier wine-growing regions. It has a substantial aboriginal population and also a considerable tourist trade – Kangaroo Island has an incredible concentration of Australian wildlife, for example, as well as geological features such as the Remarkable Rocks. In Adelaide itself the contrasts can be extreme – in the restaurants, one can find kangaroo meat cooked Szechuan style on a bed of leeks, and in the streets one can find hard-bitten settlers from the Outback rubbing shoulders with chartered accountants catching the tram out to the seaside suburb of Glenelg.

Unsurprisingly perhaps, and in common with many other parts of the world, South Australia has problems with alcohol. Alcoholism among the aborigine population is much more common than among other Australians, and also there has been a worrying increase in underage drinking in recent years. In 2002, over 90 per cent of students aged 12 to 17 reported having consumed alcohol within the last week. Given that alcohol was the main drug of concern in more than half of all treatments at drug abuse units in the state, and that the abuse of alcohol tends to increase with age, the South Australian Government decided that something had to be done to nip the problem in the bud.

Other potentially dangerous activities by underage children and youths were also targeted. Use of illicit drugs, vandalism, shoplifting and underage sexual activity were growing problems as well: although it would be unfair to say that young people were getting completely out of control, the Government knew that things were moving on from occasional experimentation and boisterous behaviour, and towards a serious delinquency problem. Perhaps more importantly, it was the most vulnerable kids who were most likely to get into difficulties.

The solution was to set up the Children and Youth Health Service. This service was given the role of persuading children away from inappropriate behaviour – but the service quickly found that preaching at children wasn't going to work!

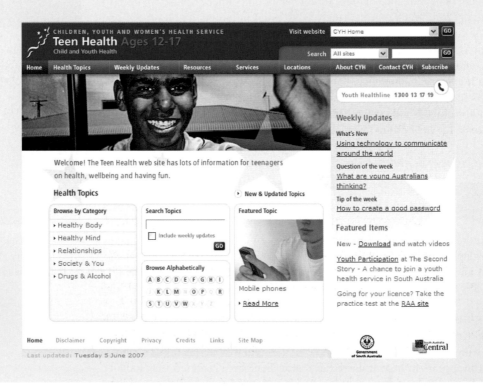

Most people prefer to fit in with the group (to a greater or lesser extent). This is either through politeness or through a desire not to be left out of things. Particularly when they are with groups of friends, people will 'go along with the crowd' on a great many issues, and will tend to adopt the group norms regarding behaviour and attitudes. Experiments conducted by Solomon Asch in 1951 demonstrated this in a graphic manner. In the experiment, subjects were asked to judge the lengths of different lines. The lines were displayed on a large board, and each person was seated with a group of strangers who were also supposed to be making judgements about the line lengths. In fact the strangers were Asch's assistants who had been instructed to agree with each other about the length of each line, but to make errors; the experimental subjects consistently agreed with these errors, even though the errors were sometimes glaringly obvious. Respondents did not make the same mistakes when there were no other people present, however. It appears from this that the fear of seeming foolish or of being the odd one out is enough to make the individual doubt the evidence of his or her eyes, or at the very least to lie about the evidence (Asch 1951).

Responses to group pressures may, in some circumstances, be gender-specific. Fisher and Dube (2003) found that men and women respond differently to emotional advertising depending on whether other people are present or not. Specifically, women show the same emotional responses to advertisements whether other people are present or not, whereas men are affected by the presence of others, especially if the emotional response is regarded as gender-specific. For example, an advertisement which causes someone to shed tears would cause the same response in a woman whether or not other people are around, whereas a man would be more likely to suppress this response if others are present (even if he were to shed a tear when in private).

Perception of what is fair and what is not also seems to be influenced by social interaction with the group one happens to be in at the time (Carlson and Sally 2002). For example, when associating with a group of middle-class professionals one might perceive welfare payments as unfair, since they are paid for by hard-working taxpayers: in the company of a more left-wing group, one might perceive welfare payments as unfair because they do not provide enough money for a dignified and comfortable lifestyle.

Talking point

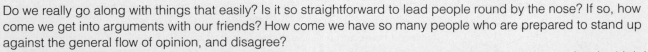

Do we really go along with things that easily? Is it so straightforward to lead people round by the nose? If so, how come we get into arguments with our friends? How come we have so many people who are prepared to stand up against the general flow of opinion, and disagree?

Asch's experiment might just show that students try to please their lecturers, or that people try to give the 'right' answers in situations which look a lot like exams. Or maybe the results are good, but only when we are in the company of strangers – does our natural politeness (and fear of a punch in the mouth) make us wary of arguing with someone we know nothing about?

Reference groups fall into many possible groupings; the following list is not intended to be exhaustive.

Primary groups are composed of those people we see most often; friends, family, and close colleagues. A primary group is small enough to permit face-to-face interaction on a regular basis, and there is cohesiveness and mutual participation which results in similar beliefs and behaviour within the group. Because people tend to choose friends who think in similar ways, and have similar interests, the primary group is often very cohesive and long-lasting. Possibly the strongest primary group is the family, but the primary groups might be close friends, colleagues in work, or people with whom we share a hobby.

Secondary groups are composed of people we see occasionally, and with whom we have some shared interest. For example, a trade association or a sports club would constitute a secondary group. These groups are correspondingly less influential in shaping attitudes and controlling behaviour, but can exert influence on behaviour within the purview of the subject of mutual interest. For example, if you are a member of a cycling club, you may be persuaded to take part in a sponsored bike ride, or perhaps a protest in favour of creating more cycle lanes. Within a secondary group, primary groups will sometimes form; there will often be groups of special friends whose shared interests go beyond those of the rest of the secondary group. For example, a cycling enthusiast might have a close friend with whom he cycles regularly: the friends might be members of a cycling club, and arrange with a few other members of the club to go on an evening out. In this example, the friends are a primary group, but met through a secondary group (the cycling club) and formed a new primary group to enjoy a different shared interest (the evening out).

Aspirational groups are the groups which the individual wants to join. These groups can be very powerful in influencing behaviour, because the individual will often adopt the behaviour of the aspirational group in the hopes of being accepted as a member. Sometimes the aspirational group will be better off financially, sometimes it will be more powerful; the desire to join such groups is usually classed as ambition. For example, a humble office worker may dream of one day having the key to the executive washroom. Advertising commonly uses images of aspirational groups, implying that use of a particular product will move the individual a little closer to being a member of an aspirational group.

Dissociative groups on the other hand are those groups which the individual does not want to be associated with. Like a backpacker who does not want to look like a typical tourist, or a Marxist who would not want to be mistaken for a capitalist, the individual tries to avoid dissociative groups. This can have a negative effect on behaviour; the individual avoids certain products or behaviours rather than be taken for somebody from the dissociative group. Like aspirational groups, the definition of a group as dissociative is purely subjective; it varies from one individual to the next.

Formal groups have a known list of members, very often recorded somewhere. An example might be a professional association or a club. Usually the rules and structure of the group are laid down in writing; there are rules for membership and members' behaviour is constrained while they remain part of the group. However, the constraints usually only apply to fairly limited areas of behaviour; for example, the Chartered Institute of Marketing lays down a code of practice for marketers in their professional dealings, but has no interest in what its members do as private citizens. Membership of such groups may confer special privileges, such as job advancement or use of club facilities, and may lead to responsibilities in the furtherance of the group's aims.

Informal groups are less structured, and are typically based on friendship. An example would be an individual's circle of friends, which only exists for mutual moral support, company and sharing experiences. Although there can be even greater pressure to conform than would be the case with a formal group, there is no written set of rules. Often informal groups expect a more rigorous standard of behaviour across a wider range of activities than would a formal group; such circles of friends are likely to develop rules of behaviour and traditions that are more binding than written rules.

Automatic groups are those groups to which one belongs by virtue of age, gender, culture or education. These are sometimes also called **category groups**. Although at first sight it would appear that these groups would not exert much influence on the members' behaviour, because these are groups which have not been joined voluntarily, it would appear that people are influenced by group pressure to conform. For example, when buying clothes older people are sometimes reluctant to look like 'mutton dressed as lamb'. Also, membership of some racial groups can influence behaviour because of the associated physical characteristics: some cosmetics are specifically designed for skin and hair types which are genetically determined.

Football fans show their loyalty by buying team strips and flags and behaving in specific ways at matches.

Virtual groups are a recent phenomenon, brought about as a result of chatrooms on the Internet (Okleshen and Grossbart 1998). The communication is virtual rather than face to face, which means that people can (in effect) be whoever they say they are. Such Internet communities are based on social interactions which can often be more open and uninhibited than would be the case in a real space rather than a virtual space (Fischer, Bristor and Gainer 1996). This allows people to express views which might be controversial, and of course since the chatrooms are not geographically based, people with unusual interests (such as collecting rare whiskies or building light aircraft) are able to share information much more easily. Satisfaction with virtual communities such as chatrooms comes from interactions with the members: the organizers of chatrooms have little influence over this (Langerak, Verhoef and Verleigh 2004). On the one hand, chatrooms allow individuals to discuss issues of common interest, and to share information about whatever topics interest them (however obscure). On the other hand, chatrooms open up possibilities for people to misrepresent themselves, perhaps for social purposes (for example to appear more interesting or desirable), or perhaps for criminal purposes such as fraud or paedophilia.

There are four types of virtual community, as follows (Muniz and O'Guinn 2001):

- *Brand communities* – These are groups who have a shared interest in a specific brand, for example owners of a particular motorcycle or classic car. These groups share experiences, help each other with obtaining peripherals, spare parts etc., and offer each other advice when things go wrong.

- *Communities of interest* – Typically these are hobby sites: people who share an interest in a sport or have a professional interest.

- *Fantasy communities* – These are based on games, whether fantasy games or ordinary games such as chess or bridge.

- *Relationship communities* – These are based on common shared problems and experience – for example support groups for those with mental illness or for crime victims, or action groups who campaign for reform.

The above categories of group are not mutually exclusive. A dissociative group could also be an informal one; a formal group can be a secondary group (and often is) and so forth.

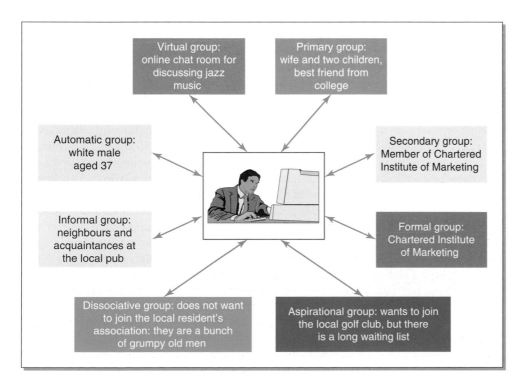

Figure 10.1

An individual and his reference groups

For example, one may not wish to become friends with a group of drunken hooligans (who see themselves as an informal group of friends having a good time). Likewise the golf club could be a place of refuge to which one retreats to have a quiet drink with like-minded people, as well as a place where golf is played.

Reference groups affect people in several ways. First, groups tend to modify members' behaviour through a process of socialization. This is a learning process for the individual, leading to an understanding of which behaviours are acceptable within the group and which are not. For example, there may be a formal set of rules laid down by a golf club regarding care of the greens, dress codes, behaviour in the clubhouse and so forth, but it is the members who will advise new members on which rules are essential and which are often ignored. More importantly, the existing members will advise new members on behaviour which is expected, but which is not in the written rules – for example, buying a round of drinks when one scores a hole in one. Going shopping with friends is an important way of learning what is appropriate and what is not, which may be one of the reasons why adolescent females spend a lot of time shopping with friends (Haytko and Baker 2004). Shopping also provides a shared activity which develops social education, companionship, and an understanding of what is safe and what is not in the adult world.

Talking point

If shopping has become a hobby, and more particularly an educational experience for young teenage girls, marketers must think they've finally struck gold! But how true is it that young girls behave in this way? Haytko and Baker's research was conducted in the United States, where 'going to the mall' is inbuilt to the culture. But does it apply in Europe, or elsewhere in the world?

Would most European shopping malls be happy for gangs of teenagers to be hanging around anyway? And is the situation in Europe different culturally? Maybe we don't rely on malls so much because there are other places for teenagers to go – but in some places we only have the street corners. Maybe malls are a better way to go after all!

Second, people develop a self-concept through their interactions within groups. How we see ourselves is a result of how others see us: feedback from others is the basis of our understanding of who we are. This is particularly apparent when the group has a specific purpose such as supporting a football team: supporters often wear uniforms to show which team they support, thus identifying with the group and also projecting their own identity, not only to the group but to any other observers. This is a way of blending one's personal identity with the culture surrounding the team (Oliver 1999). Marketers use this aspect of group behaviour to sell the uniforms, and also it is a feature of celebrity endorsement – by using a particular product, the individual associates himself or herself with the celebrity.

Third, groups affect people through conformity. This is a change in beliefs or actions based on group pressures. There are two types of conformity: compliance and acceptance. Compliance happens when an individual goes along with the behaviour of the group without really accepting its beliefs. For example, someone who is not a football supporter might accompany a friend to a match and cheer on the friend's team without actually having any long-term interest in the team's fortunes. Compliance is common in the workplace. Acceptance occurs when the individual not only adapts behaviour, but also adapts his or her beliefs to come into line with the group. This might happen if the non-supporter decides that the experience was so exciting, and the team played so well, that he (or she) decides to become a supporter. Acceptance commonly occurs through religious conversions. Overall, conformity can be considered as behaviour one adopts by observing others when confronted with membership of a new group: it is most likely to occur when the costs of conforming are outweighed by the advantages. Advantages might include self-esteem, acceptance by an aspirational group, companionship, practical benefits such as potential for earning or saving money, and so forth (Homans 1961).

Fourth, people use groups for social comparison. We evaluate ourselves by comparing our performance with others, for example when we consider our wealth or our social standing we compare ourselves with people whom we consider to be our equals on other respects.

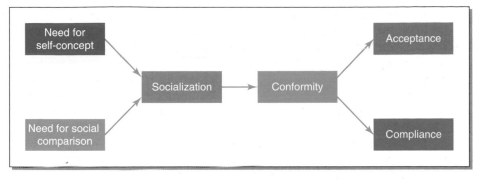

Figure 10.2
Modifying behaviour through groups

Comparisons are not necessarily made with groups with whom we have personal contact: for example, a lawyer might compare his or her salary with what other lawyers earn, or alternatively might make the comparison with other professionals such as doctors or accountants. If the groups are similar, the individual has greater confidence in the comparison (Tesser, Miller and Moore 1988), but people generally value differing views when they are themselves confident in their own ability and opinions (Wheeler *et al.* 1969). This may explain why some people opt for cosmetic surgery (nose jobs, liposuction, breast implants etc.) whereas other people are apparently quite happy to live with physical 'imperfections'.

In Figure 10.2, the need for social comparison and self-concept drive the socialization process. These are the reasons why people are prepared to accept socialization. The result of socialization is conformity, either by acceptance or by compliance.

The mechanisms by which reference groups affect consumer behaviour are shown in Table 10.1 and Figure 10.3.

Table 10.1 Effects of reference groups on consumer choice

Type of influence	Definition	Explanation	Example
Normative compliance	The pressure exerted on an individual to conform and comply.	Works best when social acceptance is a strong motive, strong pressures exist from the group, and the product or service is conspicuous in its use.	Street gangs require their members to wear specific jackets or other uniform. The members want to be accepted, the pressure to wear the jacket is great, and the jacket itself is a conspicuous badge of membership.
Value-expressive influence (Burnkrant and Cousineau 1975)	The pressure that comes from the need for psychological association with a group.	The desired outcome is respect from others; this pressure comes from the need for esteem, rather than from the need to belong.	The businessman in his pinstripe suit, the hippy in his colourful shirt, sweatband and jeans – both are seeking respect from others by expressing a set of values in the way they dress.
Informational influence (Calder and Burnkrant 1977)	The influence arising from a need to seek information from the reference group about the product category being considered.	People often need to get expert advice and opinion about their product choices. This can often be provided by the appropriate reference group.	Many professional organizations and trade bodies offer their members free advice about useful products for their businesses. Clearly a recommendation on, say, computer software for a hairdressing business would be well received if it came from the Hairdressers' Federation.

Figure 10.3

Mechanisms for controlling behaviour

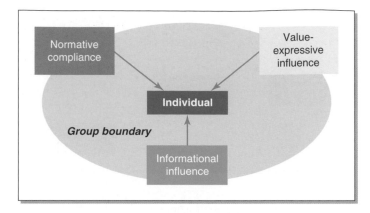

Of the above three influences, **normative compliance** is probably the most powerful. The source of normative compliance lies in **operant conditioning**; the individual finds that conforming behaviour results in group approval and esteem, whereas non-conforming behaviour results in group disapproval. Eventually the 'good' behaviour becomes automatic and natural, and it would be difficult to imagine any other way of doing things (see Chapter 6 for more on operant conditioning). The principles of good moral behaviour are not absolutes; they are the result (in most cases) of normative compliance with a reference group. Normative compliance may be less important now than it used to be for four reasons: first, the influence of the extended family (grandparents, parents, aunts and uncles) may be reducing as people move away from their home towns, and second there is strong evidence that people are becoming more inner-directed (McNulty 1985). Third, the reduction in face-to-face interaction may be leading to this move away from normative compliance; increasingly people communicate by impersonal means such as text messages and e-mail. Whether this is a cause of the paradigm shift or one of its effects is difficult to decide at present. Fourth, there is a weakening of respect for social norms, generated by a feeling of alienation from society. This is called 'anomie' by sociologists (Durkheim 1951). Some people have little or no respect for rules made by other people, and conform grudgingly or not at all, because they do not feel that they have a position within society as a whole.

Of course, the pressure to conform will only work on someone who has a strong motivation to be accepted. If the pressure is coming from an aspirational group, this is likely to be the case; if, on the other hand, the pressure is coming from a dissociative group, the reverse will be the case and the individual will not feel under any pressure to conform. For example, most law-abiding citizens would comply with instructions from the police, and would usually go out of their way to help the police. Criminals, on the other hand, might avoid helping the police even in circumstances where their own crimes were not at issue.

The conspicuousness of the product or service is also crucial to the operation of normative compliance. For example, if all your friends vote Labour you might be under some pressure to do likewise, but since the ballot is secret nobody will know if you vote Conservative instead, so there is little pressure for normative compliance. Likewise, if your friends all drink Stella Artois lager you may feel under pressure to do the same, but might be happy with supermarket own-brand when you're having a beer in the back garden at home.

Advertisers often appeal to the need to belong to an aspirational group. Advertising which shows desirable groups

Most people are happy to help the police solve crimes, as part of being good members of society.

having a good time together, all thanks to the product, are so common that they are regarded as clichés. Typically, products with a social element such as beer, entertainment and some food products are advertised in this way.

The reference group will not exert influence over every buying decision. Even in circumstances where group influence does come into play, the consumer will be influenced by other variables such as product characteristics, standards of judgement, and conflicting influences from other groups. Table 10.2 shows some of the determinants of reference group influence.

Table 10.2 Determinants of reference group influence

Determinant	Definition	Explanation	Example
Judgement standards	The criteria used by the individual to evaluate the need to conform.	Judgement standards are objective when the group norms are obvious and when the group approach is clearly the sensible course of action. The standards are subjective when it is not clear which is the most sensible course of action.	Decisions of boards of directors are often portrayed as being unanimous because it is important to present a united front when dealing with shareholders or employees. On the other hand, it is not unusual for politicians to disagree with their leaders in public in situations where controversial issues are being discussed.
Product characteristics	The features of the product that are salient to the group influence.	The two main characteristics necessary for group influence to work are that the product should be visible, and that it should stand out (non-universal ownership).	A member of a judo club will be proud to wear the black belt, since it not only denotes a high level of expertise, but it is not available to other members unless they achieve the same level.
Member characteristics	The traits of the group member which make him or her more or less susceptible to group pressures.	People vary considerably in the degree to which they are influenced by the pressures from the group. Some people remain fairly independent, where others conform habitually. Personality, status and security all seem to play major roles in determining whether an individual will conform or not.	It transpires that university students are much more likely to conform with group norms than are housewives (Manz and Sims 1981). This is possibly because the university students are young, poor and often away from home so have a greater need to belong.
Group characteristics	The features of the group that influence individuals to conform.	The power of the group to influence the individual varies according to size, cohesiveness and leadership. Once the group is bigger than three members, the power to influence levels off. This is probably because the group has difficulty reaching a consensus. Likewise, the stronger the leadership the greater the influence, and the greater the cohesiveness the stronger the influence, because the group reaches a clear decision.	Most smokers begin take up the habit as a result of peer group pressure when they are aged around 12 or 13. If a child's friends are strongly anti-smoking, the influence from advertisers and even family background is likely to be much less of an influence.

(Continued)

Table 10.2 Determinants of reference group influence (*Continued*)

Determinant	Definition	Explanation	Example
Role model	An individual whose influence is similar to that of a group.	A role model is a hero, a star or just somebody the individual respects and admires, and wishes to imitate.	Many young women seek to imitate top models by extreme dieting, to the extent that the Madrid fashion week banned all models with a body mass index below 18: Milan threatened to follow suit (BBC 2006). During the 1930s, when Clark Gable took off his shirt in a movie and showed that he was not wearing a vest, sales of vests plummeted because it became non-macho to wear one.

Modelling was briefly discussed in Chapter 2, with regard to motivation and pain avoidance. The effectiveness of the **role model** in modelling behaviour will depend on the personal characteristics of the role model. Attractive models will be imitated more than unattractive ones; successful-looking models are given more credence than unsuccessful-looking ones, and a model who is perceived as being similar to the observer is also more likely to be emulated (Baker and Churchill 1977).

There is also some evidence to show that observers are more likely to identify with role models who have some difficulty in completing the modelled task (Manz and Sims 1981). There has, of course, been debate about whether crime shows on TV encourage people to copy the behaviour which is shown in the programmes; according to the theory, modelled behaviour will be copied if the observer feels able to identify with the role model. Presumably, therefore, a programme showing young working-class men making a living from selling hard drugs might encourage other young working-class men to do the same. However, the saving grace of this scenario is that the role model must also be seen to be successful and attractive – and in most TV dramas and movies the criminal is shown as being, ultimately, unsuccessful.

Some recent research has shown that role models can be too good to be true – Superman turns out to be too super, so that people who compare themselves to Superman are less likely to volunteer to help others, simply because they feel that they do not measure up to the role model (Nelson and Norton 2004).

Figure 10.4

Factors in modelling

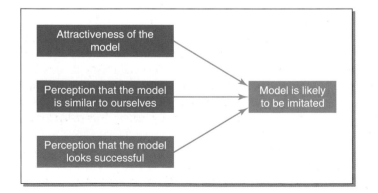

Mechanisms of personal influence

Personal influence is commonly conducted via word of mouth. Word of mouth communication is informal, and is conducted between individuals, neither of whom is a marketer. Word of mouth is therefore conducted without the ulterior motive of profiting from a sale.

Groups and individuals obviously have a strong influence on people's attitudes and behaviour through word of mouth; there are three main theories regarding the mechanisms whereby this personal influence is exerted (Figures 10.5 and 10.6, page 222). The history of the theory is not so much one of advancing knowledge about the mechanisms involved, but is rather a history of the way society has changed in the period in which the theories were evolving.

Trickle-down theory says that lower-class people often imitate upper-class people (Veblen 1899). Influence is transmitted down from the wealthier classes to the poorer classes, as the poorer groups in society seek to 'better themselves'. In fact, trickle-down is rarely seen in industrialized, wealthy countries like the UK because new ideas are disseminated overnight by the mass media and copied by chain stores within days. This is particularly true of clothing fashions, and the Punk revolution in the mid-1970s was an example of 'trickle-up' where the fashion came up from the poorer classes. What is replacing trickle-down theory is **homophilous influence**, which refers to transmission between those of similar age, education, social class, etc. in other words those who already have a lot in common. The main area in which trickle-down theory can be observed is in the cult of celebrity – famous people are frequently imitated, and marketers use this to their advantage by obtaining celebrity endorsements of products. Soap operas play an important role here, because they mimic group life in the real world, so much so that people often associate themselves with the cast of a soap opera in the same way as they would with a real group of people. This can affect people's aspirational consumption patterns (Russell and Stern 2006).

Talking point

Obviously in the early twenty-first century we are well beyond the forelock-tugging attitude of our Victorian forebears, aren't we? Or are we? We may not have much respect for the opinions of the aristocracy, but there are other opinion leaders around – rock stars, TV stars, footballers, and so forth. Even the subtle aristocracy of the TV chef has an influence on what we eat.

The plethora of 'I'm a Celebrity' TV shows, where C-list 'celebrities' whom nobody has heard of put themselves into embarrassing situations demonstrates that people still have an interest in what the famous have to say. Or is it simply that we like to see the once-famous come a cropper?

Two-step flow theory says that new ideas flow from the media to 'influentials' who then pass the information on to the rest of society (Lazarsfield, Berelson and Gaudet 1948). When this theory was first formulated in the late 1940s and early 1950s it probably had a great deal of truth in it, and there is still evidence for this view; certainly in the diffusion of innovative high-tech products there is strong evidence for it. However, there is a weakening of this mechanism due to the preponderance of mass media. In the 1940s most homes did not have TV and there was no commercial radio in the UK; the availability of commercial information was therefore more restricted to the wealthy. Also, the two-step flow assumes that the audience is passively waiting for the information to be presented, whereas in fact people actively seek out information about new things by asking friends and relatives and by looking for published information.

The multistage interaction model (Figure 10.6, page 222) agrees that some people are more influential than others, but also recognizes that the mass media affect both influential and seeker. The influential doesn't mediate the information flow, as the two-step model

Figure 10.5

Mechanisms of personal influence

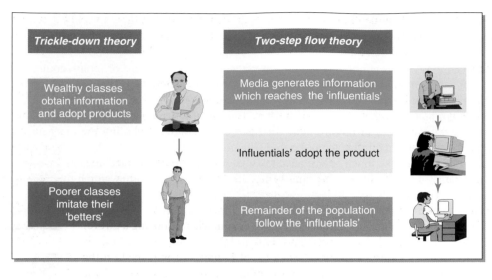

Figure 10.6

Multistage interaction model

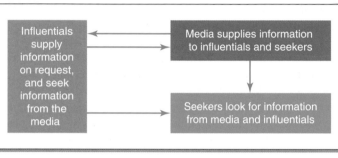

suggests, but rather acts as a mechanism for emphasizing or facilitating the information flow. Within the model, there is a continuous dialogue between marketers, seekers and influentials with many stages of influence before the new idea is adopted or rejected.

Clearly it is important for marketers to identify who the influential people are likely to be, and much research has been carried out into this area. Table 10.3 shows the main

Table 10.3 Characteristics of influentials

Characteristic	Description of influential
Demographics	Wide differences according to product category. For fashions and film going young women dominate. For self-medication, women with children are most influential. Generally, demography shows low correlation and is not a good predictor.
Social activity	Influencers and opinion leaders are usually gregarious.
General attitudes	Generally innovative and positive towards new products.
Personality and lifestyle	Low correlation of personality with opinion leadership. Lifestyle tends to be more fashion conscious, more socially active, more independent.
Product-related	Influencers are more interested in the specific product area than are others. They are active searchers and information gatherers, especially from the mass media.

characteristics of influentials which have been identified so far; this is probably not an exhaustive list, nor will it be generally applicable to all cases (Figure 10.7, page 224).

Influencers (and others) like to pass on their knowledge, and there are several reasons for doing this.

Involvement is a major force. The influencer is actually interested in the subject area, and wants to share the excitement with others. A hi-fi enthusiast who buys a new Arcam stereo will want to tell friends and colleagues all about it on Monday morning. Telling other people acts as an outlet for the pleasure of owning the equipment.

Self-enhancement is about airing one's superior knowledge. People like to appear to be 'in the know' – perhaps being able to say 'I discovered a wonderful unspoiled place for a holiday'. Appearing to be a connoisseur, whether of fine wines or works of art or classic cars is something many influencers strive for. People often ask a friend or relative to help when choosing a gift for a third party, especially where the gift giving might be risky (where little is known about the third party, or where a lot of importance is placed on the gift). This usually increases the social bonding between the giver and the adviser (Lowrey, Otnes and Ruth 2004).

Concern for others often precipitates influence. The genuine desire to help a friend to reach a good decision often prompts the expert to say 'OK, I'll come with you when you go to the shop.' This factor works most strongly when there is a strong link between the individuals concerned, and when the influencer has been very satisfied with the product or service concerned. This can have a very direct effect on consumption: there is evidence that people often feel guilty about buying themselves a treat, but if a free gift for someone else is included, the guilt is very much reduced or even disappears altogether (Lee and Corfman 2004). This implies that firms in the 'treat' or 'luxury' business would do well to offer an extra little something to 'give to a friend'. Laphroaig Whisky Distillers do this: periodically they ask established customers ('Friends of Laphroaig') to pass on the names and addresses of three friends, to whom the distillery sends a small bottle of the whisky. Naturally, people are asked to obtain permission from their friends before passing on their details, but the promotion is successful on two fronts: it rewards the loyalty of the existing customer, and it brings the whisky to the attention of the friends.

Message intrigue is the factor concerned with comments about advertising messages. If an advertisement is particularly intriguing or humorous, people will discuss it; this enhances the message by repetition. Advertisements for Guinness have often used this approach: at the time of writing, Guinness have a TV advertisement which shows young drinkers regressing backwards through evolution to the status of lungfish, and expressing their disgust at the pond water they are drinking: this implies that human evolution was driven by the need to drink something better than pond water, i.e. Guinness. This advertisement needs to be watched carefully several times for the joke to become apparent, but since it is also eye-catching and uses exceptionally good graphics people are more likely to watch it and remember.

Dissonance reduction is about reducing doubts after making a major purchase. As word-of-mouth influence this can be good or bad; sometimes the influencer will try to reassure him- or herself by telling everybody about the good points of the product; more often, though, the disappointed customer will use word-of-mouth to complain bitterly and explain how the wicked manufacturer has cheated him or her. This is sometimes a way of passing the responsibility over to the supplier rather than admitting that the influencer has made a bad decision or a bad choice.

GOOD THINGS COME TO THOSE WHO WAIT

Waiting for your Guinness to settle is one thing . . .

. . . waiting for evolution to progress is another.

Figure 10.7

Forces driving influencers

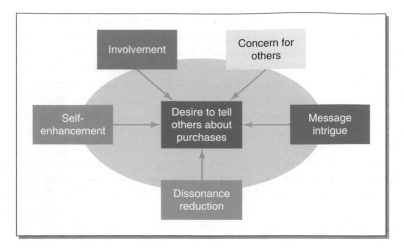

Overall, word-of-mouth influence is much stronger than advertising or other marketer-produced communications. For marketers, then, the problem lies in knowing how to use word-of-mouth to its best advantage. Table 10.4 offers some comparisons and strategies.

Interestingly, most of the reasons influencers have for passing on what they know are selfish ones. They want to show off their knowledge, pass on an interesting bit of gossip, reassure themselves that they made the right decision by persuading someone else to make the same choice, and so forth.

Only occasionally, apparently, are they motivated by concern for others – passing on a good tip to a friend, in this case. Does this tell us that people are essentially selfish? Or should we give people credit for getting their kicks by being helpful rather than destructive?

It is not usually possible to rely entirely on word of mouth, but marketers should take steps to stimulate it as a promotional tool. If the company is in a position to be able to identify influentials, it is well worthwhile offering to lend them the product (or even give

Table 10.4 Word of mouth

Strong influence	Weak influence	Tactical suggestions
Seeker initiates conversation with source	Source initiates conversation with seeker.	Advertising could emphasize the idea of 'Ask the person who owns one'. Network marketers could emphasize a more advisory role for their salespeople rather than a strongly proactive approach.
Negative information	Positive information.	Because marketers are uniformly positive about the product, the seeker is more alert to any negatives. The essential thing for marketers to do is to ensure that any complaints are dealt with immediately and thoroughly.
Verbal communication is stronger for thinking and evaluation.	Visual communication is stronger for awareness and stimulation of interest.	Where appropriate, marketers could encourage satisfied customers to show their friends the product; this tactic is often used for home improvement sales, where customers are paid a small reward or commission for introducing friends to the product. This is also the basis for party-plan selling, e.g. Tupperware and Anne Summers.

them it, if the cost is low enough) so that they can be stimulated into talking about it to friends. Advertising should be interesting and involving, perhaps even controversial, so that debate ensues. Although it is not true to say that any word of mouth will be good for a company, it is certainly true to say that controversy and debate will always increase brand awareness, even when it does not enhance brand image. For example, Harveytiles (a brand of Harvey Roofing Products Ltd., a South African roofing tile manufacturer) produces advertisements which are extremely controversial. The slogans use religious references ('A roof without Harveytiles is like being burnt in Hell without a Saviour': 'Only Heaven is covered with Harveytiles') which have proved to be extremely offensive to the committed Christians of Zambia. The result has been that everyone in Zambia has heard of Harveytiles, but of course this does not necessarily mean that people will buy the product. Some people undoubtedly boycott the product because of the religious references.

Controversial advertising stimulates word-of-mouth.

Another way of stimulating word of mouth is to allow people to try out the product. Car manufacturers usually give exceptionally generous discounts to car hire companies, taking the view that hirers might well be tempted to buy the same model at a later stage, and are also very likely to talk about the vehicle to others.

To prevent negative word of mouth, marketers should do more than merely satisfy any customer complaints. Coca Cola carried out a survey of customer communications in 1981.

Consumer behaviour in action
The Da Vinci Code

Dan Brown's climb to fame was hardly meteoric. He failed at several careers before getting into writing – and even then his earlier books hardly set the world on fire. Yet everyone needs to learn their craft, and eventually Dan hit the jackpot with *The Da Vinci Code*.

The book, which puts forward the theory that Jesus married Mary Magdalene and had children by her, was not exactly a great work of literature, but it caught the public imagination. Initially, the publishers only planned a short print run – based on the sales of Dan's other books, it seemed unlikely that the book would be a runaway best-seller. The rest, of course, is history – the book had sold 2.2 million copies by March 2005, and received another boost when the film version was released in 2006.

So how come this book sold so much better than expected? The publishers certainly didn't hype the book – after all, they weren't expecting to sell it in large enough numbers to justify a big publicity campaign. The answer lies in word of mouth. People told people about the book, and those people told other people, and so the process went on until everybody had heard of it.

Research by Nielsen Bookscan in 2005 showed that a large number of best-selling books have achieved success this way – *Captain Corelli's Mandolin, Eats, Shoots and Leaves* and *The Lovely Bones* were all cited as million-plus sellers that had succeeded almost entirely on personal recommendation.

As a result, the World Book Day organizers ran a campaign encouraging people to recommend a book to a friend – another resounding success!

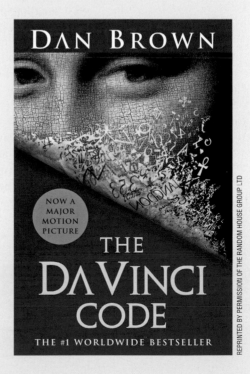

The survey was undertaken among customers who had complained to the company; here are the main findings (Coca Cola Company 1981).

- More than 12 per cent told 20 or more people about the company's response to their complaint.
- Those who were completely satisfied with the response told a median of four to five others about the experience.
- Nearly 10 per cent of those who reported being completely satisfied increased their purchases of company products.
- Those who thought their complaint was not dealt with fairly told a median of nine to ten other people.
- Of those who thought their complaint was not dealt with fairly nearly one-third subsequently boycotted company products entirely, and another 45 per cent reduced their purchases.

From these figures it follows that marketers should actually encourage people to complain, and should go beyond the call of duty in satisfying complaints, since this will actually increase the loyalty of those who complain.

Word of mouse

In recent years word of mouth has been supplemented by e-mail communications, sometimes called 'word of mouse'. E-mail is a fast and powerful communications medium, but more importantly it provides a semi-permanent record of what was actually said, so that communications can contain facts and figures which can be referred to later. Encouraging people to e-mail each other about products has become a growth area for e-marketing, and is a feature of many websites.

Word of mouse also happens in chatrooms and on blogs (see earlier in this chapter). Virtual communities are extremely powerful in promoting products – they frequently ask each other for specific recommendations about products.

Website design has moved through a number of phases, shown in Figure 10.8. During the late 1990s most websites were merely 'presence' sites, giving a brief outline of the company and its products and directing the interested potential customer to a telephone number or snail-mail address. Over the next few years, more and more sites became interactive, allowing customers to navigate around the site, place orders online and e-mail the company as appropriate for further information.

By the early twenty-first century, sites had gone a step further, and were offering the capability of involving visitors' friends. 'E-mail this site to a friend' buttons became commonplace, and eventually firms began to add value to the site by including games and puzzles, and even jokes, to encourage the site visitors to enroll their friends onto the site. This approach helped to overcome the major problem of Internet marketing – making your voice heard through the clutter of almost five billion websites worldwide.

Figure 10.8

Evolution of websites

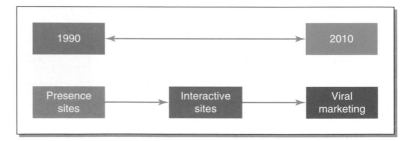

A recent development (and for many an unethical one) is the linking of marketing messages to self-replicating viruses. The virus operates by sending itself to everyone in the victim's address book, displaying the marketing message in the form of an e-mail. It then copies itself into all the other recipient's address books and sends itself out again. Soon it has sent the message to everyone on the planet (often several times). Although in most cases recipients simply ignore the message and delete it, even a tiny response rate will represent a very large amount of business for the initiating firm.

There is little doubt that word of mouse will grow as access to the Internet and consequent increased use of e-mail spreads throughout the world. Future developments (notably voice e-mail and Internet-enabled telephone systems) may bring us back to vocal delivery of messages (word of mouth) but web enabled viral marketing is likely to be an increasing force for the foreseeable future.

Summary

In this chapter we have looked at some of the interpersonal factors which influence purchasing behaviour. In particular, we have looked at the groups and individuals who most influence consumers, and at the ways the influence is exerted. Finally, we have looked at ways marketers can use these interpersonal factors to improve customer relations and customer loyalty. The key points from the chapter are as follows:

- Most people are members of several reference groups, all of which influence the individual in different ways.

- Normative compliance is probably the most powerful influence on behaviour.
- Conspicuousness is the most crucial product characteristic for normative compliance.
- Word of mouth spreads because the informant (influencer) likes to talk about the products concerned.
- Complaints can be turned to the marketer's advantage by generous handling.
- Word of mouse is likely to be a growth area in marketing communications in the twenty-first century.

Chapter review questions

1 How might companies encourage word of mouth?

2 What is the role of normative compliance in fashion marketing?

3 How might peer pressure encourage people to try new things?

4 Why is word of mouse becoming more popular with companies?

5 How can companies counteract negative word of mouth?

6 How might membership of an automatic group affect buying behaviour?

7 How might membership of an automatic group affect someone's propensity to join a secondary group?

8 How might a secondary group also be a formal group?

9 What are the defining characteristics of a primary group?

10 How might a marketer make use of a virtual group?

Preview case study revisited
Children and Youth Health Service

The Children and Youth Health (CYH) Service quickly realised that campaigns such as the 'Just say No!' anti-drug campaign in the UK would not work. Young teenagers are in a phase of their lives where they want to work out their own answers – obeying adults blindly is simply not part of their world.

The CYH Service therefore looked at the root of the problem. Peer pressure was compelling kids to try things they otherwise would not do – the need to be part of the group was outweighing their common sense, good upbringing, and fear about trying alcohol, drugs and anti-social behaviour. The CYH therefore set out to show kids how to resist peer pressure, and to stand up for themselves. Leaflets and a website (set up in 2004) gave teenagers advice such as 'Sometimes it is hard to say no to your friends – perhaps you need to learn how to keep out of situations that could lead to trouble.' The site goes on to provide tactics for avoiding peer pressure while still appearing cool – as follows:

If someone is asking you to do something that is good and won't lead to trouble for someone, they will not say things like . . .

'Everyone does it.'
'No one will know.'
'You're chicken.'
'Who's going to find out?'
'Don't be a wuss.'
'Go on I dare you.'

How to say no

These are some ways that have worked for kids who wanted to say no.

- Pretend you haven't heard and walk away.
- Make an excuse. 'Can't stop now, got to go . . .'.
- Talk about something else that they are interested in and don't let them change the subject.

- Laugh. 'I thought you said . . . You've got to be joking!' Then change the subject or leave – still laughing.
- Pretend to be shocked or amazed.
- Have a better idea.
- Give friendly advice. 'That could be a dumb thing to do. Whose idea was it? You're too smart to get into that.'
- Say 'I'm not doing this because I'm your friend and I don't want to see you get into trouble.'
- Say 'That's a bit unkind. How would you feel if someone did (said) that to you?'

The site goes on to give more advice on resisting peer pressure – it even tells young people how to recognize the physical signs that they are being pressured (butterflies in the stomach, feeling hot or cold, feeling shaky and so forth), and questions to ask oneself about the behaviour (will someone be hurt, physically or mentally? Will this break the law, or the school rules?).

The campaign has proved extremely successful so far. Between 2002 and 2005 there was a 25 per cent drop in the number of children reporting that they had consumed alcohol in the previous week, and a similar drop in binge drinking. The most spectacular fall was in the case of 12-year-old boys, previously seen as a problem group: there was a 60 per cent fall in the numbers who had consumed alcohol recently, falling from 20.2 per cent to 7.9 per cent over the period.

Similar reductions in other dangerous behaviour were also recorded. Obviously there is still a long way to go – alcohol is widely available in Australia (as elsewhere) and young people will always want to experiment and imitate their elders as well. But giving them the tools to resist peer pressure is a key plank in the platform.

Case study
UKGA.com

Private flying is often regarded as a rich man's sport, but in fact most of the private pilots in the UK are fairly ordinary people in fairly ordinary jobs. What's more, a lot of them are women. Private pilots almost always share their aircraft – they form syndicates to buy old Cessnas and Pipers, they get together with a friend to build a microlight, or they hire a club aircraft every so often and head off into the wild blue yonder.

In fact there are several hundred thousand pilots in the UK, all at various levels of experience and with different qualifications. There is a common saying among pilots that a flying licence is a licence to learn – so pilots spend a lot of time chatting to each other, meeting up to discuss their latest ideas and generally sitting around the clubhouse drinking tea and waiting for the weather to clear.

The opportunity to expand this chatting to include a wider group of people came about when UKGA.com first appeared. UKGA stands for United Kingdom General Aviation and is a website set up and operated by two pilots, Neville Kilford and Phil Murphy. They do it for free – in fact, over the years they have subsidized the site quite a lot, but still rely on voluntary contributions from the pilots who use the site. Anyone can visit the site, but many of the online facilities are only available to those who register to use the site. Registration is free, and all contact details of members are kept secret.

The site itself has a whole range of items to attract pilots and wannabes. UKGA has a guide to airfields with a search facility which allows pilots to locate airfields by name or by nearest town: the airfield guide includes technical information (runway directions and details), aerial photographs of the airfield and road maps (thus allowing pilots to get there either by road or air) and in many cases detailed reviews of the airfield written by pilots themselves. The site has aviation weather forecasts, an automatic flight planning service, a NOTAM service (Notices to Airmen) which passes on Government safety warnings about air hazards such as balloons and parachuting, and a system for maintaining one's own flying logbook electronically.

Most important of all, however, the website hosts several chatrooms. Pilots are able to ask each other questions about flying, share experiences, admit to making errors

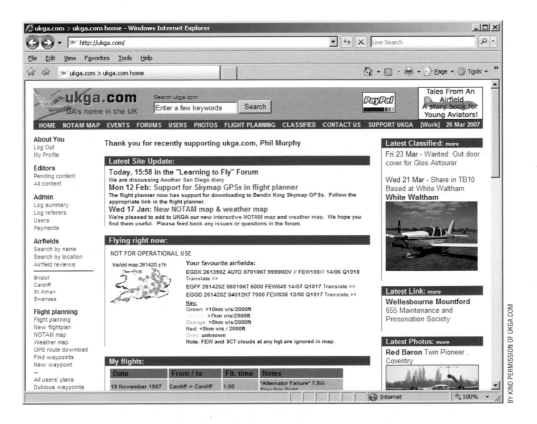

BY KIND PERMISSION OF UKGA.COM

and get advice on how to avoid problems in future, and can generally move the flying-related chit-chat out of the clubroom and into a wider arena. More experienced pilots are happy to pass on information to newer pilots, and many friendships have started as a result of chatting on UKGA. Flying clubs organize fly-outs (collectively flying to another airfield) and fly-ins (inviting others to visit their own airfield). People are able to offer lifts to each other, or to arrange days out when the costs (and the piloting) can be shared.

Neville and Phil could, of course, charge people to use the site, or at least allow advertisers onto the site. Most people who use the site pay absolutely nothing – less than 10 per cent make a contribution. But they don't want to restrict anyone from contributing – flying can be expensive, and every pound paid to UKGA is a pound less available for flying. Asking for contributions is as far as the founders want to go – they say £30 is a reasonable amount, but if

pilots think it's worth an hour's flying (which could be anything from £30 for a microlight pilot up to £150 for a Cessna pilot) then they should give that. Meanwhile, the site is free for anyone who wants to use it.

Case study questions

1 What is the role of normative compliance in Neville and Phil's request for contributions?

2 What is the informational value of joining UKGA?

3 What is the value-expressive influence of the website?

4 Why would an experienced pilot take the time and the trouble to help out a less experienced pilot?

5 How might Neville and Phil increase the number of people who contribute financially to the site?

References

Asch, Solomon E. (1951) Effects of group pressure on the modification and distortion of judgements. *Groups, Leadership and Men*, ed. H. Guetzkow (Pittsburgh, PA: Carnegie Press).

Baker, Michael J., and Churchill, Gilbert A. Jr. (1977) The impact of physically attractive models on advertising evaluations. *Journal of Marketing Research*, November: 538–55.

BBC (2006) *News*, Wednesday 13 September, 10.58 a.m.

Beardon, William O., and Etzel, Michael J. (1982) Reference goup influence on product and brand purchase decisions. *Journal of Consumer Research*, 9 (Sept): 184.

Burnkrant, Robert, and Cousineau, Alain (1975) Informational and normative social influence on buyer behaviour. *Journal of Consumer Research* (Dec): 206–15.

Calder, Bobby, and Burnkrant, Robert (1977) Interpersonal influences on consumer behaviour: an attribution theory approach. *Journal of Consumer Research*, 4 (Jun): 29–38.

Carlson, Kurt A., and Sally, David (2002) Thoughts that count: fairness and possibilities, intentions and reactions. *Advances in Consumer Research*, 29(1): 79–89.

Coca Cola Company (1981) Measuring the Grapevine: Consumer Response and Word-of-Mouth.

Durkheim, Emile (1951) *Suicide: a Study in Sociology* (New York: Free Press).

Fischer, E., Bristor, J., and Gainer, B. (1996) Creating or escaping community? An exploratory study of Internet consumers' behaviours. *Advances in Consumer Research*, 23(1): 178–82.

Fisher, Robert J., and Dube, Laurette (2003) Gender differences in responses to emotional advertising: the effect of the presence of others. *Advances in Consumer Research*, 30(1): 15–17.

Haytko, Diana L., and Baker, Julie (2004) It's all at the mall: exploring adolescent girls' experiences. *Journal of Retailing*, 80(1): 67.

Homans, G.C. (1961) *Social Behavior: Its Elementary Forms* (New York: Harcourt, Brace & World).

Koretz, Gene (1990) Economic trends. *Business Week*, 5 March.

Langerak, Fred, Verhoef, Peter C., and Verleigh, Peeter W.J. (2004) Satisfaction and participation in virtual communities. *Advances in Consumer Research*, 31(1): 56–7.

Lazarsfield, Paul F., Berelson, Bernard R., and Gaudet, Hazel (1948) *The People's Choice* (New York: Columbia University Press).

Lee, Sooyen Nikki, and Corfman, Kim P. (2004) A little something for me, and maybe for you too: promotions that relieve guilt. *Advances in Consumer Behaviour*, 31(1): 28.

Lowrey, Tina M., Otnes, Cele C., and Ruth, Julie A. (2004) Social influences on dyadic giving over time: a taxonomy from the giver's perspective. *Journal of Consumer Research*, 30: 547–58.

Manz, Charles C., and Sims, Henry P. (1981) Vicarious learning: the influence of modelling on organisational behaviour. *Academy of Management Review*, 6(1), January: 105–13.

McNulty, W. Kirk (1985) UK social change through a wide-angle lens. *Futures*, August.

Muniz, A., and O'Guinn, T. (2004) Brand community. *Journal of Consumer Research*, 27(4): 412–32.

Nelson, Leif D., and Norton, Michael I. (2005) From student to superhero: Situational primes shape future helping. *Journal of Experimental Social Psychology*, 41(4), July: 423–30.

Okleshen, C., and Grossbart, S. (1998) Usenet groups, virtual community and consumer behaviors. *Advances in Consumer Research*, 25(1): 276–82.

Oliver, Richard L. (1999) Whence consumer loyalty? *Journal of Marketing*, 63, October Special Issue (4): 33–44.

Russell, Cristel Antonia, and Stern, Barbara (2006) Aspirational consumption in US soap operas: the process of parasocial attachment to television soap characters. *Advances in Consumer Research*, 33(1): 36.

Tesser, Abraham, Miller, Murray, and Moore, Janet (1988) Some affective consequences of social comparison and reflection processes: the pain and pleasure of being close. *Journal of Personality and Social Psychology*, 54 (Jan), 1: 49–61.

Veblen, Thorstein (1899) *The Theory of the Leisure Class* (New York: Macmillan).

Wheeler, L., Shaver, K.G., Jones, R.A., Goethals, G.R., Cooper, J., Robinson, J.E., Gruder, C.L., and Butzine, K.W. (1969) Factors determining the choice of a comparison other. *Journal of Experimental Social Psychology*, 5 (April): 219–32.

Chapter 11
The family

Learning objectives After reading this chapter, you should be able to:

1 describe the different definitions of family, and explain the influences on creating the definitions

2 explain the role of culture in creating decision-making styles

3 explain the roles of family members in decision-making

4 describe ways in which conflict is generated and resolved

5 describe the process by which children become effective consumers

6 explain how brand loyalty is passed down through the generations

7 critique family lifestyle models and explain the possible alternatives

8 describe the roles family members take in the purchase and consumption process

Introduction

Of all the reference groups, the family is probably the most powerful in influencing consumer decision-making. Almost all of us are, have been or will be members of families: our parents teach us how to be effective consumers from an early age, and we influence our brothers and sisters, our parents, and eventually our own children in their purchasing choices.

The family has gone through many changes in structure, but still remains the most important social grouping. The reasons for this are as follows:

1 In the case of children, the parental influence is the earliest, and therefore colours the child's perception of everything that follows. In fact, the superego is thought to be an internalized parent.

2 In the case of parents, the desire to do the best they can for their children influences their decision-making when making purchases for the family. Clear examples are the purchase of breakfast cereals and disposable nappies, where the appeal is almost invariably to do with the comfort and well-being of the baby.

3 In the case of siblings, the influence comes either as role model (where an older sibling is looked up to by a younger one) or as carer/adviser to younger siblings.

4 Because families share a large part of their consumption, decision-making is often joint, or follows formalized rules which control consumption behaviour within the group.

Because we value the opinions of our family members, we take their advice and often conform to their norms of behaviour. Even though the structure of families has undergone major changes in recent years, it is still true to say that the family is the basic unit of society.

Defining families

The concept of what constitutes a family varies from one culture to another. In the UK and United States, families usually consist of parents and their natural or adopted children. In some other cultures, families might extend to aunts, uncles, grandparents and cousins all

Preview case study
Raising Kids

Raising children seems to be harder now than ever before. Because people often live far away from their own parents, advice can be hard to come by – and because fewer couples are having children, it can easily be the case that there are no friendly neighbours to advise, either.

On the other hand, the media seems to be determined to give too much advice. High-profile campaigns (such as that conducted by TV chef Jamie Oliver to improve school dinners), scare stories about nutritional problems and pressure on parents to buy the right toys and the right books and play the right music to their children seem to have made bringing up baby into a solemn affair where there are a thousand pitfalls to be avoided. Added to this, people are tending to have children when they are older and more established in their careers, and want to take a professional approach to child-rearing: they have more money, and fewer children to lavish it on ('only' children are the norm now, whereas 40 years ago they were a rarity) and clearly parents want to get it right first time, since there is unlikely to be a second time.

From a purchasing viewpoint, deciding which products are appropriate for children, and knowing which will be effective and reliable, is an added problem. Just knowing what a baby needs is a big consideration – new parents find themselves relying on commercial information (most of which is fairly accurate, but is of course biased towards the manufacturers). The whole process starts on the maternity ward, where new mothers are issued with Bounty bags. The Bounty bag contains free samples and information about products which are available for babies. Manufacturers pay a premium for their products to be included in the Bounty bag, so the information can hardly be said to be unbiased – on the other hand, the free samples come in handy, and the new mother is in the right place to get advice from the midwives, doctors and nurses.

New parents are often targeted by direct marketing campaigns in which companies send out information through the mail or via e-mail. All this advice is wonderful, but it tends to peter out after a few years: parents are not informed about how to deal with a fractious two-year-old, or a primary school child who won't eat the school meals, or a rebellious teenager who won't get out of bed in the morning. Some websites exist: Bounty run a very successful site, and Calpol (the painkiller for children) has a good website offering advice and information about many products other than Calpol itself. However, overall there is a shortage of real guidance for parents trying to find a way through the minefield!

It can really change your life.

Especially now it's available in liquid sachets.

Calpol Sachets

(If you've got kids, you'll understand.)

living in the same house and sharing their consumption. These extended families are becoming rare in industrialized countries, partly because of the mobility of workers: someone who finds a job in another part of the country is unlikely to find it convenient to take a large number of extended family members along.

Within the UK, a family is usually defined in narrow terms – the parents and their offspring. However, in most families there will also be influences from uncles, aunts, grandparents and cousins. While these influences are often less strong in UK households than they might be in some other countries where the extended family is more common, the influences still exist to a greater or lesser extent. For statistical purposes, Eurostat has adopted the United Nations definition of a family, which is as follows:

> The persons within a private or institutional household who are related as husband and wife or as parent and never-married child by blood or adoption. (United Nations Economic Commission for Europe 2000, section 191)

For the purposes of the definition, couples who cohabit without marrying are still regarded as a family. The European Community Household Panel defines a family household more broadly as a shared residence with common housekeeping arrangements.

From a marketing viewpoint, the level of demand for many products is dictated more by the number of households than by the number of families. For example, most households in affluent countries would have a washing machine, but hardly any would have two washing machines. The relevance of families to marketing is therefore much more about consumer behaviour than about consumer demand levels.

In terms of its function as a reference group, the family is defined by the following characteristics (Figure 11.1, page 236):

1 Face-to-face contact – Family members see each other most days, and interact as advisers, information providers and sometimes deciders. Other reference groups rarely have this level of contact.

2 Shared consumption – Durables such as fridges, freezers, televisions and furniture are shared, and food is collectively purchased and cooked (although there is a strong trend away from families eating together). Purchase of these items is often collective: children even participate in decision-making on such major purchases as cars and houses. Other reference groups may share some consumption (for example, a model railway club may hire a workshop and share tools) but families share consumption of most domestic items. In some cases products are passed on from one generation to another as a way of preserving family identity and values. Whether this means passing on great-grandmother's wedding ring or handing over the family's old car to the newly licensed eldest child, the family link is continued (Curasi 2006). The same behaviour has been found in investments, with parents passing on investments and investment advice to children (Williams 2006). Products passed on in this way can move between 'sacred' and 'profane' values (Hartman and Kiecker 2004). For example, Granny's wedding ring might be worn on a chain round the neck of a teenager: equally, Grandad's old penknife might be preserved as a family heirloom.

3 Subordination of individual needs – Because consumption is shared, some family members will find that the solution chosen is not one that fully meets their needs. Although this happens in other reference groups, the effect is more pronounced in families.

4 Purchasing agent – Because of the shared consumption, most families will have one member who does most, or all, of the shopping. Traditionally, this has been the mother of the family, but increasingly the purchasing agent is the older children of the family – even pre-teens are sometimes taking over this role. The reason for this is the increase in the number of working mothers – women who work outside the home – which has left less time for shopping. This has major implications for marketers, since pre-teens and young teens generally watch more TV than adults and are therefore more open to marketing communications. Other reference groups may well have a purchasing agent, but this is probably only for specific items rather than for all those items the group is interested in – and most informal groups would only appoint a purchasing agent for occasional purposes (for example, to send out for pizza or to book a weekend away).

Family decision-making is not as straightforward as marketers have supposed in the past. There has been an assumption that the purchasing agent (e.g. the mother) is the one who

Children learn to be consumers by shopping with their parents.

Figure 11.1

Defining characteristics of families

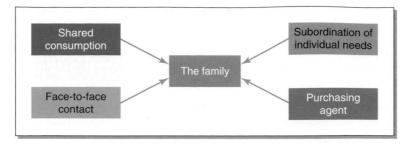

makes the decisions, and while this is often the case, this approach ignores the ways in which the purchase decisions are arrived at.

There is a problem here with terminology: traditionally, studies of the family have referred to the male partner as the husband, and the female partner as the wife. The increasing number of families in which the parents are not married has rendered this approach obsolete; the research reported in the next section was conducted in the 1970s, when the vast majority of parents were married. The validity and relevance of the research is not in question, since it refers to traditional roles; these roles may or may not actually be adopted by specific families.

Role specialization is critical in family decision-making because of the sheer number of different products that must be bought each year in order to keep the family supplied. What this means in practice is that, for example, the family member responsible for doing the cooking is also likely to take the main responsibility for shopping for food. The family member who does the most driving is likely to make the main decision about the car and its accessories, servicing, fuelling and so forth; the family gardener buys the gardening products, and so on.

Four kinds of marital role specialisation have been identified: **wife dominant** where the wife has most say in the decision; **husband dominant**, where the husband plays the major role; **syncratic** or **democratic**, where the decision is arrived at jointly; and **autonomic**, where the decision is made entirely independently of the partner (Filiatrault and Ritchie 1980). For example, the wife may have the biggest role in deciding on new curtains, the husband may have the lead role in choosing the family car, they both may decide on a home extension, and the husband alone might choose the fertilizer for the garden. Marketers need to identify which role specialization type is mainly operating within a target market in order to know where to aim the promotional activities. Some recent research indicates that, in the event of disagreement about a joint decision it is the man's decision which is likely to prevail (Ward 2006). This research was conducted exclusively in Tennessee, however, which may account for at least some of the result.

Product category affects role specialization and decision-making systems. When an expensive purchase is being considered, it is likely that most of the family will be involved in some way, if only because major purchases affect the family budgeting for other items. At the other end of the scale, day-to-day shopping for toilet rolls and cans of beans entails very little collective decision-making. Where the product has a shared usage (a holiday or a car) the collective decision-making component is likely to increase greatly. Conversely, where the product is used predominantly by one family member, that member will dominate the decision-making even when the purchase is a major one (the family chef will make most of the decision about the new cooker, for example).

Culture has a marked effect on family decision-making styles. Religion and nationality will often affect the way decisions are made; African cultures tend to be male-dominated in decision-making, whereas European and North American cultures show a more egalitarian pattern of decision-making (Green *et al.* 1983). In India, gold carries very strong family significance at weddings. The bride is thought to be purified by gifted and borrowed gold – typically her new husband's family will lend jewellery to her, as a way of binding her to the new family (Fernandez and Veer 2004).

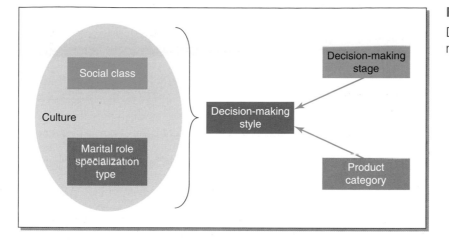

Figure 11.2

Determinants of decision-making style in families

There are two issues here for the marketer: first, what is the effect on the marketing mix of the multi-ethnic society now emerging in Europe, and second, what is the effect when dealing internationally? This is a somewhat sensitive area, and one which marketers are still getting to grips with. There is more on the general aspects of culture in Chapter 9.

Social class creates patterns of decision-making. Among very wealthy families, there appears to be a greater tendency for the husbands to make the decisions, but at the same time the norms of purchase tend to be well established and therefore discussion is unnecessary (Komarovsky 1961). Lower-class families, with low incomes, have traditionally been more matriarchal, with the wives often handling the financial decisions about rent, insurance, food bills and Christmas clubs without reference to the husbands. Poorer families will often divert a large proportion of their limited resources towards ensuring that the children are not stigmatized by poverty: often children of poorer parents will still wear the latest trainers and go on the school trips (Hamilton and Catterall 2006). Middle-class families tend to show greater democratic involvement in decision-making. These social class distinctions are gradually breaking down, however, as a result of increasing wealth and mass education.

The family may well adopt different roles according to the decision-making stage. At the problem-recognition stage of, for example, the need for new shoes for the children, the children themselves may be the main contributors. The mother may then decide what type of shoes should be bought, and the father may be the one who takes the children to buy the shoes. It is reasonable to suppose that the main **user** of the product might be important in the initial stages, with perhaps joint decision-making at the final purchase.

Other determinants might include such factors as whether both parents are earning. In such families, decision-making is more likely to be joint because each has a financial stake in the outcome. Some studies seem to indicate that family decision-making is more likely to be husband-dominated when the husband is the sole earner, whereas couples who are both earning make decisions jointly (Filiatrault and Ritchie 1980). Males also tend to dominate highly technical durable products (e.g. home computers, DVD players or TV equipment).

Talking point

In recent years we have been almost morbidly preoccupied with gender equality. Yet at the same time we have seen a rise in 'new laddism' and in 'girl power'. Women seem to be revelling in traditional female behaviour, and men seem to be reverting to traditional male stereotypes. So if women are getting together with their girlfriends to gossip, and men are swilling beer and going to the football, are we heading back to a traditional division along gender lines?

Are we going to see women fluttering their eyelashes and asking men to help them change a flat tyre? Are we going to see men refusing to change the baby? Or are we perhaps just observing a minor blip in our road to equality?

Table 11.1 Conflict resolution in families

Resolution method	Explanation
Persuasion through information exchange	When a conflict occurs, each family member seeks to persuade the others of his or her point of view. This leads to discussion, and ultimately some form of compromise.
Role expectation	If persuasion fails, a family member may be designated to make the decision. This is usually somebody who has the greatest expertise in the area of conflict being discussed. This method appears to be going out of fashion as greater democracy in family decision-making is appearing.
Establishment of norms	Families will often adopt rules for decision-making. Sometimes this will involve taking turns over making decisions (perhaps over which restaurant the family will go to this week, or where they will go on holiday).
Power exertion	This is also known as 'browbeating'. One family member will try to exert power to force the other members to comply; this may be a husband who refuses to sign the cheque unless he gets his own way, or a wife who refuses to cook the dinner until the family agree, or a child who throws a tantrum. The person with the most power is called the least dependent person because he or she is not as dependent on the other family members. Using the examples above, if the wife has her own income she won't need to ask the husband to sign the cheque; if the other family members can cook they can get their own dinner; and if the family can ignore the yelling toddler long enough eventually the child will give up.

Source: Adapted from Sak Onkvisit and John J. Shaw (1994) *Consumer Behaviour: Strategy and Analysis* (New York: John Wiley).

Gender role orientation is clearly crucial to decision-making. Husbands (and wives) with conservative views about gender roles will tend towards the assumption that most decisions about expenditure will be made by the husband. Even within this type of decision-making system, however, husbands will usually adjust their own views to take account of their wife's attitudes and needs.

Conflict resolution tends to have an increased importance in family decision-making as opposed to individual purchase behaviour. The reason for this is that, obviously, more people are involved each with their own needs and their own internal conflicts to resolve. The conflict resolution system is as shown in Table 11.1.

Influence of children on buying decisions

First-born children generate more economic impact than higher-order babies. Around 40 per cent of babies are first-born; they are photographed more, they get all new clothes (no hand-me-downs) and get more attention all round. First-born and only children have a higher achievement rate than their siblings, and since the birthrate is falling there are more of them proportionally. More and more couples are choosing to have only one child, and families larger than two children are becoming a rarity. Childlessness is also more common now than it was 30 years ago.

Children also have a role in applying pressure to their parents to make particular purchasing decisions. The level of 'pester power' generated can be overwhelming, and parents will frequently give in the child's demands (Ekstrom, Tansuhaj and Foxman 1987).

Although the number of children is steadily declining, their importance as consumers is not. Apart from the direct purchases of things that children need, they influence decision making to a marked extent. Some research (*Marketing News* 1983) has shown that pre-teens and young teens have a greater influence on family shopping choices than do the parents themselves for these reasons:

1 Often they do the shopping anyway, because both parents are working and the children have the available time to go to the shops.

2 They watch more TV, so are more influenced and more knowledgeable about products.

3 They tend to be more attuned to consumer issues, and have the time to shop around for (for example) the free-range eggs.

Children have to be taught how to be consumers, since they will (eventually) become adults and will need to manage their money and make appropriate choices in their purchasing behaviour. Children's development as consumers goes through five stages (Figure 11.3):

1 Observing.

2 Making requests.

3 Making selections.

4 Making assisted purchases.

5 Making independent purchases.

Children often do some or all of the shopping if both parents go out to work.

In the observing stage, children see how their parents go about obtaining the things they need. At this point, the child will probably not understand that money is a finite resource, but can easily understand the basic system: things that the family need are available in shops, and they can be bought with money if you know what to do. Usually children will begin to consider ways in which they might obtain goods themselves – quite young children can grasp the idea that goods must be paid for, and they will sometimes try using 'money' (perhaps play money or tokens) to pay for things.

At a very early stage children learn to make requests. Even before being able to talk, children recognize brands and favourite products and are able to reach for them or point to them. As they grow older and more able to articulate requests, they can (and do) develop 'pester power'. This means that they make insistent demands for products, sometimes throwing tantrums or continually wheedling their parents to obtain what they want. At this point parental judgement may vary – some parents will give in fairly quickly and provide the child with what he or she wants, while others will refuse to buy the product (making a judgement as to its suitability for the child). In many cases the request becomes a basis for negotiation – the parent agrees to buy the product on condition that the child behaves in a certain way.

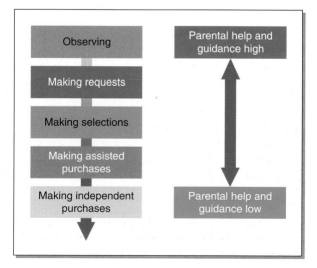

Figure 11.3

Children's stages of development as consumers

Table 11.2 Tactics used by children to influence their parents

Tactic	Explanation
Pressure tactics	The child makes demands and uses threats or intimidation to persuade the parents to comply with his or her request.
Upward appeal	The child seeks to persuade the parent by saying that the request was approved or is supported by an older member of the family, a teacher or even a family friend.
Exchange tactics	The child makes an implicit or explicit promise to provide some sort of service such as washing the car, cleaning the house or taking care of the baby in return for a favour.
Coalition tactics	The child seeks the aid of others to persuade the parents to comply with his or her request, or uses the support of others as an argument for the parents to agree with him or her.
Ingratiating tactics	The child seeks to get the parent in a good mood or think favourably of him or her before asking the parent to comply with a request.
Rational persuasion	The child uses logical arguments and factual evidence to persuade the parent to agree with his or her request.
Inspirational appeals	The child makes an emotional appeal or proposal that arouses enthusiasm by appealing to the parent's values or ideals.
Consultation tactics	The child seeks the parent's involvement in making a decision.

Children use a wide variety of tactics to influence their parents (Wimalasir 2004). These are shown in Table 11.2 and Figure 11.4.

Parenting style has an obvious effect on the likely response to such requests. Broadly, there are five basic styles of parenting (Carlson and Grossbart 1988):

1 *Authoritarian* – These parents are cold and restrictive.

2 *Authoritative* – These parents are warm and restrictive.

3 *Permissives* – These parents are warm and non-restrictive.

4 *Strict Dependent* – These parents foster dependence in their children, almost to the point of not allowing them to grow up.

5 *Indulgent Dependent* – These parents foster dependence by giving their children everything they want and need, even into adult life.

These parenting styles are not necessarily universal, in fact they happen almost exclusively in collectivist cultures (Rose *et al.* 2002). It is easy to see that authoritarian and authoritative parents are unlikely to yield easily to pester power, strict dependents would not allow the child to pester, and permissives and indulgent dependants are unlikely to need to be pestered – they would simply accede to the request the first time round.

In most cases, parents will agree to purchases subject to conditions being met. This is an important lesson, because the child needs to know that products are subject to exchange processes. In this case, the parent is demonstrating that, in order to obtain benefits, there will need to be concessions in terms of behaviour. Parents frequently use the promise of supplying (or withholding) products as a way of modifying the child's behaviour. There is evidence to suggest that this is culturally based in some respects: American parents apparently seek to develop autonomy in their children, making them into independent consumers, whereas Japanese parents maintain greater control over their children's consumption, so that the children tend to develop consumer skills at a later age (Rose 1999).

Talking point

What responsibility do marketers have for pester power? We hear all the time that wicked marketers are encouraging children to want the latest toys, games, gadgets and even fashions – so are we to blame if they then pester their parents?

On the other hand, people do have to buy things. It's the way the world works. Children have to learn to distinguish between advertising and programming – and they have to learn that they can't just demand anything they want in this life. So maybe marketers are carrying out a public service, educating the consumers of tomorrow and teaching children that they can't just have everything!

Once children reach an age when they can understand money, parents will typically provide them with pocket money so that they can learn to make their own selections. In most cases pocket money is supplied as a fixed amount: this is so that the child can learn that money is not an infinite resource, and must be spent carefully. In other cases, pocket money might be provided as a reward for specific behaviour (for example, cleaning the car or mowing the lawn) so that the child learns the concept of working for rewards. This is a further reinforcement of the exchange concept. In the early stages of having pocket money, parents will often help the child make choices, applying their own sense of value to the transaction. As time goes on, the child will be able to make choices alone, and will ultimately (perhaps during teenage years) become a fully fledged consumer by spending money earned by doing odd jobs or part-time work.

At this point, the individual is more likely to look to friends or role models for ideas on acceptable consumer behaviour (John 1999). Although younger children respond best to

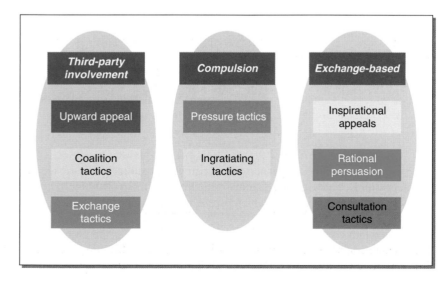

Figure 11.4

Children's persuasion tactics

Consumer behaviour in action
Teenagers and technology

The communications revolution has certainly made it much harder to monitor the behaviour of teenagers – not that it was ever easy, of course. Each generation of teenagers takes great care to prevent their parents from knowing what they are really doing, but electronic communications have made the situation much easier.

Consider the case of buying illicit drugs. One teenager called Sean entered the names of some common illegal drugs into Google and came up with a lot of information telling him not to do drugs: he also came up with a lot of information saying that small amounts of drugs would make him feel great. He used the information to decide which drugs he really wanted to try and which ones he should leave alone. He became an addict by the time he was 17 – he was only 15 when he started. Another teenager, Amy, was given a mobile phone when she was 12 years old. She found the phone extremely useful for calling her drug supplier, especially when using text. She had no fear at all of being caught: 'I knew for a fact my parents didn't have a clue about it,' said Amy. 'My parents got a cell phone four months ago and my dad is still, like, "How do you call?"'

Also consider the widespread use of electronic games. Teenagers (and even pre-teens) like to play the latest games, but some games are clearly labelled '18+' meaning that they are not considered suitable for younger children. Games such as Grand Theft Auto, which involves carnage on an unprecedented scale, is clearly not the kind of game that most parents would want their 14-year-old to play. However, it appears that (according to a 2005 survey by market researchers Modulum) most parents are concerned about the amount of time their children spend playing video games, but are less concerned about the content of the games (BBC 2005). This may be because parents are not aware of the extent to which game graphics have moved on in the last ten years or so, from jerky cartoon characters to images which are close to live actors. Parents who would not allow their children to watch films with violent or sexual content seem to have no problem with games with the same content, even though the games are interactive (which makes them more powerful) and the unsuitable content goes on throughout the game, not just for a few minutes during an otherwise acceptable film.

Since adding the '18+' symbol increases dramatically the desirability of the game, game manufacturers are not entirely displeased; however, firms know that they must, eventually, clean up their act or legislation will be brought in. Meanwhile, children will continue to wheedle and manipulate their parents into buying the latest games, suitable or not.

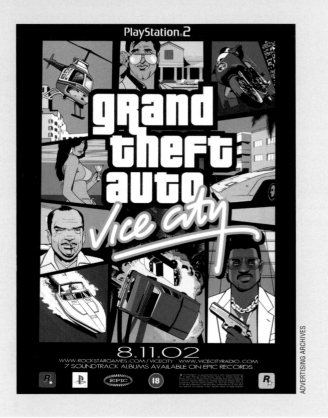

advertising in which the spokesperson is a parental or authority figure, teenagers often buy products simply because their parents disapprove of them (Rummel *et al.* 2000). This is probably part of the process by which people become independent adults, and demonstrate that they are no longer children.

Socialization continues down the generations even after the child has become a fully independent adult, however. Some research shows that brand loyalties can be passed down from one generation to another, even for three or four generations within the same family (Mandrik, Fern and Bao 2004; Olsen 1993). The reason for this is that people enjoy using the brands that they remember from their childhood: specific brands of sauces, soups, marmalade or soft drinks commonly remain popular in the family for many years after the child has grown up and left home. In some respects the family identity is carried on through the generations by these means (Epp and Arnould 2006).

As children (and of course their parents) grow older, advice on consumption begins to go the other way. Parents begin to seek the advice of their children on some aspects, particularly where new technology is concerned or where the child has acquired specialist knowledge. The evidence is that parents with a 'warm' approach to parenting are more likely to learn from their children (Grossbart et al. 2002).

The changing nature of the family

One of the changes currently occurring throughout Western Europe is the increase in the number of single-person households (office for National Statistics 2002, p. 45); there is, of course, a difference between a household and a family. A further change, coming about through the tremendous increase in the divorce rate, is the growing number of single-parent families. A second major change is the worldwide shift in attitude towards having large families. Since the advent of mass contraception, more and more women say that they would prefer to have fewer children than was the case even ten years ago. Currently, European birthrates are below the replacement rate for the population, meaning that the population would be shrinking if it were not for immigration. One UK study predicted that one in five women born between 1960 and 1990 will never have children, and the birthrate among those women will be half that of their mothers' generation (European Union 1995).

In Figure 11.5, the 1900 family has more children, but many people at that time remained single. From the seven people in the example, only five children are born. In 1960, a more typical family size would be three children, but many more people married and had children: that was an expectation of the baby boom years. Nowadays, families are smaller and many people never have children at all, so in our final example the ten people in the diagram only manage four children between them. It should be noted that these are examples only: the birthrate actually has not fluctuated quite that dramatically over the period.

Large families such as this are becoming rare.

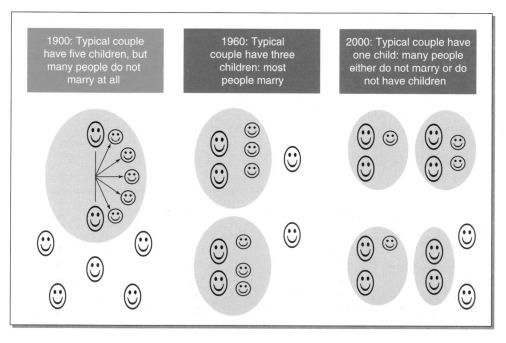

Figure 11.5
Effects of the falling birthrate

Table 11.3 The family life cycle

Stage of life cycle	Explanation
Single stage	Single people tend to have low earnings, but also have low outgoings so have a high discretionary income. Tend to be more fashion and recreation orientated, spending on clothes, music, alcohol, eating out, holidays, leisure pursuits and hobbies, and 'mating game' products. Often buying cars and items for their first residence away from home.
Newly married couples	Newly-weds without children are usually dual-income households and therefore usually well off. Still tend to spend on similar things to the singles, but also have the highest proportion of expenditure on household goods, consumer durables and appliances. Appear to be more susceptible to advertising.
Full nest I	When the first child arrives, one parent usually stops working outside the home so family income drops sharply. The baby creates new needs which alter expenditure patterns; furniture and furnishings for the baby, baby food, vitamins, toys, nappies and baby food. Family savings decline, and usually couples are dissatisfied with their financial position.
Full nest II	The youngest child is over six, so often both parents will work outside the home. The employed spouse's income has risen due to career progression, and the family's total income recovers. Consumption patterns still heavily influenced by children; bicycles, piano lessons, large-size packages of breakfast cereals, cleaning products, etc.
Full nest III	Family income improves as the children get older. Both parents are likely to be working outside the home, and both may have had some career progression; also, the children will be earning some of their own money from paper rounds, part-time jobs etc. Family purchases might be a second car, replacement furniture, some luxury items and children's education.
Empty nest I	Children have grown up and left home. Couple are at the height of their careers and spending power, have low mortgages, very reduced living costs. Often go for luxury travel, restaurants, and theatre – so they need fashionable clothing, jewellery, diets, spas, health clubs, cosmetics, hairdressing.
Empty nest II	Main breadwinner has retired, so some drop in income. Expenditure is more health-orientated, buying appliance for sleep, over-the-counter remedies for indigestion. Often buy a smaller house or move to an apartment in Spain.
Solitary survivor	If still in the workforce, widows and widowers enjoy a good income. May spend more money on holidays, as well as the items mentioned in Empty Nest II.
Retired solitary survivor	Same general consumption pattern as above but on a smaller scale due to reduced income. Has special needs for love, affection and security so may join clubs, etc.

The family is a flexible concept, and families go through life cycles. There have been various versions of the family life cycle, but most are based on the original work of Wells and Gubar (1966). Table 11.3 shows the stages of the family life cycle.

The main problem with this model is that it was originally developed in the 1960s, when couples rarely lived together without being married, there were very few single-parent families, and the divorce rate was dramatically lower than it is in the twenty-first century. Towards the end of the life cycle (from Empty Nest I onwards) it is likely that the model holds true fairly well, but it is unlikely that the earlier stages will follow the same pattern.

For example, it is now the case that single-person households represent 29.1 per cent of UK households, whereas households comprising a married couple and their dependent children only comprise 22.6 per cent of households (Office for National Statistics 2002).

The traditional nuclear family of two parents with their own children has become a minority of households: it is more likely that a household will consist of a mother with her children from her first marriage, a husband or partner who pays maintenance to his ex-wife for the children from his first marriage, and possibly a new child from the new partnership. Even more common is a childless home, either a single-person household or a childless couple living together: these represent more than half of all UK households (Office for National Statistics 2002).

It may be more realistic to consider the life cycle of the individual, and link this to possible family roles and responsibilities rather than consider different possible family structures. Here are some of the life stages an individual might have:

1 *Living alone I* – This is someone who has left home, has a job and is living alone.

2 *Cohabiting, no children I* – This would be a couple who are living together without being married, but have no children.

3 *Cohabiting, with joint children* – This couple now have a child or children, but are not married.

4 *Married, no children I* – Similar to cohabiting, no children I, but have a legal relationship as well as a romantic one.

5 *Married, with joint children* – Similar to cohabiting, but with the legal relationship.

6 *Living alone II* – This is someone who is divorced or widowed.

7 *Single, with children* – Someone who is divorced or never married, and is bringing up one or more children alone.

8 *Cohabiting, no children II* – This couple are divorced or separated from earlier partners, and are now living together.

9 *Cohabiting, with children II* – The children may be from a previous relationship, or may not live with the couple at all but may be occasional visitors at weekends or during the week.

10 *Married, no children II* – This couple have been married before, and may or may not intend having children together at some future time.

11 *Married, with children II* – This couple are second-time married, with children from earlier relationships who may or may not live with them.

12 *Married or cohabiting couple with grown-up children still at home* – This situation is becoming more common as property values rise and single people find it harder to buy a home. These households can be extremely wealthy, since three or more adults are contributing to the overall income.

There are likely to be other, more complex, situations but each of these situations impacts on family decision-making, and (particularly in the case of cohabiting or married couples with children from previous relationships) other people who are not actually part of the family will also need to be considered (in this case, ex-partners). Working out the decision rules between the various players is likely to be difficult in these cases, and in some cases special marketing activities are in place to take account of single parents who have access rights to their children on specific days. The concept of being 'a father for half an hour in McDonald's' has become familiar, and some advertising reflects this.

The divorce–remarry cycle also means dramatic surges in income. Divorce usually means a dramatic fall in disposable income as the economies of scale in shared consumption evaporate and the individuals have to set up their own homes: this can mean a boost for businesses selling furniture, household appliances and homes, of course. Later on, though, the remarry phase often leads to a sudden sharp increase in wealth as the previous single people pool their resources. When people in their forties remarry, having finished paying out for child maintenance and (often) now owning substantial equity in their homes, and combine their assets they can find themselves suddenly wealthy.

Gender roles

There are more women than men in the population, largely due to two factors: greater infant mortality among boys and greater life expectancy of women. Women's roles have changed greatly over the past 30 years or so; women make more (or most) of the purchasing decisions, earn around a third of the household income and make most of the decisions regarding the home and the children.

Major purchasing decisions are far more likely to be made jointly, and men are now much more likely to participate in decisions regarding the household expenditure. An American survey carried out in the 1990s showed that 35 per cent of couples said that they were equally responsible for food shopping; 8 per cent said the man was solely responsible; the other 57 per cent said the woman did the food shopping (Opinion Research Corporation 1990). In another survey carried out in Scotland ten years later, 30 per cent of men reported doing the food shopping (Ellaway and Macintyre 2000). Although it is still the case that the bulk of food shopping is done by women, the trend is for more men to do some (or all) of the shopping and some (or all) of the cooking.

The change in gender roles comes from the following:

1 Technology means that most jobs do not require physical strength, so more careers are open to women.

2 Mass contraception has freed women from childbearing.

3 A more ordered society has led to greater physical security; there is less need for the defence role of the male.

4 More widespread education means that women are not satisfied to stay home and do housework.

This shift in gender roles and expectations is affecting marketers, who are now changing the appeal of their advertising to meet the new conditions. For example, Flash Wipes are advertised showing a man doing the cleaning: he is portrayed as the average man, doing the cleaning and winning praise for doing so, but revealing to the audience that in fact the cleaning is really no big task. Even 20 years ago such advertisements would only have been shown for comic purposes, and even now men are frequently portrayed as being incapable of doing the housework properly.

Gender roles might also include sexual orientation, which affords another dimension to the definition of family. In the UK, civil partnerships between same-sex couples were introduced towards the end of 2005, and there was consequently a flurry of people in long-term relationships going through the ceremony. Registering a civil partnership

Ads such as this show that it's OK for men to do the cleaning.

Figure 11.6

Drivers for gender role change

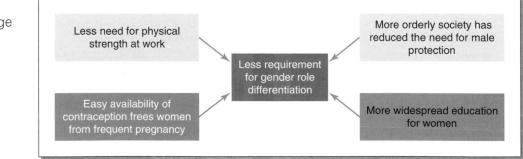

in this way gives the couple the same legal status as if they were a heterosexual married couple: giving the relationship a legal status means that such partnerships have the status of being families by the definition. No doubt the people concerned already felt as if they were families, and in many cases they have even had children either from previous heterosexual marriages or by adoption.

Gay people tend to be wealthier than heterosexuals: male homosexuals earn an average 23 per cent more than heterosexual men, have twice as many credit cards as the general population, and spend more on entertainment than average (BBC 1998). In the UK, gays' disposable income is called the Pink Pound (in the US it is called the Dorothy Dollar) and is worth around £6 billion a year. This has meant that gays have been targeted by some financial institutions and by information services, clubs and even holiday companies such as Pink Pound Travel. Since gays are estimated to account for at least 4 per cent of the population (the exact figure is hard to determine as some gays still feel that they would face prejudice or hostility if they were open about their sexuality) they represent a substantial market.

Eventually one might expect that gender role will not be an issue in advertising at all, but since advertising (at least in part) reflects society, this may still be some way off.

Other functions of the family

Families also provide economic well-being, emotional support and suitable family lifestyles (Figure 11.7). Because families share consumption, the standard of living of the members is higher than would have been the case had they chosen to live separately. In some families, economic well-being is also generated by employment in the family business. Because the overall tasks within the family are divided between the members, some members might exchange earning their own money for taking on a larger role within the family, for example staying at home to care for small children. In most cases this is a female role, but there are more cases of men becoming 'house husbands' and it is certainly an option which is open when both parents have careers.

In the majority of UK families both parents work outside the home. There is considerable debate as to whether this has a detrimental or a positive effect on children, but it certainly has a positive effect on the family's finances, increasing spending power and also (on the downside) increasing the need for labour-saving devices and behaviour, for example ready meals, child care and children's entertainment devices which leave the parents free to carry out other tasks.

In traditional societies children are expected to contribute to the family's finances, in particular teenage children are expected to work and contribute. In most Western families teenagers would be expected to retain any earnings, either to save towards their education or adult life in general, or at least to pay for their own entertainment and perhaps clothing items.

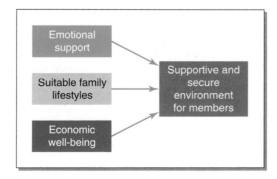

Figure 11.7

Other functions of the family

Economic well-being is also provided when (for example) parents pay for a child's education, or help with the deposit for a house. Sometimes the help goes in the other direction: grown-up children might pay for a care home or for improvements to an elderly parent's home. In either case, marketers have a role in providing facilities for this to happen.

Talking point

In less 'advanced' societies children are with their parents pretty much all the time. Little boys are with their dads, building huts or digging for crops or making things, while little girls are with their mothers collecting fruit or cooking or making clothes. In our more 'advanced' society we all go out to work and we apparently subcontract our child-rearing to nannies, child-care centres and schools.

Are we really doing ourselves any favours here? Are we raising a generation of confused kids who don't know whether the nanny is the true authority on everything, or Mummy and Daddy? Anyway, does it matter? After all, one great advantage of our way of doing things is that most children make it past five years old, most don't get eaten by lions and most don't suffer from debilitating diseases!

Emotional support is a core function of families. This can comprise love and affection, but also involves moral support and encouragement: this emotional support has formed the basis for the entire greeting-card industry. When families are unable to provide appropriate emotional support from within the group, it may turn to counselling or even psychiatric services to provide professional help for its members.

Finally, families also help to establish suitable lifestyles. Family members bear more than a physical resemblance to each other: they tend to have similar attitudes about the importance of education, about reading, about environmentalism, about home décor, about holidays and about appropriate entertainments (sport, dining out, etc.). There is a trend towards family members acting independently rather than sharing activities, but the idea of spending 'quality time' with each other has recently led to a tendency to seek out activities and experiences which can be shared. Marketers have not been slow to capitalize on this, promoting family leisure activities such as weekends away in hotels, meals out in fast-food restaurants, and so forth.

Roles in family consumption

Within families, a great deal of decision-making is collective. Even such basic decisions as buying underwear might be shared or carried out by one member of the family on behalf of another. The traditional example would be a mother buying underwear for the children of the family, but many women buy underwear for their husbands, and it is far from unknown for husbands to buy underwear for their wives, often as Valentine or birthday gifts.

Within families, consumption and purchase roles are often divided between family members. There are thought to be eight basic roles in family decision-making, as shown in Table 11.4.

Depending on the type of product being considered, family members may adopt different roles for each decision. In other words, deciders are not necessarily deciders for everything – they may be deciders for some categories of product (e.g. holidays) and gatekeepers for another category (e.g. home entertainment systems). Likewise, roles often overlap, or the same person occupies more than one role.

In Figure 11.8, the main arrows show where each individual has a major input. The fine arrows show where the individuals have a lesser input. Obviously the same individual may have more than one role in the purchase decision.

Table 11.4 Roles in family decision-making

Role	Explanation
Influencers	These are the family members who perhaps have no direct involvement in the purchase or consumption of the item, but who can offer help and advice.
Gatekeepers	These members control the flow of information to the others. A gatekeeper may be the person who reads the brochures or watches the advertising on TV.
Deciders	These members have the final say on the product being bought or consumed. In most families, the deciders would be the parents, but this is not always the case: it depends on the product being considered.
Buyers	Family members who make the actual purchase are the buyers. It may be that a decision is made to book a particular holiday, and the member with the best IT skills is given the task of booking it online, for example.
Preparers	These members transform the product into a form suitable for the others to consume it. The obvious example is cooking food, but the concept could equally apply to one of the children of the family programming the new TV set.
Users	The family members who will consume the product.
Maintainers	The family members who will ensure that the product is in good condition for the others to use it. This not only applies to someone who mends the kitchen cupboards, it also applies to someone who cleans the house and does the laundry.
Disposers	Members who have the job of removing the used products and packaging or arranging for the sale or trade-in of products for which the family has no further use.

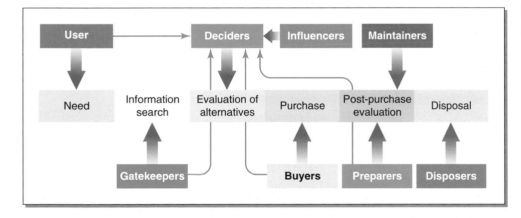

Figure 11.8

Family roles and decisions

Children appear to have a greater role in family decision-making than in the past. Research conducted by Tinson and Nancarrow (2005) shows that children themselves believe that they have considerable influence in many family purchase decisions, even including buying a car among these. The areas in which children believe themselves to be most important as decision-makers are shown in Table 11.5 (page 250).

Other research carried out in Canada indicates that children there have an even greater influence on decisions: 40 per cent of children in one study believed themselves to be the main decision-makers with respect to choice of restaurant when eating out (Labrecque and Ricard 2001). The same study showed that children underestimate their influence on the decision to go to a restaurant in the first place.

Table 11.5 How children perceive themselves to have influenced the purchase of different products

Product	Percentage influence
Casual clothes for me	91%
Trainers for me	88%
CDs for me	84%
Sweets for me	83%
Computers for me	83%
Soft drinks for me	80%
School shoes for me	80%
A family trip to the cinema	73%
Food for me for lunch at the weekend	73%
A holiday I would go on with the family	63%
Going out for a family meal	52%
A family car	37%

Figure 11.9

Communication pattern and children's influence

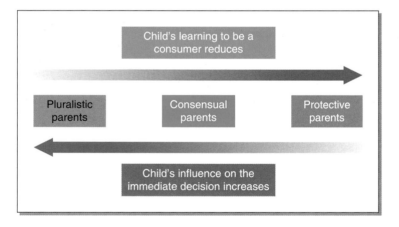

There is some evidence to suggest that the family's communication pattern is also related to the child's influence on the decision making process. Communication patterns usually fall into one or other of the following categories (Figure 11.9) (Shoham, Rose and Bakir 2004):

1 *Pluralistic parents* – These parents encourage their children to express their ideas and preferences. Not surprisingly, these families experience the greatest influence from the children.

2 *Consensual parents* – These parents encourage their children to seek harmony, but they are influenced by the children's ideas.

3 *Protective parents* – These parents believe that 'mother knows best' and in general expect children to agree to the parents' choices.

It seems probable that children with pluralistic parents would be likely to develop consumer skills early, but might also be the most likely to use pester power to get their own way. Children with protective parents might take longer to develop consumer skills, but would perhaps be more likely to adopt brands favoured by their parents in later life.

Some teenagers spend a great deal of time on the Internet, and consequently regard themselves as experts at researching information relating to major purchases. These teenagers, called Internet mavens, can contribute significantly to family decision-making, especially in the information search phase of the process (Belch, Krentler and Willis-Flurry 2005). Internet mavens are usually accepted by their parents as having more knowledge and more information-gathering skills than anyone else in the family.

Summary

Families are often said to be the building blocks of society. We are influenced more by our families than by anybody else: partly this is because the influence starts at a very early age, partly it is because we spend a large part of our lives living with our families, and partly it's because our family relationships (especially those with our siblings) are the longest-lasting relationships in our lives.

Because families share so much of their consumption, the ways in which they interact and make decisions are of great interest to marketers. Families share decision-making in many ways, and the views of family members are still important even when it is the parents who make the final decision.

There are many different patterns of family, but what they have in common is relationships by blood, marriage or adoption; shared consumption: face-to-face contact on a daily basis; emotional, economic and lifestyle support for their members; and finally shared regard for each other's welfare.

The key points from this chapter are as follows:
- 'Family' has several definitions, each of which is dependant on culture and circumstances.
- Culture has a marked effect on decision-making styles.
- All members of a family have some input into decision-making.
- Conflict is common in families because of shared consumption.
- Children have to be taught to be effective consumers.
- Brand loyalty can pass down through several generations.
- Family life cycle models are pluralistic in twenty-first century society.
- Family members often adopt specific roles in the purchase and consumption process.

Chapter review questions

1 Why is the family powerful in influencing consumption behaviour?

2 Why is the family a culturally based concept?

3 What are the main changes in the family in recent years?

4 How might family purchase roles change in the next 20 years?

5 What are the drivers for change in family purchase roles?

6 How might the change in the ethnic structure of European society affect family decision-making?

7 How do children influence decision-making?

8 How does parenting style affect children's consumption behaviour?

9 What are the main criticisms of the family life cycle concept?

10 What are the key functions of a family?

Preview case study revisited
Raising Kids

Making appropriate choices is not easy when you're a parent. Surrounded by conflicting advice, parents often lack the support networks their own parents and grandparents enjoyed – so confusion reigns supreme.

Luckily, help is at hand. A website called Raising Kids (www.raisingkids.co.uk) has everything anyone could need for raising children. Founded by parenting-skills specialist Dr Pat Spungin, Raising Kids offers advice and support online. There are blogs, advice on specific subjects, news reviews, competitions and prize give-aways. Parents can join the website: although most of the content is freely available to anyone who cares to visit, joining provides parents with access to the discussion forums (blogs) and makes them eligible for extra information and free offers.

The site funds itself by winning a small amount of advertising revenue, but it is certainly far from commercial – other sites are characterized by persistent ads and pop-ups, but Raising Kids limits the amount and type of advertising. The site allows companies to e-mail the site's members, who number over 65,000 parents, but editor Catherine Hanly insists that only one such mailing per month will be allowed. Raising Kids does not want to make a nuisance of itself to its readers!

Companies can also sponsor different areas of the site, a particularly useful promotion for some companies since they might have a particular affinity for one or another section of the site – for example, the site has special areas devoted to babies aged 0–1 year, pre-school children aged 1–4 years, and so forth. Raising Kids also offers companies the opportunity to use their members for research purposes, either through the monthly omnibus survey in which companies can buy questions, or through 'bespoke' surveys which are specially designed and conducted. These surveys enable companies to become more responsive to the needs of parents and their children – which is of benefit to everyone.

Bringing up a family is a challenge to anyone – but Raising Kids offers a way of making it all so much easier, and certainly a great deal less lonely.

BY KIND PERMISSION OF DR P. SPUNGIN WWW.RAISINGKIDS.CO.UK

Case study
Blue Kangaroo

Even ten years ago restaurants in the UK were extremely reluctant to cater for families. Some restaurants called themselves 'family' restaurants, but they were often far from child-friendly: children were supposed to be seen and not heard, and for the most part the only concessions to children were puzzle place mats (which were no use once the food arrived) and a 'children's menu' which usually consisted of a choice of fish fingers or baked beans.

This unimaginative approach to catering for children meant that families were less likely to eat out together except on special occasions. This had two immediate effects – first, and most obviously, it meant that the parents were unlikely to patronize restaurants much until their children had grown up, and second it meant a delay in teaching young people that eating out is a pleasant social occasion.

Over the last ten years or so, restaurants have become much more child-friendly. Jamie Oliver's parents run The Cricketers in Essex, where children can have a child-size portion of anything on the adult menu: there is also a more 'traditional' children's menu, but the increasing sophistication of children's palates means that they are not always going to be satisfied with beans on toast or frozen pizza. Even restaurants at tourist sites such as the Eden Project in Cornwall, or Hackney City Farm, have gone to the trouble of expanding their menus to bring children into the mainstream. In many cases restaurants offer gluten-free, diabetic, vegan or vegetarian options. Some restaurants go out of their way to encourage children to visit – the Giraffe chain (they prefer to be called a herd) of twelve restaurants in London will give a free smoothie to any child who brings in a coloured-in picture from the company website.

COURTESY OF BLUE KANGAROO RESTAURANT

The ultimate family award, though, goes to Blue Kangaroo. Blue Kangaroo is a restaurant based in Chelsea, London: it is probably the most child-friendly restaurant in the UK, as many reviews have testified (the *Guardian* reviewer said that the staff should be taken out and canonized). The restaurant has a downstairs play area where the children can go while the parents enjoy a meal, or the family can eat together and visit the play area later. The children are supervised by closed-circuit TV, so parents can monitor them on the big screen in the dining room. Alternatively, parents can eat in the Blue Kangaroo Café, which is right next to the play area and serves the same food. The play area is divided up into a soft space for babies, a toddler zone and a playframe for four to seven-year-olds.

The children's menu is imaginative without being frightening – fish fingers have become fish goujons, for example, but the children's menu includes the restaurant's famous salmon fishcakes and several vegetarian options. Penne pasta, spaghetti carbonara and organic pork sausages also feature alongside mini-burgers. Main courses for adults are around the £10 mark, while all children's meals are £5.45. Wines start from £12 a bottle, so a meal at Blue Kangaroo is hardly going to break the bank. The quality of the food is as high as anywhere in London, but most importantly the restaurant maintains the high quality when it comes to serving the children – their food is also top-quality, organic and imaginative.

Blue Kangaroo's motto is, '*We deliver exhausted and happy children to refreshed and relaxed parents*'. There are many parents in the London area who would agree with this claim.

COURTESY OF BLUE KANGAROO RESTAURANT

Case study questions

1 What might be the drivers for the increasing sophistication of children's menus?

2 Why would Giraffe actively encourage children to want to come to the restaurant?

3 Why do Blue Kangaroo offer two separate eating areas if the menu is the same in each?

4 What is the role of pester power in family decision-making about restaurants?

5 How might a restaurant such as the one at Hackney City Farm improve its child-friendliness still further?

References

BBC (1998) Business: The economy. The pink pound. *News*, 31 July.

BBC (2005) Parents 'ignore game age ratings'. *News*, 24 June.

Belch, Michael A., Krentler, Kathleen A., and Willis-Flurry, Laura A. (2005) Teen Internet mavens: influence in family decision-making. *Journal of Business Research*, 58: 569–75.

Carlson, Les, and Grossbart, S. (1988) Parental style and consumer socialization of children. *Journal of Consumer Research*, 15: 77–94.

Curasi, Carolyn (2006) Maybe it IS your father's Oldsmobile: the construction and preservation of family identity through the transfer of possessions. *Advances in Consumer Behaviour*, 33(1): 83.

Ekstrom, Karin M., Tansuhaj, Patriya S., and Foxman, Ellen (1987) Children's influence in family decisions and consumer socialization: a reciprocal view. *Advances in Consumer Research*, 14 eds Melanie Wallendorf and Paul Anderson (Provo, UT: Association for Consumer Research).

Ellaway, Anne, and Macintyre, Sally (2000) Shopping for food in socially contrasting localities. *British Food Journal*, 102(1): 52–9.

Epp, Amber M., and Arnould, Eric J. (2006) Enacting the family legacy: how family themes influence consumption behaviour. *Advances in Consumer Research*, 33(1).

European Union (1995) The population of the EU on 1 January 1995. *Statistics in Focus. Population and Social Conditions No. 8* (Luxembourg: Office for Official Publications of the European Communities).

Fernandez, Karen V., and Veer, Ekant (2004) The gold that binds: the ritualistic use of jewellery in an Indian wedding. *Advances in Consumer Research*, 31(1): 53.

Filiatrault, Pierre, and Ritchie, J.R. Brent (1980) Joint purchasing decisions: a comparison of influence structure in family and couple decision-making units. *Journal of Consumer Research*, 7 (September): 131–40.

Green, Robert T., Leonardi, Jean-Paul, Chandon, Jean-Louis, Cunningham, Isabella C.M., Verhage, Bronis, and Strazzieru, Alain (1983) Societal development and family purchasing roles: a cross-national study. *Journal of Consumer Research*, 9 (March), 4: 436–42.

Grossbart, Sanford, Hughes, Stephanie McConnell, Pryor, Susie, and Yost, Amber (2002) Socialisation aspects of parents, children and the Internet. *Advances in Consumer Research*, 29(1): 66–70.

Hamilton, Cathy, and Catterall, Miriam (2006) Consuming love in poor families: children's influence on consumption decisions. *Journal of Marketing Management*, 22(9/10): 1031–52.

Hartman, Cathy L., and Kiecker, Pamela (2004) Jewellery – passing along the continuum of sacred and profane meanings. *Advances in Consumer Research*, 31(1): 53.

John, Deborah Roedder (1999) Consumer socialization of children: a retrospective look at twenty-five years of research. *Journal of Consumer Research*, 26 (Dec): 183–213.

Komarovsky, Mirra (1961) Class differences in family decision-making. *Household Decision Making*, ed. Nelson N. Foote (New York: New York University Press).

Labrecque, J., and Ricard, L. (2001) Children's influence on family decision-making: a restaurant study. *Journal of Business Research*, 54 (November): 173–6.

Mandrik, Carter A., Fern, Edward F., and Bao, Yeqing (2004) Intergenerational influence in mothers and young adult daughters. *Advances in Consumer Research*, 31: 697–9.

Marketing News (1983) Teenage daughters of working mothers have a big role in purchase, brand selection decisions, 18 (Feb): 20.

Office of National Statistics (2002) General Household Survey (London: ONS).

Olsen, Barbara (1993) Brand loyalty and lineage: exploring new dimensions for research. In *Advances in Consumer Research*, 20, eds Leigh Macalister and Michael L. Rothschild (Provo, UT: Association for Consumer Research).

Opinion Research Corporation (1990) *Trends: 1990 Consumer Attitudes and the Supermarket* (Princeton, NJ: ORC).

Rose, Gregory M. (1999): Consumer socialization, parental style, and developmental timetables in the United States and Japan. *Journal of Marketing*, 63 (July): 105–19.

Rose, Gregory S., Dalakis, Vassilis, Kropp, Fredric, and Kamineni, Rajeev (2002) Raising young consumers: consumer socialization and parental style across cultures. *Advances in Consumer Behaviour*, 29(1).

Rummel, Amy, Howard, John, Swinton, Jennifer M., and Seymour, D. Bradley (2000) You can't have that! A study of reactance effects and children's consumer behaviour. *Journal of Marketing Theory and Practice*, (Winter): 38–45.

Shoham, Aviv, Rose, Gregory M., and Bakir, Aysen (2004) The effect of family communication patterns on mothers' and fathers' perceived influence in family decision making. *Advances in Consumer Behaviour*, 31: 692.

Timmins, Nicholas (1995) One in five women to remain childless. *Independent*, 4 October.

Tinson, J., and Nancarrow, C. (2005) The influence of children on purchases. *International Journal of Marketing*, 47(1): 5–27.

United Nations Economic Commission for Europe (2000) *Population and Housing Census Statistical Standards and Studies Number 49* (Geneva: UNECE).

Ward, Cheryl B. (2006) He wants, she wants: gender, category and disagreement in spouses' joint decisions. *Advances in Consumer Research*, 33(1): 117–23.

Wells, William D., and Gubar, George (1966) The life cycle concept in marketing research. *Journal of Marketing Research*, 3 (Nov): 353–63.

Williams, Tonya P. (2006) Money and meaning: the role of social bonds and capital in inter vivos gifting. *Advances in Consumer Research*, 33(1): 7.

Wimalasir, Joyantha S. (2004) A cross-national study on children's purchasing behaviour and parental response. *Journal of Consumer Marketing*, 21(4): 274–84.

Part four
Decisions and their aftermath

This section of the book shows how the behavioural theories outlined in previous chapters affect the actual decision-making process. The section draws on research conducted by marketing academics and others, and is the largest section of the book.

Chapter 12 examines some of the most common models of the decision-making process. It covers pre-purchase activities, information searches, making the actual choice and decision rules which might be developed and applied in choosing which brands to buy. The chapter also examines repeat purchases – issues surrounding loyalty and routine buying behaviour where there is little thought or decision-making required.

Chapter 13 is about innovation. It is a marketing cliché that 'newness' is an important motivator for buying a product, and it seems to be the case that people like to have a degree of novelty in their lives. This chapter looks at the ways in which innovations are diffused, and at how different people respond to innovative products.

Chapter 14 examines a key factor in consumer behaviour: involvement. We have all had the experience of falling in love with a product, or of being so delighted with a particular brand that we will buy no other: this chapter explains the mechanisms by which this comes about. The chapter also looks at a related topic, the purchase of unsought goods (products which we know we need but rarely seek out, such as life insurance or funeral plans).

Chapter 15 considers what happens after the purchase has occurred. A purchase is far from being the end of the story: people evaluate what they have bought, and consider how they might behave differently in future. They may be delighted, in which case a further purchase is likely as is positive word of mouth about the product, or they may be disappointed in which case they may complain and seek redress. Either way, eventually the product (or what is left of it after consumption) will need to be disposed of in some way. This in itself is a topical issue, given the environmental implications of creating more waste.

Chapter 16 is about consumer behaviour in services markets. Defining what is and is not a service is problematical in the current marketing climate, since almost all physical products have a service element and almost all services have an element of physical product, but in the twenty-first-century business climate the service element is often the most important differentiator between products. Due to the difficulties of assessing services in advance of purchase, products with a large service element do require a different decision-making approach. This chapter considers those differences.

Chapter 17 is about the ways in which marketers group consumers. Segmentation is one of the key concepts in marketing, and this chapter outlines methods of grouping people with similar needs according to their characteristics and behaviour.

Some people make purchasing decisions for a living. Chapter 18 is concerned with ways of applying consumer behaviour theory to industrial buying behaviour, highlighting the similarities and differences between buying on behalf of an organization and buying on behalf of oneself or one's family.

Chapter 19 brings together the previous chapters of the section by relating consumer behaviour to the marketing mix. The mix model used is the seven P model which was developed to include service elements: the chapter shows how marketers can use knowledge of consumer behaviour in day-to-day planning decisions.

Chapter 12
New and repeat buying behaviour

Learning objectives After reading this chapter, you should be able to:

1 describe how needs become apparent

2 explain some of the limiting factors on information searches

3 explain how assortment management affects problem-solving

4 explain the role of consideration sets

5 explain how decision rules are established and used

Introduction

This chapter is concerned with the ways in which consumers approach making purchase decisions. The methods used depend on whether the purchase is a new one, or a repeat of a previous purchase; whether the product is novel or tried and tested; whether the purchase is routine or out of the ordinary. Decision-making does not end when the purchase is made: people evaluate their purchases, and use the information in the next round of decision-making.

In fact, many decisions are made without much conscious thought. Decision-making often happens below the conscious level, but this does not necessarily mean that the processes used in a more complex decision are not followed – it merely means that the consumer is not aware of them.

Decision-making models

Decision-making models are often complex and involve many stages. The John Dewey model (Dewey 1910) outlined in the early part of the twentieth century gives the following five stages:

1 A difficulty is felt (need identification).

2 The difficulty is located and defined.

3 Possible solutions are suggested.

4 Consequences are considered.

5 A solution is accepted.

This model of decision-making is probably excessively rational, and is certainly far more complex than most purchase situations warrant. In the vast majority of purchase situations, the individual simply buys the same brand as last time, or spends very little time in evaluating choices. Life is simply too busy to spend much time agonizing over which brand of biscuit to buy.

Later, Engel, Kollat and Blackwell developed the EKB model of consumer behaviour, which later became the CDP (Consumer Decision Process) model, and which follows seven stages (Blackwell, Miniard and Engel 2006). These are shown in Figure 12.1 (on page 261), and are:

1 *Need recognition* – The individual recognizes that something is missing from his or her life.

Preview case study
Selfridge's

In 1909 Gordon Selfridge established a new department store in Oxford Street, London. He declared that Selfridge's was 'for everyone', and for the next 90 years the store lived up to that promise of being London's premier department store. Department stores meant that everything a customer needed could be found under one roof – making the search for products much simpler compared with shopping around many small stores.

By the mid-1990s, however, department stores in general and Selfridge's in particular were losing ground to smaller specialist stores, and to hypermarkets and edge-of-town retailers. Shopping in central London was losing some of its appeal – the impossibility of parking, the cost of public transport, the difficulty of carrying goods home afterwards and many other problems meant that West End shopping was becoming the prerogative of tourists. For Selfridge's, the problem was to move the store from 'famous building' status to 'famous brand' status ahead of plans to move the firm out into the regions of Britain. A key issue was to communicate the idea of shopping as entertainment, according to marketing director James Bidwell. 'We firmly believe in the power of the brand, as opposed to traditional department stores, where layout was historically dictated by product groupings,' Bidwell says.

Selfridge's needed to get back to basics – to making a store which would make shopping easier, and which

would create an attractive experience for shoppers. Helping consumers make appropriate purchasing decisions was a problem of communication and of clear positioning of the brand.

2 *Search for information* – This information search may be internal (remembering facts about products, or recalling experiences with them) or external (reading about possible products, visiting shops, etc.).

3 *Pre-purchase evaluation of alternatives* – The individual considers which of the possible alternatives might be best for fulfilling the need.

4 *Purchase* – The act of making the final selection and paying for it.

5 *Consumption* – Using the product for the purpose of fulfilling the need.

6 *Post-consumption evaluation* – Considering whether the product actually satisfied the need or not, and whether there were any problems arising from its purchase and consumption.

7 *Divestment* – Disposing of the product or its packaging or any residue left from consuming the product.

The similarity between Dewey's model and the CDP model is obvious, and similar criticisms apply, but both models offer a basic outline of how people make consumption decisions. People do not buy unless they feel they have a need (see Chapter 1 for a definition of what constitutes a need). A need is felt when there is a divergence between the

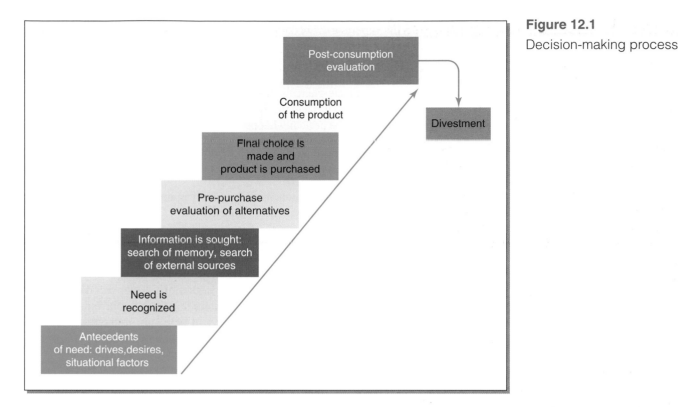

Figure 12.1

Decision-making process

person's **actual state** and their **desired state**. The degree of difference between the two states is what determines the level of motivation the person feels to do something about the problem, and this will in turn depend on a number of external factors (see Figure 12.2).

As explained in Chapter 1, need becomes apparent when there is a divergence of the desired and actual states. The motivation that arises from this depends on the level of disparity between the actual state and the desired state. For example, a driver who is late for an appointment may be thirsty, but not thirsty enough to stop the car at a motorway services. Likewise, a householder might have run out of one or two items, but still has enough food in the house to get by on; as the days go by more and more items are used up, and

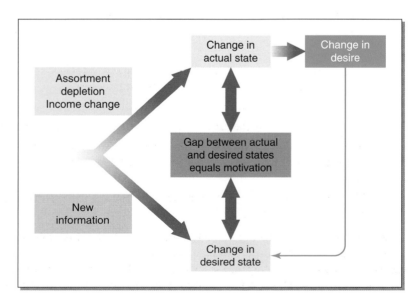

Figure 12.2

Actual and desired states

eventually a trip to the supermarket becomes essential. The disparity between the actual and desired states grows greater, in other words, and therefore the householder becomes more strongly motivated to do something about it.

There are two possible reasons for a divergence between the desired and the actual states; one is that the actual state changes, the other is that the desired state changes. In practice, it is rare for the actual states and the desired states to be the same, since this would imply that the consumer would be perfectly happy and have everything that he or she could possibly want, which is rarely the case in an imperfect world.

Causes of shift of the actual state might be taken from the following list (Onkvisit and Shaw 1994):

- *Assortment depletion* – Consumption, spoilage, or wear and tear on the stock of goods or products within the individual's assortment.

- *Income change* – This can be upwards, through a salary increase or windfall, or downwards through (say) redundancy.

Causes of shifts in the desired state are often more to do with marketing activities. This is because new information may change the individual's aspirations. If the individual sees a better car, hears a better stereo or otherwise becomes aware that there is a better solution to the problem than the one currently in use there is likely to be a shift in the desired state. From a marketing viewpoint, this approach is most effective when the consumers are not satisfied with their present products.

Changing desire is often brought on by a change in actual state; getting a new job may mean moving house, for example. Sometimes a pay increase (which is a shift in the actual state) will raise the individual's aspirations and he or she will consider purchases that previously had been out of reach and therefore not even considered. For example, a lottery win might prompt an individual to book the holiday of a lifetime somewhere.

The **psychology of complication** says that people complicate their lives deliberately by seeking new products, even though they are fairly satisfied with the old one. (This may account in part for the high divorce rate.) The psychology of complication is the opposite of the **psychology of simplification**, which says that consumers try to simplify their lives by making repeat purchases of the same old brand (Hoyer and Ridgeway 1984). Probably both these mechanisms act on consumers at different times.

Talking point

Marketers are often accused of creating needs. There is a view that somehow marketers can persuade people to want things for which they actually have no use – and of course marketers hotly deny this.

In practice, of course, marketers have very little influence over the actual state of consumers, but do they have influence over the desired state of consumers? Emphatically yes – otherwise all that advertising is just going to waste. So is it all right to seek to change people's desired state? Is it ethical? Or are we simply continuing the process that all people indulge in – advising each other about ways to make our lives more comfortable and enjoyable?

Conditions causing shifts in actual and desired states are interdependent; that is to say, a shift in the actual state (sudden redundancy, for example) will cause a shift in the desired state (instead of looking for a promotion, the individual would now be glad just to have a job at the old grade). Likewise a shift in the desired state (seeing a programme about a holiday in Sri Lanka and wanting to go there) will cause a shift in the actual state as soon as the consumer tries to save for the trip, because the individual will begin to accumulate the necessary cash to pay for the trip.

It is important to repeat that people are not automatons – much of what is written about consumer decision-making implies an almost machine-like process, whereas in the real world many decisions are made emotionally, are based on little information, are made on apparent impulse, and are often regretted afterwards. Consumers are, in fact, a lot like people.

Pre-purchase activities

Having recognized the need, the individual will undertake a series of pre-purchase activities.

The information search (Figure 12.3) comes from two sources: an internal search (from memory) and an external search (from outside sources). In both cases most of the information originates from seller-based sources, and is therefore readily available and low cost. If the internal information search is insufficient, that is to say the individual does not have enough knowledge of the product category to be able to make a choice, an external search will be undertaken.

Sources of information might be marketer-dominated (advertising, brochures, product placements in film and TV shows, websites, sales people, retail displays and so forth) or be non-marketer dominated (friends, family, influential journalists, opinion leaders, consumer organizations, government and industry reports, news stories and so forth). Most non-marketer communications use word of mouth (or e-mail, sometimes called 'word of mouse'). Word-of-mouth communications are generally more powerful than any marketer-generated communications, for the following reasons:

● Word of mouth is interactive, because it involves a discussion between two or more parties. This forces those involved to think about the communication.

● It allows for feedback and confirmation of the message in a way that one-way communications such as advertising do not.

● Because the source is a friend or family member who has no profit motive (unlike the marketer), the communication is more credible.

People often discuss products and services: they like to talk about their own recent purchases, to advise people about purchases and even to discuss recent controversial

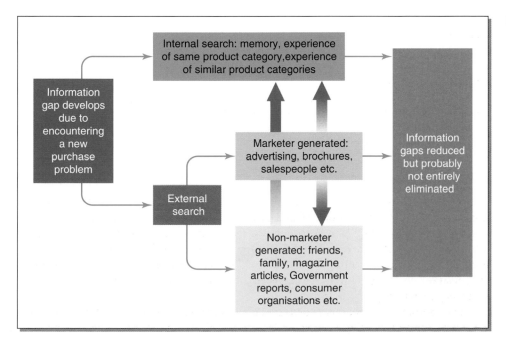

Figure 12.3

Information searching

A friend's recommendation is non-marketer-generated, but it is probably influenced by marketers.

marketing communications. It should be noted that non-marketer-generated sources are themselves influenced by marketers, and also much of the consumer's memory of the product comes from marketer-generated communications, so that even the internal search is affected by marketers.

From a marketer's viewpoint, the problem is that people will talk about products and companies whether the firm likes it or not, and may very well discuss products in negative terms. A great deal of word of mouth is negative: bad news seems to travel twice as fast as good news, and there is very little marketers can do about this.

Sometimes an individual will set out with the belief that he or she has sufficient internal information to make the purchase, but is then presented with new information at the point of purchase. For example, somebody who already owns a mobile phone but would now like to buy another might already feel familiar with the product. On entering the shop the individual might be presented with a staggering array of mobile telephones with features which were not available two or three years ago, and which might even be incomprehensible. In that case the consumer may feel the need to ask the sales staff questions in order to gain enough information to make an informed decision. In other cases, people experience 'choice paralysis' brought on by having too wide a range of possible products to choose from (Shankar, Cherrier and Canniford 2006). Because choosing involves a degree of emotional effort as well as cognitive effort (people often become quite stressed when faced with a difficult choice between expensive options) the individual might well run out of self-regulatory capacity and make a hasty choice (Baumeister 2004). In other words, if the individual is finding it hard to choose, he or she might cut the decision-making short by just grabbing the nearest product, simply to end the stress of trying to reach a decision.

Incidentally, it is common for people with limited information to base their decisions on price, simply because they lack the necessary understanding to make a judgement based on other features of the product.

Search efforts are not very extensive under most circumstances, even for major purchases like houses, because of the amount of time and effort that has to be expended. Usually consumers will continue to search until they find something that is adequate to meet the need, and will then not look any further. A US study (Formisan, Olshavsky and Tapp 1982) found that almost three-quarters of purchasers of insurance policies bought from the first company they saw, for example.

The information search is often carried out on the Internet. Some searches can be time-consuming, but as users become more adept, and as website design improves, searching is becoming much more rapid (Hogue and Lohse 1999). It is possible that people will become more price sensitive as the ease of searching becomes greater – the cost of searching is low in terms of both money and time, so it becomes easier to shop around for bargains.

Surfing behaviour has been classified as follows (Muylle, Moenart and Despontin 1998):

● *Exploratory surfing* – This is characterized by low purposiveness and low specificity. The surfer is gathering information for fun, killing time or seeking amusement. It is the Net equivalent of window-shopping.

Figure 12.4

Limits on the information search

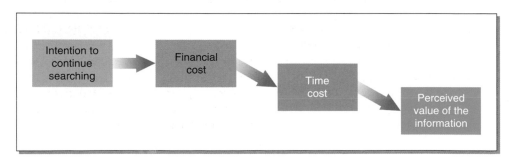

- *Window surfing* – This has medium purposiveness and low specificity. Here the surfer follows up on interesting items – perhaps visiting a website that has details of a new sports car – without necessarily having a specific purpose in mind.
- *Evolved surfing* – Medium purposiveness, high specificity. The surfer is looking for particular categories of information, perhaps surfing travel pages or car dealerships. Even though no particular purchase is intended, the information is highly specific.
- *Bounded navigation* – High purposiveness, low specificity. The individual has determined the search boundaries in advance, and is looking for any available information about the search object.
- *Targeted navigation* – This has high purposiveness and high specificity. For example, someone who is looking for cheap flights to Spain might go directly to the low-cost airlines' home pages to compare prices. This type of surfing obviously has a direct impact on price sensitivity.

In some cases, consumers will visit websites which carry complaints about companies. There is evidence that most web users are not aware of these websites, but will visit them once they become aware of their existence (Bailey 2004). In order to simplify the process, online recommenders have sprung up. Online product recommendation agents gather information from consumers, then search the Web to find products which match the consumer's needs; there is evidence to show that these agents should offer more than one solution for the consumer to choose from, which of course dilutes the advantage to some extent (Aggarwal and Vaidyanathan 2003).

The Internet is also a useful source of information through blogs and chatrooms (there is more on this in Chapter 10). Whether this can be categorized as Internet influence or as influence through a group is a matter for debate – it is, of course, something which fits into both categories.

Information search patterns are also gender-specific (Cleveland *et al.* 2003). Women in general tend to use impersonal information sources (but are much wider-reaching in their information gathering) than do men, whereas men are more likely to use sales staff as an information source, and be more specific in their questioning.

Marketing in practice
McNitemares

McNitemares websites are sites that are consumer generated and which carry scurrilous (and often untrue) stories about major firms. In some cases, firms respond to these accusations on their own websites, in others they simply ignore the statements made. In some cases the allegations are serious – the websites accuse the companies of fraud, of criminal negligence and of deliberately creating dangerous products and failing to withdraw them despite overwhelming evidence.

For the companies, the problem is that they are unable to respond effectively. If they attack the websites and sue those who spread the libel, they will be accused of oppression and stifling free speech – but if they ignore the websites, the stories will continue to be spread. Most of the sites do have feedback chatrooms, in which

supporters of the companies under attack can have their say – but of course they are just as promptly jumped on by the company's attackers. There is of course no way of proving the truth or otherwise of most of the statements made in the chatrooms.

Whether consumers believe the information on the McNitemares sites or not is only partly relevant. The sites form part of the information consumers are presented with, and there will inevitably be some effect, even if the accusations seem unlikely. Perhaps fortunately for the companies concerned, the McNitemares sites are not as frequently visited as the companies' own websites – although critics of major corporations might feel that that is also detrimental!

Figure 12.5

Programmed and non-programmed problem-solving

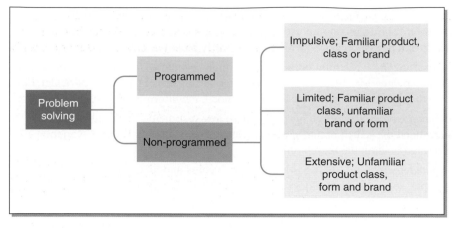

Source: Onkvisit Sak, and Shaw, John J. (1994) *Consumer Behaviour Strategy and Analysis* (New York: Macmillan): 483.

Assortment adjustment is the act of entering the market to replenish or exchange the assortment of products the consumer owns. Assortment adjustment can be programmed (habitual) or non-programmed (new purchases) (Figure 12.5). Non-programmed assortment adjustment divides into three categories. Impulse purchases are not based on a plan, and usually just happen as the result of a sudden confrontation with a stimulus. Such purchases are not always of familiar products; sometimes consumers will spend quite substantial amounts on a whim, whether it be a sudden urge to buy a particularly attractive jacket or to buy a fancy electronic gadget. Impulse buying has been further subdivided into four categories (Stern 1962): pure impulse, based on the novelty of a product; reminder impulse, which relates to a product which has been left off the shopping list; suggestion impulse, which is about products that fulfil a previously unfelt need; and planned impulse, which occurs when the customer has gone out to buy a specific type of product but is prepared to be swayed by special offers.

For example, a consumer may set out to the supermarket to buy the week's groceries, plus something for lunch today. On the way round, he sees a jar of almond-stuffed olives and decides to buy some to try (pure impulse). Next he notices the green lasagna, which reminds him he's out of pasta (reminder impulse) and also on the shelf near it a special rack for keeping lasagna separate while it's cooking (suggestion impulse). Finally, he notices that the smoked chicken is on special offer, and decides to buy some for lunch (planned impulse). This type of scenario is familiar to most people who shop in supermarkets, and indeed supermarkets will often capitalize on this in the way the shelves are stocked and in the way the store is laid out.

The other two types of non-programmed decision-making involve either limited decision-making or extended decision-making. Of the two, limited decision-making is probably the most common.

Limited decision-making takes place when the customer is already familiar with the product class and merely wants to update his or her information or fill in a few gaps revealed by the internal search. This is typical behaviour for someone who is replacing a car: since this is usually an infrequent activity, consumers often find it necessary to check out what new models are available and renew acquaintance with the price levels being charged, even though (as a driver) the consumer will have considerable knowledge of what a car is and what it can be expected to do.

Limited decision-making tends to occur when the consumer is not completely satisfied with the existing product and seeks a better alternative. Here the consumer is only looking for something that overcomes the perceived problem with the existing product.

Extended decision-making occurs when the consumer is unfamiliar with the product class, form and brand. For example, for some people a mobile telephone would be a completely new class of product and they would have to undertake a fairly extensive information search before committing to a telephone or network. Extended decision making is caused by unfamiliarity; consumers who know little about the product category, brands, etc. will tend to shop around more.

Factors affecting the external search for information

The extent and nature of the external search for information will depend on a range of factors connected with the consumer's situation, the value and availability of the information, the nature of the decision being contemplated and the nature of the individual. Figure 12.6 illustrates how these factors interrelate.

Assortment adjustment can take the form of either assortment replenishment, i.e. replacing worn-out or consumed products, or **assortment extension**, adding to the range of products owned. **Assortment replenishment** will usually require very little information searching or risk, since the product is already known. Assortment extension is more likely to lead to an extensive problem-solving pattern.

The type of problem-solving adopted will depend on the task at hand. A programmed decision pattern will lead almost immediately to purchase; these are the regular, always-buy-the-same-brand type decisions. Non-programmed decisions may still lead immediately

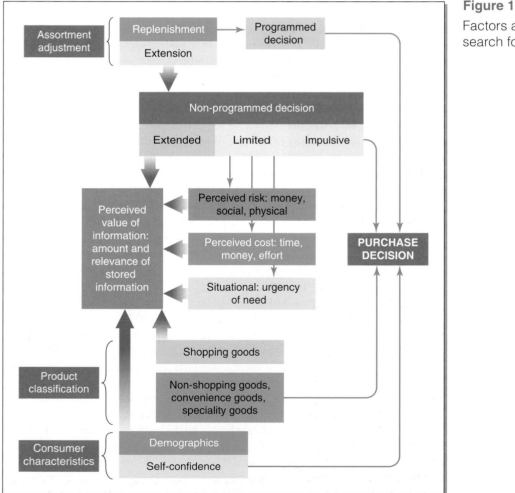

Figure 12.6

Factors affecting the external search for information

to a purchase by impulse, but this type of decision pattern will more likely lead to limited or extensive information search patterns.

The perceived value of the information is important in terms of how extensive the information search will be. In other words, the extent of the external search depends on how valuable the information is. If there is plenty of information in the 'internal files' within the consumer's mind, the extent of external information seeking will be correspondingly less; consumers who are highly familiar with the product will search less than those who are only moderately familiar (Bettman and Park 1980).

The relevance of this information is also a factor: if it's a long time since the last purchase, the stored information may not be relevant any longer. New alternatives may have developed or the product may have improved. If the consumer was satisfied with the last product (which may by now have been consumed or has worn out) the internal information will probably be regarded as relevant, and the search will be less extensive or non-existent (Kiel and Layton 1981).

Any action by a consumer produces unpredictable consequences, some of which might be unpleasant. These consequences form the perceived risk of the transaction. Financial risk is present since the consumer could lose money; for houses, cars and other major purchases the risk is great because the commitment is long term. Because the risk is reduced as knowledge increases, greater perceived risk will tend to lead to greater information search efforts, and the benefits of such a search will be correspondingly greater. If the consumer feels certain about the decision already, there will be correspondingly less benefit in carrying out a search for information.

The fear of losing face with friends and associates is the major component of social risk. It is determined in part by product visibility; consumers who buy certain Eastern European cars can risk ridicule from their friends and colleagues, and might therefore carry out a more extended information search to ensure that the car will not provoke this reaction.

Risk is often perceived as being higher when buying online. This is perhaps unsurprising, since physical inspection of the goods is difficult or impossible, and (even if there is a returns policy) a commitment has to be made and payment sent before the goods are actually received. Research shows that regular Internet users do not perceive the Internet as being any more or less risky than other forms of buying, and previous satisfaction with purchases does reduce perception of risk, at least with everyday, low-involvement purchases (Pires, Stanton and Eckford 2004). The same research found that the perceived risk for buying physical products was higher than that for purchasing services. This implies that the Internet is particularly suited to the marketing of frequently purchased items or service products (such as hotel rooms and airline seats).

Interestingly, research by Wen-yeh, Schrank and Dubinsky (2004) showed that on-line shoppers were not reassured by a well-known brand name, in fact quite the reverse: people perceived greater risk when shopping for branded goods on-line. The researchers thought that this may be due to a perceived reduction in risk caused by buying a cheaper, non-branded product on-line. The researchers also thought that the website brand might be more important than the product brand, a finding which agrees to some extent with research on the branding of retailers generally (Gonzales-Mieres, Diaz Martin and Trespalacios Gutierrez 2006).

Perceived cost is the extent to which the consumer has to commit resources to the search. People will frequently cut the search down simply because it is taking too much time, money or effort. This is because the potential loss of making a wrong purchase decision is seen as being less than the cost of making a full search.

Time is a cost relating to search. It is sometimes measured in opportunity cost, or in terms of what the person could be doing instead of spending time searching. For example, highly paid people may value their time highly because they can earn more money at a desk than they save by shopping around, so they are prepared to spend money in order to save time. Poorer consumers may be more prepared to spend time shopping around in order to save money (Urbany 1986).

Money costs are the out-of-pocket expenses of searching. Clearly a consumer who wants to buy olive oil might compare different brands in Tesco, but is unlikely to drive to Sainsbury's to check their prices, and would certainly not cross the Channel to check the prices in Carrefour in Calais (even though olive oil would almost certainly be cheaper in France).

The psychological costs of the information search include frustration, driving, chasing around to different shops, talking to shop assistants and generally giving a lot of thinking time to the search. Often the consumer will become overwhelmed with the quantity of information available and will be unable to reach a decision because of information overload.

Sometimes the reverse happens and the consumer actually enjoys the shopping experience as an entertainment. Ongoing search is different from external search in that consumers go to look for product information to augment stored product knowledge, and just for the fun of it. In other words, some people go shopping just for fun and this is often a more important motivator than a genuine need to buy something (Bloch, Sherrell and Ridgway 1986).

Talking point

Some people really do seem to enjoy shopping. In fact, most of us do at one time or another – we go to the shops when we are on holiday, we wander round High Streets trying on clothes or we wander round car showrooms looking at the cars. Browsing in bookshops, trying out new electronic equipment, even cruising the aisles of the supermarkets all provide entertainment for some people.

So where does that leave Internet shopping? How can we have a day out, when the Internet means having a day in? How can we take a friend with us for advice? How can we try on the dress, or kick the tyres convincingly when they are only on a screen?

Situational factors will also affect the product information search. The search will be limited, for example, if there is an urgent need for the product. If a driver's car has broken down the driver is unlikely to phone around for the cheapest breakdown van. Other variables might include product scarcity, or lack of available credit.

In terms of product classification, shopping goods are those for which a new solution has to be formulated every time. Non-shopping goods are those for which the consumer already has a complete preference and specification, and the consumer almost always buys the same brand (Bucklin 1960). For example, tomato ketchup is usually a non-shopping product, whereas a stereo system is a shopping product.

Consumer characteristics are those features of the consumer which affect the information search. Demographics affect the search in that outshoppers (people who shop outside the area in which they live) have higher incomes and are mobile. This factor may be product specific, since outshopping most frequently occurs when buying groceries at an out-of-town shopping centre or buying consumer durables. Outshopping can also occur in the form of a shopping trip to a major city, or even a day trip to another country to take advantage of lower prices there. There appear also to be gender differences – males tend to seek assistance from store staff more often than do females when making gift purchases (Cleveland *et al.* 2003). Psychological differences also affect information search and decision making – people who are dependent on television as an information and entertainment source are (perhaps not surprisingly) overwhelmingly more likely to buy off the screen (teleshopping) (Alcaniz, Blas and Torres 2006).

For a complete decision such as choosing a holiday, in-store assistance is often vital.

Marketing in practice
Cross-border shopping

In many parts of the world, differentials exist between prices in one country and prices in another. Sometimes these differences appear as a result of differing taxation and duty regimes between countries, sometimes they occur because one country produces the goods more cheaply than the other, sometimes they occur because of differential pricing by marketers. Frequently, if the countries are close together, the result is a regular traffic across the border – in some cases, goods are illegally smuggled across, but in many cases there are few if any border controls and shoppers can simply switch countries and save money.

Within the European Union, British consumers cross the English Channel in their thousands to take advantage of lower prices on alcohol and tobacco in France. The so-called 'booze cruises' are a major source of revenue for the ferry companies, who of course have shops on board selling alcohol and tobacco at French prices. Shoppers can even buy a ticket which allows them to park their car on the car deck of the ferry, and cross to France and back without ever going ashore – the ferry is a cheaper place to park than the multi-storey car park at Dover port.

In Brazil and Argentina, consumers often cross into Paraguay (especially near the Foz do Iguacu waterfalls) to buy cheap consumer electronic equipment, which is often half-price or less due to different customs regulations. A short bus ride, with minimal border checks (no passports needed within the Mercosur region), and consumers can carry back almost any amount of cheap goods. It is even possible to walk across the bridge over the Parana river.

In the United States, shoppers in southern states cross into Mexico to buy tequila, cheap clothing, jewellery, blankets and handicrafts. In some cases, prices are 25 per cent of US prices, and again no passport is required – a US driving licence is enough. In northern states, the flow is reversed – during August 2004 1.7 million Canadians drove south to take advantage of the strength of the Canadian dollar, crossing the border for a day's shopping. Towns like Bellingham in Washington State, and Grand Forks, North Dakota, found their car parks filling up with cars carrying British Columbia and Manitoba licence plates.

Of course, the cost of crossing the border whether by ferry or by car means that shoppers need to buy in large quantities to make the exercise economically worthwhile. On the other hand, shrewd marketers in the targeted areas recognize that they are dealing with shopping as entertainment – people are enjoying a day out, and justifying it on the basis that they are saving money.

Making the choice

Having gone through the procedures of collecting information, whether by a lengthy search or by simply remembering all the necessary facts, the consumer will make a choice based on the collected information. The first procedure is to establish a consideration set, which is the group of products from which the final choice is to be made. This consideration set will only usually contain a small subset of all the possible alternatives, so from the marketer's viewpoint it is essential to be included in the consideration set, and this is the role of much of the advertising activity undertaken.

Consumers construct the consideration set from the knowledge obtained in the information search. Consumers will often use cut-offs, or restrictions on the minimum or maximum acceptable values. Typically consumers will have a clear idea of the price range they are willing to pay, for example, and any product priced outside this zone will not be included. Incidentally, this price range may have a minimum as well as a maximum; price is often used as a surrogate for judging quality. For example, someone buying a car is unlikely to buy the cheapest available – many people are prepared to pay a little more (or even a lot more) in order to drive a more prestigious vehicle. Again, marketers need to know what the consumer's cut-off point is on given specifications; this can be determined by market research.

Signals are important to consumers when judging product quality. A signal could be a brand name, a guarantee, and even the retailer from whom the product is bought. Because

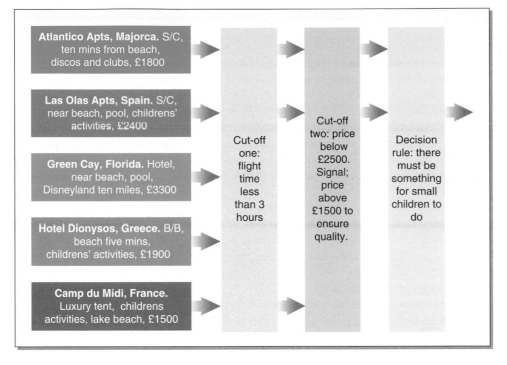

Figure 12.7
The decision-making process involved in a holiday purchase

it is common for consumers to equate quality with high price, a useful tactic for low-priced manufacturers is to undermine this perception in as many ways as possible. The use of price as a quality signal is somewhat reduced when other signals are present. For example, if the consumer is easily able to judge the quality by inspecting the product, the relationship may not apply.

Finally, consumers will often select a decision rule or heuristic. Consumers develop these rules over a period of time; for example, a rule might be always to buy the best-quality that one is able to afford at the time. Some consumers have rules about brand names, or shops they know and trust, or people whose preferences they will always respect.

Maintaining control over the decision-making process will increase satisfaction for most people (Botty, McGill and Iyengar 2003). This is because people will perceive less risk in the process, and will also avoid the feeling of being manipulated which can be a factor in any buying process where strong marketing activities are part of the scene. Heuristics are an important way to maintain control.

Figure 12.7 shows an example of a decision-making process for a holiday purchase.

According to Figure 12.7, the consumer begins with a choice of five different holidays which form the consideration set. The relevant information about each holiday has been included, and now the decision rules need to be applied. First of all, the consumer decides that a long flight would be difficult with children so he or she sets a limit of three hours. This cuts out Greece and Florida. Then there is a cut-off on cost (not to go above £2500). This cut-off has no relevance, since none of the remaining holidays costs above £2500, but the consumer also uses price as a signal to by which to judge quality, and cuts out the tent in France because it is too cheap. The remaining decision rule is that there must be something for the children to do, and this leaves only the apartment in Spain as the final choice.

Sometimes the consumer will find that applying all the decision rules cuts out all of the alternatives, so that a revision of the rules needs to take place. This can result in establishing a hierarchy of rules according to their relative importance (Bettman 1979).

There appear to be some gender differences in decision-making styles: men tend to see shopping as a chore whereas women see it as a recreational activity; men are less likely to be swayed by quality issues; men tend not to think much about their purchases or care; and men tend to stock up on items which are offered in sales (Mitchell and Walsh 2004).

Categorization of decision rules

Women are more likely than men to enjoy shopping as an entertainment.

Non-compensatory decision rules are absolute: if a product does not meet the decision rule for one attribute, this cannot be compensated for by its strength in other areas. In the holiday example above, despite the fact that the Florida location is near to Disneyland, and is therefore a very strong candidate as far as entertaining the children is concerned, the cost and the flight time rule it out. In the lexicographic approach the consumer establishes a hierarchy of attributes, comparing products first against the most important attribute, then against the second most important, and so forth. In the holiday example, the consumer might feel that availability of children's activities is the most important attribute, in which case the Florida destination might be the most attractive. Decisions can be made by elimination of aspects whereby the product is examined against other brands according to attributes, but then each attribute is checked against a cut-off; in the above example, this led to Florida being rejected on grounds of flight time and cost.

The **conjunctive rule** is the last of the non-compensatory rules. Here each brand is compared in turn against all the cut-offs; only those brands which survive this winnowing-out will be compared with each other.

Compensatory decision rules allow for trade-offs, so that a weakness in one area can be compensated for in another. The simple additive rule involves a straight tally of the product's positive aspects, and a comparison of this tally with the tally for other products. The product with the most positive attributes will be the one chosen. A variation of this is the weighted additive approach, which gives greater weight to some attributes than to others. In each case, though, the products do not necessarily have to have all the attributes in common (or, indeed, any of them).

Phased decision strategies may involve using rules in a sequence. For example, the consumer may use a non-compensatory cut-off to eliminate products from the consideration set, then use a weighted additive rule to decide between the remaining products.

Two more special categories of decision rule exist. First, the consumer may need to create a constructive decision rule. This means establishing a rule from scratch when faced with a new situation. If the rule thus created works effectively, the consumer will store it in memory until the next time the situation is encountered, and 'recycle' the rule then. Second, affect referral is the process whereby consumers retrieve a 'standard' attitude from memory. For example, a consumer may strongly disapprove of American foreign policy, and this attitude prevents the inclusion of any American products in the consideration set.

For marketers, it is clearly useful to know how consumers are approaching their decision-making. If, for example, consumers are using a weighted additive rule, it would be useful to know which attributes are given the greatest weightings. If, however, consumers are using a conjunctive rule with cutoffs at known levels, the product can be designed to fall within the cut-offs. The initial aim for marketers must be to ensure that the product becomes part of the consideration set for most consumers, and therefore it must pass at least the first hurdles in terms of the cut-offs and signals employed in the decision process.

Several attempts have been made to bring the factors in consumer decision-making together in one model. Most of these models are complex, since there are many factors which interrelate in a number of ways; an example is the Howard-Sheth model shown in Figure 12.8. This is a somewhat simplified version; the original requires one diagram to be superimposed on another.

In Figure 12.8 the solid arrows show the flow of information, the dotted arrows show the feedback effects. Essentially, the diagram deals with the way the inputs are dealt with by perception and by learning, and eventually become outputs.

Following on from the purchase, there will be an evaluation of both the product itself and the decision process. The learning process will feed back into the internal search, and new heuristics will be developed: sometimes the process of revising memories of the transaction and its aftermath result in creating false memories which inform future decision-making (Yi and Shi 2003). There is more on post-purchase evaluation in Chapter 13.

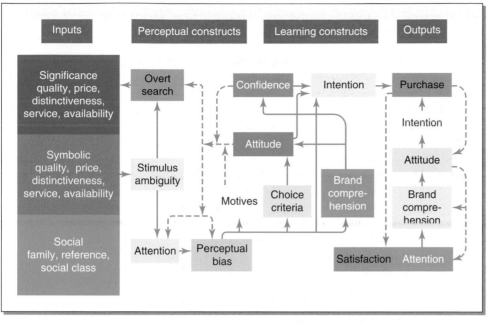

Figure 12.8

Howard-Sheth model

Source: Adapted from John A. Howard and Jagdish N. Sheth (1969) *The Theory of Buyer Behaviour* (New York: John Wiley).

Summary

This chapter has been about consumer decision-making processes. The processes often happen largely below the conscious level, and people often fall in love with a product without having much real knowledge of it, but the processes nevertheless occur, even if only at the subconscious level. The key points are as follows:

● Needs become activated when there is a divergence between the actual and the desired states.

● Any information search is likely to be limited, since there is a cost attached as well as a risk reduction aspect.

● The type of problem solving undertaken will depend in part on whether the consumer is replenishing the assortment or extending it.

● The consideration set doesn't include every possible solution.

● Most decisions involve decision rules, either pre-programmed or invented on the spot.

Chapter review questions

1 What type of information search would you expect someone to undertake when buying a new type of television?

2 What might be a suitable marketing communications approach for a shop whose main target market is composed of women?

3 What might be a suitable marketing communications approach for a shop whose main target market is composed of men?

4 Which is likely to be a more powerful motivation – assortment depletion, or assortment extension?

5 How might a compensatory decision rule operate when buying an expensive item such as a new car?

Preview case study revisited
Selfridge's

After spending £100 million on redesigning the store layout to make shopping easier and more pleasurable, the company made radical changes in its corporate identity. Selfridge's ran a major advertising campaign in the London area, based on the theme 'It's Worth Living in London'. The campaign did not feature any products at all (an unusual approach for a department store, or indeed any retailer), and the campaign was designed to communicate the idea that Selfridge's is at the heart of metropolitan life. Selfridge's share of voice (the proportion of advertising it bought compared with other firms) was 8 per cent in 1999, compared with Harrod's 18 per cent, Harvey Nichol's 2 per cent and Liberty's 4 per cent.

The company ran a series of PR events in-store, ranging from Spice Girls book signings, club nights in the car park in conjunction with the Kiss FM radio station, to collaborations with artists and designers through window displays. The store windows were turned over to establishing the Selfridge's brand, rather than the usual purpose of displaying products for sale. The store ran a series of sponsorship initiatives with art galleries such as the Serpentine, Barbican and Hayward galleries.

All this effort paid off in terms of sales. Sales increased by 6 per cent in the Oxford Street store, and by 23 per cent in the new Manchester store, compared with UK sales growth of only 2 per cent in the same period. People visiting the stores increased by 28 per cent in London and 58 per cent in Manchester, indicating further growth to come. The improvements did not go unnoticed

on the stock market, either – share value grew 35 per cent, indicating a new confidence in the store's ability to maintain its turnround.

Selfridges now has two stores in Manchester and a new store in Birmingham, and has plans to begin retailing online. From dowdy, old-fashioned department store, Selfridge's has become a central feature of the cities it operates in – truly a store for everyone.

Case study
Crossing the Channel

In 1994 the biggest civil engineering project the world had ever seen came to a conclusion with the opening of the Channel Tunnel. Making a direct connection between Britain and Continental Europe for the first time since the Ice Age, the Channel Tunnel had involved 13,000 British and French engineers for six years, digging a total of over 90 miles of tunnel. The rubble alone, dumped in the sea, increased the size of Britain by 90 acres (the area is now a park). The Chunnel, as it was then known, represented a triumph of engineering for the French and British civil

engineers who built it, and a political triumph for the governments of France and Britain.

For the ferry companies who ran the cross-Channel traffic, however, the Chunnel was a major threat. The Chunnel could not have come at a worse time for P&O Ferries: they had bought out Townsend Thoresen in 1988, immediately following the Zeebrugge ferry disaster, and were still living down the image that ferries were dangerous. The capsizing of an Estonian ferry in the Baltic in September 1994, with the loss of 1000 lives, did nothing to help this image.

P&O's main competition on the lucrative Dover–Calais route was Stena Line, the successor to the former Sealink ferries operated jointly by British Railways and SNCF, the French rail company. Stena Line and P&O had competed very effectively, offering a range of services for both freight customers and private individuals: both companies offered special day-trip deals, as well as special fares for five-day excursions and (of course) longer trips. Much of the companies' revenue came from sales of duty-free goods on board: in fact, the savings on duty-free cigarettes, spirits and wines would more than cover the cost of the fare on a day trip, so business was assured.

The sheer capacity of the Channel Tunnel would change all that. The Tunnel had cost a fortune to build, and all that finance had to be paid for, either as dividends or as interest payments. For the tunnel to become profitable, it had to take virtually the entire cross-Channel trade. The economics of the tunnel were the reverse of those for the ferries: the ferries were relatively cheap to build but expensive to run, whereas the tunnel was expensive to build but cheap to run. At first a price war raged: the ferry companies' pockets were deeper, and at one stage it appeared that the Tunnel would go bankrupt before it had ever really got started, with ferry operators offering free crossings to anyone who spent more than £30 in the duty-free shop. Eventually, though, it became apparent that bankrupting the Tunnel would not be a good idea – somebody would simply buy it from the liquidator, thus getting rid of all the debt, and would then have what amounted to a 30-mile stretch of railway line to run. Fares would drop to rock-bottom, well below what the ferry companies could afford to charge.

P&O's response was subtle but very effective. Casting back to the great days of passenger liners, P&O rebranded the company to build on a nostalgic image. Using the 1930s French song, 'J'attendrai' as its theme song, the company ran a series of successful TV ads to promote the idea of 'cruising' across the Channel rather than going through a hole in the ground. The pleasures of being able to stroll around on board, to do a little shopping, to admire the passing ships and see the White Cliffs of Dover were promoted as an antidote to the practical, get-there-quick appeal of the Tunnel.

Eventually, Stena and P&O realized that the real competition was the Tunnel, and they merged to form P&O Stena Line. Head-on competition with the Tunnel became possible, but by now was not really necessary – cross-Channel travel had increased dramatically, and while some people liked to use the Tunnel others preferred the appeal of the

ferries. The increasing popularity of the 'booze cruise' added to this – the price differential between UK and France as far as wines and spirits went was huge, making crossing the Channel a regular event for many smokers and drinkers in the UK.

Further problems arose for the ferry companies. The European Union decided to ban sales of duty-free goods on boats and aircraft moving between EU countries, on the basis that duty-free has no place in a unified market. This was a heavy blow to all the companies involved, since duty-free represented a large part of their revenues and an even larger part of their profits. Although the companies could continue to sell alcohol and tobacco at French prices, they had to pay French duty on them, which meant the profit margins were seriously cut. Fortunately, the increasing

traffic across the Channel, and some innovative special offers, enabled the ferries to maintain traffic levels and increase sales in the shops to compensate. Inevitably, fares have had to rise to compensate, so the companies have been forced to add value, and to improve the décor and facilities on board.

Meanwhile, the Channel Tunnel continues to emphasize the speed and convenience aspects of its product. From central London to central Paris (using the Eurostar express train) in three hours is no mean achievement, much quicker than flying, and offering the possibility of attending a meeting in Paris and being home again for dinner. The Eurostar also offers special deals for non-business customers – special fares for clubbers to go nightclubbing in Paris and be home for work in the morning, for example.

As long as there is a differential between Continental prices and UK prices, and as long as there is a desire to experience different cultures, there will be a demand to cross the English Channel. Ultimately, as long as that demand exists the ferries and Tunnel will be able to show a profit from providing it.

Case study questions

1 How have hedonic needs been addressed by the companies?

2 What heuristics might a cross-Channel traveller use in choosing between ferries and tunnel?

3 What role does involvement play in the decision to cross the Channel?

4 What information sources might be most relevant for travellers?

5 What should businesses on the other side of the Channel do to encourage outshopping?

References

Aggarwal, Praveen, and Vaidyanathan, Rajiv (2003) Eliciting online customers' preferences: conjoint vs. self-explicated attribute-level measurement. *Journal of Marketing Management*, 19(1/2): 157–77.

Alcaniz, Enrique Bigne, Blas, Silvia Sanz, and Torres, Francisco Toran (2006) Dependency in consumer media relations: an application to the case of teleshopping. *Journal of Consumer Behaviour*, 5 (Sept–Oct): 397–410.

Bailey, Ainsworth Anthony (2004) Thiscompanysucks.com: the use of the Internet in negative consumer-to-consumer articulations. *Journal of Marketing Communications*, 10(3): 169–82.

Baumeister, Roy F. (2004) Self-regulation, conscious choice, and consumer decisions. *Advances in Consumer Behaviour*, 31(1): 48–9.

Bettman, James R. (1979) *An Information Processing Theory of Consumer Choice* (Reading, MA: Addison-Wesley): Chapter 7.

Bettman, James F., and Park, C.W. (1980) Effects of prior knowledge and experience and phase of choice processes on consumer decision processes: a protocol analysis. *Journal of Consumer Research*, 7 (August): 234–48.

Blackwell, Roger D., Miniard, Paul W., and Engel, James F. (2006) *Consumer Behaviour*, 10th ed. (Mason, OH: Thomson Southwestern).

Bloch, Peter H., Sherrell, Daniel L., and Ridgway, Nancy M. (1986) Consumer search: an extended framework. *Journal of Consumer Research*, 13 (June): 111–26.

Botty, Simona, McGill, Anna L., and Iyengar, Sheena S. (2003) Preference for control and its effect on the evaluation of consumption experiences. *Advances in Consumer Research*, 30(1): 127–8.

Bucklin, Louis P. (1963) Retail strategy and the classification of consumer goods. *Journal of Marketing*, 27 (January): 50–5.

Cleveland, Mark, Babin, Barry J., Laroche, Michel, Ward, Philippa, and Bergeron, Jasmine (2003) Information search patterns for gift purchases: a cross-national examination of gender differences. *Journal of Consumer Behaviour*, 3(1): 20–47.

Dewey, John (1910) *How We Think* (Boston, MA: DC Heath & Co.).

Formisan, Roger A., Olshavsky, Richard W., and Tapp, Shelley (1982) Choice strategy in a difficult task environment. *Journal of Consumer Research*, 8 (March): 474–9.

Gonzales-Mieres, Celina, Diaz Martin, Anna Maria, and Trespalacios Gutierrez, Juan Antonio (2006) Antecedents of the difference in perceived risk between store brands and national brands. *European Journal of Marketing*, 40(1/2): 61–82.

Hogue, A.Y., and Lohse, G.L. (1999) An information search cost perspective for designing interface for electronic commerce. *Journal of Marketing*, 6(3): 387–94.

Hoyer, Wayne D., and Nancy M. Ridgway (1984) Variety seeking as an explanation for exploratory purchase behaviour: a theoretical model. *Advances in Consumer Research*, 11, ed. Thomas C. Kinnear (Provo, UT: Association for Consumer Research).

Kiel, Geoffrey C., and Layton, Roger A. (1981) Dimensions of consumer information seeking behaviour. *Journal of Marketing Research*, 18 (May): 233–9.

Mitchell, Vincent-Wayne, and Walsh, Gianfranco (2004) Gender differences in German consumer decision-making styles. *Journal of Consumer Behaviour*, 3(4): 331–46.

Onkvisit, Sak, and Shaw, John J. (1994) *Consumer Behaviour, Strategy and Analysis* (New York: Macmillan).

Pires, Guilherme, Stanton, John, and Eckford, Andrew (2004) Influences on the perceived risk of purchasing on-line. *Journal of Consumer Behaviour*, 4(2): 118–31.

Shankar, Avi, Cherrier, Helene, and Canniford, Robin (2006) Consumer empowerment: a Foucauldian interpretation. *European Journal of Marketing*, 40(9/10): 1013–30.

Stern, Hawkins (1962) The significance of impulse buying today. *Journal of Marketing*, 26 (April): 59–62.

Urbany, Joel E. (1986) An experimental investigation of the economics of information. *Journal of Consumer Research*, 13 (September): 257–71.

Wen-yeh, Huang, Schrank, Holly, and Dubinsky, Alan J. (2004) Effect of brand name on consumers' risk perceptions of on-line shopping. *Journal of Consumer Behaviour*, 4(1): 40–50.

Yi, Cathy, and Shi, Zang (2003) A dynamic choice process: how choices generate biased memory that influences future choices. *Advances in Consumer Behaviour*, 30(1): 109–110.

Chapter 13
Innovation

Introduction

Innovation is said to be the lifeblood of successful companies. Firms which fail to innovate are thought to become moribund very quickly, and eventually to disappear altogether because competitors introduce new products which supersede the old ones.

However, this constant stream of innovation does create problems from a consumer behaviour viewpoint. Decision-making and information-gathering are at their most complex when consumers are considering an innovative product. Thousands of new products are launched onto the market every year, with varying success rates; the vast majority never recoup their development costs. (Estimates of new-product success rates vary, largely due to the difficulty of defining what constitutes success.)

The product life cycle

Products are constantly being superseded by newer, more effective products. For this reason firms seek to develop new products; those firms that fail to innovate will, eventually, only be producing products that are obsolescent. The product life cycle illustrates the process of introduction, growth, maturity and obsolescence in products.

Products tend to lose money when they are first introduced, because the amount of marketing support they need is not justified by the initial sales as the product tries to become established in the market. As the product moves into a growth phase, profits begin to come in, and when the product becomes well established (i.e. mature) the profits are also at a peak. Eventually, the product will go into decline as competing products enter the market, or fashions change, or the market becomes saturated.

In fact, the situation is often much more complex than this, so the basic product life cycle or PLC (as shown in Figure 13.1) does not always describe what actually happens in practice.

The product life cycle is a useful concept for explaining what happens to products, but it suffers from a number of weaknesses. First, the model is no use for making predictions, because there is no good way of knowing what the length of the maturity phase will be: for a fashion item, the maturity phase might only last a few months, whereas for a product such as pitta bread the maturity phase has already lasted several thousand years and shows no sign of changing.

Second, the model ignores the effects of marketing activities. If a product's sales are declining, marketers might decide to reposition the product in another market, or might

Preview case study
Wind turbines

For many years now European governments have been encouraging the construction of wind farms to generate electricity. Wind power is clean, does not emit greenhouse gases and appears to be sustainable in the long term – at least in windy countries such as the UK and the Netherlands.

There is, of course, a downside to everything. Wind farms create some noise pollution, which may not affect many human beings given that the turbines are established in rural areas, but which certainly does affect the navigation systems of bats and some birds. Then again, the wind does not always blow, and when it does it doesn't always blow consistently.

Then there is the cost of building and maintaining the turbines, and the cost of laying cables to remote areas to collect the electricity – not to mention protests by people who live near wind farms, or who dislike the appearance of these giant structures.

On the other hand, governments are committed to reducing greenhouse gas emissions, and in some countries (notably the UK) the reliance on imported fuel is likely to become a hot political issue. The answer? Home wind turbines.

The idea is a simple one. Homeowners would be offered financial incentives to put small wind turbines on their roofs. The electricity generated would go directly into the house's ring main, and would supplement electricity from the National Grid. Any surplus electricity could be sold to the electricity supplier, thus reducing bills for power 'imported' from the Grid in times of heavy usage.

Unfortunately, the cost of a wind turbine for domestic use was around the £3000 mark in 2005, meaning that (for most people) the payback period (the length of time it would take for the savings on electricity bills to exceed

the cost of the installation) would be unrealistically long, especially given that the life of the turbine system itself was only expected to be around ten years.

The result of this was that relatively few people installed turbines – those who did were usually committed 'greens' or at least wanted to appear to be so. In a BBC article published in October 2005, wind turbines were described as 'the new handbags', in other words a fashion item only, with limited real value. At that time, 7000 households had taken advantage of a Government grant scheme and installed the turbines. But would there be more to follow?

Figure 13.1

The product life cycle

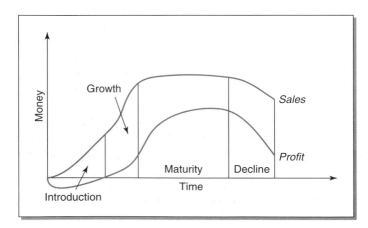

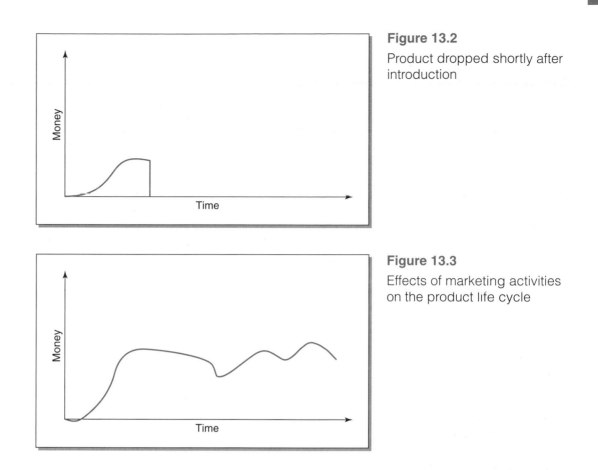

Figure 13.2
Product dropped shortly after introduction

Figure 13.3
Effects of marketing activities on the product life cycle

run a major promotional campaign, or might decide to drop the product altogether and concentrate resources on another product in the portfolio. These alternatives are shown in Figures 13.2 and 13.3.

Talking point

It is not unusual for products to disappear almost as soon as they are launched: test marketing sometimes shows disappointing results, so the product is taken off the shelves. But the product life cycle tells us that products often lose money at first – and some products are 'sleepers' which do nothing for several years, and then suddenly take off for no apparent reason.

There are also products which appear to be eminently sensible, and which do not find a market, possibly through a lack of professionalism on the part of the marketers. So should there be a marketer's life cycle instead? If the product doesn't perform, should we keep the product and fire the managers?

Third, the model does not account for those products which come back into fashion after a few years in the doldrums. Recent examples include the Mini Cooper, the Volkswagen Beetle and the yo-yo (which seems to undergo revivals every ten to fifteen years).

Fourth, the model does not take account of the fact that the vast majority of new products fail. This would give a life cycle such as that shown in Figure 13.4 (page 282), where the product never moves into profit.

Finally, the PLC only looks at one product, whereas most marketing managers have to balance the demands of many different products, and decide which of them is likely to yield the best return on investment (or perhaps which one will take the company nearest to achieving its strategic objectives).

The product life cycle can be explained in terms of consumer behaviour. In the introduction and growth stage, the more innovative consumers are adopting the product. In the maturity phase, the more cautious consumers buy the product, until finally another

Innovative, exciting new product . . .

. . . or re-hashed old design?

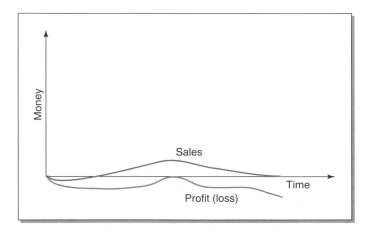

Remote controls for TVs have obvious advantages – as long as we know how to use them.

product comes along which has more benefits or which does a better job, and the consumers switch to the new product. The basic problem for marketers lies in knowing how long the maturity phase will last; the PLC does tell us, though, that all products eventually fade and die, and marketers should therefore develop new products to replace the old ones as these products fall out of favour with consumers.

Although we can be reasonably sure that all old products will eventually fail, we cannot by any means be sure that a new product will succeed. The lack of a good predictive system for forecasting product success wastes resources since producers will spend time and effort making things that consumers do not want to buy. The ideal outcome for a producer is to develop products that become **culturally anchored** – that become part of modern life. Recent examples are the mobile telephone, cable television and the personal computer – none of which would have been part of the average household 30 years ago, but which now would be difficult to manage without. In practice such breakthroughs are hard to achieve. Understandably, with so much at stake for firms, there has been a great deal of research interest in innovation, with many researchers trying to determine what are the critical factors in new product success.

The process of **adoption** of innovation is much more to do with communication throughout the population than with individual decision-making. Each individual will make decisions by the processes already outlined for existing products; the main difference is that there will be many fewer sources of information about an innovative product, since few people will have any experience of it as yet.

Figure 13.4
Failed product

Table 13.1 Attributes necessary for adoption

Attribute	Explanation	Examples
Relative advantage	The product must have some advantage over the products already on the market. It must offer the consumer a better range of benefits than the existing solution, in other words.	Before the Sony Walkman was launched, the only way to listen to stereo-quality music was to carry a 'ghetto-blaster' on your shoulder. The Walkman replaced this cumbersome and anti-social device within a few years.
Compatibility	The product must fit in with the consumer's lifestyle.	At one time, the Welsh Valleys had the highest rate of VCR ownership in the world. This was due to the high unemployment and lack of entertainment facilities in the area, making a video recorder a very convenient way of providing entertainment.
Complexity	The product must not be too complex for the consumer to understand.	The One for All Video Programmer is a remote control which simplifies programming VCRs. The firm's strap line is, 'So easy to use, even an adult can work it.'
Trialability	Products which can be tried out are more likely to succeed.	Whenever a motor manufacturer launches a new vehicle people are invited to test drive it.
Observability	The more observable the product, the quicker the diffusion process. If other potential consumers are able to see the product in use, this is bound to raise interest in it.	Part of the reason for the Walkman's worldwide success is that it can clearly be observed in use. Likewise, new fashion ideas seem to catch on very quickly; this is due to the high level of observability.

Everett M. Rogers (1983) postulated that products would be adopted if they possessed most of the attributes shown in Table 13.1.

There have been several models of the adoption process, most of which assume a somewhat complex process of assessing the new product. In the case of radically new products (those which will alter the user's lifestyle) this may well be the case, but since most products which are classified as new are, in fact, adaptations of existing products, it might be safe to assume that the consumers do not necessarily carry out a lengthy evaluation of the type assumed by most researchers. Five adoption models are shown in Figure 13.5 (page 284).

Talking point

It's all very well to talk about making products which will become culturally anchored – but how do we do this in practice? It's easy to think that something will come along which will become essential to daily life, but in fact most such 'whizzo ideas' fail dismally.

Even when there is a clear advantage people might not be ready for it. What happened to the video telephones of the 1960s? Why have they suddenly made a comeback in the 3G phones of the twenty-first century? What happened to the Philips laserdisc system, and why did it flop in the 1980s but re-appear as the DVD system in the 1990s?

So how can it be useful to talk about getting our products to be culturally anchored? It's pure luck if it happens, surely!

The AIDA model is probably among the oldest models in marketing. It is commonly quoted when considering promotions, but it applies equally well to adoption of innovation. The model is somewhat too simplistic, however: it implies that the process is mechanical, without any conscious thought on the part of the individual who adopts the

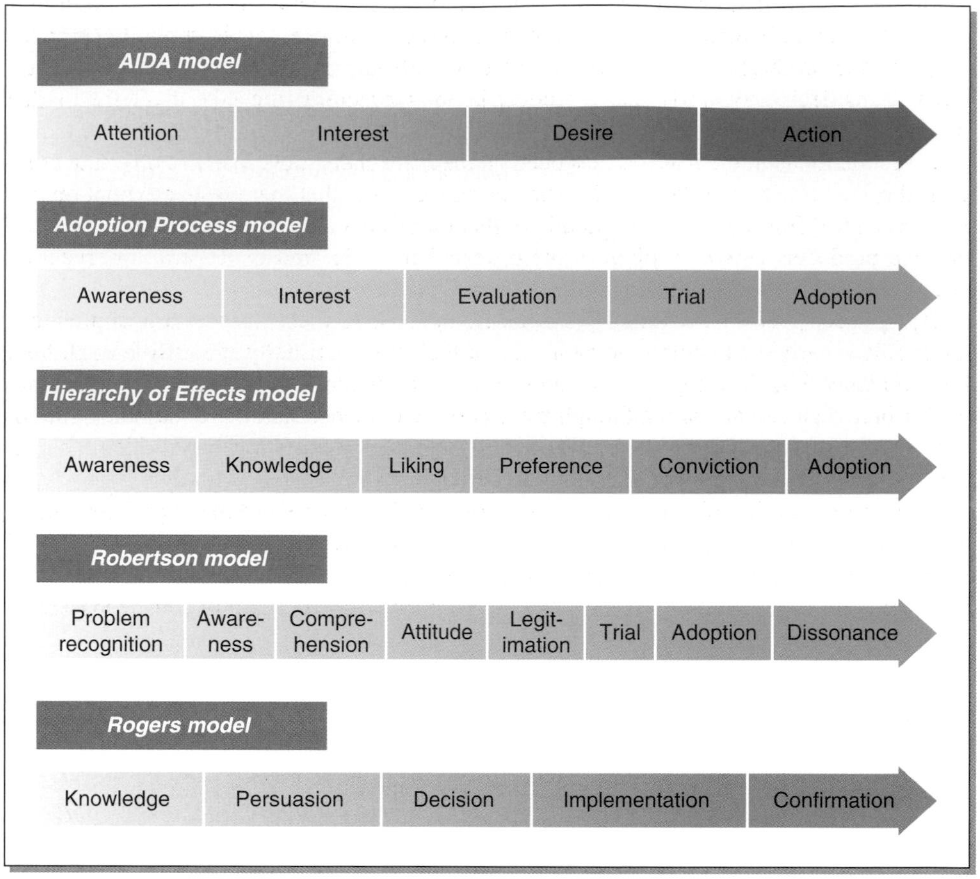

Figure 13.5

Models of the adoption and diffusion process

product. There is also the view that the model implies something being done *to* consumers (leading them through a process) rather than something that is done *for* them (meeting a need).

The Adoption Process model includes some thought on the part of the customer. In this case, becoming interested in the product leads to some serious evaluation before trial and adoption. This model portrays adoption as a sequence which the individual follows, using conscious thought and interaction with the product to come to the adoption decision.

The Hierarchy of Effects model suggests that each stage of the process leads the customer closer to the decision – as each stage is passed, the individual is further up the hierarchy and therefore becoming more committed. Obviously an individual might drop out of the model at any stage, and thus the sale will not happen, but the model implies that people must normally pass through each stage in the correct order if a sale is to result. This is a suspect proposition, since people are likely to skip stages or even buy the product on impulse without any real evaluation at all.

Robertson's (1967) model is by far the most complex, seeking to break down the process into more stages. Robertson shows how the attitude is formed rather than simply subsuming it into a category of 'liking'. This model provides more of an insight into the internal workings of the adopter's mind, rather than simply describing behaviour.

Rogers (1983) includes the concept of persuasion in his model. Persuasion does not necessarily come from outside, however – it may just as easily come from within the individual. Persuasion is clearly of interest to marketers, whether it is marketing generated or whether it is produced socially via peer pressure (normative compliance).

The main feature that all these models have in common is that they imply that adoption of innovation is a linear process, following logical steps. This may or may not be true – individuals may follow a straight line, or they may be diverted by circumstances. The models also show that innovations take a long time to be adopted. This means that it may be a year or more before a new product begins to show a return; this is implicit also in the shape of the product life cycle curve, where the introduction phase shows a slow start. Often firms decide too early that a product is not succeeding and take it off the market before consumers have completed the evaluation process.

A second focus in the research has been on the consumers most likely to buy new products; the **innovators**, in other words. The reason for this is that there is an assumption that innovation is diffused by word of mouth, or that innovators are likely to influence others to buy the products. This is implicit in the product life cycle, and in Rogers' observability criterion (Rogers 1983).

It is perfectly feasible to classify consumers in terms of their attitude to new products; the problem with identifying innovators is that they are not usually innovative in all their buying habits. That is to say, an innovator for hi-fi equipment is not necessarily an innovator for breakfast cereals, and although there is some evidence that there may be a kind of super-innovator who likes virtually everything that is new, these people are difficult to find, and it is debatable whether they are likely to influence other buyers anyway.

Everett Rogers classified consumers as innovators (2.5 per cent of the population), early adopters (13.5 per cent), early majority (34 per cent), late majority (34 per cent), and laggards (16 per cent) (Figure 13.6, page 286). These classifications were originally devised from agricultural product adoptions, but have been widely accepted as applying to consumers

Consumer behaviour in action
Optical recording systems

In 1973 the giant Dutch Philips corporation announced a radical new system for recording and playing back movies. It was the videodisc system, which used laser technology to burn information onto a disc which was about the size of a vinyl LP.

The system was at prototype stage, but by 1978 the system was up and running, and in collaboration with MCA and Pioneer Electronics Philips appeared ready to take the world by storm. At about the same time, the first home video recorders were also appearing on the market – heavy and clunky to use, and with relatively poor picture quality, the new VCRs were expensive. However, they had one major advantage over the videodisc system – they could record programmes from the TV for later replay. Consumers rejected the videodisc system in favour of the VCR, and eventually the JVC VHS system became the standard means of watching movies at home.

By 1981, technical teething problems and consumer apathy about the videodisc system had combined to kill the project almost entirely. Philips continued to market machines produced by MCA and Pioneer, but essentially the whole idea of selling laser-recorded movies for home viewing was regarded as a complete flop. Even IBM's vast resources could not keep the project afloat.

In 1989, Pioneer bought up all the Philips patents on the technology and went into business producing DVDs. Although these were hardly a roaring success initially, eventually they became the format of choice – especially when systems for burning DVDs at home became available.

Now it appears that DVD systems, based on the original videodisc technology, are taking over from VHS. Some retailers no longer sell VHS systems, instead concentrating on DVDs and recordable DVDs. It is hard to explain why the videodisc system failed in 1980, and yet 25 years later has proved to be the innovation success story of the decade. Perhaps it is due to consumer fickleness, or perhaps it is due to the existence in 1980 of several competing systems – people were hardly likely to adopt all the available systems, and VHS won at that time. Perhaps now that everyone has a VCR using VHS technology, they feel ready to move on to the next exciting innovation. Whatever the reason, executives at Philips must feel frustrated at the outcome.

© iStockphoto.com

Figure 13.6

Classification of innovators

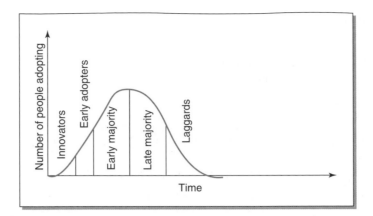

equally well. The percentages given are arbitrary; everybody is at some point along a continuum, and Rogers decided that those whose scores lay more than two standard deviations from the mean would be classed as innovators, those whose scores lay between one and two standard deviations would be early adopters, and those whose scores lay within one standard deviation from the mean would be the early majority. Scores below the mean were classified in the same way: those within one standard deviation of the mean were classified as the late majority, and everyone else as laggards. This means that Rogers' classifications involve circular reasoning: people are innovators because they innovate, and laggards because they are slow to innovate. The classification tells us nothing about the characteristics of the people involved.

Innovativeness is the degree to which a person tends to adopt innovations earlier than other people. It can be measured very simply using the Goldsmith-Hofacker Innovativeness Scale, which uses six questions to determine an individual's innovativeness in respect to a particular product category (Goldsmith and Hofacker 1991). The Goldsmith-Hofacker Scale is, in a sense, too simplistic because it merely asks what the individual's behaviour is, without finding out what it is about people that makes them into innovators. In order to try to discover what it is that makes somebody an innovator, studies have been carried out into known innovators to find out what they have in common.

Three main groups of variable have been identified thus far: socioeconomic factors, personality factors, and communication behaviour (Figure 13.7). It should be noted, again, that all these studies are based on limited product categories, and are therefore not necessarily generally applicable.

Socioeconomic variables which are positively related to innovativeness are as follows:

● education
● literacy
● higher social status

Figure 13.7

Variables which affect innovativeness

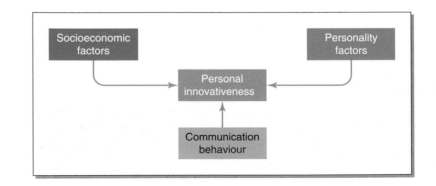

- upward social mobility
- larger-sized units
- commercial rather than subsistence orientation
- more favourable attitude towards credit
- more specialized operations

Clearly, higher-income people are in a much better position to take the risk of buying new products. Those who are educated and literate are also more likely to hear about new products before other people do.

Personality and attitude variables associated with innovativeness are as follows:

- empathy
- ability to deal with abstractions
- rationality
- intelligence
- favourable attitude towards change
- ability to cope with uncertainty
- favourable attitude towards education
- favourable attitude towards science
- achievement motivation
- high aspirations

There some personality traits that militate against innovativeness, however:

- dogmatism
- fatalism

M.J. Kirton (1986) showed that consumers can be classified as either adapters or innovators. Adapters tend to take existing solutions and adjust them as necessary to fit the current need problem; innovators tend to look for radical solutions. Kirton's Adaption-Innovation Index has proved to be a very reliable measure of innovativeness.

Cognitive innovators tend to be those who seek out new intellectual experiences, whereas sensory innovators are those who seek new sensory experiences. In both cases the innovators are seeking something new for its own sake; and there is ample research to indicate that novelty is an attractive feature of a product in its own right.

Communication variables that are positively associated with innovativeness are as follows (Figure 13.8, page 288):

- social participation
- interconnectiveness with the social system
- cosmopolitanism
- change agent contact
- mass media exposure
- exposure to interpersonal communication channels
- knowledge of innovations
- opinion leadership
- belonging to highly interconnected systems

Although innovators for one product group are not necessarily innovators for other groups, there are some correlations. For example, technophiles are people who like technology for its own sake, and who are prepared to take an interest in (and even buy) new computers, electronic gadgets, GPS equipment and so forth, whereas technophobes have a loathing for such devices.

Figure 13.8

Communication variables associated with innovativeness

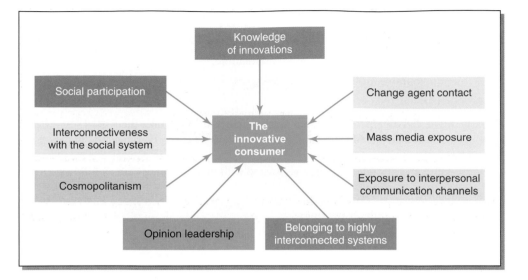

Feick and Price (1987) identified a group of influencers they called 'market mavens'. A market maven is someone who has an intense interest in, and a high level of knowledge about, a specific category of product. Mavens are able to provide price and availability information to others, as well as information about the products themselves: in effect, they act as an extension of the gatekeeper role in disseminating information about new products. Mavens are usually motivated by the desire to share information, to show off their knowledge and to help others in reaching the right decisions (Walsh, Gwinner and Swanson 2004). Mavens are also sometimes known as 'infomediaries', particularly when they operate predominantly online: many chatrooms and weblogs are inhabited by such experts, who enjoy helping others with purchasing decisions.

From the viewpoint of a marketer, it would appear that there is a demand for newness per se. In other words, as a general rule people like new things and like to feel that the product they buy now is better than the one they bought ten years ago. On the other hand, consumers are not necessarily prepared to take the risk of buying products that are radically different from their existing purchases.

In terms of the effect on the consumer's lifestyle (and consequently the risk to the consumer), innovations can be classified under three headings (Figure 13.9) (Robertson 1967):

1 **Continuous innovation** – a relatively minor change in the product, for example the packaging or the styling.

2 **Dynamically continuous innovation** – changes which materially affect the core functioning of the product. An example might be a coupe version of a family saloon.

3 **Discontinuous innovation** – A product which is new to the world, and changes the lifestyles of those who adopt it. In recent years the mobile telephone and the MP3 player have changed people's lives radically.

A study by Calentone and Cooper (1981) found that the most successful new products were, in fact, only incremental improvements on existing products rather than radically new products; this study also emphasized the need for the product to have a marketing synergy rather than be simply a wonderful idea which the engineering department thought might succeed.

In this connection, the recent trend towards **benchmarking** is likely to lead to even more 'me-too' or incremental product offerings. Benchmarking is the process by which firms compare their activities with the best in the industry, and try to match the best practice of their competitors in each area. The aim is to become the best of the best. To this end, motor manufacturers buy their competitors' cars and strip them down to see how they are made and what their features are, then try to emulate the best of them in their

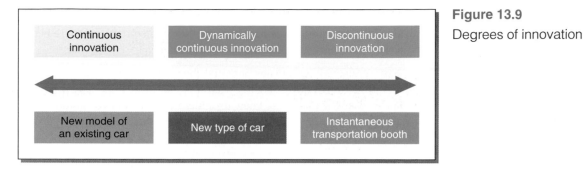

Figure 13.9
Degrees of innovation

own product offerings. This is called 'reverse engineering'. Inevitably this will lead to more copying of competitors' products if the philosophy is applied to new product development.

Talking point

If the most successful products are me-toos, and the easiest and cheapest way of refreshing the product range is to copy someone else's designs, why does any firm bother to take the risk to innovate at all? Why do we have people like Akio Morita developing the Walkman in the face of opposition from his marketing people? Why do we have loopy inventors banging on manufacturers' doors demanding to be allowed to show their latest gadget?

Is it perhaps because we just get carried away with the fun of inventing something new, and then we have to find a market for it? Or is it that being first to market with a radical, life-changing new product could mean making millions, instead of just rubbing along showing a decent profit?

Part of the problem for manufacturers is that there is no generally agreed upon definition of newness. For the purposes of marketing, manufacturers really have to rely on the consumer's perception of what is new and what is not. Since this is very much a subjective and individualistic perception, the manufacturer frequently finds him- or herself in a marketing minefield.

Marketing approaches to new product launches

Combining decision-making theory and diffusion theory, it is possible to come up with some broad recommendations for launching new products.

1 *Need recognition* – Marketers should activate the needs by mentioning them in advertising. The advertising needs to make people aware of what's new, and how it will have a relative advantage over current competitors.

2 *Prepurchase activities or search* – Information sources are strongly linked to marketing strategy; brochures, product information adverts, leaflets, PR activities, and salespeople all contribute to the process. Marketers should ensure that there is an emphasis on the product's compatibility with the target market's lifestyles and aspirations.

3 *Evaluation and purchase decision* – Salespeople have a strong contribution to make to this part of the process; marketers must ensure a high quality of presentation of information materials, and the salesforce must be able to guide consumers through the complexity of the product.

4 *Act of purchase and consumption* – The product has to be right for the task, and fulfill the manufacturer's claims. Allowing the customer to try the product out is a good means of reducing the risk, so trialability is a key issue in this context.

5 *Post-purchase evaluation* – After-sales service has strong role to play here, and ideally there should be some **observability** in the product if there is to be rapid diffusion of the product to the broader market.

Some new products have greater potential than others for consumer acceptance. Sometimes it is difficult to analyze exactly what it is that makes one new product more acceptable than another – if marketers knew this, there would be fewer failures of new products. There is, after all, no point in trying to market a product for which consumer acceptance will be limited.

One route around the acceptance problem is mass customisation. Here customers are able to design the product themselves from a range of possible options: the application of this concept ranges from Subway sandwiches through to Dell computers. The advantage is that customers are able to design something which meets their own needs very closely indeed, and do not have to accept (or pay for) features which are only present because most people want them. At first sight, it would seem that a driver for mass customization would be that customers can save money by only paying for features which they actually need, but in fact research shows that such customers are actually prepared to pay a substantial premium, in some cases more than double the ordinary price, in order to design something to their own specification (Schreier 2006). This may be due to a better perceived fit, it may be due to perceived uniqueness of the product, or it may be simply pride of authorship – the pleasure of knowing that one has created something unique.

Resistance to innovation can come from several sources (see Figure 13.10), as can facilitation of innovation. First, channels of communication might create a barrier: as we saw in Chapter 10, communications received from respected opinion leaders will be taken seriously and often acted upon, whereas communications from a member of a dissociative group will be ignored or will tend to militate against action. Poorly executed advertising can create negative attitudes about the product, as can other poorly executed approaches such as insensitive salespeople, over-persuasive direct mailshots or negative press coverage. On the other hand, some forms of communication have greatly aided the adoption of innovation – the Internet has provided a wide variety of online forums which have enabled people to exchange information rapidly about new products. Likewise, mobile telephones have provided people with rapid interpersonal communication (as opposed to landlines, which only provide communication from one place to another). Text messages, and in particular commercial permission-based text messages, have greatly increased the rate at which information about new products is disseminated. Although the rate at which bad news travels will also increase, the net result is that those who are likely to adopt the product hear about it much faster than they might have done a few years ago.

The social system can also create a barrier. The social system is the physical, cultural and social environment within which decisions are made: for marketers, it usually corresponds to the market segment (or target market). For example, there is a social system which functions in most jobs or professions: lawyers discuss cases, Young Farmers Societies organize social events, academics have conferences, and students have student unions. Social systems might have traditional values, in which case innovation is likely to be stifled, or they

Figure 13.10

Barriers to innovation

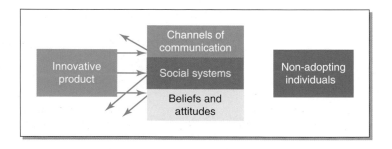

may have modern values, in which case innovation is likely to be stimulated. Modern social systems have the following characteristics (Rogers and Shoemaker 1971):

- A positive attitude towards change.
- An advanced technology and skilled labour force.
- A general respect for education and science.
- An emphasis on rational and ordered social relationships rather than on emotional ones.
- An outreach perspective, in which members of the system frequently interact with outsiders.
- A system in which members can easily see themselves in different roles.

Consumer behaviour in action
Effects of new technology on society

So far we have looked at ways in which consumer behaviour affects adoption of new technology. However, technology also affects consumer behaviour, creating new possibilities for social interaction, new possibilities for entertainment and new possibilities for improving one's standard of living. These improvements are, of course, the motivation for adopting new products, but in many cases marketers are taken by surprise by consumer responses to new products.

For example, take the telephone. In the late nineteenth century, when the telephone was first introduced, suppliers assumed that the main customers would be sophisticated, relatively wealthy city dwellers. From a telephone company's viewpoint, these would be easier to connect than would rural dwellers – the length of cable required would clearly be a great deal shorter, apart from any other considerations. However, it transpired that farmers were the most keen to acquire the new technology, because they were so isolated otherwise. Before the telephone, the only way a farmer could hear a voice other than that of his immediate family and a few farmhands was to saddle up a horse and ride to the nearest town. The telephone also provided a lifeline in case of emergencies. In the cities, on the other hand, most people could not see an immediate use for a telephone, and the telephone companies had to spend considerable sums of money on persuading people that they would find a telephone useful.

Other uses for the telephone disappeared almost without trace. In 1895 the Electraphone was introduced in London. This used the telephone lines to 'broadcast' live concerts and even church services to subscribers. After 12 years of operation there were only 600

subscribers, so the system was abandoned: interestingly, a similar system introduced in Budapest was a runaway success, perhaps because it also broadcast the news.

Consider also the trend towards text messages. The result of this is that younger people now have stronger, more agile thumbs than the older generation, but they also report to doctors with repetitive strain injury due to excessive texting. The fear of radiation from mobile phones still worries some people, in the same way that Victorians feared catching tuberculosis from telephone mouthpieces. Texting is having an effect on the language as well – children commonly use the shorter 'text' forms of words in their school essays.

Other innovations have wrought even greater social changes. The development of cheap commercial flights has contributed to an explosion in holiday home purchases, which has had a dramatic effect on the culture in some countries: in France there are whole villages which are now British, and in coastal Spain the local culture has (in some places) been overwhelmed by an influx of foreign holiday-home owners and retirees. Likewise, the Internet has further reduced the number of people who use reference libraries, and the invention of weblogs has increased possibilities for people to contact complete strangers, for good or ill.

Each new technological advance carries with it the possibility of social change. This is what science fiction is concerned with. In the long run, a society is defined by its technology as much as by its members – the available tools will determine how people behave, what resources become available to them and how much time they have to act out and develop their lives.

Social systems can be of any size, up to and including entire countries. The prevailing social climate has already been discussed in Chapter 9, but it clearly has relevance for innovation, as it does for any other consumer behaviour.

Finally, adoption may be blocked because the individuals concerned object to the product and its use: for example, an environmentalist would not respond favourably to a new low-cost airline or a new model of four-wheel drive car. Nor would a vegetarian be likely to adopt a new type of snack sausage. Such people may well be innovative in adopting the stances they adopt, but not be innovative in terms of product purchases.

Summary

Adoption of new products is a somewhat hit-and-miss affair. Companies need to introduce new products regularly in order to avoid being left with an obsolete product portfolio, but on the other hand it is extremely difficult to predict consumers' responses to innovative products. Many firms therefore simply make minor incremental changes to their products rather than make radical innovations.

On the other hand, most people like some novelty in their lives, and many people like a lot of novelty. This means that at least some people will be open to the idea of buying a new product, or of trading in an existing product for something different. The problem for marketers lies in knowing which new products would be acceptable to which target market segments.

The key points from this chapter are as follows:

● The product life cycle shows that all products eventually become obsolete and must be replaced.

● Innovators are usually educated and relatively well off, as well as being well connected socially.

● Innovators for one product category are not necessarily innovators for any other product category.

● The most successful products are often me-toos or continuous innovations.

● Mavens have a high level of interest in specific product categories, and enjoy airing their knowledge.

● Innovation can be continuous, dynamically continuous, or discontinuous.

● Resistance to innovation can come from many sources.

Chapter review questions

1 What is the role of mavens in word-of-mouth communication?

2 What barriers to adoption might there be for a new type of alcoholic drink?

3 How does trickle-down theory relate to adoption of new products?

4 What is the key difference between a dynamically continuous innovation and a discontinuous innovation?

5 Why is the PLC difficult to use as a predictor?

6 How might a marketer speed up the adoption process?

7 Why do most new products fail?

8 Why do most new products lose money at first?

9 What can marketers do to help overcome barriers to adoption?

10 What are the main criticisms of Everett Rogers' classification of consumers?

Preview case study revisited
Wind turbines

In 2006 the move towards generating electricity at home took a major boost when the price of gas rose dramatically across Europe. In the UK, this was a mixed blessing – on the one hand, revenues from North Sea gas fields rose, but on the other hand the price to consumers also rose. Additionally, North Sea gas fields were becoming exhausted, and the UK became a net importer of gas, relying on pipelines from the former Soviet Union. The pipeline system of Eastern Europe passes through some fairly volatile countries, so a Government concern about security of supply came to the fore, especially during the winter of 2006–7 when supplies ran dangerously low. For the UK especially this could have been a major problem: other European countries maintain large strategic reserves of gas in order to meet energy shortfalls caused by extreme weather or interruptions in supply, but the UK has only very small reserve storage facilities, due to the availability (in the past) of North Sea reserves.

The basic problem was that the cost of the generators was too high for the general public, and the only way prices could come down would be if the Government (or some other large organization) was prepared to buy the equipment in large enough quantities to bring the price down. After all, the technology itself is hardly rocket science – but how could people be persuaded to take the initial step?

In fact, circumstances overtook the debate when electricity prices rose by as much as 50 per cent within a year from some suppliers. The rise in the cost of energy was a wake-up call where the greenhouse effect had been widely ignored. People began to look for energy savings as a way of cutting their bills rather than as a way of reducing emissions – as usual, market forces were at work, and they generated their own solution.

B&Q, the giant DIY and hardware store, announced in the autumn of 2006 that they would now stock wind turbine kits and solar collectors for heating water. The turbines cost around £1500, including installation, and would pay back the installation costs within about seven years, assuming electricity prices remained the same. Of course, electricity prices are likely to rise even further – so the payback period would probably be even shorter. The idea was that, as more people bought the turbine systems, prices would fall (due to economies of scale in manufacture). On the back of the adoptions of turbines, competitors would enter the market and (eventually) it was expected that most homes in Britain would have their own electricity generators.

In practice, some doubt has been cast on the feasibility of using wind power for domestic electricity generation. Most British people live in cities, where the buildings create complex wind patterns which would dramatically reduce the efficiency of the turbines (or even damage them). Perhaps other solutions need to be sought – but at least people are taking the topic seriously!

© iStockphoto.com

Case study
Strange New Products

The age of the wacky inventor is not yet passed. Strange New Products is a website (www.strangenewproducts. com/) that is devoted to products which are new on the market – and are also strange.

For example, in 2006 the website listed the Dry Air Louse Killer, a scary-looking machine that uses exceptionally dry air to kill head lice. The lice are simply dehydrated within a few seconds by the air, which means that school children with head lice can be treated on the spot, without having to be sent home. The inventor, Dale Clayton, had the idea while studying bird lice – when he moved to Salt Lake City, which is in a salt desert, his research became difficult because the dry desert air killed the lice.

So far a very useful and not too weird idea. But how about Season Shot? Season Shot is a shotgun shell filled with seasoning, so that the game bird is killed by having the seasoning fired into it in flight. This means that the bird can be cleaned and cooked with no need to remove shotgun pellets, and it arrives at the table ready-seasoned. If the idea of killing birds with a blast of Cajun spices appeals to you, this is your product: www.seasonshot.com/About.com is the website.

Moving on, Strange New Products features poop soap. This is soap shaped like, well, poop. It is coffee-scented, and is just the thing for washing children's mouths out when they swear. www.nopeitssoap.com is where you can order some.

Sue Stipanovich is a dog-lover who was horrified to see a dog leaning out of a lorry window. Dogs love to have their heads out of the car window, but is it safe? Sue invented the BreezeGuard dog cage which fits over the car window so that the dog can stick its head into the breeze without being able to fall (or jump) out.

From Slovakia we find anti-haemorrhoid toilet paper. Impregnated with special soothing herbs, Hemo-Roll will ease that itching, burning sensation and help prevent piles.

The motorized toilet seat, the hair colouring for pubic hair and the water bottle (complete with filter) made out of corn plastic which biodegrades in 80 days are all interesting products with an unlikely market: however, for sheer yuk value, it's hard to beat Moco de Gorila. This is a Mexican hair gel product, already on the market and selling well. The brand name translates as Gorilla Snot, and the package has a picture of a gorilla with its nose running.

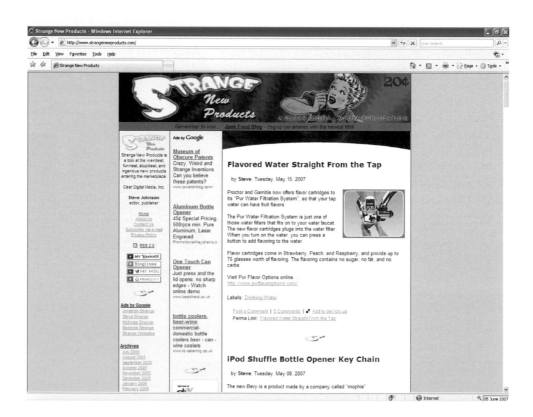

Gourmet oxygen is another product that is already out there and selling well. Intended for athletes, it provides pure oxygen in a small pressurized can (about 30 to 40 breaths' worth). The oxygen will take the pain away from oxygen-starved muscles in moments, and apparently works much better than an energy drink.

On the lunatic fringe, there is a hat which has a bottle-opener built in. This is very much a guy product – a hat that will open a beer bottle is perfection in clothing, just the thing for sporting events and fishing.

All these products fulfil a need of some sort – and most of them will fail. Perhaps they would be laughed off the market (can anyone seriously imagine going hunting with a bunch of hairy macho guys, and using a shotgun shell full of seasoning to kill the birds?) or perhaps they would be rapidly super-seded by other products. Maybe they would fulfil a need – but only for a very small number of people. Whatever the reason, it's good to know that not everything has been invented yet.

Case study questions

1 A hat with a bottle-opener built into it appears to meet a need. In terms of Rogers' criteria for new-product adoption, what would you expect the product's success rate to be?

2 Why would someone buy Moco de Gorila?

3 What would be the main barriers to adoption of the Dry Air Louse Killer?

4 What is the appeal of the Strange New Products website?

5 How might Sue Stipanovich improve the adoption rate of her BreezeGuard?

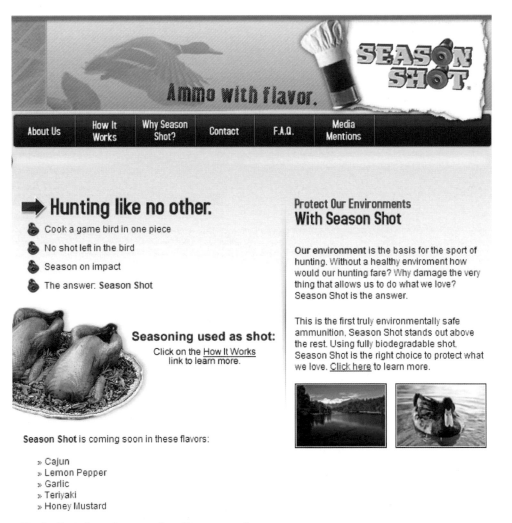

References

Calentone, Roger J., and Cooper, Robert G. (1981) New product scenarios: prospects for success. *American Journal of Marketing*, 45 (spring): 48–60.

Feick, L.F., and Price, L.L. (1987) The market maven: a diffuser of marketplace information. *Journal of Marketing*, 51: 83–97.

Goldsmith, R.E., and Hofacker, C.F. (1991) Measuring consumer innovativeness. *Journal of the Academy of Marketing Science*, 19(3): 209–22.

Kirton, M.J. (1986) Adapters and innovators: a theory of cognitive style. In *Innovation: A Crossdisciplinary Perspective*, eds K. Gronhaugh, and M. Kauffman (New York: John Wiley).

Robertson, Thomas S. (1967) The process of innovation and the diffusion of innovation. *Journal of Marketing* (January): 14–19.

Rogers, Everett M. (1983) *Diffusion of Innovation* (New York: Free Press).

Rogers, Everett M., and Shoemaker, F. (1971) *Communication of Innovation* (New York: Macmillan).

Schreier, Martin (2006) The value increment of mass-customised products: an empirical assessment. *Journal of Consumer Behaviour*, 5 (Jul–Aug): 317–27.

Walsh, G., Gwinner, K.P., and Swanson, S.R. (2004) What makes mavens tick? Exploring the motives of market mavens' initiation of information diffusion. *Journal of Consumer Marketing*, 21(2): 109–22.

Chapter 14
High involvement purchase behaviour

1. explain the relationship between involvement and information processing
2. show how involvement relates to end goals and values
3. describe how dimensions of involvement can be used to segment markets
4. explain the role of word of mouth in high-tech purchase behaviour
5. explain what is meant by 'unsought goods'

Introduction

Involvement is the degree of importance individuals place on buying the correct brand or product. This chapter is about those purchases which carry the highest levels of emotional commitment. High-involvement purchases, self-image purchases, purchases of unsought goods and purchases of complex, high-tech items all stretch the consumer's emotions and energy.

Involvement is an important concept in consumer behaviour because it relates to the values and goals of consumers: from a marketer's viewpoint, it also relates to brand loyalty and frequency of purchase.

Involvement

Involvement is a person's perceived relevance of the object based on the person's inherent needs, values, and interests (Zaichowsky 1985). It is about the degree to which the individual feels attached to the product or brand, and the loyalty felt towards it. Involvement has both cognitive and affective elements: it acts on both the mind and on the emotions.

Involvement is sometimes seen as the motivation to process information (Mitchell 1979). Someone who is closely attached to a product will probably tend to process information about the product much more readily than will someone who has no such association. At a low level of involvement, individuals only engage in simple processing of information: at high levels of involvement, people will link incoming information to their pre-existing knowledge system, in a process called 'elaboration' (Otker 1990). The degree of involvement will lie somewhere on a continuum from complete **inertia** (someone who makes decisions out of habit, lacking the motivation to consider alternatives) through to high involvement where we might expect to find an intensity of feeling which borders on the religious. At the extreme, we would expect to find people who worship celebrities, or who have a brand tattooed onto their skin (Harley Davidson owners have been known to do this). Such people have often become involved with cult products such as Harley motorcycles, Barbie dolls, sports teams or rock bands.

Figure 14.1 shows the continuum in action. Someone who has no real interest in the product category only makes routine purchases of generic products (or no purchases at all) exhibits inertia. Someone with a mild interest in the product exhibits a willingness to listen to explanations or advice about the product. Someone who is involved at a medium level would take an interest in anything he or she happens to see concerning the product, and someone who is highly committed would actively seek out information. Finally, someone who is totally committed to the brand identifies with it to the point of obsession.

BLACK STAR/ALAMY

Bikers define themselves by a product or brand.

Preview case study
Wii

In the early part of 2006, Nintendo (the Japanese electronic games manufacturer) announced that profits were down by 19 per cent on the previous year. Other manufacturers such as Sony (with their flagship Playstation product) and Microsoft (the Xbox 360) were grabbing market share away from Nintendo. Sony and Microsoft were able to cross-subsidize new product development and marketing outlays from their other businesses, but Nintendo only produce games, so they had nowhere to go in terms of recouping profitability – except by producing a new, and very exciting, breakthrough in electronic games.

Up until now, electronic games had been essentially passive. Players would sit motionless except for their fingers, peering intently at a screen. The adrenaline generated by the game had nowhere to go, so the players had a certain degree of unease about remaining virtually motionless, and of course to many people electronic gaming represented the ultimate in unhealthy lifestyles. The new Nintendo technology was set to change all that.

Nintendo developed a wireless interface which enabled the individual to be physically involved in the game. Remote controls somewhat like a TV remote control unit use motion sensors to register movement by the player, and these are translated onto a TV screen. The player is able (for example) to take a golf swing and watch the ball's trajectory, or to participate in a fencing match, or to be involved in a police shoot-out. The remote can even be used as a 'scalpel' for players to pretend to be doctors in an emergency room.

The launch date was set for late 2006, with a roll-out starting in Japan and gradually covering the world. The price of the new system was to be set comfortably below that of either Playstation 3 or Xbox, since Nintendo were seeking to capture a large part of the market quickly before competitors could react – the Wii system had already been demonstrated in September 2005, so competitors had been given plenty of time to produce their own systems.

The problem now was to see whether customers would buy the targeted 6 million systems by March 2007!

Involvement is not always confined to products. People can experience message-response involvement or advertising involvement in which they become eager to process information obtained from advertising (Batra and Ray 1983). In some cases the messages are passive (as in the case of TV advertising) whereas in other cases messages involve more effort on the part of the observer (for example print advertisements) and some marketing communications require a great deal of interaction (some mailshots and some Internet advertising).

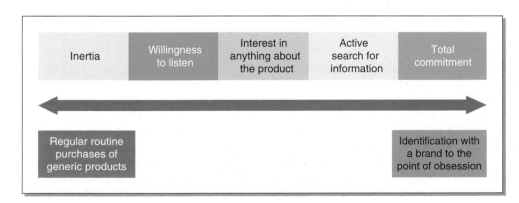

Figure 14.1

Involvement continuum

Figure 14.2

Categories of involvement

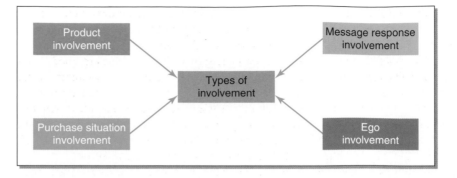

Purchase situation involvement is about the different contexts in which purchase takes place. For example, if one were buying an expensive gift for a new girlfriend or boyfriend, one might be extremely involved in the purchase since there would be a high social risk involved if a mistake is made. If, on the other hand, the gift-buying is almost obligatory (e.g. buying a birthday gift for a relative one has little liking for and rarely sees) the involvement level will be considerably lower.

Ego involvement is about the importance of the product to the individual's self-concept. Making a mistake in purchase could lead to a high social risk – the individual's self-concept might be damaged, to embarrassing effect. For example, a committed vegan would be horrified to find that a supposedly vegan product contained animal fat.

Figure 14.2 illustrates these categories of involvement.

High product involvement is driven by the degree to which the individual feels that the product's attributes are linked to end goals or values. Lower levels of involvement occur if the attributes only link to function, and very low levels of involvement occur if the product attributes are irrelevant to consequences.

In other words, high-involvement products are those which figure strongly in the individual's lifestyle. They involve decisions which it is important to get right, preferably first time. In most cases, these products are ones the consumer knows a lot about, and about which he or she has strong opinions. This means that high-involvement consumers are hard to persuade: they will not easily be swayed by advertising, or even by persuasive sales pitches. For example, an amateur chef might favour using a specific type of oil for cooking. If the oil is unavailable, he or she is unlikely to be persuaded that another oil is 'just as good': an attempt by a salesperson to persuade in those circumstances would just make the salesperson appear stupid. The discrepant information is ignored or disparaged, so the source of the information (the salesperson) will lose esteem in the eyes of the consumer.

Talking point

Do we really become that emotionally attached to products? Surely we are not so shallow that the most important thing in our lives is a brand of cooking oil! People might be in the habit of saying, 'I really love my car!' but isn't that just a figure of speech? Saying that we like something a lot is not the same as saying we love it, and saying that we think a product is the best available does not mean that we cannot live effectively without it.

In the course of a long life we fall in love with many people and things – surely we are not so blinded by love that we cannot be aware of the possibility of changing the brand of underwear we buy!

Levels of involvement are influenced by two sources: **personal sources** and situational sources. Personal sources (also called '**intrinsic self-relevance**') are derived from the means-end knowledge stored in the individual's memory, and are influenced both by the person and by the product. People who believe that the attributes of the product link to important end goals are likely to be more heavily involved with the product because the importance of the end goal means that it is more important to be right first time. Even in products such as snacks can have personal involvement issues: pre-teen girls have been shown to have very specific requirements for snacks, based on what friends find acceptable

(Dibley and Baker 2001). Involvement does not necessarily depend on the outcome being positive: sometimes involvement might be greater if the possible outcomes are negative, since the consumer will take care to choose products which will avoid negative outcomes.

There is always a risk with any purchase behaviour, but high-involvement goods carry the greatest perceived risk since these are the purchases which are most important to the consumers. This means that consumers are more likely to engage in extended problem-solving behaviour when considering high-involvement goods. People are therefore unlikely to switch brands in the case of high-involvement goods unless forced to (for example, if the product is taken off the market). When brand switching becomes unavoidable, the individual needs to go through the same extended decision making behaviour as before.

Situational sources of involvement are concerned with aspects of the immediate social or physical surroundings of the individual. Sometimes a change in social circumstances will increase involvement: most people will give considerable thought to how they dress when going on a first date, for example. Physical environment issues are about the circumstances that arise in the surrounding environment rather than those arising from people. For example, a climber might revise her view of the importance of reliability if a climbing-rope were to fail halfway up a mountain. Likewise, experience of cold weather might cause an individual to become strongly involved with a ski jacket.

Marketers may be able to manipulate some of the environmental aspects in order to increase consumer involvement in some way. For instance, a salesperson might explain the possible consequences of buying the wrong type of double glazing (showing that not all double glazing has the same insulating properties, for example). This may make the customer aware that the end result (having paid out a lot of money for windows that do not keep the heat in) could be highly self-relevant.

Dimensions of involvement

Laurent and Kapferer (1985) developed a five-factor model for assessing the dimensions of involvement. The factors were as follows, and as shown in Figure 14.3:

- The personal interest a person has in the product category, its personal meaning or importance.
- The perceived importance of the potential negative consequences associated with a poor choice of product (risk importance).
- The probability of making a bad purchase.
- The pleasure value of the product category.
- The sign value of the product category (how closely it relates to the self).

The researchers found that buying a product such as a vacuum cleaner scored high on the risk dimension (because vacuum cleaners are likely to last for many years) but low on the

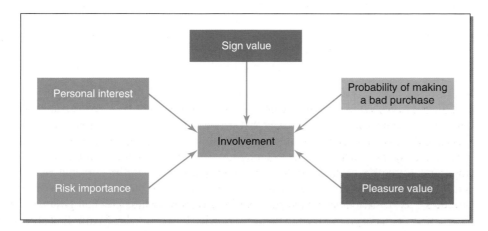

Figure 14.3

Dimensions of involvement

Consumer behaviour in action
Dinner parties

Inviting friends to eat with us is a great pleasure for most people, and it is a particularly human thing to do as well. Although all humans share food with their friends (unlike most other creatures, who will tend to push their fellows aside rather than share) the rules surrounding the process are very different between cultures.

In Britain, few people would serve traditional British food at a dinner party. It would be the norm to provide something foreign. In France the reverse would be the case – even if the host entertained at home, instead of inviting friends to a restaurant, traditional French recipes would be on the menu. What is served reflects on the host in most countries – in Brazil, it would be regarded as almost insulting to serve bananas for dessert, since bananas are so cheap it would mark the host out as a mean person.

In Hawaii, dinner guests would bring small snacks (puu puus) and in many parts of the United States it would not be unusual for guests to bring substantial quantities of food if invited to dinner. In Britain, this would be seen as a criticism – the sign value of offering interesting and exotic food to one's guests is so important within the culture that many indifferent cooks will either not host dinner parties at all, or will hire caterers to provide the food.

The very fact of hosting a dinner party carries sign values as well as pleasure values. Some people like to be known as good dinner party hosts: keen amateur chefs like to show off their skills, to the extent that there are several TV programmes dedicated to the amateur chef. Cookery programmes are a perennial favourite on British TV, something which would be surprising in some other countries.

Pleasure and sign values are the main elements in dinner parties, but not the only ones. Some hosts spend large amounts of money on ingredients, simply to be sure that the quality of the food will be as high as can be managed. There is a considerable risk, of course, in having an amateur chef dealing with very expensive ingredients. In a sense, it seems crazy that people should be so involved (and anxious) about something which is so straightforward – meeting up with friends and sharing some food!

pleasure and sign value dimensions. On the other hand, chocolate scores high in terms of pleasure, but low on sign value and risk value. The evidence is, therefore, that different products may be high involvement for different reasons.

It is possible to use these dimensions of involvement to segment the market for a given product. For example, for some people an iPod might have a strong sign value, while for others it has a strong pleasure value: the approach to each of these groups would be different in terms of marketing communication. Such factors would also be different between different countries, and this is especially true of food and drink items. A food which is an everyday purchase in one country might be a luxury only available in delicatessens in another country, and therefore the sign value of serving the product to friends or guests is very different.

iPods have strong sign values for some people.

Involvement with brands

People often develop relationships with brands. Typical examples might be favourite perfumes, jeans, cars, cigarettes, and even coffee. Research by Brann Consulting showed that people are more likely to think of their brand of coffee as a friend than they are to think of their bank this way: banks are acquaintances at best, enemies at worst. This may seem surprising considering that banks are composed of people, whereas coffee is inanimate, but it is perhaps due to the fact that coffee is consumed at home or with friends whereas bank services are often regarded as an unpleasant necessity.

Table 14.1 Categorizing consumers according to involvement

Brand loyalists	Strong affective links to a particular brand. Usually these people tend to link the product category to the provision of personally relevant consequences. These people buy the 'best brand' within the category, but also feel that the product category itself is an important part of their lives.
Routine brand buyers	These people have low personal sources of involvement, but have a favourite brand. They are more interested in the types of consequences associated with regular brand purchases, and will not necessarily look for the 'best' brand: a satisfactory brand will do. For these consumers, it is easier to buy the same brand each week, and even if it is not the 'best' it is at least reliable.
Information seekers	These consumers have positive means-end information about the product category, but no one brand stands out as superior. This means that they will use a great deal of information to help them find a suitable brand from within the product category.
Brand switchers	These people have low brand loyalty and low personal involvement. They do not believe that the choice of brand has any important consequences, even if the product category is interesting. Usually they do not have a strong relationship with the product category either, which means that they are easily affected by environmental factors such as sales promotions.

Source: Adapted from Peter, J. Paul and Olsen, Jerry C. (1994) *Understanding Consumer Behaviour* (Burr Ridge, IL: Irwin).

It is, of course, the brand that the individual has the relationship with, not the product. In blind taste tests, most smokers are unable to distinguish their favourite brand from other similar brands, but it would take considerable persuasion to make them switch brands: likewise, drivers often develop affectionate relationships with their cars. Someone's first car is often personalized with stickers and accessories, and not infrequently given a name. Drivers even talk to their cars (sometimes in less than flattering terms). Involvement also has an influence on decision-making styles (Bauer, Sauer and Becker 2006).

Involvement can be considered in terms of attachment theory, specifically avoidance and anxiety factors. Avoidance factors are those which make people shun relationships due to a fear of intimacy (or, for brands, read fear of becoming too dependent) while anxiety factors are those which make people fear loss, anxiety or rejection. People who are low or high on both dimensions report high satisfaction with brands, whereas people who are high on one dimension and low on the other report low satisfaction rates (Thompson and Johnson 2002). Presumably this means that people with a fear of becoming dependent, and a fear of loss, will be less likely to form relationships with brands and will therefore have no problems with them, whereas people who have no fear of becoming dependent and also no fear of loss will have many favourite brands. There are gender differences in brand relationship formation: when considering the two propositions 'I understand the brand' and 'The brand understands me' women use both dimensions to judge their closeness to the brand, whereas men judge only by their own actions towards the brand (Monga 2002).

For any given product category, people can be classified according to their level of involvement, as shown in Table 14.1 and Figure 14.4 (page 304). Even when the product has other products associated with it, the involvement may only apply to one of the products: for example, someone might be staunchly loyal to a brand of whisky without caring much which brand of soda goes in it. While it is true that some people may be heavily involved in several brands, there is no evidence that high involvement in one brand will lead to high involvement in another brand from a different product category.

Involvement does not necessarily equate to price. A high-involvement product is not necessarily a high-priced one, nor is a low-involvement product always a cheap one. Beer drinkers can be heavily committed to their brand of beer, costing only a few pounds a pint, whereas other people might not care

The actual beers may be similar, but people develop strong feelings about the brand.

Figure 14.4

Categorizing consumers

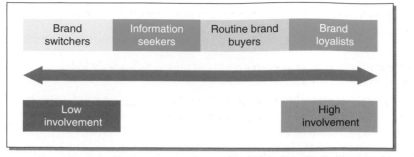

what make of car they drive as long as it gets them from A to B. Equally, someone might spend a large amount of money on a computer without being a computer enthusiast – such an individual might simply be intending to work from home. In other words, there might be no affective element in the purchase, and hence little involvement except regarding the end result. High involvement always has a strong affective component, and this does not necessarily mean a high cost commitment – people also fall in love with cheap products.

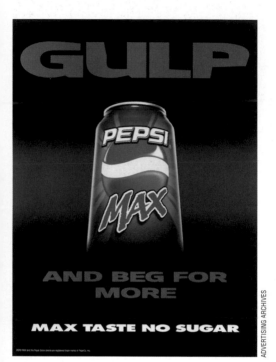

Pepsi Max appeals to hedonic needs.

Increasing involvement levels

From a marketer's viewpoint, increasing consumers' involvement levels is clearly a priority. Marketers will try to increase consumer involvement with the products whenever it is possible to do so, since this will make communications easier and loyalty levels higher. There are various techniques available to marketers for encouraging consumers to process relevant information, shown in Figure 14.5, as follows (Stewart and Furse 1984):

- Appeal to hedonic needs. Advertising which appeals to the senses generate higher levels of attention (Holbrook and Hirschman 1982). There is evidence that the pleasure of shopping tends to increase involvement with clothing (Michaelidou and Dibb 2006).
- Use unusual stimuli to attract attention.

Figure 14.5

Increasing involvement

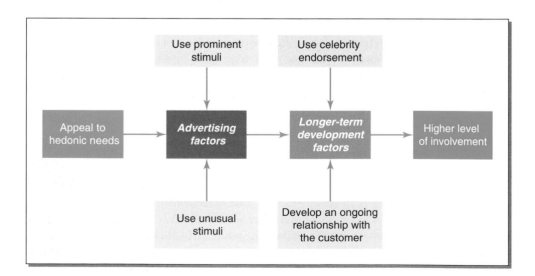

- Use celebrity endorsement. The viewer's involvement with the celebrity is likely to transfer to the product, although there are dangers with this approach.
- Use prominent stimuli such as fast action or loud music. This will help to capture the viewer's attention.
- Develop an ongoing relationship with consumers. This can often be done by using a well-designed interactive website to generate involvement.

Ultimately of course consumers develop their own ideas about involvement, and will only become involved in products which appeal to their innermost selves. Marketers can only facilitate a process which would have happened (at least to some extent) in any case.

Even fictional celebrities can endorse products.

Loyalty

Involvement with a brand should, in the vast majority of cases, lead to feelings of loyalty. In recent years, marketers have taken the view that it is better to generate loyalty and therefore retain customers than it is to keep recruiting new customers. This view has been expressed most clearly by Ehrenberg, who proposes the 'leaky bucket' theory. In the past, most companies have operated on a 'leaky bucket' basis, seeking to refill the bucket with new customers while ignoring the ones leaking away through the bottom of the bucket. According to research by Gupta, Lehmann and Stuart (2004) a 1 per cent improvement in customer retention will lead to a 5 per cent improvement in the firm's value. A 1 per cent improvement in marginal cost or customer acquisition cost only make 1 per cent increase in firm value respectively. In other words, according to Gupta *et al.*, customer retention is five times as effective as cutting costs.

Satisfaction is not necessarily enough to generate loyalty, however. East, Hammond and Gendall (2006) found no evidence that satisfaction breeds loyalty, but have found evidence that satisfaction leads to personal recommendations and therefore to recruitment of new customers. In fact, in many ways people are not loyal, and their loyalty cannot be bought: only a small percentage of loyalty card holders actually are loyal (Allaway *et al.* 2006), and the existence of loyalty cards has had minimal impact on market structures because every store issues them now, and most people carry several cards (Meyer-Waardn and Benavent 2006).

If loyalty can be generated, though, it does increase profitability (Helgesen 2006). Since companies are often not good at acquiring new customers, loyalty becomes important (Ang and Buttle 2006). It also has the effect of reducing the evaluation of brand extensions – people tend to assume that the extension will be as good as the original brand (Hem and Iversen 2003).

Purchasing high-tech consumer durables

Defining what is a high-tech consumer durable is somewhat difficult. In general, the category includes most recent electronic devices such as mobile telephones, digital cameras, computers, DVD recorders and so forth. Such products are frequently high-involvement purchases because there is usually a high level of personal relevance when someone is contemplating buying an expensive and highly visible piece of equipment. This could be because of the social values applied (friends being envious or admiring) or perhaps because of a situational change. Someone contemplating a high-tech purchase is likely to have acquired, or be acquiring, extensive means-end knowledge.

Factors in the decision-making process include the following:

- *Self-image considerations* – The potential buyer needs to ask him- or herself whether the piece of equipment fits into the kind of image the buyer has of him- or herself, or (perhaps more importantly) the kind of image the buyer would like to project to others.

- *Situational sources of involvement* – These are the considerations surrounding the immediate need. For example, a laptop computer purchaser might need to ensure that the machine will run software which is compatible with that used in work.

- *Product-related considerations* – Issues such as the reliability and durability of the equipment will come into play here. Consumer durables are usually only purchased every few years, perhaps only once a decade, so there is a strong incentive to buy products that will suit the purpose for a long period.

- *Information considerations* – Purchasers will probably be information seekers, since frequency of purchase is low, and high-tech products (almost by definition) develop rapidly. Personal sources of information (i.e. information held in memory) are likely to obsolete.

- *Financial risk* – This is fairly high, since high-tech goods are usually fairly expensive. Mobile telephone providers found a way round this by building the cost of the telephone into the cost of the 'line' rental, with the intention of expanding the market rapidly. The thinking was that consumers would be unlikely to commit the true cost of the telephones 'up front'.

- *Social risk* – This can also be high, since the purchaser may have friends who know more about the product category than does the purchaser. A friend may even be a maven (see Chapter 13) and might be contemptuous of a poor purchase decision.

- *Rational approaches to marketing communications* – Marketers will often adopt an informative, rational communications strategy because the consumers are likely to be information seekers. For example, makers of hi-fi sound equipment often produce very detailed, highly technical brochures and information. Occasionally consumers criticise these for being too complex, but many hi-fi enthusiasts not only understand all the jargon, but welcome it as an indication of their membership of an elite group.

In Figure 14.6, the self-image of the individual leads to rational information processing and an assessment of the financial and social risk. This happens within the context of the product itself, and the overall situation.

Figure 14.6

Factors in decision-making for high-tech products

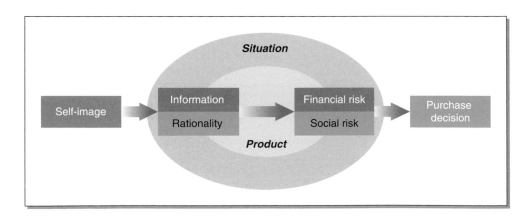

Word of mouth plays a strong role in the purchase of high-tech consumer durables, because purchases tend to be infrequent. In this context, mavens may play an important role (see Chapter 13) since they make a hobby out of knowing about such products, and are more than willing to share their knowledge.

Unsought goods

So far, we have looked at consumer behaviour when seeking out goods to meet a specific, recognized need. While most products fall into the category of being sought out as a way of meeting a need, there is a category of **unsought goods** which consumers do not look for.

Unsought goods are those goods for which consumers will recognize a need, but which they nevertheless tend to avoid buying. Examples are life insurance, wills and funeral plans (because people prefer not to contemplate their own deaths), and home improvements (because major capital expenditures can always be postponed).

If consumers do not seek out these products, two questions arise: first, why do people not seek out these products when they have already recognized a need for them, and second, how are such products marketed?

The possible reasons for not seeking out the products are as follows:

- People do not like to think about the reasons for needing the products. Because people do not like to think about old age and death, they prefer not to think about pensions and insurance.

- The products are expensive or require a long-term commitment, and people do not like to risk making a mistake.

- There is no urgency about seeking a solution. Retirement may be a long way off, or the roof may last another year or two.

- The consumer may not see any immediate benefit. In the case of life insurance, the insured person never benefits directly, since the policy only pays out on proof of death.

- Some unsought goods are new on the market, so the level of knowledge about them is low and the individual automatically rejects any marketing approach because the benefits are not obvious. Trust in both the product and the brand needs to be established first before information can be transferred.

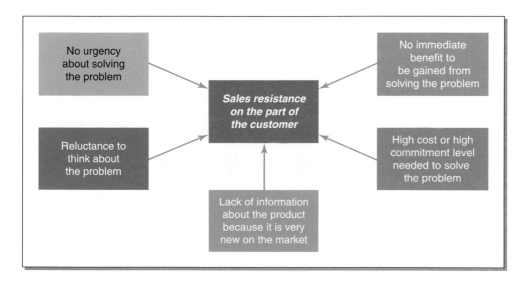

Figure 14.7

Reasons for postponing purchase of unsought goods

Marketers can overcome these problems with a series of tactics, but the main one is to use salespeople to explain the benefits of the product and close the sale. These salespeople usually have to overcome an initial resistance to the idea of spending time listening to a presentation, since the consumer of unsought goods is not engaged in an information search and is therefore unlikely to want to spend time and resources on listening to a sales presentation. The salesperson will therefore need to employ a tactical device to gain the customer's attention for long enough to activate the need for the product.

Talking point

OK, we all put things off, and we know there are things we ought to do. Equally there are things we would like to do, but maybe a little later. So who are these salespeople to come along and try to cajole us into doing things we evidently don't want to do? Surely if we wanted to buy some home improvements, or make our wills, we would do it immediately?

There must be other ways to inform people of new developments. Do we really need salespeople banging on our doors, telling us about new products? Half the time they are only telling us what we already know anyway! Not to mention that customer need is supposed to be the cornerstone of marketing – and what needs are being met?

Insurance salespeople often do this by using the referred-name method. The salesperson will ask an existing customer (or a friend or acquaintance) for the name of somebody who might be interested in the product, and will then call up the person on the telephone with a view to making an appointment. The recipient of the telephone call is put at ease because of the friend's involvement, and there is also a certain amount of social obligation to hear the salesperson's story.

Table 14.2 and Figure 14.8 show some tactics for overcoming initial reluctance on the part of the customer.

The next stage in the selling process is to activate the need. The salesperson needs to bring the problem to the forefront of the customer's mind, and the customer must recognize that something must be done about the problem. Once the need is activated and the

Table 14.2 Tactics for overcoming sales resistance

Tactic	*Explanation*
Salespeople sometimes offer a small gift in exchange for listening to a presentation. This tactic is often used by insurance companies and timeshare salespeople.	The gift helps towards compensating the customer for what he or she thinks of as a waste of time: the gift also puts the customer under a small social obligation to hear the salesperson out.
The salesperson might make an appointment for the presentation, and leave some literature with the customer. This is often used in circumstances where the appointments are made by cold-calling.	This prepares the potential customer for the information search procedure. The literature is there to whet the customer's appetite and activate the need.
The salesperson tries to ensure that all decision-makers are present. This is used in virtually all home-improvement sales calls.	This ensures that there is no need to repeat information, or waste the customer's time by calling back. It also ensures that decisions can be taken immediately and questions answered.
Salespeople sometimes seek recommendations for people to contact from each customer. This is a common ploy in insurance and pensions selling.	A recommendation from a friend helps to reassure the new customer that the salesperson is honest and reliable.

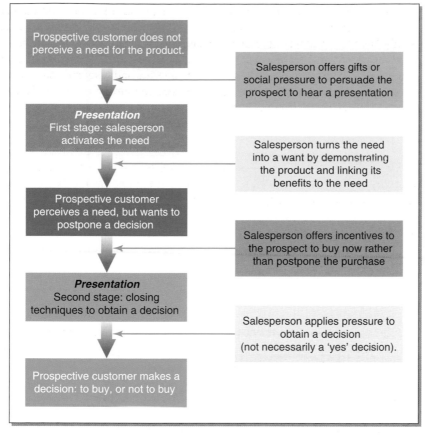

Figure 14.8
Overcoming sales resistance

The flowchart contains the following boxes:

- Prospective customer does not perceive a need for the product.
  - Salesperson offers gifts or social pressure to persuade the prospect to hear a presentation
- **Presentation** First stage: salesperson activates the need
  - Salesperson turns the need into a want by demonstrating the product and linking its benefits to the need
- Prospective customer perceives a need, but wants to postpone a decision
  - Salesperson offers incentives to the prospect to buy now rather than postpone the purchase
- **Presentation** Second stage: closing techniques to obtain a decision
  - Salesperson applies pressure to obtain a decision (not necessarily a 'yes' decision).
- Prospective customer makes a decision: to buy, or not to buy

customer admits to having a need for the product, the salesperson is able to present a solution. In some cases, the presentation will take a considerable time: in many business-to-business situations the presentation may be extended to days rather than hours.

Unsought goods highlight the difference between want and need. For unsought goods, the need is not there because it is not perceived: however, once a salesperson has activated the need, the need may be there without having a corresponding want in place. The salesperson's job is to activate the need, and then provide a want to satisfy it. Since the customer does not want to continue thinking about these unpleasant things, he or she is unlikely to do much shopping around: for this reason the bulk of unsought goods are sold on the first or second visit.

Because salespeople are compelled to use various closing techniques to persuade people to make decisions in these difficult areas, consumer groups and others have raised objections to what are seen as high-pressure techniques. This has, in turn, led to legislation in many countries which allows consumers a cooling-off period of several days during which they can cancel the agreement without penalty. Often consumers will have second thoughts, and often these thoughts are based more on a fear of commitment than on any reasoned objection to the product. This is called 'buyer's remorse'.

The double glazing market (see Consumer Behaviour in Action box) has now matured, and therefore the need for high-pressure sales techniques has reduced dramatically. The same effect has been observed in the timeshare market in the United States and in the solar heating market in Greece. Over a period of time, novel products which are also expensive will tend move from being unsought goods to being sought goods. This is shown diagrammatically in Figure 14.9.

Solar heating was an unsought good at one time – now it is commonplace in many countries.

Figure 14.9

Movement from unsought to sought goods

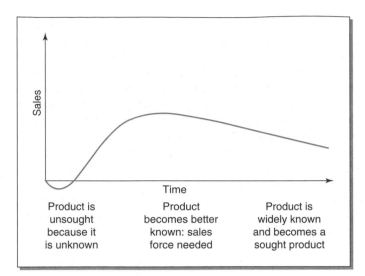

Consumer behaviour in action
Double glazing

When a new invention appears on the market it is likely to be an unsought good, particularly if it is expensive. Double glazing first appeared in the UK in the 1960s, at which time people had not heard of it and so were unlikely to seek it out. Since the product was new, there were no existing owners, so there was no opportunity for people to try it out or see the advantages. Double glazing is almost always made to fit the actual house: it therefore has no second-hand value, and there is no going back once it is fitted. This raises the risk greatly for the consumer, and since one's home is always a high-involvement good the risk is even greater.

Consequently, the only way double glazing could be sold at first was by door-to-door salesmen. These salesmen would go from house to house during the day making appointments for the evenings: the evening presentations would last anything from two hours to five hours, since the product was a total unknown to the householders and the salesman (almost all of them were men) would need to explore the householder's needs. Most of these salesmen were paid on a commission-only basis: if they didn't sell, they didn't earn any money, so they were under some pressure themselves to bring in the sales. Householders were encouraged to agree the purchase on the first visit – in fact it was rare for anyone to buy the windows as a result of a second or third visit.

Closing techniques included offering 'tonight only' discounts, and some closing techniques were aggressive. In some cases, prospective customers had great difficulty getting the salesman to leave their homes – in at least one case the salesman only left when the police were called.

As the double glazing market matured, the majority of homes in the UK were (eventually) fitted with double glazing. During this time, many companies switched over to heavy advertising, and used the line that 'no salesman will call' to reassure customers that they would not be subjected to a high-pressure sales call in their own homes. Where salespeople continued to operate, the approach was greatly toned down: after all, there is no need to pressure somebody who actually wants the product, except in the sense of encouraging them to make the decision now rather than postpone it.

Now that the market is fully mature, and a home without double glazing is regarded as an anomaly, householders without double glazing are regarded as environmentally unfriendly: Government grants are available for home insulation, and it would be difficult to sell a home which is not double glazed. However, double glazing salesmen are still used as the prime example of high-pressure selling – even though there are now relatively few of them around.

When the product is first introduced, the industry marketing norm is to operate on a 'scattergun' principle, offering the product to everyone without segmenting the market. This is because there is little information on which to base a segmentation policy. At this stage salespeople will use 'high pressure' techniques, first to persuade the potential buyer to listen to a presentation, and second to persuade the individual to make a purchase decision. Note that the decision is not necessarily positive – persuading someone to make a decision one way or the other is the key to the process. As the product becomes more established, the market can be segmented and the sales effort can be targeted more accurately.

Once the product category is fairly widely known, it is possible to use low-pressure techniques (for example advertising special offers). Even further along in the process it is possible to identify segments in the market and advertise accordingly. For example, Pilkington's K glass™ has a special coating which reflects heat back into the room, but since the coating would quickly rub off with ordinary cleaning it can only be used on double-glazed windows. This means that there must be a well-established double glazing industry for the product to be viable.

Unsought goods present a problem for marketers, since they do not at first appear to conform with accepted consumer behaviour theory. On closer examination it is clear that consumers follow the same stages of purchase behaviour, with the difference that the process is managed almost entirely by the marketers. This is illustrated in Table 14.3.

The selling techniques used for unsought goods have attracted a great deal of adverse publicity, but it is worth bearing in mind that the vast majority of double-glazing owners are perfectly happy with the product, as are the vast majority of timeshare owners. Generally speaking, people are not stupid enough to commit large sums of money to products they do not want and do not see a need for.

Pilkington K glass is specifically intended for double glazing.

Table 14.3 Decision-making model for unsought goods

Stage	Techniques for management
Need recognition	Sales representatives activate the need by asking questions about the individual's current circumstances.
Information search	The sales representative performs a lengthy presentation, explaining the product's features and benefits. Questions and objections are dealt with as they arise.
Evaluation of alternatives	The salesperson 'no-sells' competitors by pointing out ways in which their products are inferior.
Choice decision	The salesperson closes the sale by using a phrase or technique which elicits a yes or no decision.
Post-purchase evaluation	The company may follow up on the sale by sending comments forms, the salesperson may call back to elicit feedback, or a sales manager might call back. In the case of buyers' remorse, there will be a return visit by the salesperson or by a sales manager.

Summary

Making a major purchase is very different from buying something on an everyday basis. Whether the purchase is an infrequent one, or is a major financial commitment, or is one which might have repercussions on one's self esteem or social standing, or is even one about which one has very little information, major purchases require a great deal of emotional and mental effort on the part of the individual. This may take the form of an extended information search, it may take the form of a reliance on word of mouth, or it may require sitting through a lengthy sales presentation but in any event the individual is motivated to process a large amount of information.

Some of the information that the individual processes is marketer-generated, other information is acquired from friends and family via word of mouth. For marketers, encouraging involvement in the product category and (eventually) the brand can only be a good thing, since it increases loyalty and frequency of purchase.

The key points from this chapter are as follows:

- Involvement is the motivation to process information.
- High involvement is linked to end goals and values.
- Dimensions of involvement can be used to segment markets.
- Word of mouth is a strong factor in high-tech purchases.
- Unsought goods are those for which people recognize a need, but still avoid buying.

Chapter review questions

1 What factors cause people to become involved in products or brands?

2 How might a marketer increase involvement?

3 How can marketers reconcile the sale of unsought goods with the marketing concept?

4 Why is word of mouth strong in high-tech purchases?

5 What is the role of mavens in encouraging purchase?

6 Where might someone obtain information about a product with which they are heavily involved?

7 Why are people often reluctant to buy life insurance?

8 How might a marketer use an understanding of the dimensions of involvement?

9 What causes a product to move from being an unsought good to being a sought good?

10 Why might someone become involved with a brand, rather than with the benefits of the product itself?

Preview case study revisited
Wii

Wii launched in the UK on 7 December 2006, comfortably in time for Christmas. The rush to buy Wii sets was so great, though, that shops quickly sold out and queues formed: almost immediately, Wii sets began to appear on Internet auction sites such as eBay, where they sold for anything up to £500 (as opposed to a list price of £180). Nintendo told prospective purchasers that the company could not

guarantee delivery before Christmas, and in fact were expecting to ship more games into the UK some time in January.

Some commentators thought that perhaps the gap between supply and demand had been engineered by Nintendo to increase the publicity impact of the game's launch, an allegation which Nintendo hotly denied. The fact was, though, that the Wii featured on national

TV news and in the press as the hottest new product on the market for 2006.

Although the product appeared to be easy to use (one quickly learns to move appropriately to control the figure on the screen) some problems quickly became apparent. First, some gamers complained of muscular pains, joint strain, backache and so forth due to the unaccustomed physical activity caused by the game. Second, over-enthusiastic gaming caused some people to let go of the remote control, smashing their TV sets or damaging their furniture. Reports began to come in of broken windows, smashed light fittings, exploded TV sets and even (in one case) a remote slammed so hard into a dividing wall that it left a bulge on the other side of the wall. The retaining strap on the remote was evidently not strong enough to hold, so Nintendo fitted stronger straps and also issued advice to people to wipe their hands if they became sweaty. People still managed to smash their knuckles on furniture and walls, and hospital casualty departments became used to seeing former couch potatoes coming in with sporting injuries.

In the United States, a special website (Wii Have A Problem) was constructed (www.wiihaveaproblem.com). The website catalogued all the disasters that had befallen boisterous Wii players: ten-pin bowlers who had forgotten that they were not supposed to let go of the remote at the end of the swing, basketball players who had leapt up too enthusiastically and collided with the light fittings, and baseball players who threw the remote through the TV screen. The remotes largely came away unscathed, and those that were damaged were replaced immediately by Nintendo, but the borderline between game and reality was evidently seriously blurred – a tribute to the realism of the games.

As a way of getting couch potatoes to move around, Wii was a roaring success. It was also a roaring success in terms of reviving the flagging fortunes of Nintendo – the company reported vastly improved results in its next end-of-year financial statement.

Case study
Critical illness insurance

Many people have life insurance to provide for their families in the event of their death – but what happens if you don't actually die? For many people, that is actually a worse scenario. Being seriously ill, perhaps with a stroke or cancer, might mean being unable to earn a living but still needing to live. One's husband, wife or partner might have to give up work and take up full-time caring, so the net result would be a drop in income and an increase in outgoings.

There are, of course, firms which will buy the rights to a life insurance policy and will (in return) pay out the bulk of the benefits immediately, so that the individual can use the money for care in his or her final days, but the payouts are considerably less than the value of the policy (after all, there is some risk on the part of the company – the patient might recover). The survivors would still need some money to keep going, after all.

Into this gap in the market stepped critical illness insurance. Basically, if a policyholder is diagnosed with a serious illness such as a stroke, cancer or a serious heart condition which renders the person unfit to work, the company pays out on the policy. This should (if the sums add up) be enough for the individual to maintain the lifestyle they have been used to, and more importantly to provide the care they will need, whether this comes from an institution such as a hospice or nursing home, or whether it comes from a family member who has to give up work to

care for the patient. Critical illness cover pays out even if the patient is eventually cured – being cured after two or three years of intensive treatment might be wonderful, but at the same time the patient might have been unable to work for all that time, and is very likely going to find it difficult to pick up the threads of an interrupted career.

Nowadays, most insurance companies offer some form of critical illness cover, and there is a well-established group of brokers who are available to sell it to the general public. The difficulty is, of course, persuading people to take the plunge and actually sign up for the cover. After all, no one likes to think too closely about the possibility of falling seriously ill. Equally, some illnesses are not covered, or may only be covered in special circumstances – AIDS is an example. Most companies will only cover patients for AIDS contracted as the result of an assault, a blood transfusion or an occupational hazard such as working in an accident and emergency unit, where blood is likely to be spread around. Some diseases are considered to be self-inflicted: smokers are unlikely to be covered against lung cancer, emphysema or stroke for example.

Given all the restrictions and exclusions, it's almost surprising that anyone takes out the insurance at all, but the cover it provides (and the reassurance it gives) are invaluable. The whole process of marketing the cover was reviewed by the UK's Financial Services Authority in May 2006.

The FSA found the following positive aspects of the marketing of critical illness policies:

- Intermediaries (brokers) typically undertook a detailed review of the individual's personal circumstances before making a recommendation to buy a policy. This usually included a review of the individual's mortgage and other financial commitments as well as the person's priorities in terms of what should be covered.
- Firms had good controls in place to minimize the risk of mis-selling (i.e. selling someone an inappropriate policy). This was a key factor, since there had been a number of scandals in the UK over the mis-selling of pensions and insurance.
- There was little or no evidence of brokers using scare tactics to persuade people to buy policies, nor was there evidence of high-pressure sales tactics.
- Customers were typically shown other products which might meet their needs as well or better than critical illness cover.

On the negative side, the FSA found that:

● Brokers did not always ensure that people disclosed all relevant information about their medical and family history. This resulted in approximately 25 per cent of claims being rejected by the insurers.

● Brokers often did not explain the cover properly – what it would cost, what benefits could be expected, and so forth.

● Documentation needed to be clearer. The documents were often couched in complex legal language, with the key limitations and exclusions far from clear.

● Firms did not always justify the sales advice given. Often people were just told that the policy would pay out if they developed a serious illness – the wording in the documents was too standardized, and did not give people sufficient information about their individual circumstances.

● Brokers typically encouraged people to go for the cheapest option rather than the one which gave more features and benefits.

Critical illness insurance has been in decline in recent years. The reasons for this are unclear – it is possible that people have heard too many stories about claims being refused, or it may be that restrictions on high pressure sales techniques in the insurance industry have allowed people to put serious illness to the backs of their minds. The fact that it is not a compulsory insurance cover when taking out, for example, a loan or a mortgage might also be a factor. The fact remains that, given that people are living longer and are therefore more likely to meet with a serious illness, critical illness cover is likely to be more important than life insurance in the twenty-first century.

Case study questions

1 Why do the brokers take particular care to discuss the prospective customer's total financial situation?

2 Why might brokers not take care that customers have made a full disclosure of their medical history?

3 What reasons might there be for a fall in the amount of critical illness insurance being sold?

4 Why would someone fail to disclose an adverse family history?

5 Why would a broker encourage customers to go for the cheapest option?

References

Allaway, Arthur W., Gooner, Richard M., Berkowitz, David, and Davis, Lena (2006) Deriving and exploring behaviour segments within a retail loyalty card programme. *European Journal of Marketing*, 40(11/12): 1317–39.

Ang, Lawrence, and Buttle, Francis (2006) Managing for successful customer acquisition: an exploration. *Journal of Marketing Management*, 22(3/4): 295–317.

Batra, Rajeev, and Ray, Michael L. (1983) Operationalising involvement as depth and quality of cognitive responses. *Advances in Consumer Research*, eds Alice Tybout, and Richard Bagozzi (Ann Arbor, MI: Association for Consumer Research): 309–13.

Bauer, Hans H., Sauer, Nicola E., and Becker, Christine (2006) Investigating the relationship between product involvement and consumer decision-making styles. *Journal of Consumer Behaviour*, 5 (July–Aug): 342–54.

Dibley, Anne, and Baker, Susan (2001) Uncovering the links between brand choice and personal values among young British and Spanish girls. *Journal of Consumer Behaviour*, 1(1): 77–93.

East, Robert, Hammond, Kathy, and Gendall, Philip (2006) Fact and fallacy in retention marketing. *Journal of Marketing Management*, 22(1/2): 5–23.

Ehrenberg, A. (1988) *Repeat Buying: Facts, Theory and Applications* (New York: Oxford University Press).

Gupta, Sunil, Lehmann, Donald R., and Stuart, Jennifer Ames (2004) Valuing customers. *Journal of Marketing Research*, 41(1): 7–18.

Helgesen, Oyvind (2006) Are loyal customers profitable? Customer satisfaction, customer (action) loyalty and customer profitability at the individual level. *Journal of Marketing Management*, 22(3/4): 245–66.

Hem, Leif, and Iversen, Nina M. (2003) Transfer of brand equity in brand extensions: the inmportance of brand loyalty. *Advances in Consumer Research*, 30(1): 72–9.

Holbrook, Morris B., and Hirschman, Elizabeth C. (1982) The experiential aspects of consumption: consumer fantasies, feelings and fun. *Journal of Consumer Research*, 9 (Sept): 132–40.

Laurent, Gilles, and Kapferer, Jean-Noel (1985) Measuring consumer involvement profiles. *Journal of Marketing Research*, 22 (Feb): 41–53.

Meyer-Waarden, Lars, and Benavent, Christophe (2006) The impact of loyalty programmes on repeat purchase behaviour. *Journal of Marketing Management*, 22(1/2): 61–88.

Michaelidou, Nina, and Dibb, Sally (2006) Product involvement: an application in clothing. *Journal of Consumer Behaviour*, 5 (Sep–Oct): 442–53.

Mitchell, Andrew (1979) Involvement: a potentially important mediator of consumer behaviour. *Advances in Consumer Research*, ed. William L. Wilkie (Provo, UT: Association for Consumer Research): 191–6.

Monga, Alokparna Basu (2002): Brand as a relationship partner: gender differences in perspectives. *Advances in Consumer Research*, 29(1): 41.

Otker, Ton (1990): The highly involved consumer: a marketing myth? *Marketing and Research Today* (Feb): 30–6.

Stewart, David W., and Furse, David H. (1984) Analysis of executional factors in advertising performance. *Journal of Advertising Research*, 24: 23–6.

Thompson, Matthew, and Johnson, Allison R. (2002) Investigating the role of attachment dimensions as predictors of satisfaction in consumer-brand relationships. *Advances in Consumer Behaviour*, 29(1): 42.

Zaichowsky, Judith L. (1985) Measuring the involvement construct in marketing. *Journal of Consumer Research*, 12 (December): 341–52.

Chapter 15
Post-purchase behaviour

Learning objectives After reading this chapter, you should be able to:

1. explain how the attributes of a product and the relationship between supplier and consumer contribute to the perception of quality

2. explain how satisfaction and dissatisfaction are generated

3. show how complaints develop

4. explain the advantages and disadvantages of various supplier approaches to complaint handling

5. show how consumers might reduce dissonance

6. explain the different routes open to consumers when disposing of used or unwanted products

7. describe how lateral recycling works

Introduction

For some marketers, the job appears to be finished once the sale is made. For consumers, the purchase is only the beginning of the consumption experience. The post-purchase behaviour of consumers determines (ultimately) whether they will buy again, whether they will come back and complain, or (in the worst case) whether they will tell their friends, family, and even consumer protection organizations about their bad experience with the product.

Post-purchase evaluation and behaviour are therefore key issues for marketers, particularly in a relationship marketing context. Within this evaluation, expected and actual quality of the products plays a role in leading to a decision as to whether the product represents value for money or not: a product which falls below the expected quality will create dissatisfaction, but the problem for marketers lies in deciding what consumers believe quality actually is.

Disposal of used products (and even of products which still have some useful life left in them) has become central to the cause of environmentalism in recent years. Recycling, using products to the full and exercising care in disposal into the environment have been near the top of the agenda, and consumer behaviour in these areas has come under considerable scrutiny.

Quality

Following on from a purchase, people will evaluate whether the purchase has worked out well or not. This is a process of comparing the outcome with the previous expectation of the product: the result is an estimate of the quality of the product.

Quality is a complex construct subject to varying definitions. In many cases, marketers use the term as a substitute for the word 'good' – high quality means very good, poor quality means bad. In fact this is an over-simplification. Here are some definitions of quality in current use:

> Quality is defined as fully satisfying agreed customer requirements at the lowest internal price. (Bank 1992)
> Quality means conforming to requirements. (Crosby 1984)
> Quality is about fitness for use. (Juran 1982)
> Quality can only be defined by customers and occurs where an organization supplies goods or services to a specification that satisfies their needs. (Palmer 1998)

Clik2complaints.co.uk is a website dedicated to moaning. It exists to give consumers an opportunity to voice their complaints about companies and organizations – and it is very effective indeed. Consumers can post their complaints about companies on the website, and the website editors will even forward the complaints to the companies concerned for their reaction, so responses are often extremely rapid once the offending company knows that a third party has become involved.

The website is funded entirely from the pockets of the editorial team, who are keen to improve consumer experiences and to offer a way of putting things right for disgruntled consumers. Complaints are categorized by industry: people can complain about financial services, holidays, gadgets, furniture and DIY, small business, utility companies, and many other categories of business. Companies are given the opportunity to reply on the website, so that consumers can see that the company has (or has not) dealt with the complaint fairly. In some cases companies do not respond, of course, and there is not a great deal Clik2complaints can do about that – consumers then need to resort to lawyers.

Of course, not every complaint can be resolved, and not every company cares much about either its customers or its reputation. Equally, a site which only exists for people to complain may appear to be somewhat one-sided after a while – there should be room for praise as well! For this reason Click2complaints includes a 'thumbs up' section which allows people to praise companies from whom they have obtained really good service.

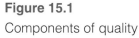

There have been attempts to distinguish between subjective and objective measures of quality. Swan and Combs (1976) defined two elements of service quality. First, they referred to instrumental quality, which describes the physical aspects of the product or service; and second, they referred to the expressive dimension, which is about the intangible or psychological aspects. Although the authors were talking about services in particular, there appears to be no reason why the same dimensions should not apply to physical products. Gronroos (1984) identified technical quality and functional quality as the components of overall quality, with technical quality being the quantifiable aspects of the quality construct, and functional quality being those aspects which arise through the interaction between consumer and supplier.

Figure 15.1 shows how the interaction between supplier and customer leads to functional quality, which then combines with technical quality to generate the overall quality.

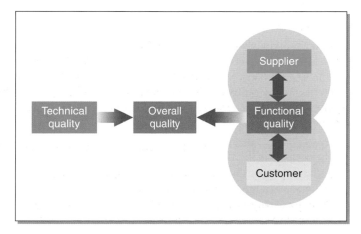

Figure 15.1
Components of quality

Reliable delivery of mail can be measured as an aspect of service quality.

Because technical quality can be easily measured it is something that both the supplier and the consumer can agree on. For example, the reliability of delivery of mail is a technical aspect of the Post Office service: the percentage of letters which arrive on time can be calculated, and (provided the statistics are honest) both parties can agree that this is, in fact, the technical quality of what is happening. What cannot be agreed is the degree to which individual consumers regard reliable delivery as important. For some, a next-day delivery is of lesser importance than a convenient delivery time in the morning, or perhaps a lower cost of postage.

People are also influenced by how the benefits are delivered to them. This is what Gronroos calls 'the functional quality', and it cannot be measured objectively because it is a function of the individual's needs and expectations. This problem of assessing quality is much harder in services markets, because the functional quality forms a much greater proportion of the total product experience. This means that effective communication with consumers becomes more important as we move towards the 'service' end of the product continuum.

In summary, quality seems to relate to the extent to which a product's performance meets customers' expectations and requirements, so it would appear to be a construct between what the marketers provide and what the customer receives. This is, of course, subjective: there is therefore no absolute measure of quality.

Talking point

In recent years, especially in the UK, we have heard a great deal about offering people choice. This has been particularly the case in public services such as schools and hospitals, where formerly people were simply sent to the nearest school or hospital whatever their personal preferences or, indeed, needs.

Now we have league tables for schools and universities, published statistics for hospitals, and choices about where and when we receive these services. Yet is that actually improving the situation for the consumers? If there is a league table, doesn't that simply place added burdens on already overstretched teachers and administrators?

Wouldn't it be better if we just ensured that all the local services worked efficiently and effectively? If we get the technical quality right, surely for most people the functional quality will not lag far behind!

Post-purchase evaluation

An evaluation of the product's performance against the consumer's pre-purchase expectation will result in several possible outcomes (Figure 15.2). In most cases, people are satisfied with their purchases to a greater or lesser extent. In some cases, people may be dissatisfied to a greater or less extent, and in a few cases they will be extremely dissatisfied. Equally, in a few cases the individual will be more than satisfied, perhaps even delighted, with the product.

Satisfaction has been described as the full meeting of one's expectations (Oliver 1980), but there are probably degrees of satisfaction, i.e. points at which the individual feels less than completely satisfied, but would still feel that reasonable expectations have been met. From a marketing viewpoint, customer satisfaction is regarded as the most important factor in developing the business and meeting corporate goals: satisfied customers are more likely to generate positive word of mouth, they are more likely to return and buy again, and they are more likely to increase the quantities purchased.

Satisfaction does not necessarily mean that the customer will always return; dissatisfaction almost certainly means that the customer will not return, however, provided there are other options available. Therefore satisfaction is necessary but not sufficient for developing loyalty in customers.

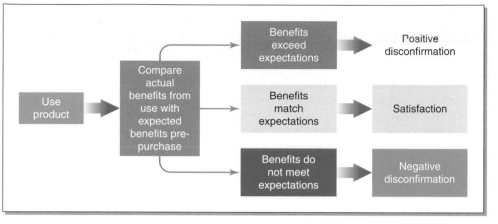

Figure 15.2

Post-purchase evaluation

In choosing between products, customers are likely to anticipate the level of satisfaction they will obtain from making a particular purchase. In anticipating satisfaction, people are more likely to pay attention to product attributes that are 'vivid' in nature (i.e. are easy to visualize, and easy to imagine as experiences) than they are to less vivid attributes (Shiv and Huber 2000). For example, someone who is thinking about buying a new outfit is likely to concentrate more on how it will look when worn, and possibly on how easy it is to keep clean, than on what materials it is made of or even what it costs to buy. After owning the clothes for a while, the individual might find that the material wears out quickly, or stretches out of shape. Anticipated satisfaction is therefore related to how the individual thinks the product will function rather than to the actual performance of the product in use.

Measuring satisfaction and dissatisfaction relies on what is called the disconfirmation paradigm. The two variables in this paradigm are pre-purchase expectations and post-purchase disconfirmation. Expectations are matched by either positive disconfirmation (the product performs better than expected) or negative disconfirmation (the product performs worse than expected). The greater the **positive disconfirmation**, the greater the satisfaction (Churchill and Surprenant 1982), and if the difference between the two is large enough the consumer feels delighted (Oliver 1997). Managing expectations is therefore a key factor in managing overall satisfaction – raising unrealistic expectations will lead to **negative disconfirmation**, even though low expectations may well mean that the initial purchase is less likely.

Santos and Boote (2003) describe four post-purchase affective states, as follows:

1 *Delight* – This occurs either when performance of the product falls between the individual's ideal and desired level of performance (a disconfirmed experience of delight) or when the consumer expected to be delighted (a confirmed experience of delight).

2 *Satisfaction (or positive indifference)* – This occurs when product performance falls between desired and predicted level (a disconfirmed experience of satisfaction), or when the person expected to be satisfied (a confirmed experience of satisfaction). This is probably a fairly common experience.

3 *Acceptance (or negative indifference)* – Acceptance occurs when product performance falls between the person's predicted and minimum tolerable level of expectation (a disconfirmed experience of acceptance) or when the person expected the performance to be no more than satisfactory (a confirmed experience of acceptance).

4 *Dissatisfaction* – When product performance falls between the minimum tolerable and the worst imaginable levels of expectation there will be a disconfirmed experience of dissatisfaction. If the consumer expected to be dissatisfied, there will

be a confirmed experience of dissatisfaction. For example, if a holidaymaker is setting off on a booked package holiday and the weather forecast is extremely bad, he or she is expecting not to enjoy the holiday – the thunderstorms and gales will come as no surprise, but will still lead to dissatisfaction.

The psychological impact of loss is often greater than the impact of a comparable gain (Hankuk and Agarwal 2003). Interestingly, these researchers found that loss of quality takes precedence over loss of price – in other words, if people feel that they have overpaid for something this is less important than if they feel that they have bought something which is of poor quality. This implies that firms need to make a large reduction in price if people are to be happy with a poor-quality product.

Interestingly, people often evaluate other people's purchases, and often take pleasure from seeing other people's purchases fail (Sundie *et al.* 2006). Pleasure at the downfall of another is called 'schadenfreude' and may not be the noblest of human emotions, but it does exist. According to Sundie *et al.*, schadenfreude is greater when a high-status product fails than when a low-status product fails: in other words, when your friend's new Porsche breaks down you will feel a certain secret delight, whereas when his new yard brush snaps you simply feel sorry for him.

Consequences of post-purchase evaluation

How people act following on from their evaluation of the consequences of their purchases is of course of intense interest for marketers. Typically, post-purchase behaviour falls into the following categories:

- repurchase
- complaint
- word-of-mouth recommendation
- no change of behaviour at all

Repurchase is almost always a clear indicator that the customer was satisfied with the product. Repurchase is perhaps best explained by the operant conditioning model discussed in Chapter 6: an action which has a positive outcome (consuming the product) is likely to be repeated (buying another of the same). Repeat buying behaviour has already been discussed in more detail in Chapter 12.

Figure 15.3 shows the possible consequences of post-purchase evaluation, in other words how evaluation might translate into behaviour. Note that the first three options are not mutually exclusive – it is perfectly possible for someone to complain, but still repurchase

Figure 15.3

Consequences of post-purchase evaluation

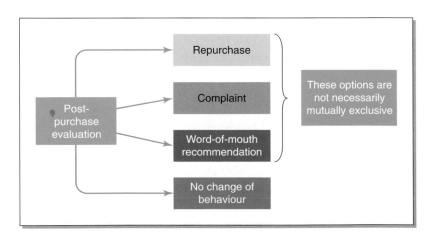

(for example, if the complaint is handled to the individual's satisfaction). This might in turn lead to positive word-of-mouth recommendation. Clearly no change of behaviour rules out the other three since they are behaviours.

Complaining behaviour may take one of three forms (Singh 1988). These are as follows:

1 *Voiced complaints* – These are complaints made directly to the supplier, and are probably the best outcome from the supplier's viewpoint (apart of course from complete satisfaction with the product) since they provide an opportunity for the supplier to redress the problem. Such complaints should be dealt with promptly and effectively, since there is some evidence to indicate that customers whose complaints are dealt with to their complete satisfaction may become more loyal than customers who did not have a complaint in the first place.

2 *Third-party complaints* – In this case, the complainer goes to a lawyer, a consumer rights champion, or even the news media to make the complaint. This can create serious problems for the supplier, although to be fair most third parties would check with the supplier first and give them a chance to make amends before taking further action.

3 *Private complaints* – Here the complainer tells friends, family, work colleagues and anyone else who will listen about the failure on the part of the supplier. This negative word of mouth can be destructive for the supplier, depending on how far it reaches and whether it is passed on further. In recent years, there have been examples of negative word of mouse (Internet or e-mailed complaining behaviour).

People do not always complain, even when dissatisfied. Complaining behaviour will only occur when some or all of the following conditions apply (Figure 15.4):

1 *The consumer blames someone else for the problem* – If the individual attributes blame to themselves (perhaps knowing that the purchase decision was a mistake) there is no one to complain to.

2 *The experience was particularly negative* – A minor problem is likely to be overlooked, for example slow service in a restaurant might not be worth complaining about: the customer simply does not eat at that restaurant again.

3 *There is a reasonable chance of some kind of redress being forthcoming* – There is no point in complaining if the customer believes that the supplier either will not, or cannot, make amends: if people do not think that their complaint will be taken seriously, they are more likely simply to switch brands than to complain (Richins 1987). For example, if the product was purchased in a closing-down sale and the shop has since gone out of business there is really no point in complaining. Note that this behaviour is likely to extend to private complaints as well as voiced or third-party complaints. The complaining activity will be possible within the level of the individual's time and money resources. There is no point in complaining about a product bought in a duty-free shop at Istanbul airport if one is now at home in Manchester. At a less obvious level, a packet of biscuits which turn out to be

When someone's expensive car breaks down, we sometimes experience schadenfreude.

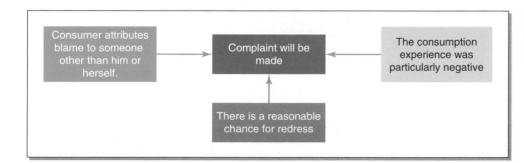

Figure 15.4

Factors in complaining behaviour

Consumer behaviour in action
Shadow websites

In 1996, partly in response to the longest-running libel case in British legal history, a new website started up. Called McSpotlight, the website was started by the McInformation Network, a group of anti-McDonald's, anti-globalization, possibly anti-capitalist activists based in 16 countries. McSpotlight is dedicated to attacking McDonald's on every front – providing information about McDonald's 'exploitation' of meat animals, about the company's low wages, about dubious marketing practices, about the endless stream of litigation which McDonald's has engaged in and about the health hazards of fast foods. The website owners say that they are not especially against McDonald's, but are rather against what McDonald's represents in terms of globalization, environmental damage and exploitation of consumers.

The Anti-Nuclear Alliance of Western Australia also runs a website on which it attacks Rio Tinto (the mining corporation) among others. In particular the site attacks Rio Tinto's Namibian uranium mining operations, attacking exploitation of workers and environmentally damaging mining methods.

In New York, the Killer Coke campaign uses a website to allege that Coca Cola uses strong-arm tactics to break up union activities in Colombia and elsewhere. The website is detailed in its allegations – and the authors of the website have no problem revealing their address.

Toys R Us fell victim (or put themselves in a bad position, depending on your viewpoint) to a website calling itself Roadkills R Us. This was a spoof website, founded by one Miles O'Neal in 1988: it existed merely to exercise O'Neal's chaotic sense of humour, and had no products, no finances, no premises and in fact no existence outside cyberspace. Toys R Us threatened O'Neal with legal action unless he closed down his 'company', but under US law (and that of most other countries) running an obviously satirical website is not against the law. The result? O'Neal started a counter-campaign, publicizing Toys R Us and their 'sledgehammer' approach. The Roadkills site still exists, but now it has a great deal to say about Toys R Us.

McSpotlight also have a website dedicated to Shell Oil, offering similar opportunities for people to attack the company. There is little that Shell can do about this – the website operates from several countries, and therefore it is difficult or even impossible for Shell to locate the perpetrators, let alone sue them (bearing in mind that different countries have different rules about libel and freedom of speech).

Many large companies have attracted the attention of people who are Net-literate enough to create a counter-website. As a way of complaining about a company it certainly puts the customer in charge – if the website is named carefully, and the right keywords are chosen, it should come up within the first ten or so sites and therefore will be seen by anyone accessing the corporation's legitimate site. From the corporation's viewpoint, this is probably not good, but of course most people are aware that the Internet is not a reliable source of information – after all, anyone can say anything on there without much fear of reprisals.

The companies which do respond do so at their peril – being seen as humourless, bullying or just plain stupid probably does more to damage the corporate image than being pilloried by a small group of people with very limited resources.

© NICK COBBING

almost all broken is unlikely to be worth complaining about, even if the grocery shop is a few hundred yards away.

The current thinking is that marketers should actively encourage people to complain: people who are dissatisfied are more likely to spread the bad news to friends and family in private responses than they would to spread good news if they were satisfied (Schibrowsky and Lapidus 1994). Also, it turns out that people whose complaints are completely satisfied feel even better about the supplier than they would if nothing had gone wrong in the first place (Speer 1996). This may seem surprising, but actually it makes sense: consumers know that we do not live in a perfect world, and things will occasionally go wrong, so knowing that a supplier will put things right promptly is reassuring. Another supplier represents an unknown quantity on this dimension. Of course, good complaint handling is no substitute for providing a good service in the first place (Liljander 1999).

However, there is a downside to encouraging complaint behaviour. First, it can lead people to believe that there are likely to be problems, and consequently the initial purchase becomes less likely. Second, it can lead to a 'complaining culture' in which people complain at the slightest excuse. At the extreme, it can lead to the 'professional complainer' who deliberately searches out something to complain about in order to obtain a price reduction or a free gift of some sort. Professional complainers are known to exist in the package holiday industry, for example (see the Consumer Behaviour in Action box).

Obviously the existence of professional complainers creates a problem for suppliers, in that they need to judge whether a complaint is genuine, frivolous or fraudulent. Making a mistake could lead to serious consequences, so (at present at least) most suppliers would rather pay out the occasional fraudulent or frivolous claim rather than risk annoying a genuine customer or being sued for a genuine claim.

Most service companies provide an easy process for handling.

Talking point

There was once a cartoon in which a very large man with a cudgel was shown standing underneath a sign saying 'Complaints Department'. Like most jokes, this was funny because it stated a real truth in many companies – complaining will only result in verbal abuse, and being tossed onto the street.

Nowadays we expect our complaints to be taken seriously, because the law is on our side and anyway it's only fair. So if we take a new suit or dress back to the shop, we expect a refund of our money, even if there is nothing wrong with the item except that we changed our minds. We expect the shop to change it even if we wore it to go out for an evening. Because that's what's right, right?

No, it isn't right. People who complain are adding to the cost of products which other people buy. If our complaints department is a large man with a cudgel, our costs will drop – and they would drop even further if we didn't have a complaints department at all, as is the case with some cheap airlines. Those savings can be passed on to customers who do not complain, who accept that the world is not perfect, and who accept that life is risky!

Sometimes the staff in retail stores can feel threatened by customers' complaining behaviour. If the complainant becomes aggressive, staff will sometimes become angry themselves: if they are unable to release the anger, considerable stress may result. In some cases, staff members have organized their own ways of relieving their feelings – there is a website for staff called 'Customers Suck' for example, where staff can post stories about unpleasant, aggressive or even violent customers. The webmasters make it clear that the vast majority of customers present no problems – but the site still provides a valuable safety-valve for staff who deal with the problem cases.

Figure 15.5 offers some ideas for dealing with complaints. In the case of a genuine complaint, the supplier should put matters right, but should perhaps also offer some extra compensation as a reward for bringing the problem to the firm's attention. In the case of frivolous complaints, the supplier should explain why the complaint is not going to be addressed, and should reject it. In the case of attempted fraud, the complaint should be rejected and also the firm should consider blacklisting the customer, since this is clearly someone that the firm should not be doing business with in future.

www.customerssuck.com

Sometimes staff need to complain about customers.

Consumer behaviour in action
Tourist complaints

Tour operators used to say that Brits were the least likely to complain. If it turned out that the hotel was overbooked, the Swedes and Germans would bang on the counter and demand to be accommodated, while the Brits would shrug meekly and get back on the tour bus. In recent years, though, consumer protection organizations have been plugging the idea of complaining if things are not entirely satisfactory – with the result that some people seem to think that complaining is compulsory.

Airtours, a major UK holiday tour operator, deals with 17,000 complaints a year: the company now provides its reps with a catalogue of the more bizarre complaints so that they can prepare themselves for dealing with the lunatic fringe of complainers. Some examples follow.

No one told us there would be fish in the sea. The children were startled . . .

My fiancé and I booked a twin-bedded room and we were placed in a double-bedded room. We now hold you responsible for the fact I find myself pregnant. This would not have happened if you had put us in the rooms that we booked . . .

The brochure stated: 'No hairdressers at the accommodation'. We're trainee hairdressers, will we be OK staying here . . .?

It took us nine hours to fly to Jamaica from England – it only took the Americans three hours . . .

It is your duty as a tour operator to advise us of noisy or unruly guests before we travel . . .

I compared the size of our one-bedroom apartment to our friends' three-bedroom apartment and ours was significantly smaller . . .

I was bitten by a mosquito – no one said they could bite . . .

Some people apparently did not realize that there would be foreigners abroad.

There were too many Spanish people. The receptionist spoke Spanish. The food is Spanish. Too many foreigners.

Since this person was, technically, holidaying in Spain this situation was scarcely surprising.

The issue for the tour operator is, of course, planning how to deal with the ridiculous, stupid or even malicious complaint. It is hard to believe that someone would seriously complain that the sand on the beach was white

rather than the yellow depicted in the brochure, or that there was no air conditioning outside their hotel, but the holiday reps on site have had to deal with exactly those complaints. The rep has to decide whether the customer is being merely stupid, in which case the response needs to be extremely tactful, or whether the customer is trying to gain some refund or other advantage unfairly. In some cases it must be difficult not to laugh, but each complaint must be dealt with as if it were serious – the world has become much more ready to rush off to the lawyers. For example, one couple cancelled a two-week holiday in Majorca because of the SARS epidemic. The tour operator pointed out there was no SARS epidemic within 7000 miles of Majorca, and charged a cancellation fee: the couple are now suing for compensation.

Airtours do not say whether the above complaints ever resulted in compensation being paid, but they are warning holidaymakers not to waste their reps' time with frivolous or vexatious complaints. The problem here is that it might discourage the person with a genuine problem from complaining – but this might be a small price to pay for not having to deal with bizarre complaints from obvious crackpots.

Better by smiles

Customer satisfaction 97%

We ask all our holidaymakers to tell us exactly what they think of us by completing a Customer Satisfaction Survey at the end of their holiday. Year on year, they tell us that the quality and value of our holidays just gets better and better. In our latest survey an impressive 97% rated their holiday overall as good or very good. To put a smile on your face, ask your local Going Places or Airtours Recommended Agent for an Airtours Summer 2003 brochure, or call 0870 900 8639 quoting ref. MAIL 5

That's a breath of fresh *Airtours*

ADVERTISING ARCHIVES

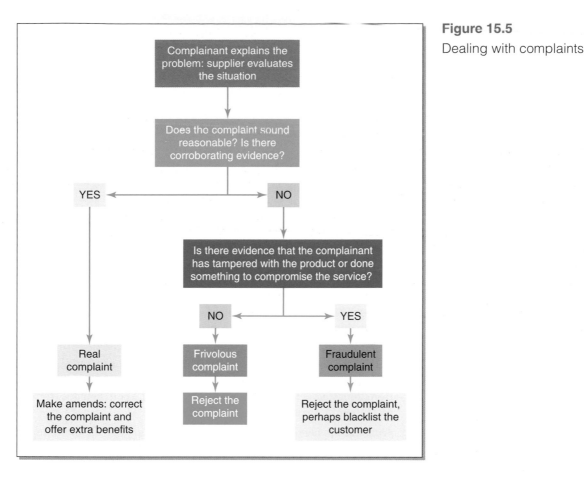

Figure 15.5
Dealing with complaints

Complaining behaviour is a way of relieving one's feelings, releasing the anger and frustration that is often felt when a purchase does not go according to plan. This is a way of reducing cognitive dissonance, which will be discussed in the next section of this chapter.

Word-of-mouth recommendation often occurs when people are satisfied, either because friends or family ask about the product, or because the individual is sufficiently delighted to want to share the positive experience. Research from Germany indicates that people who have recently switched to a new energy supplier exhibit higher levels of word-of-mouth activity than people who have been loyal to the energy supplier for a long time; in other words recent 'converts' like to tell people about their new supplier. This is perhaps not surprising – people who have been with the company for a while have probably already told anybody who might be interested all about their experiences. However, people who have switched as the result of a recommendation from someone else (referral switchers) have higher satisfaction levels, are more loyal, and give more positive word of mouth than any other group (Wangenheim and Bayon 2004).

From this it would seem that, if we want to be satisfied with the things we buy, we should listen to our friends' recommendations.

Cognitive dissonance

Cognitive dissonance is the psychological tension which results from holding two conflicting ideas at the same time. The term came originally from work by Carl Festinger in the late 1950s, in which he experimented on people's motivation to lie. Festinger recruited students to perform a tedious task (specifically, putting pegs into holes, rotating the pegs a quarter-turn, then removing the pegs). He then told the students that he needed more recruits for the tests, and asked them to 'sell' their friends on the idea of helping with the tests by telling them that the experiment was really interesting and good fun. He offered some students a dollar for telling this lie, and others $25 (a considerable sum in 1957). Interestingly, the ones who were only paid a dollar actually began to believe the lie themselves: Festinger's explanation for this was that they could not justify their statements on the basis that they were being paid to make them, so therefore the statements had to be true (Festinger 1957).

In the realm of consumer behaviour, post-purchase dissonance arises when the idea that a product was going to be a good purchase turns out to be wrong. The new information (that the product was not a good purchase) conflicts with the existing information, and the individual needs to resolve the dissonance.

Dissonance reduction is not always straightforward. Essentially, there are four basic strategies, as follows:

1 *Ignore the dissonant information and seek consonant information* – For example, if one has just made a major purchase and a friend says that the supplier has a bad reputation, one could ignore the new information altogether (perhaps rationalizing this by thinking that the friend is just jealous) and one could perhaps search online for reports to confirm the good reputation of the supplier.

2 *Distort the dissonant information* – Here one might agree with the friend's statement, but rationalize it by thinking that the supplier's bad reputation arises from things which would not affect the product's performance (for example, a reputation for treating its workers badly).

3 *Minimize the importance of the issue* – One might agree that the supplier has a bad reputation, but also believe that this is not important in the context of the product itself, which is manifestly perfectly all right.

4 *Change one's behaviour* – In this case, one might take the product back for a refund, or not make further purchases in future.

Cognitive dissonance is a motivator to process information or to act, because the individual is driven to reduce dissonance wherever possible. Dissonance can occur at any point in the purchase cycle: when considering a major purchase, pre-purchase dissonance can easily affect the way decisions are arrived at, and in particular can easily delay the final purchase as the individual spends time reducing dissonance. Inevitably some doubt will remain, of course.

In Figure 15.6, the gap between the expected outcome and the actual outcome is what causes the post-purchase dissonance. The actual outcome is used as the benchmark for choosing which route to go in reducing the dissonance, and the end results of the dissonance-reducing activity is fed back into the dissonance itself to cause the reduction.

Figure 15.6

Dissonance reduction strategies

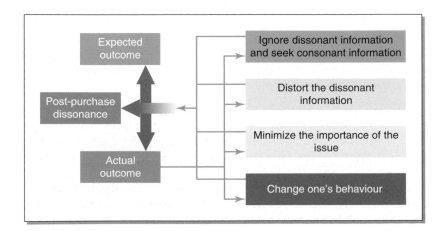

One very effective way of reducing dissonance is to complain. Complaining allows the individual to release negative feelings and to talk through the information which has led to the dissonant feelings. It often elicits new information from the person being complained to: for example, someone making a private complaint to a friend will almost certainly find that the friend will offer suggestions for redressing the problem. A voiced complaint to the supplier might reveal that the individual is not using the product correctly, or has been supplied with a faulty product which can be replaced. A third-party complaint to a consumer protection organization might reveal that other people have met with the same problem, and that there is a way of putting matters right. In any event, the complainant will gain some moral support from the complaining behaviour, which in itself is reassuring.

Disposal

After a product has been used up, the consumer has the problem of disposing of whatever remains. In some cases, what is left still has value – the second-hand car market is an obvious example. In other cases, the product has been so totally used up that virtually nothing remains, as is the case with most food products.

In some cases, people form strong attachments to products (see Chapter 14 for a description of high-involvement products) and find it difficult to 'let go'. Favourite clothing, much-loved cars, and even now-obsolete vinyl records may be kept until there is really no further possibility of using them any longer. Such possessions are our links with our past, and giving them up removes one of the anchors of our identities (Belk 1989). People who retain possessions have been defined as **packrats**, whereas people who regularly dispose of their possessions have been defined as purgers (Coulter and Ligas 2003). Packrats attach more meaning to their possessions, and see themselves as thrifty: they usually do not mind giving possessions away to other people or to charities, but they hate waste. Purgers, on the other hand, think packrats are messy and disorganized, and do not attach much significance to their possessions.

No matter how assiduously some of us might try to hoard our possessions, sooner or later everything must go. When the object is no longer of any use, the individual has a choice of three options (Figure 15.7, page 330):

1 *Keep the item* – This may mean putting the item away in a safe place – a loft or a garage – or it may mean re-using the product in some way. For example, an old bath might be recycled as a garden pond, or a broken radio might be incorporated into an artwork.

2 *Temporarily dispose of the item* – Christmas decorations might be put away for use the following year, for example. Equally, products might be lent to someone else, or even rented to someone. For example, someone who will be working abroad for a year might rent out his or her house rather than sell it.

3 *Permanently dispose of the item* – This could be achieved by selling the item, giving it away, putting it into the refuse disposal system, or by some other permanent means such as burning it.

In recent years, there has been an increasing emphasis on recycling items which are no longer of any use. In some cases the recycled article can be renovated, cleaned or donated as itself: for example, used spectacles can be collected and sent to Third World countries to be worn by people who otherwise could not afford glasses. Since individuals' eyes deteriorate over time, everyone needs new spectacles with a different strength from time to time, so glasses which are still perfectly useable need to be disposed of. Equally, bottles can be cleaned and re-used as bottles rather than being smashed in a bottle bank and melted down. Before the 1970s virtually all bottles were re-used in this way.

Figure 15.7

Disposal options

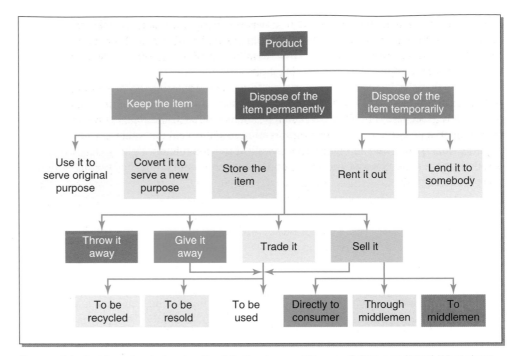

Source: Adapted from Jacob Jacoby, Carol K. Berning, and Thomas F. Dietvorst (1977) What about disposition? *Journal of Marketing*, 41 (Apr): 23.

Clothing, books, and used household items are often contributed to charity shops where they are sold to new users. Clothing which is completely beyond re-use can be processed for paper-making: high-quality writing paper uses recycled fabric fibres (known in the trade as 'tramp's trousers') to strengthen the paper.

In the 1950s everything was recycled. People took bottles back to the shop and were refunded a small deposit, milk bottles were given back to the milkman (and he would get pretty nasty if he didn't get his bottles back), and food scraps were collected by pig-keepers. Ashes were spread on gardens or made into building blocks, paper and scrap wood were burned in household boilers to heat water, clothes were repaired, darned and eventually re-cut or unpicked and re-knitted to make new clothes. Newspapers were used to wrap food (notably in the UK, fish and chips), and in some households were used as toilet paper.

So where do our twenty-first-century consumers get off, telling us to recycle? Sending newspapers away to be re-pulped instead of simply using them as packaging? Breaking bottles and re-melting them instead of re-using them as bottles? Packing milk in one-way, non-recycleable plastic containers instead of in multi-use glass bottles?

Since the environmental movement started, we seem to have become *less* environmentally responsible than we were before!

Some countries place a greater emphasis on recycling than do others, and there is also some debate over which recycling options are worthwhile and which are not. In some cases, the cost of collecting and recycling used items (including the energy used) may mean that it is less environmentally damaging to use new materials rather than to attempt to recycle. One study showed how specific instrumental goals were linked to abstract terminal values, and thus to recycling behaviour. Lower-order goals which were identified were 'avoid filling up landfills', 'reduce waste', 're-use materials', and 'save the environment'. These were linked to terminal values of 'promote health and avoid sickness', 'achieve life-sustaining ends', and 'provide for future generations'. The perceived effort of recycling turns out to be the best predictor of whether people will actually take the trouble at all. In other words, even when people are sold on the idea of recycling and believe it to be important, difficulty in actually recycling will often outweigh their motivation to do so (Bagozzi and Dabholkar 1994).

There is some evidence that the eagerness to recycle is levelling off somewhat and is certainly far from embedded in people's consciousnesses. Much depends on culture and on the availability of recycling schemes – Germans appear to be far more recycling-conscious than, for example, Spaniards or Britons. There is some evidence that women are more environmentally conscious than men, but this is based on American research and may not be true for other countries (Iyer and Kashyap 2007). These authors conclude that recycling will not succeed unless people are offered incentives and are reminded regularly about the need to recycle. Interestingly, they also found that recycling attitudes and behaviours correlate weakly with environmental attitudes and behaviours – in other words, having environmentally friendly attitudes in some areas (cycling rather than driving, using eco-friendly products) does not necessarily mean that one also believes in recycling.

'Lateral recycling' is the term given to selling goods on, donating them to others or exchanging them for other items. Car boot sales (also called flea markets) exist to facilitate this process, as do charity shops. A more recent arrival in the lateral recycling market is eBay and similar websites, on which people can sell almost anything. eBay has become an international institution of its own, with people selling and buying in an almost compulsive manner – the website has rules about what can and cannot be sold, but even so some very dubious items have appeared from time to time.

going, going, gone-on-line.

You can buy and sell anything on eBay. **eBaY**.CO.UK

e-bay facilitates lateral recycling.

Selling used products has become a lucrative business for some people – clearly antique dealers and the like can make their livings from selling off previously unwanted products, but even dedicated car-boot-sale attendees and eBayers can make substantial amounts of money from buying and selling. Reclaimed architectural products such as Victorian fireplaces, antique tiles, decorative roofing features, stained glass windows, and so forth are often traded both on- and offline.

Given the huge increase in wealth in developed countries over the past 30 years or so, and the correspondingly dramatic increase both in number of possessions per household and in quantities of rubbish produced, disposal is becoming one of the hot issues of the twenty-first century. People can no longer simply throw things away – in the words of one researcher, there is no longer an 'away' to throw things to (Sherry 1990). Marketers are likely to find that, if they do not address the issue of disposal and find ways to tap the potential of recycling in all its forms, they will be forced to do so by legislation. Already the European Union (largely at the instigation of Germany) is moving towards legislation which will require companies to take cradle-to-grave responsibility for their products.

Summary

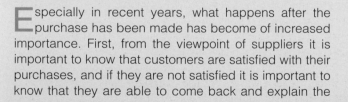

Especially in recent years, what happens after the purchase has been made has become of increased importance. First, from the viewpoint of suppliers it is important to know that customers are satisfied with their purchases, and if they are not satisfied it is important to know that they are able to come back and explain the problem so that it can be dealt with at source in future, thus reducing the potential for further dissatisfaction.

Disposal of used-up products, packaging, accessories and so forth has become a key issue in the environmental movement. There simply are not enough landfill sites to absorb the quantities of materials being thrown away, and at the same time the world's supply of raw materials cannot keep up with the demands of producers. Recycling has therefore become an essential part of the twenty-first century consumer behaviour repertoire.

The key points from this chapter are as follows:

- Technical quality refers to quantifiable aspects of the product: functional quality refers to the interaction between consumer and supplier.
- Satisfaction and dissatisfaction are measured by disconfirmation, which may be positive or negative.
- Complaints will only occur if the consumer blames someone else, the experience was particularly negative and there is a good chance of redress.
- Encouraging complaints helps prevents bad word of mouth, but may encourage frivolous complaints.
- Dissatisfied customers will act to reduce dissonance.
- There are three options for disposal: keep and store the article, dispose of it temporarily or dispose of it permanently.
- Lateral recycling (passing the product on to someone else for re-use) is a growing phenomenon.

Chapter review questions

1 How might a company minimize the number of fraudulent or false complaints, without discouraging genuine complaints?

2 Why might a company encourage environmentally friendly disposal of its products?

3 What methods exist for customers to reduce dissonance?

4 How does disconfirmation theory affect complaining behaviour?

5 What are the basic routes for disposal of used products?

6 What are the drivers for lateral recycling?

7 How might a company encourage positive word of mouth from people whose complaints have been satisfactorily dealt with?

8 Why would someone only complain if he or she can blame someone else for the problem?

9 Why is quality not an absolute?

10 How can firms improve the customer's perception of the quality of their products?

Preview case study revisited
Clik2complaints.co.uk

The website's mission statement is very clear – the site exists to provide a forum for complaints. It does not exist to provide somewhere for people to post complimentary messages about companies (although this does sometimes happen, of course) and it does not exist to give companies a chance to put their side of the case (although again this does happen). The site does, however, aim to give people the chance to talk to each other about their experiences, whether good or bad, through online forums. Recent forum topics included a debate on whether it is better to buy all one's security software as a single bundle, or to buy each item separately, and a debate on the rights of an individual who has been supplied a defective mobile telephone.

There is no doubt that the website provides a useful outlet for consumers to complain, and also to pass on useful advice about companies and products. Although at first sight it may seem that the site encourages complaints, in fact most people are perfectly satisfied with the products and services they buy – only when things go wrong do they become motivated to go online. Less frequently, people may be motivated to pass on news of truly excellent service, but the merely satisfactory is unlikely to be mentioned since (in general) people expect to be satisfied with the products they buy.

One interesting aspect of the forums appeared in December 2006, continuing into January 2007. The forums are moderated by one of the website owners (as is usually the case with this type of website) and the debate on the rights of mobile telephone subscribers became somewhat heated, following the entry of a mobile telephone retailer who wanted to put the industry case. At one point the moderator decided to edit out one posting and lock the thread, but then re-opened the discussion. At that point the retailer came back with a strong complaint about the thread being closed and questions remaining unanswered: the moderator then closed the thread again. The thread was closed because (in the moderator's words) 'Sadly, certain people have used defamatory remarks against this site'. The thread was closed on 11 January 2007, apparently because someone complained about the site itself – an interesting outcome for a site dedicated to the complaint.

Given the somewhat one-sided nature of Clik2complaints.co.uk, one might wonder why companies do not set up counter-websites which allow them to complain about customers. On the other hand, Clik2complaints does offer a valuable safety-valve and the occasional chance to win redress from companies which have fallen short of the ideal in their customer service operations.

Case study
Recycling

Governmental attitudes to recycling vary greatly, even within the European Union. Germany, for example, has the Verpackvo, a law which allows consumers to return packaging to retailers, who are in turn required by law to return the packaging to the manufacturers. Manufacturers and suppliers assume responsibility for dealing with this packaging, which in practice means recycling. People are encouraged to return packaging to recycling bins: visitors to Germany are often surprised to see four separate slots on street rubbish bins to accommodate plastics, paper, metal and miscellaneous rubbish. Recycling bags are supplied by an organization set up by 400 major companies, and consumers are encouraged to separate out their rubbish for recycling.

Austria and Sweden also have comprehensive recycling systems. In Austria, potentially hazardous refuse such as batteries, old refrigerators and old computers must by law be returned to retailers for recycling or treatment. Householders typically sort their waste into separate components for recycling or disposal. In Sweden industry has established a special company to handle recycling, and in Finland 35 per cent of household waste is recovered. The rate for industry is much higher, at over 60 per cent. Finns also recycle bottles: 98 per cent of bottles in Finland are returned for refilling, rather than being smashed for re-melting or (worse) sent to landfills (virtual.finland.fi).

In the United States, each citizen produces 730 kilos of household refuse per annum, compared with just over 500 kilos per annum in Europe. America now has an official America Recycles Day, but recycling policy is left to each state to legislate. Some states, notably Oregon, have very strict environmental protection laws, and retailers are required to charge a small deposit on soft drink cans. Because each state has its own laws, however, the deposits vary from one state to another, and therefore it is theoretically possible for someone to pay a 5¢ deposit in one state, cross the state line, and have 10¢ or even 15¢ returned. The USA has an Environmental Protection Agency which has the power to enforce environmental legislation, but the somewhat chaotic nature of the law in each state means that relatively little of each citizen's 730 kilos of refuse actually is recycled.

Much of the thrust towards recycling comes from the cost of using landfill. In the UK, landfill costs are relatively low at $30–35 a ton, compared with the USA at $50 a ton and Austria at $140 a ton (Kanari, Pineau and Shallari 2003). This may in part account for the UK's poor record on recycling.

Recycling is not a free option. Energy, time and effort are expended in returning materials and rendering them fit for re-use. Public acceptance of recycled (as opposed to all-new) products is still somewhat patchy. Often the materials sent for recycling need to be re-sorted since people are not always as careful as they might be about separating the refuse correctly – an example is metal bottle-caps, which often find their way into glass-only recycling bins. In many cases it is still cheaper to use new materials rather than recycle, disregarding the effect on the environment in the long term.

Case study questions

1 How might governments encourage citizens to recycle more?

2 Why might some countries (and even some states within the US) be more concerned with recycling than others?

3 What barriers exist to recycling, in terms of consumer behaviour?

4 What incentives might companies need in order to facilitate recycling programmes?

5 Why might goods made from recycled materials be perceived as inferior?

References

Bagozzi, Richard P., and Dabholkar, Pratibha A. (1994) Consumer recycling goals and their effect on decisions to recycle: a means-end chain analysis. *Psychology and Marketing*, 11 (July/August): 313–40.

Bank, John (1992) *The Essence of Total Quality Management* (Harlow: Prentice Hall).

Belk, Russell W. (1989) The role of possessions in constructing and maintaining a sense of past. *Advances in Consumer Research*, 17, eds Marvin E. Goldberg, Gerald Gorn, and Richard W. Pollay (Provo, UT: Association for Consumer Research): 669–76.

Churchill, G.A., and Surprenant, C. (1982) An investigation into the determinants of customer satisfaction. *Journal of Marketing Research*, 19 (November): 491–504.

Coulter, Robert A., and Ligas, Mark (2003) To retain or to relinquish: exploring the disposition practices of packrats and purgers. *Advances in Consumer Research*, 30(1): 38.

Crosby P.B. (1984) *Quality Without Tears* (New York: New American Library).

Festinger, L. (1957) *A theory of Cognitive Dissonance* (Palo Alto, CA: Stanford University Press).

Gronroos, C. (1984) A service quality model and its marketing implications. *European Journal of Marketing*, 18(4): 36–43.

Hankuk, Taihoon Cha, and Agarwak, Praveen (2003) When gains exceed losses: attribute trade-offs and prospect theory. *Advances in Consumer Research*, 30(1): 118–24.

Iyer, Easwar S., and Kashyap, Rajiv K. (2007) Consumer recycling: role of incentives, information and social class. *Journal of Consumer Behaviour*, 6 (Jan–Feb): 32–47.

Juran, J.M. (1982) *Upper Management and Quality* (New York: Juran Institute).

Kanari, N., Pineau J-L., and Shallari, S. (2003) End-of-life vehicle recycling in the European Union. *Journal of Metals*, August: 15–19.

Liljander, Veronica (1999) Consumer satisfaction with complaint handling following a dissatisfactory experience with car repair. *European Advances in Consumer Research*, 4, eds Dubois, Lowrey, Shrum, and Vanhuele: 270–5.

Oliver R.L. (1997) *Satisfaction: a Behavioural Perspective on the Consumer* (New York: McGraw-Hill).

Oliver, R.L. (1980) Cognitive model of the antecedents and consequences of satisfaction decisions. *Journal of Marketing Research*, 17 (November): 460–9.

Palmer A. (1998) *Principles of Services Marketing*, 2nd ed. (Maidenhead: McGraw Hill).

Richins, Marsha L. (1987) A multivariate analysis of responses to dissatisfaction. *Journal of the Academy of Marketing Science*, 15 (Fall): 24–31.

Santos, Jessica, and Boote, Jonathan (2003) A theoretical exploration and model of consumer affective expectations, post-purchase affective states, and affective behaviour. *Journal of Consumer Behaviour*, 3(2): 142–56.

Schibrowsky, John A., and Lapidus, Richard S. (1994) Gaining a competitive advantage by analyzing aggregate complaints. *Journal of Consumer Marketing*, 11(1): 15–26.

Sherry, John F. (1990) A sociocultural analysis of a Midwestern American flea market. *Journal of Consumer Research*, 17 (June): 13–30.

Shiv, B., and Huber, J. (2000) The impact of anticipating satisfaction on consumer choice. *Journal of Consumer Research*, 27(2) September: 202–17.

Singh, Jagdip (1988) Consumer complaint intentions and behavior: definitions and taxonomical issues. *Journal of Marketing*, 52 (January): 93–107.

Speer, Tibbett L. (1996) They complain because they care. *American Demographics*, (May): 13–14.

Sundie, Jill M., Ward, James, Chin, Wynne W., and Geiger-Oneto, Stephanie (2006) Schadenfreude as a consumption-related emotion: feeling happiness at the downfall of another's product. *Advances in Consumer Research*, 33(1) 96–7.

Swan, J.E., and Combs, L.J. (1976) Product performance and consumer satisfaction: a new concept. *Journal of Marketing*, April: 25–33.

Wangenheim, Florian, and Bayon, Tomas (2004) Satisfaction, loyalty and word of mouth within the customer base of a utility provider: differences between stayers, switchers, and referral switchers. *Journal of Consumer Behaviour*, 3(3): 211–20.

Chapter 16
Services markets

Learning objectives After reading this chapter, you should be able to:

1. explain the differences between services and physical products from a purchasing perspective
2. explain the role of word of mouth in both purchase decisions and in after-purchase behaviour
3. describe ways in which consumers reduce their risk when buying services
4. describe the role of involvement in service purchases
5. explain sales promotion in a service context
6. describe the role of service levels
7. describe ways of minimising dissatisfaction, and ways of handling it when it does occur

Introduction

Services are a major part of the developed world's economies. In Western Europe we manufacture relatively little compared with 100 years ago, and we earn our living through providing services such as finance, tourism, insurance, education and (of course) marketing.

Even our consumption patterns are heavily skewed towards services. We eat out more than we did 50 years ago, we enjoy travel, we play more sports, we enjoy more entertainment, and most of us work in service industries. Even our gift-giving is moving more towards the service sector, with the giving and receiving of 'experience' gifts such as weekend breaks, trial flights in light aircraft, motor-racing days, and so forth (Clarke 2006). Marketing literature is gradually catching up to this reality, and emphasizing service products more and more, but the focus still remains firmly on the marketing of physical products. This chapter is intended to redress the balance somewhat by discussing some differences in people's behaviour when choosing services.

Services – products or not?

From the consumer's viewpoint a service is as much a bundle of benefits as is a physical product. The consumer is paying money for the purpose of getting something back; the fact that the product is not actually something that can be held in the hand is irrelevant.

For example, consider the difference between a pizza bought from a supermarket, and one bought in a pizza restaurant. The supermarket pizza will be pretty much identical to the one next to it in the freezer, and may have been produced weeks beforehand; the purchaser may not consume it for several more weeks, if he or she is stocking up the freezer. The individual is buying the pizza in order to have a convenient meal at some later date.

In a pizza restaurant, though, the benefits go far beyond merely satisfying hunger. Often the individual will be with friends (or on a date), thus satisfying social needs as well. The restaurant provides a pleasant atmosphere, and does the washing-up, and even panders to esteem needs by waiting on customers. The actual pizza will vary from one customer to another – partly because the pizzas are made to order, and partly because the chef may not use exactly the

Other people in a restaurant are part of the total product.

Preview case study
Choosing a restaurant

Although choosing a restaurant is hardly a life-threatening decision, it can be important on several levels. If one is planning a special celebration like a birthday or anniversary, the restaurant needs to be able to cope well: but even if the meal is simply a lunch stop or a 'can't be bothered to cook' event the diners need to feel confident that they won't come away with food poisoning.

In New Jersey, one of the local restaurant reviewers (using the pen-name 'The Artful Diner' has produced a three-page guide to choosing a restaurant. The Artful Diner suggests that calling a friend for a recommendation has its good points, but also points out that 'asking for a personal recommendation is like playing Russian roulette with your innards' if the word of mouth is coming from an untrustworthy mouth. The reviewer recommends calling in to see the restaurant – in the United States (as in many other countries) it is perfectly possible to call in for a cocktail after work and check the place out, although this is not usually an option in the UK. In Spain one can go even further, because restaurants are usually bars as well and will serve small samples of the food on offer as tapas.

Further recommendations from the Artful Diner include checking out the toilets. If these are clean and fragrant, the kitchen will also be clean and fragrant. In some countries it is even acceptable to visit the kitchens. Interestingly, the Artful Diner is sceptical of restaurant reviewers ('hired bellies' as he calls them) and points out that they are only human, and in any case make their recommendations on a purely personal basis. He is particularly scathing of 'local yokel' reviewers, who he says often become excited by the mere fact that there is a restaurant in their neck of the woods.

How do people actually choose a restaurant? A survey conducted in 2004 by Londoneats.com found that 29.4 per cent of Londoners thought that cuisine was the most important factor, 20.8 per cent thought that recommendation was most important, 18.3 per cent thought price was most important, ambiance and service tied at 10.7 per cent each, and finally location accounted for the remaining 10.2 per cent. It should be said that online surveys such as this are not necessarily a very good reflection of the whole population, but personal recommendation does seem to come very high up the list.

However, when it comes to actually rating a restaurant, we come up against the two major problems of reviewing: first, the opinions of the diners are just opinions, and one man's meat is another man's poison; second, restaurant service and even food is variable. If the chef leaves or the head waiter is off sick the experience may be very different for the next diner!

The *Artful* Diner

Talking point

same quantities of the various ingredients each time, or it may be a different chef each night. Clearly, though, the bulk of what the customer is paying for in a restaurant is the intangible part of the transaction: the atmosphere, the socializing, the attention of the waiter. The pizza is certainly part of it, but it probably represents less than 20 per cent of the final bill.

Usually services cannot be tested before the individual agrees to purchase them, because the only way to test is to actually use the service. For instance, someone who bought

Isn't the difference between a pizza bought in a supermarket and a pizza bought in a restaurant a somewhat artificial distinction? After all, someone had to assemble the supermarket pizza, probably by hand, and probably for a minimum wage. Likewise the average fast-pizza place operates the same way – the staff manufacture the pizzas by hand, probably also for minimum wage.

Surely there is still a big services component in each pizza? Even the fact that it is sold in a supermarket contributes to the service element! So how do we draw the line between a product with a little bit of service and one with a large amount of service?

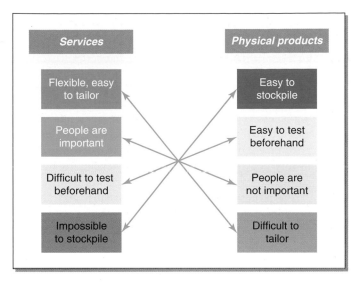

Figure 16.1

Services vs. physical products

the pizza from supermarket could take a good look at it first, read the ingredients list, and see if it looked like an appealing brand: in a restaurant, the pizza will have been ordered, cooked and served before the individual has a chance to examine it. Likewise, some of the peripheral aspects of the restaurant pizza (such as the ambience of the restaurant itself, the quality of the waiters and waitresses, and even the attitude of the other diners) can affect the overall experience. Unfortunately, if a diner does not like the waitress in the restaurant, this is difficult to complain about (unless there is something seriously wrong with the way the meal has been served). The customer in these circumstances can only pay up and smile, perhaps leaving a smaller tip than he or she had intended to. Refusal to pay afterwards only works if the service is very seriously poor.

From the supplier's viewpoint, a further problem is apparent. Services cannot be stockpiled in the same way as physical products. If the restaurant has a quiet night, the waiters and chefs still have to be paid: the service they would have provided has not been sold, but the cost of employing them remains. Conversely, if the supermarket does not sell the frozen pizza today, it can be sold tomorrow. Services are, therefore, highly perishable compared with physical products.

We can see, then, that services are distinguished from physical products by the following characteristics (Figure 16.1):

1 They are intangible.
2 Production and consumption usually happen at the same time.
3 There is a lack of trialibility.
4 Services are variable, even from the same supplier.
5 Services are perishable.

This naturally leads to problems for the consumer, since buying a service will inevitably look like buying a pig in a poke. In effect, consumers are buying a promise; the service provider is offering certain benefits which may or may not appear, and the consumer has little redress if the service does not come up to expectation. This means that the decision-making process is affected considerably when someone is buying a product with a high service component.

In practice, of course, very few products are either entirely physical or entirely service-based. Most products appear at some point along a continuum, having characteristics of service and of physical products in varying degrees. The further towards the service end of the spectrum a product is, the greater it will show the characteristics of intangibility, perishability and so forth: equally, the greater the uncertainty for the consumer, and therefore the greater the tendency for the consumer to exhibit behaviours associated with choosing service products.

Lawyers often say which aspects of law they specialise in.

GARY ROEBUCK/ALAMY

Consumer approaches to information gathering

In services markets consumers rely much more on word of mouth than is the case with physical products. Because of the intangibility of the product, the consumer is unable to carry out many of the usual processes of information gathering: advertising is less verifiable, the suppliers are often unable to be specific about the service and the quality thereof, and most services are less subject to close regulation by government or trade bodies. Prospective consumers of a service are therefore likely to rely heavily on personal recommendations by friends and colleagues. This is particularly true for services such as hairdressing and restaurants.

For professional services, the consumer may also ask questions about the qualifications and credentials of the service provider. For example, someone who is looking for a solicitor to handle a divorce case will naturally want to seek out a specialist in family law, and will look into this aspect of the solicitor's experience. Professional services rely heavily on referrals from other professionals; estate agents recommend solicitors, who recommend accountants, and so forth.

Because the service is hard to assess, prospective customers are likely to use surrogates when choosing a service provider. For example, solicitors might be judged on the quality of their office accommodation, hairdressers on the location of their salons, and restaurants on their prices. People often spend more time on the information search for a service than would be the case for a physical product, simply because of the greater risks involved.

Figure 16.2 shows some of the effects of good sources of communication. The individual will obtain reassurance that the decision is the right one, will reduce risk, will develop new criteria for choosing and may develop useful long-term heuristics for making similar decisions in future.

Risk and uncertainty

Consumers will naturally want to minimize risk. Risk involves not only the possible loss of the purchase price of the product, but also some consequential losses. In the case of purchase of services, these consequential losses can be quite substantial; for example, poor legal advice could conceivably result in the loss of a large amount of money, or even one's liberty. Even the injudicious purchase of a restaurant meal could result in food poisoning.

Table 16.1 illustrates some of the risks and the possible remedies.

Of course, there is a risk attached to the purchase of physical products as well, but usually the risk is confined to the purchase price (no doubt there are many exceptions to this

Figure 16.2

Sources of information

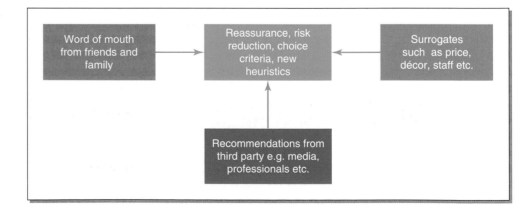

Table 16.1 Risks and remedies in services

Type of risk	Possible consumer response	Possible supplier remedy	Explanation
Consequential loss	Lawsuit	Ensure that risks are explained beforehand; use disclaimers in contracts; carry public or professional liability insurance.	Consequential losses arise when a service goes wrong and causes damage to the customer. For example, if a train is late and the customer misses a vital business meeting, there may be a big consequential loss. British Rail have disclaimers on the back of the ticket for this type of loss.
Purchase price risk	Refuse to pay	Correct the fault; check with the customer during the service provision that everything is all right.	It is too late afterwards to ask if everything's all right (although this should be done). Checking during the service (a) makes it less likely that things will go wrong and (b) makes it harder for the consumer to claim that the service went wrong in order to avoid paying.
Misunderstanding about what was wanted	Complain, perhaps refuse to pay	Before providing the service go through everything carefully and explain exactly what's going to be done, when and why. Perhaps even explain why the job can't be done the way the consumer would like it to be done.	One of the commonest problems in service provision is lack of real communication. This is particularly true in professional services, where the professional perhaps rightly feels that the customer wouldn't understand the finer technical details of the job. It is worthwhile providing an explanation, however, since there is otherwise a potential for post-purchase dissonance.

general rule) and in the event of buying a faulty product, it is possible to obtain a replacement or a refund. Consumers therefore need to weigh up the purchase decision for both value for money (assuming the service the consumer expects when agreeing to the purchase is what is actually obtained) and also the possible consequential loss if the service offering goes wrong. Because of the risk of consequential loss, consumers will frequently avoid the cheapest services, on the assumption that there 'must be something wrong with it'. Though this phenomenon is also noticeable for purchases of physical products, it is far more common with the purchase of services. For example, ladies' hairdressing is not price sensitive, and consumers often show perverse price sensitivity (deliberately going to a more expensive salon, all other aspects being equal).

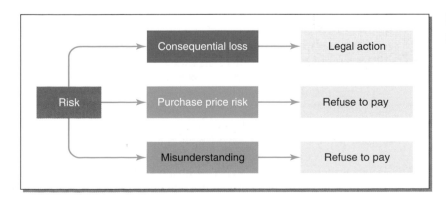

Figure 16.3

Consumer responses to risk

Naturally consumers will still expect to see value for money, having made the decision to opt for the higher-price alternative.

Consumers are faced with a greater degree of uncertainty when purchasing services, in that the service is (a) intangible and (b) variable. Even the supplier of the service cannot always guarantee that the outcome will be to the consumer's satisfaction: this is particularly true of professional services, such as lawyers and accountants. Lawyers still expect to be paid even if they lose the case, and likewise an accountant will still expect a fee even if the profit-and-loss account isn't as healthy as the client would like, or the tax authorities do not allow all the deductions. Equally, if the restaurant is not as romantic as the customer expected and his or her date is displeased, the waiter will still expect the customer to pay for the meal.

Talking point

Life is risky – for sure, nobody gets out of it alive. So are we perhaps blinded by our fear of loss so much that we cannot see where our best interests lie? Are we really prepared to pay well above the going rate for a service, in the hope that in some way there will be a relationship between a high price and good service?

After all, there is no rational reason to suppose that a high price has anything whatever to do with a good product. There are plenty of products around that are both expensive and no good – and there are certainly plenty of lawyers, accountants, mechanics, financial advisers and so forth who are hopelessly incompetent but also expensive. Why do we assume that expensive equals good, when we have overwhelming evidence to show that the relationship between high prices and good quality is the same as that between chalk and Wednesday – i.e. no relationship at all!

An expensive hair style does not guarantee looking cool.

This is, of course, outside the scope of errors or misunderstandings. If someone ordered a mild curry and got a spicy one instead, he or she would have cause to complain: the problem arises when what is described in good faith turns out differently from what was expected. The uncertainty usually arises from the gap between what the consumer is expecting in the way of benefits, and what the service provider can actually provide.

For example, it is well known in ladies' hairdressing that some clients expect to come out looking like their favourite movie star or pop singer. While it is sometimes (though by no means always) possible to recreate the appropriate hairstyle, it is not possible to carry out plastic surgery, and the particular hairstyle may not suit the customer's facial or physical features. Not unnaturally this causes post-purchase dissonance; either the stylist must explain to the customer why the hairstyle will not work, or the stylist has to reproduce the hairstyle and handle the customer's disappointment.

Consumers may seek to reduce uncertainty by looking for guarantees from the service provider; unfortunately, since services are perishable and not reclaimable, the supplier is rarely able to recoup anything from a 'returned' service. This makes suppliers reluctant to offer money-back guarantees, and therefore the consumer would normally be faced with a greater level of uncertainty.

Purchase of a service differs slightly from purchase of a physical good. Figure 16.4 illustrates the differences between the two.

The fact that the service is frequently not paid for until after it has been delivered and consumed means that the consumer is offered a considerable degree of reassurance. Also, because the service is being consumed as it is being produced, the supplier and the consumer have ample opportunity to confirm that what is being supplied is meeting the consumer's expectations.

This is why waiters will typically check with diners that their meals are OK; this reduces the risk that the consumer will complain after the meal has been consumed.

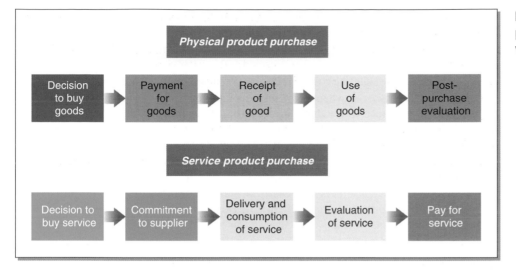

Figure 16.4 Comparison of purchase of physical products vs. services

Reducing the risk for the consumer will, of course, increase it for the supplier. Suppliers often have problems with customers who do not pay up on time, and it can be difficult for the supplier to recoup the loss; it is not possible to repossess a dinner for two or a haircut, and suing clients for non-payment for professional services such as accountancy can prove problematic, since the client can easily claim that the service was inadequate in some respect. Service industries tend to lose more money this way than physical product suppliers lose through pilfering.

Involvement

Involvement is the perceived importance or personal relevance of an object or event (see Chapter 14). Because of the greater risks and uncertainty attached to purchase of services, consumers are likely to become more involved with the service provider (Figure 16.5), and therefore more brand-loyal. In other words, having found a restaurant which provides a reliable meal in the right atmosphere, the consumer will tend to keep returning there rather than risk going somewhere new.

This is particularly true in the case of personal services, such as hairdressing. Loyalty to the service provider is extremely strong, because of the personal contact necessary for carrying out the service, and typically extends beyond loyalty to the salon. The loyalty is usually extended to the actual hairstylist providing the service. In many cases, the relationship between the hairstylist and the customer becomes a lifetime one, only breaking down when the hairstylist retires.

For comparison, consider how loyal the average motorist is to a car manufacturer. Despite car purchase being used by textbook authors as a prime example of a high-involvement purchase, most motorists will have tried several different manufacturers, and certainly many different models, over a lifetime's driving. It would be difficult for car

People sometimes commit to a service provider at an early age.

Figure 16.5 Services and involvement

manufacturers to find customers who always buy their brand, yet it has been fairly straightforward for Frizzell Insurance to find a group of customers who have always insured their cars through them. Frizzell have successfully used these customers in advertising campaigns.

This is true of most services, from restaurants to banking. Consumers are reluctant to switch bank accounts, even when problems become apparent with their current bankers; likewise people will tend to use the same solicitor rather than switch. For this reason, solicitors tend to operate from practices large enough to accommodate the various specialist functions (family law, criminal law, conveyancing, etc.) because the client who originally came to the firm for a house purchase is likely to return when he needs to be defended on a drunk-driving charge, or needs to sue somebody for a debt.

Likewise, although consumers will readily switch brands of baked beans in order to take advantage of sales promotions, they will buy the beans from their usual supermarket. This is because the consumer knows where everything is in the supermarket, knows what the store's policy is on returned goods, knows which credit cards are acceptable, knows what the store's own brands are like, and so forth. Supermarkets worldwide encourage this by the use of loyalty cards.

The reason for this is not that the supermarkets have suddenly become aware of the involvement phenomenon, but rather that the technology of **EPOS** (electronic point-of-sale) equipment has become sophisticated enough to handle the amount of data involved. In future, supermarkets will be able to keep complete records of each customer's buying pattern and act accordingly; for example, it would be quite feasible in future to remind customers at the checkout that they are running low on, say, tomato ketchup – and to know the brand and size that the customer usually buys (Evans 1994). In fact, although the technology to do this already exists, it is unlikely to happen because consumers are likely to regard it as an unwarranted invasion of privacy (Patterson, O'Malley and Evans 1997).

Consumer behaviour in action
Endsleigh Insurance

Anybody who has ever been a student is familiar with Endsleigh Insurance. The company specialized in the specific needs of students, who are often living away from home for the first time, in shared accommodation, surrounded by strangers who may have less than honest backgrounds. Generations of students have had good reason to be grateful to Endsleigh when their rooms have been burgled or their stereo equipment, guitar, laptop or mobile phone has mysteriously disappeared. Endsleigh also offer travel insurance for backpacking and Inter-railing, car insurance for old bangers, cover for studying abroad, and bicycle insurance.

What many people are less aware of is that Endsleigh will continue to look after their customers long after the graduation ceremony. Endsleigh look to establish a lifetime relationship with their customers – a sensible move in view of the fact that graduates earn more than people without degrees, and will therefore typically drive more

expensive cars, live in more valuable houses and own more possessions – especially the portable possessions beloved of thieves.

Endsleigh therefore offer winter sports insurance, multi-trip travel insurance including business travel, very high-value home and contents insurance, and extreme activities cover. In fact, everything the rising young executive needs in terms of insurance.

Endsleigh retain a high proportion of their former student customers: after all, if the service has been good and the costs reasonable, why go elsewhere? Starting by servicing the student community has proved to be a very successful strategy: Endsleigh now employs over 1000 people throughout the UK and is one of Britain's best-known insurers. Additionally, the company has carved out a market among people who are not only well off, but are also less likely to make a claim – which is insurance heaven!

Sales promotion

Promotion schemes for services are therefore somewhat problematic; customers are less likely to switch merely because of a temporary price reduction or 'special offer'. It is possible, as we have seen, to encourage existing customers to stay (and in fact this is likely to be the most cost-effective way of doing business, as it is in the case of physical products) but it is harder to bring in new customers.

Typically, service providers focus on problems which they have identified with the competition. For example, some bank customers feel strongly about banks who invest in countries with oppressive regimes; the Co-Operative Bank has been able to capitalize on this by promising that they will never do so. In this case the bank is playing off one involvement (with the customer's existing bank) against another (the customer's involvement with a social cause).

Likewise, First Direct has based its entire existence on the fact that most working people cannot get to a bank during normal banking hours; the bank has made deep inroads into the personal banking sector by offering 24-hour telephone and Internet banking.

Many service providers make good use of the consumer's need to belong by offering 'club' membership. This ranges from the 'exclusive flight deals' offered by RCI, the timeshare exchange company, through to the 'Friends of the Theatre' benefits offered by some theatres and theatrical companies. Museums and galleries often offer season tickets, as (of course) do transport services such as trains and buses.

Perhaps the biggest phenomenon in loyalty schemes for regular customers is the frequent-flyer programmes, which began in the USA during the late 1970s and early 1980s. Following the deregulation of US airspace, many companies sprang up to compete with the majors; routes were no longer the exclusive province of the big airlines, and government-sanctioned monopolies no longer applied, with the result that fierce price wars broke out. Airlines which had previously not had to compete at all in any real sense suddenly found themselves scrambling for business; the result was a burgeoning frequent-flyer programme, by which airlines gave free flights to loyal customers.

This type of programme now exists among all the world's major airlines, and usually also covers 'associate' airlines; for example, 21 airlines have formed the Star Alliance, which now operates almost 17,000 flights every day. The member airlines do not compete on the same routes, but they do operate a single frequent-flyer programme so that flights on one airline can contribute to free flights on another. This ensures that customers flying with any of those airlines can still obtain frequent-flyer points for the entire journey, so that the airline prevents competitors from offering a more comprehensive route coverage and thus luring customers away. Each airline benefits, since they don't compete directly with each other; also the small airlines have a better chance of surviving in an industry dominated by the big players.

This type of loyalty programme should be distinguished from promotions such as air miles. Since air miles can be collected from a large number of outlets and suppliers, they cannot be considered as a loyalty programme; the air miles system is intended as a sales promotion exercise, to persuade customers to use one supplier rather than another.

Telephone banking is not only convenient – it can also be very informal.

Service levels

The **service level** refers to the degree to which the customer's needs are met. For example, an airline might aim for a service level criterion of ensuring that 95 per cent of flights leave within ten minutes of the scheduled time. Or perhaps a pizza delivery service might

Service providers need to make explicit promises.

Virgin trains emphasise speed of service rather than price.

guarantee that pizzas will be delivered within 30 minutes, or the pizza is free. (This particular type of guarantee was outlawed in Dublin because it resulted in too many road accidents caused by over-hasty pizza delivery drivers.)

The UK Government's efforts to establish Citizen's Charters for various government departments is an example of trying to improve service levels. In effect, there has been a recognition that taxpayers are actually paying for a service, and Her Majesty's Revenue and Customs, DSS, National Health and other departments are there to provide that service. Clearly it cannot always be the case that the service is provided to the complete satisfaction of the client (nobody is happy to pay the Inland Revenue) but at least the service can be run in a sympathetic way that minimizes inconvenience to the customer.

Here are some examples of firms seeking to raise service levels:

● Aurora Energy of Tasmania will pay $80 to anyone who experiences more than 12 power cuts in a year, or whose power stays off for more than 12 hours.

● Tesco supermarket guarantees that, if there is one other person in front of you, they will open another checkout, unless all the checkouts are open already.

● Virgin Trains will provide vouchers to the value of 25 per cent of the fare if the train is delayed for more than an hour, and will refund the fare in full if the train is delayed more than two hours.

● Post Office Counters guarantee that 95 per cent of clients will be dealt with within five minutes.

The decision about service levels will depend mainly on economic factors and the value-for-money perception of the clients. This reverts back to the problem examined earlier, that clients will often pay more for a service because they believe that this will mean, in itself, that they will get a better service; disappointment may creep in afterwards. Put another way, someone who is paying £200 a night to stay in a five-star hotel will expect the room service to be comprehensive, polite and prompt. The same person staying in Mrs Boggins' Bed and Breakfast for £30 a night will not expect any room service at all. Conversely, small B&B guest houses have a reputation for providing a good, filling, old-fashioned British breakfast, and guests will be expecting this as part of the service.

The service level must relate to something that the customer feels is important. A supermarket that ensures that shopping trolleys are returned to the pick-up point within ten minutes of the previous customer abandoning them at the other end of the car park is unlikely to be of much help to the customer. Guaranteeing never to be out of stock of certain essential items is probably far more relevant.

Likewise, the service level set must be within the firm's powers to achieve. Guaranteeing sunshine for a holidaymaker clearly is beyond the control of a tour operator (but a cash rebate for every day when the sun doesn't shine is within the supplier's control, and might be highly relevant).

It is important to understand here that the service level must be appropriate to meet expectations, not at the maximum. A consumer paying a low price will be expecting drawbacks: people who are only prepared to pay the lowest prices for services do not expect to be looked after very well, and may become suspicious if the service is too good. In other words, it is possible to make your customers think that there must be a catch somewhere.

The early experience of Safeway supermarkets in the UK markets bore this out. In the USA, Safeway (in common with most other supermarkets) employ packers to pack customers' purchases into carrier bags, and even carry the bags to the customer's car (usually in the expectation of a tip). There is no charge for this service. When Safeway entered the UK market, the company followed the same practice, but UK shoppers (who are not used

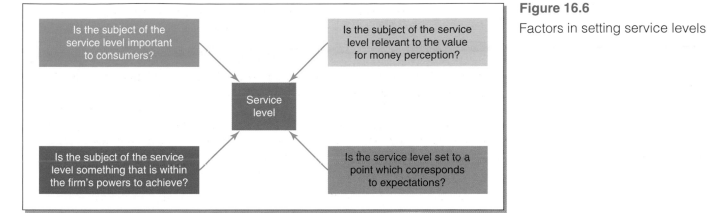

Figure 16.6

Factors in setting service levels

to this level of service) became suspicious and assumed that the shop's prices must be higher in order to pay for the higher service level. Safeway eventually discontinued the practice, although packers are still available on request.

Likewise, customers shopping at discount stores such as Lidl expect that the goods will be less attractively displayed and that the checkout queues will be longer. The store management deliberately keep the surroundings less attractive than the mainstream supermarkets so that the customer's perception is that the prices must be much lower. Aldi, on the other hand, maintain a pleasant shopping environment while still keeping prices extra-low; this may, in the long run, prove counter-productive as it runs counter to the common perception.

To sum up this section, the main decision criteria regarding service levels are as follows (Figure 16.6):

1 The service level must relate to a benefit the customer feels is important.

2 The service level must be achievable.

3 The service level must be appropriate rather than optimal.

Handling dissonance

Of course, sometimes things go wrong and the customer is not happy with what has been provided. In other words, what was delivered is not what was expected, and the service provider has to attempt to make amends in some way. Following on from a service failure, people adopt coping strategies: service recovery (which means going back to the supplier and trying to obtain redress), re-evaluation of the brand's trustworthiness, apportioning blame, or re-interpreting the brand into stereotypes (Chung and Beverland 2006). For example, someone who has had a disappointing service from a builder might ask the builder to come back and do the work again, might decide that the builder is not very good or reliable, might blame the poor work on the pre-existing state of the building, or might simply decide that modern builders are not the craftsmen their fathers and grandfathers were.

As we have seen in Chapter 15, consumers will tend to express their dissatisfaction in one of three ways (Singh 1988):

1 Voice responses, in which the customer comes back and complains.

2 Private responses, which would include telling friends about the poor service.

3 Third-party responses, such as taking legal action.

Figure 16.7 Complaint routes and damage limitation

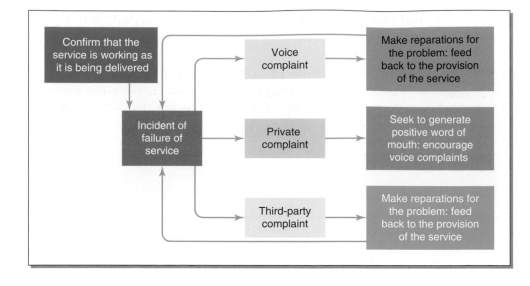

The majority of service providers try to ensure that this does not happen, by using the following methods:

1 Explaining the service in great detail beforehand and explaining what the possible drawbacks might be.

2 Checking with the client during the provision of the service that everything is satisfactory.

An example of the first type of dissonance-reduction technique would be the initial consultation with a lawyer regarding a court case; the lawyer will typically warn the client that the outcome of any court case cannot be guaranteed, that the client may incur substantial court (and lawyer) costs without actually winning the case, that the opposition may come up with some line of defence (or attack, as the case may be) which is unanticipated, and so forth.

An example of the second approach would be in an aircraft first-class cabin, where the flight attendants check regularly with the passengers to ensure that all is well. This approach is often used where the service is carried out over a period of time where the client is present throughout the service provision; medical procedures, air travel, hairdressing, beauty treatments, etc.

It is always worthwhile checking that the client fully understands what is being provided, whether the supplier is a doctor explaining the prognosis for a surgical operation, or a waiter explaining that the dish being ordered is extra spicy. This is why detailed descriptions of ingredients, and even the cooking instructions, are usually given on restaurant menus.

Even so, things can go wrong, sometimes because the variability of the service leads to a failure to provide the service at the level expected. Even the service provider can be surprised at the outcome in these cases.

The remedy has, of course, to fit the circumstances. Because the customer's loss falls into two categories, loss of the service and consequential loss, it may be necessary to lay down specific rules beforehand to limit the supplier's liability.

For example, photographic development services usually limit their liability to the cost of a new roll of film. This means that they can avoid the possibility of being sued for the loss of, say, irreplaceable wedding photographs or holiday snaps.

Services fall into the following categories, for the purpose of correcting complaints:

1 Services where it is appropriate to offer a repeat service, or a voucher. Examples are dry cleaners, domestic appliance repairers, and takeaway food outlets.

2 Services where giving the money back will usually be sufficient. Examples here would be retail shops, cinemas and theatres, video rental companies.

3 Services where consequential losses (those which go beyond the fees paid) may have to be compensated for. Examples would be medical services, solicitors, and hairdressers.

The above categorizations are not necessarily exclusive, in the sense that (in most cases) giving disappointed theatre-goers their money back is sufficient, but sometimes they may sue for travelling costs (or even for injury, in the event of an accident during a performance). For this reason, service providers usually carry public liability insurance, and the third category of service providers usually also have professional liability insurance which covers for consequential losses.

Talking point

Obviously no company can guarantee that things will never go wrong. The question is, where do we draw the line and decide on liability? Naturally the customer will tend to think that liability lies with the supplier – but in the case of services, the product is so variable it would be almost impossible for a supplier to be able to guarantee anything.

Hence the small print. But who ever reads the small print? Who among us actually reads the Terms and Conditions before we tick the box saying that we have read the Terms and Conditions? Any of us? And even if we did read them, how much sense would they make, given that they are usually written in obscure legal language?

The bottom line is whether the supplier and the customer can agree between them whose fault it is when something goes pear-shaped: standing on the strict letter of the small print might be legal, but it isn't necessarily good business! So we're back to finding some way of drawing a line, of negotiating an agreement about liability, and (ultimately) dumping the small print!

Unlike compensation for the failure of a physical product, it is often difficult to quantify an appropriate level of compensation for a failed service. For example, if a new iPod breaks down in the first week, it can be replaced with an identical model or the customer's money can be returned. If, however, a perm is not quite tight enough for the client, a repeat service may not be possible (due to the risk of over-processing the hair) and clearly the service is only a partial failure. In this case, returning the money may be an over-compensation, but still something needs to be done. In an extreme case, where (for example) a hairdressing client's scalp is damaged permanently by chemicals, substantial compensation might be ordered by a court, or (more likely) paid out by the hairdresser's insurers. These situations require careful judgement as to the degree of the client's dissatisfaction, and the best way of compensating the client; this will often require some skilful negotiation, and will be best carried out by somebody with a high level of authority.

Because service provision relies heavily on word of mouth, it is even more important that complaints are dealt with to the complete satisfaction of the customer than would be the case with physical products. As with physical products, consumers tend to be more prone to use negative word of mouth than positive word of mouth, but complaints correctly handled will generate more positive word of mouth than will a good service in itself. This means that a dissatisfied customer who is pleased with the compensation offered will be more likely to speak positively of the service provider than would a customer whose expectations had been met in the first place. (See Chapter 15 for a more complete discussion of post-purchase dissonance.)

For this reason it is important to ensure that dissatisfied customers voice their dissatisfaction, and the service provider answers the problem effectively. Airlines, tour operators and theatres frequently ask consumers to fill in market research questionnaires to determine satisfaction levels for various aspects of the service provision, but this is somewhat harder to do for restaurants and personal services; here it is more usual to rely on discussion between the service provider and the customer, rather than formal research.

Summary

This chapter has been about consumer attitudes towards service provision. Although there is some debate in academic circles about the differences between physical products and services, and whether the differences are real enough to alter marketing strategy, there are distinct differences in approach as far as consumers are concerned. Products which have a high service component will almost always engender a different approach in terms of customer behaviour, if only because the risk element is higher: this necessitates a different approach from suppliers.

The key points from the chapter are as follows:

- A service is as much a product as is a physical item, even though it can't be handled; this is because a service provides a bundle of benefits to the consumer, in exchange for payment.
- Consumers rely much more on word of mouth when choosing services, and will be more prone to using word of mouth after purchasing a service – whether to praise or condemn.
- Consumer risk is greater when buying a service than when buying a physical product, particularly as regards consequential losses.
- Some of this risk is reduced because consumers usually pay for services after consuming them.
- Consumers tend to be more loyal to service providers than to physical product suppliers, because there is often greater involvement.
- Sales promotion schemes tend to focus on comparisons with the competition, rather than on 'money off' deals.
- Service levels need to be appropriate, not optimal.
- Dissonance can be reduced by careful prior explanation of the service, and by monitoring during consumption.
- It is worthwhile encouraging customers to express dissatisfaction, rather than waiting for them to use word of mouth to damage your business.

Chapter review questions

1 What are the main problems in establishing appropriate service levels?

2 What is the difference between a sales promotion and a loyalty programme?

3 Why is purchasing a service more risky than purchasing a physical product?

4 How can service providers reduce risk for customers?

5 What is the role of involvement in service purchase?

6 What is the role of word-of-mouth in service provision?

7 How can a professional service provider such as a lawyer or accountant improve customers' perception of service quality?

8 Why has services marketing become more important in recent years?

9 Why are people important in the service experience?

10 How can service providers minimize post-purchase dissonance?

Preview case study revisited
Choosing a restaurant

One of the problems of following restaurant reviewers' recommendations is that everybody else does the same – a good review means that the restaurant becomes swamped, a bad review means that the restaurant becomes deserted (often people who were previously satisfied with the restaurant end up going elsewhere).

The Artful Diner therefore recommends going with one's own instincts – recommendations are not recommended, in other words. This is amply illustrated by one set of online reviews, posted by restaurant customers on Londoneats.com. These are as follows (the name of the restaurant has been changed, for obvious reasons).

I have often passed this restaurant on the train and decided to try it on a busy Saturday evening and was pleasantly surprised.

Delicately prepared Indian dishes, good size portions for the price I thought and beautifully presented; not your average tandoori but something a bit special! Airy décor and friendly staff made for a lovely evening. Would definitely go back for their seafood curry! (This reviewer gave the restaurant 8 out of 10.)

I went to The Raj only by chance as I heard they've changed management. The portions of the starter was very small but the chicken was succulent.

The main course was as close to India as you can get! I felt the portions were small but it could just be my appetite.

Great news for smokers! You can have a fag downstairs!

Also, I've noticed a change in décor, there's lots of real art hanging in there which is really cheerful on a grey and rainy day.

Will come back for the Sunday buffet! (This customer also scored the restaurant as an 8.)

Unfortunately the promising menu and glitzy appearance did not match the actual experience. Service was very slow and almost rude. We were expected to share a menu and then wait 20 minutes for our order to be taken and a further 30 for the cold starter. The main meal was actually quite bland and again not too hot with the portions small and nowhere near as fancy as they describe. Certainly not good value for money but definitely dreadful service and disappointing food. Try the Mirch Masala in Tooting for a better experience on all counts. (Not surprisingly, this customer only gave the restaurant a score of 1.)

I'm afraid to say I disagree with Sean Richardson. Although he is clearly a sophisticated and knowledgeable man, I felt the atmosphere was poor, service was slow and unwelcoming and the food tasted as though it had been waiting to be delivered to my table for hours (a possibility with this level of service).

Furthermore, I felt the atmosphere was horrible, Herne Hill seemed dilapidated and lacking in any character. In fact my meal was disrupted by yobs banging on the window. Luckily the evening was saved with a walk through Dulwich Village (or more specifically Winterbrook Road) after my meal.

My recommendation would be to somewhere such as the Bombay Bicycle on Nightingale Lane, and to avoid this area for dining in future. (Again, this disappointed diner only gave a score of 1.)

This place is one of the hotspots in south London if not the whole of London. The food is really good and the area is just amazing. This place is well worth a visit and Herne Hill is so much better than an area like Clapham Junction or Common. The Raj was Brilliant! (This somewhat excitable diner scored the restaurant at 10.)

Obviously the reviewers here are a self-selected group of 'experts' and there is no way of knowing whether any of them are actually the restaurateurs themselves seeking to boost business by posting a false review. Having said that, the discrepancy between those who thought the restaurant was wonderful and those who thought it was terrible is only too obvious – this is probably the major problem with reviews in general, and one can understand why the Artful Diner suggests avoiding recommendations altogether!

Case study
Care for the elderly

In Western Europe and indeed in most of the developed world life expectancy has risen so rapidly that caring for elderly people has moved high up the agenda for politicians. It is also high on the agenda for individuals – whereas 40 years ago one might expect to retire at 65 and have perhaps four or five years of retirement, people now reasonably expect to be retired for 10, 15 or even 20 years. Naturally at some point these people will be in need of help with the daily tasks of living, and many of them will need to be cared for entirely in residential units, or old folks' homes. For most, this is a distasteful or even frightening prospect, so residential homes become an unsought good – one which people know they need, but which nobody wants to buy.

In these circumstances, planning ahead is obviously the right thing to do, but hardly anybody does so. The British United Provident Association (BUPA), a private medical charity, operates care homes (among its many other activities) and has a wealth of advice for people on choosing their home. BUPA recommend talking to friends and relatives to find out whether they know of somewhere good, asking one's doctor, asking the local authority social services department, and talking to the industry organizations (such as the Registered Nursing Home Association). BUPA advise visiting several homes, and they even supply a checklist of questions to ask, even if the individual is not considering a BUPA home. Some questions are perhaps obvious – is the home convenient for friends and family to visit, for example – while others are less so. For example, 'Does the home smell pleasant?' and 'How often will your care needs be reviewed?'

Even given this level of help and advice, most people still do not go through a complex decision-making process when choosing a care home. According to a Government report published in 1999, most elderly people choose a care home as the result of a crisis, for example the death of a carer or a diagnosis of a serious illness. They then become bogged down in a mass of bureaucracy, and find that they are often expected to fund their own care. For many

older people, this seems like a betrayal – they have paid their National Insurance contributions in the belief that they would be cared for 'from the cradle to the grave', and they now find that this is substantially not the case. The Government report states the following:

> Even though they pay the bill this often does not feel like a conscious purchase decision. It is often rushed, and by definition made at a time of personal crisis. It also involves using a rather unwieldy asset – their homes – to pay for care. (Health Committee 1999)

This lack of choice, and feeling of uncertainty, often strikes people at a point when they are least able to make informed, reasoned decisions. A report by the UK's Audit Commission (1997) contained this quote:

> I had a sister taken into care. She had just lost an invalid husband and was tricked into a care home. All she needed was a home help. She was fit and talkative but stripped of all she had and I tried to get her out of the bullying, neglectful home. She died after about one and a half years in this horrific place and I think I made it worse by complaints. They lied about everything. I am still haunted . . .

From the viewpoint of the Government, it would be a great deal easier if people were to exercise the choice that exists, but in many case they do not do so. From the viewpoint of elderly people themselves, the situation is worrying and frustrating – worrying because they cannot always see how their lives are going to be affected in future by having to go into care, and frustrating because they need to pay for something which they already feel they have contributed to in taxation. Whatever the rights and wrongs of the situation, the increasing number of old people in the UK and indeed in the rest of Europe will continue to exercise influence on Government policy, since they represent a large number of voters.

Case study questions

1 Why are people reluctant to prepare for going into care by arming themselves with the facts in good time?

2 How might the Government encourage people to find out the facts in advance?

3 Why might BUPA be so helpful in providing information on choosing a care home, considering that people might well use the information to choose a competing home rather than a BUPA one?

4 How might residential homes counter the scare stories?

5 What factors would increase the acceptability of going into care?

References

Audit Commission (1997) *The Coming of Age: Improving Care Services for Older People.* (London: Audit Commission).

Chung, Emily, and Beverland, Michael (2006) An exploration of consumer forgiveness following marketer transgressions. *Advances in Consumer Research*, 33(1): 98–9.

Clarke, Jackie R. (2006) Different to 'dust collectors'? The giving and receiving of experience gifts. *Journal of Consumer Behaviour*, 5 (Nov–Dec): 533–49.

Evans, M. (1994) Domesday marketing? *Journal of Marketing Management*, 10(5): 401–31.

Health Committee (1999) *The Long-Term Care of the Elderly* (London: TSO, House of Commons papers, session 1998/9, HC 318).

Patterson, M., O'Malley, L., and Evans, M.J. (1997) Database marketing: investigating privacy concerns. *Journal of Marketing Communications*, 3(3): 151–74.

Singh, Jagdip (1988) Consumer complaint intentions and behavior: definitions and taxonomical issues. *Journal of Marketing*, 52 (January): 93–107.

Chapter 17
Behavioural segmentation

Learning objectives After reading this chapter, you should be able to:

1. explain the need for segmentation
2. explain the development of the segmentation idea
3. explain the role of ownership of core benefits in segmentation
4. describe how segments can be identified
5. explain how the viability of a segment is determined
6. describe the relationship between size of segment and premium customers will pay
7. describe the main ways of segmenting markets
8. show how different segmentation bases relate to each other
9. explain the role of the changing demographic profile of the developed world
10. describe different methods of segmenting by behaviour
11. explain how to segment industrial markets
12. describe the different strategic options in segmenting markets

Introduction

Segmentation is concerned with grouping consumers who have similar needs. This chapter is about ways in which this is done, and methods of assessing whether segments are economically worth pursuing.

Reasons for segmenting markets

Market **segmentation** is the process of identifying a group of consumers with similar needs and producing a product that will meet those needs at a profit. It has a simple basis in logic; it is that no single product will appeal to all consumers.

Before the advent of mass production there was a pent-up demand for basic, simple products, and this is still the case in some parts of the world, for example Eastern Europe and the Third World. This meant that manufacturers could produce standardized products using long production runs to keep costs (and prices) as low as possible. In these circumstances **undifferentiated marketing** approaches work well because people are prepared to put up with standardized goods and lack of choice rather than do without. Costs of mass production are so much less than the costs of hand production that the prices can undercut anything custom-made, so that if the only choice is between one type of mass-produced article and a much more expensive hand-made version, consumers are often prepared to accept a product that is less than perfect for their needs.

Figure 17.1 shows how segmentation has developed. At first, there is pent-up demand for simple, one-size-fits-all products. This leads to undifferentiated marketing (i.e. the same marketing approach is taken towards all customers), and thus to the production

Preview case study
Alcohol-powered cars

As long ago as 1975 the Brazilian government realized that their country's dependence on imported fuel would, in the long run, create problems for the balance of payments and the country's national security. On the plus side, Brazil has very extensive sugar-cane farms and other sources of carbohydrates which can be turned into alcohol – in fact, far more alcohol than is needed for the national drink, cachaca.

The solution was obvious – use the alcohol to run motor vehicles. By 1980, alcohol was being added to petrol in a 20/80 ratio: cars can run on this without major adaptation. As more alcohol was added, cars needed minor adjustments to the carburettor and fuel systems, but apart from a tendency towards difficult starting in cold weather (not a major problem in a country which largely lies within the tropics), the cars could still run perfectly well. However, the Brazilian government set a goal that all cars should be able to run on pure (or near-pure) ethanol – which meant that motor manufacturers needed to consider serious adaptations of their products.

The Brazilian market represents a large number of motorists. With a population of 140 million people, and a high standard of living in much of the country, Brazilian motorists represent a substantial part of the world market for cars, certainly enough for motor manufacturers to go to some lengths to capture their share of the market.

The main contenders in the Brazilian market, General Motors and Volkswagen, immediately began researching the necessary adaptations.

concept and a selling orientation, in which persuasive sales people move the product using high-pressure techniques. Next, as people become more wealthy and consequently more demanding, firms need to segment the market, using a customer orientation and adopting the marketing concept. Later, firms develop niche markets, taking an overall awareness of the market (including competitors, future developments, and so forth as well as customers)

Figure 17.1

Development of segmentation

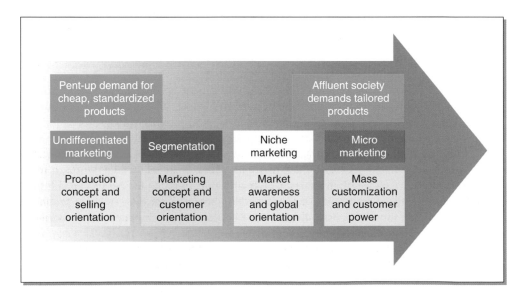

and may be driven towards a global orientation in order to obtain the necessary production economies. Finally, customer power compels firms to adopt a mass customization approach, leading to **micro marketing**.

For example, consider the manufacture of clothing. Prior to the industrial revolution most cloth was woven at home, or by hand in small factories. Clothing would be made to measure by tailors, and most people would perhaps only own one change of clothing since the work involved in making each item by hand made the price high in comparison to people's earnings. With the advent of steam-powered looms, sewing-machines and production lines, the cost of producing clothing fell to around one-tenth of the hand-made price. Although the new clothing was made to standard sizes the cost was so much lower that people could own several changes of clothing, even if this meant putting up with a less than perfect fit. Even when British manufacturers had virtually eliminated domestic competition from hand-loom producers, the rest of the world had yet to industrialize and therefore there was little or no competition in export markets.

This led to the development of **mass markets** and firms using **production orientation**. Under these conditions, the way to succeed in business was to ensure that the production costs (and hence the prices) were kept as low as possible. The greater the number of people who would buy the product, the greater the standardization and the longer the production run, so the greater the profits.

Clearly this approach works very well during times when choices are limited, and when production cannot keep up with demand. In First World countries in the twenty-first century this approach is no longer viable, because machine manufacturing is now so widespread that there is almost always another company elsewhere in the world with even lower production costs. Mass marketing still works in countries where there is very little outside competition (for example the former Soviet Bloc countries, and some Third World countries where imports are severely restricted), but for most purposes it is true to say that there are very few mass markets left in Western industrialized countries.

Mass production of standardized clothing brings prices down.

Talking point

Everybody loves a bargain – and consequently most towns in Britain have at least one 'cheap shop' selling seriously cheap items. OK, they're often not very well made or even well designed, but millions upon millions of cheap photo frames, ornaments, kitchen scales, flimsy radios, even flimsier tents, second-rate tools and out-of-date sauce mixes are shifted by these stores every day.

Does that mean that we'll buy anything as long as it's cheap? Do we really come away from these stores loaded down with items that we'll probably never use? Well, actually, perhaps it means exactly that! What drives us to buy yet another all-in-one tool set which just sits at the bottom of a cupboard gathering dust? Or a spirit level that actually doesn't show a proper level? Maybe it's just the hunter-gatherer joy of finding a bargain – or maybe it's just that we aren't too concerned with being part of a segment!

Undifferentiated marketing is less effective than segmented marketing in economies where most consumers already own the core benefits of the product. In other words, if most families already own a TV set, they have the core benefits of being able to receive TV programmes. Each family will have other needs; perhaps for cable stations, or DVD recording functions, or stereo sound. Segmentation deals with finding out how many people are likely to want each benefit, roughly how much they will be willing to pay for it and where they would like to buy it from. In this way, the firm approaching a segmented market is able to offer more functional benefits and more attention to hedonic needs, i.e. the products are more fun.

Figure 17.2

Four levels of segmentation

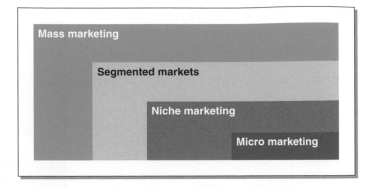

Segmentation operates at four levels, shown in Figure 17.2, as follows:

1 *Mass marketing* – This is an attempt to produce something which virtually everybody will want, and produce it in such large quantities that the production costs can be minimized and thus the price can be kept low. This approach appeals to production engineers, but is virtually impossible to carry out in the modern world because people prefer a more individual, tailored product which suits their needs more precisely.

2 *Segmented markets* – Here the firm seeks to find groups of people with similar needs. This is a compromise position for both the producer and the customer: for producers, the production runs will be shorter than would be the case for mass marketing, and for the consumer the product is unlikely to be exactly what is wanted.

3 *Niche marketing* – Niche marketers focus on one sub-group within the larger segments. Some niche marketers concentrate on a product category rather than on a specific type of consumer – Sock Shop and Tie Rack are examples. At first sight, this appears to be a product-orientated paradigm, but in fact it is consumer-orientated in that it reduces search time for people looking for the specific product category. This type of niche marketing is the direct opposite to the department-store or supermarket approach to retailing: instead of stocking a few products in a wide range of categories, niche marketers stock a wide range of products in a single category.

4 *Micro marketing* – This is the practice of tailoring products and marketing programmes to suit specific individuals and circumstances. Even mass-production operations such as motor manufacturers can offer new-car buyers a very wide range of options, but the ultimate in micro marketing is probably Dell Computers. Each computer is built to the customer's specification, using plug-in components. Mass customization is the ability to produce individual, custom-made products using mass-production techniques, for example producing prescription spectacles on-site, as Vision Express do. Customers are able to choose frames, have an eye test and walk out with the finished spectacles within an hour. In many cases people are not prepared to pay the increased cost of such service, however (Bardacki and Whitelock 2004).

Bespoke tailors produce clothes which fit exactly – at a price!

In large markets, such as the USA (298 million consumers), the European Union (457 million consumers) or Japan (127 million consumers), there are often enough consumers with a specific need in common for manufacturers to be able to obtain the economies of scale enjoyed by British manufacturers in the mid-nineteenth century. Marketers now are able to treat consumers more as individuals, with individual wants and needs; in most industries we are not yet at the point where we can provide individual attention for individual consumers, so we need to identify groups of people with similar interests and design our approach to fit those groups. This is what segmentation seeks to achieve.

Table 17.1 Evolution of cars

Product type	Core benefits	Other benefits and drawbacks
Horse and carriage	Basic transportation for owner, passengers and goods	Easy to maintain, but unreliable, slow, not suitable for long-distance travel, and expensive. Could be tailor-made for the individual owner. Only the most prosperous people could afford one.
Model T Ford	Basic transportation for owner, passengers and goods	Faster, more reliable, expensive. Standard engine, seating, colour ('Any colour you want as long as it's black'), and standard components so servicing is cheap.
Modern Ford vehicle range	Basic transportation for owner, passengers and goods	Reliable, cheap to buy and run, easy to maintain, fast and suitable for long-distance travel. Available in several hundred different combinations of body versions and engine sizes, according to individual preference, with a wide range of payment options to make it easy to buy. Optional extras include everything from wind spoilers to upgrade in radio equipment.

PICTORIAL PRESS LTD/ALAMY

Table 17.1 shows how a basic product has gone through a series of changes over the course of a hundred years or so.

Although people were prepared to buy the Model T Ford in huge numbers when it first appeared, it became apparent that it was not fitting consumers' needs. This was evidenced by the fact that consumers were taking the basic model and adapting it themselves to suit their individual needs; cutting off the body and replacing it with a truck bed, altering the engine by drilling out the cylinders to make it more powerful, adding windows or removing the roof. The Ford Motor Company realised that they could make more money by offering these alterations as factory alternatives and charging the customers a little more for them. Since this still worked out cheaper than doing the alterations themselves, customers were prepared to pay the extra money. Looked at from another angle, the options offered by the company made the product more desirable and therefore increased sales, despite the extra cost to the consumer.

The end result of this process is the modern range of Ford cars, which continually adapt in order to compete with other manufacturers who are carrying out a similar process of continual adaptation in response to consumer needs. The manufacturers' orientation has shifted from trying to produce cars as cheaply as possible towards trying to produce cars that are as desirable as possible.

Figure 17.3

Adaptation of products

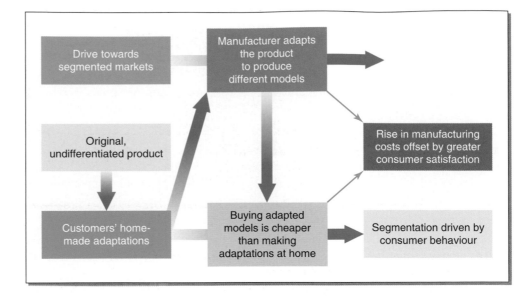

Are you still a Johnson's baby? Baby products might meet the needs of other market segments.

Consumers are usually prepared to pay a premium price for a product that fits their needs more closely. This is because the cost-benefit relationship is more favourable if the benefits are much greater. By tailoring the products more nearly to consumers' needs, manufacturers are able to charge a little more, thus offsetting the extra costs of producing non-standardized products, and actually increasing profits as well.

Segmentation is an essential precursor to most marketing activities (Figure 17.3). Identifying a target group and knowing their needs allows us to **position** the product correctly in the target group's minds, and to adopt an appropriate promotional strategy, designing ads that appeal to the particular group. A well-known example of this is the Johnson's Baby products campaign. Johnson's became aware that more baby lotion and talcum powder was being sold than could be accounted for by the number of babies in the country; research showed that mothers were using the products on their own skins, believing that the products would be less harmful than those made for adults. This knowledge led Johnson's to reposition the products as an adult range, using the slogan 'Are you still a Johnson's baby?'

If we know where our target group shop, we can develop a distribution strategy, and knowing what the segment think of as good value will dictate our pricing strategy.

Over the last 20 years there has been tremendous growth in **database marketing**, in which details of the consumer's purchases, lifestyle and behaviour can be used to tailor the marketing approach exactly, potentially to a 'segment of one' (Larson 1991). The foundation of database marketing is the possibility for marketers to hold information about their customers on computer files. In some cases this information is very detailed; EPOS and EFTPOS systems in supermarkets hold details of every grocery purchase made by the consumer, and with the increasing use of loyalty cards the supermarkets can identify which consumers buy which combination of products. This data can be used to segment markets behaviourally (Duchessi, Schaninger and Nowak 2004).

Increased computing capability gives (at least theoretically) the ability to combine the records of databases held by different marketers, each of which hold information about the purchases of individual consumers, so as to provide a more complete picture of each person's behaviour and characteristics. The resulting database could hold, under each consumer's name and address, an almost complete picture of the consumer's purchasing behaviour. If information from credit card companies and bank computer files could be added, the consumer's income and expenditure could be defined exactly. It may even be possible, eventually, to anticipate an individual consumer's needs and make a direct approach with a solution for those needs (Evans 1991). There are two major limitations on this scenario, however: first, legislation in most European countries limits the degree to

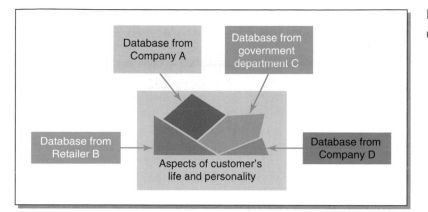

Figure 17.4
Combining databases

which companies can share data, and second, there is considerable consumer resistance to what is widely seen as an invasion of privacy.

In Figure 17.4, the various companies, retailers and government departments contribute different information about aspects of the customer's life. The separate pieces fit together like a jigsaw puzzle to provide an overall understanding of the customer's life, personality and buying behaviour.

The aim of segmentation is to form a mental picture of the organization's ideal customer, and plan everything around that person. In order to do this, the organization must be able to judge the size of the segment so as to form an opinion as to whether it is worthwhile producing a specialist product just for those people.

Segments vary in size according to the following criteria:

1 *Narrowness of definition of need* – For example, there may be a segment who prefer the product in blue, but this can subdivide further into metallic blue, dark blue, sky blue, etc. The narrower the definition, the smaller the segment.

2 *Complexity of the product in terms of features available* – The more features a product has, the more segments it will appeal to and therefore the smaller the individual segments.

3 *Consumer involvement with the product category* – If the product category generally attracts high-involvement consumers, the segments are likely to be small and loyal.

Clearly the bigger the segment, the greater the profit potential as the benefits of standardization and long production runs will be greater. On the other hand the consumer's satisfaction with the product is likely to be less, as Figure 17.5 illustrates.

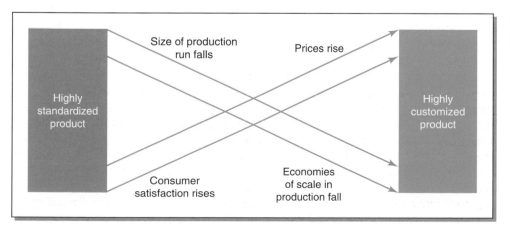

Figure 17.5
Segmentation trade-offs

As Figure 17.5 shows, the production run gets smaller as the product becomes more customized, but the customer satisfaction gets greater; a highly standardized product is cheaper to produce, but really pleases nobody.

Segmentation increases profitability when the value to the consumer of the improvements is greater than the cost to the manufacturer of providing them. This is because the manufacturer is able to charge a price higher than the cost of making the changes, but still less than it would cost the consumer to make adaptations after purchase.

For comparison, it is possible to buy clothes from a chain store that almost fit, and then take them home and alter the seams slightly so that the fit is perfect. It might be worthwhile, however, to pay a little extra at a different shop to buy something that already fits perfectly.

Markets can be segmented according to many different factors; in the above example, the catalogue company will segment according to dress size as a matter of course, and will have carried out research to find out how many of each size they are likely to sell so that they can order the appropriate quantities. Apart from that, though, the company will also be segmenting according to consumer preference for dress styles, and this is a rather more complicated exercise.

For example, the clothing market could be segmented demographically (according to age, income, family size, occupation, etc.), psychographically (according to behaviour patterns, attitudes, expectations), geographically (according to the area in which the people live, which may be relevant to a catalogue company since more northerly customers will need warmer clothing) or even behaviourally (perhaps according to whether they already buy from other catalogues).

Suppose for example the company segments demographically. This may mean aiming the catalogue at a particular age group (perhaps 25- to 35-year-olds) or a particular income group, or perhaps both. If the company segments behaviourally, they may decide to aim at party-lovers and offer clubbing and party wear. (Some catalogues specialize in outdoor wear for the hikers and mountaineers; others specialize in smart business wear for the career person.)

A mail-order company is likely to be particularly interested in using database marketing, since this enables the company to send only those mailings which will interest the consumer they are aimed at. This will substantially cut the costs of sending out 'junk mail', since only those mailings of direct interest will be sent, and also the response rate from mailings should increase with more accurate targeting.

In practice, no single segmentation method is likely to effective. Most firms would need to use several different methods in order to identify a precise target market, since virtually all the 'easy targets' have long since been hit. Figure 17.6 shows the process in action.

In the example shown in Figure 17.6, the company (which is assumed to be a firm specializing in products for middle-aged outdoor enthusiasts) begins by looking at everyone in the country. Demographic segmentation reduces the market to people over 40 years old, behavioural segmentation reduces the number still further to people who enjoy mountain activities such as hill walking and mountaineering, geographical segmentation reduces the

Figure 17.6

Using multiple segmentation bases

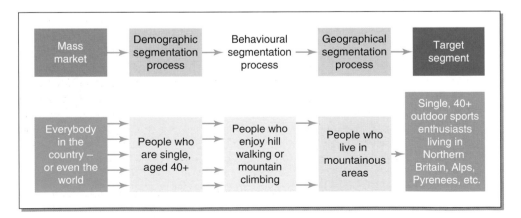

numbers to people who live in mountainous areas, and finally the target segment is identified. This company would now be in a position to target its marketing activities, for example using appropriate models in its advertising, advertising in magazines which are read by the target market, and distributing its products in the areas in which these people live.

There are many other ways of segmenting markets, but all the methods serve the same function; they allow the company to specialise in what they can do best, and spend their marketing budget in the most effective way rather than spread it too thinly by trying to please everybody.

Choosing a segment

For a segment to be viable, it must have the following characteristics:

1 *Measurability* – It must be possible to find out how many people there are in the segment, and where they are, otherwise there is no way of knowing how big the market is going to be.

2 *Accessibility* – It must be possible to approach them in some identifiable way. For instance, if it is a geographical segment, is there a retailer in the area who would carry our product? If the segment defined in terms of behaviour (say, golfers) is there a suitable magazine to advertise in?

3 *Substantiality* – Is the segment big enough to be economically worth while? This is a complex issue, because it is not just a matter of saying whether there are enough people in the segment to make a viable market. There is also the question of whether their needs are sufficiently unmet by their existing products for them to be prepared to pay a little more for our product.

4 *Congruity* – The needs of the target group must be similar, otherwise our product will meet with the same problems as the existing one: it won't meet everybody's needs well enough.

What firms are looking for is a group of people whose needs are not being met, and who are prepared to pay extra (a premium price) for a product that will meet those needs better than the product they are currently using. The equation for determining the viability of a segment is the number of people in the segment multiplied by the premium they are prepared to pay.

Firms can make good profits from a few people who are prepared to pay a lot extra to get exactly what they want, or from a lot of people who are prepared to pay a little extra to get what they want. The most profitable segments, of course, are those which have many members who are prepared to pay a high extra premium for the benefits of a product which more exactly meets their needs. Note that the product must meet the consumers' needs sufficiently better to remain good value for money.

The computer software industry follows exactly this approach. The production cost of software is huge in terms of setting-up costs; writing new software takes many hours of highly skilled (and highly paid) work. Once the software is written, though, the cost of putting it onto CDs is tiny by comparison; a blank CD costing 20p to produce is worth £90 or more to the consumer once the software is on it. Consider the advent of desktop publishing. Before DTP, anybody wanting to produce camera-ready artwork, or produce a small newsletter with attractive typefaces and illustrations, would have to pay a graphic artist and a printer several hundred pounds to produce the work. With DTP, the consumer can do most of that work at home or in the office. Consumers are therefore prepared to pay £90 for the software because it will save them hundreds of pounds in wasted time and fees to printers.

What Bill Gates of Microsoft has managed to achieve is to tap into a market where there are literally hundreds of millions of people all over the world using his software, paying big premiums to do so because the previous solutions (typewriting, paying printers, etc.) were very cumbersome and expensive, and the net production cost, while high in absolute terms, is low when spread over the size of market the software has.

Segmenting a market

It is important when segmenting a market not to use arbitrary assumptions, but there is often no simple way to determine the best way to segment. The first decision will be to determine the basis of the segmentation – whether demographically, geographically, behaviourally or psychographically, or a combination of bases. Within these bases there will be subdivisions, as shown in Figure 17.7 and Table 17.2.

Figure 17.7

Viability characteristics of segments

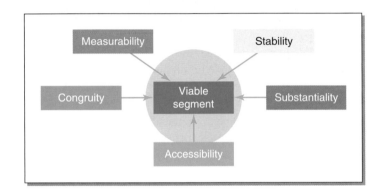

Table 17.2 Segmentation bases

Segmentation types or bases	Examples
Geographic segmentation	
Region	Scotland, north of England, south-east England, West Country, Wales
City size	Up to 100,000; 100,000 to 500,000; 500,000 to 1 million; 1 million +
Population density	Urban, suburban, rural
Climate	Warm, cold
Demographic segmentation	
Age	<12, 13–19, 20–39, 40–59, 60–69, 70–79, 80+
Gender	Female, male
Household size	1, 2, 3, 4, 5 or more
Income	Up to £15k per annum; £15,001 to £25k, £25,001 to £35k, £35,001 to £45k, £45,001+
Occupation	Professional, blue-collar, retired, unemployed
Education	GCSE, A-level, college, university, higher degree

Table 17.2 Segmentation bases (*Continued*)

Segmentation types or bases	Examples
Sociocultural segmentation	
Culture	European, Asian, African, Caribbean
Subculture: religion	Catholic, Jewish, Islamic, Protestant
Subculture: national origin	British, Indian, Chinese, Sudanese, Jamaican
Subculture: race	Asian, Caucasian, Afro-Caribbean
Social class	Aristocracy, upper class, middle class, working class
Marital status	Single, married, divorced, widowed, co-habiting
Psychographics	Achievers, strivers, strugglers
Affective and cognitive segmentation	
Degree of knowledge	Expert, novice
Benefits sought	Convenience, economy, prestige
Attitude	Positive, neutral, negative
Behavioural segmentation	
Brand loyalty	None, divided, undivided loyalty
Store loyalty	None, divided, undivided loyalty
Usage rate	Light, medium, heavy
User status	Nonuser, ex-user, current user, potential user
Payment method	Cash, credit, hire purchase
Media usage	Newspapers, magazines, TV
Usage situation	Work, home, on holiday

Source: Adapted from Peter, J. Paul and Olson, Jerry C. (1994) *Understanding Consumer Behaviour* (Burr Ridge, IL: Irwin): Chapter 3.

Geographic segmentation may be carried out for a number of reasons. First, the nature of the product may be such that it really only applies to people living with a specific area or type of area. There is really no point in trying to sell air-conditioning to Eskimos when there is a ready market among Spaniards. (In fact the old story about the salesman who could sell sand to the Arabs only shows that the salesman in question hasn't heard of segmentation!) The market may also be segmented geographically if the company's resources are limited, so the firm starts out in a small area and later rolls out the product nationally. A third reason might be that the product itself does not travel well. This is true of sheet glass, wedding cakes and most personal services like hairdressing.

Because geography is often more relevant than age, **ACORN** classifications are widely used. ACORN stands for A Classification Of Residential Neighbourhoods, and seeks to group consumers according to the type of housing they live in, in other words by geographical area.

The ACORN classifications are as shown in Table 17.3.

Table 17.3 ACORN classifications

Category	Group	Type
A: Thriving	Wealthy achievers, suburban areas	1 Wealthy suburbs, large detached houses
		2 Villages with wealthy commuters
		3 Mature, affluent home-owning areas
		4 Affluent suburbs, older families
		5 Mature, well-off suburbs
	Affluent greys, rural communities	6 Agricultural villages, home-based workers
		7 Holiday retreats, older people, home-based workers
	Prosperous pensioners, retirement areas	8 Home-owning areas, well-off older residents
		9 Private flats, elderly people
B: Expanding	Affluent executives, family areas	10 Affluent working families with mortgages
		11 Affluent working couples with mortgages, new homes
		12 Transient workforces, living at their place of work
	Well-off workers, family areas	13 Home-owning family areas
		14 Home owning family areas, older children
		15 Families with mortgages, younger children
C: Rising	Affluent urbanites, town and city areas	16 Well-off town and city areas
		17 Flats and mortgages, singles and young working couples
		18 Furnished flats and bedsits, younger single people
	Prosperous professionals, metropolitan areas	19 Apartments, young professional singles and couples
		20 Gentrified multi-ethnic areas
	Better-off executives, inner-city areas	21 Prosperous enclaves, highly qualified executives
		22 Academic centres, students and young professionals
		23 Affluent city centre areas, tenements and flats
		24 Partially gentrified multi-ethnic areas
		25 Converted flats and bedsits, single people
D: Settling	Comfortable middle agers, mature home-owning areas	26 Mature established home-owning areas
		27 Rural areas, mixed occupations
		28 Established home-owning areas
		29 Home-owning areas, council tenants, retired people

Table 17.3 ACORN classifications (*Continued*)

Category	Group	Type
	Skilled workers, home-owning areas	30 Established home-owning areas, skilled workers
		31 Home owners in older properties, younger workers
		32 Home-owning areas with skilled workers
	New home-owners, mature communities	33 Council areas, some new home owners
		34 Mature home-owning areas, skilled workers
		35 Low rise estates, older workers, new home-owners
	White-collar workers, better-off multi-ethnic areas	36 Home-owning multi-ethnic areas, young families
		37 Multi-occupied town centres, mixed occupations
		38 Multi-ethnic areas, white-collar workers
F: Striving	Older people, less prosperous areas	39 Home owners, small council flats, single pensioners
		40 Council areas, older people, health problems
	Council estate residents, better-off homes	41 Better-off council areas, new home owners
		42 Council areas, young families, some new-home owners
		43 Council areas, young families, many lone parents
		44 Multi-occupied terraces, multi-ethnic areas
		45 Low-rise council housing, less well-off families
		46 Council areas, residents with health problems
	Council estate residents, high unemployment	47 Estates with high unemployment
		48 Council flats, elderly people, health problems
		49 Council flats, very high unemployment, singles
	Council estate residents, greatest hardship	50 Council areas, high unemployment, lone parents
		51 Council flats, greatest hardship, many lone parents
	People in multi-ethnic, low-income areas	52 Multi-ethnic, large families, overcrowding
		53 Multi-ethnic, severe unemployment, lone parents
		54 Multi-ethnic, high unemployment, overcrowding
	Unclassified	55

Source: © CACI Ltd (2005). ACORN is a registered servicemark of CACI Ltd.

OK, we all know that birds of a feather flock together, as the saying goes – but is it really the case that we can be defined so accurately simply by where we live? What happens if a run-down inner-city neighbourhood becomes 'gentrified' by wealthy incomers? What happens if a formerly 'posh' area becomes unfashionable? What happens as local residents move through different life cycle stages – having children, growing older, becoming sole survivors, perhaps divorcing or re-marrying along the way?

Are we all supposed to move house every time our lives change? Or perhaps people actually *do* move house every time their lives change? Or (perhaps even more subtly) our basic purchasing behaviour and attitudes do not change much, despite what life throws at us!

Demographic segmentation is the most commonly used method of segmenting markets. Demographics is the study of the 'shape' of the population, and is concerned with areas such as age, occupation, salary, and lifestyle stage.

The argument in favour of using demography as a segmentation variable is that people are the foundation of marketing analysis. We therefore need to ask ourselves:

1 How many are there/will there be?
2 What is/will be the age distribution?
3 Where do/will they live?
4 How long do they/will they live?

Population trends are fairly reliable statistically; we can predict how many 40-year-olds there will be in ten years' time because we know how many 30-year-olds we have now, and we know fairly accurately what the death rate is for people in their thirties. Even natural disasters, wars, plagues etc. may not affect the figures too much, depending on the scope of the study. The biggest variable is likely to be births rather than deaths; of the three variables (births, deaths and immigration) births is the most volatile.

The number of births is dependent on several factors. **Birthrate** is the number of live births per thousand population in a given year. **Fertility rate** is the number of live births per thousand women of childbearing age. **Completed fertility rate** is the total number ever born to women of a specific age group (an indication of family size). **Total fertility rate** is the number of children a woman would expect to have in her lifetime if she passed through all the average completed fertility rates. This is a complex concept, but it gives an idea of how many children women are currently having. The current TFR is less than 1.8 for the UK; 2.1 will maintain the population, so if we were only relying on births to replace people who die the population would be falling. TFR is not to be confused with **natural increase**, which is the surplus of births over deaths, or **growth rate**, which includes migration effects.

The population of the European Union is increasing at present, but natural increase is actually negative, that is to say the death rate exceeds the birth rate. The difference is being made up by immigration, which means that there will be ethnic and cultural shifts in the population. There are ethnic differences in fertility rates and birthrates and this is also affecting the mix of population; partly these differences are cultural, because some cultures have a strong imperative towards large families, and partly it is because migrants are predominantly of child-bearing age but often have not yet started their families. Clearly once a couple have children it becomes much more difficult to switch countries. This again is leading to substantial cultural shifts within the host countries.

There are four variables in the birth rate: age, family structure, social attitudes and technology. Age distribution of the population affects birthrate, since an aging population is likely to have fewer children per thousand than a younger population. Segmentation by age is problematic: although it would be true to say that people become more interested in pensions and investments as they grow older, and some physical characteristics (such as greying hair, wrinkled skin, weight increase and reduced mobility) may also affect buying decisions, it is dangerous to make too many assumptions about age-related buying. Adventure holidays for the over-fifties, gym memberships and adventure sports such as flying and motorcycling have all proved to be of great interest to older age groups. In fact, many older people could not afford to learn to fly, or could not afford the insurance rates for sports cars and motorbikes, in their younger days. Marketers have tended in the past to bypass older consumers, but this trend is changing (Szmigin and Carrigan 2001).

Talking point

They say that youth is wasted on the young, but are we heading into an era where everybody expects to be young forever? Has it become the norm for people to be snowboarding at 70, abseiling at 80 and white-water rafting at 90? Does nobody stay at home and knit any more?

Realistically, though, how many older people do any of us know who actually do these things? By contrast, we most of us know younger people who spend all day watching daytime TV and most of the evening sitting around scratching themselves, so maybe it's a generation thing? Are older people simply from a generation which likes to get out and do stuff, while younger people are from a generation which likes to let other people do the running about?

A more subtle effect of age is that different age groups have markedly different life experiences. People in their eighties remember living through the Second World War; people in their seventies were teenagers during the 1950s; people in their sixties remember Vietnam War protests and were teenagers during the 1960s; people in their fifties remember Flower Power and the 1970s; people in their forties spent their early working lives in Thatcherite Britain; people in their thirties grew up with the telecommunications revolution, and people in their twenties are faced with a longer working life than any previous generation. These life experiences can be used in marketing communications: playing music from the specific era is often used in advertising, and of course some products rely directly on nostalgia: compilation CDs, DVDs of newsreel footage and various 'commemorative' products rely on people's feelings about their own pasts. Segmentation by age is generally considered to be too simplistic – the relationship between age and behaviour is far from linear (Simcock, Sudbury and Wright 2006).

Family structure concerns areas such as marriages, women's employment outside the home and the average age at first marriage. As more women are following careers they are postponing having children (or even dropping the idea altogether) and therefore tending to have fewer of them. Fewer people are marrying now than previously, and many are marrying much later, so that the one-child family is becoming far more common.

Gender segmentation is not as clear-cut as it once was. Gender roles have shifted dramatically in the last 30 years, with men taking on a greater share of housework and women carrying out traditionally 'male' tasks such as maintenance jobs around the house. Research by Mintel shows that 28 per cent of men now take responsibility for cooking, 20 per cent take responsibility for the laundry and 40 per cent of men aged 55 and older do at least half the grocery shopping. Men still take the bulk of the responsibility for gardening and home maintenance tasks, but women are encroaching on these traditional male preserves.

It seems likely that these trends will continue. In older households the traditional gender division of household tasks continues, but most younger couples have a more equal division of housework and certainly younger women have an expectation of having a career rather than a 'pin money' job. This means that household tasks have to be shared more equally. The statistics may be skewed by the number of women who remain home to care for small children, since they would typically carry out more of the housework.

Astute marketers have taken note of these changes. Power-tool manufacturers now offer smaller, lightweight power tools with women in mind: instructions for assembling flat-pack furniture now no longer assume that the reader has studied woodwork in school, and men are shown shopping, cleaning and cooking in TV advertisements. There are, of course, products which are gender-specific simply because there are physical differences between the genders: likewise, some products are aimed at specific genders because of social mores. In Western Europe, facial make-up for men is still somewhat rare, and relatively few women take up boxing, but even these distinctions are being eroded.

The gender debate also includes issues of sexual orientation. Homosexual people have specific characteristics from a marketing viewpoint: in general, gay people tend to be wealthier, and have greater disposable income since they are less likely to have dependent children (see Chapter 11). Estimates vary, but current thinking is that gays represent about 4 per cent of the UK population – the difficulty with this type of estimate is that many gays are still reluctant to 'come out' due to fear of abuse or even physical attacks, and also that the distinction between 'gay' and 'straight' is by no means clear-cut, so there are problems of definition.

Attitudes towards issues such as illegitimacy have relaxed. Marriage and family is emphasized less nowadays, and there is a far weaker cultural imperative to reproduce. Even thirty years ago couples were under great pressure from their families and friends to have babies; nowadays the pressures are less, even when the prospective grandparents are eager for the couple to 'get started'.

Technology is mostly about the availability of contraception. As contraceptive techniques have improved, the birthrate has fallen because more people have been able to exercise choice in reproduction. This is not true in every country in the world; in third-world countries contraception is not widely available (or at least is not widely affordable) and therefore the birthrate remains high.

It is possible to identify shifts in attitude and behaviour that have come about due to rises and falls in the national birthrate.

The **Baby Boomers** were born in the 15 years or so after the Second World War. This was a time of rising prosperity, when returning soldiers (and war-weary civilians) felt confident about starting families. The Baby Boomers are now aged around 50–65. Born and

Consumer behaviour in action
Pink Cloud Travel

Pink Cloud Travel was founded in 2000 as a subsidiary of Dorado Reisen AG, a Swiss travel company. Pink Cloud supplies holidays specifically for homosexual people. The organization taps into the problems often encountered by gay people when on holiday – homosexuality is not tolerated in some countries (in some it is actually illegal) and gay couples frequently find themselves subject to verbal and even physical abuse. Pink Cloud Travel operates through airlines and other tour operators and offers trips to the Caribbean and the Mediterranean, city breaks and ski holidays. The company works closely with organizations in destination countries to ensure that its clients have a hassle-free holiday: not always easy, given the overt hostility often encountered by gay people.

Rival company Outlet4Holidays began life as a London agency dedicated to finding accommodation for lesbian and gay couples – often discriminated against by landlords. Now there are four companies in the group, including the holiday division: here the company has taken on some bold initiatives, for example booking out an entire ski resort so that only gay and lesbian holidaymakers can be found on the slopes.

Although it says a great deal about the world's lack of tolerance for sexual orientation, there is a definite need for this type of product – as witness the fact that both these companies are thriving on providing hassle-free (though by no means cheap) holidays for their unique market segment.

brought up in periods of rising prosperity, increasing personal freedom, and rising expectations, they tend to pay cash for their purchases (although they used to use credit, interest rates are deterring them now they are richer). They tend to buy more and save less than previous generations, and banks will make less on providing them with credit over the next few years, but more on providing pensions and savings schemes.

Baby Busters were born between 1964 and 1980 – a time of falling birthrates. There were also falling standards of living, oil crises, more social dislocation caused by the rise in one-parent and both-parents-working families. Baby Busters tend to be heavy consumers, hard workers, educated, ambitious, selfish and determined to succeed financially. These are the generation that produced the yuppie.

Woopies are well-off older people. Not all the over-65s are living in poverty; many have generous occupational pensions, low outgoings, and substantial savings and investments. They spend more than the average on holidays, their homes and financial services. Many retired teachers, engineers, doctors and middle managers are in this position, and they now form a substantial market. Companies such as Saga Holidays have tapped into this market very successfully by providing holidays that are specifically tailored for elderly people; for example, Saga ensure that their clients rarely (if ever) have to carry their own luggage any distance, since elderly people might have difficulty with this. Saga holidays are not cheaper than others, in fact they are often considerably more expensive: they simply cater for the over-50s.

The population is ageing rapidly, due to two factors; falling birthrate and increased longevity. By 2050 more than a quarter of Europe's population is expected to be aged over 65 (compared with 8.2 per cent in 1950) (IIASA 2006). This has several effects:

1 Relationship marketing is more important if the relationship between company and consumer might last 50 years or more.

2 More leisure time per head of population means more spending on leisure pursuits.

3 The possibility of living to be very old may encourage younger people to look after themselves better, so there may be an upsurge in sales of health and fitness products.

4 The lack of new consumers makes it important for marketers to look after existing ones better.

Marketers are facing new challenges from shifting demography, not least the problem of zero population growth, which in theory means static or even shrinking markets. This inevitably means that marketers can no longer rely on the natural increase of the population to expand the company's business. They must instead be able to compete better for the consumer's money.

Income is widely used as a segmentation base, but is not as simple as might first be assumed (see Figure 17.8). For example, high income might be associated with high outgoings, and vice versa, meaning that a high earner might have very little disposable income, or a low earner might have substantial funds to play with. Equally, high earnings do not tell us anything about an individual's tastes and interests, or what the individual regards as value for money. Wealthy people are frequently extremely careful about what they spend money on – understandably, since this is probably the attitude that enabled them to become rich in the first place. Some firms have managed to succeed very well by catering to the less well-off in society: retailers such as Aldi and Lidl target less affluent consumers, using a lean organization, cheap store locations and an absence of frills to minimize costs.

Ethnicity is also a demographic method of segmenting markets. Religion and nationality are also (in part) included in ethnicity, which is concerned with culture as well as race. In fact, though, the influence of these factors is less than might be expected. For example, religious belief has an effect on purchases of religious artifacts, and in some religions it also has an effect on purchases of food and drink: Muslims and Jews avoid pork, Buddhists avoid meat in general, Jains and Parsees are strictly vegetarian, and many Catholics still eat fish on Fridays even though this is no longer a requirement of the Church. Apart from these

Saga have carved out a successful niche catering to older holidaymakers – often by providing more adventurous holidays.

Figure 17.8

Disposable income

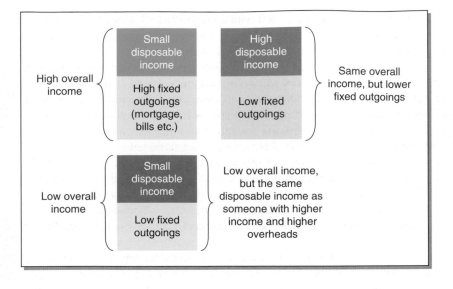

factors, though, the bulk of the consumption behavior of these groups is likely to be very similar – they will live in similar houses, enjoy similar entertainments, drive similar cars, and so forth.

Some physical characteristics may affect purchasing behaviour, notably in the areas of cosmetics and hair care, but in most other respects differences between ethnic groups have been considerably eroded in recent years. Ethnic segmentation has become blurred due to culture swapping, especially in the areas of food and fashion: ethnic segmentation for these products is therefore no longer realistic (Jamal 2003). In global markets it is common to segment by nationality, even though nationality is a legal state rather than an ethnic one. The reason for this is that different countries have different laws regarding products. There is a limited number of products which are nationality-dependent: patriotic products such as flags and national symbols, and some legal services.

The segmentation bases described above are not necessarily mutually exclusive; it is perfectly feasible to aim for 20–30-year-old men of Asian background who are expert motor mechanics and live in towns of less than 100,000 population. This would use demographic, sociocultural, geographic and cognitive segmentation. Naturally the number of men fitting into this category would be small, but (presumably) if such a segment were to have very similar needs their level of interest in a product that would meet those needs would be correspondingly high. In fact, current thinking on segmentation is that a single method is unlikely to be adequate.

Generally speaking, the narrower the segment, the more loyal and interested the consumers will be, but the fewer of them there are. Marketers therefore have to make strategic decisions about which segment should be approached.

From the viewpoint of consumer behaviour, the most relevant segmentation bases are the psychographic and the behavioural. These will be examined in greater depth in the following sections.

Psychographic segmentation

Psychographic segmentation has the drawback that it is difficult to measure consumers' psychological attributes on a large scale. This means that this type of segmentation often fails on the grounds of accessibility. For example, market research may have shown that there is a substantial number of consumers who are afraid of having their pets stolen for medical experiments. The problem now is that there is no obvious medium to advertise our new security system for pets in; if there were a magazine called *Pet Security Monthly* we would have no problem. We are therefore left with mass media such as television, which is probably far too expensive for the purpose. Some of the most creative ideas in marketing have revolved around ways of gaining access to such segments.

People can be divided into groups according to their lifestyles. Lifestyles both are created by products, and dictate which products will be bought and used: someone who owns a penthouse flat has a different psychology (and lifestyle) from someone who chooses to buy a smallholding and be self-sufficient, but both dwellings are products as well as lifestyle determinants. Incidentally, it is likely that the cost of each type of home will be similar: the choice is about lifestyle, not about financial considerations.

Lifestyle segmentation has the major advantage that it relates directly to purchasing behaviour. It has been said that marketing delivers a lifestyle, so considering consumers on the basis of their chosen lifestyles is certainly logical. The VALS model discussed in Chapter 2 is an example of lifestyle segmentation: consumers are divided into nine lifestyle positions, determined by their attitudes to other people and (to an extent) by their level of wealth.

Personality characteristics appear, at first sight, to be an extremely useful way of segmenting markets because personality changes relatively slowly. Unfortunately, it is difficult to measure personality traits on a mass scale, so it is difficult to identify groups of people with similar traits. For example, an insurance company might like to target people who are excessively afraid of burglary, but who are also wealthy and have many possessions. Such people might be expected to be careful about locking their houses, and would have burglar alarms, and would also invest in security locks. The result would be a group of people who are unlikely to make a claim against their policies – the ideal customers for insurance companies. There is, however, no easy way to target such a group: there is no single advertising medium directed at these people, and therefore the insurance company would have no alternative but to use mass marketing approaches, which is an expensive and wasteful policy.

As we saw in Chapter 4, psychologists have developed many ways of categorizing people according to psychological characteristics. In theory, these categorizations could be used to segment markets, but in practice the only realistic way of approaching these groups is by allowing them to self-select against a mass marketing communications approach. For example, our hypothetical insurance company above would need to model the product's use using actors who portray the particular personality traits which are of interest.

Behavioural segmentation

Behaviour can be a useful and reliable way of segmenting. At its most obvious, if we are marketing to anglers we are not interested in how old they are, what their views are on strong drink or where they live. All we care about is that they go fishing, and might therefore be customers for our new type of rod. Accessing the segment would be easily undertaken by advertising in the *Angler's Times*. At a deeper level we might be interested in such issues as where they buy their fishing tackle, how much they usually spend on a rod, what kind of fish they are after, and so forth but this information is easily obtained through questionnaire-type surveys.

The main behavioural bases for segmentation (see Figure 17.9) are as follows:

All we need to know about anglers is that they enjoy fishing.

1 *Benefits sought* – Different people look for different things in each product purchase. Sampson (1992) divided people into three groups: functionality seekers who look for the simple, practical aspects of ownership; image seekers, who look for products which will enhance their self-image in various ways; and pleasure seekers, who look for the hedonic aspects of owning products. For example, someone who

Figure 17.9

Behavioural bases for segmentation

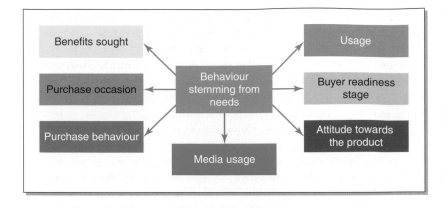

buys a car as simple transportation for themselves, their family and their luggage would be classified as a functionality seeker. Someone who buys an upmarket car for its prestige value, to show off to the neighbours, is an image seeker, while someone who simply enjoys driving or looks for a car which has exceptional comfort is a pleasure seeker.

2 *Purchase occasion* – Some products are bought on a regular basis, whereas some others are bought as an occasional treat. More importantly, the same product might be a regular purchase for some people, but a treat for others – for example, someone on a strict diet may only buy a chocolate bar very occasionally, whereas someone else might regard a chocolate bar as a normal element in the weekday lunchbox. Likewise, 50 years ago chicken was regarded as an occasional Sunday lunch treat (beef was the usual Sunday lunch roast in the UK) but intensive farming has brought the relative price of chicken down to the point where it is one of the cheapest meats available. Even in the 1950s many people ate chicken regularly, either because they were wealthy enough to do so or because they considered the extra cost to be worthwhile – as is the case with lamb in the twenty-first century. Another aspect of purchase occasion relates to gift giving: the vast majority of sales of aftershave are made to women. Relatively little aftershave is bought by men for their own use. Purchase occasion might also relate to situational factors: buying a new car battery may come about because of a growing awareness that the existing battery is getting old, or it might be as a result of a sudden failure of the battery far from home. Different versions of the same product might also be purchased at different times – someone travelling for business purposes may decide to stay in a four-star business-class hotel, but when on holiday might prefer a crumbling old bed-and-breakfast because such places have more character. Going to a restaurant because one is too tired to cook results in a different choice of restaurant from that chosen when celebrating a wedding anniversary or a birthday, and even the choice between a romantic restaurant with cosy corners (for a wedding anniversary or first date) and a lively restaurant with entertainment for celebrating a birthday with friends is an example of purchase occasion differences.

3 *Purchase behaviour* – Relates to time of purchase, place of purchase, quantities bought on each occasion, degree of willingness to buy innovative products, and so forth. For example, books might be bought from a bookshop, second-hand from a charity shop, online from retailers such as Amazon, or even in a street market. Each type of behaviour relates to the consumer concerned, but may not relate to other characteristics: someone might enjoy shopping online, whereas another person might prefer the bargain-hunting aspects of browsing in a second-hand book shop. The same person might enjoy both ways of buying books – online for practical, work-related purchases; second-hand for personal books for leisure reading. The individual's motivation may or may not be concerned with saving money: many people shop online because it is more convenient than shopping in retail stores

(for example because the individual lives in a remote area, or is housebound, or whose working life makes it difficult to get to a bricks-and-mortar retailer). Brand loyalty is also an element in purchase behaviour: high involvement with the brand means that the marketer will try to identify and recruit those customers, whereas brand switchers can only be lured by sales promotions.

4 *Usage* – Some customers use the product more frequently and in higher quantities than do others. Users are usually divided into heavy users, medium users, light users, ex-users and non-users. The aim of the marketers is to move people from being non-users to being heavy users if possible. Non-users are not, of course, consumers of the product but they may present an opportunity if the product is appropriate for their needs – clearly there will always be some people who will never buy the product under any circumstances. Light users and medium users can be encouraged to use more of the product, and although this is probably a great deal easier than recruiting new customers most firms still spend the greater part of their effort on recruitment rather than development. A neglected area of marketing has been customer win-back, which is the re-enrolling of former customers. These people represent a good opportunity – they already know the company and its products, and in many cases defected to another company for fairly trivial reasons. In many cases, firms seek to recruit heavy users from their competitors, but this can be a dangerous tactic if it provokes heavy competitive responses.

5 *Buyer readiness stage* – Some people may be on the verge of buying the product, whereas others may never have heard of it. Still others may have an interest in the product but do not have any money, others might be aware of the product but are not yet interested, others might be interested but do not at present have a need for the product, and so forth. Marketers need to be aware of these stages and be prepared to act at the appropriate time: for example, a couple who have just bought their first house will not currently be in the market to buy another, but very well might be in five to seven years' time, when perhaps they have started a family or are earning more money. Contacting people at the wrong time (when they are not ready to buy) is irritating for the customer and a waste of resources for the company, whereas contacting people at the right time (when they are considering another purchase) is helpful and productive in terms of generating business.

6 *Attitude towards the product* – In some cases, the non-user's attitude towards the product is so hostile that there is really no point in trying to change it. Political parties know that many of their supporters will be loyal no matter what happens, and that the same is true of their opposition: efforts are usually concentrated on the 'floating voters' who might be persuaded one way or the other. Likewise, Disneyland Paris know that about 20 per cent of the population of Europe would never visit the theme park – their values and lifestyles simply would not permit it.

7 *Media usage* – The types of media the individual consumes are clearly of interest since (as marketers) we need to communicate with our target audience. Additionally, the quantity of media consumed is relevant – an individual who reads several newspapers, or who watches a wide range of TV channels, will be exposed to a great deal more advertising than one who rarely opens a newspaper or watches very little TV.

8 *Preferences* – Research among Norwegian teenagers found four preference types: food lovers, fish haters, fish lovers, and dislikers. Within these preferences the teenagers chose specific products: the conclusion was that family-related attitude and lifestyle variables explained segment membership much better than demographic variables (Honkanen, Olsen and Myrland 2004).

Segmenting markets according to the behaviour of the customers within them makes perfect sense since our interest in customers lies ultimately in how they behave. What people do is a great deal more important than who they are or what they think, at least in terms of marketing. For example, motor vehicle users can be segmented much more effectively in terms of whether they prefer to lease their cars or buy them outright than by demographic characteristics (Trocchia, Beatty and Hill 2006).

Life events can have a profound effect on brand preferences (Mathur, Moschis and Lee 2003). Adjustments to new life situations brought about by moving to a new place, a bereavement, a major conflict with a family member, a change of job or financial status, and so forth may lead to a change of favourite brand. The authors believe that life events and life status changes might prove better predictors of behaviour and hence be a better base for segmentation, but it is hard to see how such a segmentation base could be quantified or the actual segments identified.

Segmenting business markets

Segmentation methods and criteria differ between consumer markets and business-to-business markets, for the following reasons:

1 Consumer markets are characterized by customers who are either the end user of the product or are very close to the end user. Business markets are characterized by buyers who do not themselves use the product.

2 The number of potential customers in business markets is almost always smaller, so there is likely to be a greater degree of customization necessary.

3 Psychographic and demographic variables are almost entirely inappropriate.

Business marketers should be careful about applying consumer segmentation techniques directly to business markets. Unrefined use of consumer segmentation techniques can lead a business marketer in the wrong direction.

Many firms define a market segment by product type or product size. This overly simplistic approach can have dire consequences, because it is product focused rather than customer focused. In the US computer hard disk drive (HDD) industry, suppliers identified customers for 14-inch drives as mainframe computer manufacturers, users of 8-inch drives as mini computer makers, customers for 5.25-inch drives as personal computer manufacturers and for 2.5-inch drives as portable and laptop suppliers. Many firms focused on one or few segments and were unable to move into new segments as technology converged. A number of leading US HDD firms such as Memorex, Control Data and DEC were eventually forced to leave the HDD business. In the HDD business, the leading Japanese firms continue to be the major suppliers, as they have been for the past 20 years (Chesbrough 2003).

Another common error business marketers make in segmenting is simply accepting the definition of an entire industry as one segment. For instance, a manufacturer of train control equipment might say 'We sell to electrified railways' and classify the Santiago Subway or London Underground in the same category as a surface electrified railway in India. The most obvious differences (such as the product being used underground as opposed to being used in full exposure to the elements) would thus be ignored. Some managers err on the other side of the spectrum, thinking about their segments in too narrow a fashion. They may think only about a particular industry dominated by a few major firms and not about new segments which could use their product that are entirely unrelated to the primary target segment.

Talking point

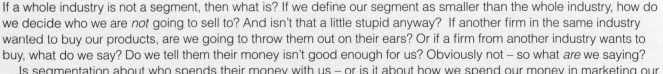

If a whole industry is not a segment, then what is? If we define our segment as smaller than the whole industry, how do we decide who we are *not* going to sell to? And isn't that a little stupid anyway? If another firm in the same industry wanted to buy our products, are we going to throw them out on their ears? Or if a firm from another industry wants to buy, what do we say? Do we tell them their money isn't good enough for us? Obviously not – so what *are* we saying?

Is segmentation about who spends their money with us – or is it about how we spend our money in marketing our products?

Segmentation variables

Business marketing segmentation variables can be divided into two main categories (see Table 17.4).

In the first category called identifiers by Day (1990), firms attempt to pre establish segments *a priori* – that is, before any data is collected. These are the more traditional segmentation variables because the data is easier to obtain through observation of the buying situation or from secondary sources. Some researchers call these 'macro variables'. As can be seen from Table 17.4, they include demographic, operations, product required and purchasing situation variables related to current or potential customer market segments. Day (1990) also identified response profile characteristics, 'unique to the product or service . . . based on attributes and behaviour toward the product category or specific brands and vendors in that category' (p. 101). These include specific vendor attributes such as overall value offered, product quality, vendor reputation, on-time delivery and so on. In addition, customer variables such as the make-up of the decision-making unit (or buying centre), the importance of the purchase to the subject segment and the innovativeness of the firms in this potential segment are examined. Another important aspect of the response profile technique is to review applications to determine how products are used. Finally, personal characteristics may be included to define a particular segment. These include variables related to individuals in the buying centre such as risk tolerance, loyalty, age, education and experience.

Table 17.4 Segmentation variables

Identifier (a priori)	Response profile (a posteriori)
• **Demographic** – Industry classification – Firm type – OEM, end user, aftermarket (MRO) – Company size – Geographic location – Financial info/credit rating	• **Vendor product attributes** – Overall value – Product quality – Vendor reputation – Innovativeness – On-time delivery – Lowest cost
• **Operations** – Technologies used – Level of use – heavy, light, non-user – Centralized/decentralized purchasing	• **Customer variables** – DMU (buying centre) make-up – Purchase importance – Attitude toward product – Corporate cultural characteristics (innovativeness)
• **Product required** – Custom ↔ standard	• **Application** – End use – Importance of value in use
• **Purchasing situation** – Buying situation – new task, modified re-buy, straight re-buy – Current attitude toward our firm – Relationships	• **DMU/buying centre personal characteristics** – Risk tolerance – Loyalty to current vendor – Age – Experience – Education

Source: Adapted from: Kotler (2003), Day (1990), Rao and Wang (1995), Malhotra (1989), Cardozo (1980).

These variables are often referred to as *a posteriori,* or after the fact variables in which a 'clustering approach' is used to gather like customers together based on their particular needs. Some researchers call these 'micro variables'.

Looking at the usefulness of the two basic segmentation approaches as measured against the tests for a good segment, Malhotra (1989) claims the identifier approach is better than the response profile approach in terms of measurability and accessibility since it is easy to find and reach the segments which already have established data classifications. He feels this method is particularly good for institutional markets where the number of establishments is small and the number of variables is large. On the other hand, Malhotra believes that using the response profile or clustering approach will produce more responsiveness from a particular segment since the marketing mix will be closely tailored to the specific needs of the segment identified.

Generally speaking, business marketers have used identifiers in segmenting their customers. The major reason for this is simplicity. With the Internet, it is easy to get the kinds of information needed to segment markets using the identifier approach.

The use of the response profile approach is a subject of much discussion in the literature. While there is general agreement that the customer's view of vendor attributes, how the decision-making unit is constituted or the risk tolerance of key members of the DMU is invaluable segmentation information, there is little agreement about how widespread this approach is.

Dibb and Simkin (2001) point out that although much has been written about segmentation, there is limited guidance for managers attempting to implement a true market segmentation process. They identified three major categories of barriers to segmentation: infrastructure, process and implementation. These can be further subdivided into culture, structure and resources.

Infrastructure barriers include the support (or lack of support) from senior management, lack of intra-functional communications, entrenched organizational structures and the lack of financial and human resources. Process issues include the lack of practical advice on how to actually implement segmentation, the unwillingness to share ideas and data, the lack of a fit with corporate strategy, and the misuse of the process because there is poor understanding of it. Implementation barriers include the difficulty of changing present segmentation in the firm. Since industries are often organized around product categories or distribution channels it is extremely difficult to develop segments which are not congruent with those existing divisions. These barriers also include poor identification of responsibility and poor communications and lack of senior management involvement. In the end, the test is aligning budgets and assignments with the segmentation solutions. If this isn't accomplished, the entire process is a waste of time. A summary of the key segmentation barriers and recommended treatments is included as Table 17.5.

Dibb and Simkin recommend treatments or solutions to the problems identified. As can be seen from Table 17.5, prior to the process it is important to find important data, identify the people and the skills required to get the segmentation process done. Senior management must strongly support the process, develop the proper communications channels, establish adequate budgets and set up training for people who will be assigned to do the process but may not have the necessary education or skills.

During the process, it is important to identify the segmentation steps, get the education gaps filled, then collect the data through internal and external sources (here a firm may employ a number of secondary and primary data techniques). It is also important to establish regular meetings for communications or progress and for senior management to be sure that the segmentation is going to fit into the overall corporate strategy.

Finally, to facilitate implementation the authors recommend identifying the specific audiences to whom the findings will be communicated and then to do that, to make changes to plans and programmes congruent with the new segmentation solutions and to identify changes that are required in the culture and the structure of the firm; then to specify responsibilities, budgets and timing to make the segmentation work and finally to set

Table 17.5 Diagnosing and treating key segmentation barriers

Problems	Infrastructure	Process	Implementation
Culture	• Inflexible, resists new ideas • Not customer focused • Doesn't understand segmentation rationale	• Not committed to sharing data/ideas • Lack of 'buy in' • No fit with corporate strategy planning	• Product focus • Insufficient belief in the process • Unwillingness to change current segmentation
Structure	• Lack of intra-functional communications • Low senior management interest or involvement • Entrenched organizational structures	• Misuse of segmentation process	• Poor demarcation of responsibility • Ineffective communications of segmentation solution • Poor senior management involvement
Resources	• Too few or untrained people • Insufficient budgets	• Inadequate data available • Insufficient budgets • Too few or untrained people	• Lack of alignment of budgeting with segmentation • Insufficient time allowed
Solutions	**Prior to process:** • Find available data • Identify people/skills • Get senior management support • Develop communications • Establish adequate budgets • Train people – basic segmentation skills	**During process:** • Specify segmentation steps • Fill gaps in education/skills • Collect data – internal and external • Establish regular communications meetings • Review for fit with corporate strategy	**Facilitate implementation:** • Identify and communicate findings • Make changes to plans and programmes • Identify changes required to culture and structure • Specify budgets, responsibilities and timing to roll out solutions • Develop method for monitoring roll out

Source: Based on Dibb, Sally, and Simkin, Lyndon (2001) Market segmentation: diagnosing and treating the barriers. *Industrial Marketing Management*, 30(8): 609–25.

up a monitoring process to see whether the segmentation process is being implemented and whether this implementation is effective.

The most widely accepted approach to segmentation is that proposed by Bonoma and Shapiro (1984). They describe the nested approach, starting with very general, easily available information and moving to the most specific variables which, incidentally, are the most difficult to obtain information about. See Figure 17.10.

The first and most obvious step is to group companies by industry classification. In the United States, the most common industry classification has been the Standard Industrial Classification (SIC), which was replaced in 1997 by the North American Industrial Classification System (NAICS). The NAICS was created to rationalize data among the three NAFTA countries (members of the North American Free Trade Agreement) – United States, Canada and Mexico. Other classification systems include the SITC System established by the United Nations in 1950. The US also participates in the Harmonized Commodity Description System, known simply as the Harmonized System, which has been used to classify goods in international trade since 1 January 1989. This system is in common use in more than 50 countries.

Industry classifications give a firm a start on a grouping of customers and prospective customers into potential segments.

Figure 17.10

The nested approach to segmentation

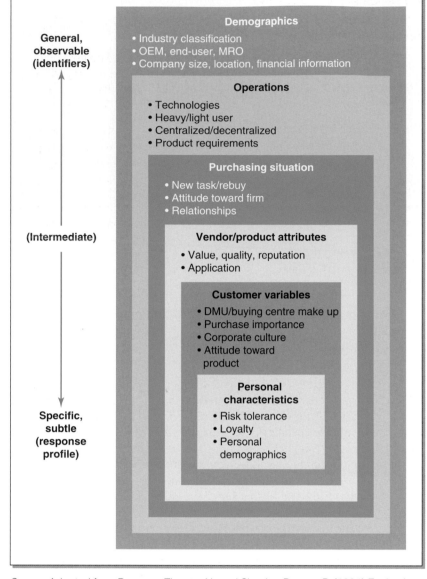

Source: Adapted from Bonoma, Thomas V., and Shapiro, Benson P. (1984) Evaluating market segmentation approaches. *Industrial Marketing Management*, 13(4): 257–68.

Many firms simply divide their customers into heavy, medium and light users, the so-called A-B-C division. This may be useful for assigning salespersons to particular accounts, but is a poor substitute for the full segmentation process. Using firm demographics also includes dividing customers into types (OEM, user and aftermarket or MRO) and also to group them by company size, geographic location and by specific financial factors such as credit worthiness.

Classifying customers according to OEM, end user or aftermarket (maintenance, repair and operations) (Table 17.6) gives important clues to their commonalities. An OEM or original equipment manufacturer buys components, systems, equipment and materials. In the case of components, these enter the OEM's final product while materials are consumed in the manufacturing of their products. Systems and equipment are used to make the products. OEMs often purchase many different items to develop a particular product and frequently brand the product with their own name. Users obviously put the product to use. For instance, John Deere tractors are used by farmers while Deere itself is an OEM (Hlavacek and Ames 1986). The aftermarket, also called MRO, includes firms who offer

Table 17.6 Classification of customers

Type of customer	Description
OEM	Original equipment manufacturer. These customers buy manufacturing equipment, raw materials and components to make into finished products. Examples would be car manufacturers or consumer durables manufacturers.
End user	These customers use up the product entirely in the course of running the business. For example, a company will use cleaning materials, energy, copier paper, office furniture and so forth without incorporating any of these items into the finished products which it sells.
Aftermarket (MRO)	Maintenance, repair and operations companies provide services to companies and consumers. For example, a computer repair company will use spare parts, tools and transport to repair or replace defective parts.

add-on products, repair services or replacement parts. Often, a producer may sell his product or services to all three of these firm types, but each is a separate and different segment since requirements will probably be quite different.

A second step involves more understanding of customer operations. In this step, the marketer would determine what technologies potential customers are employing, whether they are heavy or light users of the product to be offered, whether they purchase in a centralized or decentralized way, and specifically what product requirements customers have, ranging from standard to custom products.

A third step is to look at the purchasing situation – whether for this firm this purchase is a new task, a straight re-buy or a modified re-buy, whether the potential customer has positive attitudes toward the firm and what relationships have been established by the marketing firm with potential customers.

The fourth step is to determine what commonalities there are among potential customers related to particular attributes by an offering firm. For instance, a customer group may be quite price sensitive where another emphasizes delivery and still a third product quality defined in some specific manner. As an example, a firm supplying chemicals to an ink maker might find that colour consistency was of primary importance and far outweighed price or delivery as a purchasing attribute. Another aspect of the vendor attribute would be the application in which the product may be used.

A more refined and more difficult set of variables to gain are identified in Figure 17.10 as customer variables. First and most important would be the make-up of the buying centre or DMU. Included here would be the importance of this purchase to the firm, the corporate culture including the attitude toward innovation and finally the attitude toward the product area. A final and most difficult set of characteristics which may be used for segmentation are personal characteristics of individuals in the DMU. These include age, experience and education, loyalty to current vendor and risk tolerance. A common saying used in many firms is: 'No one ever got fired for buying IBM.' Individuals with low-risk tolerance would tend to choose a vendor like IBM since the chances of negative consequences for an individual who chooses the pre-eminent supplier in any market are far lower than if that individual chooses a rather unknown supplier. In nearly every industrial market, firms tend to stay with vendors who have satisfied them. So, important segmentation characteristics will be the attitude toward the firm as well as loyalty and tolerance for risk.

Robertson and Barich (1992) proposed a simple approach to segmentation based only upon the purchase decision process. In this case, the authors claim identifying potential customers as **first-time prospects, novices** and sophisticates yields all the segmentation information needed. First-time prospects are firms who see a need for the product, have started to evaluate possible suppliers, but have not yet purchased. Novices are customers who have purchased the product for the first time within the last 90 days and sophisticates have purchased the product before and are ready to re-buy or have recently repurchased. First-time prospects are seeking honest sales reps who know and understand their business, and a vendor who has been in business for some time; they will wish to have a trial period.

Novices are looking for technical support, training and knowledgeable sales reps. Sophisticates are seeking compatibility with existing systems, customized products, a successful record from the vendor, speed in fixing problems and post-sales support. The main advantage of this simplified approach is the ability to implement it with the sales force, which is often the major hurdle for effective segmentation implementation.

Segmenting by customer benefits is recommended as the most effective approach and Rao and Wang (1995) found that identifiers do not correlate very well with profile or benefit sought variables. While these authors endorsed the nested approach to segmentation, they emphasized the importance of understanding specific customer benefits for the most effective segmentation.

Need to re-segment

Since business market segments change quickly, it is important to re-segment frequently. Some have suggested resegmenting at the beginning of a new stage of the product life cycle, but this is too difficult to determine. Nevertheless, changes in competition, technological advances, economic downturns or upswings and consolidation of an industry make re-segmentation very important. Once a firm begins to look at its existing segmentation on a regular basis, it may find it necessary to establish new segments for the most effective use of its marketing efforts. Managements should avoid being 'married' to the current segmentation and hold open the possibility of resegmenting. It is a management task to consistently ask questions, re-examining the basic assumptions which underlie the current segmentation.

Global segmentation

Segmentation strategy is not limited to any one country. Sophisticated business marketing firms look across countries for commonalities of market segments. For instance, ICI Nobel Explosives offers mining explosives across various countries to similar customer types, coordinating its activities in each country by segment and offering product and sales activities accordingly (Gillespie, Jeannet and Hennessey 2004). The same segmentation procedure described in Figure 17.10 can be used across various countries except that the data is much more difficult to get and developing common measures is often a real obstacle. Despite this, Schuster and Bodkin (1987) found that more than 40 per cent of firms they surveyed gathered segmentation information for the following macro variables: geographic location, company size, usage, buying strategy, end market and decision-making stage. More than 40 per cent of firms gathered data for the following micro variables: product attributes, purchase importance, attitudes and personal characteristics.

In business markets, it is not unusual to find commonalities among customers throughout the world. Electric utilities require the same products whether they are located in Kuala Lumpur or Caracas. A firm selling switchgear to electric utilities must look to a worldwide customer base in order to get the economies of scale necessary to be a global competitor. According to Yip (2003), customers can be segmented according to their purchasing patterns. Global customers are quite willing to purchase products outside their domestic markets and tend to have global control of purchasing from headquarters. Another important variable for segmenting these customers is the way in which the products are used. Yip defines national global customers who use suppliers from around the world but employ the products in one country. Multinational global customers also buy from suppliers in many countries, but they use the products in many countries as well. Management should look for commonalities among customers using the segmentation process described in the earlier part of the chapter rather than accept that minor differences make serving one segment across countries too difficult to achieve. There are many benefits to serving multinational customer segments not only including economies of scale, but also moving rapidly to world class product and service offerings, making further expansion even easier.

A study of the purchasing decision process in a region of the United States, Sweden, France and five south-east Asian countries found some differences in the decision-making process and the structure of the buying centre (Mattson and Salehi-Sangari, 1993). This study also found differences in the most important purchase decision variables used by the decision-making unit for the same products. In short, this study serves as a caution that care must be taken in segmenting markets across countries. However, the benefits of international segmentation are worth the effort required.

In global consumer markets, some segments have been identified (for example, the global youth segment) but such segmentation is still in its infancy, not least due to the difficulties of conducting research on a global basis. Some commentators suggest that segmentation by 'coming of age' experiences rather than birth date is more relevant in a global context (Schewe and Meredith 2004), while others doubt that a global youth market exists at all, suggesting instead that young people are not being offered alternatives (Kjeldgaard and Askegaard 2004).

Strategic options

Having segmented the market, there are three basic strategic options open to marketers. In reality, these are points on a continuum; segmentation is not exact, and therefore targeting a segment will not be an exact process.

1 **Concentrated marketing** (single segment, or few segments). This is about **niche marketing**: Tie Rack and Sock Shop follow this approach. The marketer who adopts a concentrated strategy aims to be the very best within a single tiny segment.

2 **Differentiated marketing** (multi-segmented) means to concentrate on two or more segments, offering a differentiated marketing mix for each. Trusthouse Forte run the most prestigious hotels in the country, but also run Motor Lodges at motorway services, with a different marketing strategy for each type of hotel. The hotels all carry the THF logo, even though the service levels and prices are very different.

3 **Undifferentiated marketing** is about using a 'scattergun' approach. Coca Cola used to do this: the company had one product, one approach and one ad to appeal to all ages and personality types. Although the company now has a wide range of products and approaches, the original Coca Cola brand still tends to use 'world' advertising, running the same advertisement worldwide and only changing the language (or using no words at all).

The decision regarding which strategy to adopt will rest on the following three factors: the company's resources, the product features and benefits and the characteristics of the segment(s). Clearly if resources are limited the company will tend to adopt a concentrated marketing approach. This is the approach taken by High and Mighty, the menswear retailer. This company specializes in clothing for exceptionally tall and exceptionally large men, and has become highly successful even though their market (men over six foot four inches in height, or over 25 stone in weight) is actually small (numerically!) in absolute terms. The reason for the success is that men of this size are not catered for at all by the big chain retailers, and the alternative used to be to have everything tailor-made. High and Mighty are able to produce in sufficient quantities to keep prices reasonable (though still considerably higher than chain store prices) while still catering for their segment.

Coca-Cola uses the same advertising whatever the language.

Figure 17.11

Levels of resource and segmentation strategy

High-resource company		
Type of product	High differentiation consumers	Low differentiation consumers
Mass market	Differentiated	Undifferentiated
Specialist market	Differentiated	Concentrated

Low-resource company		
Type of product	High differentiation consumers	Low differentiation consumers
Mass market	Concentrated	Differentiated (perhaps geographically)
Specialist market	Concentrated	Concentrated

A higher level of resourcing coupled with a range of segments to approach will lead to a differentiated approach, and a simple made-for-everybody type product will lead to an undifferentiated approach. Figure 17.11 shows this in action.

Companies with a small resource base are unable to attack large, mass markets simply because they cannot afford the level of promotional spend needed to make their voices heard above the big firms. They therefore need to differentiate, perhaps by starting out in a small area of the country and gradually spreading nationwide as resources become available.

Summary

This chapter has been about dividing markets into groups with similar needs. The key points from the chapter are as follows:

- There are few, if any, mass markets left.
- Segmentation, as a concept, has developed as markets have become more sophisticated.
- If most consumers already own the core benefits of a product, the market must be segmented if success is to follow.
- Segments must be measurable, accessible, substantial and congruous.
- The profitability of a segment is calculated as the number of people in the segment multiplied by the premium they are willing to pay.
- The narrower the segment the fewer the customers, but the greater the satisfaction and the greater premium they are willing to pay.
- There are many ways to segment a market, in fact as many ways as there are groups with congruent needs.

- No single segmentation base is likely to be sufficient.
- The UK population is rapidly ageing due to low birthrate and greater longevity. This is affecting the size and nature of traditional segments, and also may mean that age is not a reliable segmentation base.
- The viability of a segment is a function of the size of the segment and the premium its members are willing to pay.
- Behavioural segmentation is direct and easy to measure.
- Industrial markets segment differently from consumer markets.
- The nested approach is often used in industrial market segmentation.
- Segmentation strategy can be concentrated, differentiated or undifferentiated.

Chapter review questions

1 How might a company segment the market for shoes?

2 Why do firms need to use more than one segmentation base?

3 What is the purpose of segmentation?

4 Why is age becoming less reliable as a segmentation base?

5 What is meant by the nested approach to segmentation?

6 When might a concentrated segmentation strategy be more effective than a niche strategy?

7 What type of company would pursue a niche strategy?

8 What are the main problems associated with psychological segmentation bases?

9 When should a firm *not* segment the market?

10 The bigger the segment, the less the product meets the customers' needs. Discuss.

Preview case study revisited
Alcohol-powered cars

Motor manufacturers were aware that they would need to adapt the product substantially, but realised that there would be spin-offs in terms of marketing their products elsewhere in the world – with an eye to the day when oil runs out, car makers know that (sooner or later) motorists will have to rely on biofuels, or give up their cars.

First, the motor manufacturers' engineers increased the compression ratio of the engines to take account of the higher 'octane' rating of alcohol. Alcohol can take a 15:1 compression ratio, but manufacturers only took the engines up to 10.5:1 initially since higher ratios would require much more expensive forged components.

Second, alcohol-powered cars preheat the intake air. This prevents ignition ping and gives more power under acceleration.

Third, the carburettors were recalibrated to give a 9:1 fuel-air mixture as opposed to petrol's 14:1 ratio. The main jets, idle circuits, power valves and (in some cases) the accelerator stroke also needed to be altered – in effect, virtually new carburettors needed to be developed.

Fourth, the valve seats needed to be hardened to compensate for the fact that alcohol does not contain the lubricating impurities that petrol does.

Fifth, the intake manifolds were heated to improve the evaporation of the alcohol in the carburettor.

Sixth, the fuel system components were bronzed to prevent corrosion. Alcohol tends to absorb water, so it is likely to be more corrosive than petrol.

Seventh, the ignition timing was advanced four to eight degrees and the distributor advance curve is adjusted. 'Hotter' spark plugs are used, and a high-intensity ignition coil is used.

Eighth, cold start systems needed to be fitted for use in temperatures below about 12 degrees centigrade. This may not be needed in the tropical north of the country, but was certainly necessary in the temperate south, and in the mountains where temperatures can fall below freezing.

All these adaptations meant that alcohol-fuelled cars became extremely popular – at one point they represented 85 per cent of new cars sold in Brazil. Unfortunately, in recent years the Brazilian government has had to reduce the tax incentives for the cars: alcohol is a less efficient fuel, so the extra cost of getting fewer miles per gallon had to be offset by tax breaks which the government has no longer been able to afford since the financial crisis of the 1990s. At first sight, this would seem to destroy the entire segment – but in fact the technology is not wasted since there is likely to be a future market for biofuelled cars.

Meeting the needs of a substantial segment may often require firms to go to considerable effort, as has been the case with motor manufacturers in the Brazilian market. In the long run, the world market will need these cars – and motor manufacturers are hoping that their research investment will pay off when other countries move to alcohol-fuelled vehicles. Meanwhile, the smell of half-burnt rum which pervades most Brazilian cities will be temporarily replaced by the smell of petrol fumes.

Case study
Continental Tyre AG

Tyres are often regarded as boring. Even people in the industry think so – after all, about the only time anyone thinks about their car tyres is when they go flat. Yet the tyre industry is remarkably complex: after all, there are over a thousand different tyre sizes currently in use in the UK, and as motor manufacturers seek new ways to improve performance, the bit of the car that joins it to the road is often seen as a key area for innovation. Continental turns over almost £7 thousand million a year – no small sum of money.

Continental Tyre is a German-based company which operates throughout the world. 75 per cent of the firm's business is in tyres, and while the company may not be as well known to the general public as Pirelli, Dunlop or Michelin, it has a very substantial share of the market in supplying to motor manufacturers. BMW, Volkswagen and Mercedes are big customers for Continental tyres, but Continental also supplies tyres to tractor manufacturers, truck builders, and bicycle manufacturers. Continental see the original-equipment market as not only profitable in its own right, but also as a way of encouraging car owners to fit Continental as replacements when the original tyres wear out or are damaged.

There are three key areas for success in the tyre industry: managing the supply chain, branding and customer segmentation. Tyres have to be sold through dealers because they have to be fitted – there is no DIY market for tyres. In order to meet the needs of distributors, OEMs and end users, Continental produces a wide range of tyres under several brand names. The two main brands are Continental (Conti for short) in the premium sector and Uniroyal in the quality sector. The company also produce economy and budget brands – Semperit is the firm's mid-range brand, acquired when Continental took over the Austrian company of that name in 1985. Continental even produces own-name brands, sold under the brand names of the fitting companies themselves. In all, Continental have 11 brands.

Because Continental have to work through dealers all the time, the firm carries out a lot of 'push' activity: incentive programmes, training programmes for tyre fitters, education about how to market tyres and move customers up the 'brand ladder' and fit Continental tyres rather than simply buy the cheapest available. Segmenting the dealers is also not easy – there are national dealers, regional dealers, car dealers, car fleet dealers, and so on. Also, of course, the OEM market divides into car manufacturers, agricultural machine manufacturers, truck manufacturers and even bicycle manufacturers. On a global level, the number of different segments the company is trying to serve is staggering.

Tyres are often seen as a distress purchase – people only buy them when they have to, because they are worn out or damaged. Continental would like to change that perception. Advertising aimed at car owners used the theme, 'Taking care of the one you love', using the strap line: '80 per cent of men have a secret love affair – with their car.' Whether or not this is true, the ads proved very successful.

Continental did not ignore women when planning the campaign. Forty per cent of tyres are bought by women, so the marketing people at Continental ran women-only focus groups to test the appeal of the advertising. The ads tested favourably with women, so the campaign ran.

Continental certainly have a number of challenges to meet. Balancing performance against cost is the least of their problems – ensuring that they understand the end users as well as the intermediaries is the key to dealing in a complex market. As UK head of marketing Antonio Betes says, 'I firmly don't agree that tyres are boring. Anything that costs as much as tyres is not boring.'

Case study questions

1 Why does Continental have so many brands?

2 What basis does Continental appear to be using for segmenting the market?

3 What type of motorist do you think would react favourably to Continental's advertising?

4 If tyres are a distress purchase, why do Michelin and Pirelli spend large amounts of money on supporting their brands?

5 Is Continental's segmentation policy realistic?

References

Bardacki, Ahmet, and Whitelock, Jeryl (2004) How ready are customers for mass customization? An exploratory investigation. *European Journal of Marketing*, 38(11/12): 11396–496.

Bonoma, Thomas V., and Shapiro, Benson P. (1984) Evaluating market segmentation approaches. *Industrial Marketing Management*, 13(4): 257–68.

Cardozo, Richard N. (1980) Situational segmentation of industrial markets. *European Journal of Marketing*, 14(5/6): 264–76.

Chesbrough, Henry W. (2003) Environmental influences upon firm entry into new sub-markets: evidence from the worldwide hard disk drive industry. *Research Policy*, 32: 659–78.

Day, George S. (1990) *Market-Driven Strategy: Process for Creating Value* (New York: The Free Press).

Dibb, Sally, and Simkin, Lyndon (2001) Market segmentation: diagnosing and treating the barriers. *Industrial Marketing Management*, 30(8): 609–25.

Duchessi, Peter, Schaninger, Charles M., and Nowak, Thomas (2004) Creating cluster-specific purchase profiles from point-of-sale scanner data and geodemographic clusters: improving category management at a major US grocery chain. *Journal of Consumer Behaviour*, 4(2): 97–117.

Evans, M.J. (1991) Domesday marketing? *Journal of Marketing Management*, 10(5): 409–31.

Gillespie, Kate, Jeannet, Jean-Pierre, and Hennessey, H. David (2004) *Global Marketing: An Interactive Approach*. (Boston, MA: Houghton Mifflin Company).

Hlavacek, James D., and Ames, B.C. (1986) Segmenting industrial and high-tech markets. *Journal of Business Strategy*, 7(2): 39–50.

Honkanen, Pirjo, Olsen, Svein Ottar, and Myrland, Oystein (2004) Preference-based segmentation: a study of meal preferences among Norwegian teenagers. *Journal of Consumer Behaviour*, 3(3): 235–50.

IIASA (International Institute for Applied Systems Analysis) (2002) *European Ageing Projections* (Vienna: IIASA).

Jamal, Ahmed (2003) Marketing in a multicultural world: the interplay of marketing, ethnicity and consumption. *European Journal of Marketing*, 37(11): 1599–620.

Kjeldgaard, Dannie, and Askegaard, Soren (2004) Consuming modernities: the global youth segment as a site of consumption. *Advances in Consumer Research*, 31(1): 104–5.

Kotler, Philip (2003) *Marketing Management* (Upper Saddle River, NJ: Prentice-Hall).

Larson, Jan (1991) A segment of one. *American Demographics*, (Dec): 6–17.

Malhotra, Naresh K. (1989) Segmenting hospitals for improved management strategy. *Journal of Health Care Marketing*, 9(3): 45–52.

Mathur, Anil, Moschis, George P., and Lee, Euehun (2003) Life events and brand preference changes. *Journal of Consumer Behaviour*, 3(2): 129–41.

Mattson, Melvin R., and Salehi-Sangari, Esmail (1993) Decision making in purchases of equipment and materials: a four-country comparison. *International Journal of Physical Distribution and Logistics Management*, 23(8): 16–30.

Peter, J. Paul, and Olson, Jerry C. (1994) *Understanding Consumer Behaviour* (Burr Ridge, IL: Irwin).

Rao, Chatrathi P., and Wang, Zhengyuan (1995) Evaluating alternative segmentation strategies in standard industrial markets. *European Journal of Marketing*, 29(2): 58–75.

Robertson, Thomas S., and Barich, Howard (1992) A successful approach to segmenting industrial markets. *Planning Review*, Nov–Dec: 4–48.

Sampson, P. (1992) People are people the world over: the case for psychological market segmentation. *Marketing and Research Today*, November: 236–45.

Schewe, Charkes D., and Meredith, Geoffrey (2004) Segmenting global markets by generational cohorts: determining motivations by age. *Journal of Consumer Behaviour*, 4(1): 51–63.

Schuster, Camille P., and Bodkin Charles D. (1987) Market segmentation practices of exporting companies. *Industrial Marketing Management*, 16(2): 95–102.

Simcock, Peter, Sudbury, Lynn, and Wright, Gillian (2006) Age, perceived risk, and satisfaction in consumer decision-making: a review and extension. *Journal of Marketing Management*, 22(3/4): 355–77.

Szmigin, Isabelle, and Carrigan, Marylyn (2001) Learning to love the older consumer. *Journal of Consumer Behaviour*, 1(1): 22–34.

Trocchia, Philip J., Beatty, Sharon E., and Hill, William H. (2006) A typology of motor vehicle consumers using motives for leasing versus financing. *Journal of Consumer Behaviour*, 5 (Jul–Aug): 304–16.

Yip, George S. (2003) *Total Global Strategy II*. (Upper Saddle River, NJ: Prentice Hall).

Chapter 18
Organizational buying behaviour

geographic distance, and even time zone differences are often more important (Pressey and Selassie 2003). Within the national culture is the corporate culture, sometimes defined as 'the way we do things round here'. Corporate culture encompasses the strategic vision of the organization, its ethical stance, and its attitudes towards suppliers among other things. In addition, many businesspeople act in accordance with their professional culture (Terpstra and David, 1991). Each of these will affect the way business is done.

Talking point

The expansion of the European Union in 2004 was hailed (rightly) as an historic event, reuniting Europe peacefully for the first time in its long and bloody history. For business, the expansion was expected to bring great rewards in terms of bigger markets and greater choice of suppliers.

Yet many firms still preferred to deal with countries thousands of miles away, where the technical standards are the same. So why not create closer links with these countries? Why did Britain, for example, join the EU and reject its former empire just at the time when transportation costs had fallen dramatically? Surely the wider range of climate, availability of raw materials, and greater diversity of the Commonwealth made it a better bet?

Or perhaps the Commonwealth countries (for the most part) are so poor that they have no choice but to sell to us anyway – and we need to ally ourselves with the rich rather than with the poor!

Organizational factors derive from corporate culture, as well as from strategic decisions made by senior management within the firm. Organizational policies, procedures, structure, systems of rewards, authority, status and communication systems will all affect the ways buyers relate to salespeople. Figure 18.3 shows the main categories of organizational influences on the buyers' behaviour.

Buying tasks differ greatly between firms, but may also differ significantly within firms. For example, the buying task for a supermarket clearly differs from that for a manufacturing company, since the supermarket intends to sell the vast majority of its purchases unchanged, whereas the manufacturer is largely concerned with sourcing components and raw materials. The supermarket has other, internal, variations in the buying task: buying canned goods will be totally different from buying fresh produce such as vegetables or fresh fish. Equally, the manufacturer will have a different approach when buying basic raw materials to when buying components, and yet another set of approaches when buying lubricating oil or business services or new factory premises. The different purchasing tasks affect the buyer's thinking and negotiating approach, so firms will usually have separate buyers for each type of buying task.

Structure of the organization falls into two categories: the formal structure is what shows on the organization chart, the informal structure is the network of personal relationships which dictates staff behaviour in most cases. The formal organization structure

Supermarkets source goods globally, but sell them on virtually unchanged.

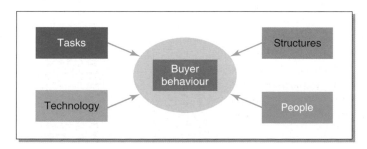

Figure 18.3

Organizational influences on buyer behaviour

determines such issues as the degree of centralization in purchasing decision-making, the degree to which buying decisions follow a formal procedure (i.e. how constrained by the rules the buyers are), and the degree of specialization in buying for different purposes or different departments in the organization.

The informal structure dictates such issues as rivalry between buyers, recognition by management, cooperation between buyers in maintaining each other's status in the eyes of the boss, and so forth. The maze of informal relationships can be extremely complex, especially for a salesperson observing it from the outside, is likely to be crucial in the success or failure of key-account selling. In the global context, the informal structure is subject to many cultural influences – the Oriental concern with gaining or losing face, for example, can be a crucial factor in doing business. The informal structure is also the major factor in determining who will be the most important influencers in the decision-making unit; some colleagues' opinions may be regarded as more trustworthy than others, for example.

The organization's technology base also affects the buyers' level of control over purchasing. For example, computer-controlled stock purchasing, particularly in a just-in-time purchasing environment, can limit the buyer's ability to negotiate deals and in many cases removes the buyer from the process altogether. Models for inventory control and price forecasting are also widely used by buyers, so that in many cases the negotiating process is virtually automated with little room for manoeuvre on the part of the buyer. If this is the case, the selling organization needs to go beyond the buyer to the other members of the DMU in order to change the rules or find creative ways round them. Technology-minded companies are likely to use electronic communications systems (e-mail being only one example) to a greater extent than other firms: research shows that technology-mediated communications have a positive, direct effect on future intentions to buy, but of course this is still affected considerably by factors of trust and commitment (McDonald and Smith 2004). E-commerce in business-to-business marketing relies on the following factors (Claycomb, Iyer and Germain 2005):

1 Compatibility with existing systems.
2 Cooperative norms with customers.
3 Lateral integration within the firm.
4 Technocratic specialisation.
5 Decentralization of information technology.

The characteristics of the people involved in the organization will determine the organization culture, but will in any event control the interpretation of the rules under which the purchasing department operates. At senior management level, the character of the organization is likely to be a function of the senior management, and in many cases the organization's founder will have set his or her personality firmly on the organization's culture. Virgin is clearly an offshoot of Richard Branson's personality, as The Body Shop is an offshoot of Anita Roddick's.

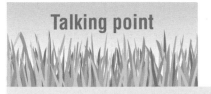
Talking point

We frequently hear about the global village, and about the convergence of cultures, and about a new world order in which we accept and understand each other's cultures. So why is it necessary to consider cultural issues when we are marketing products and services? Surely the goods themselves speak for themselves – does crude oil have a cultural value, or does a stamp mill have a cultural connotation?

Shouldn't buyers be prepared to accept and understand cultural differences? Otherwise how are we to do business? Or perhaps the buyers arrogantly believe that the sellers should adapt their approach to meet the buyers' culture – thus possibly missing out on getting the best deals for their organizations.

If we get clashes between corporate cultures within the same country, how much worse will the clashes be in globalized markets?

Classifying business customers

A business customer is one who is buying on behalf of an organization rather than buying for personal or family consumption. In everyday speech, we usually talk about organizations as the purchasers of goods, but of course this is not the case: business customers, in practice, are human beings who buy on behalf of organizations.

Organizations might be classified according to the types of buying and end use they have for the products. Table 18.1 shows the commonly accepted classifications.

Business and commercial organizations

Business and commercial organizations can be segmented as original-equipment manufacturers (OEMs), users and aftermarket customers. OEMs buy foundation, entering and facilitating goods including machinery and equipment used to make products, and products which are incorporated directly into the final product. For example, computer manufacturers may buy machine tools to make computer cases and also buy silicon chips from specialist producers: the chips are incorporated into the final product, but the same type of chip might be incorporated in computers from several different OEMs. The Intel Pentium chip is an example.

For OEM buyers, the key issue will be the quality of the products or services. Such buyers are usually operating to fairly exact specifications laid down by their own production

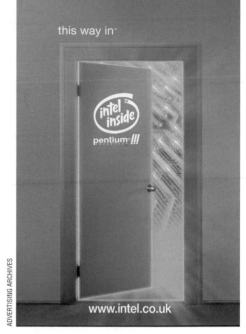

Intel chips are used by most computer manufacturers.

Table 18.1 Classification of buying organizations

Type of organization	Description
Business and commercial organizations	These organizations buy goods which are used to make other goods, and also those items that are consumed in the course of running the organization's business. These organizations buy foundation goods and services (goods used to make other products), facilitating goods and services (those which help an organization achieve its objectives) and entering goods and services (those which become part of another product).
Re-seller organizations	Re-sellers buy goods in order to sell them on to other organizations or to final consumers. Typically, re-sellers will be wholesalers or retailers, but they may also be agents for services, for example travel agents or webmasters who act as facilitators for other firms.
Governmental organizations	Governments buy everything from paper clips to submarines through their various departments. Because national and local government departments operate under specific rules which are often rigid, negotiations can be difficult to conduct: buyers are often severely constrained in what they can do. Contracts are often put out to tender, with the lowest bidder being awarded the contract.
Institutional organizations	Institutional organizations include charities, educational establishments, hospitals and other organizations that do not fit into the business, re-seller or government categories. These organizations may be in the market for almost any kind of product, but they are used to achieve institutional goals which probably do not include profit.

2001 Electronic Components Ltd is an electronic components supplier based in Stevenage, Hertfordshire. The company supplies all types of components direct to industry, and acts as a wholesaler for many of the world's leading manufacturers. For this small company in a specialized market, reaching the decision-makers is a real problem – so the company uses press releases as an effective tool for reaching users.

Using press releases is, of course, cheaper than advertising since the journals print the releases free, as news. Credibility is greater, and the target audience are more likely to read the releases. The company has a sophisticated website which potential buyers are directed to, and offers high-speed online ordering. Everything is geared to making it easy for buyers to buy – but it is the press releases which bring in the buyers in the first place!

engineers and designers: it is unlikely that the supplying firm will be able to do very much to have the specification changed, except by approaching the designers during the design process. This means that introducing a new product to an OEM will be a lengthy process, since the supplying company will need to establish a long-term relationship with the customer in order to become involved at the design stage for new products.

User customers buy products which are used up within the organization, either as components in their own equipment or to make the equipment perform properly, for example lubricating oils or cleaning products. These products are not re-sold, but may be bought in considerable quantities. Many of these user products are services – accountancy or legal services, cleaning services, and maintenance or building services are all contained within the firm and not resold.

Aftermarket customers are those involved in the maintaining, repairing and overhauling (**MRO**) of products after they have been sold. For example, central heating systems are likely to be maintained by independent contractors rather than the original manufacturers or installers. The reason for this is that maintenance requires an investment in expensive testing equipment and different training from that required for installation or manufacture. These contractors buy the components, supplies and services they need from the most convenient supplier.

The classification split between **OEM**, users and aftermarket customers is only relevant to the supplier. OEMs can also be user customers for some suppliers. For example, a plastic moulding company may sell components to an OEM and plastic tools to a user as well as plastic replacement parts to an aftermarket organization: in some cases these may even be the same organization. Buying motivations for each type of purchase are clearly very different, and the supplying firm is likely to be dealing with different buyers for each category of product, if the customer company is a large one.

In Figure 18.4, the same suppliers sometimes provide goods or services for several firms in the supply chain. In some cases there will be considerable crossover between firms.

Re-seller organizations

The majority of manufactured goods are sold through **re-seller organizations** such as retailers and wholesalers. Intermediaries provide useful services such as bulk breaking, assortment of goods, and accumulation of associated product types: due to increased efficiencies resulting from these services, intermediaries tend to reduce overall prices for the final consumer. Cutting out the middle man, rather than reducing prices, usually reduces

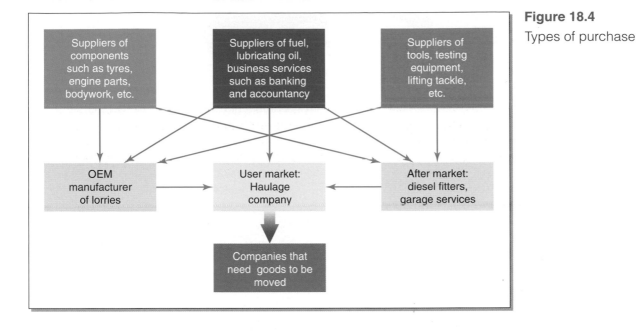

Figure 18.4
Types of purchase

efficiency and tends to increase prices: if this were not so, intermediaries would be unable to justify their existence and firms would simply bypass them.

Re-seller organizations are driven almost entirely by their customers. This means that they will only buy products which they believe will sell easily: there is therefore a premium on employing buyers who have a clear understanding of customer needs. Unlike the OEM buyers, there is little need for re-sellers to understand the technical aspects of the products they buy – they merely need to feel confident that the ultimate consumers will want the products.

Re-seller organizations carry out the following basic functions:

1 Negotiations with suppliers.
2 Promotional activities such as advertising, sales promotion, providing a salesforce, etc.
3 Warehousing, storage and product handling.
4 Transportation of local and (occasionally) long-distance shipments.
5 Inventory control.
6 Credit checking and credit control.
7 Pricing and collection of price information, particularly about competitors.
8 Collection of market information about consumers and competitors.

For manufacturers, this places a premium on establishing close long-term relationships with resellers. Shared information, as part of an integrated channel management strategy, becomes crucial to forward planning.

Government organizations

Government and quasi-government organizations are major buyers of almost everything. In some markets, the government is heavily involved in industry. For instance, all insurance in India is a government monopoly and the oil industry in Mexico is controlled by PEMEX, a quasi-government entity. Governments are thought to be the largest category of market in the world, if all levels of government are included in the equation (see Figure 18.5). The structure of government varies from one country to another: for example, in

B&W Speakers is a company well-known to hi-fi enthusiasts. The company produces state-of-the-art loudspeakers which are sold worldwide: technical excellence is maintained by its research and development facility in the south of England.

The challenge for B&W is maintaining close relationships with manufacturers, retailers and the hi-fi media in the 70 countries in which it operates. The company is relatively small, and operates in a specialist area where maintaining contact by the traditional method of sending sales representatives to customers regularly is difficult or impossible.

B&W have therefore developed a sophisticated extranet which enables customers and others to log onto a special website. Each customer has a password, so the system can offer each one a personalized greeting and can also record the interactions for marketing research purposes. Distributors have access to all areas of the extranet, but retailers have less access and the media have their own section on the site. This helps to maintain confidentiality and protect corporate secrets. The extranet is multilingual so that each customer, no matter what their native language, is able to access information much more easily than would be the case by using (for example) the telephone.

The result of using the extranet is increased service levels for all parties, and enhanced communication with all relevant stakeholders. The extranet offers added value for distributors and retailers because the services provided are relevant to them and they have access to all relevant information instantly. B&W benefit because they have much more accurate and timely information about their distributors and retailers, and also have a more loyal group of customers.

Figure 18.5

Tiers of government and their typical purchases

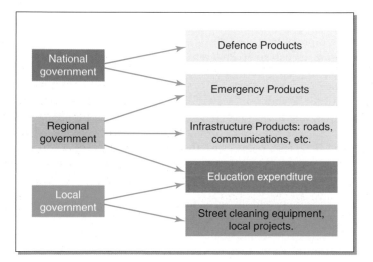

Spain there is the national government based in Madrid, the regional governments (e.g. the Junta de Andalucia), the provincial governments (e.g. Provincia de Granada) and the local town halls (e.g. Ayuntamiento de Ugijar). Sometimes these local town halls group together to form an alliance which carries out mutually beneficial activities such as tourism marketing or funding a local swimming pool, but frequently they act independently of one another within the frameworks of their own jurisdictions.

Because of the strict rules under which most government organizations operate, special measures are often needed to negotiate deals. In particular, government organizations almost always put contracts out for tender, so that firms are asked to bid for contracts. The contract is usually offered to the lowest bidder, unless there are overwhelming reasons to do otherwise. From a supplier's viewpoint, this is likely to be problematic, since the lowest price is likely to be the least profitable price, so selling firms will often try to circumvent the process by ensuring that they become involved before the tender is finalized. In this way it may be possible to ensure that the tender is drawn up in a way that favours the proactive firm over its competitors (for example by including features which competitors cannot offer) thus ensuring that competitors either do not bid at all, or bid at too high a price.

In some cases, governments need to purchase items which are not available to the general public or to other businesses. Military hardware is an obvious example: clearly ordinary businesses are not allowed to buy submarines or nuclear bombers. On a more subtle level, goods such as handguns are not permitted for private organizations in the UK, but can be sold to the Army or the police force. Some types of computer software are only appropriate for use by the tax authorities, and academic research is paid for largely by the government in the UK. From a marketing viewpoint, these specialist markets present an interesting challenge, since in some cases the products need to be tailored to a specific government or a specific government department. This may mean that there is considerable scope for negotiation, but since the contract might still have to go out to tender, the company may find that it has spent a lot of time developing a specification for a contract which is then awarded to another firm.

In some circumstances, governments may issue a 'cost-plus' contract, in which the organization is given a specific task to carry out and charges according to the cost of the contract plus an agreed profit margin. In the early days of space research this type of contract was common, since it was impossible to predict what the costs might be when dealing with an unknown set of circumstances. More recently these contracts have fallen into disrepute since they reward inefficiency and waste.

Buyer behaviour in practice
The European Union

The European Union is intended to provide a 'level playing field' for companies within its borders. This has extended to tendering for government (and even local government) buying. In the past, orders for such items as desks, computers, office supplies and so forth were commonly given to local companies within the government's own country. This was seen as a way of supporting local firms, reducing imports, and securing jobs. Under EU rules, though, this type of selective purchasing is anti-competitive and is now banned.

Currently, any government organization within the EU must offer all contracts for tender throughout the EU, if the contract is above a specific value (currently around £100,000 for services and supplies, and £4m for works). Contracts are advertised in the *Journal of the European Communities,* and also online at http://ted.publications.eu.int/. Local business organizations such as Chambers of Commerce also monitor tenders and pass them on to interested parties.

The end result of this process is that end users (the taxpayers, in the last analysis) get better value for money, and the most efficient companies have wider opportunities to expand their businesses.

Firms which supply drilling equipment may find a lucrative market among Third World charities.

Institutional organizations

Institutions include charities, universities, hospital trusts and non-profit organizations of all types, schools, and so forth. In some cases these are government-owned but independent for purposes of purchasing and supply (for example, secondary schools), in other cases they are totally independent (for example, registered charities). The traditional view of these organizations is that they are chronically under-funded and therefore do not represent a particularly wealthy market, but in practice the organizations actually have a very substantial aggregate spending power.

Because budgets are almost always very tight, the marketing organization may need to be creative in helping the institution to raise the money to buy its products. For example, a firm which produces drilling equipment may find that it has a substantial market at Oxfam, since Oxfam drills wells in many arid regions of the Third World. Oxfam relies on public generosity to raise the money to buy the equipment, so the manufacturer may find it necessary to part-fund or even manage a fundraising campaign in order to make the sale.

Suppliers are often asked to contribute to charities, in cash or in products. This may not always be possible, since the supplier's only market might be the charities, but in some cases firms may find it worthwhile to supply free products to charities in order to gain PR value, or sometimes in order to open the door to lucrative deals with other organizations. For example, a Third World charity might be prepared to field-test equipment which could then be sold to a government department in the same country.

Talking point

We are often told that marketing is about managing the exchange process, yet government departments and many institutions seem to lay down the ground rules from the start. Marketers have to play by the buyer's rules to be in the game at all – so how can they possibly be managing the process? Pushed from one set of constraints to the next, it would seem that the average marketer is just a pawn in the buyers' hands!

Yet maybe that is how it should be, if customers are at the centre of everything we do. Not to mention that the management process itself could be construed as a clearing house for pressures rather than as a directive force – in a sense, no manager is actually in control, so why should marketers be any different?

Figure 18.6

Factors in institutional marketing

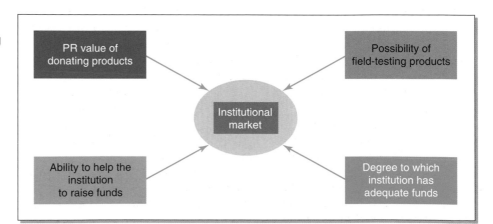

Buyers' techniques

Buyers use a wide variety of techniques according to the buying situation they are faced with (Figure 18.7). The buying situations are generally divided into three types:

1 **Straight re-buy** – Most organizational buying is routine: for example, a car manufacturer needs to buy much the same number of wheel nuts each month. A straight re-buy is a situation where the buyer is buying the same product in very much the same quantities from the same supplier. In these circumstances the buyer needs no new information, and does not need to engage in much negotiation either. Prudent buyers may occasionally look at other possible sources of components in order to ensure that no new technology is available or that other suppliers are not able to supply the same components more cheaply, but in general the order placement is automatic. In some cases the whole process is automated through an electronic data interchange (EDI) link with a supplier, or there may be an automatic buying procedure facilitated through the Internet without any human involvement. If the product is of minor importance, or represents a low commitment in terms of finance or risk, the buyer will probably not undertake any information search and will simply order the goods. This is called 'causal purchasing', because it results automatically from a cause such as low stock level. For example, a buyer for a large engineering firm probably spends very little time deciding on brands of paper for the photocopier. On the other hand, buying copper cable might be a routine purchase, but the buyer might monitor the market for alternatives occasionally. Such buying is called 'routine low-priority buying' because it has a lower priority than would be the case if an entirely new situation were being faced. The company is unlikely to get into serious trouble if it pays 10 per cent more than it should for cable, for example.

2 **Modified re-buy** – In this situation, the buyer re-evaluates the habitual buying patterns of the firm with a view to changing them in some way. The quantities ordered, or the specification of the components, may be changed. Even the supplier may be changed. Sometimes these changes come about because the buyer has become aware of a better alternative than the one currently employed (perhaps through environmental scanning), or sometimes the changes come about because competing suppliers succeed in offering something new. Internal forces (increases or decreases in demand for components) might trigger a renegotiation with suppliers or a search for new suppliers. In such circumstances the buyer is faced with a limited problem-solving scenario in which he or she will need to carry out some negotiation with existing or new suppliers, and will probably need to seek out new information as well. The buyer may well require potential suppliers to bid against each other for the business; the drawback of this approach is that it often results in damaging a well-established relationship with existing suppliers.

3 **New task** – This type of buying situation comes about when the task is perceived as being entirely new. Past experience is therefore no guide, and present suppliers may not be able to help either. Thus the buyer is faced with a complex decision process. Judgemental new task situations are those in which the buyer must deal with technical complexities of the product, complex evaluation of alternatives, and negotiating with new suppliers. Strategic new task situations are those in which the final decision is of strategic importance to the firm – for example, a bank looking for software for online banking will be investing (potentially) hundreds of thousands of pounds in retraining staff, and in transferring existing records, not to mention the risks of buying software which lacks the necessary security features or which fails under high demand. In these circumstances, long-range planning at director level drives the buying process, and the relationship with the suppliers is likely to be both long term and close.

Figure 18.7

Trade-offs in type of buying situation

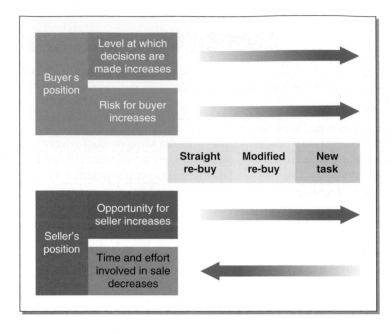

From the viewpoint of the business marketer, the main chance of winning new customers will come in the new-task situation. The risks for buyers involved in switching suppliers are often too great unless there is a very real and clear advantage in doing so: such an advantage is likely to be difficult to prove in practice. In the new task situation, potential suppliers may well find themselves screened out early in the process, and will then find it almost impossible to be reconsidered later.

The buy-grid framework

Organizational buying can be seen as a series of decisions, each of which leads to a further problem about which a decision must be made (Cardozo 1983). From the viewpoint of the supplying firm, it would certainly be valuable to be able to diagnose problems by examining the sequence of decisions. The difficulty here is that the decision sequence is probably not known to the marketer unless the firms involved already have a close relationship. If the sequence can be known, marketers can identify the stage at which the firm is currently making decisions, and can tailor the approach accordingly.

The industrial buying process can be mapped against a grid, as shown in Figure 18.8.

The most complex buying situations occur in the upper-left portion of the framework and involve the largest number of decision-makers and buying influences. This is because new tasks require the greatest amount of effort in seeking information and formulating appropriate solutions, but also will require the greatest involvement of individuals at all levels of the organization. The more people who are involved, the more complex the decision process because each individual will have a personal agenda.

The buy-grid framework has been widely criticized, however. Like most models it tends to oversimplify the case. As in consumer decision-making, the sequence may not be as clear-cut and events may take place in a different order in certain circumstances. For example, a buying firm may not be aware that it has a problem in a particular area until a supplier approaches the firm with a solution, thus cutting out several stages of the process: the firm may well recognize the need and the problem, but will probably not need to acquire proposals and select a supplier since the supplier is already offering a solution. Second, suppliers go to great lengths to differentiate themselves from competitors as effectively as

Figure 18.8

The buy-grid framework

Stage	Buying situations		
	New task	Modified re-buy	Straight re-buy
Anticipation or recognition of a problem (need) and a general solution			
Determination of characteristics and quantity of needed item			
Description of characteristics and quantity of needed item			
Search for and qualification of potential sources			
Acquisition and analysis of proposals			
Evaluation of proposals and selection of supplier(s)			
Selection of an order routine			
Performance feedback and evaluation			

Source: From the Marketing Science Institute Series, *Industrial Buying and Creative Marketing*, by Patrick J. Robinson, Charles W. Faris, and Yoram Wind. Copyright 1967 by Allyn and Bacon, Inc. Boston.

they can, so that the buyer is unlikely to have any other potential suppliers of the exact product on offer. Third, the model assumes a rational approach to purchasing which is often simply not there. Finally, the boundaries between new task, modified re-buy and straight re-buy are by no means clear-cut.

Because buyers are influenced by both rational and emotional considerations, the potential supplier needs to be aware of the personal agendas of each member of the decision-making unit. Even at a rational level, each member of the DMU will apply different criteria for judging which suppliers should be included and which excluded (Kelly and Coaker 1976): the finance director might emphasize low prices, whereas the chief designer might be concerned with product quality and the production engineer with reliable delivery. The buyer might be concerned with the relationship with the supplier's sales people. In many cases, brand equity is less important than issues of price and delivery (Bendixen, Bukasa and Abratt 2004). At the personal, emotional level, office politics, rivalries, jockeying for promotion, liking or disliking the salesperson and many other factors will affect different members of the DMU in different ways.

In the case of key-account management, this problem of dealing with different members of the DMU is often overcome by taking a team approach to the sale. While the **key-account manager** handles the initial contact and the management of the process, other specialists are brought in to deal with financial aspects, technical aspects, and so forth. In this way each member of the DMU is speaking to someone with whom he or she has a common language and a common understanding of the conceptual environment within which each specialty operates. In some cases the number of people working on the account can become large: when IBM were dealing with Lloyd's Bank (one of the Big Four UK banks) they had over 100 people working on the account, and set up a special branch office in the Canary Wharf area to be near Lloyd's head office.

There are three types of business net (Moller and Svahn 2004):

1 *Stable* – These are networks which are perhaps still growing, but they are following a predictable course.

2 *Established* – These networks are fixed and relatively unchanging: the rules are known by the members.

3 *Emerging* – These networks are still growing and changing.

The internal culture of the firm (and the external culture, in an international context) affects the nature of each of these network types.

Managing the network means identifying the key network, developing a strategy for managing the individuals who operate within the network and developing methods at the operational level for managing those actors (Ojasalo 2004). The responsibility for managing the actors is often divided between the members of the selling team.

Value analysis

Value analysis is a method of evaluating components, raw materials and even manufacturing processes in order to determine ways of cutting costs or improving finished products. 'Value-in-use' is defined as a product's economic value to the user relative to a specific alternative in a particular application (Kijewski and Yoon 1990). Value-in-use is the price that would equate the overall costs and benefits of using one product rather than using another.

For example, consider long-life light bulbs. These bulbs are usually between five and ten times as expensive as ordinary tungsten-filament bulbs to buy, but last five times as long and use only 20 per cent of the electricity. For a domestic consumer, this represents a considerable saving, more than enough to cover the initial outlay for the bulbs, but for a business customer the saving is even greater, since the cost of paying someone to replace blown light bulbs is significant. Assuming the life of a tungsten-filament bulb as being 1000 hours on average, compared with 5000 hours for a long-life bulb, the calculation would run as shown in Figure 18.9.

Using this calculation, the company can make an immediate saving of just under £1400 a year by switching to long-life bulbs. In fact, the capital cost of changing all the bulbs in the building would be recovered in the first year, although in practice the firm would probably only replace the tungsten-filament bulbs as they fail in use: in this way the labour cost of replacing the bulbs would be no higher than normal.

Because some buyers do use this type of calculation to assess alternative solutions to existing problems, a good salesperson will be prepared with the full arguments in favour of

Figure 18.9

Long-life bulb vs. tungsten-filament bulb

1. Annual cost of existing product:	
250 replacement light bulbs × 45p	£112.50
Cost of electricity: @ 6.7p per kilowatt × 60 watts × 150 bulbs × 10 hrs per day × 250 days a year:	£1507.50
Cost of replacing bulbs assuming 10 minutes per bulb @ £10 per hour:	£416.00
TOTAL COST PER ANNUM:	**£2036.00**
2. Cost of using long-life bulbs:	
50 replacement bulbs per annum × £3 =	£277.00
Cost of electricity @ 6.7p per kilowatt × 11 watts × 150 bulbs × 2500 hrs a year =	£277.00
Cost of replacing bulbs assuming 10 minutes per bulb @ £10 per hour =	£83.20
TOTAL COST PER ANNUM:	**£637.20**

the new solution, including all the relevant factors which make the product more attractive. On the other side of the coin, astute purchasers will involve potential suppliers in the discussions and in the value analysis process (Dowst and Raia 1990).

Evaluating supplier capability

Purchasers also need to assess the capability of potential suppliers to continue to supply successfully. This is a combination of assessing financial stability, technical expertise, reliability, quality assurance processes, and production capacity. In simple terms, the purchasing company is trying to ensure that the potential supplier will be in a position to keep the promises it makes. Business customers can gain competitive advantage from tracking the performance of suppliers because they are better able to manage the supply chain (Bharadwaj 2004).

Table 18.2 illustrates some of the ways in which buyers can assess potential suppliers.

These methods rely (in most cases) on judgement on the part of the purchaser, who may not in fact have the necessary expertise to understand what the supplier's capability really is.

Talking point

The methods of assessment shown in Table 18.2 all rely on some kind of judgement on the part of the buyer. Even the financial figures filed at the company record office require interpretation – and may even have been 'massaged' to make the company look more financially viable than it actually is.

So why bother with what is, after all, a somewhat time-consuming exercise? Presumably a rogue supplier would have little difficulty in pulling the wool over the eyes of a buyer who probably lacks the engineering training to understand what is in front of him or her. On the other hand, an honest supplier would probably provide the 'warts and all' picture that might well lose the contract. Maybe buyers would be better advised to go for the supplier who looks the worst – at least we know they are being honest with us!

Table 18.2 Assessing suppliers

Attribute	Assessment method
Technical capability	Visit the supplier to examine production equipment, inspect quality control procedures, and meet the engineering staff.
Managerial capability	Discuss systems for controlling processes, meet the managerial staff and become involved in planning and scheduling supplies.
Financial stability	Check the accounts filed at Companies House or other public record office, run a credit check, examine annual reports if any.
Capacity to deliver	Ascertain the status of other customers of the supplier – would any of these take priority? Assess the production capacity of the supplier, warehouse stocks of the product, reputation in the industry.

Evaluating supplier performance

Even after the contract is awarded, the purchasing company will probably re-examine the supplier's performance periodically. In some cases, suppliers have been known to relax and reduce their service level once the contract is awarded, and of course the circumstances of the buying organization are likely to change over time. If the relationship with the supplier is to continue, then (like all other human relationships) it must adapt to changing circumstances.

The basic evaluation methods are as outlined in Table 18.3.

All of these methods involve some degree of subjectivity: in other words each method requires buyers to make judgements about the supplier. Expressing the evaluations numerically makes the method appear more credible, but if the basic assumptions are incorrect, no amount of calculation will generate the right answer. Those involved in evaluation exercises of this nature should be aware that the evaluation exercise itself should be evaluated periodically, and the (usually subjective) criteria used by the various individuals involved need to be checked.

Talking point

Much of the emphasis in the preceding sections has been on the purchaser's evaluation of suppliers. But what about the other way round? Customers are not always plaster saints – some are late payers, some impose unreasonable restrictions, some reject supplies for the flimsiest of reasons, and some are just plain unpleasant to deal with.

So should suppliers have their own systems for assessing purchasers? Should we just grovel at the feet of any organization willing to buy our goods – or should we stand up and be counted? After all, without supplies no company can survive – so presumably we are equally important to one another.

Maybe this is really the purpose of segmenting our markets – and what is really meant by segmentation.

In fact, suppliers tend to adapt more often than do purchasers when there is an ongoing relationship (Brennan, Turnbull and Wilson 2003). This is due to the relative power each has (buyers being more powerful in most circumstances), and managerial preferences. Suppliers which are market-orientated tend to develop a greater customer intimacy, which also may drive suppliers to change (Tuominen, Rajala and Moller 2004). Buyers which are

Table 18.3 Evaluation approaches

Approach	Explanation
Categorical plan	Each department having contact with the supplier is asked to provide a regular rating of suppliers against a list of salient performance factors. This method is extremely subjective, but is easy to administer.
Weighted-point plan	Performance factors are graded according to their importance to the organization: for example, delivery reliability might be more important for some organizations than for others. The supplier's total rating can be calculated and the supplier's offering can be adjusted if necessary to meet the purchasing organization's needs.
Cost-ratio plan	Here the buying organization evaluates quality, delivery and service in terms of what each one costs. Good performance is assigned a negative score, i.e. the costs of purchase are reduced by good performance: poor performance is assigned a positive score, meaning that the costs are deemed to be greater when dealing with a poor performer.

themselves market-orientated tend to become more loyal to their suppliers (Jose Sanzo *et al.* 2003). Having said that, suppliers do sometimes end unprofitable relationships: many B2B relationships are unprofitable, and often companies lack the skills to make relationships profitable, so they simply end them (Helm, Rolfes and Gunther 2006).

Summary

Buyers have a large number of influences on their decision-making. At the very least, buyers have their own personal agendas within the companies they work for: in the broader context, a wide range of political, environmental and technological issues will affect their decision-making. The end result is likely to be a combination of experience, careful calculation, and gut feeling.

The key points from this chapter are as follows:

- Buyers are subject to many pressures other than the simple commercial ones: emotions, organizational influence, politics, and internal structures are also important factors.
- The decision-making unit (DMU) or buying centre is the group of people who will make the buying decision. Roles and composition of DMUs vary widely.
- Business and commercial organizations are likely to be swayed most by past experience with a vendor, product characteristics and quality.

- Re-sellers are driven by their customers.
- Government markets are large, and almost always use a tendering system.
- Institutional markets may need special techniques to help them afford to buy the products.
- Markets can be divided into those buyers who buy products designed to make other products or who will incorporate the purchase into their own products (original equipment manufacturers); those who consume the product in the course of running their businesses (user markets) or those who serve the aftermarket.
- A purchase may be a straight re-buy, a modified re-buy or a new task. These are given in order of increasing complexity, and do not have discrete boundaries.
- A team approach to buying usually dictates a team approach to selling.

Chapter review questions

1 How would you expect a government department to go about buying a new computer system?

2 How might internal politics affect a buyer's behaviour?

3 What factors might be prominent in the buying decision for cleaning materials?

4 What factors might a supplier take into account when evaluating a purchasing company?

5 How might the directors of a company go about setting standards for evaluating suppliers? What objective criteria are available?

6 What are the main problems with evaluating supplier performance?

7 How should a seller approach a government department?

8 What are the main differences between marketing to commercial organizations and marketing to charities?

9 How might a seller find out who the influencers are in the DMU?

10 How might a seller act to reduce the risk for the buyer?

Preview case study revisited
CMS Webview

Given the very small number of potential customers worldwide, CMS Webview needs to exercise considerable caution in the way it approaches its market. Buying decisions are made by a large number of individuals in most of these organizations, and the order values are high – committing to the right supplier is crucial for stock markets, since a mistake in the software could damage the reliability of the system and hence the validity of the market.

CMS Webview is therefore doing the right thing by opening its Chicago office, since it is on hand to provide a reassuring back-up service in the event of any failure in the system. In practical terms, of course, software suppliers can be based anywhere in the world, and can carry out maintenance and even training via the Internet or by secure remote servers, but in practice customers like to know that there is a human presence available if needed.

However, this does create some potential problems. Should the company have an office near every one of its customers? In the future, would this mean having 100 offices to serve 150 customers? In practice the situation is not quite that bad, since most of the quote vendors will be located near the exchanges they serve. The probability is that locating an office near each of the world's major exchanges (Chicago, New York, London, Tokyo and possibly Frankfurt) would be adequate.

Perhaps the biggest threat to the company would come from its larger rivals. CMS Webview does not have deep enough pockets to fight off a determined campaign by a major company, although a takeover bid is more likely than a competitive war. All in all, CMS Webview are providing an efficient and cost-effective service, and have managed to acquire some prestigious customers who are unlikely to allow bad things to happen to their computer wizards – after all, a failure of CMS might be a failure of the exchange.

Case study
Aircraft carriers

In January 2003 the UK Government announced that the £2.8 billion contract to build two new aircraft carriers for the Royal Navy would be split between British company BAE Systems and Thales, its French arch-rival. When maintenance work and upgrades are considered, the deal is worth approximately £9.2 billion over the lifetime of the vessels.

Celebrations were, however, somewhat muted at BAE. The company will be getting two-thirds of the business, but will (under the terms of the deal) have to build the ships to Thales' designs. In other words, BAE are taking the lion's share of the risk, since they will be responsible for any cost overruns and design corrections, but will not have the power to vary the designs. Even though the UK taxpayer will pick up 10 per cent of cost overruns, this still leaves BAE vulnerable in some respects. The situation is worsened by the fact that the companies who were involved in the bidding process were told that the outcome would be a 'winner takes all' contract. On the other hand, BAE may be lucky to have been offered anything at all. In December

2002 the company's shares dropped dramatically after it announced cost overruns on other Ministry of Defence deals, then on 15 January Geoff Hoon, the Defence Secretary, announced that he thought BAE was 'no longer

THALES UK

British'. Then, as late as 21 January, the national organizer of the Transport and General Worker's Union, Jack Dromey, revealed that senior civil servants were recommending that the contract should be awarded to Thales in its entirety.

Final details need to be worked out, and it is fairly certain that BAE will be pressing for a better deal on the overruns, since the company is already in dispute with the Ministry of Defence about cost overruns of up to £1 billion on the Nimrod aircraft and Astute submarine deals. Industry reaction to the deal was one of astonishment – one senior defence executive said, 'Thales won this on design and price, but BAE got the prime contractor role because of politics.'

The political issues are by no means simple. Under European Union rules, contractors throughout the EU must be given the opportunity to bid on government contracts within any of the member states – in other words, national governments are not allowed to play favourites by awarding contracts to their own suppliers. The problem is that this law is more honoured in the breach than in the observance – although Thales have apparently come in with a lower price and a better design, it would be impossible for a UK government to award the contract entirely to the French, knowing that there is no possibility of the French allowing British companies to compete on an equal footing in France.

Defence Secretary Geoff Hoon dismissed such allegations as being 'the kind of anti-European, anti-French rhetoric that's come to characterise the modern Conservative party . . . It's a disgrace.' Meanwhile Lord Bach, the procurement minister, and Sir Robert Walmsley, Chief of Defence Procurement, were examining the extent to which the taxpayer would carry the risk in terms of cost overruns. Government policy has been to move these risks away from the taxpayer and towards the contractor, but of course the higher the risk the contractor is expected to take, the higher the overall cost of the contract, so the Government will almost certainly need to compromise.

City analysts believe that the contract represents a Pyrrhic victory for BAE. Although the contract will contribute £30 million to annual profits, this is a relatively small amount

of money – the total contract only represents 2 per cent of sales for BAE. In exchange for this, the company has given Thales a stronger foothold in the UK, building on its acquisitions of defence companies such as Racal, Pilkington Optronics and Shorts Missile Systems. Some City analysts believe that BAE would have been better off if the company had lost the prime contract to Thales and had instead concentrated on low-risk subcontracting work at its shipyards.

Meanwhile, the Royal Navy eagerly awaits delivery of the ships. Captain Simon Williams, Assistant Director of Strategy at the naval staff, says that the current carrier fleet is designed primarily for protecting the Navy from attacks while at sea. The new carriers will have the capability to attack shore installations. 'If you put one of these carriers in international waters off another country it becomes a very flexible tool and it focuses the mind of the people we are trying to influence,' he said. The ships will be equipped with the new F-35 fighters, the replacement for the Harrier Jumpjet, now nearing the end of its useful service life.

Whatever the outcome, the Unions are pleased. Bill Morris, General Secretary of the Transport and General Workers' Union, said, 'I believe our quality British workforce will deliver a quality British product. The challenge is now for BAE Systems to deliver on time and on budget.'

Case study questions

1 How has the political environment affected the purchasing process?

2 Who were the influencers, deciders, buyers, gatekeepers and users in the DMU?

3 What effect does the UK Government's previous experience of the suppliers have?

4 If the potential profits on the deal are so low, why would BAE be interested in bidding for the contract?

5 What effects might the deal have on the long-term relationship between BAE and Thales?

References

Bendixen, Mike, Bukasa, Kalala A., and Abratt, Russell A. (2004) Brand equity in the business to business market. *Industrial Marketing Management*, 33(5), July: 371–80.

Bharadwaj, Neeraj (2004) Investigating the decision criteria used in electronic components procurement. *Industrial Marketing Management*, 33(4): 317–23.

Brennan, Ross D., Turnbull, Peter W., and Wilson, David T. (2003) Dyadic adaptation in business-to-business markets. *European Journal of Marketing*, 37(11): 1636–65.

Cardozo, Richard N. (1983) Modelling organisational buying as a sequence of decisions. *Industrial Marketing Management*, 12 (Feb): 75.

Claycomb, Cindy, Iyer, Karthik, and Germain, Richard (2005) Predicting the level of B2B e-commerce in industrial organisations. *Industrial Marketing Management*, 34(3): 221–34.

Dowst, S., and Raia, E. (1990) Teaming up for the 90s. *Purchasing*, 108 (Feb): 54–9.

Hawes, J.M., and Barnhouse, S.H. (1987) How purchasing agents handle personal risk. *Industrial Marketing Management*, 16 (November): 287–93.

Helm, Sabrina, Rolfes, Ludger, and Gunther, Berndt (2006) Suppliers' willingness to end unprofitable customer relationships. *European Journal of Marketing*, 40(3/4): 366–83.

Jose Sanzo, Maria, Leticia Santos, Maria, Vasquez, Rodolfo, and Alvarez, Luis I. (2003) The role of market orientation in business dyadic relationships: testing an integrator model. *Journal of Marketing Management*, 19: 73–107.

Kelly, P., and Coaker, J.W. (1976) Can we generalise about choice criteria for industrial purchasing decisions? *Marketing 1776–1976 and Beyond*, ed. K.L. Bernhardt (Chicago, IL: American Marketing Association): 330–3.

Kijewski, V., and Yoon, E. (1990) Market-based pricing: beyond price-performance curves. *Industrial Marketing Management*, 19 (Feb): 11–19.

Loudon, David L., and Della Bilta, Albert J. (1993) *Consumer Behaviour: Concepts and Applications* (New York: McGraw Hill).

McDonald, Jason B., and Smith, Kirk The effects of technology-mediated communication on industrial buyer behaviour. *Industrial Marketing Management*, 33(2): 107–16.

Moller, Kristian, and Svahn, Senja (2004) Crossing east-west boundaries: knowledge sharing in intercultural business networks. *Industrial Marketing Management*, 33(3), April: 219–28.

Ojasalo, Jukka (2004) Key network management. *Industrial Marketing Management*, 33(3): 195–205.

Pressey, Andrew D., and Selassie, Habte G. (2003) Are cultural differences over-rated? Examining the influence of national culture on international buyer–seller relationships. *Journal of Consumer Behaviour*, 2(4): 354–68.

Ronchetto, John R., Jr., Hutt, Michael D., and Reingen, Peter H. (1989) Embedded influence patterns in organizational buying systems. *Journal of Marketing*, 53(4): 51–62.

Terpstra, Vern, and David, Kenneth (1991) *The Cultural Environment of International Business* (Cincinnati, OH: South-Western Publishing Company).

Tuominen, Matti, Rajala, Arto, and Moller, Kristian (2004) Market-driving versus market-driven: divergent roles of market orientation in business relationships. *Industrial Marketing Management*, 33(3): 207–17.

Webster F.E., and Wind Y. (1972) *Organisational Buying Behaviour* (Englewood Cliffs, NJ: Prentice Hall).

Further reading

There are many books on business-to-business marketing, including:

Chris Fill, and Karen Fill (2004) *Business to Business Marketing: Relationships, Systems and Communications* (London: FT Prentice Hall). This is a comprehensive, readable textbook written from a marketing management perspective.

Jim Blythe, and Alan Zimmerman (2005) *Business to Business Marketing Management* (London: Thomson Learning). This book takes a global perspective on B2B marketing.

Mark Whitehead, and Chris Barrat (2004) *Buying for Business: Insights into Purchasing and Supply* (Chichester: John Wiley). This is a view from the other side. Written as a guide for practitioners, the book takes the buyer's viewpoint.

Chapter 19
Consumer behaviour and the marketing mix

Learning objectives After reading this chapter, you should be able to:

1 explain the importance of hedonism as opposed to utilitarianism in consumer behaviour

2 show how price goes beyond purchase cost

3 explain how price relates to what people will pay

4 explain the motivators for shopping behaviour

5 explain the weak and strong theories of advertising

6 explain the role of interaction in advertising effectiveness

7 describe the advantages of radio, cinema and ambient advertising

8 explain the use and effectiveness of ambient advertising

9 explain the role of social interaction in evaluating services

10 describe the importance of getting service levels right

11 show how physical evidence is used as a surrogate for judging quality of services

Introduction

Most of this book has been concerned with the theories behind consumer and buyer behaviour, and the influences on their decision-making in purchasing and consumption situations. Eventually, however, marketers need to develop practical tactics for launching new products, expanding existing markets, raising the profile of brands and so forth and must therefore apply their knowledge of how consumers make decisions.

Marketing decision-making areas have for many years been divided according to the four P model (product, price, place and promotion). During the 1980s this categorization was expanded to include a further three factors – people, process and physical evidence (Booms and Bitner 1983).

Although the expanded seven P model is probably far from comprehensive in terms of explaining what marketers do, it does provide a degree of structure and is a convenient 'shorthand' device.

Consumer behaviour and products

A product is a bundle of benefits, but those benefits are likely to go far beyond the physical item itself. The overt features and benefits of a product are based on the individual's cognitive faculties, but many aspects of the product will appeal to the individual's affective and conative aspects. The following aspects of products go beyond the rational decision-making process:

1 *Branding* – The brand may increase the observability of the product and strengthen the individual's self-image. Wearing the right brand of clothing and driving the right brand of car are both ways of telling the world who one is: getting it wrong can lead to social disaster.

Preview case study
J.D. Wetherspoon

In 1979, law student Tim Martin decided he wanted to own a pub. Unlike most students with the same ambition, Martin actually went ahead and bought the pub he usually drank in. From the beginning, Martin decided that Wetherspoon's was going to be different from the other pubs around.

For one thing, Wetherspoon's has no music. There is no juke box, no live bands and no piped music anywhere in any Wetherspoon's pub. Second, Wetherspoon's has a wider range of beers than do most pubs – and it is the beer that makes the profits. Wetherspoon's operate by keeping the price of the beer relatively low, but offering a quiet atmosphere, no-smoking areas and all-day food.

Each pub has its own name, but operates under the overall Wetherspoon brand: the pub name and the company name appear prominently on each of the 640 Wetherspoon pubs in Britain. The company was floated on the London Stock Exchange in 1992, and continues to expand throughout the UK. In recent years the company has also diversified into J.D. Wetherspoon Lodges and Lloyd's nightclubs. Each of these operations has the same philosophy as the central J.D. Wetherspoon brand.

One of the difficulties of the licensed trade is that the customer experience is not entirely under the control of the management – the pub atmosphere, one of the main selling points, is largely controlled by the people who drink there. Where alcohol is being served, there can be boisterous and threatening behaviour – even violence – which can quickly destroy a pub's reputation (not to mention destroy the pub's fixtures and fittings). This is one of the problems which Wetherspoon's seeks to solve by their approach to running the pub.

PHILIP WOLMUTH/ALAMY

2   *Styling* – The appearance of many products adds to the hedonic aspects of the product. For example, a sports car may stand out for its styling rather than for its road performance or brand.

3   *Manufacturer's reputation* – Although reputation is often part of the cognitive aspects of ownership, the reputation also colours the affective aspects. For example, a manufacturer might have a good reputation for socially responsible business practices, or may have been exceptionally helpful on a previous occasion.

As we saw in previous chapters, the affective aspects of purchase often outweigh the cognitive. For example, motorcycle manufacturers know that they are largely selling on a self-image platform: the majority of bikers are middle-aged men who can afford the bike and afford the insurance. These men buy the bikes to re-live a dream of youth: this has virtually nothing to do with the practical need for economical transportation which was the motorcycle's original reason for existence.

Being the first to own a new product can be a powerful motivation for an individual. Again, this can be an esteem issue: showing off to one's friends can be powerful. Equally there is a degree of pleasure in just owning something which very few other people have – exclusivity is a powerful factor not only in buying new products, but also in buying expensive ones. Equally, buying a 'tailor-made' product has a powerful appeal – hence the explosion in mass customization in recent years, accompanied by a sharp rise in subjectivity (Addis and Holbrook 2001).

From the viewpoint of a supplier, offering a product which appeals to self-image, self-esteem and aesthetic needs is at least as important as offering one which meets practical needs.

As we have seen elsewhere, the brand is an important factor in judging products. Bengtsson (2003) has suggested that the personification of brands by consumers is a result of marketing activities, specifically the discourse from marketers about relationship marketing. This may or may not be true, but it raises interesting issues about how marketers may be able to manipulate opinion. People often conceive a dislike of brands, sometimes because of what the brand symbolizes or because of a dislike of the corporation rather than the actual product characteristics (Dalli, Romani and Gistri 2006) so firms would be well advised to avoid manipulative behaviour. On that topic, there is research evidence to show that companies which carry out socially responsible initiatives which do not appear to have any connection with the firm are often distrusted – perhaps because people perceive it as a 'tick the box' exercise or an attempt to 'whitewash' the firm (Becker-Olsen and Cudmore 2004).

A problem for marketers lies in whether or not to extend a successful brand. In some cases, brand extensions will strengthen the overall brand, but in other cases a brand extension might actually damage the brand. According to recent research, applying the brand name to a lower-quality product does not appear to damage the brand (Heath, McCarthy and Chatterjee 2006), but the reasons for this are not clear. Other researchers have found that the position of a specific product within the overall brand is more important to consumers than the differences between brands (LeClerc, Hsee and Nunnes 2002). This may be a function of brand loyalty.

Price

The price of something is the total cost of adopting the product. This includes the purchase price, the cost of switching from an existing product to the new product and the cost of maintaining and using the product. The balance between these various elements of the total cost will vary from one product to another, of course, but the astute supplier will recognize that (in some cases) prices can be adjusted in one area to take account of costs in another.

Delivery is part of the product, because it removes the cost of collection and thus reduces the price.

Costs to the customer include internal costs (learning to use the product, time spent buying it and getting it to work properly, disposing of the product after use), acquisition costs (purchase price, delivery, installation etc.) and costs related to risk. The total of these costs will be taken into account when assessing whether the benefits outweigh the price. Note that not all these costs can be expressed in financial terms, and not all of the price asked by the supplier is monetary. For example, a supplier might expect a customer to accept a greater part of the risk in exchange for a lower price, as is the case when someone buys a 'stand-by' airline ticket. In exchange for a lower price, the customer accepts that the ticket may not be honoured at the desired time – the supplier has traded off the risk of not being able to sell the seat against getting a lower monetary price.

As can be seen in Figure 19.1, customer benefits fall into functional, operational, financial and personal categories. The functional are those that come to mind most readily, related to the physical aspects of the product – these often relate closely to the individual's cognition of the product. In the longer term, operational benefits such as reliability and durability, financial aspects such as savings made over the period of ownership and personal benefits such as feelings of well-being and of ownership will assume greater importance.

Customer costs include acquisition costs such as the initial price plus delivery, fitting etc.; internal costs, such as learning to use the product, lost time in buying it and getting it to work properly and disposal; and finally, costs related to risk. Not all of these costs are financial, and not all of the price charged by the supplier is expressed financially, either. Suppliers might expect customers to accept a higher level of risk as part of the price of obtaining the product.

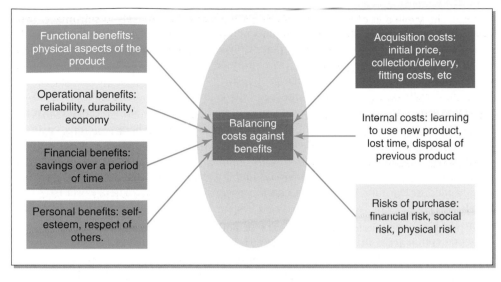

Figure 19.1
Cost-benefit trade-offs

Consumers need to balance these factors carefully in order to arrive at a final evaluation of the product's worth. Provided the benefits exceed the costs, the consumer will be happy with the outcome; if the costs exceed the benefits, the consumer will not be happy with the outcome. In the long term, marketers should seek to ensure that benefits always outweigh costs, but either side of the equation can be adjusted: if the marketer can offer greater benefits without increasing the cost to the consumer, this is a valid way of achieving value for money. If benefits cannot be improved, then the only way to improve value for money is to reduce the costs – not necessarily the initial acquisition price, but (possibly) the other costs.

Price sensitivity

Establishing the needs of each segment is a precursor to developing appropriate pricing for each segment. In some cases, a product can be customized to meet the specific needs of a segment and priced at a premium because of the customization. In setting prices for specific segments, the marketing director must estimate the price sensitivity of that particular market segment. Dolan (1995) listed factors that affect customer price sensitivity; these are listed in Table 19.1.

Table 19.1 Factors affecting customer price sensitivity

Economics
• Percentage of total expense
• Type of consumer
• Level of involvement
Search and usage
• Cost of information search
• Ease of comparing competitive alternatives
• Switching costs
Competition
• Differentiation
• Perception of price

The major categories are customer economics, search and usage and competition. Customers will be more sensitive if the percentage of the particular item is large in comparison to the total expense that the customer is making to achieve a particular end. Should the item be of extreme importance to the consumer, price sensitivity will tend to decline because reliability becomes paramount.

Reviewing the search and usage category, customers will be more price-sensitive if information search is easy and cheap, and competitive offerings are easily compared. In addition, the customer's price sensitivity is increased substantially where switching costs are low. Switching costs are all the costs associated with changing from one particular product or service to another. For example, a consumer might become persuaded that Apple Mac software is better than Microsoft, but would find it difficult to change because of the extra time needed to learn the new system and to convert existing files. These costs may outweigh the benefits seen from a potential new system. Finally, price sensitivity is decreased where the manufacturer's offering is clearly differentiated from its competition and where price perception gives an aura of quality to a particular product. In general, people are less sensitive to a downsizing in pack size than they are to a price increase: this is presumably an error of perception on the part of the individual, but for routine purchases a slight reduction in quantity is apparently less noticeable than an increase in price (Gourville and Koehler 2003).

Price sensitivity has also been shown to be affected by changing currencies. Research conducted in Germany following the replacement of the deutschmark with the euro showed that people perceived the quality of the products to be higher when priced in deutschmarks because the number of deutschmarks was higher than the number of euros, although the actual price had not changed (Molz and Gielnik 2006).

Price sensitivity can be affected by marketing, and especially selling, approaches. In some cases customers have an unrealistically low expectation of prices. Salespeople will sometimes therefore suggest (in a subtle manner) that the price might be very high indeed so that the real price comes as a pleasant surprise. This technique is also used by some catalogue marketers: by including extremely high-priced articles in the catalogue, marketers can 'price-condition' potential customers into believing that other products in the catalogue represent a bargain (Krishna, Wagner and Yoon 2002).

Some pricing methods take no account of customers at all. Cost-plus pricing, in which the total costs of manufacturing the product are totalled up and a profit margin added on, is still commonly used by manufacturers even though it takes no account of what the customers are prepared to pay. The result of this exercise will hardly ever be a price which a consumer would recognise as 'correct': it will almost certainly either be too high or too low. If the price is too high, people will not pay it: if it is too low, people may be suspicious of the quality of the product or at the very least the firm will be foregoing a surplus profit.

Customer-based pricing methods

The various approaches to customer-based pricing do not necessarily mean offering products at the lowest possible price, but they do take account of customer needs and wants.

Customary pricing

Customary pricing is customer orientated in that it provides the customer with the product for the same price at which it has always been offered. An example is the price of a call from a coin-operated telephone box. Telephone companies need only reduce the time allowed for the call as costs rise. For some countries (e.g. Australia) this is problematical since local calls are allowed unlimited time, but for most European countries this is not the case.

The reason for using customary pricing is to avoid having to reset the call boxes too often. Similar methods exist for taxis, some children's sweets, and gas or electricity pre-payment meters. If this method were to be used for most products there would be a steady reduction in the firm's profits as the costs catch up with the selling price, so the method is not practical for every firm.

Demand pricing

Demand pricing is the most market-orientated method of pricing. Here, the marketer begins by assessing what the demand will be for the product at different price levels. This is usually done by asking the customers what they might expect to pay for the product, and seeing how many choose each price level. This will lead to the development of the kind of chart shown in Table 19.2.

As the price rises, fewer customers are prepared to buy the product, as fewer will still see the product as good value for money. In the example given above, the fall-off is not linear, i.e. the number of units sold falls dramatically once the price goes above £5. This kind of calculation could be used to determine the stages of a skimming policy (see below), or it could be used to calculate the appropriate launch price of a product.

For demand pricing, the next stage is to calculate the costs of producing the product in the above quantities. Usually the cost of producing each item falls as more are made (i.e. if we make 50,000 units, each unit costs less than would be the case if we only make 1000 units). Given the costs of production it is possible to select the price that will lead to a maximisation of profits. This is because there is a trade-off between quantity produced and quantity sold; as the firm lowers the selling price, the amount sold increases but the income generated decreases.

The calculations can become complex, but the end result is that the product is sold at a price that customers will accept, and that will meet the company's profit targets. Table 19.3 shows an example of costings to match up with the above figures.

Telephone companies change prices by reducing the time for a call – resetting the coin boxes is an expensive operation.

Table 19.2 Demand pricing

Price per unit	Number of customers who said they would buy at this price
£3 to £4	30,000
£4 to £5	25,000
£5 to £6	15,000
£6 to £7	5,000

Table 19.3 Costings for demand pricing

Number of units	Unit cost (labour and materials)	Tooling-up and fixed costs	Net cost per unit
30,000	£1.20	£4000	£1.33
25,000	£1.32	£4000	£1.48
15,000	£1.54	£4000	£1.81
5,000	£1.97	£4000	£2.77

Table 19.4 Profitability at different price bands

Number of units sold	Net profit per unit	Total profit for production run	Percentage profit per unit
30,000	£2.17	£65,100	62
25,000	£3.02	£75,500	67
15,000	£3.61	£54,150	66
5,000	£3.73	£18,650	57

The tooling-up cost is the amount it will cost the company to prepare for producing the item. This will be the same whether 1000 or 30,000 units are made.

Table 19.4 shows how much profit could be made at each price level. The price at which the product is sold will depend on the firm's overall objectives; these may not necessarily be to maximize profit on this one product, since the firm may have other products in the range or other long-term objectives that preclude maximising profits at present.

Based on these figures, *the most profitable price* will be £4.50. Other ways of calculating the price could easily lead to making a lower profit from this product. For instance, the price that would generate *the highest profit per unit* would be £6.50, but at this price they would only sell 5000 units and make £18,650. The price that would generate *the highest sales* would be £3.50, but this would (in effect) lose the firm almost £10,000 in terms of foregone profit.

Demand pricing works by knowing what the customers are prepared to pay, and what they will see as value for money.

Product-line pricing

Product-line pricing means setting prices within linked product groups. Often sales of one product will be directly linked to the sales of another, so that it is possible to sell one item at a low price in order to make a greater profit on the other one.

Polaroid chose to sell its instant cameras very cheaply (almost for cost price) for the US market and to take their profit from selling the films for a much higher price. For Europe, the firm chose to sell both films and cameras for a medium-level price and profit from sales of both. Eventually this led Kodak to enter the market with its own instant camera, but this was withdrawn from sale in the face of lawsuits from Polaroid for patent infringement.

Skimming

Skimming is the practice of starting out with a high price for a product, then reducing it progressively as sales level off. It relies on two main factors: first, that not all customers have the same perception of value for money, and second, that the company has a technological lead over the opposition which can be maintained for long enough to satisfy the market.

Skimming is usually carried out by firms who have developed a technically advanced product. Initially the firm will charge a high price for the product, and at this point only those who are prepared to pay a premium price for it will buy. Profit may not be high, because

Where sales of one product depend on sales of another, the manufacturer can choose to make the bulk of the profit from the dependent product.

Consumer behaviour in action
Gillette razors

King C. Gillette, the inventor of the safety razor, was faced with something of a problem in marketing the product. He realised very early on that the revolutionary disposable blades in the razor would be expensive to manufacture unless he could produce them in their millions – but without a large, established market to sell to he would not be able to obtain those economies of scale. The razors themselves were a revolutionary idea, and consequently each prospective purchaser needed to be persuaded to try the new system, but this was simply too time consuming.

Gillette had, in his youth, been a salesman. He applied his knowledge of customers to the problem and came up with a new idea which is still in use today, over 100 years later. He simply adjusted the pricing so that the up-front cost of adopting the product was low, and the ongoing maintenance cost relatively higher than it would otherwise have been. He gave away the razors, so that customers could try the new system for free: Gillette knew that hardly any of them would return to using cut-throat razors after using the disposable blades, and he made his money selling the blades.

Safety razors became so well established in the market that, only a short while later, cut-throat razors are virtually unheard-of. Gillette's company successfully used the same marketing ploy some 80 years later to intro-duce a multi-blade system, but this system was quickly overtaken by disposable razors, which are regarded as the norm nowadays.

the number of units sold will be low and therefore the cost of production per unit will be high. Once the most innovative customers have bought, and the competition is beginning to enter the market, the firm can drop the price and 'skim' the next layer of the market, at which point profits will begin to rise. Eventually the product will be sold at a price that allows the firm only a minimum profit, at which point only replacement sales or sales to late adopters will be made.

Figure 19.2 shows how skimming works. At each price level, the product shows a standard product life cycle curve: as the curve tops out and begins to fall back, the company lowers the price and the cycle starts again with a new group of consumers. The process continues until either the market is saturated or the company decides that it cannot make any further price reductions.

The advantage of this method is that the cost of developing the product is returned fairly quickly, so that the product can later be sold near the marginal cost of production. This means that competitors have difficulty entering the market at all, since their own development costs will have to be recovered in some other way.

Skimming is commonly used in consumer electronics markets. This is because firms frequently establish a technological lead over the competitors, and can sometimes even protect their products by taking out patents, which take some time for competitors to overcome. An example of this was the Sony Walkman, which cost over £70 when it was first introduced in the early 1980s. Allowing for inflation, the price is now around one-tenth of

Figure 19.2

Skimming

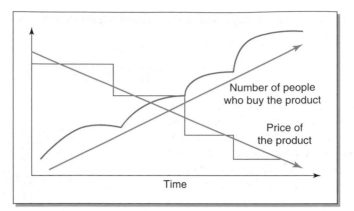

what it was then. Recent research shows that customers are aware of skimming in the electronics markets, and are delaying purchases of new electronic devices until the prices drop. This may affect the way firms view skimming in the future.

Skimming requires careful judgement of what is happening in the marketplace, both in terms of observing customer behaviour, and of observing competitive response. Market research is therefore basic to the success of a skimming policy, and very careful monitoring of sales to know when to cut the price again.

Psychological pricing

Psychological pricing relies on emotional responses from the consumer. Higher prices are often used as an indicator of quality, so some firms will use prestige pricing. This applies in many service industries, because consumers are often buying a promise: a service that does not have a high enough quality cannot be exchanged afterwards. Consumers' expectations of high-priced restaurants and hairdressers are clearly higher in terms of the quality of service provision; cutting prices in those industries does not necessarily lead to an increase in business. **Odd-even pricing** is the practice of ending prices with an odd number, for example £3.99 or $5.95 rather than £4 or $6. It appears that consumers tend to categorise these prices as '£3 and a bit' or '$5 and change' and thus perceive the price as being lower. The effect may also be due to an association with discounted or sale prices; researchers report that '99' endings on prices increase sales by around 8 per cent (Schindler and Kirby 1997).

Recent research has shown that odd-even pricing does not necessarily work in all cultures (Suri, Anderson and Kotlov 2004). In Poland, for example, the effects are negligible. Odd-even pricing also has effects on perceptions of discounts during sales. Rounding the price to (say) £5 from £4.99 leads people to overvalue the size of any discount that is then applied, which increases the perception of value for money (Gueguen and Legoherel 2004). Thus the positive effect on sales of using a 99 ending can be negated when the product is on offer in a sale. There is also evidence that rounding prices up to an even amount encourages trial of products (Bray and Harris 2006).

In China, there is evidence to suggest that prices ending in 8 are more effective than prices ending in 4, because 8 is a lucky number and 4 is unlucky (Simmons and Schindler 2003).

Online retailers have found that 'bundling' the price and including 'free' shipping and handling appears to work effectively as a purchasing incentive, leading to more favourable memories and fewer product returns (Roggeveen, Lan and Monroe 2006). A similar effect may exist in hire-purchase or credit deals: people relate the benefits they gain from the product to the actual payments they are making at the time. This means that, as the product gets older and the benefits reduce (for example, a car becomes more expensive to maintain and does not run as well), the customer perceives the payments as worse value for money

(Seigyoung and Chuan-Fong 2006). This perhaps means that hire purchase companies should reduce the payments over time.

Second-market discounting

Second-market discounting is common in some service industries and in international markets. The brand is sold at one price in one market, and in a lower price in another; for example, museums offer discounts to students, some restaurants offer discounts to elderly people on week-nights, and so forth. Often these discounts are offered to even out the loading on the firm; week-night discounts fill the restaurant on what would otherwise be a quiet night, so making more efficient use of the premises and staff.

Happy Hour discounts increase demand at a quiet time.

Figure 19.3 shows how second-market discounting works. At the bottom of each column is the amount of full-price business a retailer does on each day. Friday and Saturday are the busiest days, so on the other four days of the week the firm offers various discounts. On Monday the retailer offers 10 per cent off to all customers, which boosts business that day to a level higher than that of the weekend trade. Tuesday is senior citizen day, and Wednesday and Thursday are student discount days. These days are aimed at people who are able to shop mid-week.

Obviously these discounts may cannibalize sales on other days: a senior citizen might have been willing to shop on a Saturday and pay the full price (or might even have shopped on a Tuesday anyway, simply because the shop is quieter).

In international markets products might be discounted to meet local competition. For example, Honda motorcycles are up against strong local competition in India from Royal Enfield, so the price of their basic 100 cc motorcycle is around Rs 39,000 (about £600). A similar Honda motorcycle in the UK costs around £2000. The specifications of the motorcycles do differ somewhat – but it is difficult to see any difference that would account for a £1400 price differential.

Pricing in business markets

In business markets, pricing has a somewhat different role because the purchasing process tends to be more rational, and is often much more price-sensitive. Pricing policies include deciding upon list price and discount levels, allowances, rebates, and geographic differences (standardization vs. differentiation).

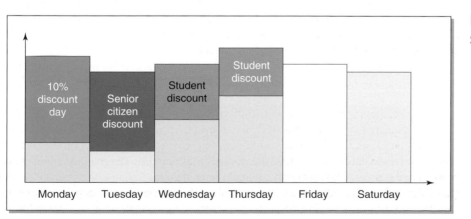

Figure 19.3

Second-market discounting

The question of list price varies by industry. In some industries, list prices are set in such a way that no customer ever pays that price. The list prices for a product line are set in order to provide various levels of discounts. Discounts can be given for volume purchases, whether cumulative or based on individual order, or based on time of order.

Allowances and rebates are simply price reductions given to dealers or distributors to help them promote a particular manufacturer's product. Some firms give advertising allowances to their distributors in order to encourage them to promote their particular product or even for identifying their facilities such as show rooms or service vehicles with a particular brand name. A firm may choose to offer a trade-in allowance for older products in order to replace them with newer versions. A rebate is a fee paid to a purchaser once the product is bought and installed.

Competitive bidding

Business-to-business sales are often completed through competitive bids. This is especially true for government institutions and non-profit organizations such as hospitals. Some non-governmental firms also use competitive bids. In some cases, a firm may require a bid to a particular specification and then reserve the right to negotiate further with the winning bidder. Firms use specification buying especially for large projects. These firms develop detailed specifications either based on the performance or description of a particular product, service or a combination of both. Firms supplying military products or large power stations or other major projects need to develop an expertise not only in the bidding process, but also in the specification process. 'Specmanship' means a firm's sales force is expert at helping a customer develop specifications which will limit the bidders. The most successful salespeople can develop specifications with requirements that can be met only by their firm. When faced with a potential competitive bidding situation which will be based on specifications to be developed by a large customer, it is necessary to spend the required time to gain the most favourable specifications possible before bidding documents are released.

The purpose of setting up a competitive bidding or tendering process is, in theory, to ensure that the customer organization gets best value for money. In practice, suppliers often circumvent the system by encouraging buyers to include specific factors in the specification, or by charging exorbitant amounts for any variations on the contract. For example, a firm contracted to refit an office building might put in a very low bid on the contract, but charge large sums for changing the location of office doors from those specified on the original plans, or for relocating power points. Such minor variations might not actually cost the fitters anything at all, but are simply a way of showing a profit on an otherwise unprofitable low-bid contract.

In some cases, government organizations have become more sophisticated in their dealings with contractors, and take greater care over their specifications to ensure that all external factors are taken into account. For example, the UK Highway Agency now charges road builders a 'rental' for the piece of road they are working on, so that there is an incentive to complete the work more quickly. This was in response to a common practice in the construction industry of agreeing to a large number of contracts at the same time in order to ensure a flow of work for months at a time.

Place

'Place' refers to the location where the exchange takes place. The place element of the marketing mix goes beyond mere convenience: often the place is, in effect, part of the product because it provides hedonic benefits of its own. For example, consider the purchase of antiques. Some antique buyers will scour car-boot sales, house clearance sales, auction rooms and so forth in the hope of picking up a bargain. Others will go to antique shops where most of the searching has already been done, while others will visit upmarket antique galleries where the pieces will be artfully displayed and the customer will be offered a glass of wine and a canapé while browsing.

In the course of the antique's passage from car-boot sale to gallery the price may well have risen from £5 to £2000, yet at each stage of the process the purchaser has bought a bargain. The reason is that the place element has added value in some way or another. The car-boot bargain hunter may have spent weeks or months trawling through junk to find the valuable item, and may also have spent a great deal of money on items which turned out to be worthless. However, the hedonic aspects of bargain hunting make the search worthwhile. At the other end of the chain, the wealthy collector enjoying a glass of wine at the gallery is enjoying having someone explain the history of the item, and is able to invest a substantial amount of money in something which he or she knows is of real value. The reputation and skill of the gallery ensures that the product is the genuine article – something the average car-boot bargain hunter cannot be sure of.

Buying goods from a catalogue, online, from a street market or from a retailer each has its hedonic aspects: marketers need to balance the place utility (cognitive) aspects against the hedonic (affective) aspects of the point of purchase.

Shopping behaviour

People have many motives for shopping, going beyond a simple need to obtain goods and services. These can be divided into social motives and personal motives, each of which determine the choice of retailer, the time spent shopping, and much of the effort which is expended.

Social motives include the following:

- *Social experience outside the home* – Talking to shop assistants, going shopping with a friend or friends, getting out of the house for a while all constitute motives for shopping.
- *Communication with others who have a similar interest* – Whether shopping for clothes or computers, people enjoy taking a friend along, especially if the friend has a specific expertise which can be used.
- *Peer group attraction* – Going to specific shops means mingling with people from a similar social background. This is reassuring in terms of self-image.
- *Status and authority* – Being a customer is a pleasant experience – the shop assistants (if they are well trained) are attentive and interested in the customers' needs, which means that customers enjoy the warm glow of being looked after.
- *Pleasure of bargaining* – In some situations in every country, bargaining is acceptable, and in some countries it is normal practice almost everywhere. The bargaining process is enjoyable because it has the elements of power, of exercising skill, and of getting a bargain.

Personal motives include the following:

- *Role playing* – Playing the part of the customer is a pleasant experience: some people even adopt a new persona when shopping, in order to enhance their own self-esteem.
- *Diversion* – Looking at new products is an entertainment in itself, and browsing around the shops can be a relaxing way of spending some time.
- *Self-gratification* – Meeting one's own needs by buying goods relieves the tensions set up by lacking something which is regarded as essential.
- *Learning about new trends* – Learning is, in itself, a pleasurable thing. Being the first to know about new products is important for some people's self-esteem.

● *Physical activity* – Often people have sedentary lives: going for a walk round the shops can relieve this. Often people experience this motivation when on holiday – relaxing on the beach or by the pool quickly becomes boring.

● *Sensory stimulation* – Simply exposing one's senses to new sensations is pleasurable, and shopping fulfils this role admirably.

Shoppers can be categorized according to their shopping behaviour, as shown in Table 19.5.

Choice of retailer is determined by the proximity of the store (the closer, the better), the store design and physical facilities, the merchandise on offer, advertising and sales promotion activities, store personnel, customer service and the other clients. This last is an interesting example of a factor over which the store does not have direct control, but it clearly has an influence on the image of the store, and the shopping experience. A store with an upmarket clientele and image will attract people who associate themselves with that image: a store with a downmarket image and a disreputable clientele will repel more upmarket clients.

Table 19.5 Shopper profiles

Profile	Explanation
Yesteryears	Approximately 17% of shoppers fit this profile. Yesteryears are insecure, conservative, somewhat anti-social and are risk avoiders. They are typically older females, and are looking for low prices, guarantees, convenient retailer location and speedy service. They are light consumers who like chain stores and discount stores.
Power purchasers	Representing about 15% of shoppers, this group are self-indulgent variety seekers. The are risk-takers and big spenders, and tend to be young. They are looking for friendly salespeople, easy-to-find merchandise, high quality and fast service, and are brand-conscious. They are very heavy consumers, and like department stores, chain stores and speciality shops.
Fashion foregoers	These are fashion laggards, and are unconcerned about image or style. They tend to be mundane and anti-social, and are typically single men living alone. They look for low prices, ease of finding merchandise, convenient location, and a wide selection of products. They are light consumers who shop infrequently, and they like DIY outlets. They represent around 16% of shoppers.
Social strivers	This group are style-conscious fashion experimenters who like shopping, are social people and are brand-aware. They are young, female, often somewhat down-market, and are heavy consumers. They like guarantees, friendly salespeople, a wide selection of goods and high quality. Typically they shop anywhere and everywhere (except DIY stores) and shop as often as possible. Because of this, they represent 20% of shoppers.
Dutifuls	16% of the country's shoppers, these people are sacrificial, practical risk avoiders. They are comparison shoppers (they like to shop around). Typically, they are downmarket mid-life households or down/middle-market older households. They look for low prices, guarantees, ease of finding merchandise, convenient location, friendly salespeople and speed of service. They shop relatively infrequently, and are light consumers.
Progressive patrons	These are self-confident, artistic, variety-seeking, open-minded, risk-taking, innovative and imaginative people. They are often male, but may also be middle to upmarket mid-life families. They look for ease of finding merchandise, high quality, wide selection and specific brands. They are very heavy consumers, and like speciality stores, catalogue outlets, convenience stores and DIY outlets. They account for the remaining 16% of shoppers.

Promotion

As we saw in Chapter 5, promotion is about creating appropriate perceptions in consumers' minds. However, people also consume marketing messages through the media – they enjoy watching some advertisements, they enjoy watching films which have brands placed in them, and they enjoy reading informative articles about product categories with which they are involved.

How advertising works (and occasionally whether advertising works) has been a topic for debate in marketing academia for a number of years now. Part of the problem is that there is no way of telling whether something works unless one first defines what it is that one is trying to achieve. Since there are many possible objectives for an advertising campaign, ranging from increasing purchases through to reinforcing attitudes, there can be no single explanation for whether advertising works (Wright and Crimp 2000).

Two general theories about advertising have emerged from the debate (Figure 19.4). The strong theory suggests that advertising is a powerful force which can change attitudes and make a significant contribution to people's knowledge and understanding. The weak theory of advertising suggests that advertising can only 'nudge' people in the direction in which they are already moving, in other words it reinforces rather than persuades (Ehrenberg 1992).

The main criticisms of the strong theory of advertising are (first) that there is little evidence to show that consumers develop a strong desire for the brand before trying it; and second, the model only considers non-buyers who become buyers. In most markets, advertising is intended to affect people who have already tried the product, either with a view to informing them about changes in the product, or to remind them about the product, or to encourage increased purchases of the product. The strong theory tends to be more prevalent in the United States, and it is of course possible that American experience is different from European experience: the weak theory tends to have more adherents in Europe. Research in FMCG (fast-moving consumer goods) markets shows that people are not usually loyal to one brand, and it is extremely difficult for

Advertising close to the point of sale is likely to be the most effective.

Consumer behaviour in practice
Measuring advertising in Australia

The Australian government, in conjunction with six universities and the state governments of Victoria and Queensland, has established the National Information and Communications Technology of Australia organization. NICTA, as it is known, has the role of encouraging excellence in research into communications technology.

One of NICTA's inventions is a software system which can recognize faces and determine which direction they are looking. Linked to a camera, this system allows advertisers to know how many people look at their billboards, and even which area of the billboard has attracted their attention. The software, Targeted Adver-

tising Based on Audience Natural Response or TABANAR, offers advertisers a golden opportunity to fine-tune their billboard ads and also to have a direct measure of audience response. This is likely to be much more accurate than traditional methods of measuring response, which involve (for example) coupon returns, calls made to free telephone numbers, or returned text messages.

In some countries there may be issues of privacy involved with putting secret cameras on billboards and recording people without their consent, but the system itself uses remarkable technology to provide information which has been previously unobtainable.

Figure 19.4

Strong and weak theories of advertising

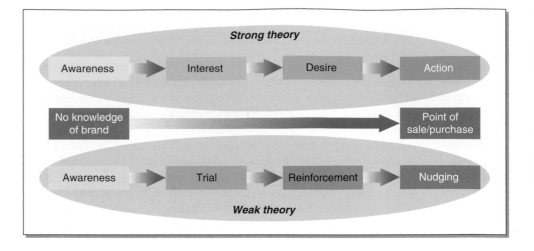

Talking point

a new brand to become established in the portfolio of brands which people buy. In these circumstances, most advertising is intended to improve brand loyalty and therefore defend the brand; this would tend to support the weak theory, because it implies that the main people to be affected by the advertising are existing customers for the brand.

If advertising is only a weak force, and doesn't persuade anybody, why is so much money spent on it by companies? Surely they wouldn't pay out billions of pounds, dollars, yen, and euros every year just on the chance that it might work?

On the other hand, when was the last time you saw an advert and then went rushing out to buy a product? Have you *ever* been persuaded by an advertisement? Are advertisements like the bumble bee – in theory too aerodynamically unsound to fly, but in practice it still flies?

Level of involvement has a role to play in determining the effects of advertising, and may also have a bearing on when the strong theory applies, and when the weak theory predominates (Jones 1991). In the case of a high-involvement purchase, consumers are more likely to access sought communications (Blythe 2003; also see Chapter 14) and are likely to be more affected by advertising since they will be actively seeking out advertising messages. In the case of low-involvement purchases, consumers are less likely to seek out advertising and are therefore only likely to be moved slightly by the **unsought communications** around them.

When there are many competing advertisements for similar products (for example in specialist magazines such as sport or hobby magazines) varying the context in which the advertisement is seen will increase its memorability (Unnava, Rajagopal and Raju 2003). In other words, if some method exists for repeating the advertisement in a different context (for example by putting a copy of the advertisement on a notice board at a sports club) it is more likely to have an impact on the target audience.

Active media: TV, radio and cinema

Radio, TV and cinema are powerful media because they are active (Figure 19.5) – they actually do something. TV and radio are probably the most pervasive media in most countries – in Western Europe, TV ownership is almost 100 per cent, and many homes have several television sets. Radio ownership is at least as widespread. People watch TV while eating, doing housework, relaxing or even while entertaining friends. In some homes the set is rarely switched off. Significantly, the biggest-selling consumer magazines in most Western European countries and in the United States are the TV programme guides.

Because television advertising is an unsought communication (people rarely, if ever, switch on the TV in order to see a favourite advertisement) it works best for activating

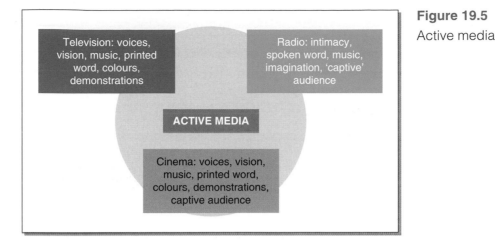

Figure 19.5
Active media

needs or providing information for the internal search. In most case advertisers are aiming to build the image of their product or firm, and to a large extent these aims can be met by television (McKechnie and Leather 1998).

TV advertising has the advantages shown in Table 19.6 (page 430) (Jefkins 1994).

There are, of course, disadvantages of television as a medium. These are shown in Table 19.7 (page 430).

Research at the London Business School shows that people do not necessarily watch the advertisements even if they are still in the room when the advertisement airs (Ritson 2003). The researchers identified a total of six behaviours which occur while the advertisement is on-screen; these are shown in Figure 19.6 and Table 19.8 (page 431).

The first three activities are interesting in that the standard method of measuring advertising on TV, which is the people meter, would have shown that people were in the room and would therefore have assumed that they were watching the advertisement. In fact, in each of these three cases, presence in the room does not mean observation of the advertising.

Interestingly, there is research evidence that advertisements which are zapped are more likely to have a positive effect on brand purchase than those which are not (Zufryden, Pedrick and Sankaralingam 1993). This is presumably because the viewer has to watch at least part of the advertisement and process the content before knowing that it is a candidate for zapping.

Fast-paced advertisements appear to have a positive effect on involuntary attention – in other words they are more eye-catching – but have little effect on involuntary attention (they are no more likely to be watched actively) (Bolls, Muehling and Yoon 2003). Furthermore, fast-paced advertisements tend to focus people on the style of the advertisement,

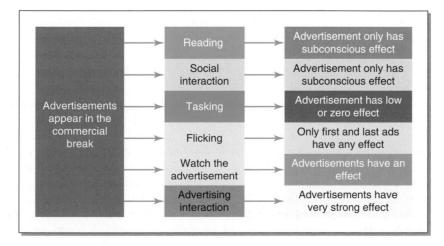

Figure 19.6
Activities in commercial breaks

Table 19.6 Advantages of TV advertising

Advantage	Explanation
Realism	It is possible to show the product in use in a typical and realistic way. Because the audience can see how to use the product, and can see the kind of person who is using it, advertisers can position the brand appropriately. Often viewers are able to identify the social class of the person in the advertisement by their accent and clothing, which helps position the brand.
Receptive audiences	TV advertisements are often seen as entertainment: many are produced to high standards, by world-class directors. Many advertisements tell a story, with surprising or amusing twists at the end.
Repetition	Advertisements can be repeated until sufficient of the audience have had an opportunity to see it. Agencies monitor this using published audience figures for each programme the advertisement appears in.
Appeal to retailers	Most retailers have a strong belief in the power of television, and are more likely to give the product prominence on their shelves if they know a TV campaign is planned. Of course, the fact that the product has more shelf space might in itself increase sales, so there is no way of being sure that the advertisement actually increased consumers' propensity to buy.
Zoning and networking	In the UK and most other countries it is possible to localize advertising to the immediate TV region, or to 'go national' with advertisements which are broadcast throughout the network.
Links with other media	Further information, coupons and order forms can be printed in other media and the TV advertisement can direct people to look for them. Printing such items in TV guides is a useful ploy: this combines the strengths of both media.

Table 19.7 Disadvantages of TV advertising

Disadvantage	Explanation
Lack of selectivity	Television is a mass medium: it is hard to segment, even though some programmes appeal more to some people than to others. This means that advertisers are probably wasting the majority of their expenditure in talking to people who have no need for the product.
Impermanent medium	Once the advertisement has been aired, it has gone forever (barring repeat airings). It is difficult for viewers to take note of where products are available, or to note down telephone numbers and so forth.
Zapping and zipping	Remote controls allow audiences to 'zap' advertisements, either by muting the sound or by switching channels. If programmes have been recorded on a VCR, the viewers can 'zip' past the ads by using the 'cue' button. Zapping has been called 'The greatest threat to capitalism since Karl Marx' (Kneale 1988).
Clutter	In some countries TV advertising rates are so low that frequent, and lengthy, advertising spots are sold: the USA and Italy are examples of this. Viewers become bored with the sheer volume of advertising, and frequently leave the room.
Audience fade-out	Audiences often leave the room while the advertisements are on, so although the ratings for the show might be high, the advertisements may not actually have been seen.

(Continued)

Table 19.7 Disadvantages of TV advertising (*Continued*)

Disadvantage	Explanation
Cost	TV advertising can be very expensive. Although it reaches a large audience, and therefore the cost-per-thousand-viewers might be low, the audience may not be composed of the right target group. The entry threshold is high: in the UK, which is admittedly one of the most expensive countries in the world for TV advertising, a nationally networked advertisement can easily cost £300,000 for one 30-second exposure.
Long lead times	Booking air time can be a lengthy process, taking weeks or even months. Additionally, production times for a commercial are likely to be long.
Restrictions on content	Most broadcast regulatory authorities take a conservative view on what can be shown in TV advertising. Sexual imagery, swearing and some categories of product (tobacco and condoms being two examples) are absolutely banned in UK advertising (despite being common in programmes). Restrictions vary from one country to another – for example, in France it was illegal until recently for retailers to advertise on TV, and in Germany toys cannot be advertised during children's TV programmes.
Dilution of audiences	As the number of available channels increases due to satellite and cable provision, plus DVD and VCR usage, the number of available viewers for any one programme has fallen. Also, high-quality programmes are spread across more channels so that the average quality of programming has fallen. This has led to a reduction in time spent watching TV and an increase in other activities. This trend may be peaking out – there have been instances recently of cable TV channels going bankrupt, which indicates that there may be a limit to the number of channels audiences are prepared to support.

Table 19.8 Behaviours in commercial breaks

Behaviour	Explanation
Social interaction	People often talk about their day, discuss household problems, or gossip while the commercial break runs.
Reading	Many people watch TV with a book or magazine at hand, to read during the breaks. Sometimes the reading will be a TV guide.
Tasking	The commercial break often affords an opportunity to load the dishwasher, clean the house, do the ironing, pay bills or make telephone calls.
Flicking	Jumping from one channel to another appears to be mainly a male activity. Flicking falls into two categories: almost random surfing across a number of other channels while waiting for the programme to restart, or alternatively going to a 'visit channel' such as a news channel for a specific length of time before returning to the programme.
Watching an advertisement	In many cases, advertisements are actually watched, and often commented on by the family members.
Advertising interaction	The final behaviour involves not only watching the advertisement, but commenting on it, singing along with the jingles, and even playing a game in which family members score 'points' by being the first to recognize the brand.

not on its content: people remember the advertisement, but not the brand. Mood affects people's response to advertisements, so placing the advertisement in an appropriate programme may have a critical effect on its success or otherwise (Bakamitsios and Siomkos (2003).

There is a clear relationship between liking the advertisement and subsequent sales, but this is not always a positive relationship. Liking the advertisement seems to be related to whether the product is meaningful and relevant to the person at the time (Biel 1990), and there is evidence that advertisements relating to food and drink are more likely to be liked than are non-food advertisements (Biel and Bridgewater 1990). Liking is usually linked to a positive view of the product, which in turn is likely to lead to sales (Biel 1990: Stapel 1991). This situation is sometimes reversed when dealing with (for example) insurance products and the like, where the advertisement might contain shocking imagery as a 'cautionary tale' to show people what can go wrong if they do not have insurance.

It may be difficult to deconstruct all the factors involved, since a truly unpleasant advertisement is likely to be ignored, so that the viewer is less likely to process the information cognitively. Such 'cautionary tale' advertisements are difficult to produce because the affective element is likely to repel the customer, whereas the cognitive element is likely to attract. Products can be placed on an approach–avoidance continuum, with products which are inherently attractive (food and beverages) at one end, and products which are inherently unattractive and which are only bought out of dire necessity (pensions, life insurance) at the other (Wells 1980).

Talking point

If people tend to 'switch off' from unpleasant advertisements, why produce them at all? Why show people scenes of crashed cars and devastated homes in order to frighten them into buying insurance? Maybe the school bully could frighten children into handing over their pocket money – but we're all grown-ups now!

Or maybe people have to be terrorized into buying insurance – otherwise they just keep putting it off until after they have been burgled or crashed the car! After all, in most countries it is a legal requirement to have car insurance – so doesn't this prove that people won't buy it unless they are threatened with jail?

Off-the-screen commercials (direct-response TV) appear to be a type of television advertising that breaks all the rules. These advertisements have high copy content, are extremely informative, and they aim to obtain a direct response from viewers by getting them to call an order line and buy the product directly. In the United States, off-the-screen selling has gone a step further with the infomercial, a (typically) half-hour programme consisting of entertainment and news about a specific product. For example, an infomercial about a new type of fishing lure might show anglers using the device, show people catching fish, give tips about the most effective locations for using the lure, and so forth. Infomercials are illegal on terrestrial TV in the UK, but they make up approximately 25 per cent of the programming on US cable stations (Steenhuysen 1994). Infomercials provide advertisers with enough time to inform and persuade people about the product's benefits: from the cable TV company's perspective, infomercials fill up air time which would otherwise have to be filled with paid-for programmes.

Radio advertising

Radio is the Cinderella of advertising, often ignored in favour of the higher profile of television. And yet, according to research conducted for Red Dragon Radio, commercial radio has a strong impact on people's lives. According to Red Dragon:

● 44 per cent of radio listeners wake up to a radio alarm;

● 27 per cent of people listen to radio in the bathroom, and 43 per cent of the 15–24 age group do so;

● 72 per cent of adult listeners listen to radio in the kitchen;

- 44 per cent of car drivers listen to the radio while driving;
- 44 per cent of employees listen to the radio in the workplace;
- 53 per cent of adults aged 15–24 listen to their radios in the garden.

Radio is a powerful medium because it is intimate: people listen to the radio in private situations, for example in the bathroom or while in bed, and predominantly while driving. Radio acts as a substitute for human company. Radios are cheap and portable, and listening does not require the audience's full attention, so people can do other things (drive, do housework, put on make-up and so forth) while listening.

Cinema advertising

For many years the cinema was the only visual advertising medium. Television meant that cinema audiences declined dramatically in the 1950s and 1960s, but in recent years the trend has reversed. A combination of 'blockbuster' movies which have attracted audiences, and the emergence of comfortable, well-equipped cinemas in entertainment complexes, has led to a resurgence of cinema attendance as part of a night out.

From the advertiser's viewpoint, cinema has all the advantages of television plus one other: it is impossible to zip, zap or leave the room while the advertisements are on. Consequently, cinemas provide an unrivalled opportunity to speak to a captive audience. UK Film Council statistics show that cinema attendances have risen from 34 million per annum in 1988, to 167.3 million visits in 2003: no small audience for advertising. Another factor in rising cinema attendance is the relatively poorer quality of television programming.

Typical cinema audiences are young people in their teens and early twenties: 56 per cent of cinema-goers are aged 15 to 24, although they represent only 18 per cent of the UK population aged over seven (Cinema Advertising Association 1997). The audience is also strongly ABC1 in socio-economic profile. In some Third World countries (notably India) cinema attendance is widespread because of the relatively low level of television ownership.

Ambient advertising

Traditional marketing communications techniques are becoming less effective as markets fragment, costs increase, audiences diminish, and clutter worsens (Evans, O'Malley and Patterson 1996). Therefore, new routes for communicating with customers and consumers are being sought.

Ambient advertising is somewhat difficult to define, although plenty of examples of it are around: in general, it is advertising which becomes part of the environment, where the message becomes the medium. For example, for one campaign an underarm deodorant manufacturer arranged to replace the hanging straps in London Underground carriages with empty bottles of the deodorant. Strap-hanging commuters are acutely aware of underarm odours, and holding onto the bottles instead of the usual straps meant that they had already assumed the position one uses when applying the deodorant. Another development is the invention of a device which converts shop windows into loudspeakers so that window can 'talk' about the products on display (Grapentine 2003).

Ambient advertising offers the following advantages:

- It is often cheaper than sales promotions, and when used near the point of purchase gives a good incentive without the loss of profit associated with sales promotion discounts.
- Well-executed ambient campaigns enhance brand image and cut through clutter.
- Novel ambient campaigns often create press coverage: some ambient campaigns are designed with this in mind.
- They are very effective for activating needs.

ADVERTISING ARCHIVES

Kelloggs used ambient advertising to promote Nutri-Grain.

Ambient advertisers need to consider the relationship between the medium being used, the advertised product or service, and the proximity to the point of sale as well as the basic objectives of the campaign. Ambient advertising works best when it is either close to the location of problem or close to the point of purchase. For example, Kellogg's Nutri-Grain bar was promoted as a snack for commuters who had missed breakfast, so Kellogg's arranged for advertisements for the product to be printed on bus and train tickets. Many travellers were reported to have bought the bars as a result, buying them from station news-stands or kiosks near bus stops.

Consumers tend to exhibit little pre-purchase decision-making for low-involvement purchases (Foxall and Goldsmith 1994), and some studies have shown that 70 per cent of all decisions to purchase specific brands are made inside the store (POPAI 1995). Trolley advertising makes around 19 per cent difference to the purchase of specific brands (Shankar 1999a) which demonstrates the power of ambient advertising to nudge consumers. Table 19.9 maps ambient advertising against Ehrenberg's ATRN model of advertising effects (the weak theory) (Ehrenberg 1997; Barnard and Ehrenberg 1997).

Ambient advertising is difficult to measure. First, the creativity of some campaigns is such that no advance predictions can be made. Second, research into the effects of ambient advertising has been relatively small as yet, so suitable test instruments have not been devised. Third, there is no industry-wide evaluation system: there is no estimating system to find out how many people picked up a particular petrol nozzle and therefore saw the advertisement, for example (Shankar 1999b).

In the future, it seems likely that ambient advertising will grow. Although greater creativity is involved in developing campaign, the impact is high and the cost is relatively low, especially considering the potential spin-off in terms of news coverage. Ambient advertising fits well within an integrated marketing communications approach because it both supports and is supported by other communications tools.

Table 19.9 Mapping of ambient advertising against the ATRN model

Stage	Explanation	Role of ambient advertising
Awareness	Consciousness of a new brand is followed by interest.	Consciousness is developed by a high-impact, innovative campaign, e.g. replacing straps with deodorant bottles.
Trial	Trial purchase of the brand may occur, perhaps with the consumer in a sceptical frame of mind.	Ambient advertising close to the point of sale may be enough to nudge the consumer towards one brand rather than another.
Reinforcement	Satisfactory use of the brand will encourage further purchase, or even establish a habitual propensity to buy the brand.	Ambient advertising only has a reminder role to play at this stage, and may be no more effective than other advertising.
Nudging	Propensity to buy may be enhanced or decreased by the nudging effect of advertising – either the firm's own or that of competitors.	Ambient advertising is thought to be better than other advertising for nudging consumers, since it has greater proximity both to the problem and to the point of purchase.

Internet advertising

A recent development in Internet advertising has been the use of viral spam programmes. Virus writers have been hired by spammers to develop viruses which will propagate spam messages through the address books of infected computers. In 2007 such viral spam programmes were used to promote 'penny shares'. Infected computers spread the spam around the world, with some users receiving five to ten copies of the advertisement per day. Clearly such tactics are unethical, and will almost certainly be banned: the difficulty is that the Internet is largely unregulated, messages can originate anywhere in the world, and therefore legislation will need to be ratified by virtually every nation on earth if unethical practices are to be stamped out entirely. It may be possible in the future for ISPs to be forced to develop ways of filtering spam from unregulated countries, but in the current state of the art this is extremely difficult, and many ISPs would regard such measures as being counterproductive since the whole point of the Internet is that it offers worldwide access.

Research into consumer attitudes towards the Internet and the advertising on it is still somewhat sparse, due to the newness of the medium. What is becoming certain is that the Internet has empowered consumers to a greater extent than ever before – the ease with which people can research suppliers and are able to switch between them has made suppliers rethink their approach and become much more interactive (Pires, Stanton and Rita 2006). There is evidence that people use various tactics for self-empowerment, as follows (Henry and Caldwell 2006):

1 Resignation.
2 Confrontation.
3 Withdrawal.
4 Engagement.
5 Concealment.
6 Escapism.
7 Hedonism.
8 Spirituality.
9 Nostalgia.
10 Creativity.

Regarding Internet tactics, people frequently feel afraid that they will lose control of their inboxes and will be swamped by unsolicited e-mails: this leads them to use tactics such as setting up different e-mail accounts with Internet service providers or giving false details when buying products. The desire to retain control over what is seen as a private medium is strong, and therefore people go to some lengths to avoid becoming victims of clever marketing tactics.

People

As we saw in Chapter 16, some service industries develop strong customer loyalties. These loyalties are almost always based on loyalty to the people working in the industry – whether the business is a hairdressing salon, a butcher's shop or a restaurant, the customer's loyalty is a function of the personal relationship he or she has with the stylist, the butcher or the waiter.

Consumers will tend to use the social interaction as a surrogate measure for judging the quality of the service. A friendly waiter, a confident hairdresser or a knowledgeable butcher will tend to inspire confidence in the overall outcome of the service provision, although there is really no guarantee that the actual competence of the supplier relates in any way to these subjective social factors.

Company employees may be divided into four groups (Judd 1987):

1 *Contactors* – These are the people who have frequent, daily contact with customers. Usually, their jobs are marketing-related; they might be salespeople, customer service employees or telesales operators. They are usually trained in customer relations techniques, and are often motivated to deal with customers in an effective and friendly way.

2 *Modifiers* – These people deal with customers regularly, but have no official marketing role. Receptionists, drivers, telephonists, progress chasers and some warehouse personnel deal with customers on an occasional basis and may need to have some idea of the organization's marketing policies. It is helpful if modifiers have good people skills, but they may not need special training in this.

3 *Influencers* – These people have some role within marketing, but have little actual contact with customers. For example, a designer may have the role of styling the product to make it as attractive as possible to consumers, without actually ever dealing with consumers.

4 *Isolateds* – These people have no customer contact and little or nothing to do with marketing. Accountants, personnel managers, office cleaners and so forth have important support roles within the organization but are unlikely ever to do anything which directly impacts on customers. Their role is to help create the right conditions for everyone else to carry out their roles.

A major influence which employees have on customers comes through word of mouth. Employees all go home at the end of the working day, and talk to family and friends about work. This means that each person helps in creating an overall corporate image, which in turn contributes to the customers' perception of the organization (Maxham and Netemeyer 2003).

The natural variability among human beings will, of course, mean that companies will not always be able to provide optimal service: firms therefore need to be prepared to work to recover from service mistakes when they do occur (Rasmusson 1997). This is often done by empowering contactors and modifiers to make amends immediately. Because the employee is the company (from the viewpoint of the consumer) this approach strengthens the social bonding which is the cornerstone of service provision.

Process

In services markets, the consumers can sometimes be seen as a co-producer of the service. For example, live theatre clearly has serious drawbacks over television: it cannot hope to provide the same level of special effects and scenes, and the actors' performances may not always be perfect (whereas on TV an imperfect performance is simply re-shot). Additionally, going to the theatre involves booking seats, going out in the cold and finding one's way to the theatre, sitting in what are often uncomfortable seats, not being able to have a drink or a snack during the performance, and not being able to press the pause button. The theatre does not allow one to change channels if the play is boring, it does not allow one to turn up the volume if the actors are speaking too quietly and it does not allow one to watch the play wearing a dressing-gown. For this experience people pay for a ticket – so what is the attraction? The main attraction is that there is an atmosphere in the theatre, generated by the presence of an audience – the other consumers. A half-empty theatre seems bleak: a theatre full of people responding to the show helps generate a response in the person watching the play.

As with any other question in marketing, the starting point for developing a service process is the customers' needs. In some cases the needs can be presented as a hierarchy –

for example, an aircraft manufacturer may not require new engines to be delivered urgently, but probably would need spare parts to be delivered quickly, as a grounded aircraft is an expensive item. The aero engine manufacturer would therefore see the supply of engines as being less important than the supply of spare parts, and would therefore seek to ensure that the stock of spares is kept up to an appropriate level even if this delayed the completion of new engines.

Service processes fall into three general categories:

1 *Before-sales service processes* – These might include helpful sales staff, readily available information, availability of samples and availability of supplies.

2 *During-sales processes* – These might include progress-chasing of orders, prompt and reliable delivery and helpful delivery staff.

3 *After-sales processes* – Courtesy calls, prompt attention to complaints, warranties and service agreements would all be after-sales services.

These processes all involve human interaction, so they all provide opportunities to improve customer loyalty. Unfortunately, they are also easy to copy, and not very difficult to exceed, so it may not be easy to maintain competitive advantage. Also, there is a trade-off between service level and cost: some firms (as we saw in Chapter 16) have been successful by cutting back dramatically on service and reducing prices accordingly. Retailers, low-cost airlines, and some restaurants offer minimal service, but have streamlined processes which reduce cost and deliver the core product efficiently. In some cases, the streamlined process might actually be preferable to the more staff-intensive process it replaces – many people find that booking flights on the Internet is a great deal easier than going through a travel agent.

Setting the right level of service can therefore be a source of competitive advantage. The emphasis here is on setting the right level – too high a level of service, and the price will have to rise or the profits will have to fall. Too low a level, and many customers will go elsewhere. Many firms still try to provide a high level of service for a low price – often at the expense of their employees – but this can only be done by shaving profits or otherwise acting in ways which reduce longer-term competitiveness. Note that segmentation still applies – some people are happy to pay for an enhanced service, while others prefer to buy the cheapest. Indeed, individuals often shift between the two levels, depending on the occasion – a couple going out for their twenty-fifth wedding anniversary dinner will not eat at the same restaurant they might go to for a quick lunch during the working week.

Physical evidence

The intangibility of most of the benefits of a service means that consumers do not have any evidence that the service ever took place. The evidence might be useful to show to other people (a certificate from a training course, a life insurance policy to show to a bank) or it might be simply something to act as a reminder of the pleasure the consumer obtained from the service (a souvenir of a holiday, a menu from a restaurant, a travel kit from an airline). **Physical evidence** might also be used as a way of assessing the quality of a product before committing to a purchase (the bank branch's décor or the menu in the window of a restaurant).

In some cases the physical element of the product itself is sufficient to act as physical evidence. A meal in a restaurant fulfils this: the food, the surroundings, the quality of the crockery and cutlery all convey evidence about the quality of the experience, even though the greater part of the bill will be absorbed by the chef's time in cooking the food and the waiter's time in delivering it (not to mention the washing up). In other cases, for example life insurance or other financial services, the physical evidence is likely to be much less or

Talking point

lacking altogether, in which case the firm may need to produce something which will provide evidence, for example a glossy brochure or policy document. For practical and legal purposes, most insurance documents could be printed on one or two sheets of paper, but for marketing purposes the document needs to be much more substantial.

It's commonly said that you can't judge a book by the cover – yet apparently we are expected to believe that we can judge a bank by its décor. Are we really as naive as that? Do people seriously think that reading the menu gives any idea of the quality of the food?

There again, what else do we have to go on? We can hardly go into the restaurant and taste the food first! Maybe restaurants should try this as an experiment – let people have a small taste of the food before they commit to buying a meal. This is, after all, what happens in Spain, in many tapas bars.

Some people might think that banks would be better spending their money on reducing their charges or improving their service – but the evidence is that having a smart interior really does affect people's decisions about where to bank. So maybe we really *are* judging the book by the cover!

There are four generic ways to add value through physical evidence (Figure 19.7):

1 Create physical evidence which increases loyalty.
2 Use physical evidence to enhance brand image.
3 Use physical evidence which has an intrinsic value of its own, e.g. a free gift.
4 Create physical evidence which leads to further sales.

Airlines use their frequent-flyer programmes to increase loyalty: the physical evidence of the flights taken is the regular newsletter which is sent out, and the plastic card which the frequent flyer uses to gain access to the executive lounges at airports en route. Some airlines (KLM for example) also issue special plastic baggage tags which let the baggage handlers know that they are dealing with a very important suitcase: what effect this has on the baggage handlers is unknown, but the effect on the customer is a feeling of importance. At each level of membership of KLM's frequent-flyer programme (Blue Wing, Silver Wing and Gold Wing) the colour of the card changes, as do the benefits to which the holder is entitled. These physical elements of the service are intended to encourage the customer to fly more often with KLM: failure to fly a set number of times a year with the airline will result in a downgrade to a lower level. An intangible benefit of membership for the customer is the occasional free flight – membership points can be exchanged for free flights at a set rate per distance travelled, or for upgrades into business class.

Brand image can be enhanced by using physical evidence which fits in with the brand's essential qualities. For example, an insurance company which wishes to convey a solid, respectable image will produce a glossy policy document full of high-flown legal phrases and reassuring photographs of solid corporate headquarters. A company aiming to convey

Figure 19.7

Adding value through physical evidence

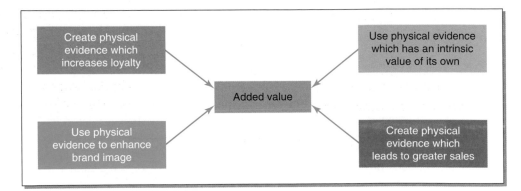

a more down-to-earth, welcoming image might produce a policy couched in simple language, with photographs of smiling staff and policyholders. Physical evidence need not always be up-market: most low-cost airlines emphasize the cost-cutting aspects of their businesses by requiring passengers to print off their own tickets on their computers, or by having no tickets at all. This is about as basic as physical evidence can get, but it does emphasize the point that the airline does not waste passengers' money on anything which is not absolutely necessary.

Physical evidence which has an intrinsic value of its own would include free gifts: this is a common ploy in the financial services industry. Clocks, pen sets, DVD players, radio alarm clocks and so forth are often given out to people who take out insurance policies or pension plans. Clearly very few people would take out an insurance policy simply to win a carriage clock, but the existence of the clock on the policyholder's mantelpiece is good evidence of the existence of the policy.

Physical evidence which leads to further business might include reminder cards sent out by garages to let drivers know that their cars are due for a service. Dentists, opticians, hairdressers and some hospitals use reminders like this to tell people they need check-ups: the physical evidence of the previous visit serves to generate more business. Some business gifts fulfil a similar function: a desk calendar, notepad or pen given away at the conclusion of a sale may serve as a reminder when a future need arises.

Summary

The marketing mix offers us a useful 'shorthand' tool for analyzing the activities of marketers. Every activity carried out by marketers can only be carried out in cooperation with consumers and customers – customers can end the relationship simply by choosing to spend their money elsewhere, a point which sometimes eludes marketers.

The interplay between marketers and customers is what generates business, and (in the last hundred years or so) has generated the highest standard of living in human history. People's daily needs, from food and shelter through to entertainment and education, are met by marketers eager to please and prepared to go to considerable lengths in serving customers. All the efforts of marketers, and consequently every aspect of the marketing mix, is designed to meet customer needs more effectively, whether those needs are for better information or for better products or even for more convenient delivery.

The key points from this chapter are as follows:

- The hedonic aspects of products are often more important than the practical, utilitarian aspects.
- Price has more components than the simple purchase cost.
- Pricing should always take account of what people are prepared to pay.
- Place provides many of the benefits of buying the product: shopping should be a pleasurable experience.
- Advertising is probably only a weak force, nudging people rather than persuading.
- Interaction with advertisements always increases effectiveness, even if the advertisement is 'zapped'.
- Radio is a powerful medium because it is intimate.
- Cinema advertising appeals mainly to younger audiences.
- Ambient advertising works best when it is close to the point of purchase.
- Ambient advertising is particularly good for 'nudging' consumers when they are close to the point of purchase.
- Consumers often use social interactions as a surrogate for judging quality in service situations.
- Service levels should be correct for the target market, not necessarily maximal.
- Physical evidence is often used as a surrogate for judging quality of services.

Chapter review questions

1 Why is cost-plus pricing dangerous?

2 Why is shopping pleasurable?

3 Why might someone ignore an advertisement, even though it is about a product of interest?

4 Why might advertisements which are 'zapped' be more effective than ones which are not?

5 What are the main advantages of radio as an advertising medium?

6 Why do ambient advertisements work well when they are close to the point of purchase?

7 What are the advantages of cinema advertising?

8 How might someone judge the quality of a restaurant they have not visited before?

9 How should service level be decided?

10 What is the difference between skimming and demand pricing?

Preview case study revisited
J.D. Wetherspoon

Maintaining a pleasant, safe atmosphere is central to Wetherspoon's policies. The company has removed all financial incentives for customers to 'trade up' to larger or more alcoholic drinks: for example, most pubs sell a double measure of spirits for less than the cost of two separate singles, but Wetherspoon's have removed this because they see it as an incentive for customers to buy more alcohol than they otherwise might. Strange behaviour – most companies seek to encourage people to buy more of their product. The company also sell their soft drinks at much lower prices than most other pubs or restaurants

John Hutson, managing director of Wetherspoon's, says:

> We believe that a combination of food served all day, reasonably priced soft drinks, an absence of financial incentives to 'trade up' to larger quantities of alcohol, combined with good facilities and a heavy emphasis on staff training are the right direction for the pub industry to take.
>
> No company which serves alcohol can be immune from bad behaviour from time to time, but these policies should help to reduce its effects and, as a company, we will, as in the past, continue to consider sensible policies for our business and the community in this complex area.

In another somewhat surprising development, Tim Martin called on the government to ban smoking in all pubs. Citing the Californian experience, where all smoking in public places was banned in the 1990s, he says that a significant number of people now avoid pubs because of the smoky atmosphere:

> I believe that a total ban would be the best way forward, and not result, for example, in a situation where customers can smoke in pubs in Newcastle, but not in nearby Gateshead, because neighbouring councils have different agendas. However, it would be commercial suicide for a pub company to prohibit smoking in the absence of a nationwide ban by the Government. Going it alone, in my opinion, is not a viable option in the pub world.

Despite this, Wetherspoon's did try to ban smoking for a short period in their pubs, but experienced a rapid decline in business as smokers went elsewhere, so were forced to reinstate smoking.

Eventually, the UK government heeded the suggestion, and smoking in pubs is now banned throughout the UK. It is (at the time of writing) too early to say what effect the ban will have, but there is no doubt at all that the smoke-free atmosphere is a major improvement as far as non-smokers are concerned. Since smokers are now a minority, it would seem likely that the ban will be a positive move rather than a negative one.

The UK is a pub culture, like Ireland: much of Britain's social life revolves around drinking, and the corner pub is often the cornerstone of the community. What J.D. Wetherspoon has done is recapture the old atmosphere of the pub – a place for conversation, perhaps some food, and a comfortable and safe environment. In a period when the licensed trade is facing difficult times, Wetherspoon's represents a remarkable success story.

Case study
Low-cost airlines

Prior to 1987, air travel within Europe was heavily regulated and was largely the province of the rich. National airlines of European Union member states had developed a highly complex set of agreements about who could fly where, how many seats were allowed on each aircraft, and what fares could be charged. All these decisions were made by the national airlines in negotiation with each other – so that, for example, Alitalia might not allow British Airways to fly from London to Milan unless Alitalia could be given a route from Rome to Manchester.

In essence, the national airlines regarded the skies of Europe as their personal property: the only exception was private charter flying, which of course they were powerless to prevent, and which gave rise to the cheap package holiday. Prior to 1987, it was often cheaper for a business traveller to buy a package holiday to (say) Rome and then stay in another hotel rather than buy a scheduled flight with BA or Alitalia.

All this changed in 1987 when the European Union agreed that the skies should be liberalized for any carriers. Over the protests of the national airlines, licences were granted for operators to fly scheduled routes from anywhere to anywhere, subject of course to air traffic control regulations and agreement with the airports concerned. Thus the possibility for cheap, no-frills airlines was opened up.

The first airline to enter the market (and still one of the best-known) was Ryanair. This airline operates a very effective website which has served as the pattern for other cheap airlines. Seat prices are not fixed, but are controlled by demand using sophisticated computer software: as demand rises, so does the price of the seat, which means that early booking makes economic sense. Sometimes seats are sold well below cost – seats for £1 (plus airport taxes) are not unusual, and it is certainly common for an air fare from Dublin to (say) Venice to be cheaper than the rail fare from Dublin to Limerick.

Other airlines quickly followed, often as subsidiaries of major carriers. KLM set up their own Buzz no-frills carrier, British Midland set up BMI Baby and MyTravel (the tour operator) set up MyTravelite. Other European countries quickly followed suit – Germany (Germanwings and HLX), Italy (Volareweb) and Holland (Basiq Air). No doubt more will follow.

The basis of a low-cost airline is that the company reduces its costs to an absolute minimum, and does not provide the level of service that a full-fare carrier would provide. For example, there are no in-flight meals (although most no-frills airlines will happily sell you a sandwich), there are no tickets (everything is done over the Internet, so passengers use their own paper and ink to print tickets) and in some cases there are no boarding-cards, merely plastic tokens. Check-in procedures often do not include reserving seats: passengers find a seat once on board, which sometimes results in an unseemly rush to board the aircraft in order to grab the best seats. Passengers buy

each ticket as a one-way option: there are no reductions for buying a return, so it is easy for someone to travel out via one airport and return via another, or even to fly a triangular trip using different airlines.

Turnround times on the ground are also usually very fast. The aircraft is tidied up quickly, the pilots talk to the ground engineers via radio so that they do not need to leave the cockpit, and the plane is often ready to go again with the same crew on board within 20 minutes. Some of the no-frills airlines have even reduced the number of toilets on board the aircraft in order to fit in extra seats. The aircraft will not wait for late passengers, even if they have already checked in – turnround times are too tight. Even the cabin-crew uniforms are basic – jeans and a T-shirt is typical.

From the passengers' viewpoint all this is fine. The standard of service is low, but so is the fare – no one expects great service if they are paying less for the flight than they paid for the taxi to the airport. On a short flight, the lack of enough toilets or an in-flight meal is hardly a problem, and no one really expects a fashion parade from the cabin crew. Where the major carriers have been able to compete is on the actual destinations: because low-cost carriers typically use cheaper regional airports, passengers are often faced with lengthy journeys to get to their final destinations. Major airlines also do well from business flyers, because the price is not an issue when the company is paying. Low-cost airlines have also (so far) had very little impact on long-haul flying: a ten-hour flight without a meal and with few toilets is not as appealing as a one-hour flight in the same conditions.

Ultimately, low-cost airlines are unlikely to take the whole market. They offer the opportunity for people to travel by air where previously they might have travelled by road, rail, or bus, or (more likely) stayed at home. There are threats on the horizon, too – the surface transport lobby objects to the fact that aircraft fuel is tax-free whereas road fuel is heavily taxed, and the European Union has recently clamped down on airports offering special deals to low-cost carriers in order to encourage more passengers, and thus increase business through airport shops, restaurants and bars. Also, the massive increase in air traffic in Europe has stretched air traffic control systems to breaking point, especially in the peak summer season. Meanwhile, passengers continue to enjoy low prices, hotels are enjoying unprecedented levels of tourism, and airports are burgeoning as a result of the spending-power of passengers coming through the gates.

Case study questions

1   The service element in the budget airline business is conspicuously absent. How do you account for the popularity of the airlines?

2   How can low-cost airlines compete with each other, since they cannot all be the cheapest and they do not appear to have any other differentiating features?

3   Apart from price, why else might someone choose to fly with a budget airline?

4   Why have cabin staff at all?

5   Why might companies be prepared to pay higher fares for their employees to travel on major airlines?

References

Addis, Michela, and Holbrook, Morris B. (2001) On the conceptual link between mass customisation and experiential consumption: an explosion of subjectivity. *Journal of Consumer Behaviour*, 1(1): 50–6.

Bakamitsos, George, and Siomkos, George J. (2003) Context effects in marketing practice: the case of mood. *Journal of Consumer Behaviour*, 3(4): 304–314.

Barnard, N., and Ehrenberg, A. (1997) Advertising: strongly persuasive or nudging? *Journal of Advertising Research*, 37(1), Jan–Feb: 21–31.

Becker-Olsen, Karen, and Cudmore, B. Andrew (2004) When good deeds dilute your equity. *Advances in Consumer Research*, 31(1): 78–9.

Bengtsson, Anders (2003) Towards a critique of brand relationships. *Advances in Consumer Research*, 30(1): 154–8.

Biel, A.L. (1990) Love the ad. Buy the product? *ADMAP*, September (299): 21–25.

Biel, A.L., and Bridgewater, C.A. (1990) Attributes of likeable television commercials. *Journal of Advertising Research*, 30(3): 38–44.

Blythe, Jim (2003) *Essentials of Marketing Communications*, 2nd ed. (London: FT Prentice Hall).

Bolls, Paul D., Muehling, Darrel D., and Yoon, Kak (2003): The effects of television commercial pacing on viewers' attention and memory. *Journal of Marketing Communications*, 9(1), March: 17–28.

Booms, B.H., and Bitner, M.J. (1981) Marketing strategies and organisation structures for service firms. *Marketing of Services*, eds J. Donnelly and W.R. George (Chicago, IL: American Marketing Association).

Bray, Jeffrey Paul, and Harris, Christine (2006) The effect of 9-ending prices on retail sales: a quantitative UK based field study. *Journal of Marketing Management*, 22(5/6): 601–617.

Cinema Advertising Association (1997) *UK Cinema Audience Profile* (London: Cinema Advertising Association).

Dalli, Daniele, Romani, Simona, and Gistri, Giacomo (2006) Brand dislike: representing the negative side of consumer preferences. *Advances in Consumer Research*, 33(1): 87–95.

Dolan, Robert J. (1995) How do you know when the price is right? *Harvard Business Review*, 73(5), Sept–Oct: 174–83.

Ehrenberg, A.S.C. (1992) Comments on how advertising works. *Marketing and Research Today*, August: 167–9.

Ehrenberg, A. (1997) How do consumers buy a new brand? *ADMAP*, March.

Evans, M., O'Malley, L., and Patterson, M. (1996) Direct marketing communications in the UK: a study of growth, past present and future. *Journal of Marketing Communications*, 2 (March): 51–65.

Foxall, G., and Goldsmith, R.E. (1994) *Consumer Psychology for Marketing* (London: Routledge).

Gourville, John, and Koehler, Jay (2003) Downsizing price increases: a differential sensitivity to price over quantity. *Advances in Consumer Research*, 30(1): 106–7.

Grapentine, Terry (2003) Window shopping. *Marketing Research*, 15(4), winter: 5.

Gueguen, Nicolas, and Legoherel, Patrick (2004) Numerical encoding and odd-ending prices: the effect of a contrast in discount perception. *European Journal of Marketing*, 38(1): 194–208.

Heath, Timothy, McCarthy, Michael S., and Chatterjee, Subimal (2006) The effect of line extensions up and down in quality on initial choice and subsequent switching tendencies. *Advances in Consumer Research*, 33(1): 75.

Henry, Paul Conrad, and Caldwell, Mary Louise (2006) Self-empowerment and consumption: customer remedies for prolonged stigmatisation. *European Journal of Marketing,* 40(9/10): 1031–48.

Jefkins, F. (1994) *Advertising* (London: M & E Handbooks).

Jones, J.P. (1991) Over-promise and under-delivery. *Marketing and Research Today*, November: 195–203.

Judd, V.C. (1987) Differentiate with the fifth P. *Industrial Marketing Management*, 16: 241–47.

Kneale, D. (1988) Zapping of TV ads appears pervasive. *Wall Street Journal*, 25 April.

Krishna, Aradhna, Wagner, Mary, and Yoon, Carolyn (2002): Effects of extreme-priced products on consumer reservation prices. *Advances in Consumer Research*, 29(1): 87–8.

LeClerc, France, Hsee, Christopher K., and Nunnes, Joseph C. (2002) Best of the worst or worst of the best? *Advances in Consumer Research*, 29(1): 59–60.

Maxham III James G., and Netemeyer, Richard G. (2003) Firms reap what they sow: the effect of shared values and perceived organisational justice on customers' evaluation of complaint handling. *Journal of Marketing* 67(1): 46–62.

McKechnie, S. and Leather, P. (1998) Likeability as a measure of advertising effectiveness: the case of financial services. *Journal of Marketing Communications*, 4: 63–85.

Molz, Gunter, and Gielnik, Michael (2006) Does the introduction of the Euro have an effect on subjective hypotheses about the price-quality relationship? *Journal of Consumer Behaviour*, 5 (May–Jun): 204–210.

Pires, Guilherme D., Stanton, John, and Rita, Paulo (2006) The Internet, consumers empowerment, and marketing strategies. *European Journal of Marketing*, 40(9/10): 1013–30.

POPAI (1994): Point of purchase consumer buying habits study. *Advertising, Promotion and Supplemental Aspects of Integrated Marketing Communications*, 4th ed., by T.A. Shimp, 1997 (Fort Worth, TX: Dryden Press).

Rasmusson, E. (1997) Winning back angry customers. *Sales and Marketing Management* (October): 131.

Ritson, M. (2003) *Assessing the Value of Advertising* (London: London Business School).

Roggeveen, Anne L., Lan, Xia, and Monroe, Kent B. (2006): How attributions and the product's price impact the effectiveness of price partitioning. *Advances in Consumer Research*, 33(1): 181.

Schindler, R.M., and Kirby, P.N. (1997) Patterns of right-most digits used in advertised prices: implications for nine-ending effects. *Journal of Consumer Research*, September: 192–201.

Seigyoung, Auh, and Chuan-Fong, Shi (2006) Balancing giving-up vs. taking-in: does the pattern or payments and benefits matter to customers in a financing decision context? *Advances in Consumer Research*, 33(1): 139–45.

Shankar, A. (1999a) Ambient media: advertising's new opportunity? *International Journal of Advertising*, 18(3), August.

Shankar, A. (1999b) Advertising's imbroglio. *Journal of Marketing Communications*, 5(1), March: 1–17.

Simmons, C. Lee, and Schindler, Robert M. (2003) Cultural superstitions and the price endings used in Chinese advertising. *Journal of International Marketing*, 11(2): 101–11.

Stapel, J. (1991) Like the advertisement, but does it interest me? *ADMAP*, April: 30–1.

Steenhuysen, J. (1994) Adland's new billion-dollar baby. *Advertising Age*, 11 April: S8–S14.

Suri, Rajneesh, Anderson, Rolph E., and Kotlov, Vassili (2004) The use of 9-ending prices: contrasting the USA with Poland. *European Journal of Marketing*, 38(1): 56–72.

Unnava, H. Rao, Rajagopal, Priyali, and Raju, Sekar (2003) Reducing competitive ad interference by varying advertising context: a test of network models of memory. *Advances in Consumer Research*, 30(1): 45–6.

Wells, W.D. (1980) Liking and sales effectiveness: a hypothesis. *Topline*, 2(1).

Wright, L.T., and Crimp, M. (2000) *The Marketing Research Process* (London: Prentice-Hall).

Zufryden, F.S., Pedrick, J.H., and Sankaralingam, A. (1993) Zapping and its impact on brand purchase behaviour. *Journal of Advertising Research*, 33 (Jan/Feb): 58–66.

Glossary

Abstraction The process whereby lower-level goals help to determine what the higher-level goals must be if there is to be overall goal consistency.

Accommodation of the new attitude Accepting new information and using it to re-form an existing attitude.

Acculturation The process of adopting a new culture.

ACORN A Classification of Residential Neighbourhoods.

Actual state The condition in which the person happens to be at a given time.

Adaptation The process by which goals are influenced by contextual issues.

Adoption The process of building an innovative product into one's daily life.

Affect The emotional element of attitude.

Affective state The physical or psychological condition of an individual which may lead to an interruption in planned behaviour.

Ambient advertising Commercial messages which are designed to become part of the environment.

Apprehender Someone who is the target for a communication.

Aspirational group A group of individuals which one wishes to join.

Assortment adjustment The process of substituting some possessions for others in order to improve one's overall position.

Assortment depletion The reduction in one's overall quantity of possessions.

Assortment extension Increasing one's overall quantity of possessions.

Assortment replenishment Replacing possessions which have worn out or been used up.

Atmospherics The factors which create the overall ambience in a retail environment.

Attitude A propensity to respond in a consistent manner to a given stimulus or object.

Attitude splitting The process of protecting an attitude by accepting only part of a new piece of information which conflicts with the attitude.

Audience fade-out The tendency for TV viewers to leave the room or otherwise cease to pay attention during advertising breaks.

Automatic group A group of people to which an individual belongs by reason of race, gender or other non-changeable factor.

Autonomic decision-making A type of decision which is made by the individual without recourse to others.

B2B Business to business.

B2C Business to consumer.

Baby Boomer An individual born between 1945 and 1965, a period of exceptionally high birth-rates in Europe and the United States.

Baby Busters Individuals born between 1964 and 1980 during a period of low birth-rates.

Backward conditioning A situation in which the unconditioned stimulus is presented before the conditioned stimulus.

Behavioural segmentation Dividing up a potential market according to the behaviour of its members.

Benchmarking Measuring the firm's performance against that of other firms across a wide range of factors.

Bias The factor which affects the processing of information as a result of a pre-existing mindset.

Birthrate The number of babies born per annum, expressed as the number of live births per thousand women.

Brand community A group of people who identify themselves with a specific brand.

Brand loyalists People who will only buy a specific brand, often refusing to switch even if their usual brand is unavailable.

Brand switchers People who do not show any brand loyalty, usually buying whichever brand is convenient or cheap.

Buyers Those with the responsibility of making the actual purchase of a product, often (in the industrial context) working to a specific brief.

Categorization The pigeonholing of information in order to prejudge events and products.

Category group *See* Automatic group.

Cautionary-tale A story which is intended to illustrate the possible negative outcomes of a particular course of action.

Central route A route to attitude change which relies on reasoned argument: an appeal to cognition, in other words.

Chunking The learning process by which items of information are grouped in the brain.

Class The social and economic grouping of individuals.

Classical conditioning The learning process characterised by repeating a stimulus at about the same time as a given behaviour occurs, with the aim of creating a permanent association between the stimulus and the behaviour.

Clutter Excessive information, especially applied to advertising: a situation in which the recipient is presented with a large number of stimuli at the same time.

Code switching The action of changing from one set of communication parameters to another.

Cognition Thought processes: the element of attitude derived from conscious thought or knowledge.

Cognitive dissonance The tension caused by holding two conflicting pieces of information at once.

Cognitive effort The amount of work needed to consider a course of action or understand a set of issues.

Cognitive innovators Those who seek new intellectual experiences.

Cognitive learning Acquiring and retaining new information through a conscious effort of thought.

Cognitive structure The way the individual thinks, and the way new information is fitted into existing knowledge.

Community of interest A type of virtual community based around a hobby or other shared interest.

Compatibility The degree to which a new product matches the individual's existing lifestyle, attitudes, and possessions.

Completed fertility rate The total number of children born to women in a specific age group.

Complexity The degree to which a new product requires extensive learning before it can be used effectively.

Conation The behavioural intentions which arise from attitude.

Concentrated marketing A strategy aimed at being the best supplier within a very small or specialized market.

Conditioned response The behaviour which results from classical conditioning.

Conditioned stimulus The stimulus which is applied to generate a conditioned response in classical conditioning.

Conformity The social pressure to behave in similar ways to other people.

Conjunctive rule A heuristic by which brands are compared to all the cut-offs until only a few surviving brands remain.

Consumer Someone who enjoys the benefits of a product.

Contactors People within an organization who have daily interaction with customers.

Continuous innovation A new product which follows closely on from a previous product, and which has a clear relationship to the previous product.

Cue An external trigger which encourages learning.

Cultural anchoring The process by which an innovation becomes part of everyday life.

Culture The set of beliefs, behaviours, customs and attitudes which are common to a large group of people.

Culture shock The discomfort which arises from being displaced from one's normal cultural milieu.

Customary pricing Retaining the same price for a product over a long period, perhaps adjusting the quantity provided as a way of maintaining profitability.

Customer Someone who makes the decision to buy a product.

Customization Redesigning a product to make it fit a customer's needs more exactly.

Database marketing Communicating, often interactively, with a computer-mediated list of customers.

Deciders Members of a decision-making unit who have the responsibility for making the final purchase decision.

Decision-making unit A group of people who influence, control or carry out purchasing activities.

Demand pricing Calculating the price of a product according to consumer demand at different price levels.

Democratic decision-making *See* Syncratic decision-making.

Demographic segmentation Dividing up a market according to people's age, income and social standing.

Demographic fracture The disparity between old and new socioeconomic structures encountered when moving from one culture to another.

Depth (guided) interview Open-ended interviews conducted with a small sample of respondents in order to assess their innermost thoughts and feelings.

Desired state The condition in which the individual would like to be.

Differentiated marketing The act of supplying different products to different market segments.

Differentiation Providing a product with features which distinguish it from competing products.

Diffusion The process of adoption of an innovation throughout the market.

Discontinuous innovation Developing a new product which relates only distantly, or does not relate at all, to previous products.

Discrimination The process by which people distinguish between stimuli.

Disinhibition Removal of the internal inhibitors which constrain behaviour.

Disposal Divestment of a product when it is worn out or used up.

Disposers Those who are responsible for divestment of used-up products.

Disruption This is damage to the message caused by circumstances and (sometimes deliberate) misconstruction of the message.

Dissociative group A social group to which one does not wish to belong.

Dissonance A mental state which arises when outcomes do not match with expectations.

Distortion A change in the meaning of the message caused by outside forces.

Drive The basic force of motivation which arises when the individual's actual state diverges from the desired state.

Dutifuls Sacrificial, careful and conservative shoppers who are practical and avoid risks.

Dynamically continuous innovation The development of a new product which differs radically from its predecessors while still retaining some commonality.

Early adopters Those who, although not first to buy a new product, do so very shortly after its introduction.

Early majority Those who adopt a new product after it has been on the market for a while, but before most people have adopted it.

Economic choice The choice made when one is unable to afford to buy both alternatives.

Economics The study of demand.

Ego The conscious self.

Ego-defensive function The function of attitude which enables the individual to maintain stability of the conscious self.

Elaboration The structuring of information within the brain, relating it to existing memory.

Elasticity The degree to which demand is affected by other factors, for example price changes.

Emotional fracture The sense of loss of emotional support encountered when moving from one culture to another.

End user The person or organization which finally obtains the benefits of the product.

EPOS Electronic Point of Sale.

Equitable performance The level of product quality that the consumer would expect, given the price paid and the other circumstances of purchase and use.

Equivocation Of a communication, to have more than one meaning.

Ethnicity The cultural background of the individual.

Ethnocentrism The belief that one's own culture is 'correct' and other cultures are derived from it.

Expectation The existing information and attitudes which make people interpret later information in a specific way.

Expected performance The level of product quality that the individual anticipates.

Experiment A controlled activity in which a given stimulus is offered to respondents in order to discover their reactions.

Extinction The process of forgetting a conditioned reflex.

Extrovert Someone who demonstrates his or her personality traits in a strongly overt or obvious manner to other people.

Family A group of people who exhibit shared consumption and who are bound by ties of genetic relationship or adoption.

Fantasy community A group of people who share a common dream world.

Fashion foregoers People who have little regard for fashion or appearances, and who are often 'loners' who look for low prices rather than fashion.

Fertility rate The number of children born per thousand women of childbearing age.

First-time prospects Firms which have identified a need for a product and have started to evaluate possible suppliers, but have not yet placed an order.

Focus group A group of people assembled for the purpose of gathering their collective views about a given issue.

Formal group A group of people with a known, recorded membership and a set of (usually written) rules of membership.

Forward conditioning A circumstance where the conditioned stimulus comes before the unconditioned stimulus.

Functional fracture The disparity between old and new systems for daily living encountered when moving from one culture to another.

Functional risk The possibility that the product will not prove to be fit for purpose.

Gatekeepers People who control the flow of information to a decision-making unit.

Generalization The tendency for a conditioned stimulus to lead to a wider than intended set of conditioned reflexes.

Geographic segmentation Dividing a market into smaller groups based on location.

Goals Specific targets towards which consumption behaviour is directed.

Growth rate The total increase (or decrease) in population including births, deaths and migration effects.

Halo effect The tendency for an individual to believe every aspect of something is good, based on a belief that some aspects are good.

Hedonism The cult of pleasure.

Heuristic A decision-making rule.

Homophilous influences Transmission of ideas between people of similar standing in the community.

Husband-dominant decision-making A situation in which the male of the household has the most power in consumption decisions.

Hygiene factors Those aspects of a product which consumers would expect as a basic feature of any product in the category.

Icon A sign which stands for an object.

Id The unconscious part of the mind responsible for basic desires.

Ideal performance The best possible outcome of buying a given product.

Identifiers Factors used as an initial segmentation base before data is collected on individual firms.

Implication The expected consequences that are attached to a message by the recipient.

Incentives Reasons for action.

Index A sign that relates to an object by causal connection.

Indifference curve The graph which shows the points at which one product will be regarded as a suitable substitute for another.

Inertia Making decisions out of habit rather than from any conscious loyalty.

Inference Extra detail added to a message by a recipient, based on a meta analysis of the message.

Influencers People who exert an advisory role to members of a decision-making unit.

Infomercial A (typically) half-hour television programme about a specific product.

Informal group A group of people which has no recorded membership and no written rules.

Information seekers People who enjoy finding out about products.

Informational influence The aspect of group behaviour concerned with exchanging knowledge.

Initiators The members of a decision-making unit who first identify a need.

Innovation A new product or service: the act of adopting a new product or service.

Innovativeness The degree to which an individual or firm creates or adopts new products.

Innovators People who are first to try a new product.

Instrumental function The aspect of attitude which enables the individual to obtain the best use from a product.

Interference Intelligent messages which disrupt communication.

Interrupt Something which diverts an individual away from a goal, usually temporarily.

Intrinsic self-relevance Sources of involvement derived from means-end knowledge stored in the individual's memory.

Introvert Someone who is withdrawn from other people.

Invention A new product, usually developed by an individual.

Involvement The degree to which an individual is attracted to, and defined by, a product or brand.

Isolateds Employees who have little or no contact with customers.

Key-account manager A salesperson who has the responsibility of dealing with the most important customers of a firm.

Knowledge function The drive to seek clarity and order.

Laggards People who are the last to adopt a new product.

Late majority People who only adopt a new product after most people have already done so.

Lateral recycling Donating goods to others, selling them on, or otherwise transferring ownership to someone who will obtain further use from the goods.

Learning Changes in behaviour which come about through experience.

Least dependent person The individual within a buying group who has the highest degree of autonomy.

Loyalty The degree to which an individual will repeat purchase of a product.

Macro environment Those environmental elements which are common to all firms in a given industry.

Maintainers A family member who has the task of ensuring that a shared product is in good condition for the other members to use.

Market maven Someone who is a self-appointed expert about a particular product category or market.

Mass market A situation in which a standardized product is purchased by a very large number of people.

Maturation The process of growing to adulthood.

Message intrigue The element of a message which arouses the interest of the recipient.

Metacommunication Communication which goes beyond the immediate meaning of the symbols used.

Micro environment Those elements of the environment which affect the individual firm.

Micro marketing Targeting customers within a very narrow segment.

Miscalculation Incorrect decoding of a message caused by errors of cognition.

Modified re-buy A purchase which, although similar to previous purchases, has been changed in a minor way.

Modifiers People who deal with customers regularly, but who have no specific marketing role.

More An element of culture.

Motivation The internal force which encourages people to act in specific ways.

MRO A company which carries out maintenance, repair and overhaul.

Natural increase The degree to which a population increases: the degree to which births exceed deaths.

Need A perceived lack of something.

Negative disconfirmation A state of affairs in which the expected outcome is disappointing or fails in some way to satisfy.

New task A type of purchase for which previous experience does not exist.

Niche marketing Targeting a small group of customers.

Non-compensatory decision rule A heuristic which cannot be offset by other factors.

Normative compliance The force which compels people towards agreeing with the rest of the group.

Novices Customers who have purchased the product for the first time within the last 90 days.

Observability The degree to which the purchase of a new product can be seen by others.

Odd-even pricing The practice of ending prices with '99p' or '99¢'.

OEM Original equipment manufacturer.

Operant conditioning The learning process in which the learner is rewarded for correct action, and in which the learner plays an active role.

Optimum stimulation level The point at which a need has become strong, but before it has become unpleasantly so.

Packrats Individuals who tend to keep their possessions for a long time.

Paralanguage Communication carried out in a manner other than through words.

Peer group Those people who are near to being one's equals.

People The element of the marketing mix concerned with employees and other consumers.

Perceived instrumentality The degree to which an action or product is thought to be useful in a practical way.

Perception The process of creating a mental 'map' of reality.

Peripheral route Using emotional appeals in order to change the affective component of attitude.

Personal sources Sources of involvement derived from means-end knowledge stored in the individual's memory.

Personal transformation The degree to which an individual is changed by a learning experience.

Personality Those factors which make up the individual's mental processes.

Pester power The ability of children to influence their parents by means of repetitive requests.

Physical evidence The element of the marketing mix concerned with the tangible aspects of the product or service.

Place The element of the marketing mix concerned with the location where the exchange takes place.

Positioning The act of placing a brand in the appropriate place in the consumer's mind relative to competing products.

Positive disconfirmation An unexpectedly good outcome of a purchase.

Power purchasers Self-indulgent variety seekers who are big spenders and risk takers.

Preparers A family member responsible for transforming a product into a condition suitable for other members to use it.

Price That which is given in exchange for receiving the benefits of a product.

Primary group The group of people we see daily, and to whom we feel closest.

Private response Complaining behaviour directed at friends or acquaintances rather than at the perpetrator of the problem.

Process The element of the marketing mix concerned with the overall delivery of a service.

Product A bundle of benefits: the response to a need.

Production orientation The belief that business success will arise from manufacturing in very large quantities in order to minimize costs.

Product-line pricing Pricing which takes account of the price of related products.

Progressive patrons Self-confident, artistic, variety-seeking, risk-taking, open-minded consumers.

Projective test A research technique whereby respondents are asked to give an opinion of what they think someone else's attitude or feelings might be on a given topic.

Promotion The element of the marketing mix concerned with communication.

Proxemics The use of physical space to convey a perceptual stimulus.

Psychographic segmentation Dividing a market according to the psychological profiles of potential customers.

Psychographics Using behavioural tendencies to infer personality traits.

Psychological pricing Applying prices to goods based on perceptual issues such as quality.

Psychology The science of the mind.

Psychology of complication The tendency for people to make their lives more complex, and therefore more interesting.

Psychology of simplification The tendency for people to make their lives less complex and therefore less stressful.

Psychosocial risk The danger of looking foolish, or being embarrassed.

Purchasing agent Someone who has the task of making purchases on behalf of a group, usually the family.

Purgers People who regularly discard their possessions.

Reference group A group of people who act as the yardstick for our behaviour.

Reinforcement The process of consolidating classical conditioning.

Relationship community A group of people who are bound by strong social ties.

Relationship marketing Marketing in such a way as to generate a long-term partnership with customers.

Relative advantage The degree to which a new product is superior to the one it replaces.

Re-seller organizations Companies such as retailers and wholesalers which sell goods on without altering them in any way.

Response The reaction the consumer makes to the interaction between a drive and a cause.

Retention The stability of learned material over time.

Rite of passage An event or action which marks a change in an individual's life circumstances.

Role The place one has within a group.

Role model An individual who acts as a reference point for judging one's own behaviour.

Routine brand buyers People who normally buy the same brand every time.

Salient belief A belief which is key in the formation of an attitude.

Schadenfreude Pleasure felt at the downfall of another.

Secondary group A group of people whom we do not necessarily see every day, and who are not our closest friends, but to which we belong nonetheless.

Second-market discounting Charging a lower price for one group of people in order to even out demand.

Segmentation The act of dividing up a market into groups of people with similar needs.

Selectivity That part of perception which deals with rejecting unnecessary stimuli.

Self-actualization The need to become the ideal self.

Self-completion questionnaire A survey instrument whereby the respondent fills in the answers without the intervention of an interviewer.

Self-concept The belief one has about oneself.

Self-enhancement The practice of airing one's superior knowledge in order to create a better image.

Self-gratification Giving pleasure to oneself.

Self-image The image of oneself one wishes to present to the world.

Self-knowledge An understanding of one's own personality, beliefs and attitudes.

Self-monitoring The regulatory mechanism which controls behaviour, without outside intercession.

Semantics The study of meaning.

Semiotics The study of sign systems.

Sensory innovators Those who seek new sensory experiences.

Service level The target a firm sets for providing customer satisfaction through intangible benefits.

Shadow websites Websites which offer an opportunity to post negative stories about specific companies or brands.

Simultaneous conditioning In classical conditioning, a state of affairs whereby the conditioned stimulus and the unconditioned stimulus are presented at the same time.

Skimming Setting prices high when a product is launched, then gradually lowering them as competitors enter the market.

Social strivers Style conscious fashion experimenters who like shopping.

Socialization The process of becoming an effective and integrated member of society.

Socioeconomic variables Those factors which derive from an individual's class and income.

Sociology The study of human behaviour in groups.

Sophisticates Established regular purchasers of a product.

Species response tendencies Instinctive reactions to stimuli, distinct from learned responses.

Stimulus rejection The process of protecting an attitude by ignoring information which conflicts with it.

Straight rebuy A situation in which a previous order is simply repeated in its entirety.

Subculture A set of beliefs and attitudes which, while part of a main culture, represents a distinctly separate set.

Sub-goal A target which forms part of a greater aim, and which needs to be achieved before the main goal can be achieved.

Subjectivity Judging everything from a personal viewpoint.

Subliminal perception Perception which occurs below the conscious level.

Superego The component of mind which acts as a restraint on behaviour.

Symbol A method of converting thought into something which can be transmitted in a message.

Symbolic fracture The disparity between old and new communication paradigms encountered when moving from one culture to another.

Syncratic decision-making (democratic decision-making) In group decision-making, the type of decision which is made on the basis of consultation.

Syntactics The study of the structure of communication.

Synthetic That which is constructed from disparate components. In perception, an overall view which is derived from grouping together a set of stimuli.

Technophiles People who like new technology for its own sake.

Technophobes People who are fearful of new technology.

Third-party response In complaining, the act of involving someone other than the complainer or the supplier, for example a lawyer or consumer rights campaigner.

Total fertility rate The number of children the average woman would expect to have in her lifetime.

Trait A component of personality.

Transactional marketing Marketing in which the marketer focuses on the individual sale, not on the long-term relationship with the customer.

Trialibility The degree to which a product can be tested before the customer needs to commit to its adoption.

Trickle-down theory The belief that innovations are adopted by wealthy, educated people first and eventually 'trickle down' to people in lower socio-economic groups.

Unconditioned response A natural response to a stimulus.

Unconditioned stimulus A stimulus which occurs without the intervention of an experimenter.

Undifferentiated marketing Offering one type of product to all possible segments.

Unsought communications Messages which have not been looked for by the recipient.

Unsought goods Products which are bought as a result of coercion rather than through desire.

Users Those members of a buying group who will actually make use of a product (not necessarily consumers).

Utilitarianism The cult of practicality.

Value analysis The process of calculating the worth of a purchase in terms of the returns made from its use.

Value importance The level of satisfaction the individual gains from the achievement of a particular value.

Value-expressive function The factor in group behaviour which allows the members to display their own beliefs and attitudes.

Value-expressive influence The factor in normative compliance which causes group members to adopt the values of the group.

Virtual group A social group which is mediated by the Internet.

Voice response A type of complaint in which the complainer returns to the supplier to seek redress.

Want A specific satisfier for a need.

Wife-dominant decision-making Decisions which are left to the female adult of a family.

Woopies Well-off older people.

Word of mouse Electronically mediated personal communications about brands and products.

Yesteryears Insecure, conservative risk avoiders.

Zapping Using the TV remote control to avoid advertisements, often by switching to another channel.

Zipping Using the remote control of a VCR to fast-forward through advertisements on a recorded programme.

Index